MW01640037
2003 International Building Code®
Study Companion
ICC
INTERNATIONAL CODE COUNCIL®

2003 International Building Code Study Companion

ISBN 1-58001-154-3

Acquisitions:	Mark Johnson
Cover Design:	Lisa Jachymiak
Illustrator:	Mike Tamai
Layout Design:	Alberto Herrera
Project Editor:	Roger Mensink
Publications Manager:	Mary Lou Luif

First Printing:	January 2004
Second Printing:	July 2004
Third Printing:	March 2005
Fourth Printing:	July 2005
Fifth Printing:	October 2005
Sixth Printing:	September 2006

Printed in the United States of America

TABLE OF CONTENTS

INTRODUCTION

This study companion provides practical learning assignments for independent study of the provisions of the 2003 *International Building Code*® (IBC®). The independent study format affords a method for the student to complete the study program in an unlimited amount of time. Progressing through the workbook, the learner can measure his or her level of knowledge by using the exercises and quizzes provided for each study session.

The workbook is also valuable for instructor-led programs. In jurisdictional training sessions, community college classes, vocational training programs and other structured educational offerings, the study guide and the IBC can be the basis for code instruction.

All study sessions begin with a general learning objective, the specific sections or chapters of the code under consideration and a list of questions summarizing the key points of study. Each session addresses selected topics from the IBC and includes code text, a commentary on the code provisions and illustrations representing the provisions under discussion. Exercises and quizzes are provided at the end of each study session. Before beginning the exercises and quizzes, the student should thoroughly review the referenced IBC provisions, particularly the key points.

The workbook is structured so that after every question, the student has an opportunity to record his or her response and the corresponding code reference. The correct answers are indicated in the back of the workbook in the answer key.

This study companion was developed by Douglas W. Thornburg, AIA, C.B.O., for the 2000 *International Building Code*. In this publication, he has updated and revised the material based on the 2003 *International Building Code*. Mr. Thornburg is currently Director of Product Development for the International Code Council. In addition to authoring numerous educational texts and resource materials, he instructs seminars nationally on both the IBC and IRC. Mr. Thornburg has over 25 years experience in the application and enforcement of building codes.

Questions or comments concerning this workbook are encouraged. Please direct your comments to ICC at *studycompanion@iccsafe.org*.

INTERNATIONAL BUILDING CODE
Study Session 1
Chapters 1, 34 and 35 — Administration

OBJECTIVE: To obtain an understanding of the administrative provisions of the *International Building Code*, including the scope and purpose of the code, duties of the building official, issuance of permits, inspection procedures, special inspections, existing buildings and referenced standards.

REFERENCE: Chapters 1, 34 and 35, 2003 *International Building Code*

KEY POINTS:

- What is the purpose and scope of the *International Building Code*?
- What are the limitations for use of the *International Residential Code*®?
- What is the relationship between the *International Building Code* and the *International Existing Building Code*®?
- When materials, methods of construction or other requirements are specified differently in separate provisions, which requirement governs?
- When there is a conflict between a general requirement and a specific requirement, which provision is applicable?
- When do the provisions of the appendices apply?
- What are the powers and duties of the building official in regard to the application and interpretation of the code? Right of entry?
- Under which conditions may the building official grant modifications to the code?
- How may alternative materials, designs and methods of construction be approved?
- When is a permit required? What types of work are exempted from permits?
- Is work exempted from a permit required to comply with the provisions of the code?
- What is the process outlined for obtaining a permit?
- Which documents must be submitted as part of the permit application process? What information is required on the construction documents?
- Which conditions or circumstances would bring the validity of a permit into question?
- When does a permit expire? What must occur when a permit expires prior to completion of a building?
- For what is a design professional responsible? When is such an individual required?
- What types of inspections are specifically required by the code? When are inspections required?
- When is a certificate of occupancy required? For what reasons is revocation permitted?
- When may a temporary certificate of occupancy be issued?
- What is the purpose of a board of appeals? Who shall serve on the board?
- Which limitations are placed upon the authority of the board of appeals?
- When should a stop work order be issued?
- How must an existing building be viewed when additions or alterations are made?
- How are nonstructural repairs to an existing building to be handled? Glass replacement?
- What should happen when there is a change in use or occupancy of an existing building?
- How should moved structures be addressed?
- What accessibility issues are encountered when an existing building is altered or when its use changes?
- How can compliance alternatives be used to evaluate an existing building's degree of safety?
- What are referenced standards? How are they used in the IBC?

Topic: Scope
Reference: IBC 101.2

Category: Administration
Subject: General Requirements

Code Text: *The provisions of the* International Building Code *shall apply to the construction, alteration, movement, enlargement, replacement, repair, equipment, use and occupancy, location, maintenance, removal and demolition of every building or structure or any appurtenances connected or attached to such buildings or structures.* See exception for dwellings and existing buildings.

Discussion and Commentary: The *International Building Code* is intended to regulate the broad spectrum of construction activities associated with buildings and structures. General provisions allow for a comprehensive overview of regulations; however, where more specific circumstances exist, any applicable specific requirements will take precedence.

Fundamental purposes of the provisions of the *International Building Code*:

- Safety of building occupants
- Stop panic
- Safety of fire fighters and emergency responders
- Safety and protection of others' property
- Safety and protection of own property

The appendices of the *International Building Code* address a diverse number of issues that may be of value to a jurisdiction in developing a set of construction regulations. It should be noted that the provisions contained in the appendices do not apply unless specifically adopted.

Topic: Dwelling Units
Reference: IBC 101.2, Exception 1

Category: Administration
Subject: General Requirements

Code Text: *Detached one- and two-family dwellings and multiple single-family dwellings (town houses) not more than three stories above grade plane in height with a separate means of egress and their accessory structures shall comply with the* International Residential Code.

Discussion and Commentary: Many residential structures are exempt from the requirements of the *International Building Code* and are regulated instead by a separate and distinct document, the *International Residential Code®*. The IRC® contains prescriptive requirements for the construction of detached single-family dwellings, detached duplexes, townhouses and all structures accessory to such buildings. Limited to three stories in height with individual egress facilities, these residential buildings are fully regulated by the IRC for building, plumbing, mechanical, electrical and energy provisions.

In addition to the general requirements, a townhouse is also limited by definition in the IRC. To fall under the scope of the *International Residential Code,* each townhouse must be a single unit from the foundation to the roof, with at least two sides open to the exterior.

Topic: Existing Buildings
Reference: IBC 101.2, Exception 2

Category: Administration
Subject: General Requirements

Code Text: *Existing buildings undergoing repair, alterations or additions and change of occupancy shall be permitted to comply with the* International Existing Building Code.

Discussion and Commentary: As an alternative to IBC Chapter 34 for the regulation of work or an occupancy change in an existing building, the provisions of the *International Existing Building Code* (IEBC®) may be utilized. The IEBC establishes minimum regulations for existing buildings using prescriptive and performance-related provisions. It is founded on broad-based principles intended to encourage the use and reuse of existing buildings while requiring reasonable upgrades and improvements. The IEBC is fully compatible with all the *International Codes*® published by the International Code Council®. The scope of the code addresses various classifications of work including repair, three levels of alterations, change of occupancy, additions, historic buildings and relocated structures.

An important portion of the IEBC is Resource A, which provides guidelines on the determination of fire ratings for archaic materials and assemblies. In addition, two appendix chapters address seismic retrofit and supplementary accessibility requirements for existing buildings.

Topic: Application
Reference: IBC 101.2.1

Category: Administration
Subject: Appendix Chapters

Code Text: *Provisions in the appendices shall not apply unless specifically adopted.*

Discussion and Commentary: The appendix chapters of the IBC address subjects that have been deemed inappropriate as mandatory portions of the code. Rather, the appendices are optional, with each jurisdiction adopting all, some or none of the appendix chapters, depending on its needs for enforcement in any given area. There are various reasons why certain issues are found in the appendices. Often, the provisions are limited in application or interest. Some appendix chapters are merely extensions of requirements set forth in the body of the code. Others address issues that are often thought of as outside of the scope of a traditional building code. Whatever the reason, the appendix chapters are not applicable unless specifically adopted.

IBC Appendix Chapters

Appendix A	Employee Qualifications
Appendix B	Board of Appeals
Appendix C	Group U — Agricultural Buildings
Appendix D	Fire Districts
Appendix E	Supplementary Accessibility Requirements
Appendix F	Rodent Proofing
Appendix G	Flood-Resistant Construction
Appendix H	Signs
Appendix I	Patio Covers
Appendix J	Grading

Appendix chapters, where not adopted as a portion of a jurisdiction's building code, may still be of value in application of the code. Provisions in the appendices might provide some degree of assistance in evaluating proposed alternative designs, methods or materials of construction.

Topic: General Requirements
Reference: IBC 104.1

Category: Administration
Subject: Duties and Powers of Building Official

Code Text: *The building official is hereby authorized and directed to enforce the provisions of* the IBC. *The building official shall have the authority to render interpretations of* the IBC *and to adopt policies and procedures in order to clarify the application of its provisions. Such interpretations, policies and procedures shall be in compliance with the intent and purpose of* the IBC. *Such policies and procedures shall not have the effect of waiving requirements specifically provided for in* the IBC.

Discussion and Commentary: It is important that the building official be knowledgeable to the point of being able to rule on those issues that are not directly addressed or that are unclear in the code. The basis for such a determination, which often takes some research to discover, is the intent and purpose of the *International Building Code.*

City of (Jurisdiction)

Department of Building Safety

Name of individual

Job function

The individual identified on the badge is a duly authorized employee of the (Jurisdiction) and is a designated representative of the Department of Building Safety.

Valid through

Date

Building Official

Identification Card
Section 104.5

Although the IBC gives broad authority to the building official in interpreting the code, this authority also comes with great responsibility. The building official must restrict all decisions to the intent and purpose of the code, with the waiving of any requirements being strictly prohibited.

Topic: Alternate Materials
Reference: IBC 104.11

Category: Administration
Subject: Duties and Powers of Building Official

Code Text: *The provisions of* the IBC *are not intended to prevent the installation of any material or to prohibit any design or method of construction not specifically prescribed by* the IBC, *provided that any such alternative has been approved.*

Discussion and Commentary: The building official is granted broad authority in the acceptance of alternative materials, designs and methods of construction. Arguably the most important provision of the IBC, the intent is to implement the adoption of new technologies. Furthermore, it gives the code even more of a performance character. The provisions encourage state-of-the-art concepts in construction, design and materials, as long as they meet the performance level intended by the IBC.

Building official may approve alternative materials, design and methods of construction, if:

- Proposed alternative is satisfactory
- Proposed alternative complies with intent of code
- Material, method or work is equivalent in:
  (1) Quality
  (2) Strength
  (3) Effectiveness
  (4) Fire Resistance
  (5) Durability
  (6) Safety

Advisable for building official to:

- Require sufficient evidence or proof
- Record any action granting approval
- Enter information into the files

The building official should ensure that any necessary substantiating data or other evidence that shows the alternative to be equivalent in performance is submitted. Moreover, where tests are performed, reports of such tests must be retained by the building official.

Topic: Research Reports
Reference: IBC 104.11.1

Category: Administration
Subject: Duties and Powers of Building Official

Code Text: *Supporting data, where necessary to assist in the approval of materials or assemblies not specifically provided for in the* IBC, *shall consist of valid research reports from approved sources.*

Discussion and Commentary: The most familiar research reports are probably the "evaluation reports" that have been issued for years by the three former model code groups (BOCA, ICBO and SBCCI). These reports are currently considered ICC Evaluation Service Reports and are maintained by ICC Evaluation Service, Inc. ICC Evaluation Service Reports are developed based upon acceptance criteria for products that are alternatives to what is specified in the code and that are structural in nature and/or affect life-safety. These reports are made available to building regulators, contractors, specifiers, architects, engineers and anyone else with an interest in the building industry or construction.

ES REPORT™

ESR-####
Issued September 1, 2003
This report is subject to re-examination in one year.

ICC Evaluation Service, Inc.
www.icc-es.org

Copyright © 2003

Page 1 of 1

Although ICC Evaluation Service Reports are generally recognized nationally as valid reports developed by an approved source, the building official can recognize the evaluation of products, assemblies and systems by other third-party agencies having the necessary credentials.

Topic: Permits Required and Exempted
Reference: IBC 105.1, 105.2

Category: Administration
Subject: Permits

Code Text: *Any owner or authorized agent who intends to construct, enlarge, alter, repair, move, demolish, or change the occupancy of a building or structure . . . shall first make application to the building official and obtain the required permit.* See thirteen exceptions where a building permit is not required. *Exemptions from permit requirements of* the IBC *shall not be deemed to grant authorization for any work to be done in any manner in violation of the provisions of* the IBC *or any other laws or ordinances of this jurisdiction.*

Discussion and Commentary: Except in those few cases specifically listed, such as small accessory structures and finish work, all construction-related work requires a permit and is subject to subsequent inspections.

Work exempt from permit:

- One-story detached accessory buildings limited to 120 square feet
- Fences not over 6 feet in height
- Oil derricks
- Retaining walls limited to 4 feet in height, unless supporting a surcharge or impounding Class I, II or III-A liquids
- Water tanks supported directly on grade, limited to capacity of 5,000 gallons and a ratio of height to diameter not exceeding 2 to 1
- Sidewalks and driveways limited to 30 inches above grade and not part of an accessible route
- Painting, papering, carpeting, cabinets, counter tops and similar finish work
- Temporary motion picture, television and theater stage sets and scenery
- Prefabricated swimming pools accessory to a Group R-3 occupancy when capacity is limited to 5,000 gallons, depth limited to 24 inches and installed entirely above ground
- Shade cloth structures used for nursery or agricultural purposes
- Swings and other playground equipment accessory to detached one- and two-family dwellings
- Window awnings supported by an exterior wall in Groups R-3 and U, where the maximum projection is 54 inches
- Movable cases, counters and partitions limited to 5 feet 9 inches in height

---

Whether or not a building permit is required by the code, it is intended that all work be done in accordance with the code requirements. It is important that the owner is responsible for all construction being done properly and safely.

Topic: Required Inspections
Reference: IBC 109.1

Category: Administration
Subject: Inspections

Code Text: *Construction or work for which a permit is required shall be subject to inspection by the building official and such construction or work shall remain accessible and exposed for inspection purposes until approved. Approval as a result of an inspection shall not be construed to be an approval of a violation of the provisions of* the IBC *or of other ordinances of the jurisdiction.*

Discussion and Commentary: The inspection function is possibly the most critical activity in the entire code enforcement process. At the varied stages of construction, an inspector often performs the final check of the building for safety-related compliance. If necessary, the building official may require a preliminary inspection of the site, building or structure to gain information that may be of assistance in the issuance of a permit.

Required inspections (where applicable):

- Footing and foundation
- Concrete slab or under-floor
- Lowest floor elevation
- Frame
- Lath or gypsum board
- Fire-resistant penetrations
- Energy efficiency
- Others as required by the building official
- Special inspections
- Final

It may be necessary to have materials removed in order to provide inspection access or observation for a portion of the building. The responsibility rests with the permit applicant to make the work available for inspection, with no expenses to be borne by the jurisdiction.

Topic: Approval Required
Reference: IBC 109.6

Category: Administration
Subject: Inspections

Code Text: *Work shall not be done beyond the point indicated in each successive inspection without first obtaining the approval of the building official. The building official, upon notification, shall make the requested inspections and shall either indicate the portion of the construction that is satisfactory as completed, or notify the permit holder or his or her agent wherein the same fails to comply with* the IBC. *Any portions that do not comply shall be corrected and such portions shall not be covered or concealed until authorized by the building official.*

Discussion and Commentary: It is important that each successive inspection be approved prior to continuing further work. This practice helps to control the concealment of any work that must be inspected, resulting in the unnecessary removal of materials that might block access.

Any request for inspection is the responsibility of the building permit holders or their duly authorized agent. They must contact the building official when the work is ready for inspection, as well as provide access to that work.

Topic: Use and Occupancy
Reference: IBC 110.1

Category: Administration
Subject: Certificate of Occupancy

Code Text: *No building or structure shall be used or occupied, and no change in the existing occupancy classification of a building or structure or portion thereof shall be made until the building official has issued a certificate of occupancy therefor as provided herein. Issuance of a certificate of occupancy shall not be construed as an approval of a violation of the provisions of* the IBC *or of other ordinances of the jurisdiction.*

Discussion and Commentary: The certificate of occupancy is the tool with which the building official can regulate and control the uses and occupancies of the various buildings and structures within the jurisdiction. The code makes it unlawful to use or occupy a building unless a certificate of occupancy has been issued for that specific use.

Certificate of Occupancy

(Address of Structure)

This (applicable portion of structure) has been inspected for compliance with the laws and ordinances of (jurisdiction) and is hereby issued a Certificate of Occupancy

Building permit number __________

Applicable edition of code __________

Use and occupancy __________

Type of construction __________

Design occupant load __________

Sprinkler system required __________

Name and address of owner __________

Special conditions __________

Building Official __________

The building official is permitted to suspend or revoke a certificate of occupancy for any of the following reasons: (1) when the certificate is issued in error, (2) when incorrect information is supplied, or (3) when the building is in violation of the code.

Topic: Existing Buildings
Reference: IBC 3403.1

Category: Existing Structures
Subject: Additions, Alterations or Repairs

Code Text: *Additions or alterations any building or structure shall conform with the requirements of* the IBC *for new construction. Additions or alterations shall not be made to an existing building or structure which will cause the existing building or structure to be in violation of any provisions of* the IBC. *Portions of the structure not altered and not affected by the alteration are not required to comply with the code requirements for a new structure.*

Discussion and Commentary: Any construction that takes place on a building will necessitate compliance with the building code in effect at the time of the work. However, only those portions being remodeled or added need comply. Existing portions of the building where no work is being performed are exempt from the current code requirements.

Conformance with the code in effect is also mandated for a change in use or occupancy. When approved by the building official, full conformance is not required where it is determined that the new use is less of a life-safety and fire-safety hazard than the previous use.

Topic: Compliance
Reference: IBC 3410

Category: Existing Structures
Subject: Compliance Alternatives

Code Text: *The provisions of Section 3410 are intended to maintain or increase the current degree of public safety, health and general welfare in existing buildings while permitting repair, alteration, addition and a change of occupancy without requiring full compliance with Chapters 2 through 33, or Sections 3401.3 through 3407, except where compliance with other provisions of* the IBC *is specifically required in* Section 3410. *For repairs, alterations, additions and changes of occupancy to existing buildings that are evaluated in accordance with Section 3410, compliance with Section 3410 shall be accepted by the building official.*

Discussion and Commentary: A thorough investigation and evaluation of an existing building can be the basis for determining the level of compliance when an existing building is altered or repaired, or when the building or portion thereof undergoes a change in use. Based on the results of the evaluation process, it can be determined if the existing building, along with any modifications, is deemed to be in compliance with the IBC.

TABLE 3410.7
SUMMARY SHEET — BUILDING CODE

Existing occupancy ____________ Proposed occupancy ____________
Year building was constructed ____________ Number of stories ______ Height in feet ______
Type of construction ____________ Area per floor ____________
Percentage of open perimeter ______% Percentage of height reduction ______%
Completely suppressed: Yes ______ No ______ Corridor wall rating ____________
Compartmentation: Yes ______ No ______ Required door closers: Yes ______ No ______
Fire-resistance rating of vertical opening enclosures ____________
Type of HVAC system ____________, serving number of floors ______
Automatic fire detection: Yes ______ No ______, type and location ____________
Fire alarm system: Yes ______ No ______, type ____________
Smoke control: Yes ______ No ______, type ____________
Adequate exit routes: Yes ______ No ______ Dead ends: ______ Yes ______ No ______
Maximum exit access travel distance ______ Elevator controls: Yes ______ No ______
Means of egress emergency lighting: Yes ______ No ______ Mixed occupancies: Yes ______ No ______

SAFETY PARAMETERS	FIRE SAFETY (FS)	MEANS OF EGRESS (ME)	GENERAL SAFETY (GS)
3410.6.1 Building Height 3410.6.2 Building Area 3410.6.3 Compartmentation			
3410.6.4 Tenant and Dwelling Unit Separations 3410.6.5 Corridor Walls 3410.6.6 Vertical Openings			
3410.6.7 HVAC Systems 3410.6.8 Automatic Fire Detection 3410.6.9 Fire Alarm System			
3410.6.10 Smoke control 3410.6.11 Means of Egress 3410.6.12 Dead ends	**** **** ****		
3410.6.13 Maximum Exit Access Travel Distance 3410.6.14 Elevator Control 3410.6.15 Means of Egress Emergency Lighting	**** ****		
3410.6.16 Mixed Occupancies 3410.6.17 Automatic Sprinklers 3410.6.18 Incidental Use		**** ÷2 =	
Building score — total value			

****No applicable value to be inserted.

In evaluating an existing building undergoing a change in use, alteration or repair, the process addresses three issues: fire safety, means of egress and general safety. Each category must be deemed satisfactory in order for the existing building to be considered compliant.

Topic: Application
Reference: IBC Chapter 35

Category: Referenced Standards
Subject: Standards

Code Text: *This chapter lists the standards that are referenced in various sections of the IBC. The standards are listed herein by the promulgation agency of the standard, the standard identification, the effective date and title, and the section or sections of the IBC that reference the standard. The application of the referenced standards shall be as specified in Section 102.4.*

Discussion and Commentary: Limited in their scope, standards define more precisely the general provisions set forth in the code. The *International Building Code* references several hundred different standards, each addressing a specific aspect of building design or construction. In general terms, the standards referenced by the IBC are primarily materials, testing, installation or engineering standards.

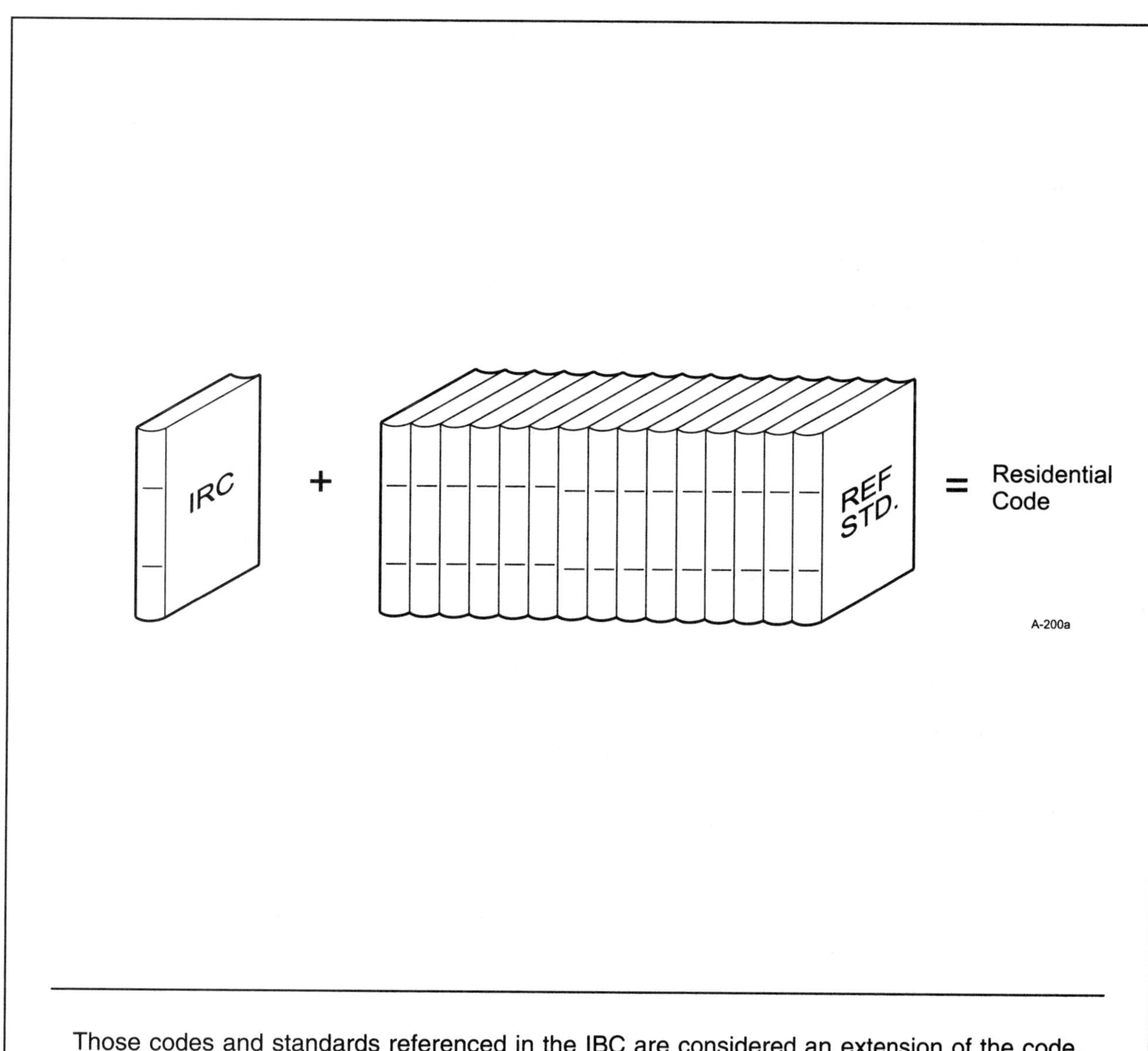

Those codes and standards referenced in the IBC are considered an extension of the code, but only to the degree prescribed by the IBC. Where there is a conflict between the provisions in the IBC and any referenced code or standard, the provisions of the IBC apply.

QUIZ

Study Session 1 — Chapters 1, 34 and 35

I. Multiple Choice

1. The *International Residential Code* is applicable to townhouses a maximum of __________ stories above grade plane in height and provided with separate means of egress.

   a. one
   b. two
   c. three
   d. four

   Reference_______________

2. Provisions of the appendix do not apply unless __________.

   a. specified in the code
   b. applicable to unique conditions
   c. specifically adopted
   d. relevant to fire or life safety

   Reference_______________

3. If there is a conflict in the code between a general requirement and a specific requirement, the __________ requirement shall apply.

   a. general
   b. specific
   c. least restrictive
   d. most restrictive

   Reference_______________

4. The __________ is considered by the code as the term to describe the individual in charge of the department of building safety.

   a. building official
   b. code official
   c. code administrator
   d. chief building inspector

   Reference_______________

5. The building official has the authority to __________ the provisions of the code.

   a. ignore
   b. waive
   c. modify
   d. interpret

   Reference_______________

6. Used materials may be utilized under which of the following conditions?

a. They meet the requirements for new materials.
b. They are limited to 10% of the total materials.
c. Used materials may never be used in new construction.
d. A representative sampling is tested for compliance.

Reference_______________

7. The building official has the authority to grant modifications to the code __________.

a. for only those issues not affecting life safety or fire safety
b. for individual cases where the strict letter of the code is impractical
c. where the intent and purpose of the code cannot be met
d. related only to administrative functions

Reference_______________

8. In order for an alternative material, design or method of construction to be considered acceptable, it must be equivalent to the code based on all but which of the following criteria?

a. durability
b. economics
c. strength
d. fire resistance

Reference_______________

9. Tests performed by __________ may be required by the building official where there is insufficient evidence of code compliance.

a. the owner
b. the contractor
c. an approved agency
d. a design professional

Reference_______________

10. A permit is not required for the construction of a one-story detached accessory structure when it has a maximum floor area of __________ square feet.

a. 100
b. 120
c. 150
d. 200

Reference_______________

11. Movable cases, counters and partitions are exempt from a building permit where they have a maximum height of __________.

a. 5 feet, 0 inches
b. 5 feet, 6 inches
c. 5 feet, 9 inches
d. 6 feet, 0 inches

Reference_______________

12. Unless an extension is authorized, a permit becomes invalid when work on the site does not commence within __________ after permit issuance.

a. 90 days
b. 180 days
c. one year
d. two years

Reference_______________

13. The building permit, or a copy of the permit, shall be kept __________ until completion of the project.

a. at the job site
b. by the permit applicant
c. by the contractor
d. by the design professional in responsible charge

Reference_______________

14. When a building permit is issued, the construction documents shall be approved as __________.

a. "Approved for Construction"
b. "Conditional Approval"
c. "Accepted as Reviewed"
d. "Reviewed for Code Compliance"

Reference_______________

15. Unless otherwise mandated by state or local laws, the approved construction documents shall be retained by the building official for a minimum of __________ from the date of completion of the permitted work.

a. 90 days
b. 180 days
c. one year
d. two years

Reference_______________

16. Which one of the following inspections is not specifically identified by the *International Building Code* as a required inspection?

a. footing inspection
b. frame inspection
c. fire-resistive construction inspection
d. energy efficiency inspection

Reference_______________

17. Whose duty is it to provide access to work in need of inspection?

a. the permit holder
b. the owner
c. the contractor
d. the owner's agent

Reference_______________

18. The certificate of occupancy shall contain all of the following information except:

a. the name of the owner
b. the name of the building official
c. the type of construction
d. the maximum height and area

Reference_______________

19. A temporary certificate of occupancy is valid for what maximum period of time?

a. 30 days
b. 60 days
c. 180 days
d. a period set by the building official

Reference_______________

20. The board of appeals is not authorized to rule on an appeal based on a claim that _________.

a. the provisions of the code do not fully apply
b. a code requirement should be waived
c. the rules have been incorrectly interpreted
d. a better form of construction is provided

Reference_______________

21. Unless in compliance with the code for new structures, alterations to an existing structure are permitted to increase the force in any structural element by a maximum of ___________percent.

a. 0, no increase is permitted
b. 5
c. 10
d. 25

Reference_______________

22. Where permitted, a fire escape must support a minimum live load of __________ pounds per square foot.

a. 40
b. 50
c. 100
d. 125

Reference_______________

23. Where alterations occur to an existing building, an access ramp with a slope of 1:8 is permitted where necessitated by space limitations, provided the maximum rise of the ramp is __________ inches.

a. 3
b. 6
c. 12
d. 30

Reference_______________

24. Which of the following categories is not specifically addressed in the evaluation of buildings under IBC Section 3410 for compliance alternatives?

a. fire safety
b. means of egress
c. general safety
d. structural safety

Reference_______________

25. ACI 318-02 is a referenced standard addressing __________.

a. structural concrete
b. wood construction
c. structural steel buildings
d. gypsum board

Reference_______________

26. A permit is required for a prefabricated above-ground swimming pool that is a minimum of _____ in depth, or where the pool has a minimum capacity of more than _____.

a. 18 inches; 4,000 gallons
b. 24 inches; 5,000 gallons
c. 30 inches; 5,000 gallons
d. 36 inches; 6,000 gallons

Reference_______________

27. The installation of window awnings is exempt from a permit, provided the awnings each project a maximum of _____ inches from the exterior wall.

a. 30
b. 36
c. 48
d. 54

Reference_______________

28. A permit may be suspended or revoked for all of the following reasons, except _____.

a. where it is issued in error
b. on the basis of incomplete information
c. where issued in violation of a jurisdictional ordinance
d. where other permits by the contractor have been voided

Reference_______________

29. Unless extended by the building official, what is the maximum time period granted for a permit issued on a temporary structure?

a. 90 days
b. 180 days
c. 1 year
d. 2 years

Reference_______________

30. The provisions of Section 3410 for compliance alternatives are applicable to all of the following occupancy classifications, except _____.

a. Group A
b. Group E
c. Group I
d. Group R

Reference_______________

INTERNATIONAL BUILDING CODE
Study Session 2
Chapter 3 — Use and Occupancy Classification

OBJECTIVE: To gain an understanding of how an occupancy is classified based on its intended use and how a building with mixed uses is addressed.

REFERENCE: Chapter 3, 2003 *International Building Code*

KEY POINTS:

- What are the ten specific occupancy groups?
- How is an occupancy that is not specifically described to be classified?
- Which types of activities are considered assembly uses? What is their general classification?
- How are small assembly uses classified where accessory to a different occupancy?
- What is the classification for restaurants and cafes? Theaters? Churches, conference rooms and libraries? Arenas? Grandstands?
- What is the primary use classified as Group B?
- Group E occupancies describe educational uses for individuals of what age group?
- Which types of day-care are considered Group E occupancies?
- Manufacturing operations fall into what occupancy group? How do the two divisions of factory-use differ from each other?
- What type of operations or materials cause a use to be considered Group H?
- How does the amount of hazardous materials affect the occupancy classification?
- Which occupancies address physical hazards? Health hazards? Semiconductor fabrication facilities?
- Which characteristics are typical of a Group I occupancy?
- In which institutional occupancies are the occupants considered incapable of self-preservation?
- For which types of institutional uses may the *International Residential Code* be utilized?
- What general type of building is considered a Group M occupancy?
- How are residential occupancies classified?
- What do storage occupancy classifications have in common with those of manufacturing uses?
- What is a utility occupancy? How does its classification differ from that of other occupancies?
- What is an incidental use area? How must such an area be separated from the remainder of the building? When is sprinkler protection required?
- What is the option to utilizing Table 302.1.1 for the separation or protection of incidental use areas?
- What is an accessory use area? What benefit is derived from such a designation?
- Which options are available for addressing multiple occupancies within a building?
- How is a mixed-use building regulated when the uses are not physically separated from each other with fire-resistance-rated construction?
- When is an occupancy separation needed? What occupancy must always be isolated from other uses by an occupancy separation?
- How is the fire-resistance rating for an occupancy separation determined? How does the presence of an automatic sprinkler system affect the required rating?
- Under which conditions may the occupancy separation be eliminated at incidental storage areas?
- How is a space that is intended to be occupied at different times for different purposes to be addressed?
- What level of separation is required between a commercial kitchen and the restaurant seating area it serves?

Topic: Occupancy Groups
Reference: IBC 302.1

Category: Occupancy Classification
Subject: Classification

Code Text: *Structures or portions of structures shall be classified with respect to occupancy in one or more of the groups listed. Where a structure is proposed for a purpose which is not specifically provided for in the code, such structure shall be classified in the group which the occupancy most nearly resembles, according to the fire safety and relative hazard involved.*

Discussion and Commentary: The perils contemplated by the occupancy groupings are divided into two general categories: those related to people and those related to content. People-related hazards include the number and density of the occupants, their age or mobility, and their awareness of surrounding conditions. Content-related hazards include the storage and use of hazardous materials, as well as the presence of large quantities of combustible materials.

Assembly	Business
Educational	Factory
Hazardous	Institutional
Mercantile	Residential
Storage	Utility

Proper occupancy classification is critical in making appropriate code determinations throughout a project. In the classification process, the building official must use appropriate judgment in the determination of the potential hazards of an affected occupancy.

Topic: Assembly Uses
Reference: IBC 303

Category: Occupancy Classification
Subject: Group A Occupancies

Code Text: *Assembly Group A occupancy includes, among others, the use of a building or structure, or a portion thereof, for the gathering together of persons for purposes such as civic, social or religious functions, recreation, food or drink consumption or awaiting transportation. A room or space used for assembly purposes by less than 50 persons and accessory to another occupancy shall be included as a part of that occupancy.*

Discussion and Commentary: The conditions related to a typical Group A occupancy suggest a moderate hazard use. This use often includes sizable numbers of people who are generally mobile and aware of the surrounding conditions. The extremely high occupant density level often present in an assembly occupancy is what distinguishes the Group A from other occupancies.

Group A-1

Motion picture theaters
Theaters
Symphony and concert halls

Group A-2

Banquet halls
Night clubs
Restaurants
Taverns

Group A-3

Amusement arcades
Art galleries
Bowling alleys
Churches
Community halls
Conference rooms
Exhibition halls
Lecture halls
Libraries
Museums
Passenger stations

Group A-4

Arenas
Skating rinks
Swimming pools
Tennis courts

Group A-5

Amusement park structures
Bleachers
Grandstands
Stadiums

Unique conditions are represented by the classifications of Groups A-1, A-2, A-4 and A-5. However, the category Group A-3 includes a variety of broad and diverse assembly uses. It is not uncommon to find high combustible loading in Group A-3 occupancies.

Topic: Business Uses
Reference: IBC 304

Category: Occupancy Classification
Subject: Group B Occupancies

Code Text: *Business Group B occupancy includes, among others, the use of a building or structure, or a portion thereof, for office, professional or service-type transactions, including storage of records and accounts.*

Discussion and Commentary: Business occupancies typically have a low to moderate fire load, a moderate density level, and occupants who are usually mobile and have a general awareness of the surrounding conditions. As such, business occupancies are grouped into a classification based upon a relatively moderate fire hazard level. Group B occupancies are not restricted by occupant load, as the number of people in a business use, such as an office, can range from one person to thousands of people.

Group B
Animal hospitals, kennels and pounds Banks Barber and beauty shops Car wash Civic administration Clinic-outpatient Educational occupancies above the 12th grade Laboratories; testing and research Motor vehicle showrooms Post offices Print shops Professional services Radio and television stations

As is the case for many of the occupancy groups, a review of the building's intended uses is necessary to determine the amount of hazardous materials that may be stored, handled or used. If the amounts exceed a specified quantity, then a Group H classification will be in order.

Topic: Educational Uses
Reference: IBC 305

Category: Occupancy Classification
Subject: Group E Occupancies

Code Text: *Educational Group E occupancy includes, among others, the use of a building or structure, or a portion thereof, by six or more persons at any one time for educational purposes through the 12th grade. The use of a building or structure, or portion thereof, for educational, supervision or personal care services for more than five children older than $2^1/_2$ years of age, shall be classified as a Group E occupancy.*

Discussion and Commentary: Educational occupancies address classroom uses for students of high school age and younger. Education facilities limited to use by older students, such as college classrooms, are classified as Group B occupancies; however, a Group A classification should be considered for lecture halls and similar large occupant load spaces.

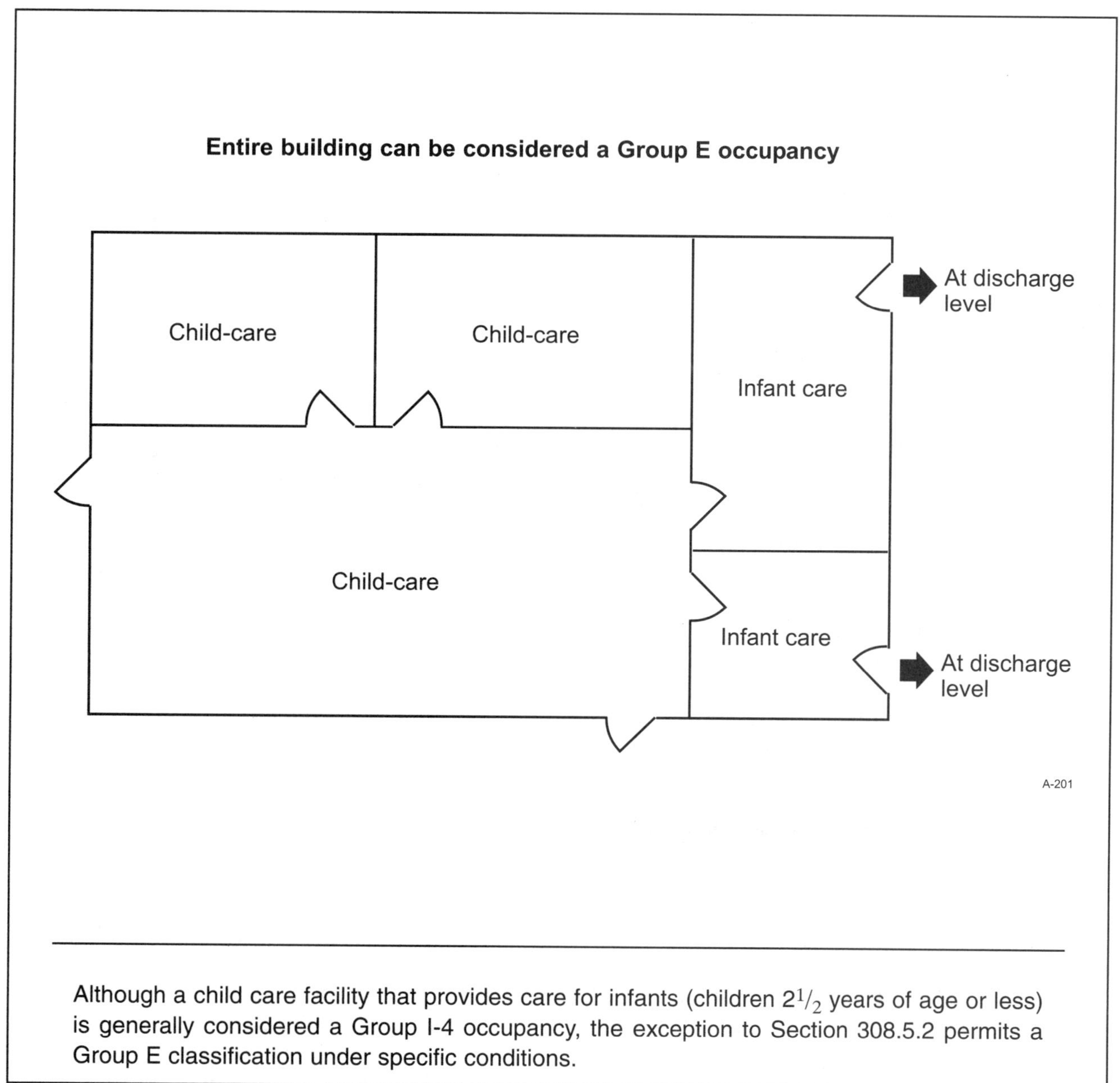

Although a child care facility that provides care for infants (children $2^1/_2$ years of age or less) is generally considered a Group I-4 occupancy, the exception to Section 308.5.2 permits a Group E classification under specific conditions.

Topic: Factory Uses
Reference: IBC 306

Category: Occupancy Classification
Subject: Group F Occupancies

Code Text: *Factory Industrial Group F occupancy includes, among others, the use of a building or structure, or a portion thereof, for assembling, disassembling, fabricating, finishing, manufacturing, packaging, repair or processing operations that are not classified as a Group H hazardous or Group S storage occupancy.*

Discussion and Commentary: Although the potential hazard and fire severity varies among the many uses categorized as Group F Occupancies, the uses still share elements in common. The occupants are adults who are awake and who generally have enough familiarity with the premises to be able to exit the building with reasonable efficiency. The presence of combustible materials in the industrial process causes a classification of Group F-1, which is by far the most common factory use.

Group F-1
Aircraft
Appliances
Automobiles
Bakeries
Business Machines
Carpets and rugs
Clothing
Electric generation plants
Electronics
Food processing
Furniture
Laundries
Millwork
Paper mills or products
Plastic products
Printing or publishing
Refuse incineration
Textiles
Woodworking

Group F-2
Brick and masonry
Ceramic products
Foundries
Glass products
Gypsum
Ice
Metal products

Classification as a Group F-2 occupancy is strictly limited because of the restrictions placed on such uses. The fabrication or manufacture of noncombustible materials, as well as the finishing, packaging or processing operations, cannot involve a significant fire hazard.

Topic: High-hazard Uses
Reference: IBC 307

Category: Occupancy Classification
Subject: Group H Occupancies

Code Text: *High-hazard Group H occupancy includes, among others, the use of a building or structure, or a portion thereof, that involves the manufacturing, processing, generation or storage of materials that constitute a physical or health hazard in quantities in excess of those found in Tables 307.7(1) and 307.7(2).*

Discussion and Commentary: There is only one fundamental type of Group H occupancy—that which is designated based solely on excessive quantities of hazardous materials contained therein. The quantities of hazardous materials that necessitate a Group H classification vary, based on the type, quantity, condition (use or storage) and environment of the materials. Where the use does not exceed the maximum allowable quantities set forth in the code, a classification other than Group H is appropriate.

Where Hazardous Materials and Processes are Involved

References

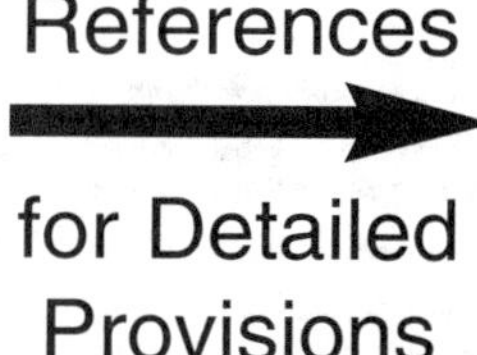

for Detailed Provisions

Although the *International Building Code* is limited to general construction regulations and occupancy-specific requirements, the *International Fire Code* sets forth special detailed provisions relating to specific materials and the specific conditions of storage, use and handling.

Topic: Exceptions to Group H
Reference: IBC 307.9

Category: Occupancy Classification
Subject: Group H Occupancies

Code Text: *The following shall not be classified in Group H, but shall be classified in the occupancy which they most nearly resemble.* See a listing of fifteen conditions under which a Group H occupancy is not warranted. *Hazardous materials in any quantity shall conform to the requirements of the* IBC, *including Section 414, and the* International Fire Code.

Discussion and Commentary: Although some degree of hazardous materials is found in most buildings, the occupancy is designated as Group H only where the quantities are excessive or the hazards are not adequately addressed. The most common condition for a non-H classification is where the amount of hazardous materials contained in the building do not exceed the maximum allowable quantities shown in Table 307.7(1) for physical hazards and Table 307.7(2) for health hazards. Footnotes to both tables can be used to increase the permitted quantities.

[F] TABLE 307.7(1)—continued
MAXIMUM ALLOWABLE QUANTITY PER CONTROL AREA OF HAZARDOUS MATERIALS POSING A PHYSICAL HAZARD[a, j, m]

MATERIAL	CLASS	GROUP WHEN THE MAXIMUM ALLOWABLE QUANTITY IS EXCEEDED	STORAGE[b]			USE-CLOSED SYSTEMS[b]			USE-OPEN SYSTEMS[b]	
			Solid pounds (cubic feet)	Liquid gallons (pounds)	Gas (cubic feet at NTP)	Solid pounds (cubic feet)	Liquid gallons (pounds)	Gas (cubic feet at NTP)	Solid pounds (cubic feet)	Liquid gallons (pounds)
Pyrophoric material	N/A	H-2	4[c, g]	(4)[c, g]	50[c, g]	1[g]	(1)[g]	10[c, g]	0	0
Unstable (reactive)	4	H-1	1[c, g]	(1)[c, g]	10[d, g]	0.25[g]	(0.25)[g]	2[c, g]	0.25[g]	(0.25)[g]
	3	H-1 or H-2	5[d, e]	(5)[d, e]	50[d, e]	1[d]	(1)	10[d, e]	1[d]	(1)[d]
	2	H-3	50[d, e]	(50)[d, e]	250[d, e]	50[d]	(50)[d]	250[d, e]	10[d]	(10)[d]
	1	N/A	NL	NL	N/L	NL	N/L	NL	NL	NL
Water reactive	3	H-2	5[d, e]	(5)[d, e]	N/A	5[d]	(5)[d]	N/A	1[d]	(1)[d]
	2	H-3	50[d, e]	(50)[d, e]	N/A	50[d]	(50)[d]	N/A	10[d]	(10)[d]
	1	N/A	NL	NL	N/A	NL	NL	N/A	NL	NL

For SI: 1 cubic foot = 0.023 m^3, 1 pound = 0.454 kg, 1 gallon = 3.785 L.
NL = Not Limited; N/A = Not Applicable; UD = Unclassified Detonable
a. For use of control areas, see Section 414.2.
b. The aggregate quantity in use and storage shall not exceed the quantity listed for storage.
c. The quantities of alcoholic beverages in retail and wholesale sales occupancies shall not be limited providing the liquids are packaged in individual containers not exceeding 1.3 gallons. In retail and wholesale sales occupancies, the quantities of medicines, foodstuffs, consumer or industrial products, and cosmetics containing not more than 50 percent by volume of water-miscible liquids with the remainder of the solutions not being flammable, shall not be limited, provided that such materials are packaged in individual containers not exceeding 1.3 gallons.
d. Maximum allowable quantities shall be increased 100 percent in buildings equipped throughout with an automatic sprinkler system in accordance with Section 903.3.1.1. Where Note e also applies, the increase for both notes shall be applied accumulatively.
e. Quantities shall be increased 100 percent when stored in approved cabinets, gas cabinets, exhausted enclosures or safety cans as specified in the *International Fire Code*. Where Note d also applies, the increase for both notes shall be applied accumulatively.
f. The permitted quantities shall not be limited in a building equipped throughout with an automatic sprinkler system in accordance with Section 903.3.1.1.
g. Permitted only in buildings equipped throughout with an automatic sprinkler system in accordance with Section 903.3.1.1.
h. Containing not more than the maximum allowable quantity per control area of Class IA, IB or IC flammable liquids.
i. Inside a building, the maximum capacity of a combustible liquid storage system that is connected to a fuel-oil piping system shall be 660 gallons provided such system conforms to the *International Fire Code*.
j. Quantities in parenthesis indicate quantity units in parenthesis at the head of each column.
k. A maximum quantity of 200 pounds of solid or 20 gallons of liquid Class 3 oxidizers is allowed when such materials are necessary for maintenance purposes, operation or sanitation of equipment. Storage containers and the manner of storage shall be approved.
l. Net weight of the pyrotechnic composition of the fireworks. Where the net weight of the pyrotechnic composition of the fireworks is not known, 25 percent of the gross weight of the fireworks, including packaging, shall be used.
m. For storage and display quantities in Group M and storage quantities in Group S occupancies complying with Section 414.2.4, see Table 414.2.4.

Where one of the fifteen exceptions is applied, the classification is based on the general use. For example, a warehouse containing quantities below the maximum allowable would simply be classified as Group S-1. A manufacturing facility would be classified as a Group F-1 occupancy.

Topic: Institutional Uses
Reference: IBC 308

Category: Occupancy Classification
Subject: Group I Occupancies

Code Text: *Institutional Group I occupancy includes among others, the use of a building or structure, or a portion thereof, in which people are cared for or live in a supervised environment, having physical limitations because of health or age are harbored for medical treatment or other care or treatment, or in which people are detained for penal or correctional purposes or in which the liberty of the occupants is restricted.*

Discussion and Commentary: The institutional uses classified as Group I occupancies are of three broad types. The first is a facility in which care is provided for the very young, sick or injured. The second category includes those facilities in which the personal liberties of the inmates or residents are restricted. The primary hazard is people related. Thirdly, supervised care facilities are regulated. Though the hazard due to combustible contents is quite low, the occupants' lack of mobility limits their egress ability.

Group I-1

Residential board and care facilities
Assisted living facilities
Halfway houses
Group homes
Congregate care facilities
Social rehabilitation facilities
Alcohol and drug centers
Convalescent facilities

Group I-2

Hospitals
Nursing homes
Mental hospitals
Detoxification facilities
Infant care (24-hour basis)

Group I-3

Prisons
Jails
Reformatories
Detention centers
Correctional centers
Prerelease centers

Group I-4

Custodial care facilities
(less than 24 hours)

Where the number of children, patients or residents in institutional uses is five or less, the hazards are similar in nature to a residential use. In most cases, an institutional facility with such a low occupant load would be considered a Group R-3 occupancy.

Topic: Mercantile Uses
Reference: IBC 309

Category: Occupancy Classification
Subject: Group M Occupancies

Code Text: *Mercantile Group M occupancy includes, among others, buildings and structures or a portion thereof, for the display and sale of merchandise, and involves stocks of goods, wares or merchandise incidental to such purposes and accessible to the public.*

Discussion and Commentary: A Group M occupancy is a retail or wholesale facility, or a store. An entire building can be classified as a Group M occupancy, such as a department store, or a portion of a building can be considered a mercantile use, such as the sales room in a manufacturing facility. A service station, including a canopy over the pump islands, is also classified as a Group M occupancy. In limited instances, a sales operation is designated as a Group B occupancy, as in the case of automobile showrooms.

Group M
Department stores Drug stores Markets Motor fuel-dispensing facilities Retail or wholesale stores Sales rooms

When classifying the occupancy of a storage area accessory to the sales area in a retail store, it is appropriate to apply the provisions that address the specific hazards of the use. In most situations, it is appropriate to classify the incidental storage area as a Group S-1 occupancy.

Topic: Residential Uses
Reference: IBC 310

Category: Occupancy Classification
Subject: Group R Occupancies

Code Text: *Residential Group R occupancy includes, among others, the use of a building or structure, or a portion thereof, for sleeping purposes when not classed as an Institutional Group I.*

Discussion and Commentary: Residential occupancies are characterized by: (1) their use by people for living and sleeping purposes, (2) a relatively low potential fire severity, and (3) the worst fire record of all structure types. Because occupants of these types of buildings spend up to one-third of each day sleeping, there is a high potential of a fire to rage out of control before the occupants awaken. After awakening, the residents will typically be disoriented for a short period of time, further decreasing the opportunity for immediate egress.

Group R-1

Boarding houses (transient)
Hotels
Motels

Group R-2

Apartment houses
Boarding houses (not transient)
Convents
Dormitories
Fraternities
Sororities
Monasteries
Vacation timeshare properties

Group R-3

One-family and two-family dwellings (unless regulated by IRC)
Adult care facilities (5 or fewer)
Child care facilities (5 or fewer)

Group R-4

Residential care facilities (6-16 occupants)
Assisted living facilities (6-16 occupants)

Detached one- and two-family dwellings, as well as townhouses, are not regulated by the *International Building Code* when limited to the conditions of the exception to Section 101.2. They are to be designed and constructed in accordance with the *International Residential Code.*

Topic: Storage Uses
Reference: IBC 311

Category: Occupancy Classification
Subject: Group S Occupancies

Code Text: *Storage Group S occupancy includes among others, the use of a building or structure, or a portion thereof, for storage that is not classified as a hazardous occupancy.*

Discussion and Commentary: Where a warehouse or other storage facility does not contain significant amounts of hazardous commodities (as determined by Section 307), it should be considered a Group S occupancy. A facility used for the storage of combustible goods is classified as Group S-1, whereas a Group S-2 occupancy shall be used only for the storage of noncombustible materials. If it is reasonable to believe that a storage building will house combustible goods for any significant period of time, it would be appropriate to consider the structure a Group S-1 occupancy, designed and constructed accordingly.

Group S-1
Aerosols, Level 2 and Level 3
Aircraft repair hangar
Bags; cloth, burlap, paper
Belting; canvas, leather
Books
Paper in rolls
Cardboard and cardboard boxes
Clothing
Furniture
Grains
Lumber
Motor vehicle repair garages
Tires, bulk storage of
Tobacco, cigars, cigarettes
Upholstery and mattresses

Group S-2
Aircraft hangar
Asbestos
Cement in bags
Chalk and crayons
Dairy products
Dry cell batteries
Electric motors
Food products
Fresh fruits and vegetables
Frozen foods
Glass
Gypsum board
Meats
Metals
Open parking garages
Enclosed parking garages

Although the goods being stored in a Group S-2 occupancy must be noncombustible, the code permits a limited amount of combustibles in the packaging or support materials. Wood pallets, paper cartons, paper wrappings, plastic trim and film wrapping are permitted for such purposes.

Topic: Utility and Miscellaneous Uses
Reference: IBC 312

Category: Occupancy Classification
Subject: Group U Occupancies

Code Text: *Buildings and structures of an accessory character and miscellaneous structures not classified in any specific occupancy shall be constructed, equipped and maintained to conform to the requirements of the code commensurate with the fire and life hazard incidental to their occupancy.*

Discussion and Commentary: Those structures not ordinarily occupied by people are classified as Group U occupancies. The fire load in these structures varies considerably but is usually not excessive. Because these types of uses are not normally occupied, the concern for fire severity is not very great, and as a group they constitute a low hazard. Several of the structures regulated as Group U occupancies are never occupied, such as fences, towers and tanks.

Group U
Agricultural buildings
Barns
Carports
Fences more than 6 feet in height
Greenhouses
Livestock shelters
Private garages
Retaining walls
Sheds
Stables
Tanks
Towers

Private garages and carports classified as Group U occupancies are generally limited to 1,000 square feet and one story in height. However, such structures are permitted to be 3,000 square feet where no repair work is done and no fuel is dispensed. The exterior wall is further regulated.

Topic: Incidental Use Areas
Reference: IBC 302.1.1

Category: Occupancy Classification
Subject: Classification

Code Text: *Spaces which are incidental to the main occupancy shall be separated or protected, or both, in accordance with Table 302.1.1 or the building shall be classified as a mixed occupancy and comply with Section 302.3. Areas that are incidental to the main occupancy shall be classified in accordance with the main occupancy of the portion of the building in which the incidental use area is located.* See exception for incidental use areas within dwelling units.

Discussion and Commentary: It is common to find uses that are typical of the general occupancy classification of the building, yet which create a hazard different from the other hazards found in the occupancy. An example would be a chemistry laboratory classroom in a high school building. The code addresses such conditions by requiring incidental areas to be separated from the remainder of the building with fire-resistance-rated construction, or to be protected with a fire-extinguishing system. As an option, the provisions for a mixed-occupancy building could apply.

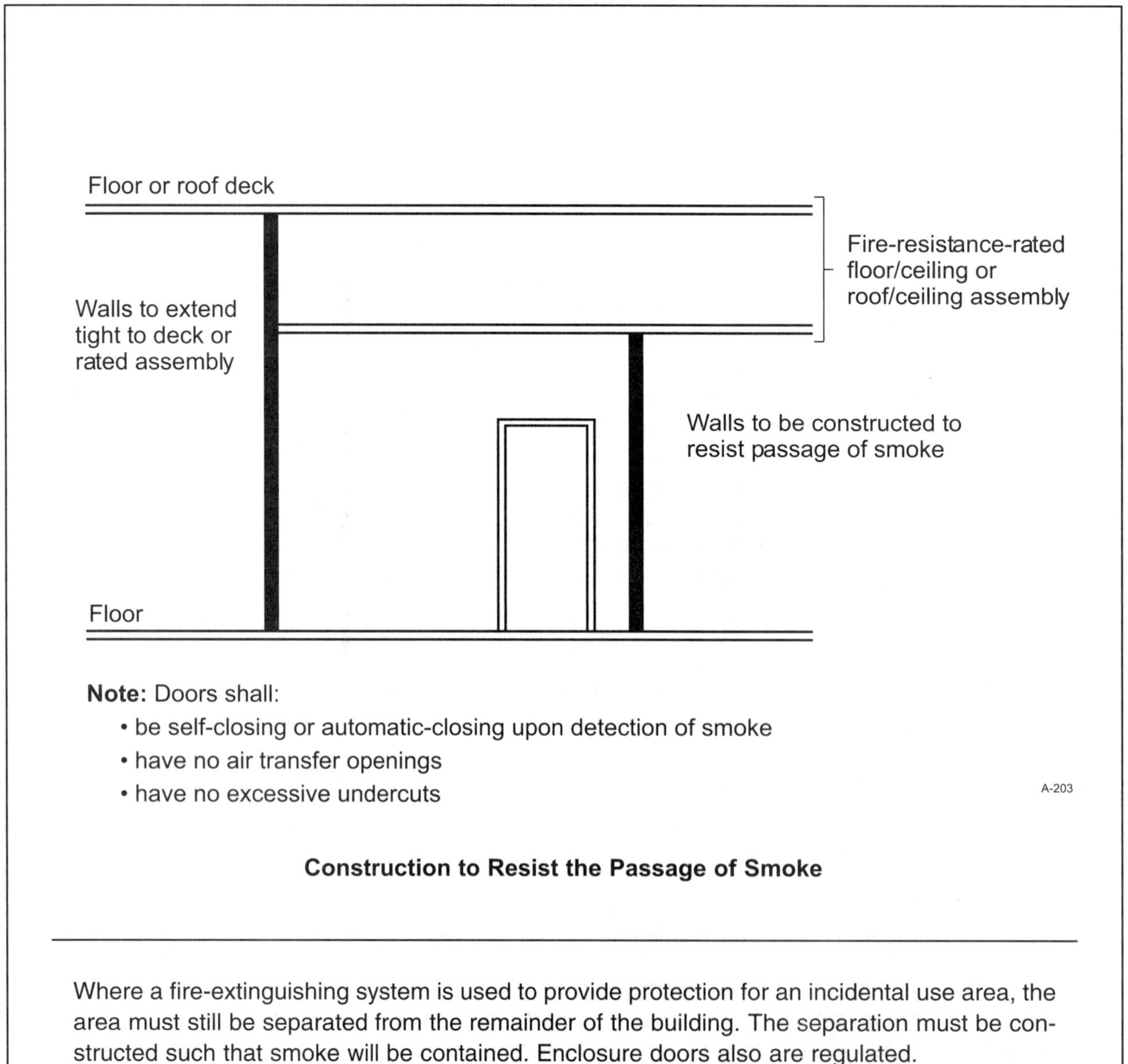

Construction to Resist the Passage of Smoke

Where a fire-extinguishing system is used to provide protection for an incidental use area, the area must still be separated from the remainder of the building. The separation must be constructed such that smoke will be contained. Enclosure doors also are regulated.

Topic: Incidental Use Areas
Reference: IBC 302.1.1.1, Table 302.1.1

Category: Occupancy Classification
Subject: Classification

Code Text: *Where Table 302.1.1 requires a fire-resistance-rated separation, the incidental use area shall be separated from the remainder of the building with a fire barrier. Where Table 302.1.1 permits an automatic fire-extinguishing system without a fire barrier, the incidental use area shall be separated by construction capable of resisting the passage of smoke.*

Discussion and Commentary: In utilizing Table 302.1.1, it is common that two options are available for addressing rooms or areas considered incidental use areas. A fire barrier may often be used to isolate the specific hazard from the remainder of the building. As an alternative, a sprinkler system or other fire-extinguishing system may be used to limit any fire in the incidental use area to that space only. By incorporating smoke containment construction, little of any smoke created would be transferred to other portions of the building.

TABLE 302.1.1
INCIDENTAL USE AREAS

ROOM OR AREA	SEPARATION[a]
Furnace room where any piece of equipment is over 400,000 Btu per hour input	1 hour or provide automatic fire-extinguishing system
Rooms with any boiler over 15 psi and 10 horsepower	1 hour or provide automatic fire-extinguishing system
Refrigerant machinery rooms	1 hour or provide automatic sprinkler system
Parking garage (Section 406.2)	2 hours; or 1 hour and provide automatic fire-extinguishing system
Hydrogen cut-off rooms	1-hour fire barriers and floor/ceiling assemblies in Group B, F, H, M, S and U occupancies. 2-hour fire barriers and floor/ceiling assemblies in Group A, E, I and R occupancies.
Incinerator rooms	2 hours and automatic sprinkler system
Paint shops, not classified as Group H, located in occupancies other than Group F	2 hours; or 1 hour and provide automatic fire-extinguishing system
Laboratories and vocational shops, not classified as Group H, located in Group E or I-2 occupancies	1 hour or provide automatic fire-extinguishing system
Laundry rooms over 100 square feet	1 hour or provide automatic fire-extinguishing system
Storage rooms over 100 square feet	1 hour or provide automatic fire-extinguishing system
Group I-3 cells equipped with padded surfaces	1 hour
Group I-2 waste and linen collection rooms	1 hour
Waste and linen collection rooms over 100 square feet	1 hour or provide automatic fire-extinguishing system
Stationary lead-acid battery systems having a liquid capacity of more than 100 gallons used for facility standby power, emergency power or uninterrupted power supplies	1-hour fire barriers and floor/ceiling assemblies in Group B, F, H, M, S and U occupancies. 2-hour fire barriers and floor/ceiling assemblies in Group A, E, I and R occupancies

For SI: 1 square foot = 0.0929 m^2, 1 pound per square inch = 6.9 kPa, 1 British thermal unit = 0.293 watts, 1 horsepower = 746 watts, 1 gallon = 3.785 L.

a. Where an automatic fire-extinguishing system is provided, it need only be provided in the incidental use room or area.

The separation and protection of incinerator rooms is unique in that both methods are required. Although a fire-extinguishing system is required within the incinerator room, it is still necessary to provide a fire-resistance-rated separation utilizing minimum 2-hour fire barriers.

Topic: Accessory Use Areas
Reference: IBC 302.2

Category: Occupancy Classification
Subject: Classification

Code Text: *Any other accessory use area* (other than a Group H occupancy or incidental use area) *shall not be required to be separated by a fire barrier provided the accessory use area occupies an area not more than 10 percent of the area of the story in which it is located and does not exceed the tabular values in Table 503 for the allowable height or area for such use.*

Discussion and Commentary: Where two or more occupancies are located within a building, it is assumed that they pose different hazards, and as such, they must be isolated from each other using fire barriers. Fire barriers are vertical and/or horizontal fire-resistance-rated elements that completely separate one occupancy from another. This provision acknowledges that an associated occupancy relatively small in floor area poses little added risk. Therefore, no fire barrier separation is required.

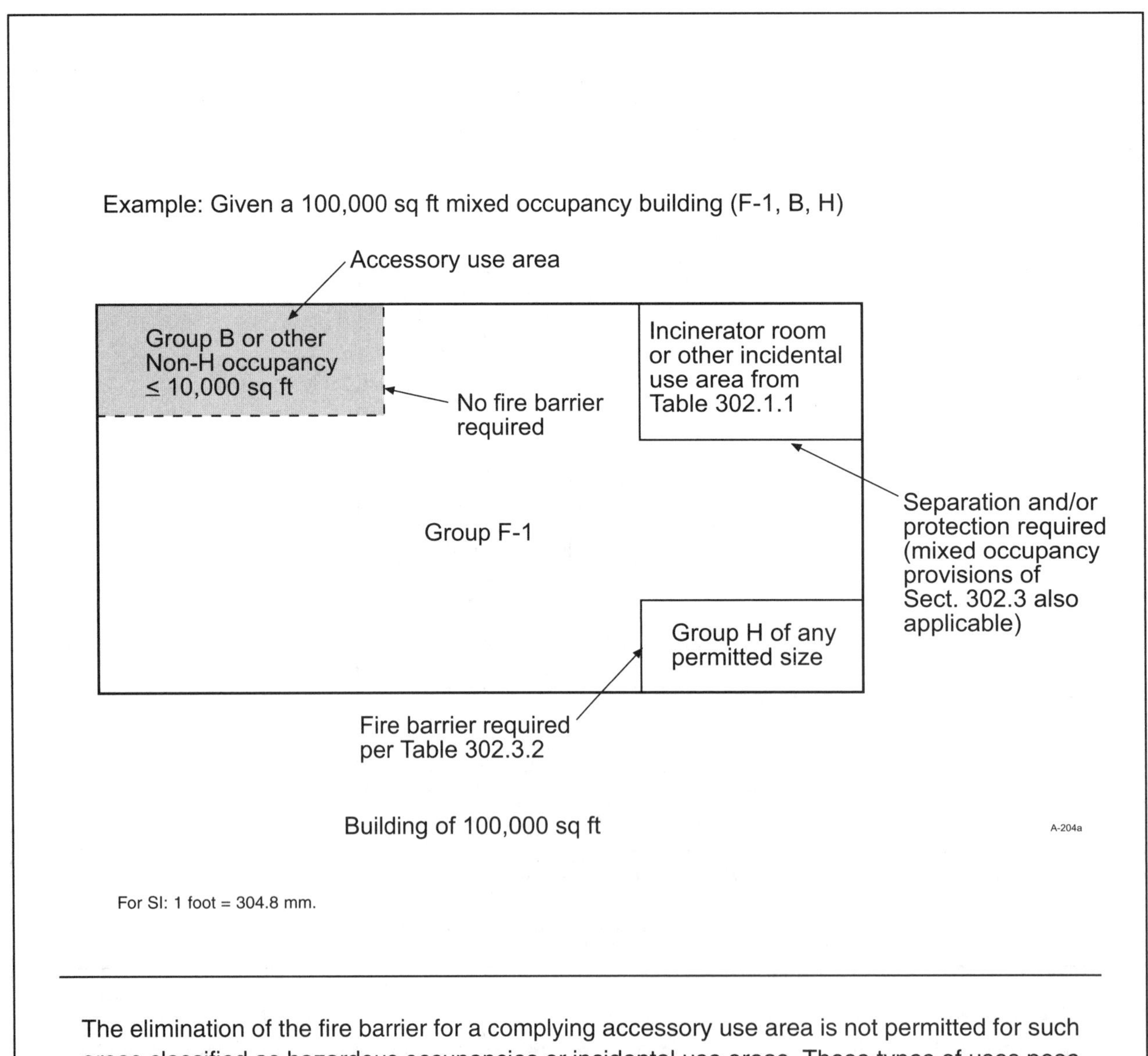

The elimination of the fire barrier for a complying accessory use area is not permitted for such areas classified as hazardous occupancies or incidental use areas. These types of uses pose unique hazards regardless of size and must be appropriately separated or protected.

Topic: Mixed Occupancies
Reference: IBC 302.3

Category: Occupancy Classification
Subject: Classification

Code Text: *Where a building is occupied by two or more uses not included in the same occupancy classification, the building or portion thereof shall comply with Section 302.3.1 or 302.3.2 or a combination of these two sections.* See exceptions for 1) occupancies regulated by the special provisions of Section 508; 2) all Group H occupancies shall be separated per Section 302.3.2; 3) Group H occupancies required to be in detached buildings; 4) accessory use areas; and 5) incidental use areas.

Discussion and Commentary: It is not uncommon for two or more distinct uses to occur within a single structure. Other than the allowance for accessory use areas, the code requires that such multiple occupancies be either 1) isolated from each other using fire-resistant separations (fire barriers), or 2) in lieu of a fire separation, regulated by the most restrictive height, area and fire protection provisions for each occupancy.

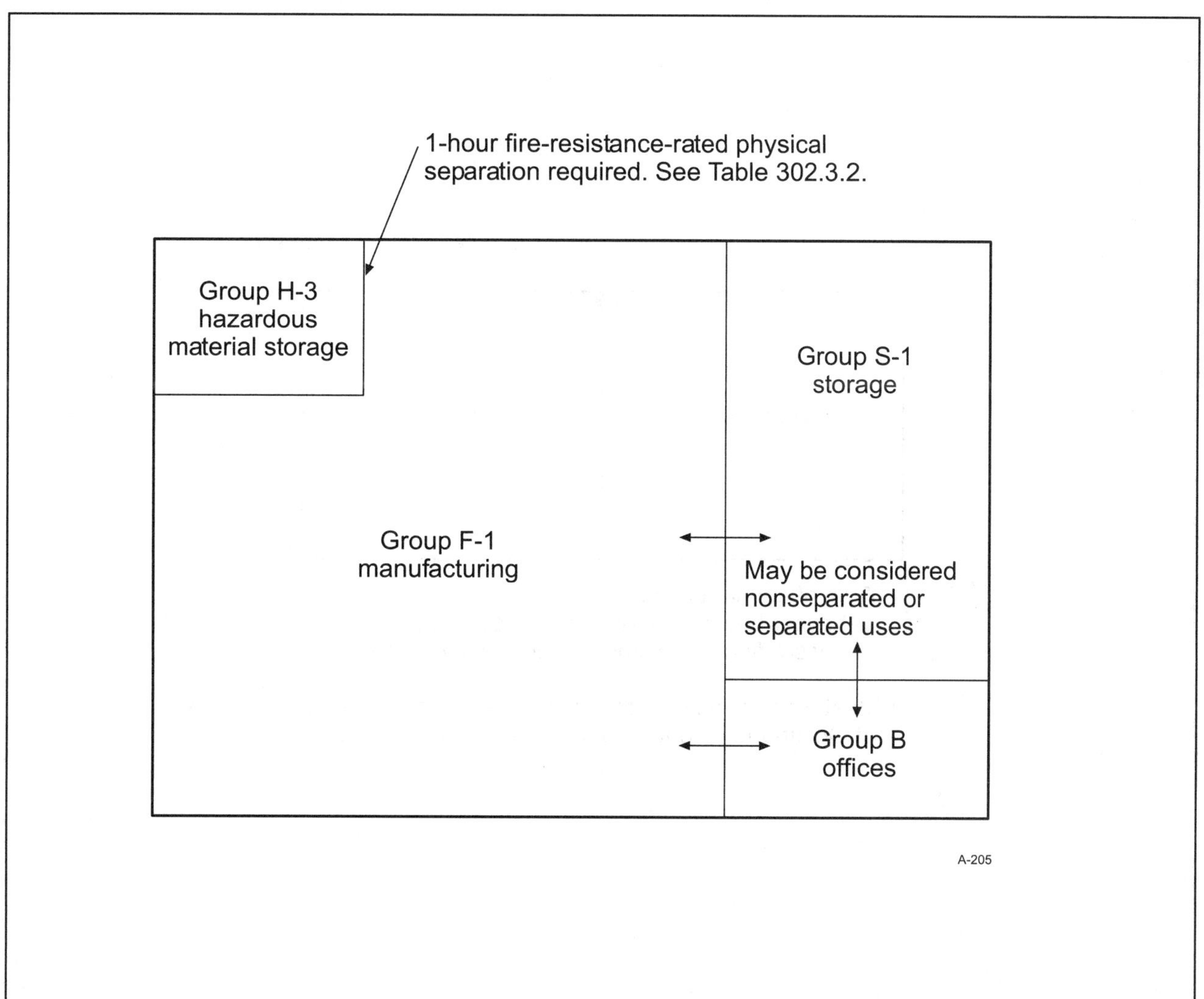

Many buildings contain what is considered a single major use or occupancy; however, where there is more than one distinct occupancy within a building, the building should be viewed as a mixed-use structure and should be regulated accordingly.

Topic: Nonseparated Uses
Reference: IBC 302.3.1

Category: Occupancy Classification
Subject: Mixed Occupancies

Code Text: *Each portion of the building shall be individually classified as to use. The required type of construction for the building shall be determined by applying the height and area limitations for each of the applicable occupancies to the entire building. The most restrictive type of construction, so determined, shall apply to the entire building. All other code requirements shall apply to each portion of the building based on the use of that space except that the most restrictive applicable provisions of Section 403 and Chapter 9 shall apply to these nonseparated uses. Fire separations are not required between uses, except as required by other provisions.*

Discussion and Commentary: The allowance for nonseparated uses, an alternative to the physical separation of different occupancies, is based on the most limiting requirements for building size and fire-protection features, such as sprinklers, standpipes and alarm systems.

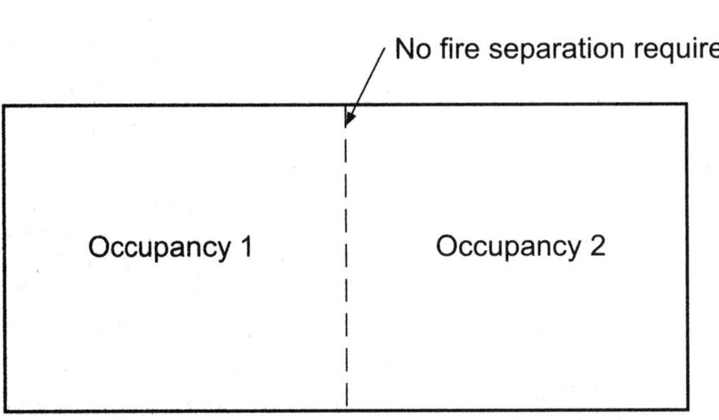

The use of this provision is not applicable to high-hazard occupancies. Those areas or spaces classified as Group H occupancies must be isolated from other occupancies within the building by fire-resistance-rated construction in accordance with Table 302.3.2 for occupancy separations.

Topic: Nonseparated Uses
Reference: IBC 302.3.1

Category: Occupancy Classification
Subject: Classification

Code Text: *The required type of construction for the building shall be determined by applying the height and area limitations for each of the applicable occupancies to the entire building.*
. . . the most restrictive applicable provisions of . . . Chapter 9 shall apply to these nonseparated uses.

Discussion and Commentary: Where the nonseparated use option is utilized to address a mixed occupancy building, it is necessary to determine the maximum building size for each of the occupancies that are not appropriately separated. Such maximum height and area would be based on the building's type of construction. In addition, any fire protective features required in any of the nonseparated occupancies would be mandated throughout the entire building. The fire protection systems that would be regulated include automatic sprinkler systems, standpipe systems, and fire alarm and detection systems.

Given: A Type VB building contains both Group B and Group E occupancies.

Determine: The height and area limitations if the occupancies are not separated under the provisions of Section 302.3.1.

OCCUPANCY	ALLOWABLE HEIGHT[1]	ALLOWABLE AREA[1]
Group B[2]	2 stories	9,000 square feet
Group E[2]	1 story	9,500 square feet

[1] Based on Table 503 assuming no permitted increases.

[2] Most restrictive fire protection requirements of Chapter 9 also applicable to entire building.

∴ Thus, for nonseparated uses the maximum building size would be 1 story and 9,000 square feet.

Nonseparated Uses

It is possible to use a combination of the various provisions of Section 302 together in evaluating a building with multiple uses. The concepts of separated uses and nonseparated uses can be combined in the same building, as can the benefits afforded an accessory use area.

Topic: Separated Uses
Reference: IBC 302.3.2

Category: Occupancy Classification
Subject: Mixed Occupancies

Code Text: *Each portion of the building shall be individually classified as to use and shall be completely separated from adjacent areas by fire barrier walls or horizontal assemblies or both having a fire-resistance rating determined in accordance with Table 302.3.2 for the uses being separated. Each fire area shall comply with the code based on the use of that space. Each fire area shall comply with the height limitations based on the use of that space and the type of construction classification.*

Discussion and Commentary: Fire-resistance-rated separations are required between certain occupancies based on the potential fire hazards they represent, unless they are regulated by Section 302.3.2 as nonseparated uses.

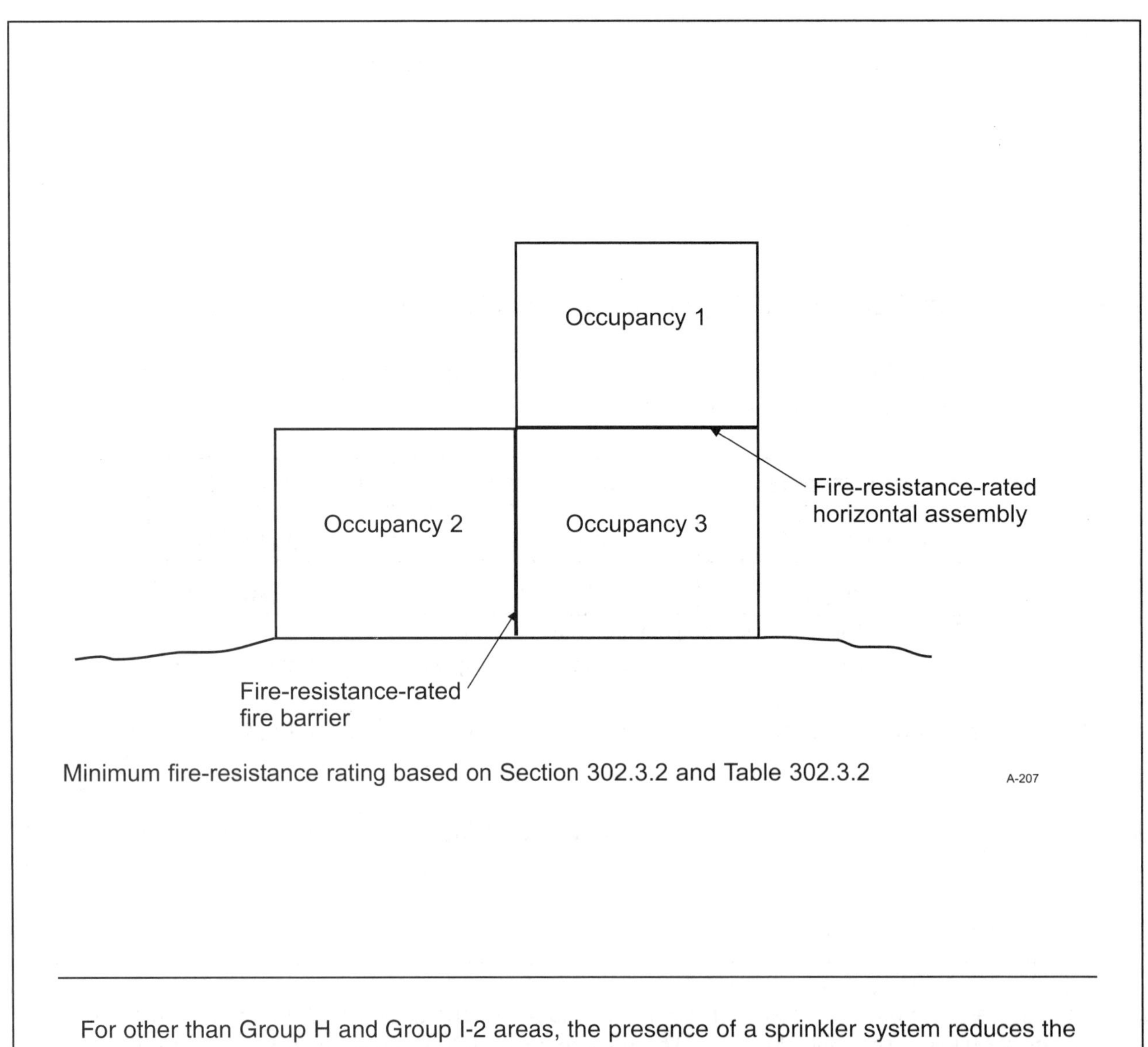

Minimum fire-resistance rating based on Section 302.3.2 and Table 302.3.2

For other than Group H and Group I-2 areas, the presence of a sprinkler system reduces the fire-resistance ratings in Table 302.3.2 by one hour. However, in no case may the required separation be less than one hour nor less than the required floor construction rating.

Topic: Separated Uses
Reference: IBC 302.3.2, Table 302.3.2

Category: Occupancy Classification
Subject: Classification

Code Text: *Each portion of the building shall be individually classified as to use and shall be completely separated from adjacent areas by fire barrier walls or horizontal assemblies or both having a fire-resistance rating determined in accordance with Table 302.3.2 for uses being separated.*

Discussion and Commentary: One of the methods for addressing multiple occupancies in a building is the physical separation of each occupancy from the others with elements of fire-resistance-rated construction. The level of separation shown in the table typically equates to the anticipated fire load of the occupancy. A two-hour separation is most often mandated, with a reduction to a one-hour fire separation permitted in a fully-sprinklered building.

TABLE 302.3.2
REQUIRED SEPARATION OF OCCUPANCIES (HOURS)[a]

USE	A-1	A-2	A-3	A-4	A-5	B[b]	E	F-1	F-2	H-1	H-2	H-3	H-4	H-5	I-1	I-2	I-3	I-4	M[b]	R-1	R-2	R-3, R-4	S-1	S-2[c]	U
A-1	—	2	2	2	2	2	2	3	2	NP	4	3	2	4	2	2	2	2	2	2	2	2	3	2	1
A-2[e]	—	—	2	2	2	2	2	3	2	NP	4	3	2	4	2	2	2	2	2	2	2	2	3	2	1
A-3	—	—	—	2	2	2	2	3	2	NP	4	3	2	4	2	2	2	2	2	2	2	2	3	2	1
A-4	—	—	—	—	2	2	2	3	2	NP	4	3	2	4	2	2	2	2	2	2	2	2	3	2	1
A-5	—	—	—	—	—	2	2	3	2	NP	4	3	2	4	2	2	2	2	2	2	2	2	3	2	1
B[b]	—	—	—	—	—	—	2	3	2	NP	2	1	1	1	2	2	2	2	2	2	2	2	3	2	1
E	—	—	—	—	—	—	—	3	2	NP	4	3	2	3	2	2	2	2	2	2	2	2	3	2	1
F-1	—	—	—	—	—	—	—	—	3	NP	2	1	1	1	3	3	3	3	3	3	3	3	3	3	3
F-2	—	—	—	—	—	—	—	—	—	NP	2	1	1	1	2	2	2	2	2	2	2	2	3	2	1
H-1	—	—	—	—	—	—	—	—	—	—	NP	NP	NP	NP	NP	NP	NP	NP	NP	NP	NP	NP	NP	NP	NP
H-2	—	—	—	—	—	—	—	—	—	—	—	1	2	2	4	4	4	4	2	4	4	4	2	2	1
H-3	—	—	—	—	—	—	—	—	—	—	—	—	1	1	4	3	3	3	1	3	3	3	1	1	1
H-4	—	—	—	—	—	—	—	—	—	—	—	—	—	1	4	4	4	4	1	4	4	4	1	1	1
H-5	—	—	—	—	—	—	—	—	—	—	—	—	—	—	4	4	4	3	1	4	4	4	1	1	3
I-1	—	—	—	—	—	—	—	—	—	—	—	—	—	—	—	2	2	2	2	2	2	2	4	3	2
I-2	—	—	—	—	—	—	—	—	—	—	—	—	—	—	—	—	2	2	2	2	2	2	3	2	1
I-3	—	—	—	—	—	—	—	—	—	—	—	—	—	—	—	—	—	2	2	2	2	2	3	2	1
I-4	—	—	—	—	—	—	—	—	—	—	—	—	—	—	—	—	—	—	2	2	2	2	3	2	1
M[b]	—	—	—	—	—	—	—	—	—	—	—	—	—	—	—	—	—	—	—	2	2	2	3	2	1
R-1	—	—	—	—	—	—	—	—	—	—	—	—	—	—	—	—	—	—	—	—	2	2	3	2	1
R-2	—	—	—	—	—	—	—	—	—	—	—	—	—	—	—	—	—	—	—	—	—	2	3	2	1
R-3, R-4	—	—	—	—	—	—	—	—	—	—	—	—	—	—	—	—	—	—	—	—	—	—	3	2[d]	1[d]
S-1	—	—	—	—	—	—	—	—	—	—	—	—	—	—	—	—	—	—	—	—	—	—	—	3	3
S-2[c]	—	—	—	—	—	—	—	—	—	—	—	—	—	—	—	—	—	—	—	—	—	—	—	—	1
U	—	—	—	—	—	—	—	—	—	—	—	—	—	—	—	—	—	—	—	—	—	—	—	—	—

For SI: 1 square foot = 0.0929 m^2.
NP = Not permitted.
a. See exception to Section 302.3.2 for reductions permitted.
b. Occupancy separation need not be provided for storage areas within Groups B and M if the:
1. Area is less than 10 percent of the floor area;
2. Area is provided with an automatic fire-extinguishing system and is less than 3,000 square feet; or
3. Area is less than 1,000 square feet.
c. Areas used only for private or pleasure vehicles shall be allowed to reduce separation by 1 hour.
d. See exception to Section 302.3.2.
e. Commercial kitchens need not be separated from the restaurant seating areas that they serve.

Note b of Table 302.3.2 eliminates the requirement for a fire separation enclosing storage areas within Groups B and M where any one of three conditions exists. The use of this allowance is acceptable in lieu of addressing the storage room as an incidental use area per Table 302.1.1.

QUIZ

Study Session 2 — Chapter 3

I. Multiple Choice

1. An institutional occupancy is typically considered Group __________.

   a. A
   b. B
   c. I
   d. R

   Reference_______________

2. A Group __________ occupancy is the general classification for miscellaneous and utility structures.

   a. A
   b. M
   c. S
   d. U

   Reference_______________

3. An "incidental use area" is to be classified __________.

   a. in accordance with the main occupancy
   b. based on its relative hazard
   c. as a Group B occupancy
   d. as an accessory use area

   Reference_______________

4. Unless protected by an automatic fire-extinguishing system, what is the minimum fire separation between a 350-square-foot laundry room and the apartment building it is incidental to?

   a. no fire separation is required
   b. one-hour fire partition
   c. one-hour fire barrier
   d. smoke barrier

   Reference_______________

5. What minimum level of protection is required for an incinerator room located in a manufacturing facility?

   a. one-hour fire partition only
   b. automatic fire-extinguishing system only
   c. one-hour fire barrier and an automatic sprinkler system
   d. two-hour fire barrier and an automatic sprinkler system

   Reference_______________

6. What minimum level of protection is required for a chemistry laboratory/classroom in a high school?

a. one-hour fire barrier only
b. automatic fire-extinguishing system only
c. both a one-hour fire barrier and an automatic fire-extinguishing system
d. either a one-hour fire barrier or an automatic fire-extinguishing system

Reference______________

7. Where an automatic fire-extinguishing system without a fire barrier is utilized for the protection of incidental use areas, what minimum level of separation is required?

a. one-hour fire partition
b. one-hour fire barrier
c. one-hour smoke barrier walls and horizontal assemblies
d. construction capable of resisting the passage of smoke

Reference______________

8. Any accessory use area classified as a Group __________ occupancy must always be separated by a fire barrier from other occupancies in the building.

a. A
b. E
c. H
d. I

Reference______________

9. Where the provisions for nonseparated uses are used for a mixed-occupancy building, the most restrictive __________ requirements shall apply to the nonseparated uses.

a. fire-protection system
b. means of egress
c. occupancy classification
d. interior finish

Reference______________

10. Where the provisions for separated uses are used for a nonsprinklered mixed-occupancy building, the minimum separation between a Group A-2 and Group B occupancy shall be a __________.

a. one-hour fire partition
b. one-hour fire barrier
c. two-hour fire barrier
d. two-hour fire wall

Reference______________

11. Where the provisions for separated uses are used for a sprinklered mixed-occupancy building, the minimum separation between a Group H-2 and Group F-1 occupancy shall be a __________.

a. one-hour fire partition
b. one-hour fire barrier
c. two-hour fire barrier
d. two-hour fire wall

Reference_______________

12. Accessory Group A-3 assembly areas are not considered separate occupancies where the floor area is a maximum of __________ square feet.

a. 120
b. 400
c. 750
d. 1000

Reference_______________

13. A lunchroom in a Group E middle school shall be separated at what minimum level from the remainder of the school building?

a. no physical separation is required
b. one-hour fire barrier
c. two-hour fire barrier
d. three-hour fire barrier

Reference_______________

14. Which of the following uses is typically considered a Group A-4 occupancy?

a. restaurant with a dance floor
b. school library
c. outdoor football stadium
d. indoor hockey arena

Reference_______________

15. Which of the following uses is not considered a Group B occupancy?

a. fire station
b. motor vehicle showroom
c. car wash
d. college classroom building

Reference_______________

16. A manufacturing facility involved in the manufacture of __________ is considered a Group F-2 occupancy.

a. soaps and detergents
b. ceramic products
c. automobiles
d. agricultural machinery

Reference_______________

17. A Class IIIA combustible liquid has a closed cup flash point at or above __________ and below __________.

a. 73°F, 100°F
b. 100°F, 140°F
c. 140°F, 200°F
d. 200°F, 212°F

Reference_______________

18. Buildings containing materials that present a deflagration hazard are typically considered __________ occupancies.

a. Group H-1
b. Group H-2
c. Group H-3
d. Group H-5

Reference_______________

19. A child-care facility providing care on a 24-hour basis to six or more infants ($2^1/_2$ years of age or less) is classified as a Group __________ occupancy.

a. E
b. I-1
c. I-2
d. R-4

Reference_______________

20. Prior to any permitted increases, the maximum allowable quantity per control area of a Class IB flammable liquid permitted in a storage condition in a one-story Group F-1 occupancy is __________ gallons.

a. 15
b. 30
c. 60
d. 120

Reference_______________

21. A facility used for supervised residential care and housing more than 16 persons is classified as a Group __________ occupancy.

a. I-1
b. I-4
c. R-3
d. R-4

Reference_______________

22. Which of the following uses is not considered a Group M occupancy?

a. wholesale store
b. sales room
c. motor vehicle showroom
d. motor vehicle service station

Reference_______________

23. A sorority house is typically considered a Group __________ occupancy.

a. R-1
b. R-2
c. R-3
d. R-4

Reference_______________

24. Which of the following uses is not considered a residential care/assisted living facility?

a. halfway house
b. drug abuse center
c. convalescent facility
d. detoxification facility

Reference_______________

25. Which of the following uses is not considered a Group S-2 occupancy?

a. open parking garage
b. enclosed parking garage
c. dry cell batteries storage
d. stable

Reference_______________

26. Where an accessory use area is not required to be separated from the major use by a fire barrier, it is limited to a maximum floor area of _____ of the area of the story in which it is located.

a. 10%
b. 15%
c. 25%
d. 33%

Reference_______________

27. Where the provisions for separated uses are utilized for a sprinkler building housing both a Group A-2 occupancy and a Group R-1 occupancy, the minimum required separation between the two occupancies shall be a _____.

a. one-hour fire partition
b. one-hour fire barrier
c. two-hour fire barrier
d. two-hour fire wall

Reference_______________

28. A public library is typically classified as a _____ occupancy.

a. Group A-3
b. Group A-4
c. Group B
d. Group M

Reference_______________

29. A manufacturing facility utilizing highly toxic materials exceeding the maximum allowable quantities set forth in Table 307.7(2) is considered a _____ occupancy.

a. Group F-1
b. Group F-2
c. Group H-3
d. Group H-4

Reference_______________

30. Aerosol storage buildings shall be classified as Group _____ occupancies when constructed in accordance with the *International Fire Code*.

a. H-2
b. H-3
c. S-1
d. S-2

Reference_______________

INTERNATIONAL BUILDING CODE
Study Session 3
Chapter 6 — Types of Construction

OBJECTIVE: To gain an understanding of how a building is classified as a specific type of construction, based on the construction materials and the various building elements' resistance to fire.

REFERENCE: Chapter 6, 2003 *International Building Code*

KEY POINTS:

- What do the various types of construction indicate?
- How are the required fire-resistance ratings of building elements determined?
- Why are exterior walls regulated by additional criteria?
- Why are exterior walls protected differently based on fire separation distance?
- At what minimum distance is the protection of exterior walls unnecessary?
- Which types of materials are required to be used as building elements of a Type I or Type II building?
- How do the two different categories of Type I construction differ in fire protection? Type II construction?
- Which types of materials are required for use in the exterior walls of a Type III structure? In the interior building elements?
- What is another name for Type IV construction?
- How shall exterior walls be constructed? Interior building elements?
- What are the minimum construction details for columns used in a building of Type IV construction?
- In Type IV buildings, what is the minimum size of heavy-timber members used in the floor and roof framing? Floors? Roofs? Partitions?
- Type V buildings may be constructed of which building materials?
- How does a Type VA building differ from a Type VB building?
- In noncombustible buildings, where may fire-retardant-treated wood be used?
- Which specific allowances are provided for combustible materials in Type I and Type II buildings?
- Which building elements are considered structural frame elements for the determination of fire resistance? Secondary members?
- When are bracing members considered part of the structural frame?
- Under which conditions may the required fire resistance of roof supports be reduced?
- At what height may the required fire resistance of roof construction be eliminated? In which occupancies is the elimination not applicable?
- For which building elements are heavy-timber members and one-hour fire-resistance-rated construction interchangeable?
- What are the limitations for the use of fire-retardant-treated wood in the roof construction of noncombustible buildings?
- How can a sprinkler system affect a building's type of construction classification?
- How are interior nonbearing walls regulated for fire resistance based on construction type? Exterior nonbearing walls?

Topic: Construction Types
Reference: IBC 602.1

Category: Types of Construction
Subject: Construction Classification

Code Text: *Buildings and structures erected or to be erected, altered or extended in height or area shall be classified in one of the five construction types defined in Sections 602.2 through 602.5.*

Discussion and Commentary: There are two major groupings based on the construction materials: noncombustible construction (Types I and II) and combustible construction (Types III, IV and V). These groupings are divided into two more categories: protected, where the major structural elements are provided with some degree of fire resistance, and unprotected, where no fire protection of the building elements is typically mandated. Protected construction is further distinguished in Type I buildings where the required protection for many structural elements exceeds a one-hour fire-resistance rating.

Noncombustible	Exterior and interior (bearing or nonbearing) walls, floors, roofs and structural elements are to be of noncombustible materials	I	A	B
		II	A	B
Combustible	Exterior walls are to be of noncombustible materials	III	A	B
		IV	HT	
		V	A	B

A-208

It is the intent of the *International Building Code* that each building be classified as a single type of construction. The construction materials and the degree to which such materials are protected determine the classification based on the criteria of Table 601 and Chapter 6.

Topic: Fire Resistance Ratings
Reference: IBC 602.1, Table 601

Category: Types of Construction
Subject: Construction Classification

Code Text: *The building elements shall have a fire-resistance rating not less than that specified in Table 601.*

Discussion and Commentary: The building elements regulated by Table 601 for types of construction include structural frame members, such as columns, girders and trusses; bearing walls, both interior and exterior; floor construction, including supporting beams and joists; and roof construction, consisting of supporting beams, joists, rafters and other members. The required fire-resistance rating for each of these elements is based on the specific type of construction assigned to the building. The required fire-resistance rating can be as high as a 3-hour or as little as a 0-hour.

TABLE 601
FIRE-RESISTANCE RATING REQUIREMENTS FOR BUILDING ELEMENTS (hours)

BUILDING ELEMENT	TYPE I		TYPE II		TYPE III		TYPE IV	TYPE V	
	A	B	A[d]	B	A[d]	B	HT	A[d]	B
Structural frame[a] Including columns, girders, trusses	3[b]	2[b]	1	0	1	0	HT	1	0
Bearing walls Exterior[f] Interior	 3 3[b]	 2 2[b]	 1 1	 0 0	 2 1	 2 0	 2 1/HT	 1 1	 0 0
Nonbearing walls and partitions Exterior	See Table 602								
Nonbearing walls and partitions Interior[e]	0	0	0	0	0	0	See Section 602.4.6	0	0
Floor construction Including supporting beams and joists	2	2	1	0	1	0	HT	1	0
Roof construction Including supporting beams and joists	$1^1/_2$[c]	1[c]	1[c]	0	1[c]	0	HT	1[c]	0

For SI: 1 foot = 304.8 mm.

a. The structural frame shall be considered to be the columns and the girders, beams, trusses and spandrels having direct connections to the columns and bracing members designed to carry gravity loads. The members of floor or roof panels which have no connection to the columns shall be considered secondary members and not a part of the structural frame.

b. Roof supports: Fire-resistance ratings of structural frame and bearing walls are permitted to be reduced by 1 hour where supporting a roof only.

c. 1. Except in Factory-Industrial (F-1), Hazardous (H), Mercantile (M) and Moderate-Hazard Storage (S-1) occupancies, fire protection of structural members shall not be required, including protection of roof framing and decking where every part of the roof construction is 20 feet or more above any floor immediately below. Fire-retardant-treated wood members shall be allowed to be used for such unprotected members.
   2. In all occupancies, heavy timber shall be allowed where a 1-hour or less fire-resistance rating is required.
   3. In Type I and II construction, fire-retardant-treated wood shall be allowed in buildings including girders and trusses as part of the roof construction when the building is:
      i. Two stories or less in height;
      ii. Type II construction over two stories; or
      iii. Type I construction over two stories and the vertical distance from the upper floor to the roof is 20 feet or more.

d. An approved automatic sprinkler system in accordance with Section 903.3.1.1 shall be allowed to be substituted for 1-hour fire-resistance-rated construction, provided such system is not otherwise required by other provisions of the code or used for an allowable area increase in accordance with Section 506.3 or an allowable height increase in accordance with Section 504.2. The 1-hour substitution for the fire resistance of exterior walls shall not be permitted.

e. Not less than the fire-resistance rating required by other sections of this code.

f. Not less than the fire-resistance rating based on fire separation distance (see Table 602).

Where a structure is separated by one or more fire walls, the code treats those individual compartments created by the fire walls as separate buildings. Thus, each separate compartment would be considered a distinct building for the purpose of classification by type of construction.

Topic: Fire Separation Distance
Reference: IBC 602.1, Table 602

Category: Types of Construction
Subject: Exterior Walls

Code Text: *Exterior walls shall have a fire-resistance rating not less than that specified in Table 602.*

Discussion and Commentary: The rationale behind exterior wall protection is that an owner has no control over what occurs on adjacent property. The property line concept provides a convenient means of protecting one building from another insofar as radiant heat could potentially be transmitted from one building to another during a fire. The requirements are based on "fire separation distance," which must be considered for all exterior walls. Where such walls are also bearing walls, the provisions of Table 601 also apply, governed by the more restrictive of the hourly ratings. Additional provisions for exterior walls are found in Section 704.

Table 602 Regulates Exterior Walls Only

- Table 602 used in conjunction with Table 601 for fire resistance of exterior bearing walls
- Only Table 602 used for nonbearing exterior walls
- Based primarily on occupancy type
- Highest required rating for exterior wall is 3 hours
- Final threshold at ≥ 30'
- Additional provisions for exterior walls and openings in Section 704

TABLE 602
FIRE-RESISTANCE RATING REQUIREMENTS FOR EXTERIOR WALLS BASED ON FIRE SEPARATION DISTANCE[a]

FIRE SEPARATION DISTANCE (feet)	TYPE OF CONSTRUCTION	GROUP H	GROUP F-1, M, S-1	GROUP A,B,E, F-2, I, R[b], S-2, U
< 5[c]	All	3	2	1
≥ 5 < 10	I-A Others	3 2	2 1	1 1
≥ 10 < 30	I-A, I-B II-B, V-B Others	2 1 1	1 0 1	1 0 1
≥ 30	All	0	0	0

For SI: 1 foot = 304.8 mm.

a. Load-bearing exterior walls shall also comply with the fire-resistance rating requirements of Table 601.
b. Group R-3 and Group U when used as accessory to Group R-3, as applicable in Section 101.2 shall not be required to have a fire-resistance rating where fire separation distance is 3 feet or more.
c. See Section 503.2 for party walls.

The "fire separation distance" is defined in Section 702.1 as the distance measured from the building face to the closest interior lot line, to the centerline of a street, alley or public way, or to an imaginary line between two buildings on the property.

Topic: Fire Separation Distance
Reference: IBC 702.1, Table 602.1

Category: Type of Construction
Subject: Exterior Walls

Code Text: Fire separation distance *is the distance measured from the building face to the closest interior lot line, to the centerline of a street, alley or public way, or to an imaginary line between two buildings on the lot. The distance shall be measured at right angles from the face of the wall.*

Discussion and Commentary: The atmospheric separation provided between a building and an adjoining structure provides resistance to fire spread due to radiant heat transfer. Many provisions throughout the IBC, such as those regulating projections and parapets, are based upon the degree of separation provided. The measurement at a right angle from the building face addresses heat transfer from the building of fire incident toward other structures and properties.

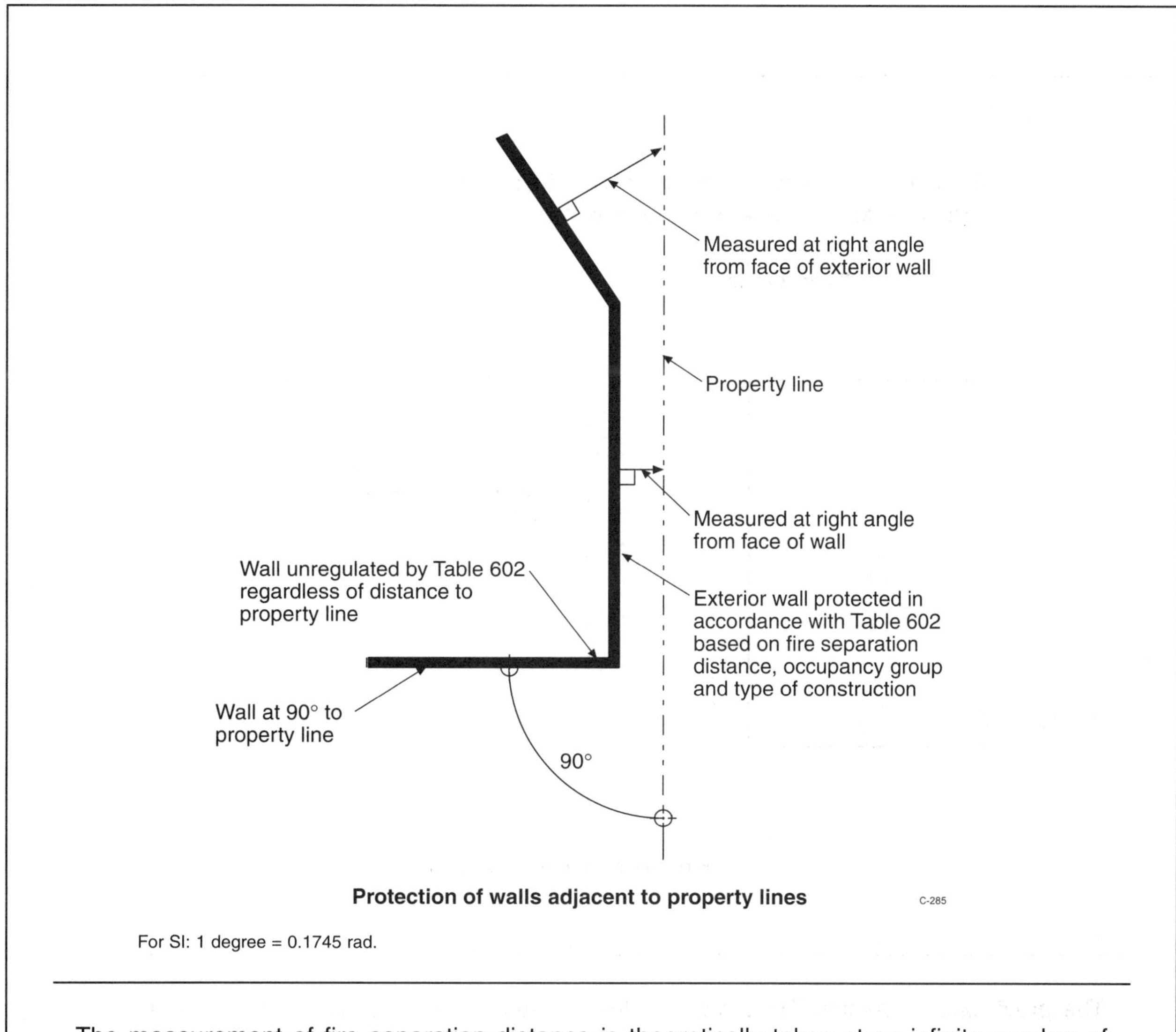

Protection of walls adjacent to property lines

For SI: 1 degree = 0.1745 rad.

The measurement of fire separation distance is theoretically taken at an infinite number of points along the exterior wall. In reality, zones are created adjacent to the building under consideration, with higher degrees of regulation mandated for those zones closest to the building.

Topic: Fire-resistance Ratings **Category:** Type of Construction
Reference: IBC T601, Note f; T602, Note a **Subject:** Exterior Walls

Code Text: The minimum fire-resistance rating for exterior bearing walls shall be *not less than the fire-resistance rating based on fire separation distance.* In addition to the fire-resistance rating requirements for exterior walls based on fire separation distance, *load-bearing exterior walls shall also comply with the fire-resistance rating requirements of Table 601.*

Discussion and Commentary: When analyzing an exterior wall for its required level of fire resistance, it is necessary to use both Table 601 and Table 602. Table 601 addresses the potential need for structural stability of exterior bearing walls under fire conditions. Exterior nonbearing walls are not regulated by this table. The concern of radiant heat transfer from an adjoining burning building results in Table 602 regulating the exterior wall rating based upon its fire separation distance (typically the distance from the building face to the property line). This concern exists for both bearing and nonbearing exterior walls.

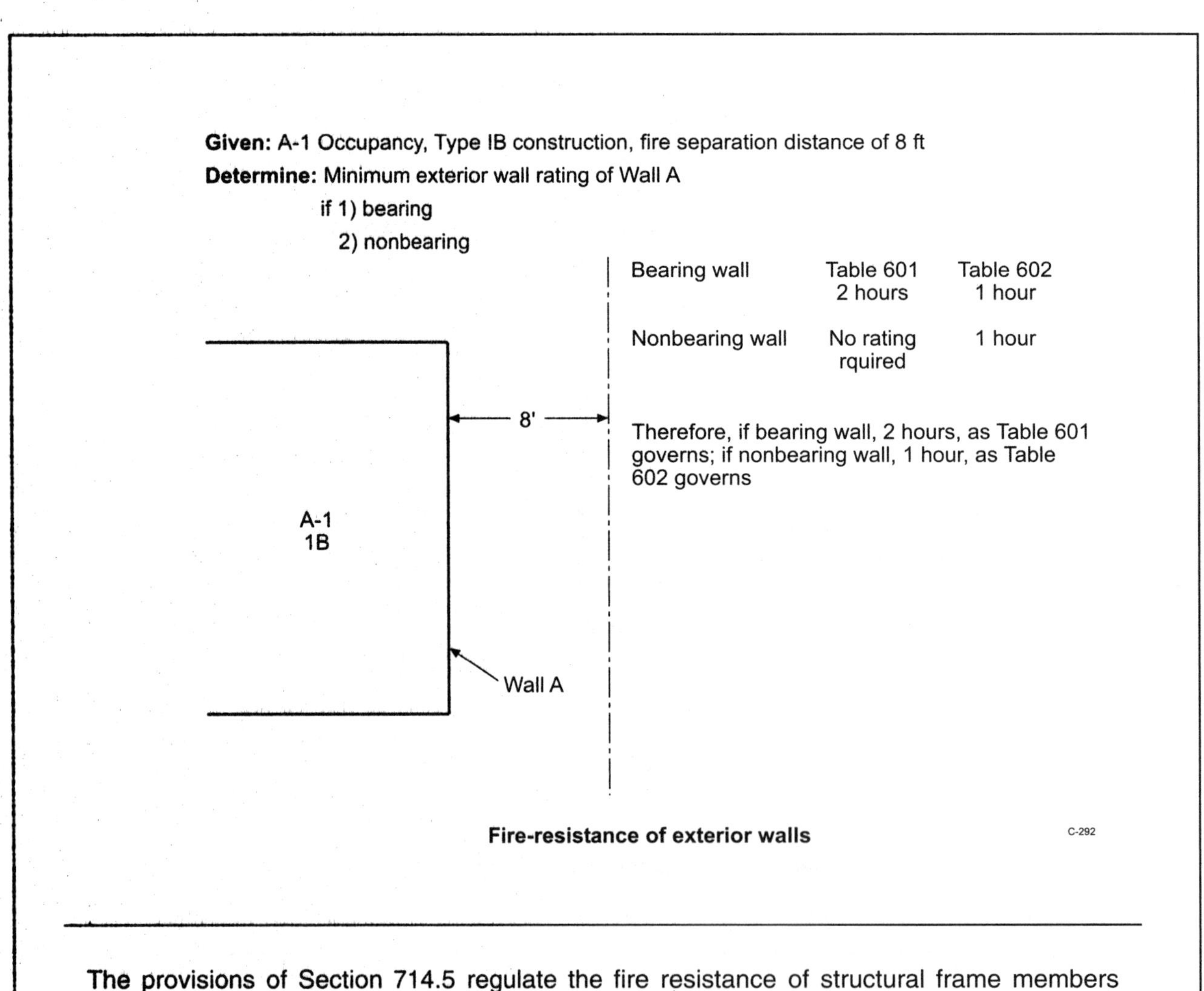

Fire-resistance of exterior walls

The provisions of Section 714.5 regulate the fire resistance of structural frame members located within nonbearing exterior walls. The required fire rating is based on the highest of ratings found in Table 601 (structural frame, exterior bearing wall) and Table 602 (fire separation distance).

Topic: Types I and II Construction
Reference: IBC 602.2

Category: Types of Construction
Subject: Construction Classification

Code Text: *Types I and II construction are those types of construction in which the building elements listed in Table 601 are of noncombustible materials.*

Discussion and Commentary: Type I buildings are noncombustible, and the building elements are also provided with a mandated degree of fire resistance. This type of construction requires the highest level of fire protection specified in the code. Type II buildings are also of noncombustible construction; however, the level of fire resistance is usually less than that required for Type I structures. Buildings of Type II construction may have a limited degree of fire resistance (Type IIA) or no fire resistance whatsoever (Type IIB).

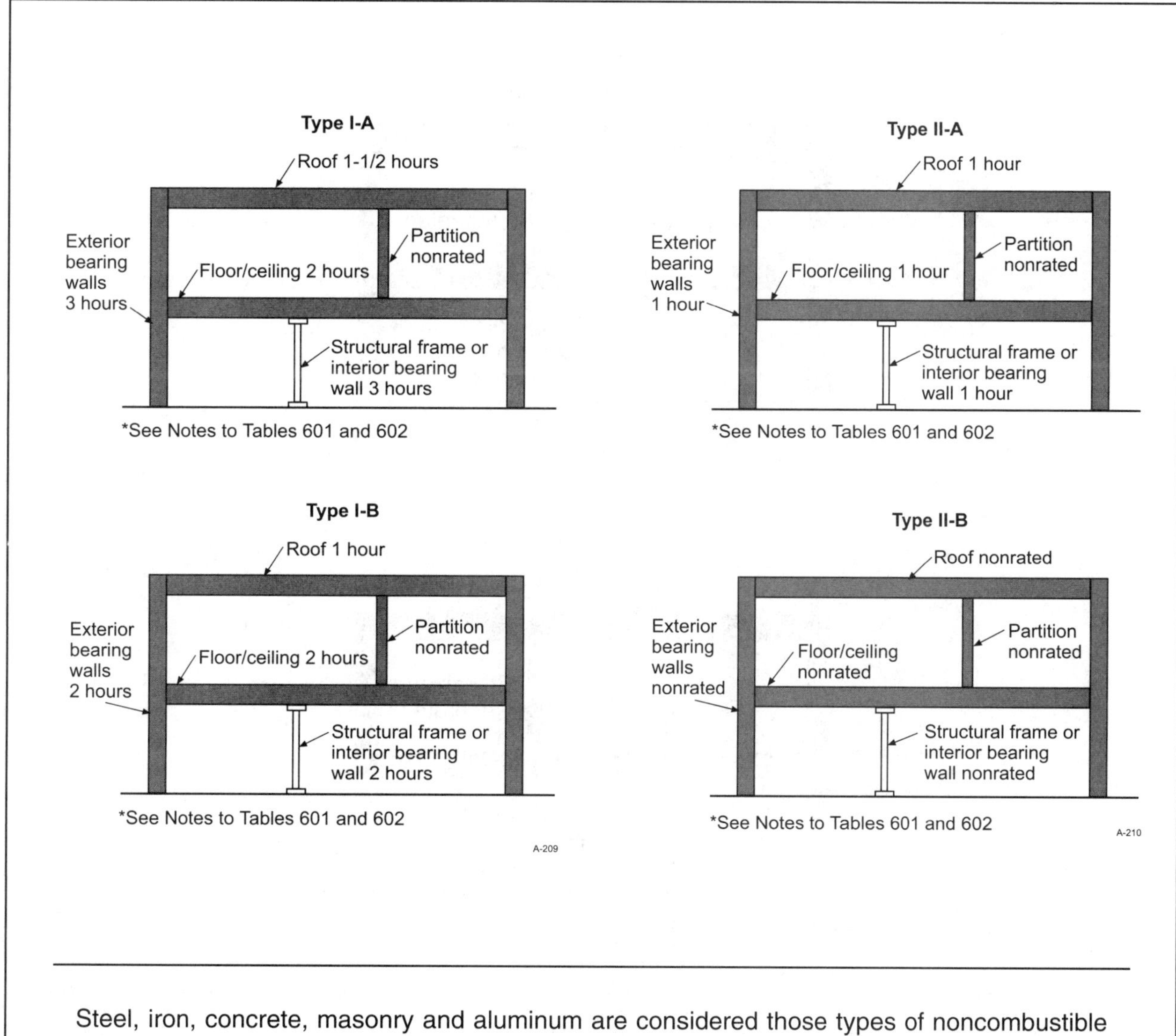

Steel, iron, concrete, masonry and aluminum are considered those types of noncombustible materials used as building elements or components of building elements, in Type I or II buildings. Section 703.4.2 also recognizes gypsum board as a noncombustible material.

Topic: Type III Construction
Reference: IBC 602.3

Category: Types of Construction
Subject: Construction Classification

Code Text: *Type III construction is that type of construction in which the exterior walls are of noncombustible materials and the interior building elements are of any material permitted by the code. Fire-retardant-treated wood framing complying with Section 2303.2 shall be permitted within exterior wall assemblies of a 2-hour rating or less.*

Discussion and Commentary: Type III buildings are considered combustible buildings and are either protected or unprotected. This building type was developed out of the necessity to prevent conflagrations in heavily built-up areas where buildings were erected side-by-side in congested downtown business districts. To limit the spread of fire from building to building, exterior walls were required to be of both noncombustible and fire-resistant construction.

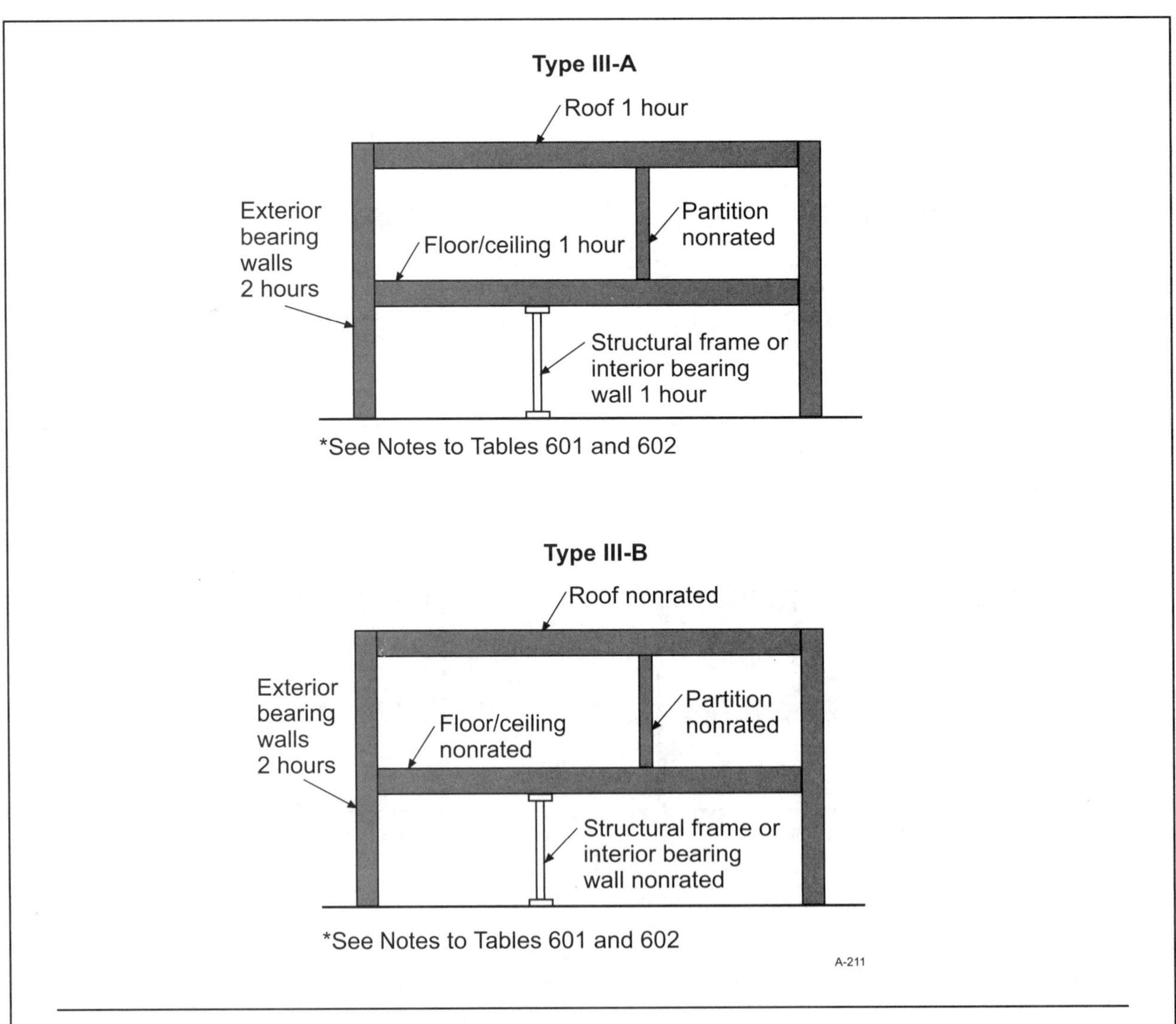

Historically referred to as "ordinary masonry construction," Type III buildings usually consist of masonry exterior walls with wood floor and roof systems. However, the IBC permits such walls to contain fire-retardant-treated wood as an element of the exterior wall construction.

Topic: Type IV Construction
Reference: IBC 602.4

Category: Types of Construction
Subject: Construction Classification

Code Text: *Type IV construction (Heavy Timber, HT) is that type of construction in which the exterior walls are of noncombustible materials and the interior building elements are of solid or laminated wood without concealed spaces. The details of Type IV construction shall comply with the provisions of Section 602.4. Fire-retardant-treated wood framing complying with Section 2303.2 shall be permitted within exterior wall assemblies with a 2-hour rating or less.*

Discussion and Commentary: Referred to as "heavy-timber," buildings of Type IV construction are essentially Type III buildings with an interior of timber members. To conform to Type IV construction, building members must be of substantial thickness. Given the characteristics of massive wood members, there is little chance for sudden structural collapse during or after a fire.

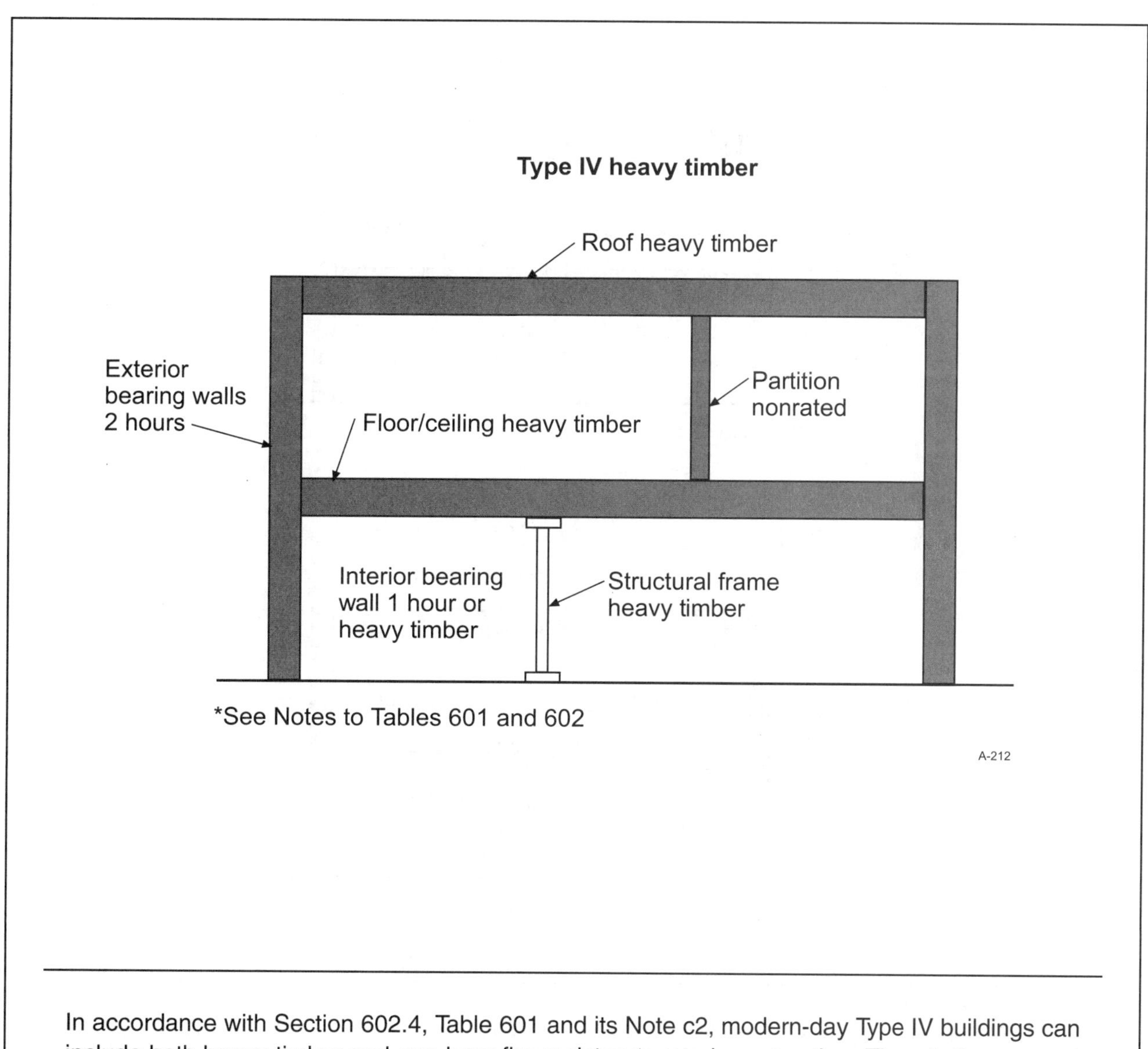

In accordance with Section 602.4, Table 601 and its Note c2, modern-day Type IV buildings can include both heavy-timber and one-hour fire-resistance-rated construction. Though they are not considered equal, both methods of construction tend to provide equivalent fire resistance.

Topic: Type V Construction
Reference: IBC 602.5

Category: Types of Construction
Subject: Construction Classification

Code Text: *Type V construction is that type of construction in which the structural elements, exterior walls and interior walls are of any materials permitted by the IBC.*

Discussion and Commentary: Type V buildings are essentially construction systems that will not fit into any of the other higher types of construction specified by the IBC. Although the construction normally considered Type V is the conventional light-frame wood building, any combination of approved materials can be considered Type V construction. Section 602.1.1 indicates that a building is not required to conform to the details of a type of construction higher than the type that meets the minimum requirements based on occupancy, even though certain features of such a building actually conform to a higher construction type.

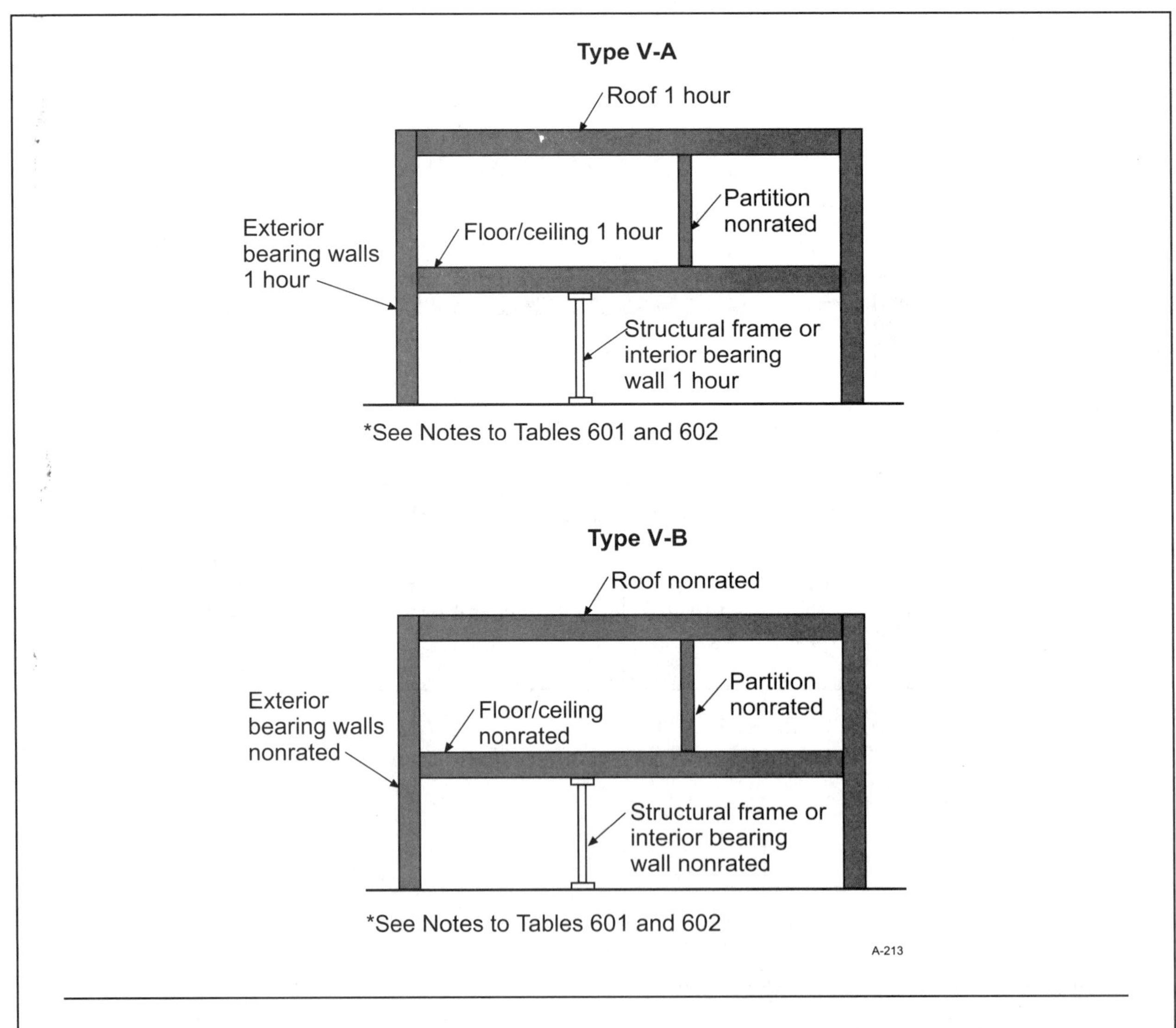

In the design and review of a building for type of construction requirements, it is wise to determine first if the structure can be built as a Type VB building, based on occupancy, location on property, height and floor area. If so, any other building type is also permitted.

Topic: Allowable Uses
Reference: IBC 603.1

Category: Types of Construction
Subject: Combustible Material in Types I and II

Code Text: *Combustible materials are permitted in buildings of Type I and Type II construction in the following applications:* (22 applications listed).

Discussion and Commentary: Materials used in the construction of buildings classified as either Type I or Type II are intended to be noncombustible, thereby not increasing the potential fire loading (fuel contribution). There are, however, a number of applications where the presence of combustible building materials is desirable in otherwise noncombustible structures. Such materials are typically permitted where they are adequately protected, limited in use or amount, or installed in accordance with the *International Fire Code®*, *International Mechanical Code®*, or other provisions of the IBC.

Combustible materials permitted in buildings of Type I and Type II construction in the following applications:

- Fire-retardant-treated wood in:
  –Nonbearing partitions with fire-resistance rating ≤ 2 hours.
  –Nonbearing exterior walls requiring no fire rating.
- Thermal and acoustical insulation with limited flame spread.
- Foam plastics per Chapter 26.
- A, B or C roof coverings.
- Interior floor finish, trim, millwork such as, doors, frames, etc.
- Platforms per Section 410.
- Blocking for handrails, fixtures, windows and door frames, etc.
- Light-transmitting plastics per Chapter 26.
- Nailing or furring strips per Section 803.3.
- Heavy timber for specific components.
- Additional applications as specified.

In Type I and Type II construction, the use of fire-retardant-treated wood is permitted in nonbearing interior partitions having a maximum 2-hour fire-resistance rating, in nonrated nonbearing exterior walls, and in roof construction of one- and two-story buildings.

Topic: Structural Frame
Reference: IBC Table 601, Note a

Category: Types of Construction
Subject: Building Elements

Code Text: *The structural frame shall be considered to be the columns and the girders, beams, trusses and spandrels having direct connections to the columns and bracing members designed to carry gravity loads. The members of floor or roof panels which have no connection to the columns shall be considered secondary members and not a part of the structural frame.*

Discussion and Commentary: To maintain stability of the building as a whole, the major structural elements are regulated for endurance when subjected to a fire. In addition to the columns, beams and girders, both interior bearing walls and exterior bearing walls are regulated to a level of fire resistance equal or greater than that of other structural elements. Secondary members, such as floor joists, roof joists or rafters are protected within the rated floor-ceiling or roof-ceiling assemblies.

Structural Frame Considered to be:

- Columns
- Girders
- Beams
- Trusses
- Spandrels

Having direct connection to the columns and bracing members designed to carry gravity loads

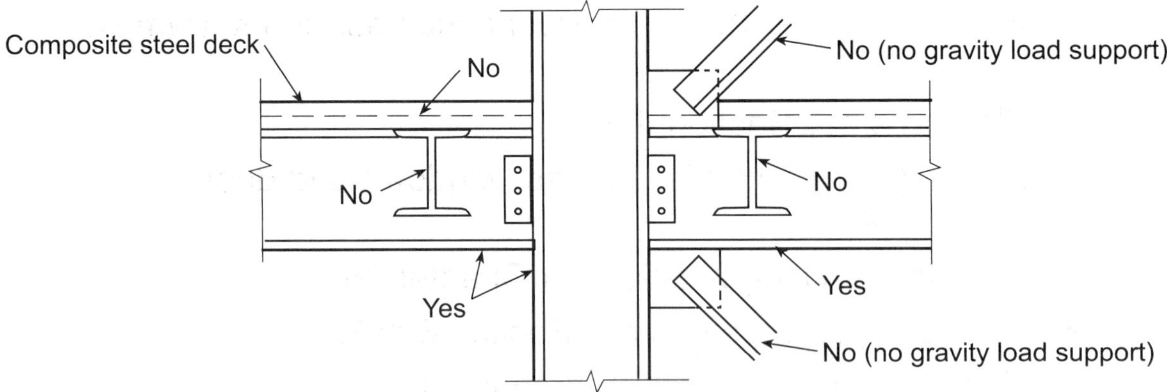

Components of structural frame

A-017

Lateral force bracing is not considered part of the structural frame where it serves no other purpose than to resist the lateral loads. For example, lateral load bracing within exterior nonbearing walls or interior partitions would be protected by the wall or partition construction.

Topic: Roof Construction
Reference: IBC Table 601, Note c1

Category: Types of Construction
Subject: Building Elements

Code Text: *Except in Factory-Industrial (F-1), Hazardous (H), Mercantile (M) and Moderate Hazard Storage (S-1) occupancies, fire protection of structural members shall not be required, including protection of roof framing and decking where every part of the roof construction is 20 feet or more above any floor immediately below. Fire-retardant-treated wood members shall be allowed to be used for such unprotected members.*

Discussion and Commentary: Where there is limited potential for a fire to be of a severe nature at the roof structure due to its height above the floor below, an elimination of the required fire-resistance rating of the roof construction is permitted. Elimination of the required fire resistance is not allowed where combustible or hazardous materials are located adjacent to the roof.

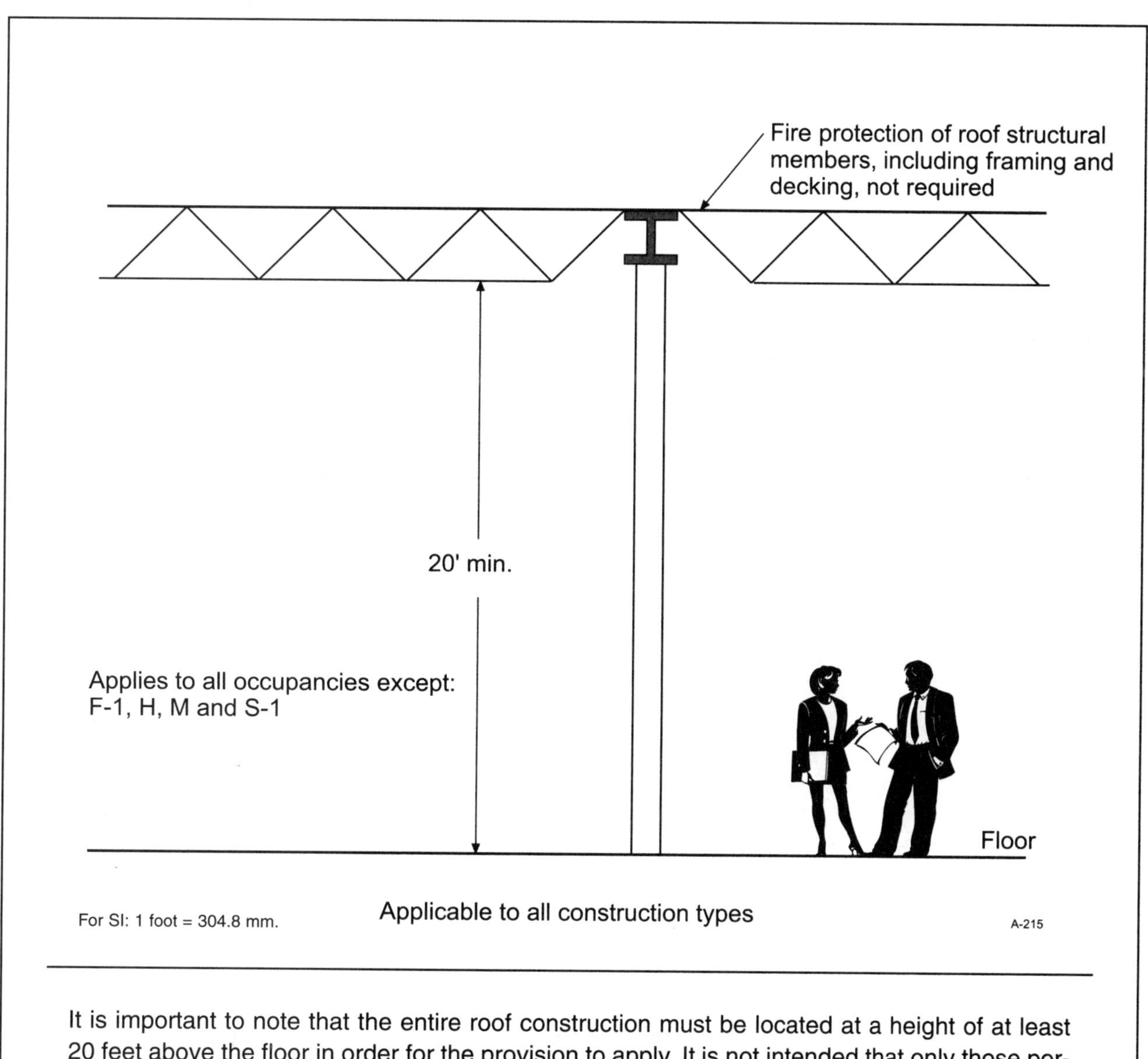

It is important to note that the entire roof construction must be located at a height of at least 20 feet above the floor in order for the provision to apply. It is not intended that only those portions of a sloping roof less than 20 feet above the floor be protected.

Topic: Fire-resistant Substitution
Reference: IBC Table 601, Note d

Category: Types of Construction
Subject: Building Elements

Code Text: *An approved automatic sprinkler system in accordance with Section 903.3.1.1 shall be allowed to be substituted for 1-hour fire-resistance-rated construction, provided such system is not otherwise required by other provisions of the code or used for an allowable area increase in accordance with Section 506.3 or an allowable height increase in accordance with Section 504.2. The 1-hour substitution for the fire resistance of exterior walls shall not be permitted.*

Discussion and Commentary: In buildings of Type IIA, IIIA or VA construction, the code allows for a reduction in the "built-in" fire protection, due to the presence of a sprinkler system that would not otherwise be required. This reduction does not apply to exterior walls, nor does it apply when a sprinkler system is used for an increase in allowable height or allowable area.

Type II-B Construction	+	Approved Automatic Sprinkler System*	=	TYPE II-A Construction
Type III-B Construction	+	Approved Automatic Sprinkler System*	=	Type III-A Construction
Type V-B Construction	+	Approved Automatic Sprinkler System*	=	Type V-A Construction

***Unless otherwise required, or used for allowable height and area increase**

The application of this note to Table 601 may be extremely limited based on the language of Section 901.2, which states that *any fire protection system for which an exception or reduction to the provisions of the code has been granted shall be considered to be a required system.*

QUIZ

Study Session 3 — Chapter 6

I. Multiple Choice

1. What types of construction are considered "noncombustible"?

a. I, II
b. I, II, III, IV
c. III, IV
d. III, IV, V

Reference_______________

2. Type III buildings shall have __________ exterior walls and interior elements __________.

a. fire-resistive, of noncombustible materials
b. noncombustible, of noncombustible materials
c. noncombustible, of any materials permitted by the code
d. combustible, of any materials permitted by the code

Reference_______________

3. A Type IV building is also described as __________ construction.

a. ordinary
b. heavy timber
c. combustible
d. provential

Reference_______________

4. In buildings of Type III and IV construction, under what condition is fire-retardant-treated wood framing permitted within exterior walls assemblies?

a. the wall has a maximum 2-hour rating
b. the fire separation distance exceeds 10 feet
c. the wall is not required to have a fire rating
d. the wall is a nonbearing element

Reference_______________

5. Where supporting floor loads, wood columns of Type IV construction shall be of what minimum nominal size?

a. 5 inches by 5 inches
b. 6 inches by 6 inches
c. 6 inches by 8 inches
d. 8 inches by 8 inches

Reference_______________

6. Where used in floor framing, wood beams of Type IV construction shall be of what minimum nominal size?

a. 4 inches by 8 inches
b. 4 inches by 10 inches
c. 6 inches by 10 inches
d. 8 inches by 10 inches

Reference_______________

7. Roofs shall be without concealed spaces in buildings of Type __________ construction.

a. I
b. III
c. IV
d. V

Reference_______________

8. A building of Type VB construction is generally considered __________.

a. noncombustible and protected
b. noncombustible and unprotected
c. combustible and protected
d. combustible and unprotected

Reference_______________

9. In a building of Type IB construction, what is the minimum required fire-resistance rating of the floor construction?

a. 3 hours
b. 2 hours
c. 1 hour
d. 0 hours (no rating required)

Reference_______________

10. Which one of the following members is not considered to be a part of the structural frame?

a. columns
b. girders
c. bracing members carrying gravity loads
d. floor joists

Reference_______________

11. In a building of Type IIB construction, what is the minimum required fire-resistance rating of the roof construction?

a. 0 hours (no rating required)
b. 1 hour
c. $1^1/_2$ hours
d. 2 hours

Reference_______________

12. In a building of Type IIIA construction, what is the minimum required fire-resistance rating of the floor construction?

a. 0 hours (no rating required)
b. 1 hour
c. $1^1/_2$ hours
d. 2 hours

Reference_______________

13. In a one-story Type IA building, what is the minimum fire-resistance rating for the interior bearing walls supporting the roof only?

a. 3 hours
b. 2 hours
c. $1^1/_2$ hours
d. 1 hour

Reference_______________

14. In Type I and II buildings limited to two stories in height, what building element is permitted to be constructed of fire-retardant-treated wood?

a. structural frame
b. bearing walls
c. floor construction
d. roof construction

Reference_______________

15. In a Type IA building housing a Group A-4 occupancy, fire protection of the roof structural members, framing and decking is not required where every portion of the roof construction is a minimum of __________ feet above the floor below.

a. 18
b. 20
c. 25
d. 35

Reference_______________

16. In a Type IIB building housing a Group I-2 occupancy, what is the minimum rating of an exterior nonbearing wall located with a fire separation distance of 8 feet?

a. 3 hours
b. 2 hours
c. 1 hour
d. 0 hours (no rating required)

Reference_______________

17. In a Type IIA building housing a Group R-2 occupancy, what is the minimum rating of an exterior nonbearing wall located with a fire separation distance of 3 feet?

a. 3 hours
b. 2 hours
c. 1 hour
d. 0 hours (no rating required)

Reference_______________

18. In a Type IIIA building housing a Group A-1 occupancy, what is the minimum rating of an exterior bearing wall located with a fire separation distance of 10 feet?

a. 3 hours
b. 2 hours
c. 1 hour
d. 0 hours (no rating required)

Reference_______________

19. In a Type VB building housing a Group B occupancy, what is the minimum rating of an exterior bearing wall located with a fire separation distance of 10 feet?

a. 3 hours
b. 2 hours
c. 1 hour
d. 0 hours (no rating required)

Reference_______________

20. Considering all occupancies and construction types, for which minimum fire separation distance is no fire rating required for a nonbearing exterior wall?

a. 20 feet
b. 30 feet
c. 40 feet
d. 60 feet

Reference_______________

21. In a building of Type I or II construction, nonbearing partitions having a maximum fire-resistance rating of __________ are permitted to be constructed of fire-retardant-treated wood.

a. 0 hours (no rating required)
b. $^1/_2$ hour
c. 1 hour
d. 2 hours

Reference_______________

22. A Group U occupancy accessory to a Group R-3 shall have a one-hour fire-resistance rating where the fire separation distance is less than __________ feet.

a. 0, no rating is required
b. 3
c. 5
d. 10

Reference_______________

23. In a building of Type I or II construction, nonbearing exterior walls having a maximum fire-resistance rating of __________ are permitted to be constructed of fire-retardant-treated wood.

a. 0 hours (no rating required)
b. $^1/_2$ hour
c. 1 hour
d. 2 hours

Reference_______________

24. Show windows may be of combustible construction in Types I and II construction where located a maximum of __________ above grade.

a. 15 feet
b. 35 feet
c. one story
d. three stories

Reference_______________

25. Which type of roof covering is not permitted on a building of Type I or II construction?

a. Class A
b. Class B
c. Class C
d. nonclassified

Reference_______________

26. Which of the following methods of construction is not permitted for partitions in Type IV structures?

a. fire-retardant-treated wood
b. 4 inches of laminated construction
c. two layers of 1-inch matched boards
d. one-hour fire-resistance-rated construction

Reference_______________

27. What is the minimum fire-resistive rating required for interior metal stud partitions in Type IIB construction?

a. 0, no rating is required
b. 1 hour
c. 2 hours
d. 3 hours

Reference_______________

28. What is the minimum vertical distance between the upper floor and the roof to permit the use of fire-retardant-treated wood in the roof construction of an eight-story Type IB building?

a. 20 feet
b. 25 feet
c. there is no minimum distance required
d. FRT wood is never permitted in such a case

Reference_______________

29. For an office building of Type IB construction, what is the minimum required fire-resistance rating for an exterior bearing wall located on an interior property line?

a. 0, no rating is required
b. 1 hour
c. 2 hours
d. 3 hours

Reference_______________

30. Heavy timber members may be used in lieu of one-hour fire-resistance-rated construction for which building element?

a. structural frame members
b. interior bearing walls
c. floor construction
d. roof construction

Reference_______________

INTERNATIONAL BUILDING CODE

Study Session 4

Chapter 5 — General Building Heights and Areas

OBJECTIVE: To gain an understanding of how a building is classified and regulated based on its floor area, height and number of stories.

REFERENCE: Chapter 5, 2003 *International Building Code*

KEY POINTS:

- How and why must buildings be identified by their address?
- How is the maximum basic floor area of a building determined? The basic height in feet and number of stories?
- What effect does the presence of one or more fire walls have on a building's permitted size?
- How is the tabular allowable building area determined?
- How is a basement viewed in the calculation of maximum allowable floor area?
- How must multiple buildings located on the same lot be handled?
- What types of special industrial occupancies are exempt from the height and area limitations of Table 503?
- What is a party wall? How shall a party wall be constructed?
- Under which conditions may the basic allowable height of a building be increased? How much of an increase is permitted?
- Which special provisions address the construction of towers, spires, steeples and other roof structures?
- What is a mezzanine?
- Under which conditions may a floor level be considered a mezzanine?
- Under what conditions is a mezzanine permitted to be enclosed or in some manner separated from the room in which it is located?
- Which conditions provide for an increase in the allowable floor areas specified in Table 503?
- What is the minimum width of a yard or public way that can provide for a floor area increase?
- How much of a building's perimeter must be considered "open" for the area increase to apply?
- What amount of area increase is permitted for sprinklered single-story buildings? For sprinklered multistory structures?
- How is the maximum total combined floor area for a multistory building determined?
- Which occupancy groups are eligible for unlimited floor area in a one-story nonsprinklered building?
- Which criteria must be met for buildings of Groups A-4, B, F, M or S to be unlimited in floor area?
- What is the minimum width required for open space surrounding an unlimited area building?
- Under which conditions may that width be reduced?
- Under what limitations is a Group A-3 occupancy permitted to be of unlimited area?
- How may high-hazard occupancies be accommodated in an unlimited area building?
- Which limitations are placed on motion picture theaters of unlimited area?
- Which special provisions address the situation where an enclosed parking garage is located below another occupancy group? Below an open parking garage?
- How may the height of buildings containing Group B, M and R occupancies be unlimited?
- What are the height limitations for apartment houses and other Group R-2 occupancies where the special provisions are met?
- How is an open parking garage regulated where located below Groups A, B, I, M or R?

Topic: General Provisions
Reference: IBC 502.1

Category: Building Heights and Areas
Subject: Definitions

Code Text: *Building area is the area included within surrounding exterior walls (or exterior walls and fire walls) exclusive of vent shafts and courts. Areas of the building not provided with surrounding walls shall be included in the building area if such areas are included within the horizontal projection of the roof or floor above*

Discussion and Commentary: The building area must be determined in order to verify that it does not exceed the maximum allowable area as determined by Section 503.1. The building area is considered, in very general terms, the "footprint" of the building, excluding those unroofed areas and any projections that may extend beyond the exterior walls. Where complying mezzanines are located within a building, they are not assumed to contribute to the building area.

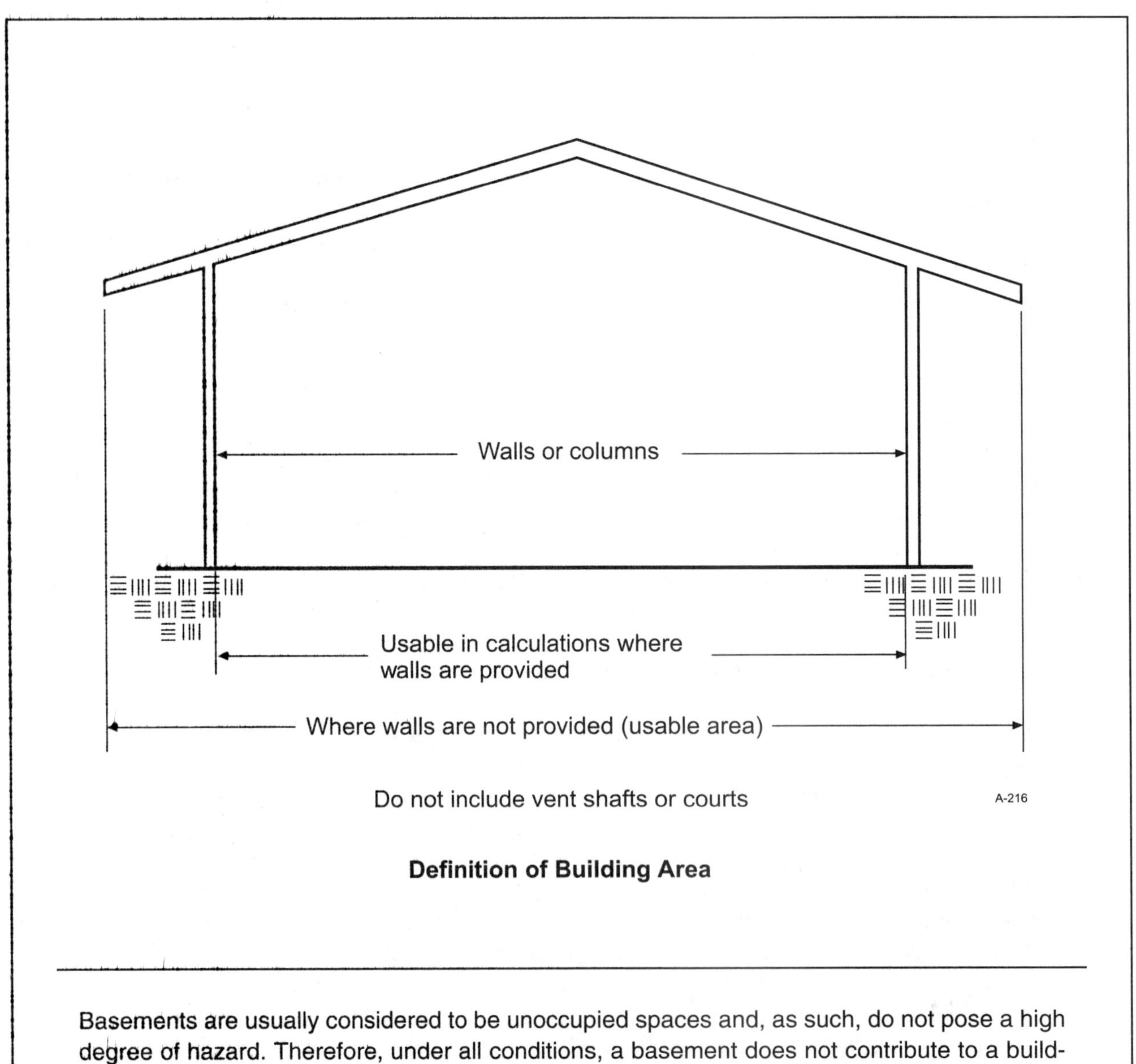

Definition of Building Area

Basements are usually considered to be unoccupied spaces and, as such, do not pose a high degree of hazard. Therefore, under all conditions, a basement does not contribute to a building's allowable height or area. However, it cannot exceed the size permitted for a single story.

Topic: Story Above Grade / Basement
Reference: IBC 202, 502.1

Category: Building Heights and Areas
Subject: Definition

Code Text: *A "story above grade plane" is any story having its finished floor surface entirely above grade plane. A basement is that portion of a building that is partly or completely below grade plane. A basement shall be considered as a story above grade plane where the finished surface of the floor above the basement is (1) more than 6 feet above grade plane, or (2) more than 6 feet above the finished ground level for more than 50 percent of the total building perimeter, or (3) more than 12 feet above the finished ground level at any point.*

Discussion and Commentary: A number of provisions in the IBC are applicable based on the location of the floor under consideration, relative to the exterior ground level. Therefore, it is necessary to define specifically the circumstances under which a floor level is considered a basement, rather than a story above grade plane.

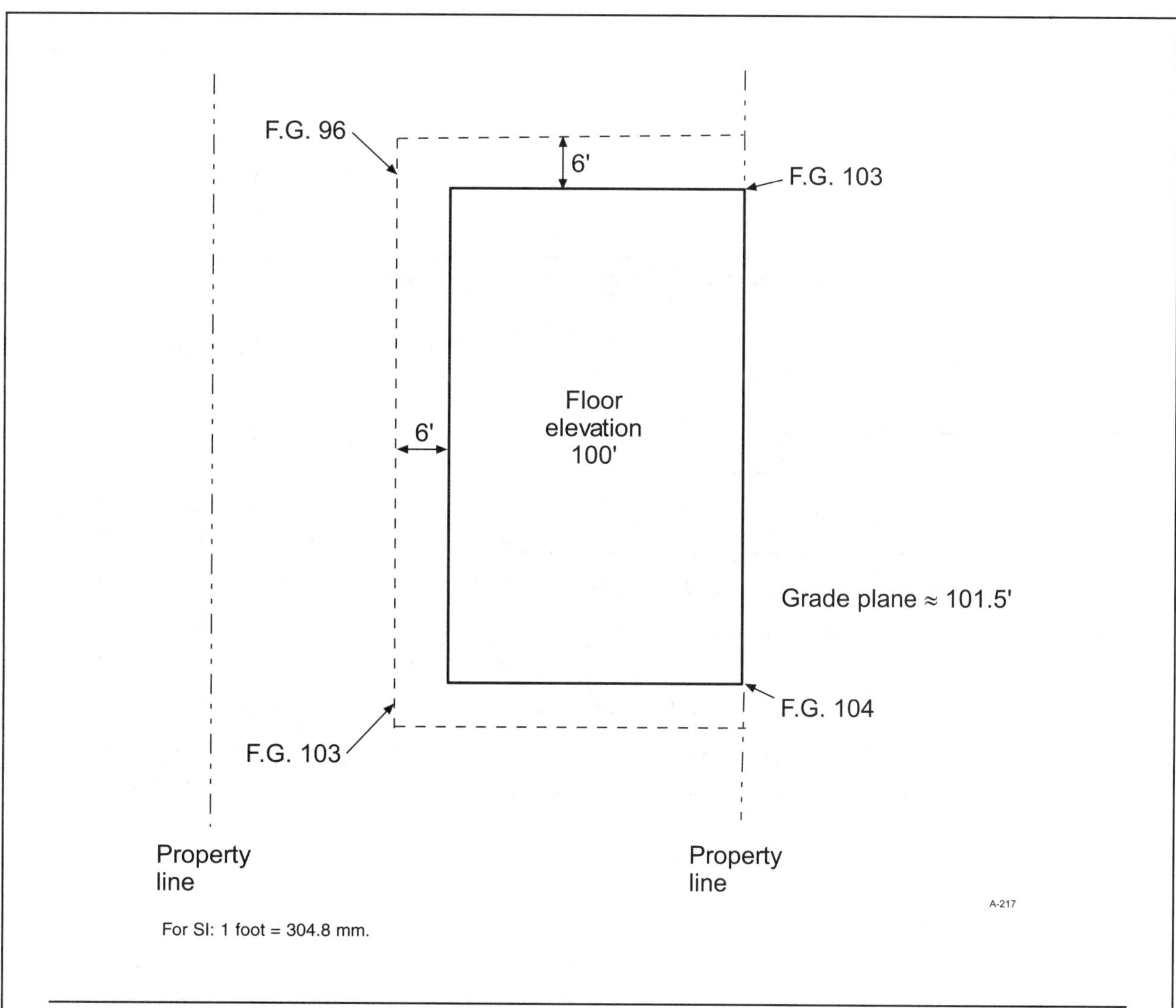

The "grade plane" is defined as a reference plane representing the average of finished ground level adjoining the building at exterior walls. It is measured at the lowest point between the building and the lot line, though never more than 6 feet from the building.

Topic: Use of Table 503
Reference: IBC 503.1, Table 503

Category: Building Heights and Areas
Subject: Height and Area Limitations

Code Text: *The height and area for buildings of different construction types shall be governed by the intended use of the building and shall not exceed the limits in Table 503 except as modified hereafter.*

Discussion and Commentary: Table 503 is the foremost code provision used in establishing equivalent risk (offsetting a building's inherent fire hazard—represented by occupancy group— with materials and construction features). Sections 504 and 506 give height and area increases to the limits of Table 503 for buildings with certain features. Table 503 has three components. The left column lists all of the occupancy classifications, the top row lists the various construction types, and each cell of the matrix contains the specific height (in stories above grade) and area (per floor) limitations for the occupancy group/type of construction combination in question.

TABLE 503
ALLOWABLE HEIGHT AND BUILDING AREAS
Height limitations shown as stories and feet above grade plane.
Area limitations as determined by the definition of "Area, building," per floor.

		TYPE OF CONSTRUCTION								
		TYPE I		TYPE II		TYPE III		TYPE IV	TYPE V	
		A	B	A	B	A	B	HT	A	B
GROUP	Hgt(feet) / Hgt(S)	UL	160	65	55	65	55	65	50	40
A-1	S	UL	5	3	2	3	2	3	2	1
	A	UL	UL	15,500	8,500	14,000	8,500	15,000	11,500	5,500
A-2	S	UL	11	3	2	3	2	3	2	1
	A	UL	UL	15,500	9,500	14,000	9,500	15,000	11,500	6,000
A-3	S	UL	11	3	2	3	2	3	2	1
	A	UL	UL	15,500	9,500	14,000	9,500	15,000	11,500	6,000
A-4	S	UL	11	3	2	3	2	3	2	1
	A	UL	UL	15,500	9,500	14,000	9,500	15,000	11,500	6,000
A-5	S	UL	UL	UL	UL	UL	UL	UL	UL	UL
	A	UL	UL	UL	UL	UL	UL	UL	UL	UL
B	S	UL	11	5	4	5	4	5	3	2
	A	UL	UL	37,500	23,000	28,500	19,000	36,000	18,000	9,000
E	S	UL	5	3	2	3	2	3	1	1
	A	UL	UL	26,500	14,500	23,500	14,500	25,500	18,500	9,500
F-1	S	UL	11	4	2	3	2	4	2	1
	A	UL	UL	25,000	15,500	19,000	12,000	33,500	14,000	8,500
F-2	S	UL	11	5	3	4	3	5	3	2
	A	UL	UL	37,500	23,000	28,500	18,000	50,500	21,000	13,000

The maximum height in feet above grade plane is shown along a top row and is based solely on construction type. Buildings must meet both the height in stories and the height in feet criteria to be considered in compliance with that type of construction.

Topic: Buildings on the Same Lot
Reference: IBC 503.1.3

Category: Building Heights and Areas
Subject: Height and Area Limitations

Code Text: *Two or more buildings on the same lot shall be regulated as separate buildings or shall be considered as portions of one building if the height of each building and the aggregate area of buildings are within the limitations of Table 503 as modified by Sections 504 and 506. The provisions of the code applicable to the aggregate building shall be applicable to each building.*

Discussion and Commentary: In general, the provisions of Section 704.3 would require an assumed property line to be located between two buildings on the same site to regulate exterior wall and opening protection, as well as roof-covering requirements. This alternate method would provide protection equivalent to that of buildings on adjoining lots.

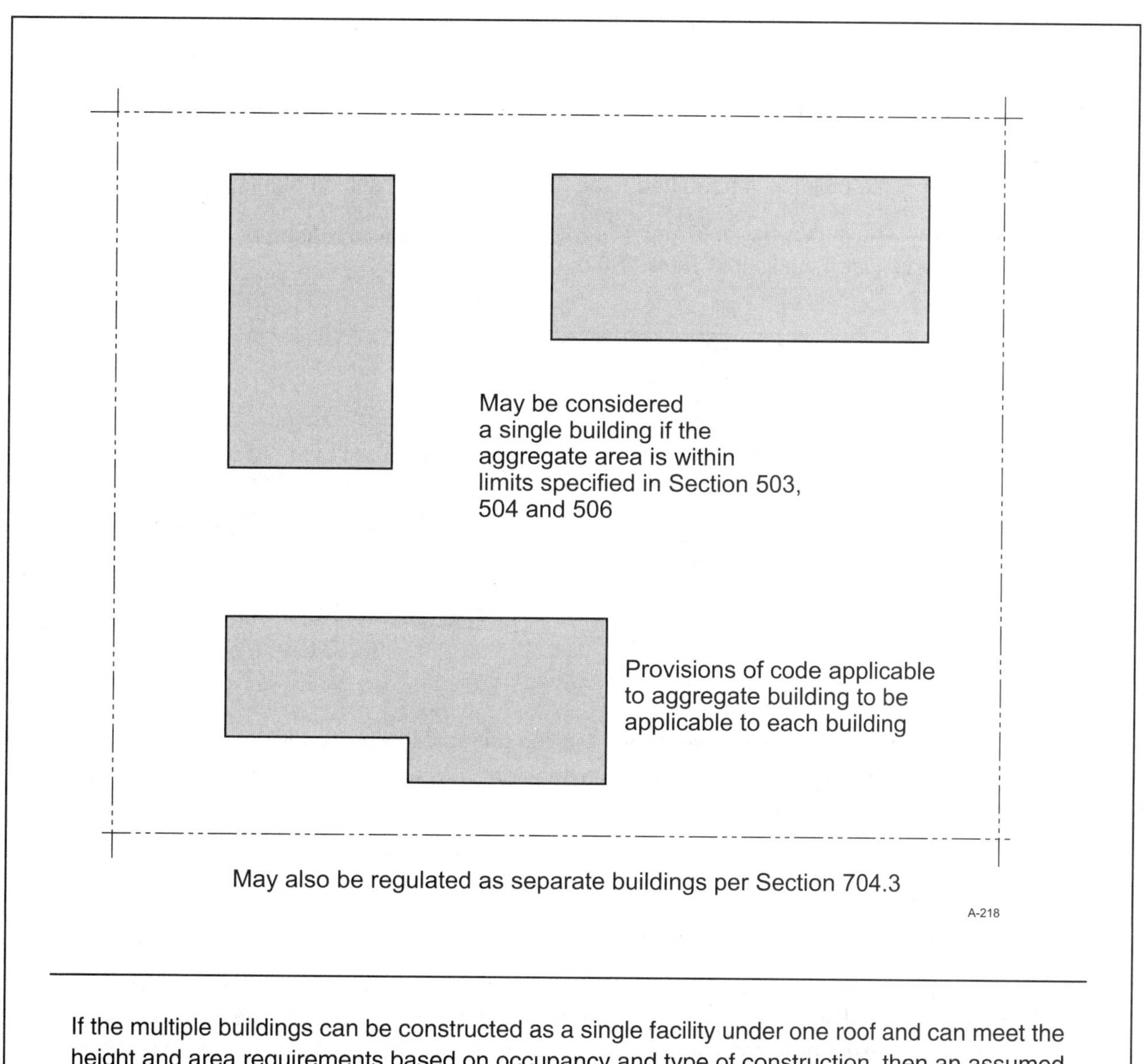

If the multiple buildings can be constructed as a single facility under one roof and can meet the height and area requirements based on occupancy and type of construction, then an assumed property line will not be required. The buildings will simply be considered a single structure.

Topic: Automatic Sprinkler Increase
Reference: IBC 504.2

Category: Building Heights and Areas
Subject: Height Modifications

Code Text: *Where a building is equipped throughout with an approved automatic sprinkler system installed in accordance with Section 903.3.1.1, the value specified in Table 503 for maximum height is increased by 20 feet and the maximum number of stories is increased by one story. These increases are permitted in addition to the area increase in accordance with Sections 506.1 and 506.3.* See exceptions for specific Group I and H occupancies and for buildings utilizing the fire-resistance-rating substitution method.

Discussion and Commentary: The installation of an automatic sprinkler system improves the fire safety aspects of a building to the degree that an increase in height is justified. The presence of a sprinkler system also can be used to provide the sizable area increase permitted in Section 506.3.

Maximum height and number of stories based upon occupancy and type of construction as set forth in Table 503.

Given: A type VA office building is permitted to be 3 stories and 50 feet in height per Table 503.

If sprinkler system installed per Section 504.2, the story limit may be increased by one story, and the height can exceed the limit in Table 503 by 20 feet.

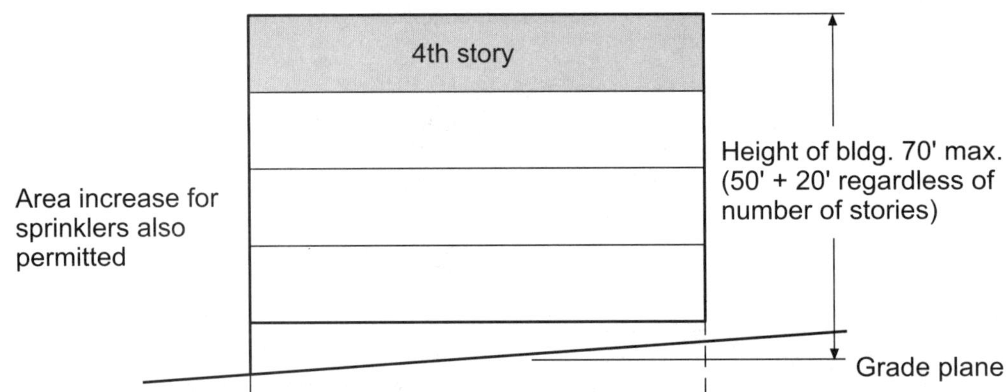

Increase does not apply when sprinkler installed under following conditions:

1. Group I-2 of Type IIB, III, IV or V construction
2. Group H-1, H-2, H-3 or H-5
3. Fire-resistance-rating substitution per Table 601, noted

A-219a

For SI: 1 foot = 304.8 mm.

In a residential building protected with an NFPA 13R sprinkler system, the increase is permitted, provided the building has a maximum height of four stories or 60 feet. The provision does not intend for a residential sprinkler system to be installed in buildings over four stories in height.

Topic: Roof Structures
Reference: IBC 504.3

Category: Building Heights and Areas
Subject: Height Modifications

Code Text: *Towers, spires, steeples and other roof structures shall be constructed of materials consistent with the required type of construction of the building except where other construction is permitted by Section 1509.2.1. Such structures shall not be used for habitation or storage. The structures shall be unlimited in height if of noncombustible materials and shall not extend more than 20 feet above the allowable height if of combustible materials.*

Discussion and Commentary: The types of structures addressed by this provision are intended to be unoccupied with no significant fire loading. It would seem logical that the height of such structures could be increased over that required for typical buildings. The only limitation occurs where the structure is of combustible materials, which would create a higher hazard.

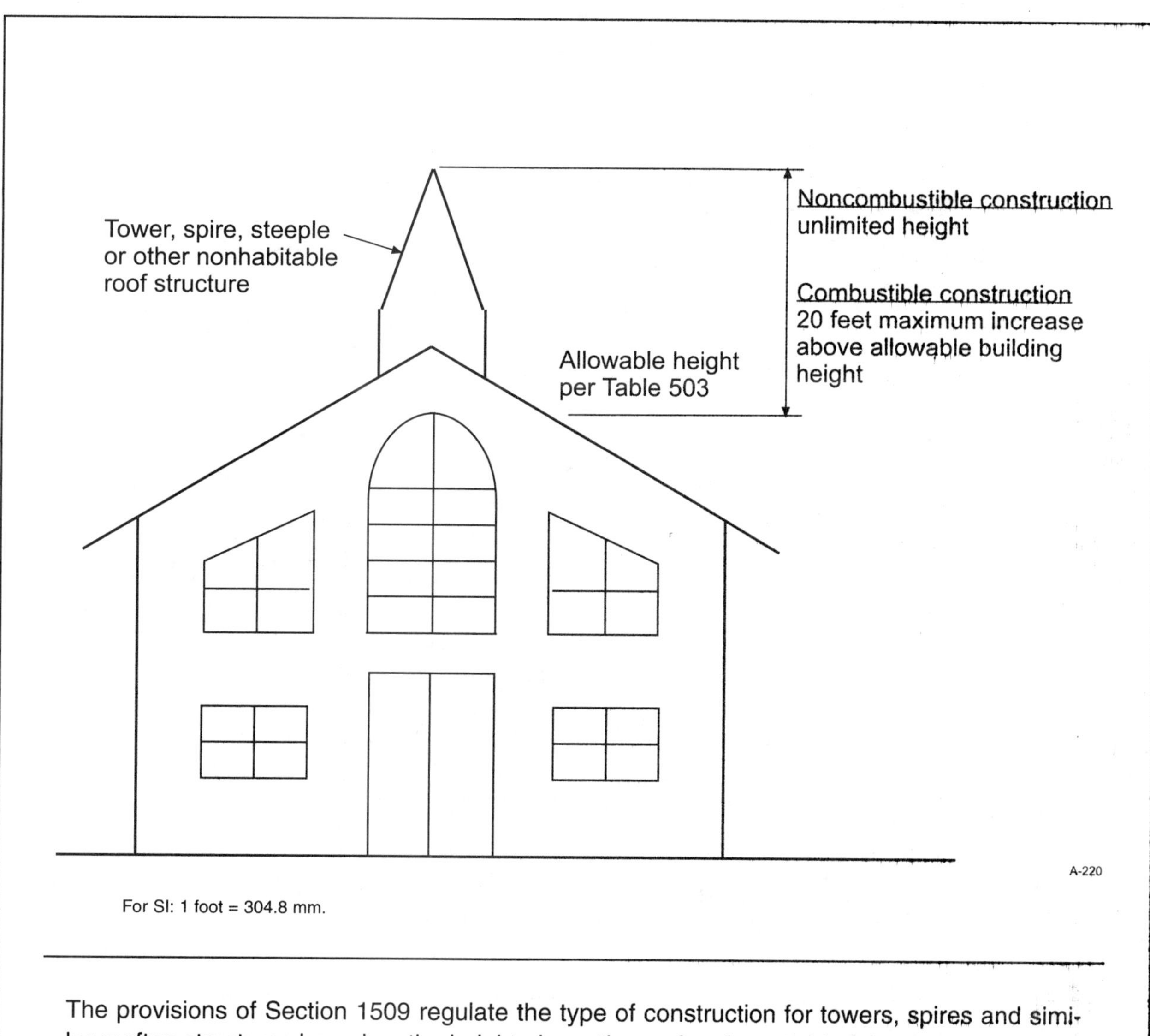

For SI: 1 foot = 304.8 mm.

The provisions of Section 1509 regulate the type of construction for towers, spires and similar rooftop structures based on the height above the roof surface, the height above grade and the largest cross-sectional dimension. Penthouses and equipment screening are also addressed.

Topic: Definition
Reference: IBC 502.1, 505.1

Category: Building Heights and Areas
Subject: Mezzanines

Code Text: *A mezzanine is an intermediate level or levels between the floor and ceiling of any story with an aggregate floor area of not more than one-third of the area of the room or space in which the level or levels are located. A complying mezzanine shall be considered a portion of the floor below.*

Discussion and Commentary: Because of size limitation and openness (a mezzanine is open to the room in which it is located, with exceptions), an intermediate floor level within a room adds minimal hazard to the building and its occupants. The occupants of the mezzanine by means of sight, smell or hearing will be able to determine if there is some emergency or fire taking place either on the mezzanine or in the room in which the mezzanine is located.

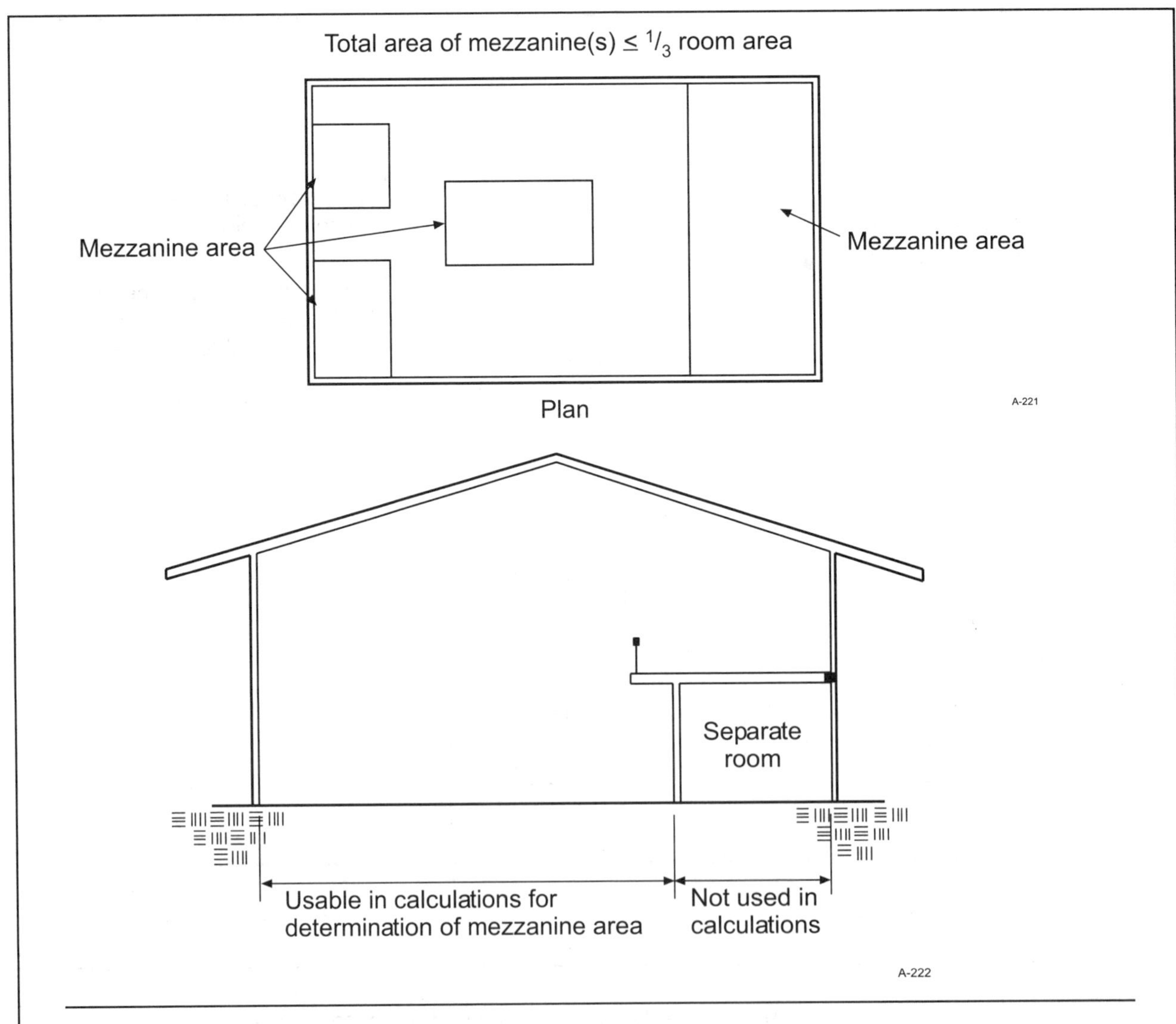

The maximum permitted floor area of a mezzanine is based on the floor area of the room in which it is located. Only those portions of the lower room that are unenclosed may be considered in the calculation of maximum mezzanine size.

Topic: Scope
Reference: IBC 505.1

Category: Building Heights and Areas
Subject: Mezzanines

Code Text: *Mezzanines shall not contribute to either the building area or number of stories as regulated by Section 503.1. The area of a mezzanine shall be included in determining the fire area defined in Section 702.*

Discussion and Commentary: There are two distinct benefits derived from the qualification of a floor level as a mezzanine. One, the mezzanine is not considered in the allowable number of stories, and two, for allowable area purposes, the mezzanine floor area does not increase the building area of the story in which it is located. However, in the determination of fire area size for sprinkler requirements, the floor area must be considered. The requirements for sprinkler systems are generally based on the fire load expected in an occupancy; thus, an increased floor area would increase the potential fire loading. The provisions of Section 505.3 also provide for a third benefit in regard to number of egress paths required.

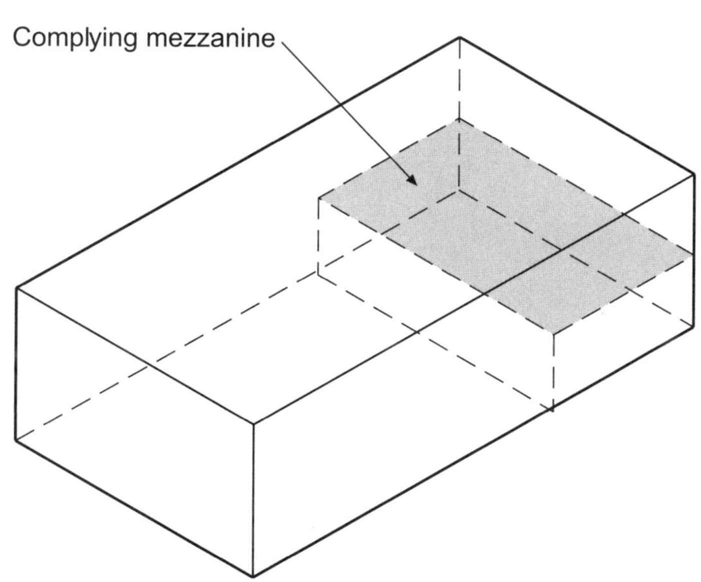

Mezzanine:

- Does not contribute to floor area for maximum allowable area
- Does not contribute as an additional story
- Does contribute to floor area for fire area size determination

Example:
For 8,000 sq ft first floor as shown with 2,000 sq ft mezzanine, building area is 8,000 sq ft, building is one story in height, and fire area is 10,000 sq ft

A-223

For SI: 1 foot = 304.8 mm.

Although it is quite possible that an individual floor level within a building can meet all of the provisions of the IBC and qualify as a mezzanine, its actual designation is the choice of the designer. It may be more advantageous to treat the floor level simply as an additional story.

Topic: Openness
Reference: IBC 505.4

Category: Building Heights and Areas
Subject: Mezzanines

Code Text: *A mezzanine shall be open and unobstructed to the room in which such mezzanine is located except for walls not more than 42 inches high, columns and posts.* See exceptions.

Discussion and Commentary: By definition, a mezzanine is intended to be open to the room or space below. This common environment allows individuals on either floor level to be aware of the conditions and hazards that may affect their safety. The IBC, through the application of one of five exceptions, permits the mezzanine to be enclosed when it has been determined that the enclosure creates little, if any concern. Where the mezzanine area houses a limited number of occupants, or where the enclosed portion is a relatively small percentage of the total mezzanine area, openness is not required. A totally glazed enclosure is also permitted in industrial facilities.

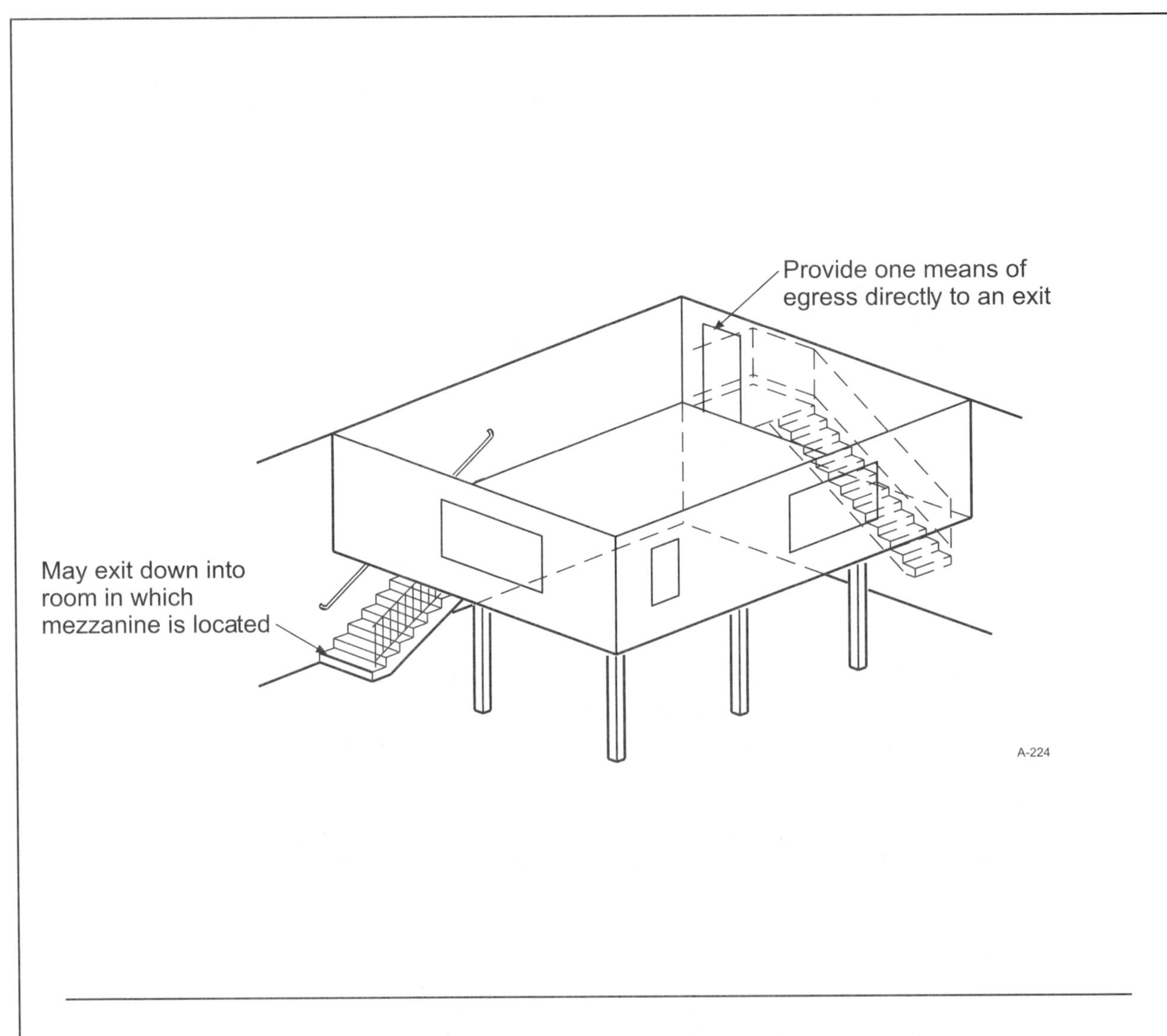

A common exception used to permit the enclosing of a mezzanine is based on egress conditions. If a minimum of two means of egress are provided from the mezzanine level, with at least one such egress path leading directly to an exit, then the mezzanine is not required to be open.

Topic: Area Determination
Reference: IBC 506.1, 506.4

Category: Building Heights and Areas
Subject: Area Modifications

Code Text: *The areas limited by Table 503 shall be permitted to be increased due to frontage (I_f) and automatic sprinkler system protection(I_s). The maximum area of a building with more than one story shall be determined by multiplying the allowable area of the first floor (A_a), as determined in Section 506.1, by the number of stories as listed: 1) for two-story buildings, multiply by 2; 2) for three-story or higher buildings, multiply by 3; and 3) no story shall exceed the allowable area per floor (A_a), as determined by Section 506.1 for the occupancies on that floor.* See exceptions for unlimited area buildings and residential buildings sprinklered with an NFPA 13R system.

Discussion and Commentary: The tabular allowable building areas set forth in Table 503 are limited on a floor-by-floor basis. The presence of sufficient open space adjacent to a building provides for an increase above the tabular value. The protection afforded by an automatic sprinkler system justifies a significant allowable area increase. The IBC permits both increases to be used to provide the maximum building area permitted per floor.

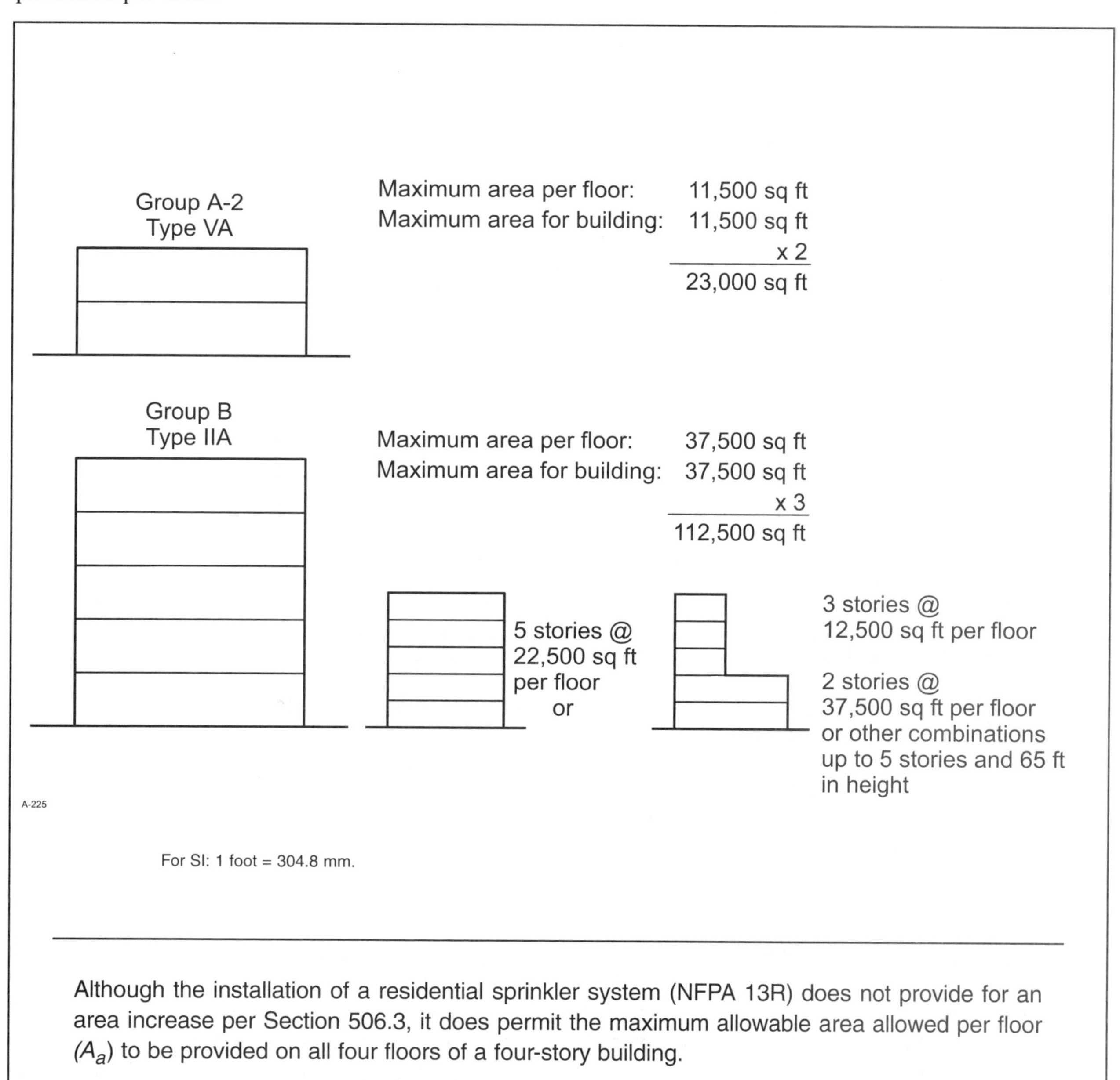

Although the installation of a residential sprinkler system (NFPA 13R) does not provide for an area increase per Section 506.3, it does permit the maximum allowable area allowed per floor (A_a) to be provided on all four floors of a four-story building.

Topic: Frontage Increase
Reference: IBC 506.2

Category: Building Heights and Areas
Subject: Area Modifications

Code Text: *Every building shall adjoin or have access to a public way to receive an area increase for frontage. Where a building has more than 25 percent of its perimeter on a public way or open space having a minimum width of 20 feet, the frontage increase shall be determined in accordance with the following:* $I_f = 100\ [F/P - 0.25]\ W/30$.

Discussion and Commentary: It is assumed that every building will adjoin a street, alley or yard on at least one side. Therefore, no frontage increase is given for the first 25% of a building's perimeter that is open. Credit is provided, however, where additional frontage is considered open (20 feet or more in width). The benefit of increased allowable building area is accrued based on better access for the fire department, as well as decreased exposure to adjoining properties.

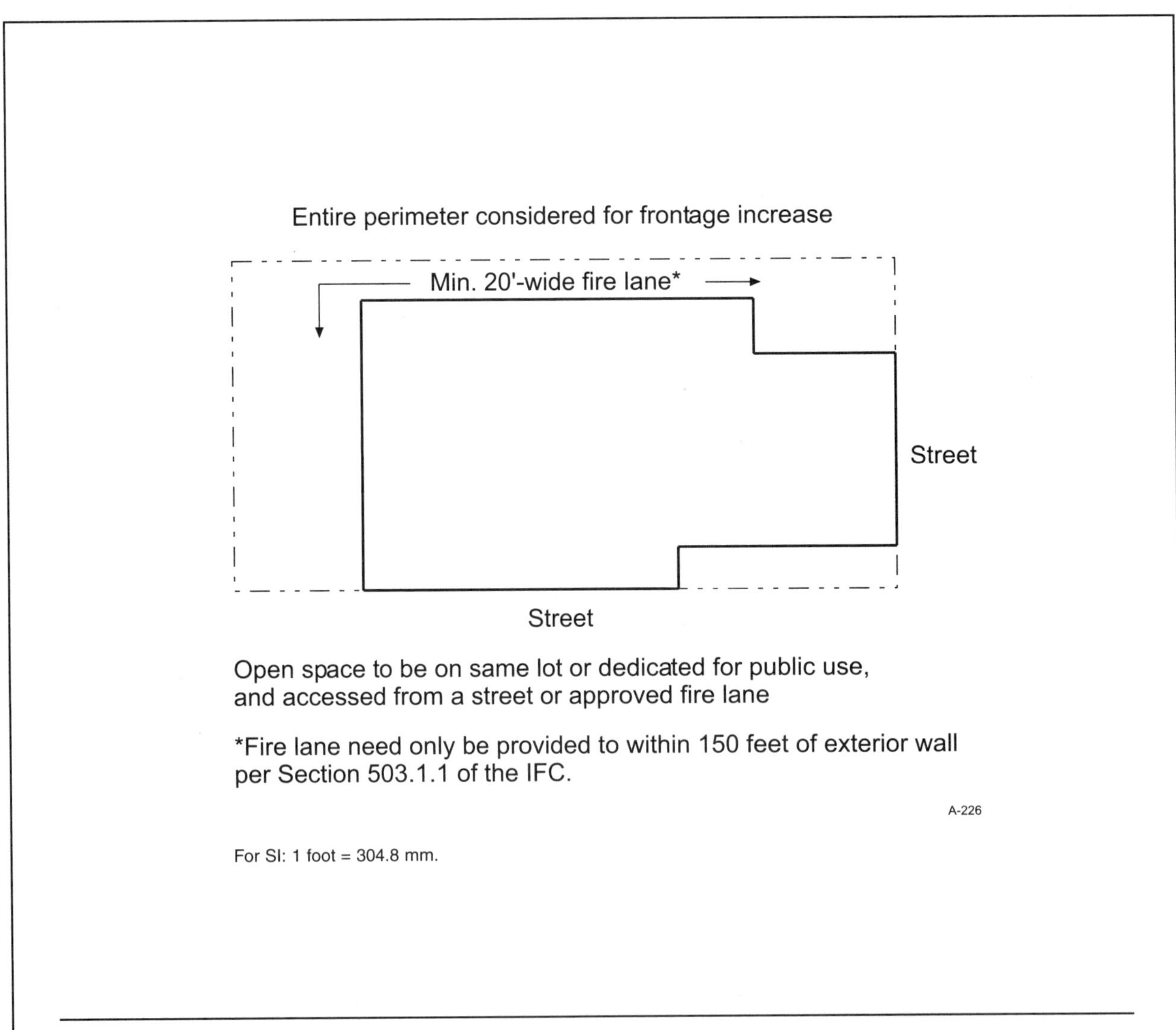

Access must be provided from a street or an approved fire lane for any open space that is used for a frontage increase in allowable floor area. The *International Fire Code* mandates that a fire lane for fire apparatus be maintained with an unobstructed width of at least 20 feet.

Topic: Sprinkler System Increase
Reference: IBC 506.3

Category: Building Heights and Areas
Subject: Area Modifications

Code Text: *Where a building is protected throughout with an approved automatic sprinkler system in accordance with Section 903.3.1.1, the area limitation in Table 503 is permitted to be increased by an additional 200 percent (I_S = 200 percent) for multi-story buildings and an additional 300 percent (I_S = 300 percent) for single-story buildings.* See exceptions for Group H-1, H-2 and H-3 occupancies, and for buildings utilizing the fire-resistance-rated substitution allowance.

Discussion and Commentary: Because of its excellent record of in-place fire suppression, an automatic sprinkler system provides for a sizable allowable area increase. The presence of the sprinkler system also allows a height increase as addressed in Section 504.2. However, sprinkler systems are considered an absolute necessity in occupancies associated with high hazard levels, such as Groups H-1, H-2 and H-3; thus, no size increases are permitted for such uses.

Examples

Given: Group B occupancy single-story
Type VB construction
No open yards available
Find: Total allowable area

Basic allowable area = 9,000 sq ft. (Table 503)
Sprinkler increase (I_s) = 27,000 sq ft. (300%)
Total allowable area = 36,000 sq ft.

Given: Same situation, however two stories in height
Find: Total allowable area

Basic allowable area = 9,000 sq ft. (Table 503)
Sprinkler increase (I_s) = 18,000 sq ft. (200%)
Total allowable area per floor = 27,000 sq ft.

For SI: 1 foot = 304.8 mm.

It is assumed that in many cases, fire department suppression activities will supplement an automatic sprinkler system. Because a multistory building presents more problems to the fire department than a single-story structure, a smaller increase in area is justified.

Topic: One-Story, Sprinklered Buildings
Reference: IBC 507.2

Category: Building Heights and Areas
Subject: Unlimited Area Buildings

Code Text: *The area of a one-story, Group B, F, M or S building or a one-story Group A-4 building of other than Type V construction shall not be limited when the building is provided with an automatic sprinkler system throughout in accordance with Section 903.3.1.1, and is surrounded and adjoined by public ways or yards not less than 60 feet in width.* Provisions also apply to two-story buildings of such occupancies other than Group A-4.

Discussion and Commentary: It is often beneficial to have very large, undivided floor areas for facilities such as arenas, office buildings, factories, retail centers and warehouses. The unlimited area provisions allow for an alternative to the higher types of construction that would normally be required. The installation of a sprinkler system and sufficient open space around the building reduce the potential fire severity to a reasonable level in these moderate-hazard occupancies.

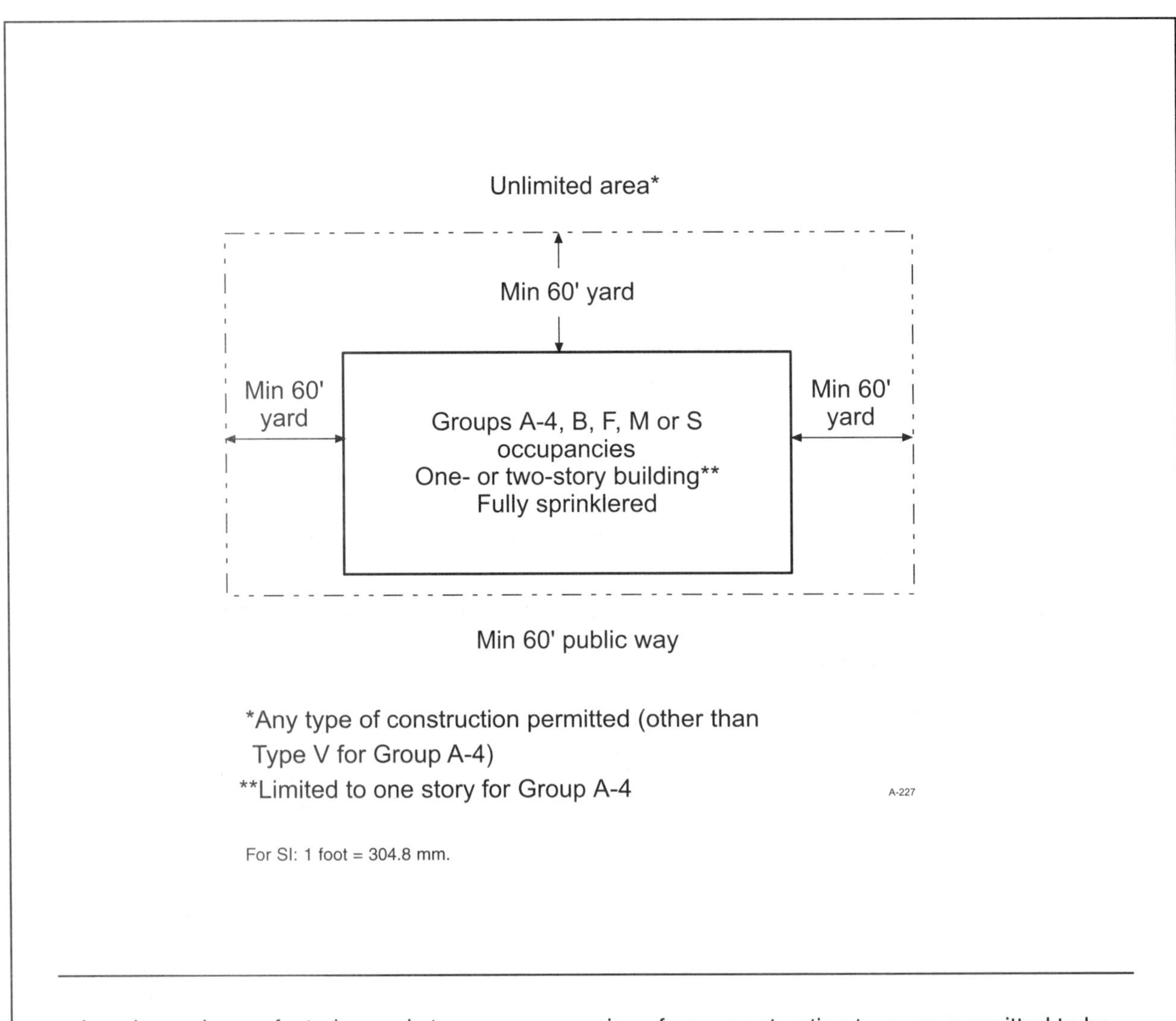

Low-hazard manufacturing and storage occupancies of any construction type are permitted to be unlimited in area where they are only one story in height and are provided on all sides with public ways or yards at least 60 feet in width. Installation of an automatic sprinkler system is not required.

Topic: Reduced Open Space
Reference: IBC 507.4

Category: Building Heights and Areas
Subject: Unlimited Area Buildings

Code Text: *The permanent open space of 60 feet required in Sections 507.1, 507.2 and 507.3 shall be permitted to be reduced to not less than 40 feet provided the following requirements are met: (1) the reduced open space shall not be allowed for more than 75 percent of the perimeter of the building, (2) the exterior wall facing the reduced open space shall have a minimum fire-resistance rating of 3 hours, and (3) openings in the exterior wall, facing the reduced open space, shall have opening protectives with a fire-resistance rating of 3 hours.*

Discussion and Commentary: When it is necessary or desirable to reduce the open space around the perimeter of an unlimited area building, the code provides an alternative. An equivalent level of protection can be provided by increasing the level of exterior wall and opening protection.

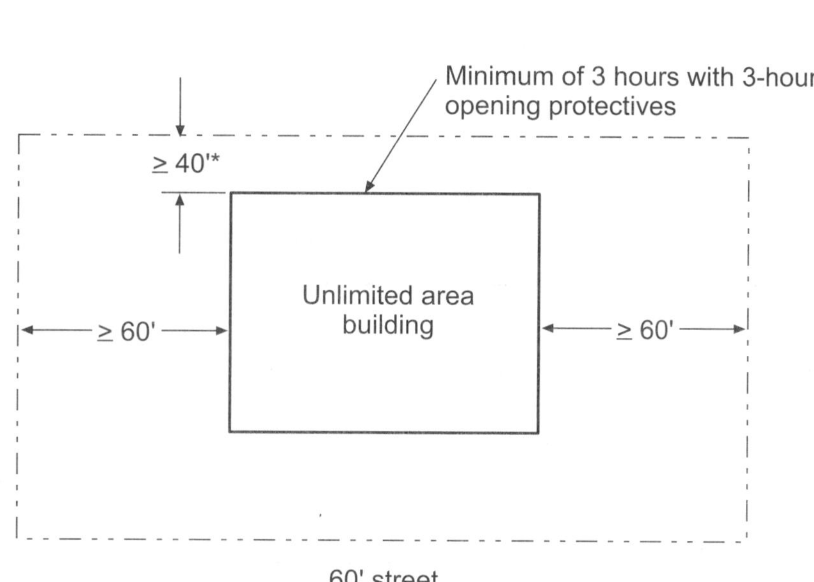

*Reduced open space permitted:

- Up to 75% of building perimeter
- Where exterior wall facing reduced open space has minimum 3-hour fire-resistance rating
- Openings in such walls are protected for 3 hours

A-228

For SI: 1 foot = 304.8 mm.

This provision is designed for warehouses, factories, retail stores and office buildings where fire resistance at the exterior wall is easily accomplished. The reduction does not apply to other buildings permitted to be unlimited in area, such as educational uses and motion picture theaters.

Topic: Group A-3 Buildings
Reference: IBC 507.5

Category: Building Heights and Areas
Subject: Unlimited Area Buildings

Code Text: *The area of a one-story, Group A-3 building used as a church, community hall, dance hall, exhibition hall, gymnasium, lecture hall, indoor swimming pool or tennis court of Type I or II construction shall not be limited when all of the following criteria are met:* See four conditions for allowance of unlimited area.

Discussion and Commentary: The Group A-3 occupancy classification includes the most diverse types of assembly uses assigned by the code. Traditionally, the allowable area of Group A occupancies is greatly limited as compared to most other occupancy groups. However, those assembly uses expected to have a relatively low fire load are permitted in unlimited area buildings subject to the special conditions prescribed by the code.

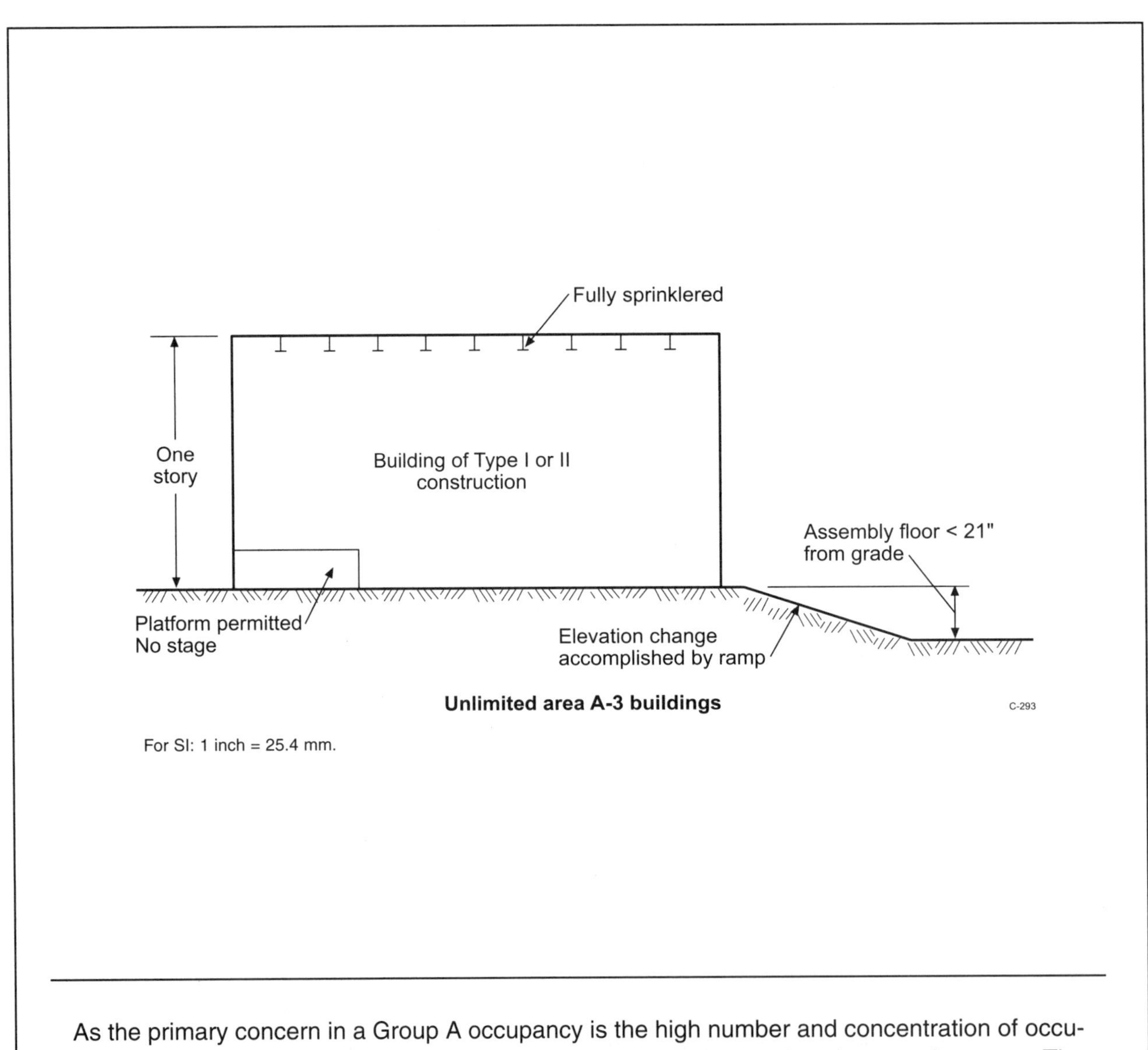

Unlimited area A-3 buildings

As the primary concern in a Group A occupancy is the high number and concentration of occupants, it is important that egress be accomplished in an efficient and unobstructed manner. The requirement for only flat or limited ramp travel assists in gaining an effective egress system.

Topic: High-hazard Use Groups
Reference: IBC 507.6

Category: Building Heights and Areas
Subject: Unlimited Area Buildings

Code Text: *Group H-2, H-3 and H-4 fire areas shall be permitted in unlimited area buildings having occupancies in Groups F and S, in accordance with the limitations of* Section 507.6. *Fire areas located at the perimeter of the unlimited area building shall not exceed 10 percent of the area of the building nor the area limitations specified in Table 503 as modified by Section 506.2, based upon the percentage of the perimeter of the fire area that fronts on a street or other unoccupied space. Other fire areas shall not exceed 25 percent of the area limitations specified in Table 503.*

Discussion and Commentary: The allowable area of the permitted Group H occupancies in a factory or warehouse is dependent on the type of construction of the building and the location of the Group H occupancy in the buildings.

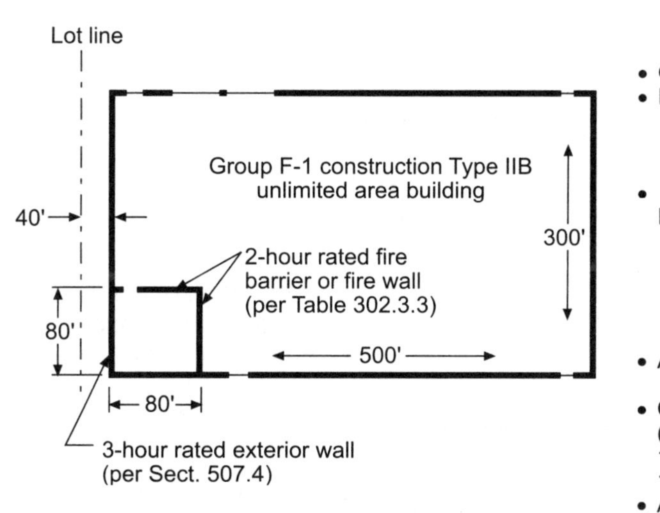

For SI: 1 inch = 25.4 mm, 1 foot = 304.8 mm.

- Group H-2
- In Equation 5-2
  F = 160 ft
  P = 320 ft
  W = 30 ft
- (The maximum per Sect. 506.2.1)
  In Equation 5-2,

$$I_f = 100\left[\frac{160}{320} - 0.25\right]\frac{30}{30}$$

$$I_f = 25\%$$

- Allowable area for H-2 = 7,000 + (0.25)(7,000)
  = 8,750 sq ft
- Check 10% of floor area criterium:
  (500)(300) = 150,000 sq ft
  150,000/10 = 15,000 sq ft
  15,000 > 8,750, ∴8,750 maximum allowable
- Actual area = 6,400, which is less than 8,750, therefore OK

Group H-2 at the corner of an unlimited area building

C-294

More ready access to the Group H from the exterior of the building provides the fire department with an opportunity to respond more effectively to an incident. As such, the allowable floor area of the Group H can be far greater than where completely surrounded by the Group F or S use.

Topic: Open Parking Garages
Reference: IBC 508.8

Category: Building Heights and Areas
Subject: Special Provisions

Code Text: *Open parking garages constructed under Groups A, I, B, M and R shall not exceed the height and area limitations permitted under Section 406.3. The height and area of the portion of the building above the open parking garage shall not exceed the limitations in Section 503 for the upper occupancy. The height, in both feet and stories, of the portion of the building above the open parking garage shall be measured from grade plane and shall include both the open parking garage and the portion of the building above the parking garage.*

Discussion and Commentary: In the more common types of occupancies, it is desirable at times to provide tiers of parking below the major use of the building. The IBC permits such a condition, provided that the upper occupancy complies with the provisions for the overall building height.

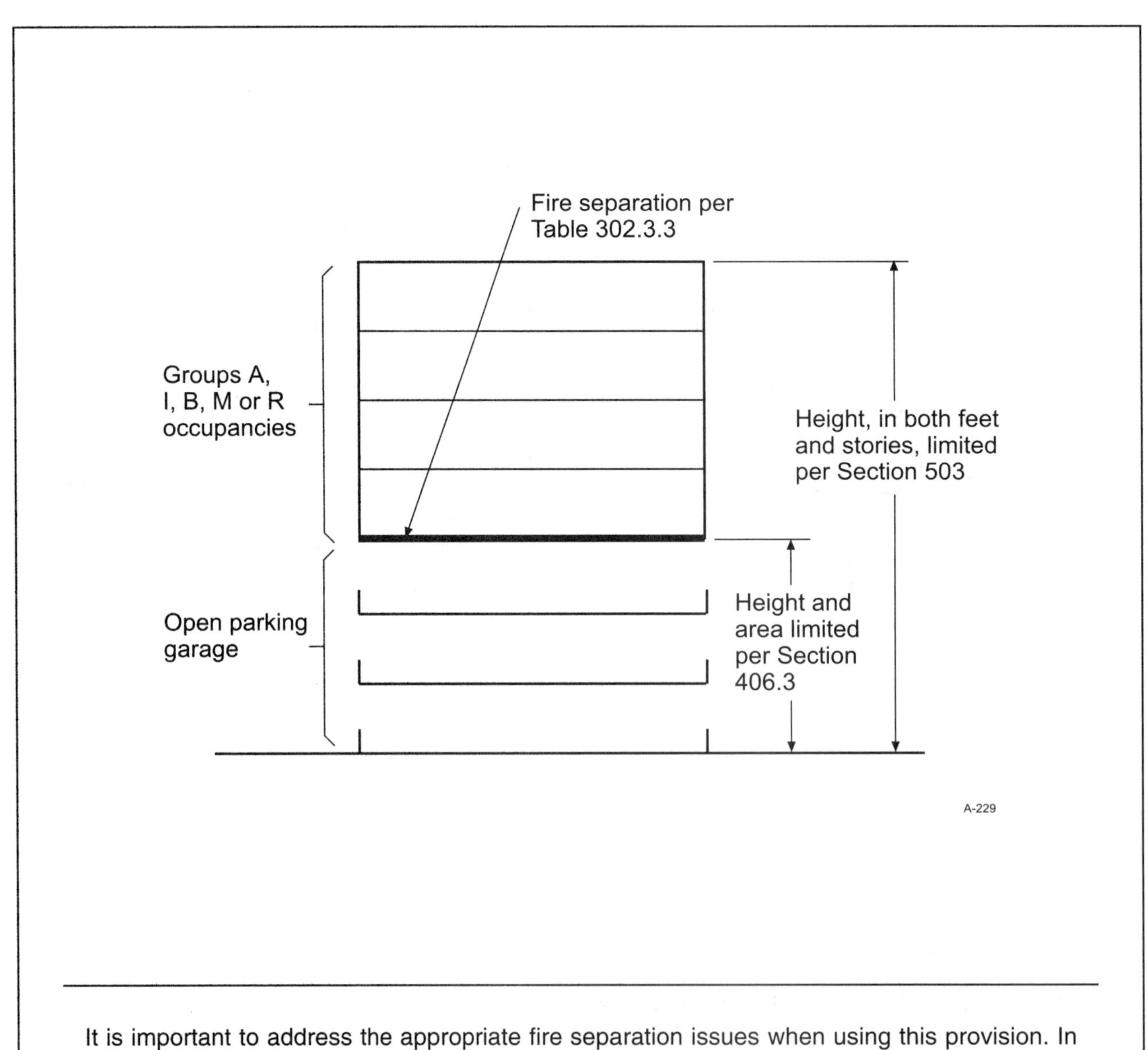

It is important to address the appropriate fire separation issues when using this provision. In addition, the structural members supporting the upper occupancy must be protected by the more restrictive fire-resistant assemblies of all of the occupancies involved.

QUIZ

Study Session 4 — Chapter 5

I. Multiple Choice

1. Premises must be identified by numbers or addresses visible from the street, with a minimum character height of at least __________ inches.

   a. three
   b. four
   c. six
   d. eight

   Reference_______________

2. The portion of a building included between the upper surface of a floor and the upper surface of the floor or roof next above is a __________.

   a. basement
   b. mezzanine
   c. story
   d. story above grade

   Reference_______________

3. The tabular allowable height and building area per floor for a Group I-2 occupancy of Type IB construction is limited to __________ stories and __________ square feet.

   a. 3, 10,000
   b. 2, 15,000
   c. 4, unlimited
   d. unlimited, unlimited

   Reference_______________

4. What is the maximum tabular height, in feet, for a Group B occupancy of Type IIA construction?

   a. 50
   b. 55
   c. 65
   d. unlimited

   Reference_______________

5. Basements need not be included in the total allowable area of a building, provided they do not exceed __________.

   a. one-third the floor area permitted for any single story
   b. the area permitted for a one-story building
   c. twice the area permitted for a single story
   d. the tabular area based on construction type and occupancy group

   Reference_______________

6. Party walls located on a property line between two adjacent buildings shall be constructed as __________.

a. fire walls
b. fire barriers
c. fire separation walls
d. fire partitions

Reference_______________

7. The maximum building area of a six-story building is limited to __________ times the allowable area permitted per floor.

a. two
b. three
c. four
d. six

Reference_______________

8. A height increase of __________ and __________ is permitted in a building housing a Group B occupancy and protected throughout with an automatic sprinkler system.

a. 15 feet, one story
b. 20 feet, one story
c. 15 feet, two stories
d. 20 feet, two stories

Reference_______________

9. An increase in allowable height is not permitted for which of the following occupancy groups located in a Type IIB building?

a. Group A-1
b. Group H-4
c. Group I-2
d. Group R-2

Reference_______________

10. Combustible steeples are limited to a maximum height of __________ feet above the allowable building height.

a. 15
b. 20
c. 30
d. 40

Reference_______________

11. The area of a mezzanine is not to be included in the determination of the __________.

a. fire area
b. building area
c. occupant load
d. plumbing fixture count

Reference_______________

12. A minimum clear height of __________ inches is required above and below mezzanine floor construction.

a. 80 b. 84
c. 90 d. 96

Reference_______________

13. In general, the aggregate area of mezzanines within a room is limited to __________ of the area of the room in which the mezzanines are located.

a. 10% b. 25%
c. $33^1/_3$% d. 50%

Reference_______________

14. Portions of a mezzanine need not be open to the room in which the mezzanine is located, provided the enclosed space is limited in size to a maximum of __________ of the mezzanine area.

a. 10% b. 25%
c. $33^1/_3$% d. 50%

Reference_______________

15. A mezzanine is not required to be open to the room in which it is located where the occupant load of the mezzanine does not exceed __________.

a. 10 b. 20
c. 30 d. 50

Reference_______________

16. An area increase for frontage is permitted where more than __________ of the building perimeter is sufficiently open.

a. 10% b. 25%
c. $33^1/_3$% d. 40%

Reference_______________

17. In order to be considered as sufficiently open for an area increase for frontage, the public way or open space must have a minimum width of at least __________ feet.

a. 10 b. 20
c. 25 d. 30

Reference_______________

18. Except for buildings permitted to be unlimited in area, a maximum increase of __________ is permitted for frontage.

a. 25%
b. 50%
c. 75%
d. 100%

Reference_______________

19. In order to gain the maximum frontage increase, the adjoining public ways and open space must be a minimum of __________ feet in width for the entire perimeter.

a. 20
b. 30
c. 40
d. 60

Reference_______________

20. The allowable building area may be increased by __________ in a multistory building protected throughout with an approved automatic sprinkler system.

a. 50%
b. 100%
c. 200%
d. 300%

Reference_______________

21. In a fully-sprinklered single-story building, the allowable building area may be increased by __________.

a. 50%
b. 100%
c. 200%
d. 300%

Reference_______________

22. Which of the following occupancy groups may be located in an nonsprinklered one-story unlimited area building of Type IIB construction?

a. Group B
b. Group F-1
c. Group S-2
d. Group U

Reference_______________

23. In order to reduce the required open space surrounding certain unlimited area buildings from 60 feet to 40 feet, walls and openings facing the reduced open space shall have a minimum fire-resistance rating of __________.

a. 45 minutes
b. 1 hour
c. 2 hours
d. 3 hours

Reference_______________

24. A complying Group H-2 aircraft paint hangar may be unlimited in floor area when limited to one story, provided the hangar is surrounded by yards or public ways having a minimum width of __________.

a. 40 feet
b. 60 feet
c. twice the height of the hangar
d. one and one-half times the height of the hangar

Reference_______________

25. Where utilizing the special provisions for height and area, an open parking garage is permitted beneath all but which of the following occupancy groups?

a. Group A-3
b. Group F-2
c. Group R-1
d. Group R-2

Reference_______________

26. What is the maximum height permitted for a noncombustible communications tower located on the roof of a Type IIB office building?

a. 55 feet
b. 65 feet
c. 75 feet
d. unlimited

Reference_______________

27. In order for a Type IIIB office building to be considered for unlimited area, it must be limited to a maximum height of _____.

a. one story
b. two stories
c. 50 feet
d. 40 feet

Reference_______________

28. A one-story Group A-3 gymnasium may be considered under the unlimited area provisions, provided the assembly floor is located a maximum of _____ above or below grade level.

a. 21 inches
b. 24 inches
c. 30 inches
d. 48 inches

Reference_______________

29. An H-3 storage room located within an unlimited area manufacturing building of Type IIB construction is limited to _____ square feet where not located on the building's perimeter.

a. 3,125
b. 3,500
c. 12,500
d. 14,000

Reference_______________

30. A nine-story apartment building of Type IIA construction shall be located a minimum of _____ feet from any other building on the lot and from all property lines.

a. 10 feet
b. 30 feet
c. 50 feet
d. 60 feet

Reference_______________

INTERNATIONAL BUILDING CODE

Study Session 5

Sections 701–704 — Fire-Resistance-Rated Construction I

OBJECTIVE: To gain an understanding of the fundamentals of fire-resistance-rated construction, the methods for the determination of fire resistance, and the regulation of exterior walls for fire-resistance rating and opening protection.

REFERENCE: Sections 701 through 704, 2003 *International Building Code*

KEY POINTS:

- Why are fire-resistance-rated materials and systems used in the construction of buildings?
- What is a fire-resistance-rating? How is such a rating determined?
- What reference standard is the basis for determining fire-resistance ratings?
- What is nonsymmetrical wall construction?
- How must interior walls and partitions of nonsymmetrical construction be tested? Exterior walls?
- Which alternative methods are available for determining the fire-resistance rating of different building elements?
- What is a prescriptive design of fire-resistance-rated building elements? What specific types of elements are addressed?
- Which types of materials can be evaluated for fire-resistance ratings through calculations?
- When is a material considered noncombustible? Is gypsum board considered a noncombustible material?
- How is a projection defined? What types of building elements are considered projections?
- What limits the extent of a projection?
- Which types of projections are permitted from walls of Type I and II buildings? Type III, IV and V buildings?
- When must combustible projections be protected? What other options are available?
- How are multiple buildings on the same lot addressed in regard to exterior wall and opening protection?
- Under which conditions must fire-resistance-rated exterior walls be rated for fire exposure from both sides?
- Under which conditions are openings in exterior walls prohibited? What are the limitations where protected openings are provided? Unprotected openings?
- How are protected and unprotected openings regulated in the same exterior wall?
- How does the presence of a sprinkler system affect the amount of unprotected openings?
- Which special provisions apply to openings in the first story of exterior walls?
- When must exterior openings in adjacent stories be protected? Where required, what methods of protection are available?
- What is a parapet? Where are parapets required?
- What fire-resistance rating is mandated for required parapets?
- What is the minimum required height of a parapet? How does the slope of the roof affect the minimum required height?

Topic: Scope
Reference: IBC 701.1

Category: Fire-Resistance-Rated Construction
Subject: Materials and Assemblies

Code Text: *The provisions of Chapter 7 shall govern the materials and assemblies used for structural fire resistance and fire-resistance-rated construction separation of adjacent spaces to safeguard against the spread of fire and smoke within a building and the spread of fire to or from buildings.*

Discussion and Commentary: There are basically two reasons for the protection of various building elements with construction resistant to fire. One, structural elements such as columns, girders, bearing walls and other loadbearing members are often required by the code to maintain their structural integrity under fire conditions for a prescribed time period. Two, horizontal and vertical assemblies are used to create compartments, including control areas, or to isolate portions of the building, such as exitways, through fire-resistant construction.

FIRE RESISTANCE. That property of materials or their assemblies that prevents or retards the passage of excessive heat, hot gases or flames under conditions of use.

In addition to limiting or resisting the spread of fire and heat within a building, certain provisions are intended to provide protection for adjoining structures. The code also uses fire-resistance-rated construction to restrict the passage of smoke to specific areas.

Topic: Materials and Systems
Reference: IBC 702, 703.2

Category: Fire-Resistance-Rated Construction
Subject: Fire-Resistance Ratings

Code Text: *Fire-resistance rating is the period of time a building element, component or assembly maintains the ability to confine a fire, continues to perform a given structural function, or both as determined by the tests, or the methods based on tests, prescribed in Section 703. The fire-resistance rating of building elements shall be determined in accordance with the test procedures set forth in ASTM E 119 or in accordance with Section 703.3* (Alternative methods for determining fire resistance).

Discussion and Commentary: ASTM E119 is the reference standard, "Standard Test Methods for Fire Tests of Building Construction and Materials." These test methods are used for the great majority of building components or assemblies that are mandated by the code to have a fire-resistance rating.

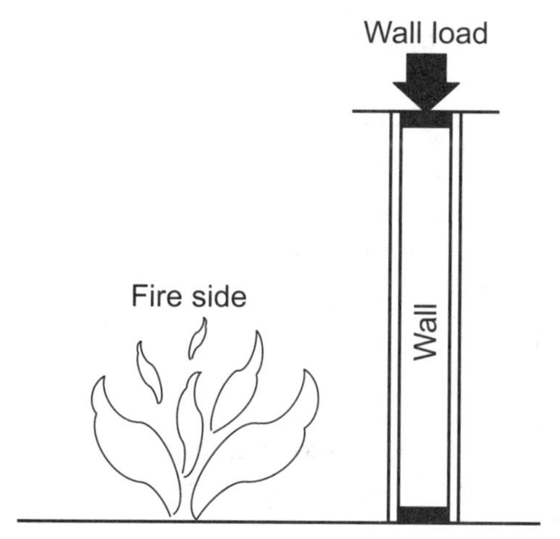

Assembly must:

sustain applied load,

have no passage of flame or gases hot enough to ignite cotton waste,

have average temperature rise on unexposed surface not more than 250°F above initial temperature or more than 325°F at any point, and

have no water pass through during hose-stream test.

Conditions of acceptance - wall fire test

A-230

For nonsymmetrical wall construction, where interior walls and partitions are provided with differing membranes on opposing sides, the IBC mandates that tests be performed from both sides. The side with the shortest test duration is the basis for the fire-resistance rating.

Topic: Alternative Methods
Reference: IBC 703.3

Category: Fire-Resistance-Rated Construction
Subject: Fire-Resistance Ratings

Code Text: *The application of any of the alternative methods listed in Section 703.3 shall be based on the fire exposure and acceptance criteria specified in ASTM E 119. The required fire resistance of a building element shall be permitted to be established by any of the following methods or procedures: (1) fire-resistance designs documented in approved sources, (2) prescriptive designs of fire-resistance-rated building elements as prescribed in Section 720, (3) calculations in accordance with Section 721, (4) engineering analysis based on a comparison of building element designs having fire-resistance ratings as determined by the test procedures set forth in ASTM E 119, or (5) alternative protection methods as allowed by Section 104.11.*

Discussion and Commentary: Prescriptive details of fire-resistance-rated building elements are contained in Section 720. Generic listings for structural parts, walls, partitions, floor systems and roof systems are addressed.

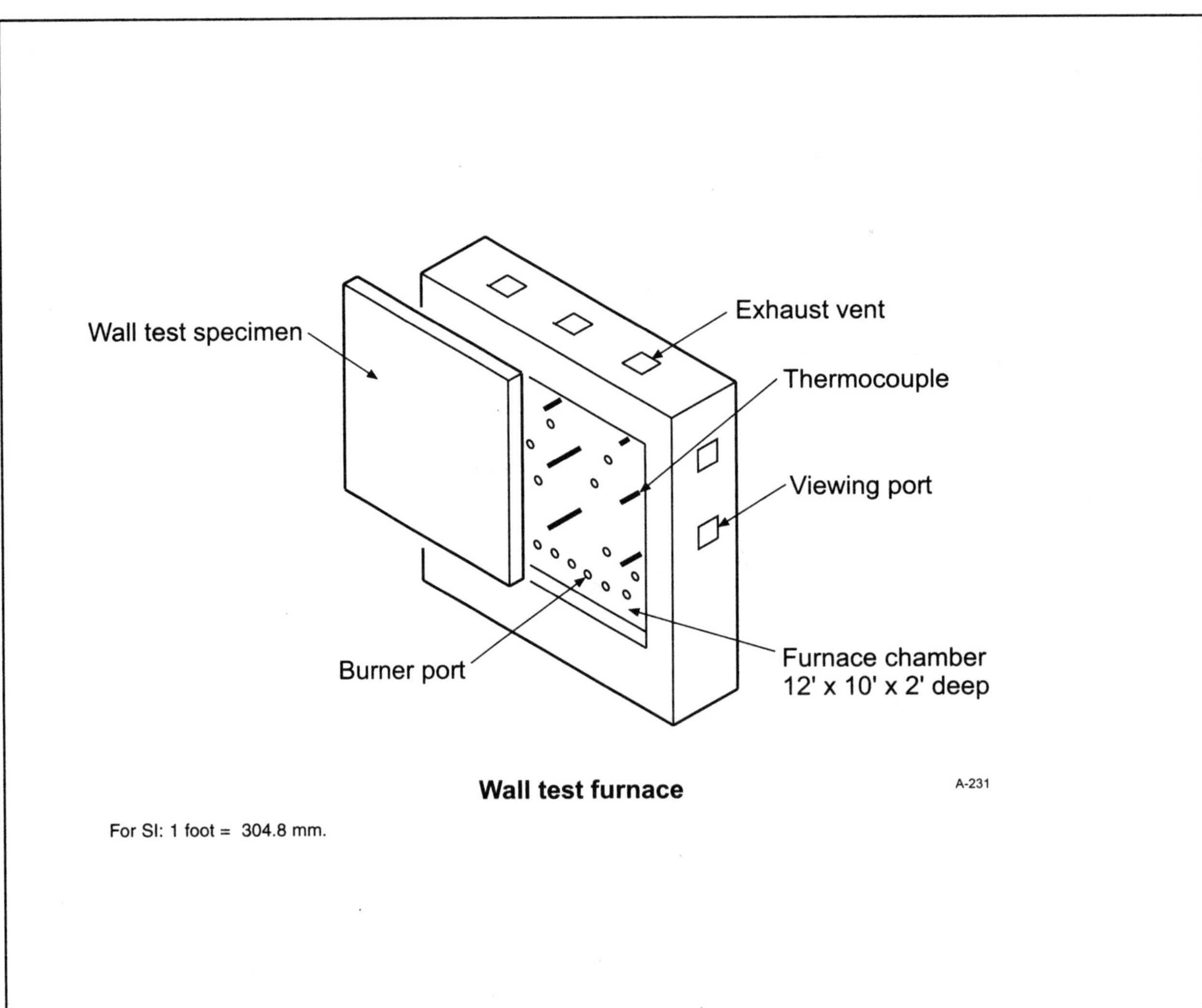

Wall test furnace

Section 721 provides methods of calculated fire resistance for concrete, masonry, steel, and wood assemblies or members. The procedures and calculations are limited to the specific information set forth in this section and are not to be used in any other manner.

Topic: Scope
Reference: IBC 720.1

Category: Fire-Resistance-Rated Construction
Subject: Prescriptive Fire Resistance

Code Text: *The provisions of Section 720 contain prescriptive details of fire-resistance-rated building elements. The materials of construction listed in Tables 720.1(1), 720.1(2) and 720.1(3) shall be assumed to have the fire-resistance ratings prescribed therein. Where materials that change the capacity for heat dissipation are incorporated into a fire-resistance-rated assembly, fire test results or other substantiating data shall be made available to the building official to show that the required fire-resistance rating time period is not reduced.*

Discussion and Commentary: The tables in Section 720 provide the details for obtaining desired fire-resistance ratings for structural parts, walls and partitions, and floor and roof systems. The methods and materials found in the tables are to be used in the same manner as any listed assembly.

Table 720.1(2)
Interior partition: Item 14-1.5

2 in. by 4 in. wood studs 16 in. on center with two layers $^5/_8$ in. Type X gypsum wallboard each side. Base layers applied vertically and nailed with 6d cooler or wallboard nails at 9 in. on center. Face layer applied vertically or horizontally and nailed with 8d cooler or wallboard nails at 7 in. on center. For nail-adhesive application, base layers are nailed 6 in. on center. Face layers applied with coating of approved wallboard adhesive and nailed 12 in. on center.

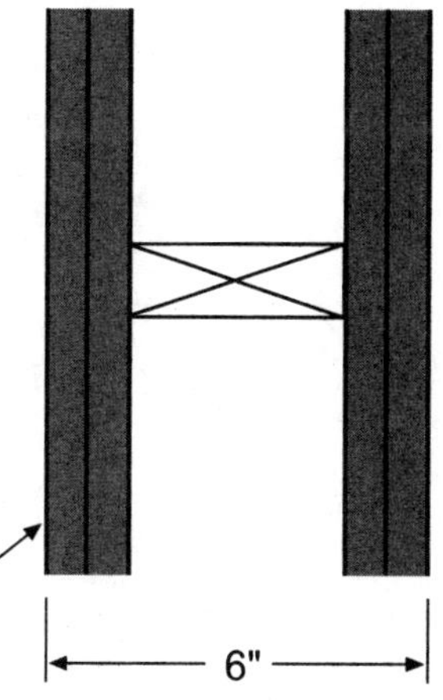

For SI: 1 inch = 25.4 mm.

When insulation or a similar material is added to a fire-resistance-rated assembly, it may change the assembly's capacity to dissipate heat. Particularly in noncombustible horizontal assemblies, the fire-resistance rating may be diminished to some degree.

Topic: Scope
Reference: IBC 721.1

Category: Fire-Resistance-Rated Construction
Subject: Calculated Fire Resistance

Code Text: *The provisions of Section 721 contain procedures by which the fire resistance of specific materials or combinations of materials is established by calculations. The procedures apply only to the information contained in Section 721 and shall not be otherwise used. The calculated fire resistance of concrete, concrete masonry, and clay masonry assemblies shall be permitted in accordance with ACI 216.1/TMS 0216.1. The calculated fire resistance of steel assemblies shall be permitted in accordance with Chapter 5 of ASCE /SFPE 29.*

Discussion and Commentary: Another method used to obtain the necessary fire-resistance ratings mandated by the code is calculation. The provisions for calculating fire resistance are applicable to concrete assemblies, concrete masonry, clay brick and tile masonry, steel assemblies and wood assemblies.

TABLE 721.6.2(1)
TIME ASSIGNED TO WALLBOARD MEMBRANES[a,b,c,d]

DESCRIPTION OF FINISH	TIME[e] (minutes)
$^3/_8$-inch wood structural panel bonded with exterior glue	5
$^{15}/_{32}$-inch wood structural panel bonded with exterior glue	10
$^{19}/_{32}$-inch wood structural panel bonded with exterior glue	15
$^3/_8$-inch gypsum wallboard	10
$^1/_2$-inch gypsum wallboard	15
$^5/_8$-inch gypsum wallboard	30
$^1/_2$-inch Type X gypsum wallboard	25
$^5/_8$-inch Type X gypsum wallboard	40
Double $^3/_8$-inch gypsum wallboard	25
$^1/_2$- + $^3/_8$-inch gypsum wallboard	35
Double $^1/_2$-inch gypsum wallboard	40

For SI: 1 inch = 25.4 mm.
a. These values apply only when membranes are installed on framing members which are spaced 16 inches o.c.
b. Gypsum wallboard installed over framing or furring shall be installed so that all edges are supported, except $^5/_8$-inch Type X gypsum wallboard shall be permitted to be installed horizontally with the horizontal joints staggered 24 inches each side and unsupported but finished.
c. On wood frame floor/ceiling or roof/ceiling assemblies, gypsum board shall be installed with the long dimension perpendicular to framing members and shall have all joints finished.
d. The membrane on the unexposed side shall not be included in determining the fire resistance of the assembly. When dissimilar membranes are used on a wall assembly, the calculation shall be made from the least fire-resistant (weaker) side.
e. The time assigned is not a finished rating.

TABLE 721.6.2(2)
TIME ASSIGNED FOR CONTRIBUTION OF WOOD FRAME[a,b,c]

DESCRIPTION	TIME ASSIGNED TO FRAME (minutes)
Wood studs 16 inches o.c.	20
Wood floor and roof joists 16 inches o.c.	10

For SI: 1 inch = 25.4 mm.
a. This table does not apply to studs or joists spaced more than 16 inches o.c.
b. All studs shall be nominal 2 × 4 and all joists shall have a nominal thickness of at least 2 inches.
c. Allowable spans for joists shall be determined in accordance with Sections 2308.8, 2308.10.2 and 2308.10.3.

Applicable to both loadbearing and nonloadbearing assemblies, the calculated fire resistance for wood-framed walls, floor/ceiling assemblies and roof/ceiling assemblies is limited to a 1-hour rating. The fire-resistance ratings of timber beams and columns may also be calculated.

Topic: Noncombustibility Tests
Reference: IBC 703.4

Category: Fire-Resistance-Rated Construction
Subject: Fire-Resistance Ratings

Code Text: *Materials required to be noncombustible shall be tested in accordance with ASTM E 136. The term "noncombustible" does not apply to the flame spread characteristics of interior finish or trim materials. A material shall not be classified as a noncombustible building construction material if it is subject to an increase in combustibility or flame spread beyond the limitations herein established through the effects of age, moisture, or other atmospheric conditions.*

Discussion and Commentary: In buildings of Types I, II, III and IV construction, specific elements are required to be constructed of noncombustible materials. Such materials are desirable because they do not aid combustion, nor do they add appreciable heat to an ambient fire. Under conditions of the test, a material may have a limited amount of combustible content and still qualify as noncombustible.

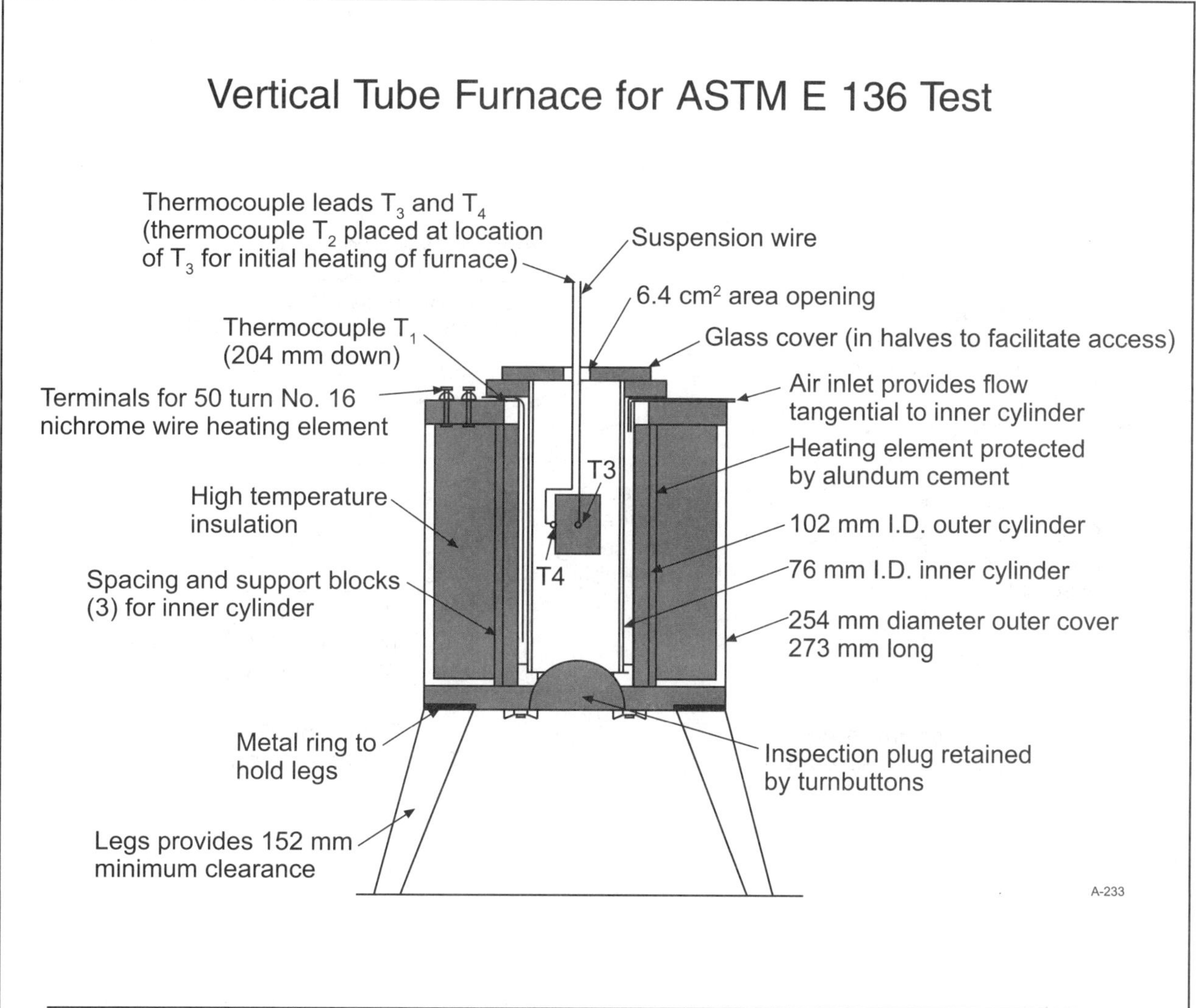

Gypsum wallboard and similar products are also acceptable as noncombustible materials. They must have a structural base of noncombustible materials, a surface material no more than $^1/_8$-inch in thickness and a maximum flame-spread index of 50.

Topic: Construction of Projections
Reference: IBC 704.2

Category: Fire-Resistance-Rated Construction
Subject: Exterior Walls

Code Text: *Projections from walls of Type I or II construction shall be of noncombustible materials or combustible materials as allowed by Sections 1406.3 and 1406.4. Projections from walls of Type III, IV or V construction shall be of any approved material. Combustible projections located where openings are not permitted or where protection of openings is required shall be of at least 1-hour fire-resistance-rated construction, Type IV construction or as required by Section 1406.3.*

Discussion and Commentary: Cornices, eave overhangs, exterior balconies and similar architectural appendages extending beyond the floor area are considered projections. Projections from noncombustible buildings are regulated to prevent a fire hazard created by inappropriate use of combustible materials at an exterior wall.

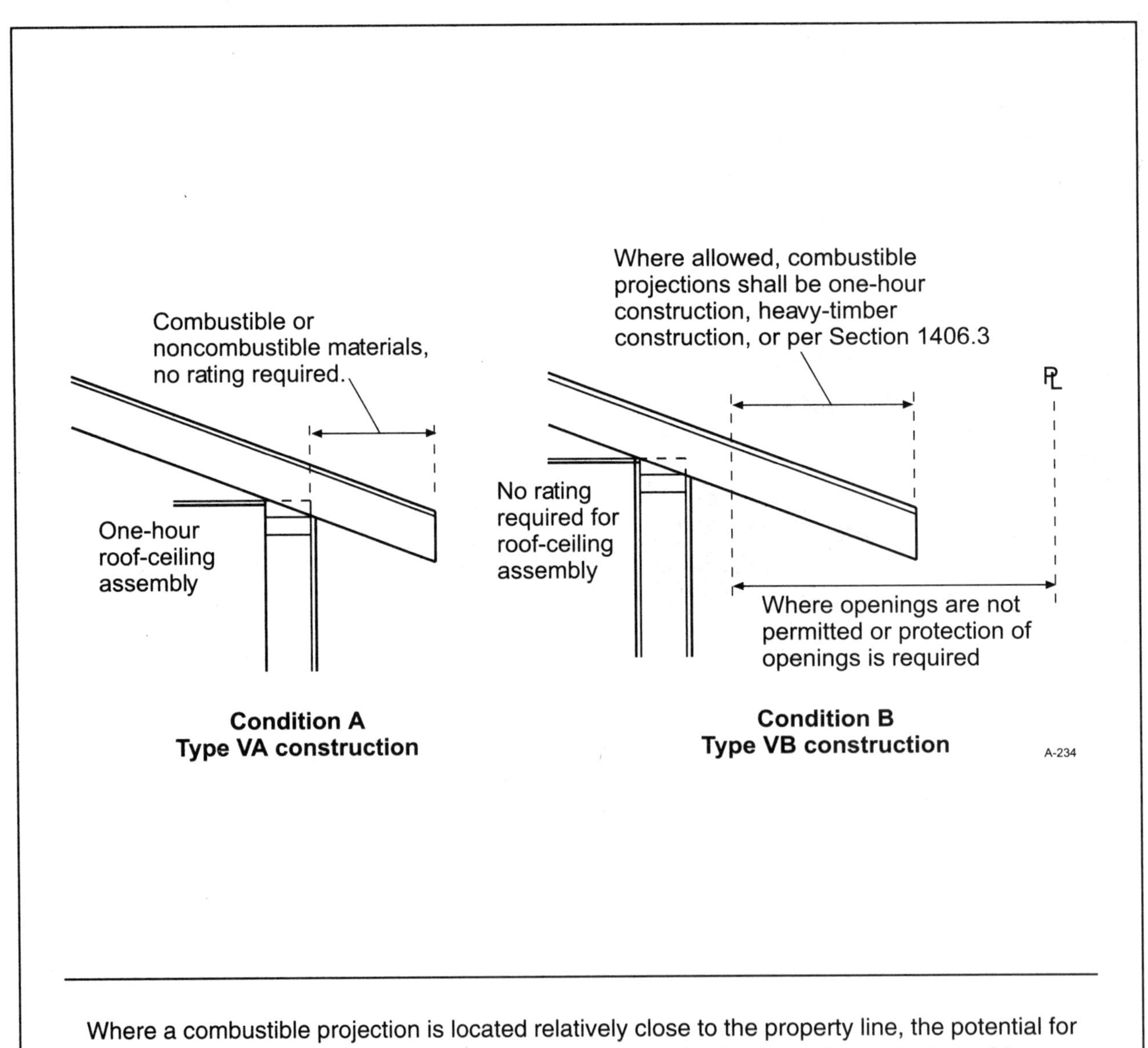

Where a combustible projection is located relatively close to the property line, the potential for severe fire exposure may exist. Accordingly, such a projection must be protected, of heavy-timber construction or regulated by Section 1406.3 for combustible materials on exterior walls.

Topic: Buildings on the Same Lot
Reference: IBC 704.3

Category: Fire-Resistance-Rated Construction
Subject: Exterior Walls

Code Text: *For the purposes of determining the required wall and opening protection and roof- covering requirements, buildings on the same lot shall be assumed to have an imaginary line between them.* See exception where aggregate area of multiple buildings is within limits specified in Chapter 5 for a single building.

Discussion and Commentary: Where two or more buildings are placed on the same piece of property, their exterior walls and openings must be regulated in the same manner as if they were on separate lots. However, if the buildings could be constructed as a single structure under one roof and meet the size requirements based on occupancy and type of construction, then an assumed property line is not required.

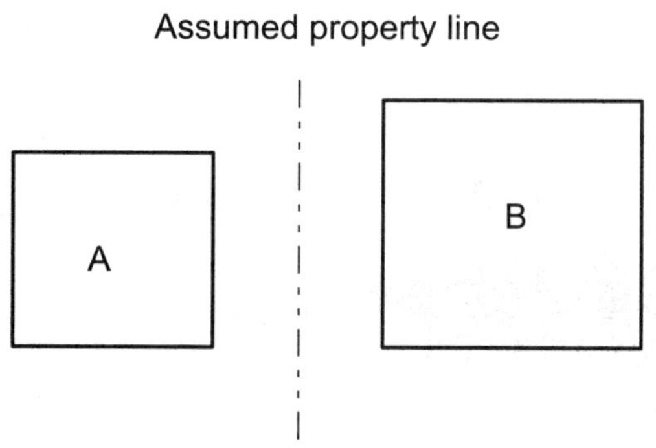

Case I: an assumed property line between buildings

A. Fire resistance and opening protection for walls adjacent to the property line must comply with the code

B. Property line may be placed to take best advantage of wall and opening protection

Case II: as a single building

A. Allowable area and type of construction are based on the most restrictive requirements for the occupancies housed

B. Total floor area may not exceed that allowed for a single building

Buildings on the same property A-235

Where a new building is to be constructed on the same lot as an existing building, the assumed property line must be placed in a location where it will not cause the exterior wall and opening protection of the existing building to become noncompliant.

Topic: Fire-Resistance Ratings
Reference: IBC 704.5

Category: Fire-Resistance-Rated Construction
Subject: Exterior Walls

Code Text: *Exterior walls shall be fire-resistance rated in accordance with Tables 601 and 602. The fire-resistance rating of exterior walls with a fire separation distance of greater than 5 feet shall be rated for exposure to fire from the inside. The fire-resistance rating of exterior walls with a fire separation distance of 5 feet or less shall be rated for exposure to fire from both sides.*

Discussion and Commentary: Exposure of the exterior wall to an interior fire does not vary based on the distance of the wall from the property line. However, exterior fire exposure decreases with an increase in the distance between the property line and the exterior wall (fire separation distance). A fire separation distance of 5 feet is considered by the IBC to be a reasonable limit of flame impingement (direct exterior fire exposure) from an adjacent building.

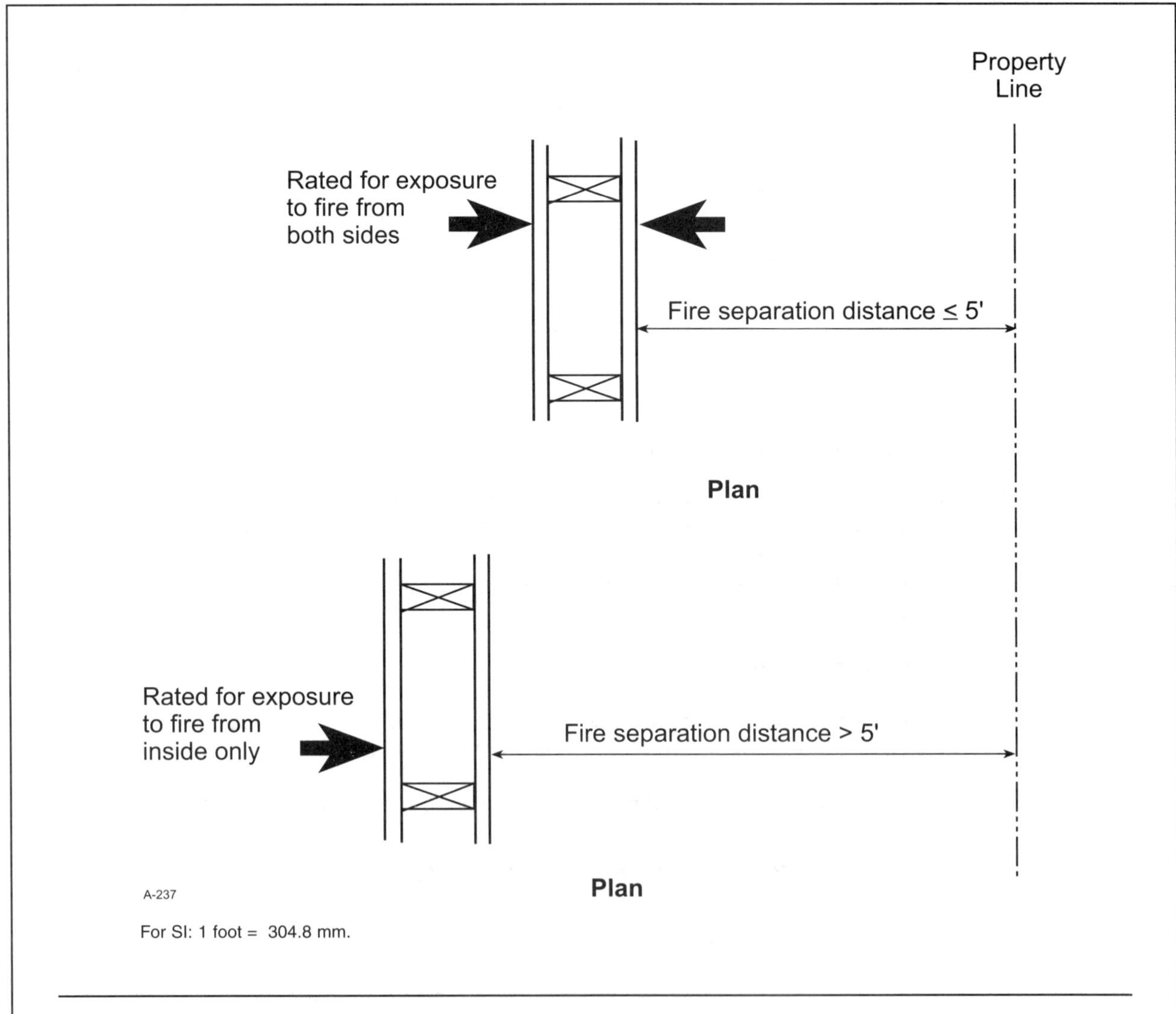

The determination of the minimum fire-resistance-rating for an exterior wall is based on two conditions: (1) the type of construction of the building, and (2) the fire separation distance. The higher of the two ratings regulates the minimum level of fire resistance.

Topic: Allowable Area of Openings
Reference: IBC 704.8

Category: Fire-Resistance-Rated Construction
Subject: Exterior Walls

Code Text: *The maximum area of unprotected or protected openings permitted in an exterior wall in any story shall not exceed the values set forth in Table 704.8. Where both unprotected and protected openings are located in the exterior wall in any story, the total area of the openings shall comply with the following formula:* $A/a + A_u/a_u \leq 1.0$

Discussion and Commentary: Based on the fire separation distance, the number of openings in an exterior wall is regulated on a floor-by-floor basis. Where all of the exterior openings are protected, a higher percentage of the exterior wall surface may be provided with openings, whereas a lesser amount is permitted if all openings are unprotected. The IBC also permits both protected and unprotected openings in an exterior wall, provided they comply with the unity formula. In a fully-sprinklered building, the maximum allowable area of unprotected openings is the same as that allowed for protected openings.

Given: the one-hour exterior wall shown is located 12 feet from an interior property line. it has protected openings as shown.

Determine: the maximum area permitted for unprotected openings.

Solution:

$$\frac{A}{a} + \frac{A_u}{a_u} \leq 1.0$$

$$\frac{83}{(45\%)(18 \times 40)} + \frac{A_u}{(15\%)(18 \times 40]} = 1.0$$

$$\frac{83}{324} + \frac{A_u}{108} = 1.0$$

$$0.25 + \frac{81}{108} = 1.0$$

81 square feet of unprotected openings are permitted

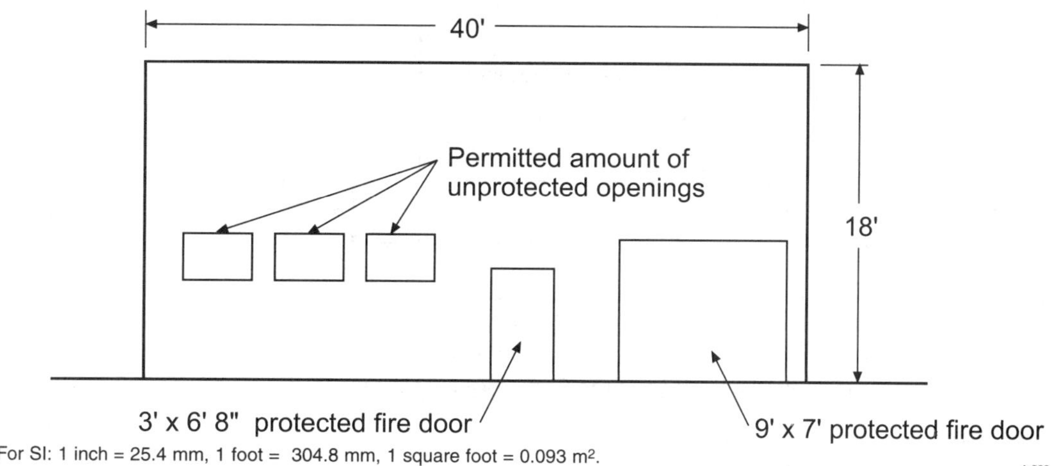

For SI: 1 inch = 25.4 mm, 1 foot = 304.8 mm, 1 square foot = 0.093 m^2.

If a building's exterior bearing wall, exterior nonbearing wall or exterior structural frame is not required to be fire-resistance rated by Table 601 or 602, then an unlimited percentage of unprotected openings is permitted regardless of fire separation distance.

Topic: First Story Walls
Reference: IBC 704.8.2

Category: Fire-resistance-rated Construction
Subject: Exterior Walls

Code Text: *In occupancies other than Group H, unlimited unprotected openings are permitted in the first story of exterior walls facing a street that have fire separation distance of greater than 15 feet (4572 mm), or facing an unoccupied space. The unoccupied space shall be on the same lot or dedicated for public use, shall not be less than 30 feet (9144 mm) in width, and shall have access from a street by a posted fire lane in accordance with the* International Fire Code.

Discussion and Commentary: Because the first story of a building is generally readily available for fire department access and manual suppression efforts, unprotected openings are not restricted, provided a moderate amount of open space is provided adjacent to the exterior wall. It is expected that the fire department can quickly mitigate the potential radiant heat exposure to surrounding buildings or structures.

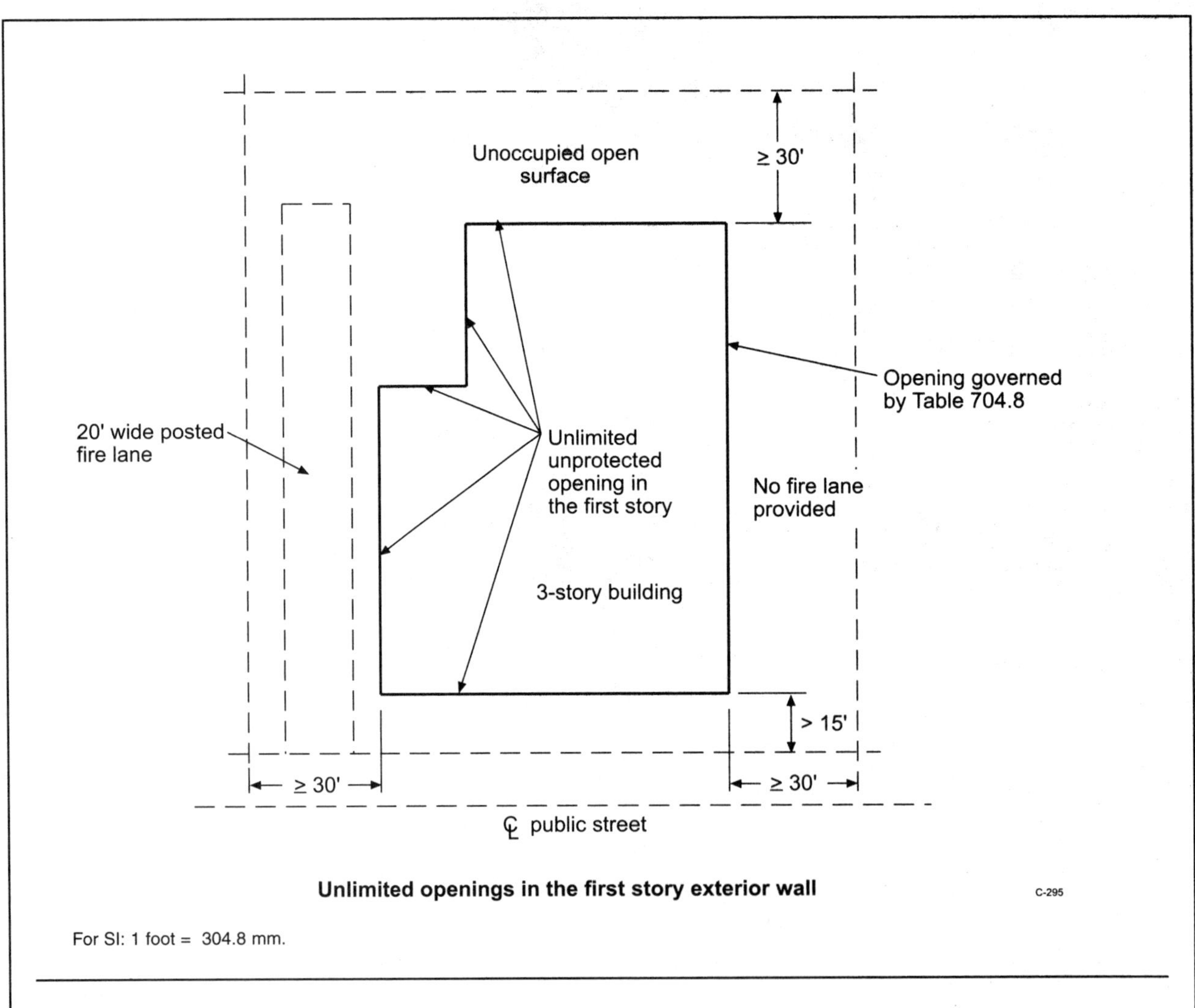

Unlimited openings in the first story exterior wall

For SI: 1 foot = 304.8 mm.

As the primary allowance for unlimited unprotected openings is the ability of the fire service to easily access and suppress at the ground level, it is critical that adequate open space be available for such purposes. Where not accessed directly from a street, a fire lane must be provided.

Topic: Vertical Separation of Openings
Reference: IBC 704.9

Category: Fire-resistance-rated Construction
Subject: Exterior Walls

Code Text: *Openings in exterior walls in adjacent stories shall be separated vertically to protect against fire spread on the exterior of the buildings where the openings are within 5 feet (1524 mm) of each other horizontally and the opening in the lower story is not a protected opening in accordance with Section 715.4.8. Such openings shall be separated vertically at least 3 feet (914 mm) by spandrel girders, exterior walls or other similar assemblies that have a fire-resistance rating of at least 1 hour or by flame barriers than extend horizontally at least 30 inches (762 mm) beyond the exterior wall.* See exceptions for buildings no more than three stories in height, buildings that are fully sprinklered and open parking garages.

Discussion and Commentary: Where unprotected openings occur in adjacent stories, a fire that breaks out of an opening in a lower story can spread vertically to upper stories of the building.

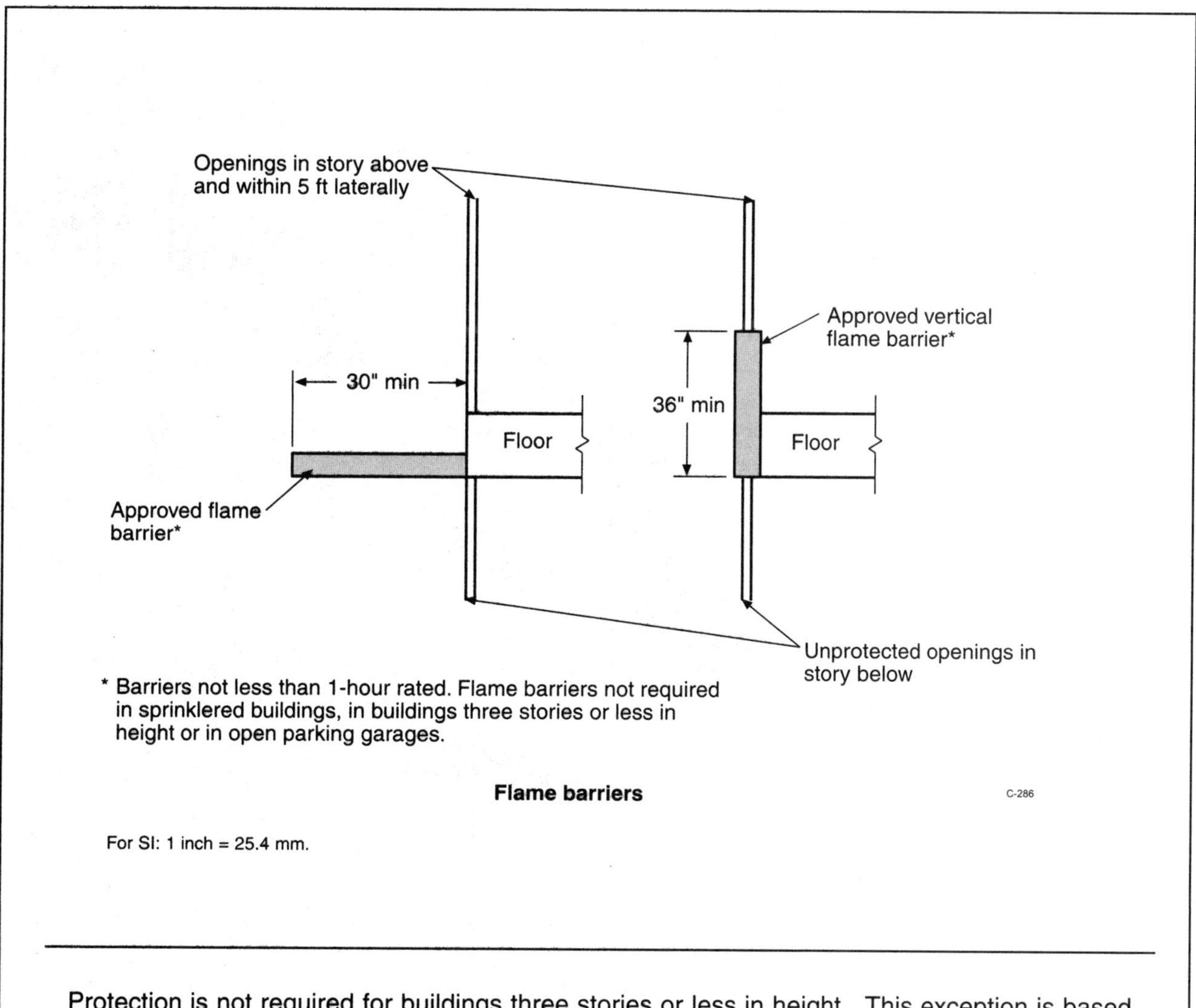

Flame barriers

Protection is not required for buildings three stories or less in height. This exception is based on Table 503, which permits buildings of three stories in height to be of unprotected construction (Types IIB, IIIB and VB) where a fire-resistance rating is not required for floor construction.

Topic: Parapets
Reference: IBC 704.11

Category: Fire-Resistance-Rated Construction
Subject: Exterior Walls

Code Text: *Parapets shall be provided on exterior walls of buildings.* See six exceptions for construction methods or locations that would eliminate the requirement for parapets. *Parapets shall have the same fire-resistance rating as that required for the supporting wall, and on any side adjacent to a roof surface, shall have noncombustible faces for the uppermost 18 inches (457 mm), including counterflashing and coping materials. The height of the parapet shall not be less than 30 inches (762 mm) above the point where the roof surface and the wall intersect.*

Discussion and Commentary: A parapet wall is defined as *the part of any wall entirely above the roof line.* Its purpose is to prevent the spread of fire from the roof of the subject building to an adjacent building and to protect the roof of a building from exposure to a fire in an adjacent building.

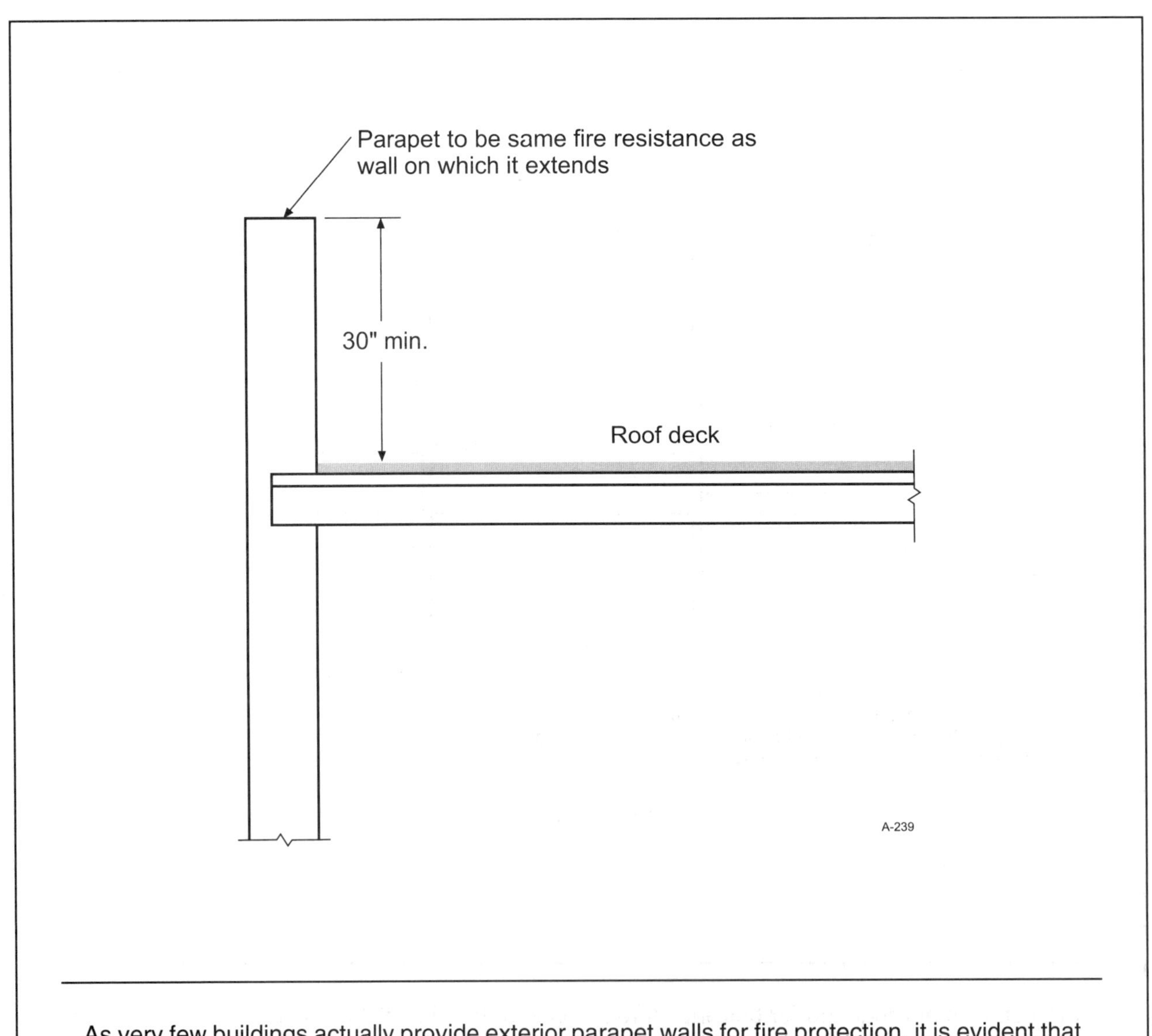

As very few buildings actually provide exterior parapet walls for fire protection, it is evident that the exceptions are widely used. In many situations, a parapet is provided only to hide the roof slope or to screen rooftop equipment, in which case the requirements do not apply.

QUIZ

Study Session 5 — Sections 701–704

I. Multiple Choice

1. An opening around a penetrating item is a(n) __________.

   a. annular space
   b. penetration
   c. through penetration
   d. joint

   Reference________________

2. A __________ is a listed device designed to limit automatically the radiative heat transfer through an air inlet/outlet opening in the ceiling membrane of a fire-resistance-rated floor/ceiling or roof/ceiling assembly.

   a. horizontal fire damper
   b. ceiling radiation damper
   c. combination fire/smoke damper
   d. horizontal access door

   Reference________________

3. The time period that a through-penetration firestop system limits the spread of fire through a penetration is considered __________.

   a. a fire-protection rating
   b. an F rating
   c. a T rating
   d. a fire-resistance rating

   Reference________________

4. All of the following building components may be used to create a fire area except __________.

   a. fire walls
   b. fire barriers
   c. exterior walls
   d. fire partitions

   Reference________________

5. The measurement between the face of an exterior wall and the closest interior lot line is described as the __________.

   a. fire separation distance
   b. fire exposure setback
   c. clearance to construction
   d. exterior fire exposure

   Reference________________

6. A __________ must have sufficient structural stability under fire conditions to allow collapse of construction on either side without collapse of the wall.

a. fire wall
b. fire separation wall
c. fire barrier
d. smoke barrier

Reference_______________

7. A smoke compartment is created by enclosure of a space on all sides by __________.

a. smoke partitions
b. smoke barriers
c. shaft enclosure construction
d. fire partitions

Reference_______________

8. The T rating for a penetration firestop system is based on a maximum temperature rise of __________ degrees F above its initial temperature through the penetration on the nonfire side.

a. 250
b. 325
c. 375
d. 400

Reference_______________

9. Unless alternate methods are used for determining the fire-resistance ratings of building elements, the procedures set forth in _________ shall be applicable.

a. ANSI Z 97.1
b. ASCE 5
c. ASTM E 119
d. UL 555

Reference_______________

10. Noncombustible building materials are required to some degree in all types of construction except for __________.

a. Type II
b. Type III
c. Type IV
d. Type V

Reference_______________

11. Composite materials with a noncombustible structural base are considered noncombustible where the surface material is limited to __________ inch in thickness and has a maximum flame spread index of __________.

a. $^1/_{28}$, 25
b. $^1/_{16}$, 50
c. $^1/_8$, 25
d. $^1/_8$, 50

Reference_______________

12. A projection is considered a building element that extends beyond the __________ of a building.

a. exterior wall
b. fire area
c. building area
d. floor area

Reference_______________

13. Projections shall never extend more than __________ inches into areas where openings are prohibited.

a. 0
b. 12
c. 30
d. 36

Reference_______________

14. In a building of Type III construction, projections shall be __________.

a. of noncombustible construction
b. of combustible construction
c. of minimum one-hour fire-resistance-rated construction
d. of any approved materials

Reference_______________

15. For wall and opening protection and roof covering requirements, an imaginary property line shall be placed between __________.

a. court walls
b. fire areas
c. buildings on the same lot
d. different occupancies

Reference_______________

16. The fire-resistance rating for an exterior wall shall be based on both interior and exterior fire exposure where the wall is located a maximum of __________ feet from the property line.

a. three
b. five
c. ten
d. twenty

Reference_______________

17. In a nonsprinklered building, what is the maximum area of unprotected exterior wall openings for a fire separation distance of 8 feet?

a. 10%
b. 25%
c. unlimited
d. unprotected openings are prohibited

Reference_______________

18. In a nonsprinklered building, what is the maximum area of protected exterior wall openings for a fire separation distance of 20 feet?

a. 25% b. 45%
c. 75% d. unlimited

Reference_______________

19. In a fully-sprinklered office building, what is the maximum area of unprotected exterior wall openings for a fire separation distance of 5 feet?

a. 10% b. 15%
c. 25% d. unprotected openings are prohibited

Reference_______________

20. In other than Group H occupancies, unlimited unprotected exterior openings are permitted in the first story of exterior walls facing an unoccupied space of a least __________ feet in width.

a. 15 b. 20
c. 30 d. 40

Reference_______________

21. Where flame barriers are required for the vertical separation of exterior openings in adjacent stories, horizontal barriers must extend at least ___________ inches beyond the exterior wall.

a. 12 b. 24
c. 30 d. 36

Reference_______________

22. Flame barriers shall have a minimum fire-resistance rating of __________.

a. 20 minutes b. 45 minutes
c. 1 hour d. 2 hours

Reference_______________

23. A parapet is not required for those buildings having a maximum floor area of __________ square feet on any floor.

a. 400 b. 1000
c. 1500 d. 3000

Reference_______________

24. Where required, parapets must extend at least __________ inches above the roof.

a. 30
b. 32
c. 36
d. 42

Reference_______________

25. The uppermost portion of a parapet wall must have noncombustible faces for a minimum of __________ inches.

a. 12
b. 18
c. 24
d. 30

Reference_______________

26. To obtain a fire-resistance rating, all nonsymmetrical walls except for _____ shall be tested with both faces exposed to the furnace.

a. fire walls
b. fire barriers
c. smoke barriers
d. exterior walls

Reference_______________

27 A roof eave, where projecting into an area where protection of openings is required, may be constructed of all of the following materials, except _____.

a. heavy-timber construction
b. noncombustible construction
c. fire-retardant-treated wood
d. one-hour fire-resistance-rated construction

Reference_______________

28. In a fully sprinklered building, the maximum allowable area of protected exterior wall openings is _____ where the fire separation distance is 12 feet.

a. 15%
b. 25%
c. 45%
d. 60%

Reference_______________

29. A parapet is not required on the exterior wall of a fully sprinklered building located a minimum of _____ feet from an interior property line.

a. > 5
b. > 10
c. > 15
d. > 20

Reference_______________

30. Unprotected openings are not permitted in the exterior wall of a Group H-3 warehouse where the maximum fire separation distance is _____ feet.

a. 3
b. 5
c. 10
d. 15

Reference_______________

INTERNATIONAL BUILDING CODE
Study Session 6
Sections 705–711 — Fire-Resistance-Rated Construction II

OBJECTIVE: To gain an understanding of the fire-resistance-rated building components such as fire walls, fire barriers, shaft enclosures, fire partitions, smoke barriers, smoke partitions and horizontal assemblies.

REFERENCE: Sections 705 through 711, 2003 *International Building Code*

KEY POINTS:

- What is the purpose of a fire wall?
- Where is a party wall located? How is it to be constructed?
- How must a fire wall perform structurally?
- Which types of materials are permitted in a fire wall? How is the minimum fire-resistance rating of a fire wall determined?
- How shall the horizontal continuity of a fire wall be accomplished? Vertical continuity?
- Which options are possible where a fire wall serves a stepped building?
- How shall the penetration of combustible framing members entering into a masonry or concrete fire wall be addressed?
- What are the limitations on openings in a fire wall?
- Where are fire barriers utilized?
- How must a fire barrier be constructed? What restrictions are placed on openings?
- What is a fire area? What is its purpose? How is the minimum fire-resistance rating for fire barrier assemblies separating fire areas determined?
- What is the purpose of a shaft enclosure? Where are such enclosures required?
- Which types of conditions permit vertical openings without enclosure?
- How does the height of a building affect the fire-resistance ratings of shaft enclosures?
- Which methods are mandated for construction of a shaft enclosure?
- Which types of openings are permitted to penetrate a shaft enclosure? How must they be protected?
- How must shafts be enclosed at the top? At the bottom?
- Which special provisions govern refuse and laundry chutes?
- Under which conditions must elevator lobbies be provided?
- Where are fire partitions required to be installed?
- What minimum fire-resistance rating is required for fire partitions? What rating is required in a sprinklered hotel or apartment building?
- To what extent must a fire partition extend above a ceiling?
- What is the function of a smoke barrier?
- What fire-resistance rating is mandated for smoke barriers?
- How must openings in a smoke barrier be protected?
- Where are smoke barriers required?
- How is a smoke partition to be constructed? How are door openings, penetrations, ducts and air transfer openings regulated?
- How is the required rating of a horizontal assembly determined?

- What is the minimum fire-resistance rating for floor assemblies separating dwelling units in apartment buildings? Sleeping units in Group R-1 occupancies?
- What weight of ceiling panel requires no additional devices for the prevention of lateral displacement?
- When may the ceiling membrane in a fire-resistance-rated horizontal assembly be omitted? Floor membrane?
- How are skylights regulated in fire-resistance-rated roof construction?

Topic: Definition and Scope
Reference: IBC 702, 705.1

Category: Fire-Resistance-Rated Construction
Subject: Fire Walls

Code Text: *A fire wall is a fire-resistance-rated wall having protected openings, which restricts the spread of fire and extends continuously from the foundation to or through the roof, with sufficient structural stability under fire conditions to allow collapse of construction on either side without collapse of the wall. Each portion of a building separated by one or more fire walls that comply with the provisions of Section 705 shall be considered a separate building.*

Discussion and Commentary: By placing one or more fire walls in a large-area building, multiple smaller-area buildings are created. Each of these smaller spaces can then be considered a unique building for code purposes. Under various conditions, fire walls can serve to reduce a structure's type of construction, eliminate a required sprinkler system or increase the permitted size of a facility under one roof.

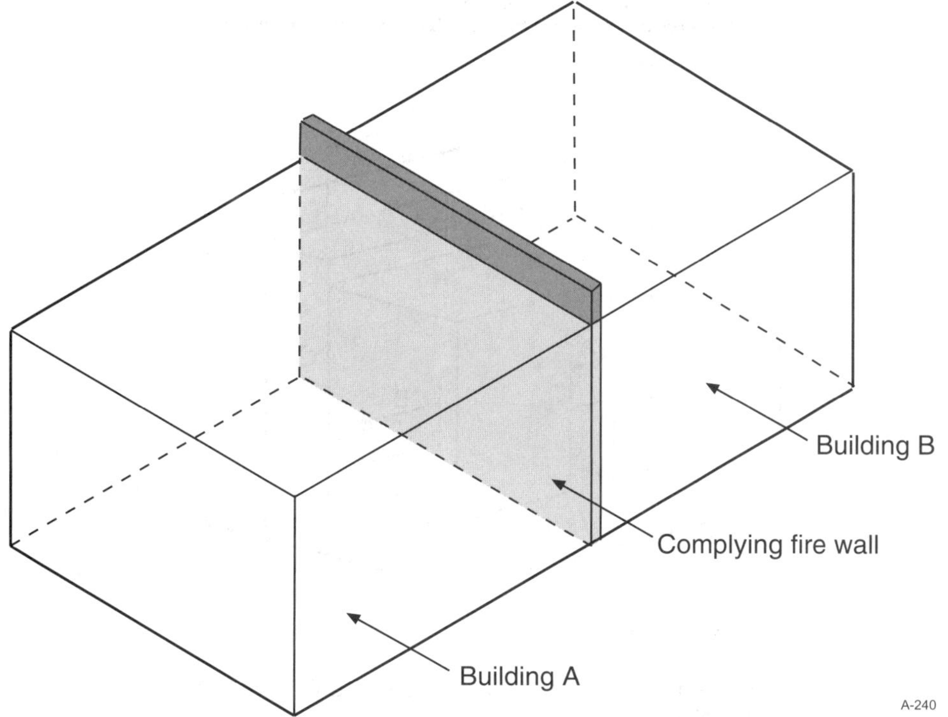

In a situation where a fire wall separates distinct occupancy groups that are required to be separated by a fire barrier wall, the most restrictive requirements of each separation apply. This includes both the wall's continuity and the required fire-resistance rating.

Topic: Construction
Reference: IBC 705.3, 705.4

Category: Fire-Resistance-Rated Construction
Subject: Fire Walls

Code Text: *Fire walls shall be of any approved noncombustible materials.* See Exception for Type V construction. *Fire walls shall have a fire-resistance rating of not less than that required by Table 705.4.*

Discussion and Commentary: A fire wall is designed to act in a manner similar to an exterior wall, as a barrier to prevent a fire in one building from spreading to the other building. Accordingly, construction of the fire wall must be commensurate with the exterior wall requirements for the construction type. In addition, the fire-resistance rating of the wall must be considerable in order to provide the necessary level of protection. The required ratings vary based on occupancy and, to some degree, type of construction.

TABLE 705.4
FIRE WALL FIRE-RESISTANCE RATINGS

GROUP	FIRE-RESISTANCE RATING (hours)
A, B, E, H-4, I, R-1, R-2, U	3[a]
F-1, H-3[b], H-5, M, S-1	3
H-1, H-2	4[b]
F-2, S-2, R-3, R-4	2

a. Walls shall be not less than 2-hour fire-resistance rated where separating buildings of Type II or V construction.
b. For Group H-1, H-2 or H-3 buildings, also see Sections 415.4 and 415.5.

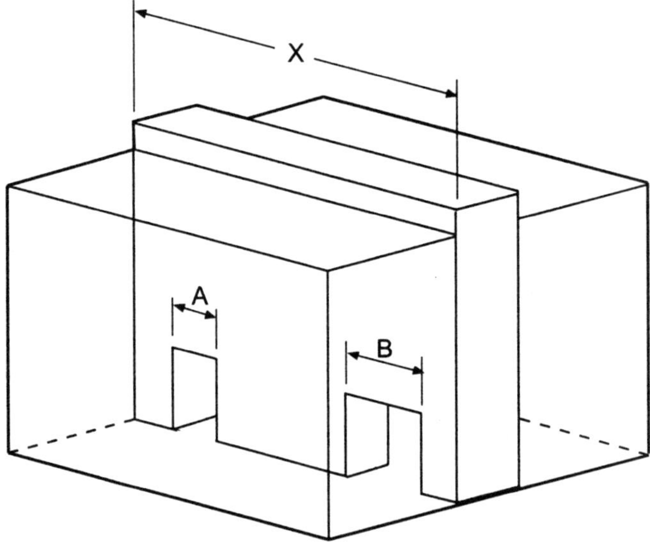

A + B ≤ 25% of X

Each opening limited to 120 square feet unless both buildings are sprinklered

Fire-protection rating based on Tables 705.4 and 714.2

A-241

Per Section 705.8, the total width of all openings in a fire wall is limited to 25 percent of the length of the wall in each story. There is no limit on the amount of total wall area containing openings; however, each opening is limited to 120 square feet in nonsprinklered buildings.

Topic: Horizontal Continuity
Reference: IBC 705.5

Category: Fire-resistance-rated Construction
Subject: Fire Walls

Code Text: *Fire walls shall be continuous from exterior wall to exterior wall and shall extend at least 18 inches (457 mm) beyond the exterior surface of exterior walls.* See exceptions for various methods of terminating the fire wall at the interior surface of the exterior sheathing or finish materials.

Discussion and Commentary: Historically, the codes have addressed the hazards of fire exposure at the fire wall only from a vertical perspective, at the roof. There is also concern of a similar hazard from the horizontal perspective, at the intersection of the fire wall and the exterior wall. The 18-inch extension is intended to abate the potential for fire to travel from one building to the other around the fire wall. The 18-inch extension must extend the full height of the fire wall.

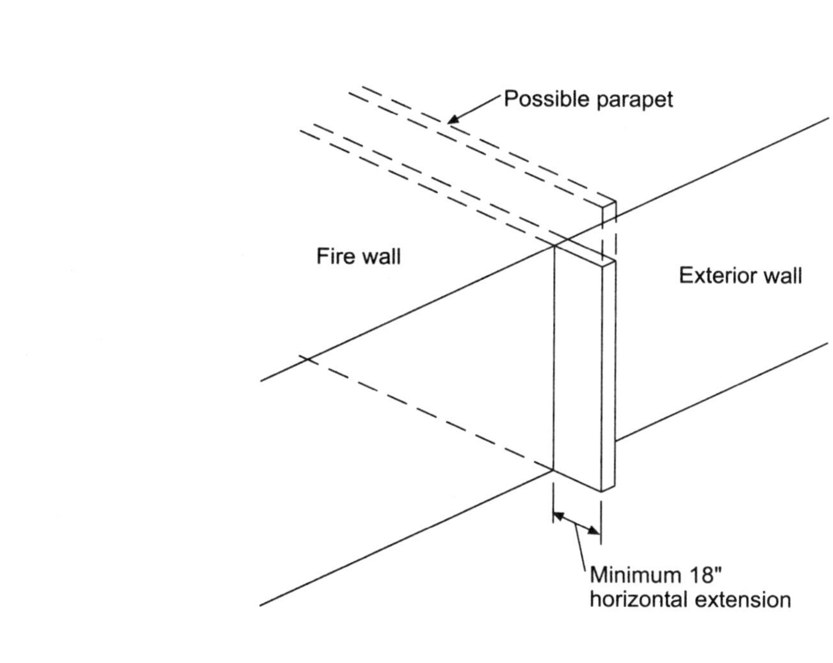

Horizontal continuity

For SI: 1 inch = 25.4 mm.

The three exceptions acknowledge the effect certain types of exterior wall construction will have on fire breaching the exterior of the building and exposing the adjacent building. These methods of protection are similar to those used at the roof construction where a parapet is not provided.

Topic: Vertical Continuity
Reference: IBC 705.6

Category: Fire-Resistance-Rated Construction
Subject: Fire Walls

Code Text: *Fire walls shall extend from the foundation to a termination point at least 30 inches above both adjacent roofs.* See exceptions for buildings with different roof levels, those with noncombustible roof construction, and those constructed under special provisions.

Discussion and Commentary: To ensure the "separate building" concept, a fire wall must be continuous vertically with no horizontal offsets from the foundation, through the roof to a point at least 30 inches above. Various exceptions to the parapet requirement allow the fire wall to terminate at the bottom of the roof deck or sheathing. According to many of the exceptions, the roof covering must be minimum Class B, and no openings in the roof are permitted within 4 feet of the fire wall.

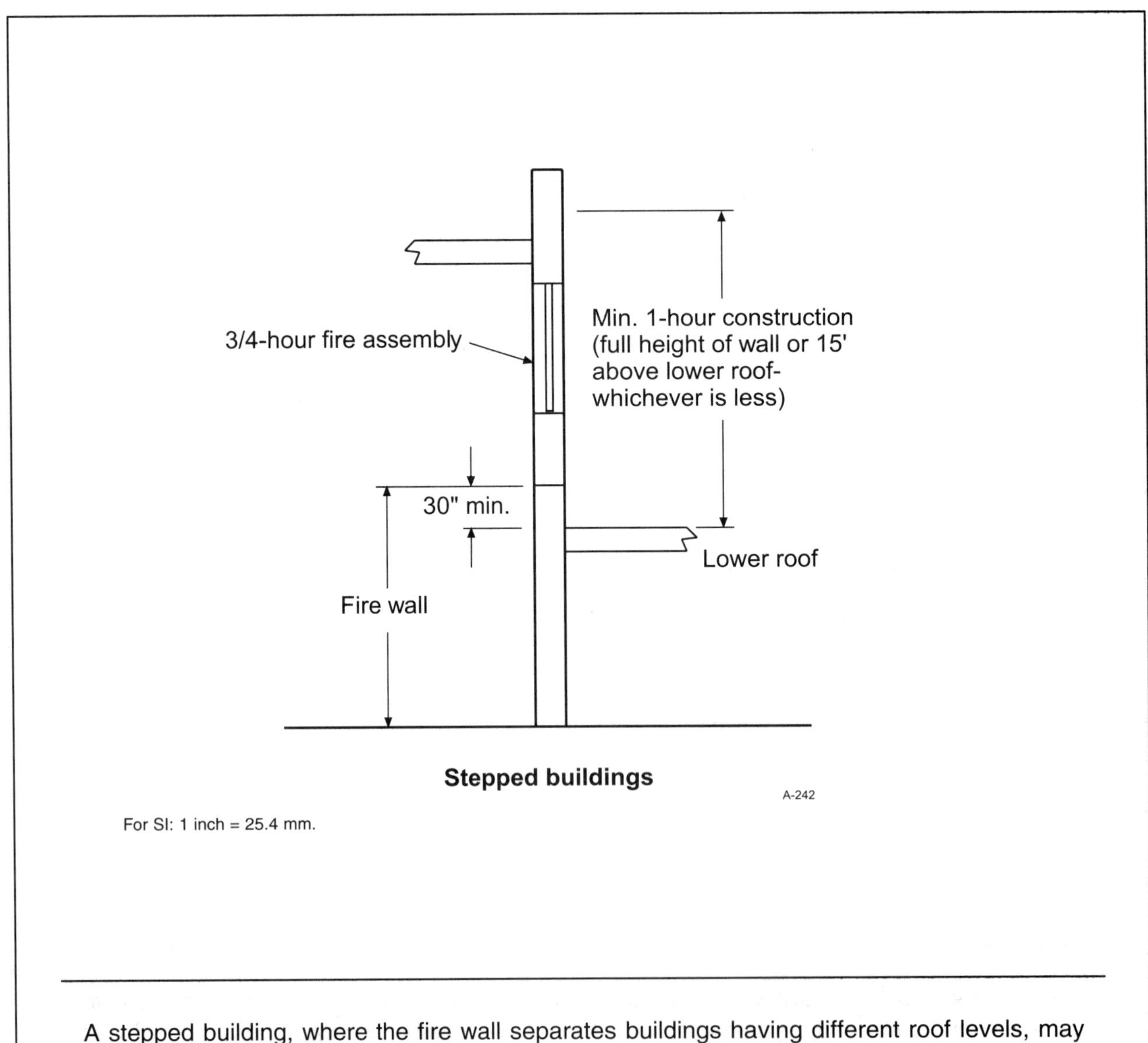

A stepped building, where the fire wall separates buildings having different roof levels, may require additional fire resistance to a point 15 feet above the lower roof. An alternative method provides for minimum one-hour horizontal protection of the lower roof assembly.

Topic: Definition and Scope
Reference: IBC 702, 706.1

Category: Fire-Resistance-Rated Construction
Subject: Fire Barriers

Code Text: *Fire barriers used for separation of shafts, exits, exit passageways, horizontal exits or incidental use areas, to separate different occupancies, to separate a single occupancy into different fire areas, or to separate other areas where a fire barrier is required elsewhere in* the IBC *or the* International Fire Code, *shall comply with* Section 706.

Discussion and Commentary: The term "fire barrier" is specific in the IBC and is used to describe a specific type of fire separation element. Fire barriers may be fire-resistance-rated floors or floor-ceiling assemblies, as well as fire-resistance-rated walls. Many of the building elements required to be constructed as fire barriers are listed in Section 706.3.

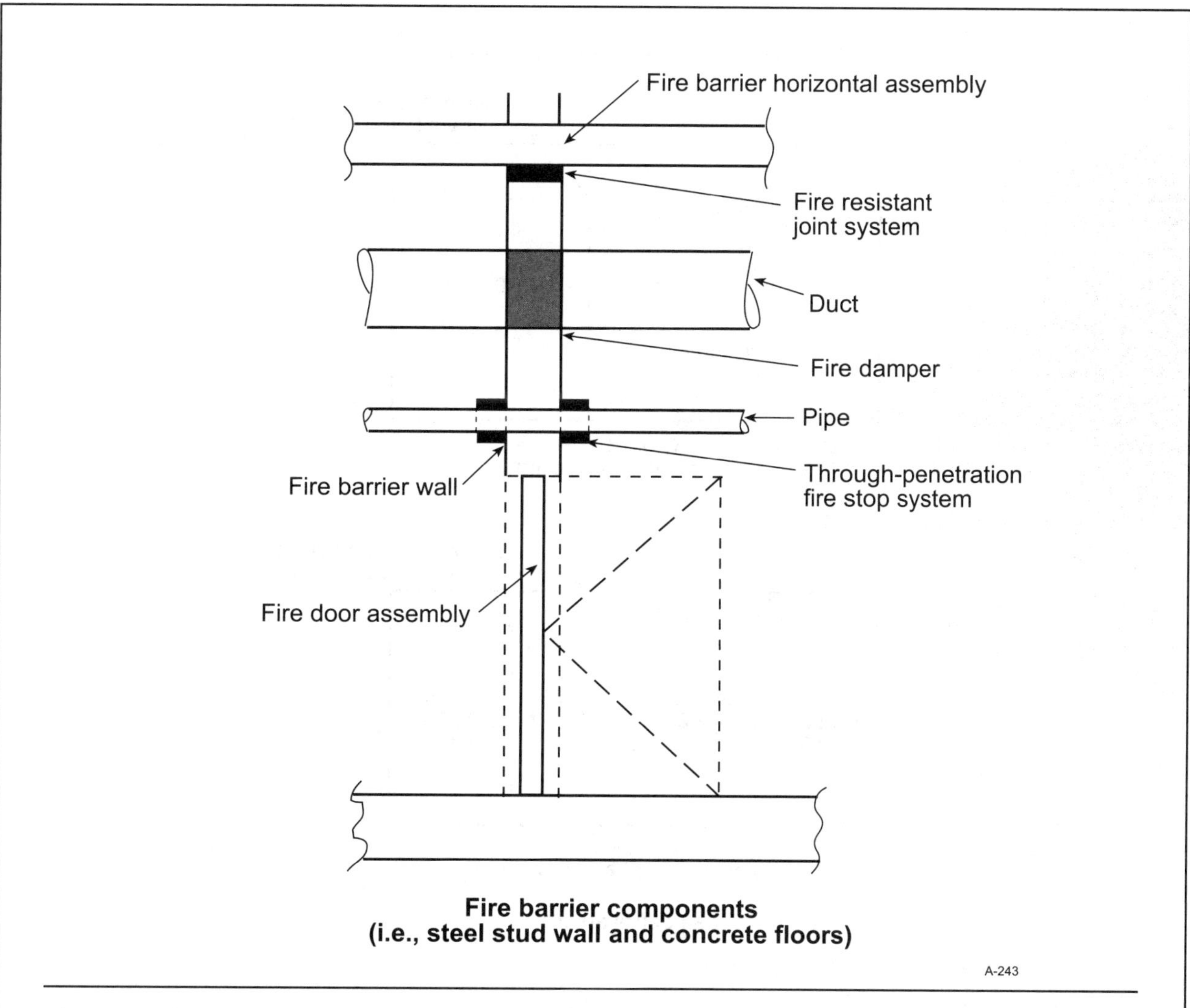

Fire barrier components (i.e., steel stud wall and concrete floors)

Fire barriers are also mandated for specific conditions not mentioned in Section 706. Throughout the IBC, as well as the other *International Codes*, fire barriers are identified as the element used to provide the necessary fire separation for compartmentation of building spaces.

Topic: Single-occupancy Fire Areas
Reference: IBC 706.3.7, Table 706.3.7

Category: Fire-resistance-rated Construction
Subject: Fire Barriers

Code Text: *The fire barrier separating a single occupancy into different fire areas shall have a fire-resistance rating of not less than that indicated in Table 706.3.7.*

Discussion and Commentary: The code recognizes that in many buildings there are two methods to limit the spread of fire, either 1) the use of an automatic sprinkler system or 2) the creation of fire-resistive compartments that contain a fire's movement (fire areas). Section 903.2 identifies those occupancies where compartmentation is an acceptable alternative to a sprinkler system. Table 706.3.7 then mandates the minimum level of fire resistance of the fire barriers utilized to separate the building into two or more compartments (fire areas). As a result, the use of Table 706.3.7 is only applicable in buildings not protected by an automatic sprinkler system.

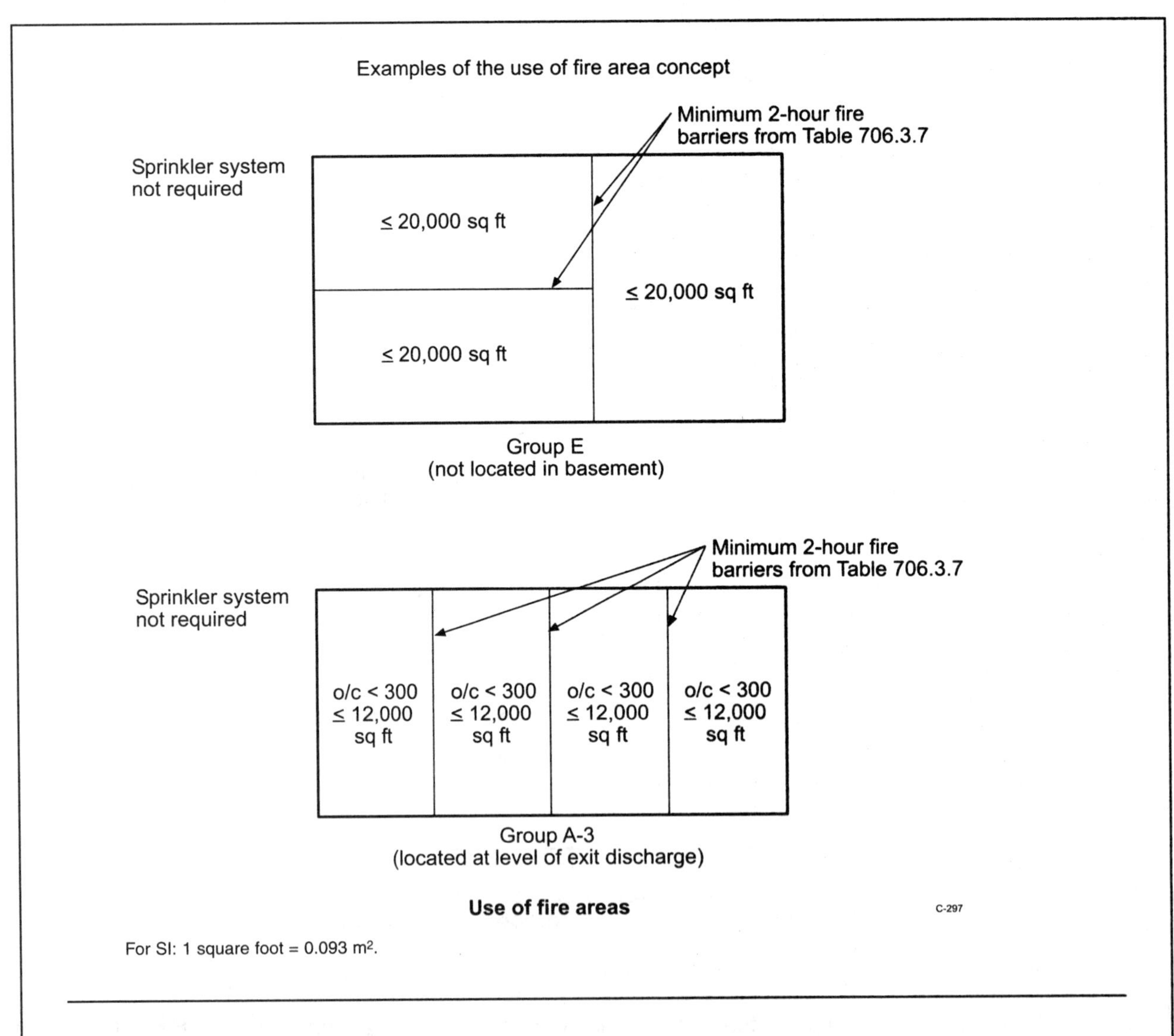

Use of fire areas

The fire area concept addressed in Section 706.3.7 only applies to those occupancies permitted by Section 903.2 to be nonsprinklered under specific conditions. Thus, the provisions do not apply to Groups A-5, B, F-2, H, I, R, S-2 and U, as fire area size is not regulated.

Topic: Continuity
Reference: IBC 702, 706.4

Category: Fire-Resistance-Rated Construction
Subject: Fire Barriers

Code Text: *Fire barrier walls shall extend from the top of the floor/ceiling assembly below to the underside of the floor or roof slab or deck above and shall be securely attached thereto. These walls shall be continuous through concealed spaces such as the space above a suspended ceiling. The supporting construction for fire barrier walls shall be protected to afford the required fire-resistance rating of the fire barrier supported except for 1-hour fire-resistance-rated incidental use area separations in buildings of Types IIB, IIIB and VB construction.* See Section 710 for horizontal assemblies used as fire barriers.

Discussion and Commentary: Where a wall is required to serve as a fire barrier, it must be tight from deck to deck in order to provide a full separation. Where a fire-resistance-rated floor/ceiling or roof/ceiling assembly is present, it remains necessary to extend the fire barrier through the entire assembly.

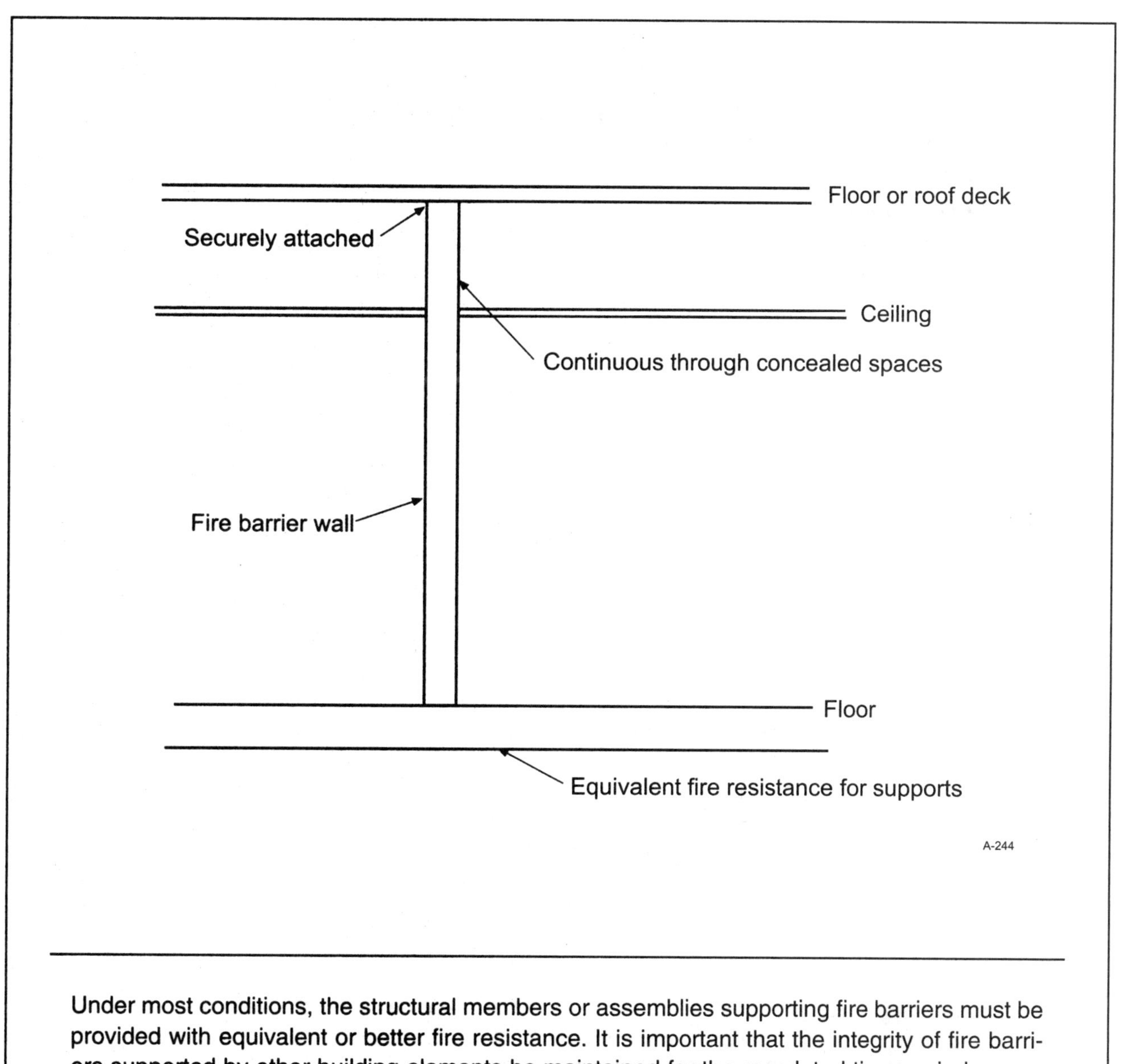

Under most conditions, the structural members or assemblies supporting fire barriers must be provided with equivalent or better fire resistance. It is important that the integrity of fire barriers supported by other building elements be maintained for the mandated time period.

Topic: Definition and Scope
Reference: IBC 702, 707.2

Category: Fire-Resistance-Rated Construction
Subject: Shaft and Vertical Exit Enclosures

Code Text: *A shaft is an enclosed space extending through one or more stories of a building, connecting vertical openings in successive floors, or floors and roof. A shaft enclosure is the walls or construction forming the boundaries of a shaft. Openings through a floor/ceiling assembly shall be protected by a shaft enclosure complying with Section 707.* See eleven exceptions identifying where a shaft enclosure is not required.

Discussion and Commentary: It is not uncommon in multistory buildings to have openings that are provided to accommodate elevators, mechanical equipment or similar devices, and to transmit light or ventilation air. Because of the potential for the rapid spread of fire, smoke and gases vertically through buildings, such openings must be protected with fire-resistance-rated shaft enclosures. There are many special and specific provisions that modify the general requirements.

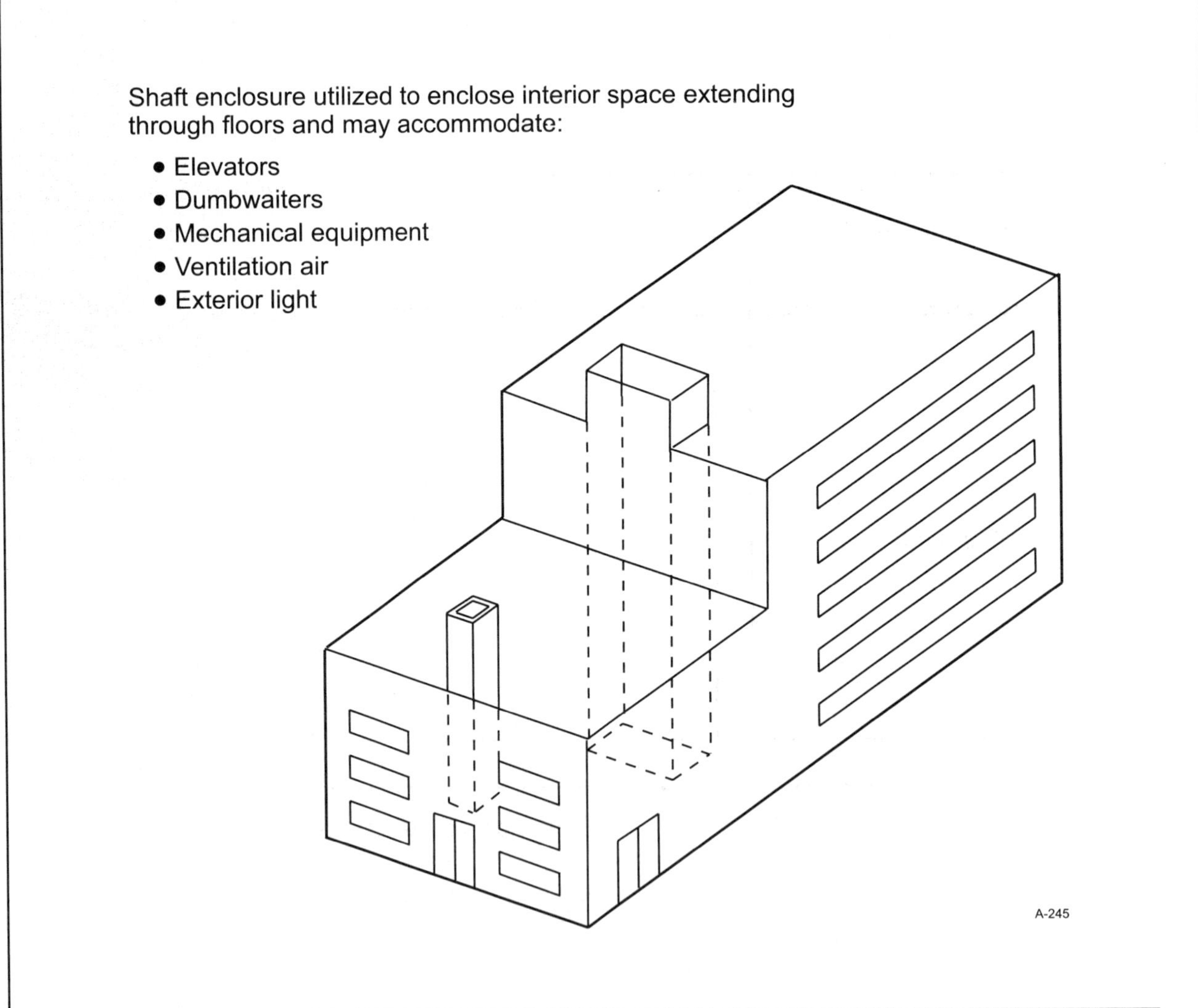

The fire-resistance rating required for a shaft enclosure is based on the building height, with 2 hours being required where four stories or more are connected. Where less than four stories are connected, 1 hour is required. The enclosure rating cannot be less than that of any floor penetrated.

Topic: Continuity
Reference: IBC 707.5

Category: Fire-Resistance-Rated Construction
Subject: Shaft and Vertical Exit Enclosures

Code Text: *Shaft enclosure walls shall extend from the top of the floor/ceiling assembly below to the underside of the floor or roof slab or deck above and shall be securely attached thereto. These walls shall be continuous through concealed spaces such as the space above a suspended ceiling. The supporting construction shall be protected to afford the required fire-resistance rating of the element supported.*

Discussion and Commentary: The general provisions dictate that a shaft be completely enclosed with fire-resistance-rated construction. However, there are conditions that modify this rule. The protection of exterior shaft walls is often unnecessary. Additionally, for those shafts that do not extend to the bottom of the building, the code provides three methods of maintaining the integrity of the shaft enclosure.

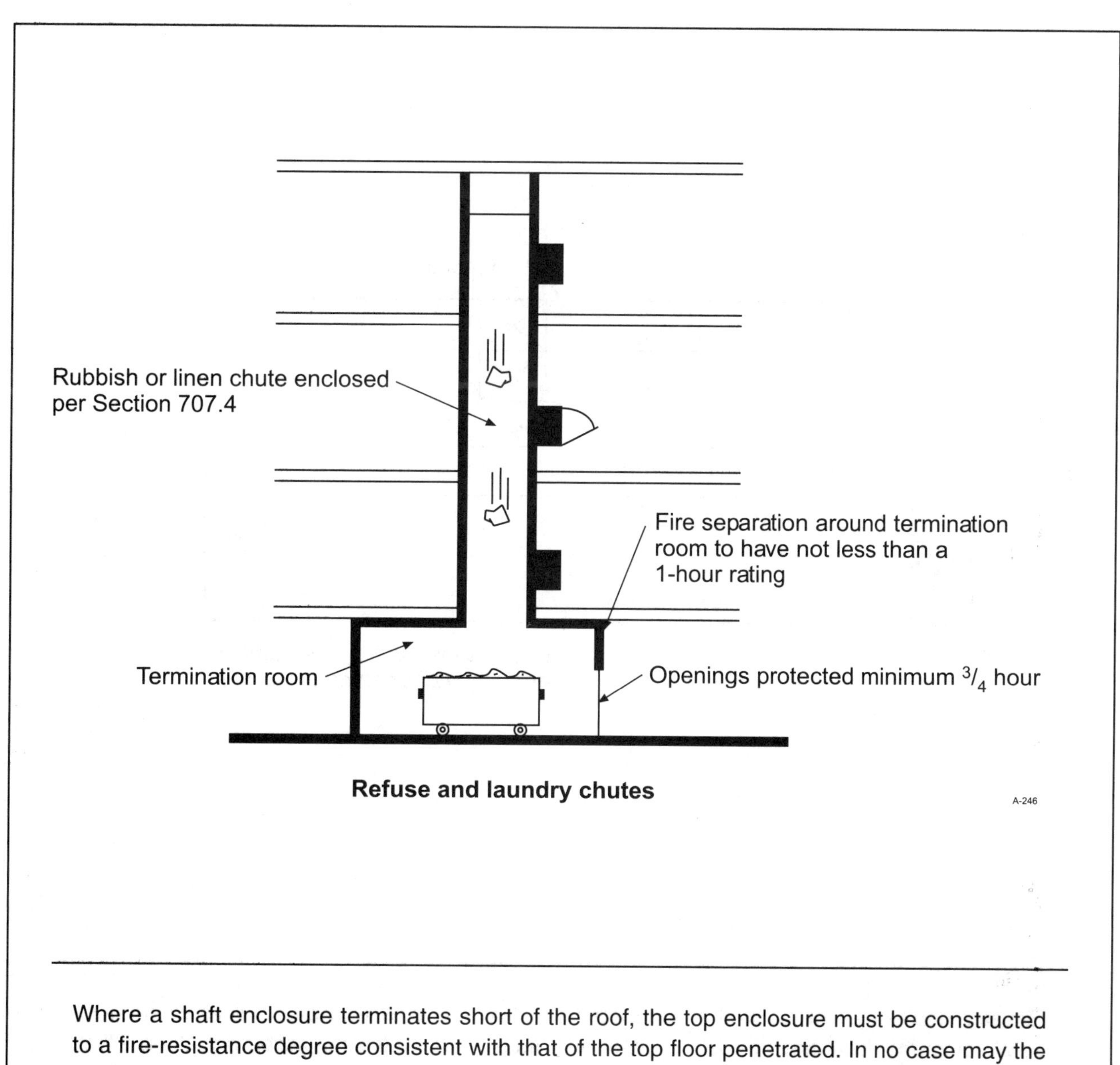

Refuse and laundry chutes

Where a shaft enclosure terminates short of the roof, the top enclosure must be constructed to a fire-resistance degree consistent with that of the top floor penetrated. In no case may the enclosure at the top be rated less than that for the remainder of the shaft enclosure.

Topic: Elevator Lobbies
Reference: IBC 707.14.1

Category: Fire-Resistance-Rated Construction
Subject: Shaft and Vertical Exit Enclosures

Code Text: *Elevators opening into a fire-resistance-rated corridor as required by Section 1016.1 shall be provided with an elevator lobby at each floor containing such a corridor. The lobby shall completely separate the elevators from the corridor by fire partitions and the required opening protection.* See four exceptions that eliminate the requirement for elevator lobbies.

Discussion and Commentary: Where an elevator opens directly into a protected corridor, the elevator shaft creates a potential breach in the integrity of the means of egress system. An elevator lobby creates an additional degree of compartmentalization that provides a buffer between the shaft and the path of exit.

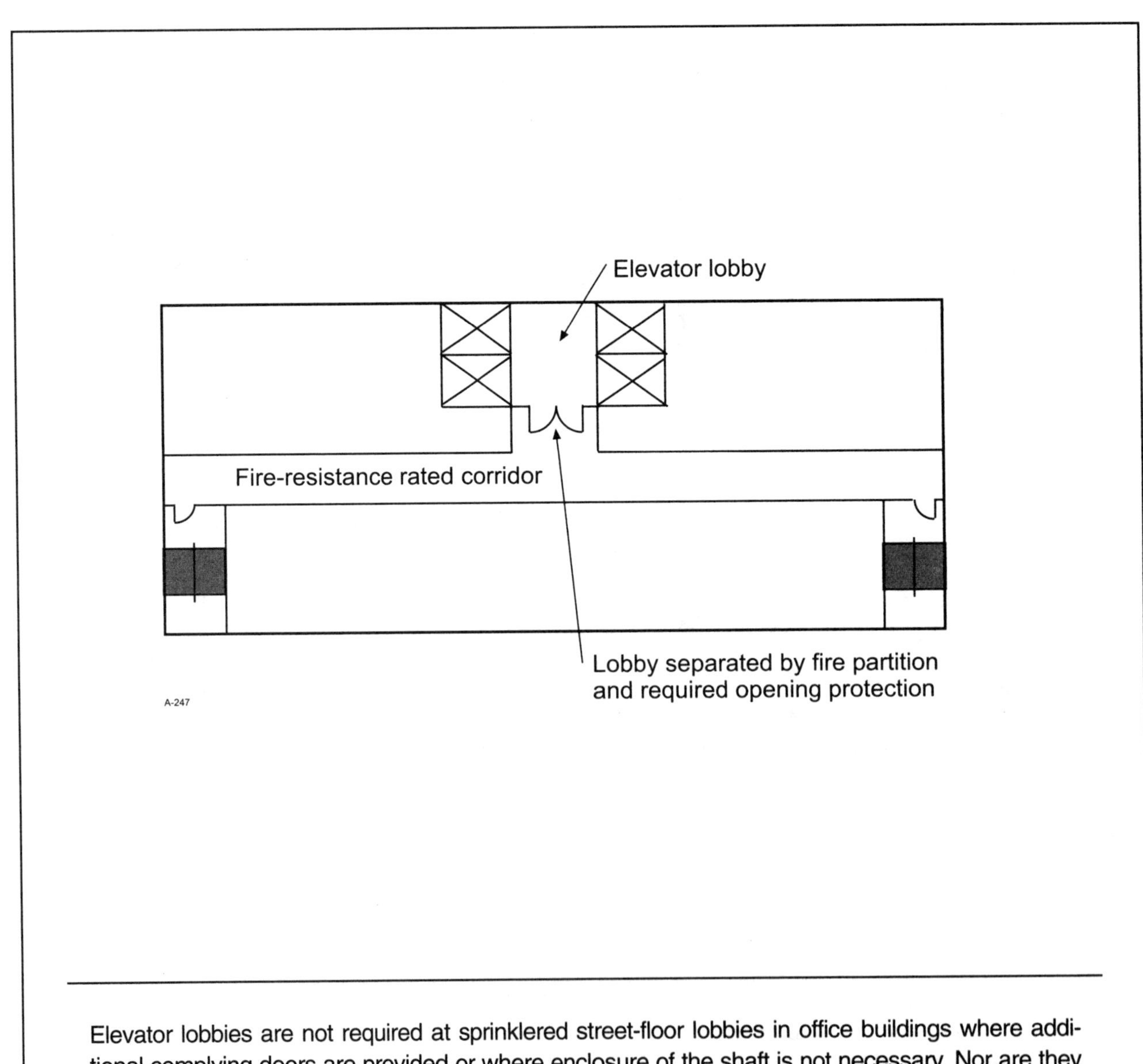

Elevator lobbies are not required at sprinklered street-floor lobbies in office buildings where additional complying doors are provided or where enclosure of the shaft is not necessary. Nor are they required in fully sprinklered buildings, other than Group I-3, that are limited to four stories.

Topic: Definition and Scope
Reference: IBC 702, 708.1

Category: Fire-Resistance-Rated Construction
Subject: Fire Partitions

Code Text: *A fire partition is a vertical assembly of materials designed to restrict the spread of fire in which openings are protected. The following wall assemblies shall comply with* Section 708: *1) walls separating dwelling units in the same building, 2) walls separating sleeping units in occupancies in Group R-1, hotel occupancies, R-2 and I-1, 3) walls separating tenant spaces in covered mall buildings as required by Section 402.7.2, and 4) corridor walls as required by Section 1016.1. The fire-resistance rating of the walls shall be 1-hour.* See exceptions for corridor walls and sprinklered buildings.

Discussion and Commentary: Required to have a fire-resistance-rating of one-hour, fire partitions provide a moderate level of separation that is necessary under certain conditions. Although fire partitions have limited applications, they are important elements in the specific uses and areas in which they are mandated.

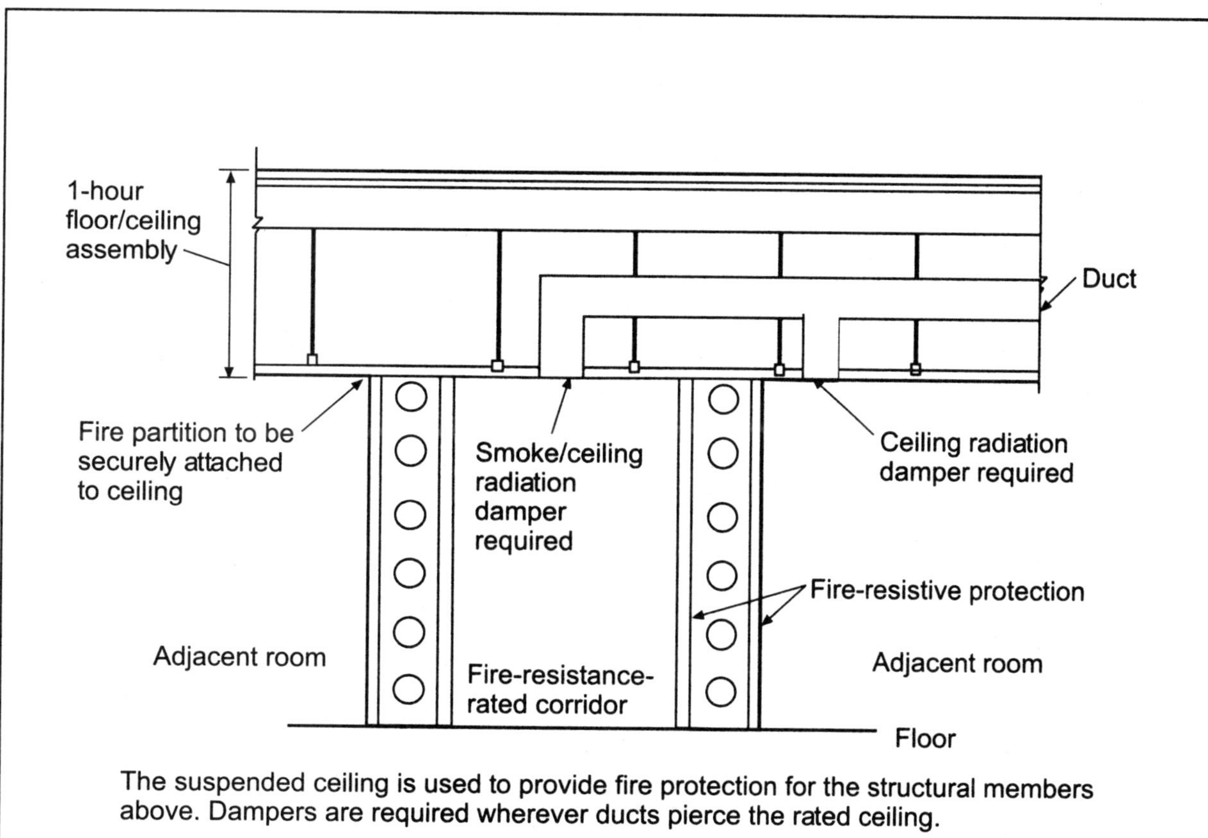

The suspended ceiling is used to provide fire protection for the structural members above. Dampers are required wherever ducts pierce the rated ceiling.

Corridor fire partitions

In sprinklered buildings of Types IIB, IIIB and VB construction, the 1-hour fire-resistance rating for dwelling unit and guestroom separations may be reduced to $^1/_2$ hour. For a typical wood-stud wall system, this separation could be satisfied with $^1/_2$-inch gypsum board on each side.

Topic: Continuity
Reference: IBC 708.4

Category: Fire-Resistance-Rated Construction
Subject: Fire Partitions

Code Text: *Fire partitions shall extend from the top of the floor assembly below to the underside of the floor/roof slab or deck above or to the fire-resistance rated floor/ceiling or roof/ceiling assembly above, and shall be securely attached thereto. If the partitions are not continuous to the deck, and where constructed of combustible construction, the space between the ceiling and the deck above shall be fireblocked or draftstopped in accordance with Sections 717.2.1 and 717.3.1 at the partition line.* See exceptions.

Discussion and Commentary: The method of continuity is a primary difference between fire barriers and fire partitions. Fire partitions need not extend through a concealed space, such as the one above a suspended ceiling, provided that the ceiling is a portion of a fire-resistance-rated floor/ceiling or roof/ceiling assembly.

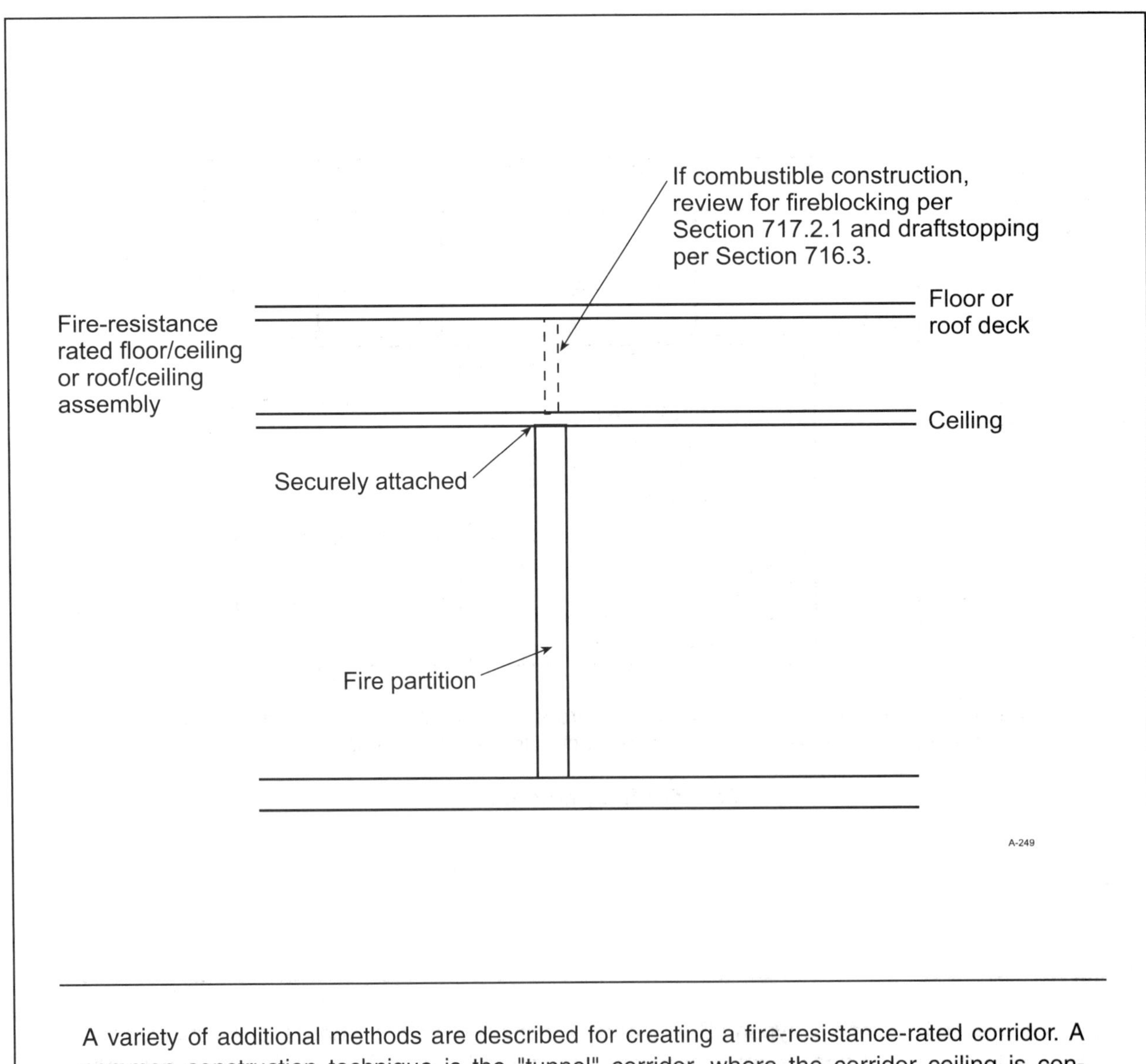

A variety of additional methods are described for creating a fire-resistance-rated corridor. A common construction technique is the "tunnel" corridor, where the corridor ceiling is constructed in a manner consistent with that of the corridor walls.

Topic: Definition and Continuity
Reference: IBC 702, 709.4

Category: Fire-Resistance-Rated Construction
Subject: Smoke Barriers

Code Text: *A smoke barrier is a continuous membrane, either vertical or horizontal, such as a wall, floor, or ceiling assembly, that is designed and constructed to restrict the movement of smoke. Smoke barriers shall form an effective membrane continuous from outside wall to outside wall and from floor slab to floor or roof deck above, including continuity through concealed spaces, such as those found above suspended ceilings, and including interstitial structural and mechanical spaces.* See exception for fire/smoke-resistant ceilings.

Discussion and Commentary: Where the primary concern of the code is the containment of smoke, the use of a smoke barrier is mandated. The locations for smoke barriers are found in various provisions in the IBC, including Section 407.4 for Group I-2 occupancies and Section 1007.6.2 for areas of refuge.

Required Use of Smoke Barriers

- Compartmentation of underground buildings (Sec. 405.4)
- Compartmentation of Group I-2 (Sec. 407.4)
- Compartmentation of Group I-3 (Sec. 408.6)
- Smoke control systems (Sec. 402.9, 404.4 and 909.5)
- Accessible means of egress (Sec. 1007.2)
- Areas of refuge (Sec. 1007.6)

A smoke barrier must have a minimum 1-hour fire-resistance rating. Openings, penetrations, joints, ducts and transfer openings must also be protected to minimize the passage of smoke through the barrier. Opening protectives must have a minimum 20-minute fire-protection rating.

Topic: General Provisions
Reference: IBC 710

Category: Fire-resistance-rated Construction
Subject: Smoke Partitions

Code Text: *Smoke partitions installed as required elsewhere in the* IBC *shall comply with* Section 710. *The walls shall be of materials permitted by the building type of construction. Unless required elsewhere in the* IBC, *smoke partitions are not required to have a fire-resistance rating. Smoke partitions shall extend from the floor to the underside of the floor or roof deck above or to the underside of the ceiling above where the ceiling membrance is constructed to limit the transfer of smoke.*

Discussion and Commentary: A smoke partition is designed for a singular purpose, to limit the movement of smoke from one area to another. Therefore, windows in smoke partitions must be sealed, doors must be tested in accordance with UL 1784 for air leakage concerns, penetrations and joints must be adequately filled and smoke dampers used to protect air transfer openings.

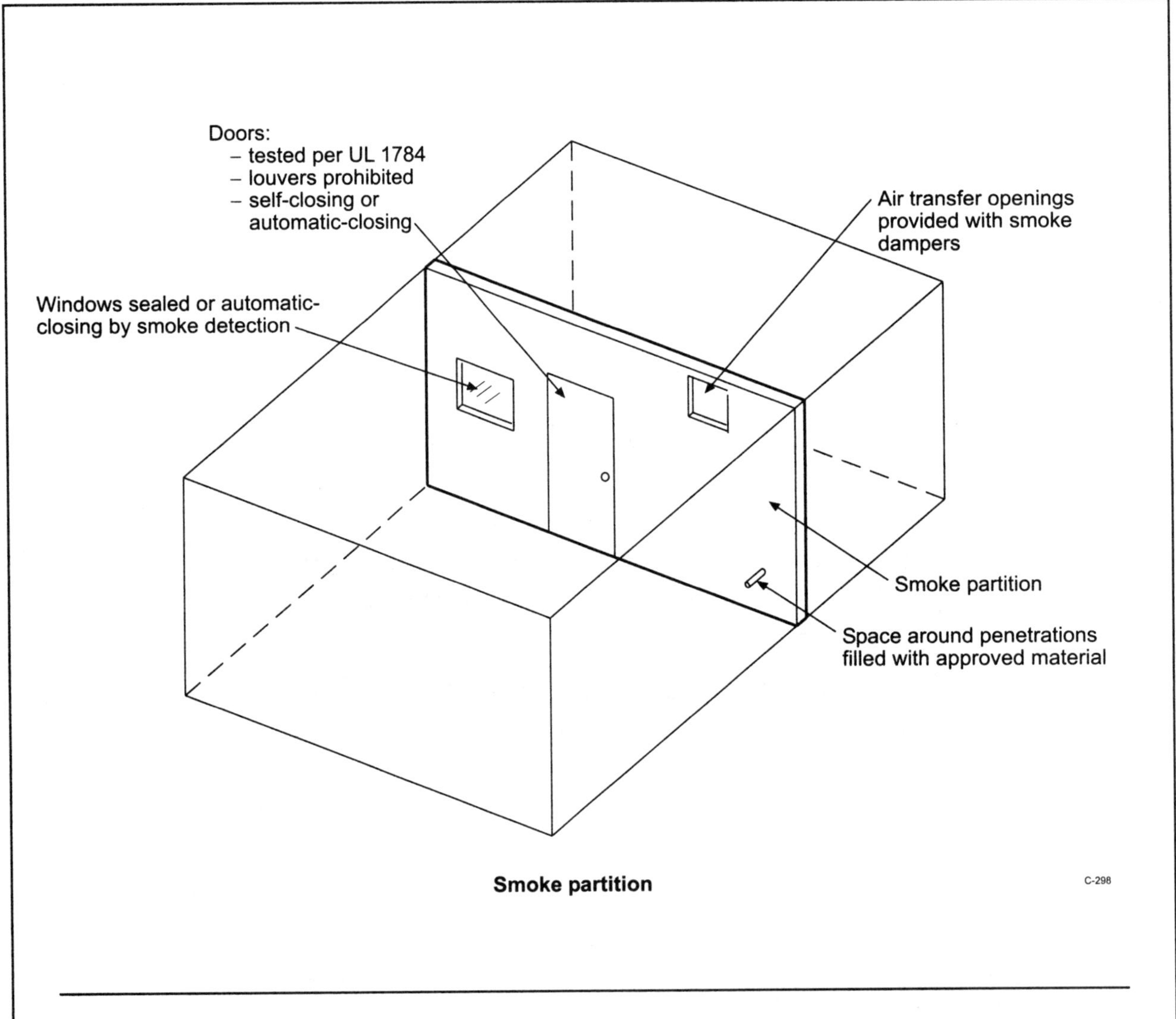

Smoke partition

Smoke partition is a specific element with specific requirements, much like smoke barriers, fire barriers, fire partitions and fire walls. Only where the code specifically mandates smoke partitions are the requirements of Section 710 applicable.

Topic: Fire-Resistance Rating
Reference: IBC 711.3

Category: Fire-Resistance-Rated Construction
Subject: Horizontal Assemblies

Code Text: *The fire-resistance rating of floor and roof assemblies shall not be less than that required by the building type of construction. Where the floor assembly separates mixed occupancies, the assembly shall have a fire-resistance rating of not less than that required by Section 302.3.2 . . . . Where the floor assembly separates a single occupancy into different fire areas, the assembly shall have a fire-resistance rating of not less than that required by Section 706.3.7.*

Discussion and Commentary: Table 601 regulates the minimum fire-resistance ratings for floor construction based on the building's type of construction. This minimum level of fire-resistance must always be maintained. Other provisions of the code must also be considered where a horizontal separation is needed within a multi-story building, such as for control areas or occupancy separations.

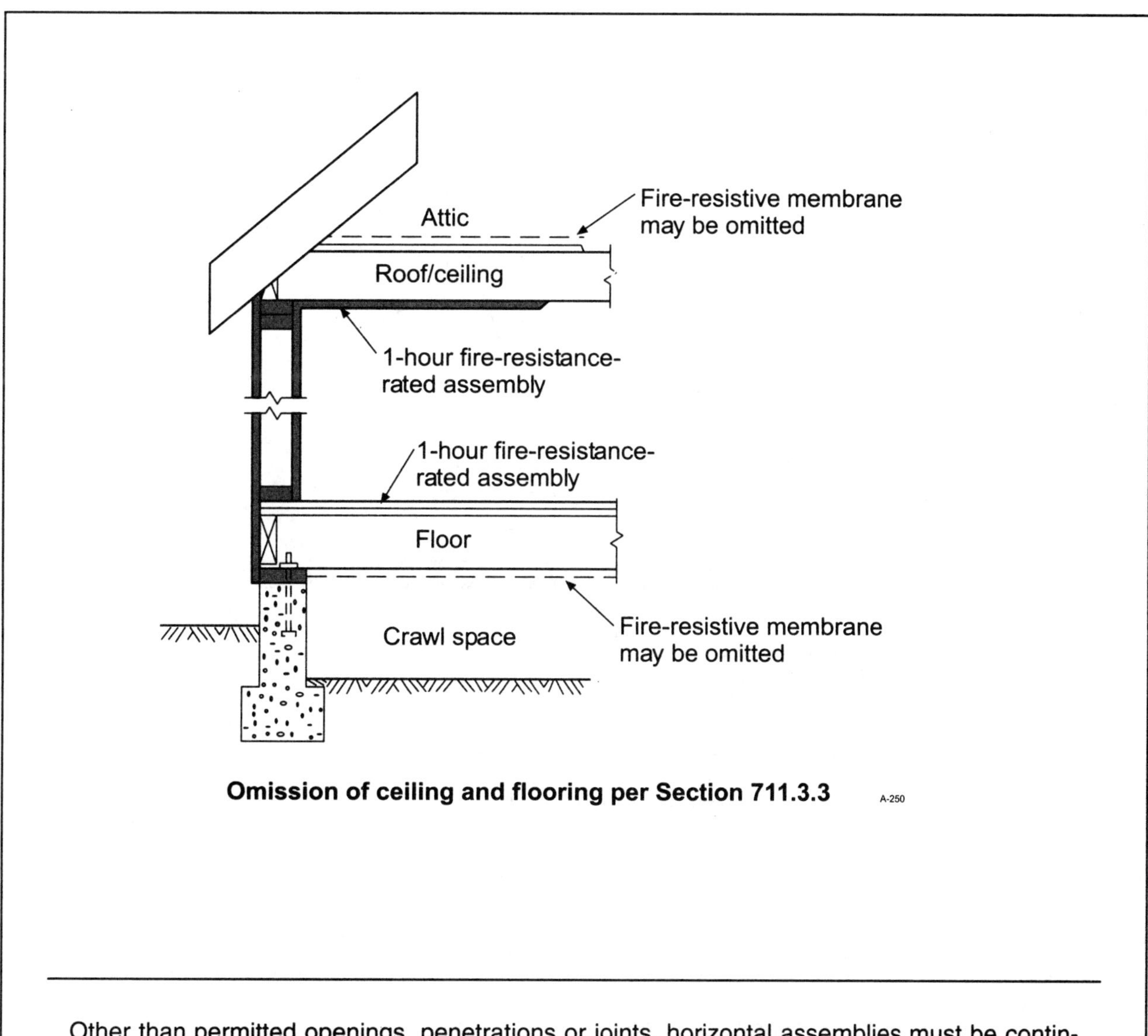

Omission of ceiling and flooring per Section 711.3.3

Other than permitted openings, penetrations or joints, horizontal assemblies must be continuous in order to isolate totally one floor from another. An allowance is permitted for fire-resistance-rated roof construction, where skylights and other penetrations may be unprotected.

Topic: Dwelling Unit Separation **Category:** Fire-resistance-rated Construction
Reference: IBC 708.1, 711.3 **Subject:** Group R Occupancies

Code Text: *The following wall assemblies shall comply with* Section 708 (fire partitions)*: 1) walls separating dwelling units in the same building, and 2) walls separating sleeping units in occupancies in Group R-1, hotel occupancies, R-2 and I-1. Floor assemblies separating dwelling units in the same building or sleeping units in occupancies in Group R-1, hotel occupancies, R-2 and I-1 shall be a minimum of 1-hour fire-resistance-rated construction.* See exception for sprinklered buildings.

Discussion and Commentary: Because of the nature of activities that occur within residential occupancies, it is necessary to mandate some degree of fire-resistant separation between dwelling units or guest rooms. By isolating each unit into an individual compartment, separated by fire-resistance-rated walls and/or horizontal assemblies, the spread of fire is greatly limited, particularly in the early stages of a fire incident, where egress of the occupants is the primary concern.

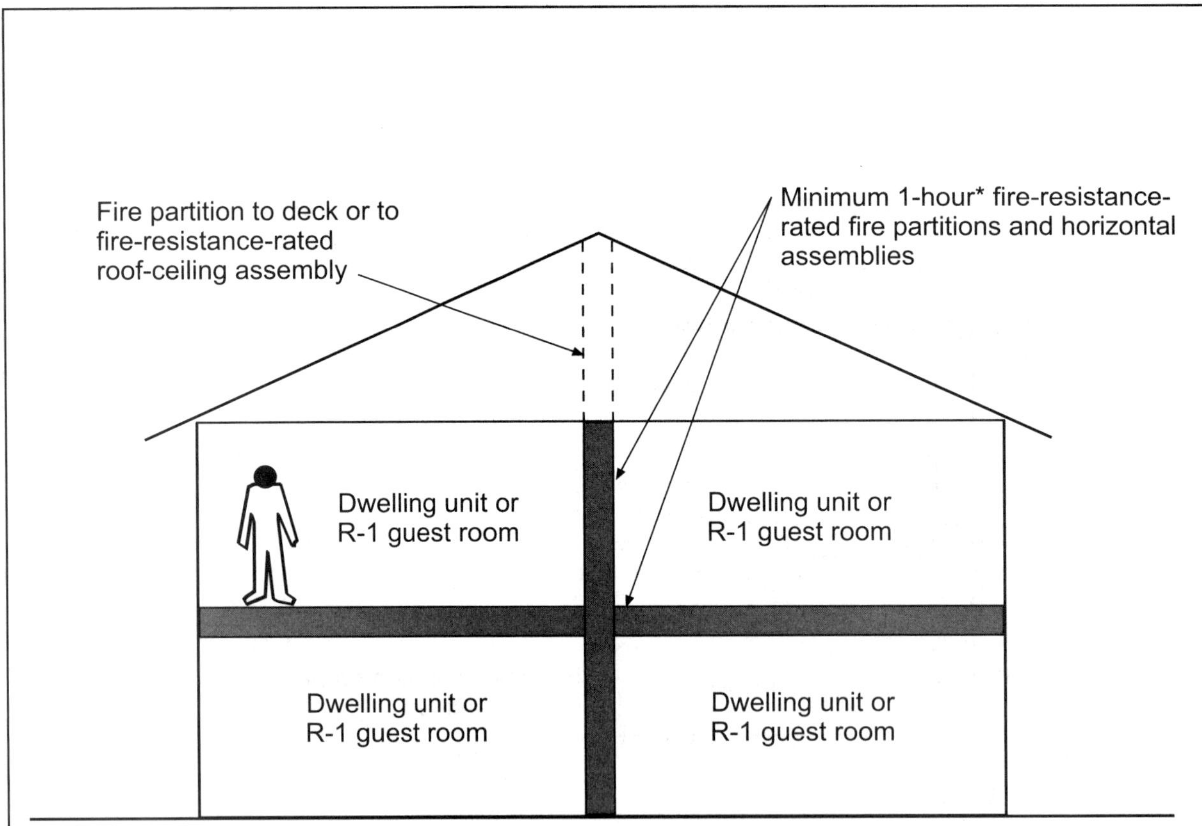

Where a wall is used to separate dwelling units or guest rooms, it must be, at minimum, a fire partition as described in Section 708. The wall must extend from the floor below to the floor deck or roof deck above, or to a fire-resistance-rated floor/ceiling or roof/ceiling assembly.

QUIZ

Study Session 6 — Sections 705–711

I. Multiple Choice

1. Fire walls must be constructed of noncombustible materials unless separating buildings of Type __________ construction.

   a. I
   b. III
   c. IV
   d. V

   Reference________________

2. A fire wall in a Type VA building housing a Group M occupancy must have a minimum fire-resistance rating of __________ hour(s).

   a. one
   b. two
   c. three
   d. four

   Reference________________

3. In a Type IIB building containing Group A-2 and B occupancies, what is the minimum fire-resistance rating for a fire wall?

   a. 1-hour
   b. 2-hour
   c. 3-hour
   d. 4-hour

   Reference________________

4. As a general provision, what minimum distance must a fire wall extend horizontally beyond the exterior surface of exterior walls?

   a. 18 inches
   b. 20 inches
   c. 30 inches
   d. 4 feet

   Reference________________

5. In general, what minimum distance above the roof must a fire wall extend?

   a. 18 inches
   b. 30 inches
   c. 3 feet
   d. 4 feet

   Reference________________

6. Where a fire wall occurs at a location where the roof heights differ, the fire wall may terminate at the underside of the lower roof slab, provided __________.

a. the lower roof is of noncombustible construction
b. the first ten feet of the lower roof assembly has a minimum one-hour rating
c. the exterior wall of the higher portion is one-hour to a height of 10 feet
d. openings in the lower roof have a minimum 45-minute fire-protective rating

Reference_______________

7. Embedded ends of combustible members entering masonry or concrete fire walls shall be separated a minimum distance of __________ inch(es).

a. 1
b. 2
c. 4
d. 6

Reference_______________

8. The aggregate width of openings in a fire wall is limited to a maximum of __________ of the length of the wall.

a. 10%
b. 25%
c. 33 $^{1}/_{3}$%
d. 50%

Reference_______________

9. Fire barriers are used for the separation of all of the following building elements, except __________.

a. shaft enclosures
b. exit passageways
c. incidental use areas
d. fire-resistance-rated corridors

Reference_______________

10. In nonrated buildings, construction supporting fire barriers need not be protected by equivalent fire resistance where the fire barriers are used for __________.

a. 1-hour occupancy separations
b. 1-hour vertical exit enclosures
c. 1-hour incidental use separations
d. 2-hour horizontal exits

Reference_______________

11. In a nonsprinklered building, any single opening in a fire barrier is limited to a maximum area of __________ square feet.

a. 20 b. 100
c. 120 d. 200

Reference______________

12. Fire doors in a fire barrier are permitted to be unlimited in area and aggregate width where the fire barrier is utilized as a(n) __________ separation.

a. exit enclosure b. horizontal exit
c. incidental use area d. exit access corridor

Reference______________

13. In a fully sprinklered hotel, under specific conditions, a stairway not considered a means of egress need not be enclosed where connecting a maximum of __________ stories.

a. 2 b. 3
c. 4 d. 6

Reference______________

14. A floor opening is permitted between a maximum of two stories without a shaft enclosure, under limited conditions, in all but which one of the following occupancies?

a. Group A-2 b. Group H-2
c. Group I-2 d. Group S-2

Reference______________

15. A shaft enclosure shall have a minimum 2-hour fire-resistance rating where connecting a minimum of __________ stories.

a. 2 b. 3
c. 4 d. 6

Reference______________

16. An elevator lobby shall be separated from a fire-resistance-rated corridor through the use of __________.

a. smoke barriers b. fire barriers
c. fire partitions d. smoke partitions

Reference______________

17. A fire partition is not the appropriate wall assembly in which of the following locations?

a. walls separating sleeping units in a hotel
b. walls separating tenant spaces in a covered mall building
c. walls separating control areas in a manufacturing occupancy
d. walls separating dwelling units in an apartment building

Reference_______________

18. What is the minimum required fire-resistance rating for a fire partition separating tenant spaces in a covered mall building?

a. 20 minutes
b. 30 minutes
c. 1 hour
d. No rating is required

Reference_______________

19. Where a fire-resistance-rated corridor ceiling is constructed as required for the corridor walls, the walls shall not terminate before reaching __________.

a. the lower membrane of the ceiling assembly
b. the upper membrane of the ceiling assembly
c. the underside of the floor or roof deck above
d. an approved fire-resistant joint system

Reference_______________

20. In other than a Group I-3 occupancy, what is the minimum required fire-resistance rating for a smoke barrier?

a. No rating is required
b. 30 minutes
c. 45 minutes
d. 1 hour

Reference_______________

21. In which of the following types of construction must a smoke barrier be supported by fire-resistance-rated construction having at least an equivalent rating to the smoke barrier supported?

a. Type IIB
b. Type IIIA
c. Type IIIB
d. Type VB

Reference_______________

22. What is the minimum required fire-protection rating for doors installed in a smoke barrier?

a. No rating is required
b. 20 minutes
c. 45 minutes
d. 1 hour

Reference_______________

23. Wire or other approved devices shall be installed above lay-in ceiling panels in a fire-resistance-rated floor/ceiling assembly to prevent vertical displacement where the weight of the panels is not adequate to resist a minimum upward force of __________.

a. 1 psf
b. 2 psf
c. 5 psf
d. 15 psf

Reference_______________

24. Under which of the following conditions may the ceiling membrane of a fire-resistance-rated horizontal assembly be omitted?

a. where usable attic space occurs above
b. where the assembly has a minimum fire-resistance rating of 2 hours
c. where the floor construction is limited to combustible construction
d. where an unusable crawl space occurs below

Reference_______________

25. Unprotected skylights are permitted through a fire-resistance-rated roof deck, provided __________.

a. the skylights were tested as a part of the roof assembly
b. the roof construction has a maximum one-hour fire-resistance rating
c. the structural integrity of the roof construction is maintained
d. they are limited to 10 percent of the total roof area

Reference_______________

26. Where a fire barrier is utilized to separate a Group M occupancy into multiple fire areas, the minimum fire-resistance rating of the fire barrier shall be _____ hour(s).

a. one
b. two
c. three
d. four

Reference_______________

27. The termination room for a laundry chute shall be separated from the remainder of the building by construction having a minimum fire-resistance rating of _____.

a. 0, no rating is required
b. $^1/_2$ hour
c. 1 hour
d. 2 hours

Reference_______________

28. What hourly rating is mandated for the construction of smoke partitions?

a. 0, no rating is required
b. $^1/_2$ hour
c. $^3/_4$ hour
d. 1 hour

Reference_______________

29. Openings in smoke partitions shall have a minimum fire-protection rating of _____.

a. 0, no rating is required
b. 20 minutes
c. 45 minutes
d. 1 hour

Reference_______________

30. In a Type IIB hotel that is sprinklered in accordance with NFPA 13, what is the minimum fire-resistance rating for the fire partitions and horizontal assemblies that separate sleeping units?

a. 0, no rating is required
b. $^1/_2$ hour
c. 1 hour
d. 2 hours

Reference_______________

INTERNATIONAL BUILDING CODE
Study Session 7
Sections 712–719 — Fire-Resistance-Rated Construction III

OBJECTIVE: To gain an understanding of the installation of fireblocking and draftstopping in combustible construction as well as the methods of protecting fire-resistance-rated building components where they contain doors, windows, ducts, air transfer openings and penetrations.

REFERENCE: Sections 712 through 719, 2003 *International Building Code*

KEY POINTS:

- Which two types of penetrations are regulated by the code?
- What are the appropriate installation details where sleeves are used in penetrating a fire-resistance-rated assembly?
- What is a through penetration? Membrane penetration?
- Penetrating items of steel, ferrous or copper may be protected in what manner?
- What is an F rating? What minimum fire-resistance rating is required of a through-penetration firestop system?
- How can the membrane penetration by a steel outlet box be addressed? A listed electrical box? A fire sprinkler?
- Which limitations are placed on noncombustible penetrating items connecting to combustible items?
- How are fire-resistance-rated horizontal assemblies penetrated? Nonfire-resistance-rated horizontal assemblies?
- What is the purpose of a fire-resistance-rated joint system? When is such a system required?
- How should the intersection of an exterior curtain wall and a fire-resistance-rated floor assembly be accomplished?
- Where must structural frame members be individually protected? How are columns protected above a ceiling?
- How is the fire-protection rating of an opening protective determined?
- What are the characteristics of a fire-resistance-rated corridor door or smoke barrier door?
- In what location must a fire door be rated to a maximum transmission temperature end point?
- What are the labeling requirements for fire doors? Smoke and draft control doors? Fire-protection-rated glazing?
- Where are self-closing door assemblies mandated? Automatic-closing assemblies?
- What is the maximum fire-protection rating assigned to fire-protection-rated glazing?
- Under which conditions is wired glass considered equivalent to $^3/_4$-hour fire-protection rated glazing?
- What is the maximum size of a fire window assembly containing a wired glass panel?
- What are the different types of dampers? How should they be actuated?
- How must fire and smoke dampers be identified and accessed?
- Where are fire dampers required? Smoke dampers? Ceiling radiation dampers?
- In what specific locations are fire dampers not required for penetrations of shaft enclosures? Where smoke dampers are not required?
- Why is draftstopping and fireblocking unnecessary in noncombustible construction?
- Where is fireblocking required to be installed? Draftstopping?
- Which materials are acceptable as fire blocks? Draft stops?

Topic: Definitions and Scope
Reference: IBC 702, 712.1

Category: Fire-Resistance-Rated Construction
Subject: Penetrations

Code Text: *A through penetration is an opening that passes through an entire assembly. A membrane penetration is an opening made through one side (wall, floor or ceiling membrane) of an assembly. The provisions of Section 712 shall govern the materials and methods of construction used to protect through penetrations and membrane penetrations.*

Discussion and Commentary: Fire-resistance-rated walls and horizontal assemblies are usually penetrated, both fully and partially, with piping, conduit, outlet boxes, cable, vents and similar penetrating items. The IBC regulates both the materials and the methods of penetration based on the specific conditions that exist. Where sleeves are used, they must be fastened securely in place, and all open space within and around the sleeve must be appropriately protected.

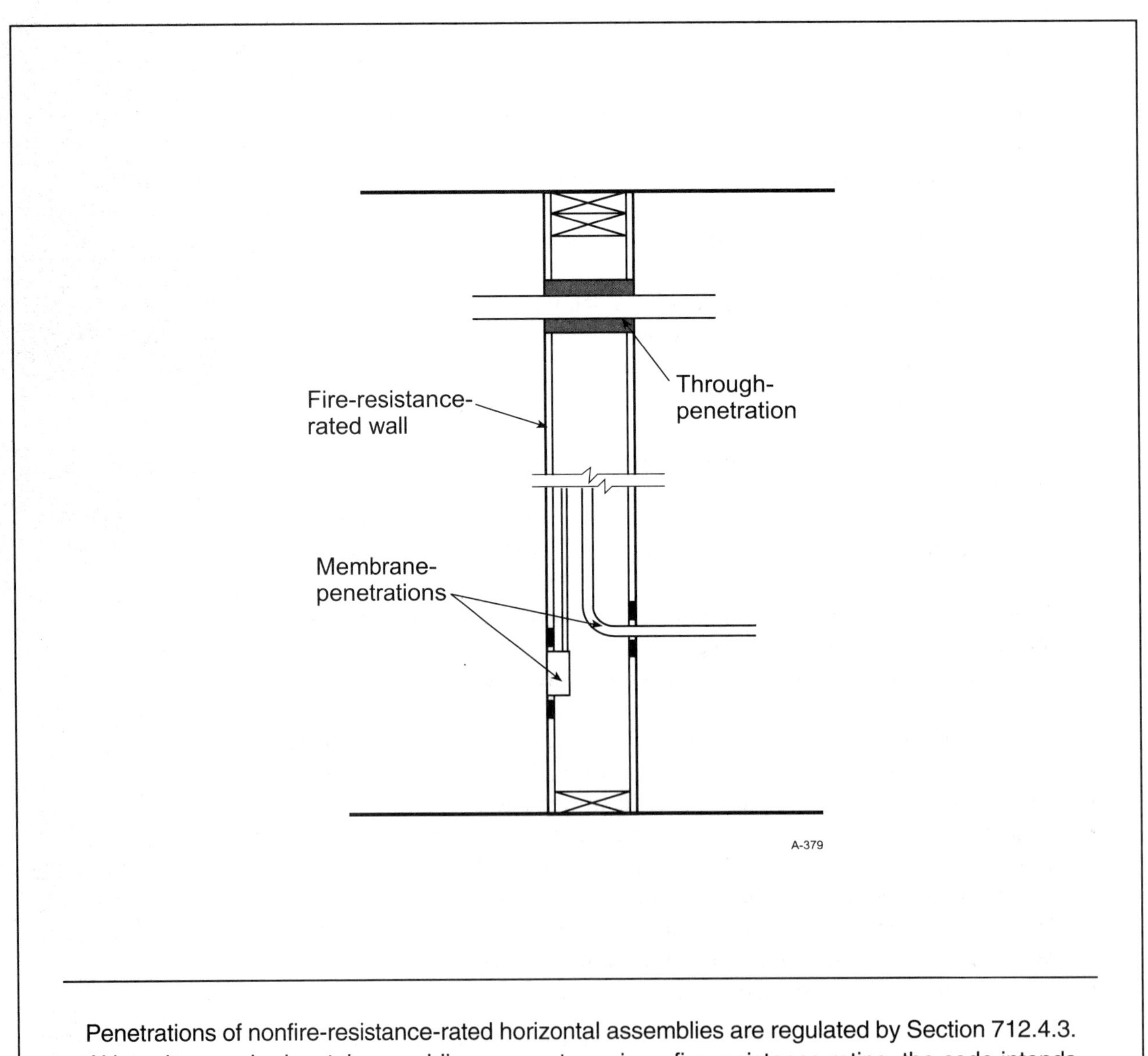

Penetrations of nonfire-resistance-rated horizontal assemblies are regulated by Section 712.4.3. Although some horizontal assemblies may not require a fire-resistance rating, the code intends that some degree of separation (compartmentalization) be provided from one story to another.

Topic: Fire-Resistance-Rated Walls
Reference: IBC 712.3

Category: Fire-Resistance-Rated Construction
Subject: Penetrations

Code Text: *Penetrations into or through fire walls, fire barriers, smoke barrier walls, and fire partitions shall comply with Section 712.3.*

Discussion and Commentary: In general, penetrations into or through fire-resistance-rated walls must be either protected with an approved through-penetration firestop system or installed as a tested component of an approved fire-resistance-rated assembly. These methods are considered proprietary, with each penetration being regulated by the specifics of the installation. Two generic methods are identified as exceptions to the general requirements; however, both methods are based on the penetration only of steel, ferrous or copper pipes or steel conduits. Under such conditions, the annular space around the penetrating items shall be filled with an appropriate material.

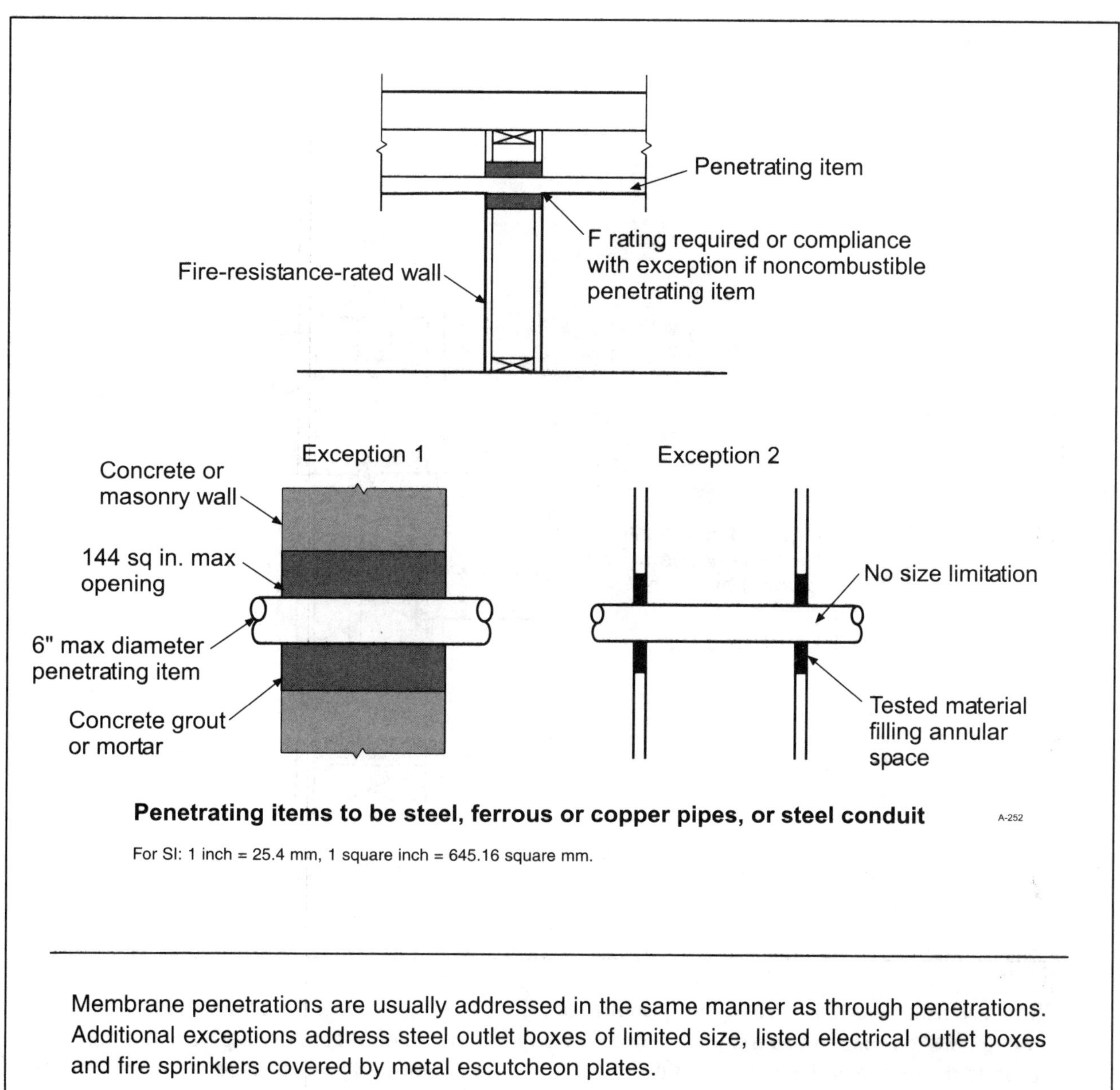

Penetrating items to be steel, ferrous or copper pipes, or steel conduit

For SI: 1 inch = 25.4 mm, 1 square inch = 645.16 square mm.

Membrane penetrations are usually addressed in the same manner as through penetrations. Additional exceptions address steel outlet boxes of limited size, listed electrical outlet boxes and fire sprinklers covered by metal escutcheon plates.

Topic: Fire-resistance-rated Walls
Reference: IBC 712.3.3, 712.3.4

Category: Fire-resistance-rated Construction
Subject: Penetrations

Code Text: *Penetrations of fire-resistance-rated walls by ducts and air transfer openings that are not protected with fire dampers shall comply with* the provisions for penetrations. *Noncombustible penetrating items shall not connect to combustible items beyond the point of firestopping unless it can be demonstrated that the fire-resistance integrity of the wall is maintained.*

Discussion and Commentary: Duct penetrations of fire-resistance-rated wall assemblies are typically protected with fire dampers in accordance with Section 716.5. However, in those locations where dampers are not required, it is still necessary to address the structural integrity of the fire-resistive-rated wall where it is penetrated. Thus, the space between the duct and the wall must be protected in a manner consistent with that used for pipes, conduits and similar items.

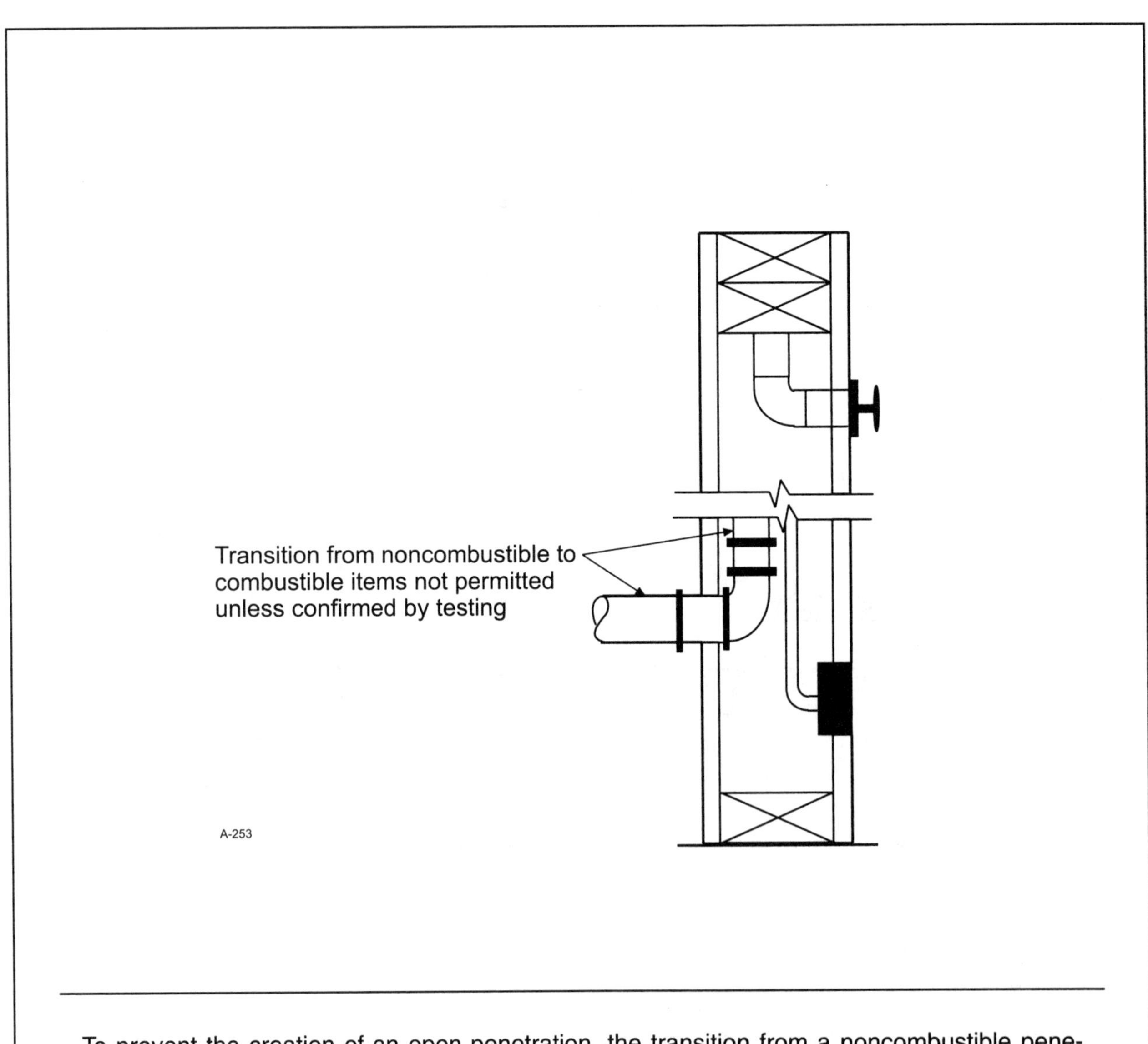

To prevent the creation of an open penetration, the transition from a noncombustible penetrating item to a combustible item is prohibited beyond the point of firestopping. Such a condition is only permitted when its suitability has been demonstrated through testing.

Topic: Horizontal Assemblies
Reference: IBC 712.4

Category: Fire-Resistance-Rated Construction
Subject: Penetrations

Code Text: *Penetrations of a floor, floor/ceiling assembly or the ceiling membrane of a roof/ceiling assembly shall be protected in accordance with Section 707. Penetrations permitted by Exceptions 3 and 4 of Section 707.2 shall comply with Sections 712.4.1 through 712.4.4.*

Discussion and Commentary: Where horizontal construction is penetrated by a pipe, tube, wire, conduit, cable, vent or similar item, the primary requirements are based on Section 707 for shaft enclosures. However, Exception 3 permits the use of Section 712.4 for both through penetrations and membrane penetrations. The provisions for horizontal assemblies are very similar to those for walls, with special allowances for steel, copper or ferrous penetrating items. In addition to the typical penetrations, the code requires that recessed fixtures in fire-resistance-rated floor/ceiling assemblies be installed so that the required fire resistance is not reduced.

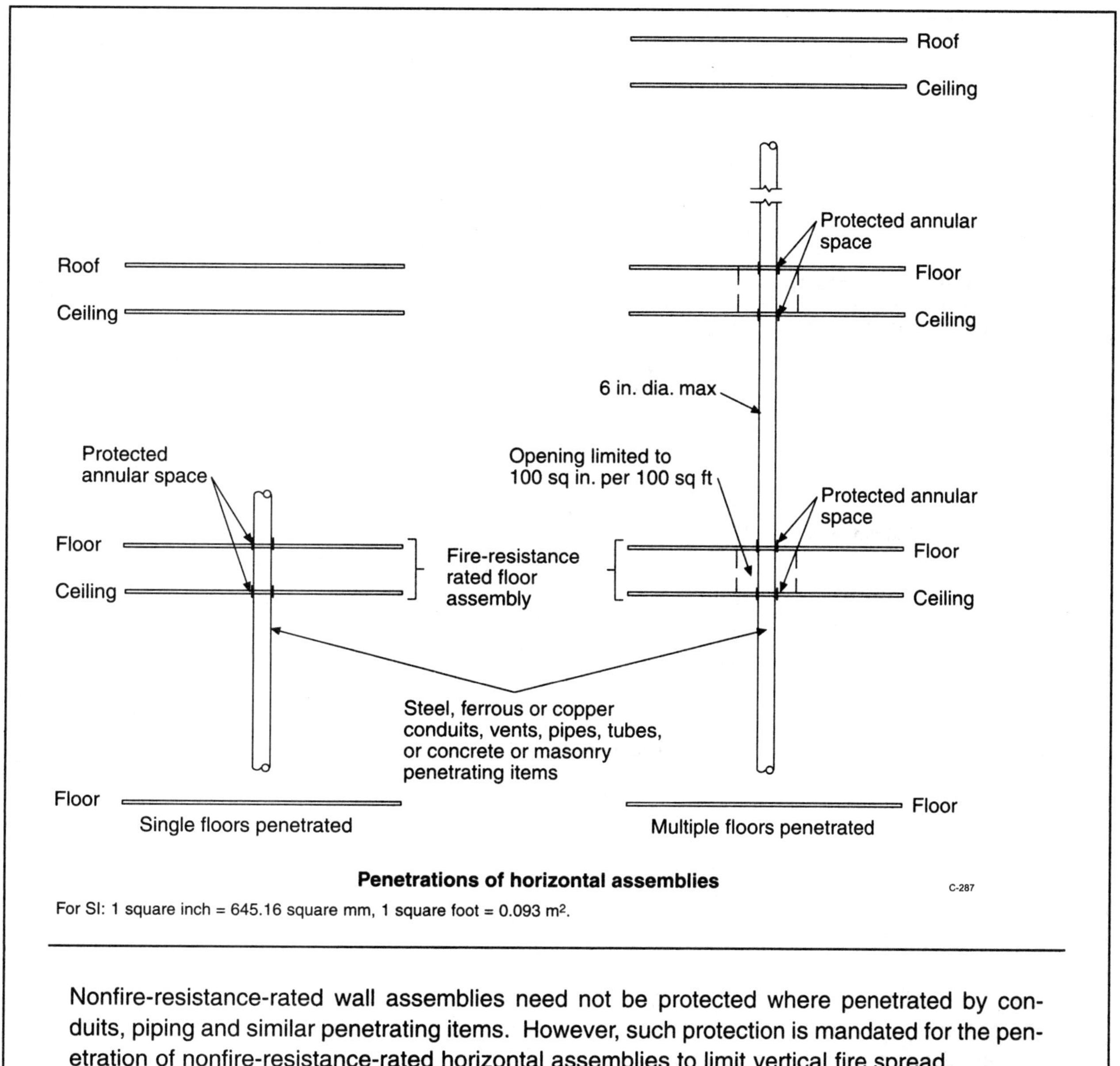

Penetrations of horizontal assemblies

For SI: 1 square inch = 645.16 square mm, 1 square foot = 0.093 m².

Nonfire-resistance-rated wall assemblies need not be protected where penetrated by conduits, piping and similar penetrating items. However, such protection is mandated for the penetration of nonfire-resistance-rated horizontal assemblies to limit vertical fire spread.

Topic: General Provisions
Reference: IBC 713

Category: Fire-resistance-rated Construction
Subject: Fire-resistant Joint Systems

Code Text: *Joints installed in or between fire-resistance-rated walls, floor or floor/ceiling assemblies and roofs or roof/ceiling assemblies shall be protected by an approved fire-resistant joint system designed to resist the passage of fire for a time period not less than the required fire-resistance rating of the wall, floor or roof in or between which it is installed. Fire-resistant joint systems shall be securely installed in or on the joint for its entire length so as not to dislodge, loosen or otherwise impair its ability to accommodate expected building movements and to resist the passage of fire and hot gases.*

Discussion and Commentary: Joints are created where the structural design of a building necessitates a separation between building components in order to accommodate anticipated structural displacements caused by thermal expansion and contraction, seismic activity, wind or other loads.

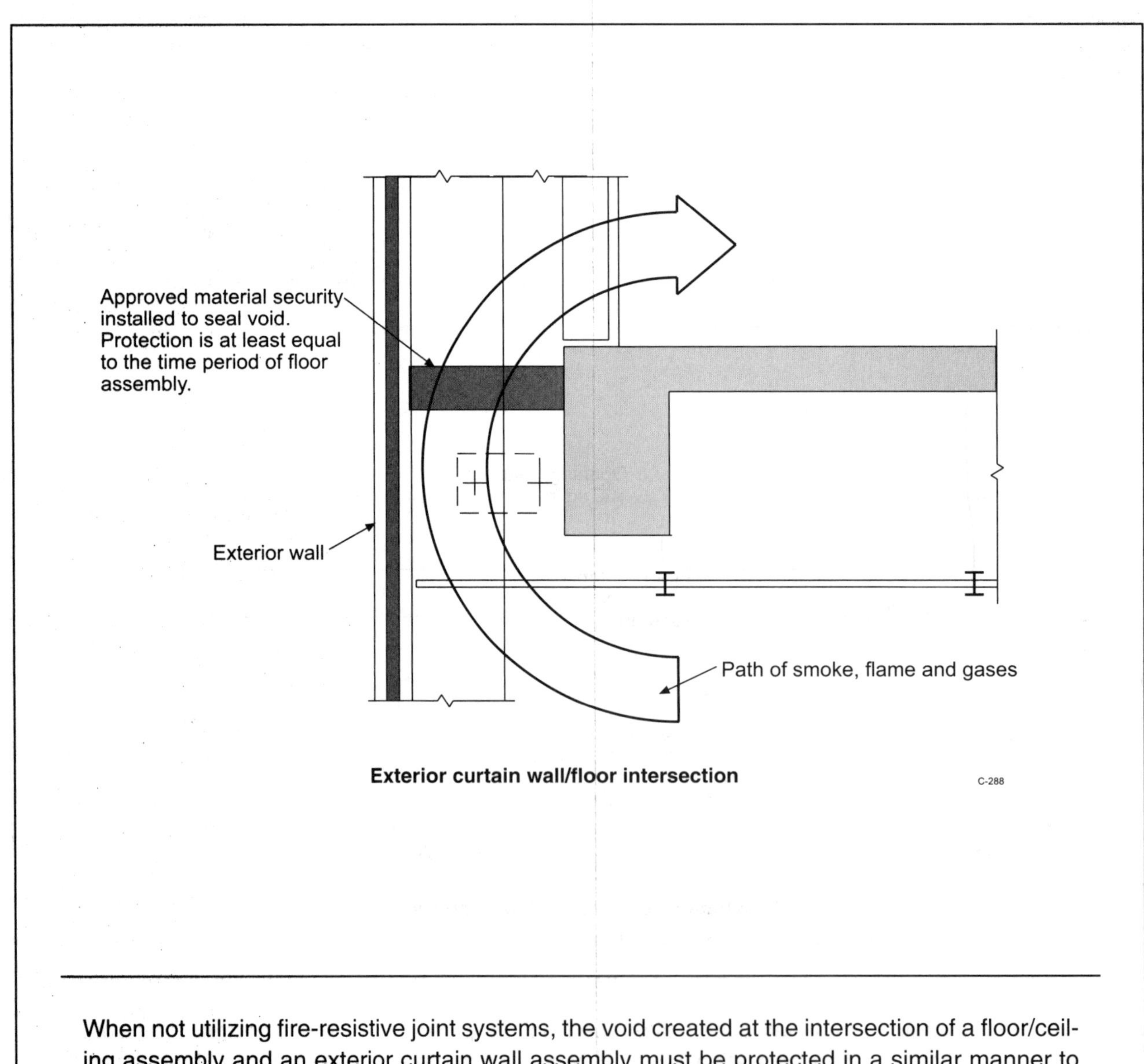

Exterior curtain wall/floor intersection

When not utilizing fire-resistive joint systems, the void created at the intersection of a floor/ceiling assembly and an exterior curtain wall assembly must be protected in a similar manner to prevent the spread of flame and hot gases vertically from floor to floor.

Topic: Individual Protection
Reference: IBC 714.2.1

Category: Fire-Resistance-Rated Construction
Subject: Structural Members

Code Text: *Columns, girders, trusses, beams, lintels or other structural members that are required to have a fire-resistance rating and that support more than two floors or one floor and roof, or support a load-bearing wall or a nonload-bearing wall more than two stories high, shall be individually protected on all sides for the full length with materials having the required fire-resistance rating. Other structural members required to have a fire-resistance rating shall be protected by individual encasement, by a membrane or ceiling protection as specified in Section 711, or by a combination of both.*

Discussion and Commentary: Because of the differences in both the testing procedure and the conditions of acceptance, structural frame members carrying significant portions of the structure cannot simply be protected by enclosure within a fire-resistance-rated wall, floor/ceiling or roof/ceiling assembly. Therefore, under specific conditions, individual encasement is mandated.

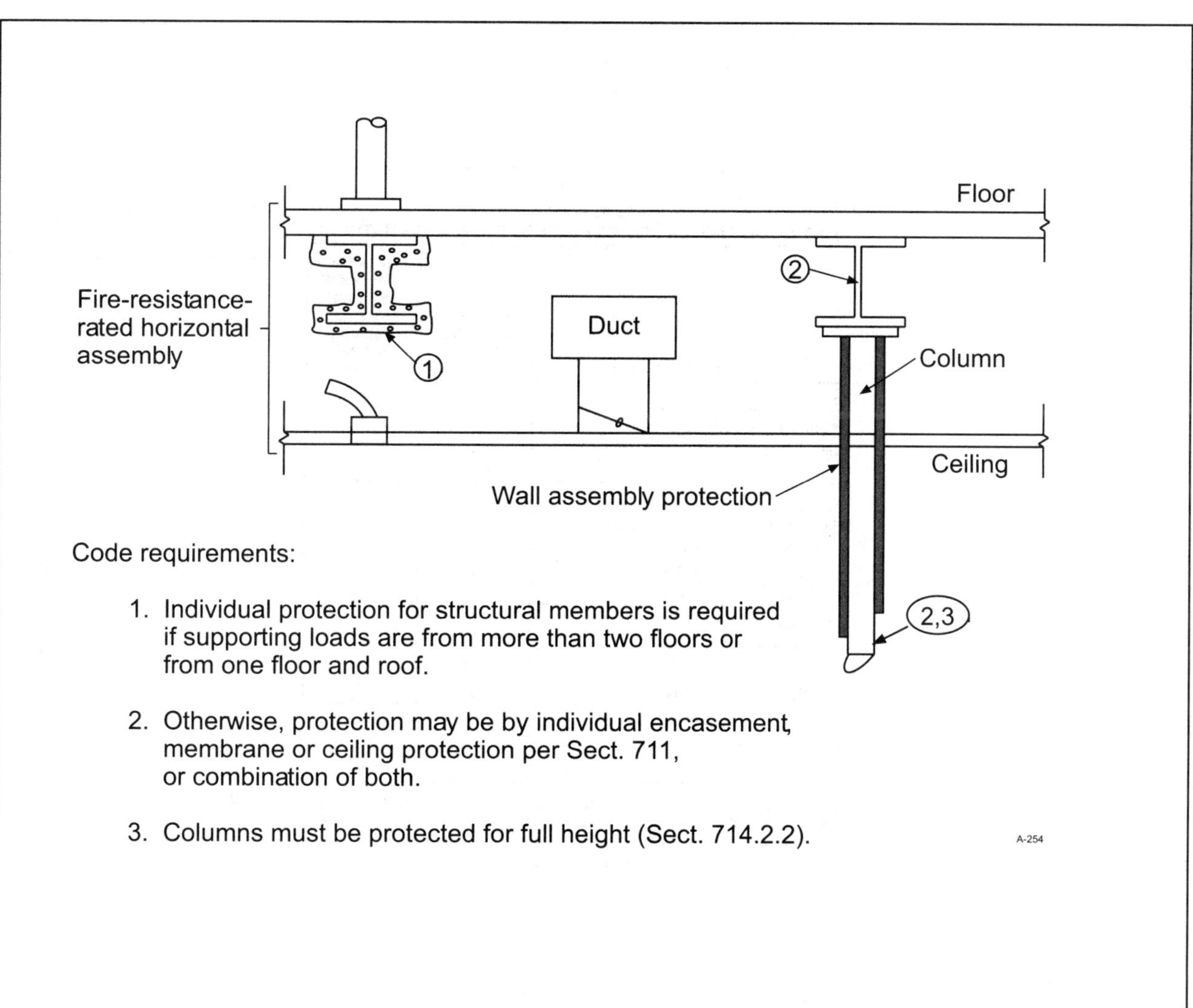

When a column requires a fire-resistance rating, it must be fully protected, including its connections to beams or girders. If the column extends above a ceiling, the fire protection must continue through the above-ceiling space to the top of the column.

Topic: Fire Door Assemblies
Reference: IBC 715.3

Category: Fire-Resistance-Rated Construction
Subject: Opening Protectives

Code Text: *Approved fire door and fire shutter assemblies shall be constructed of any material or assembly of component materials that conforms to the test requirements of Section 715.3.1* (side-hinged or pivoted swinging doors), *715.3.2* (other types of doors) *or 715.3.3* (doors in corridors and smoke barriers) *and the fire-protection rating indicated in Table 715.3.* See exceptions for tin-clad fire doors and floor fire doors.

Discussion and Commentary: The level of protection required for a fire door is commensurate with that required for the wall or partition in which it is installed. The minimum fire-protection rating varies based on the wall's required rating as well as the type and use of the wall assembly under consideration.

TABLE 715.3
FIRE DOOR AND FIRE SHUTTER FIRE PROTECTION RATINGS

TYPE OF ASSEMBLY	REQUIRED ASSEMBLY RATING (hours)	MINIMUM FIRE DOOR AND FIRE SHUTTER ASSEMBLY RATING (hours)
Fire walls and fire barriers having a required fire-resistance rating greater than 1 hour	4 3 2 $1^1/_2$	3 3[a] $1^1/_2$ $1^1/_2$
Fire barriers having a required fire-resistance rating of 1 hour: Shaft, exit enclosure and exit passageway walls Other fire barriers	 1 1	 1 $^3/_4$
Fire partitions: Corridor walls Other fire partitions	 1 0.5 1	 $^1/_3$[b] $^1/_3$[b] $^3/_4$
Exterior walls	3 2 1	$1^1/_2$ $1^1/_2$ $^3/_4$

a. Two doors, each with a fire protection rating of $1^1/_2$ hours, installed on opposite sides of the same opening in a fire wall, shall be deemed equivalent in fire protection rating to one 3-hour fire door.
b. For testing requirements, see Section 715.3.3.

A fire door installed in a corridor wall or smoke barrier must have a minimum fire-protection rating of 20 minutes. In addition, the door must pass an air leakage test to verify that it provides the necessary level of smoke protection.

Topic: Labeling Requirements
Reference: IBC 715.3.5

Category: Fire-Resistance-Rated Construction
Subject: Fire Door Assemblies

Code Text: *Fire doors shall be labeled showing the name of the manufacturer, the name of the third-party inspection agency, the fire-protection rating, and where required for fire doors in exit enclosures by Section 715.3.4, the maximum transmitted temperature end point. Smoke and draft control doors complying with UL 1784 shall be labeled as such. Labels shall be approved and permanently affixed. The label shall be applied at the factory or location where fabrication and assembly are performed.*

Discussion and Commentary: To be certain that the proper protective assembly is installed in the proper location, it is critical that the assembly be listed and labeled. Field alteration of a fire door assembly is not permitted, because the assembly is usually only listed for use in the condition it was in when it left the factory.

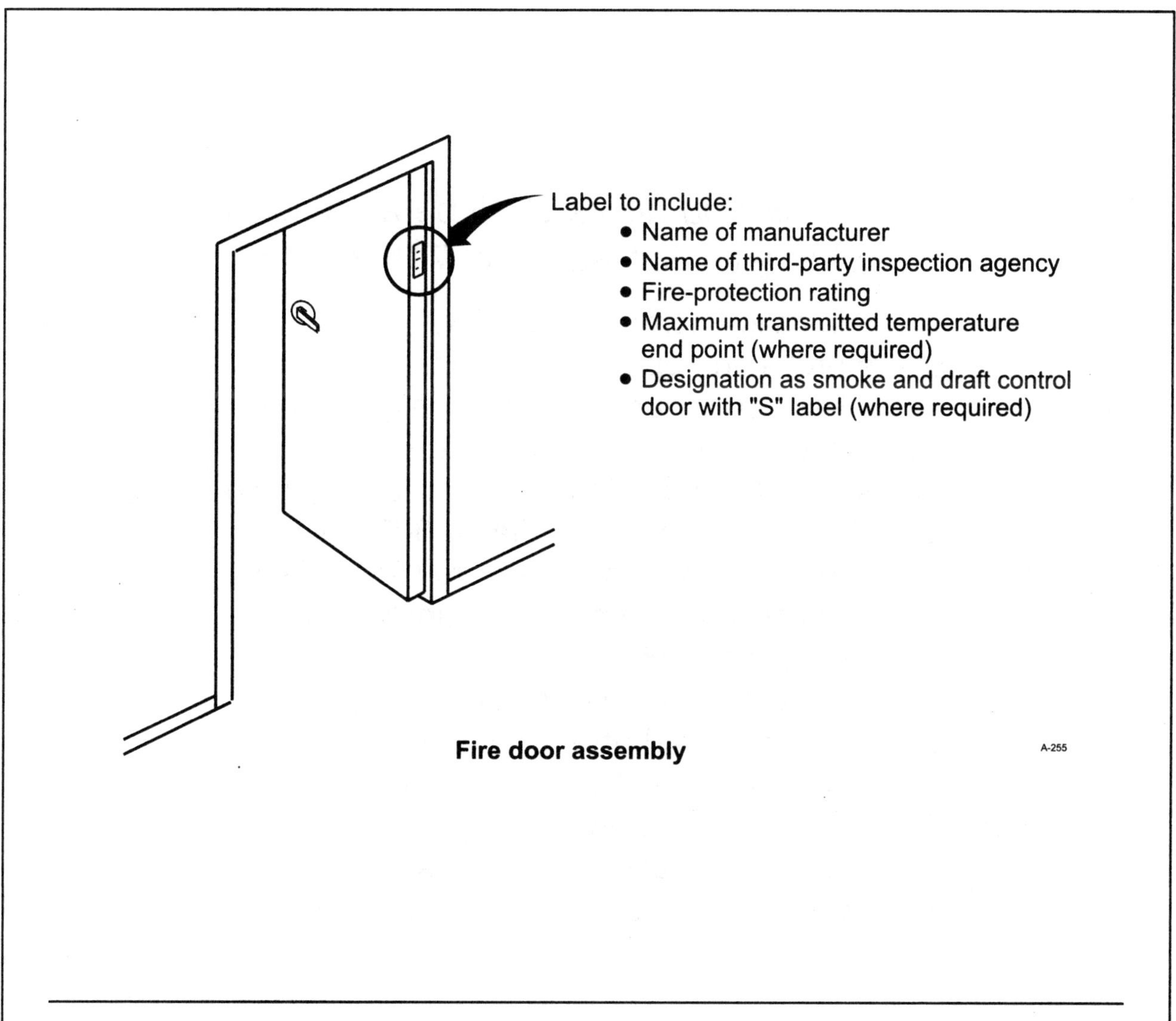

Fire door assembly

Some fire door assemblies are too large to be tested in available furnaces. Therefore, the code recognizes a certificate of inspection as proof that the oversized doors comply with the requirements for materials, design and construction for a comparable fire door.

Topic: Door Closing
Reference: IBC 715.3.7

Category: Fire-Resistance-Rated Construction
Subject: Fire Door Assemblies

Code Text: *Fire doors shall be self-closing or automatic-closing in accordance with Section 715.3.7.* See exception for fire doors in common walls between Group R-1 guestrooms. *Unless otherwise specifically permitted, single fire doors and both leaves of pairs of side-hinged swinging fire doors shall be provided with an active latch bolt that will secure the door when it is closed.*

Discussion and Commentary: Fire doors must close and latch to be effective during a fire. The expectation is that the doors will normally be in a closed position and that the self-closing device will cause the door to close after use. Where specifically mandated by the code, automatic-closing devices must be installed. Such devices are intended for doors normally held in an open position.

Automatic-closing doors shall be actuated by smoke detection at: (Sec. 715.3.7.3)

- Doors installed across a corridor;
- Doors protecting openings in horizontal exits, vertical exit enclosures and exit passageways required to be fire-resistance-rated;
- Doors in walls of incidental use areas required to be fire-resistance-rated (Table 302.1.1);
- Doors installed in smoke barriers (Sec. 709.5);
- Doors installed in fire partitions (including corridors) (Sec. 708.6);
- Doors installed in fire walls (Sec. 705.8);
- Doors installed in shaft enclosures in accordance with Section 707.7; and
- Doors installed in refuse and laundry access chutes and termination rooms in accordance with Sections 707.13.3 and 707.13.4, respectively.

Automatic-closing fire door assemblies are required only where specifically addressed, such as in Section 709.5 for cross-corridor doors in Group I-2 occupancies. Where automatic-closing fire doors are provided, including nonrequired locations, they will typically be smoke-activated.

Topic: Wired Glass
Reference: IBC 715.4.3

Category: Fire-Resistance-Rated Construction
Subject: Fire-Protection-Rated Glazing

Code Text: *Steel window frame assemblies of 0.125-inch minimum solid section or of not less than nominal 0.048-inch-thick formed sheet steel members fabricated by pressing, mitering, riveting, interlocking or welding and having provision for glazing with* $^1/_4$ *inch wired glass where securely installed in the building construction and glazed with ¼ inch labeled wired glass shall be deemed to meet the requirements for a* $^1/_4$*-hour fire window assembly. Wired glass panels shall conform to the size limitations set forth in Table 715.4.3.*

Discussion and Commentary: Fire-protection-rated glazing (fire windows) shall typically be rated for $^3/_4$ hour. This rating is based on testing in accordance with NFPA 257. The IBC permits the use of complying $^1/_4$-inch wired glass in a steel frame in lieu of a tested assembly, where a $^3/_4$-hour fire-protection rating is required.

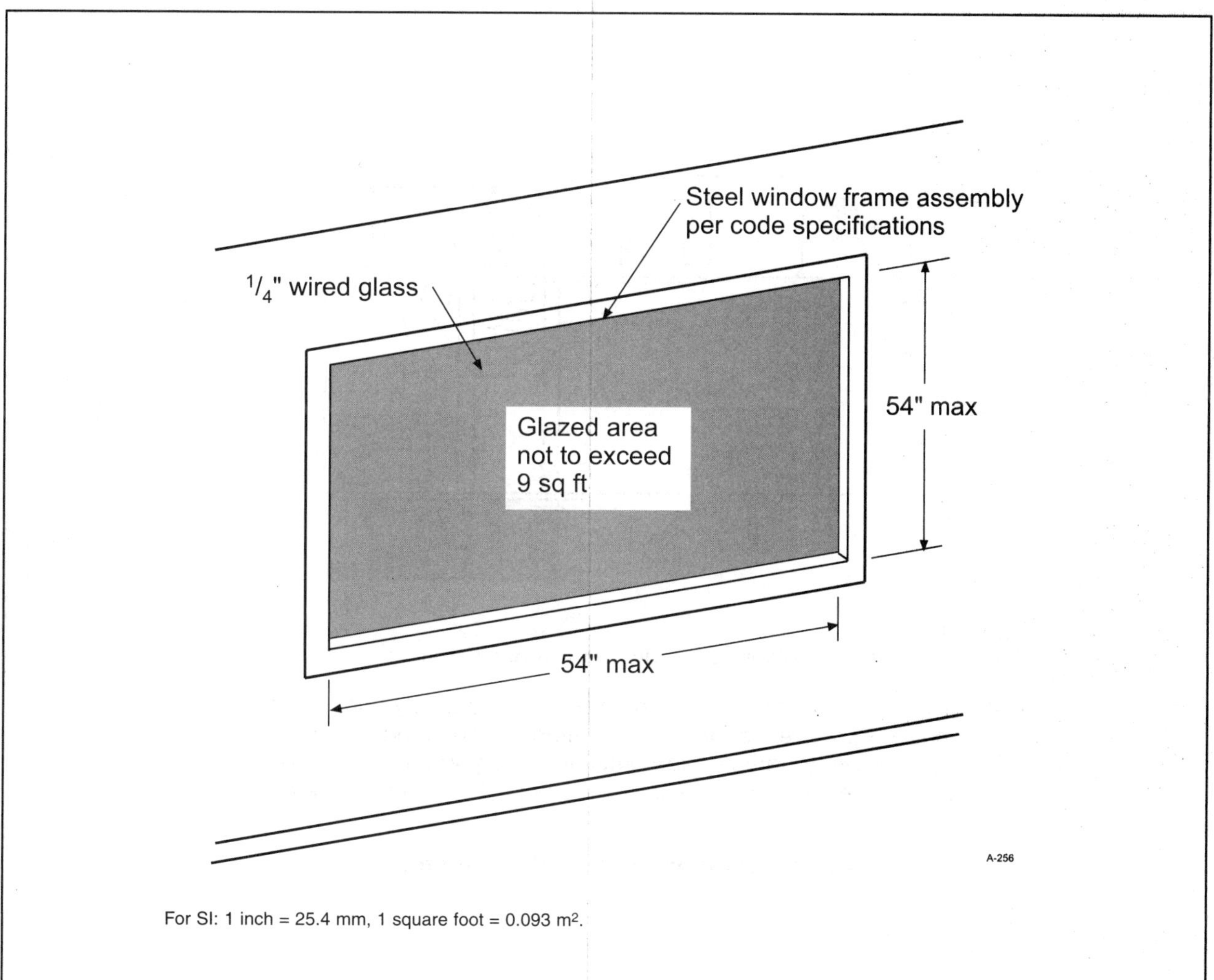

For SI: 1 inch = 25.4 mm, 1 square foot = 0.093 m².

Where fire-protection-rated glazing is installed in fire doors and fire windows located in areas subject to human impact, it also shall comply with the provisions for safety glazing as identified in Section 2406.3 (Hazardous Locations).

Topic: Definitions
Reference: IBC 702

Category: Fire-Resistance-Rated Construction
Subject: Fire and Smoke Dampers

Code Text: *A fire damper is a listed device, installed in ducts and air transfer openings of an air distribution system or smoke control system, designed to close automatically upon detection of heat, to interrupt migratory airflow, and to restrict the passage of flame. A smoke damper is a listed device installed in ducts and air transfer openings that is designed to resist the passage of air and smoke. A ceiling radiation damper is a listed device installed in a ceiling membrane of a fire-resistance-rated floor/ceiling or roof/ceiling assembly to limit automatically the radiative heat transfer through an air inlet/outlet opening.*

Discussion and Commentary: The IBC identifies several types of dampers, each of which performs a specific function. The required type of damper is based on the function of the building element that is being penetrated by the duct or air transfer opening.

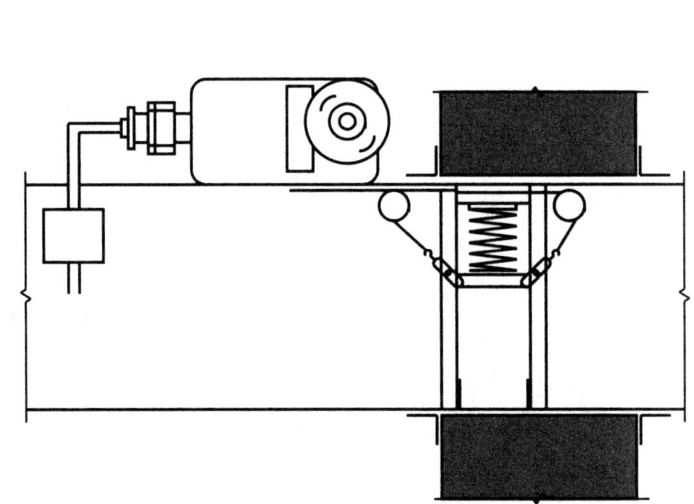

Figure courtesy
Sheet Metal and Air Conditioning Contractors National Association

Note: These illustrations are not intended to exclusively endorse or indicate preference for a combination fire and smoke damper. Two separate dampers that satisfy the requirements for the respective functions may also be used for fire and smoke control.

Combination fire and smoke dampers

A-258

Where both a fire and a smoke damper are mandated, the use of a combination damper is permitted. This type of listed device is designed to close automatically upon detecting heat and to resist the passage of air and smoke.

Topic: Damper Testing and Ratings
Reference: IBC 716.3

Category: Fire-Resistance-Rated Construction
Subject: Ducts and Air Transfer Openings

Code Text: *Dampers shall be listed and bear the label of an approved testing agency indicating compliance with the standards in Section 716.3. Fire dampers shall comply with the requirements of UL 555. Smoke dampers shall comply with the requirements of UL 555S. Combination fire/smoke dampers shall comply with the requirements of both UL 555 and UL 555S. Ceiling radiation dampers shall comply with the requirements of UL 555C. Fire dampers shall have the minimum fire-protection rating specified in Table 716.3.1 for the type of penetration.*

Discussion and Commentary: Consistent with other openings that penetrate a fire-resistance-rated assembly, fire and smoke dampers must be provided where it is necessary to maintain the integrity of the assembly. The minimum damper rating is based on the rating of the assembly penetrated.

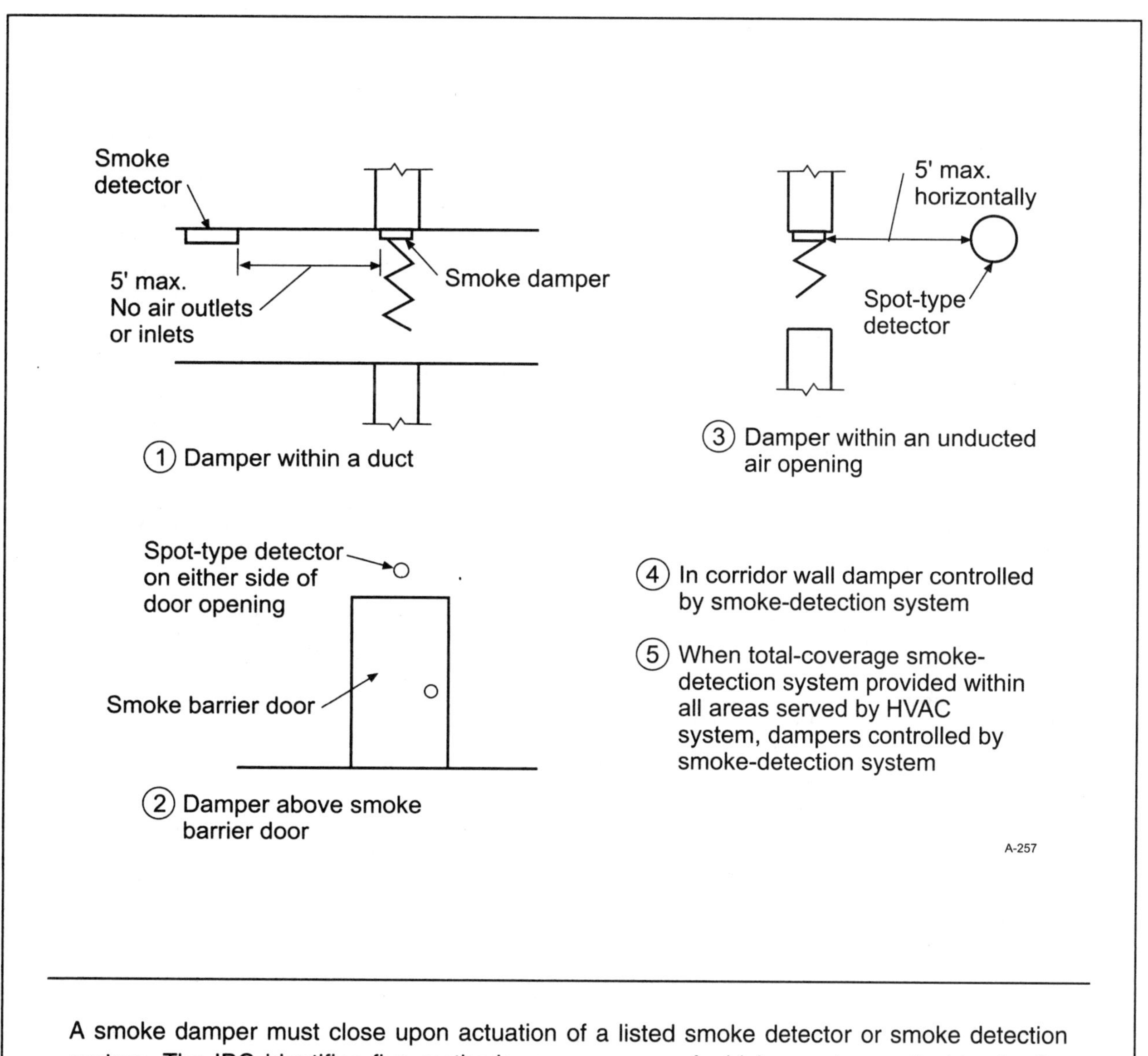

A smoke damper must close upon actuation of a listed smoke detector or smoke detection system. The IBC identifies five methods, one or more of which may be applicable, for the detector location and/or actuation.

Topic: Where Required
Reference: IBC 716.5

Category: Fire-Resistance-Rated Construction
Subject: Fire and Smoke Dampers

Code Text: *Fire dampers, smoke dampers, combination fire/smoke dampers and ceiling radiation dampers shall be provided at the locations prescribed in Section 716.5. Where an assembly is required to have both fire dampers and smoke dampers, combination fire/smoke dampers or a fire damper and a smoke damper shall be required.*

Discussion and Commentary: Only those specific building elements identified in the code need to be protected by fire and/or smoke dampers where penetrated by ducts or air transfer openings. As a general rule, fire dampers protect such openings in fire walls, fire barriers, shaft enclosures and fire partitions. Fire dampers may also be installed in some of those locations where a shaft enclosure is otherwise required. Smoke dampers are generally required for openings in shaft enclosures, smoke- and draft-control corridor enclosures, and smoke barriers.

FIGURE 715-2
2000 IBC Handbook Fire and Life Safety Provisions

Location		Fire Dampers	Smoke Dampers
Fire walls		Required	
Fire barriers		Required[1,2,3]	
Shaft enclosures[6]		Required[1,2,4,5]	Required
Fire partitions		Required[7,8]	
Corridor enclosure			Required[9,17]
Smoke barriers			Required[10]
Horizontal assemblies[11]	Through penetrations	Required[12,18]	
	Membrane penetrations	Required[13]	
	Nonfire-resistance-rated assemblies	Required[14,15,16]	

1 Not required for penetrations tested in accordance with ASTM E 119 as part of the rated assembly.
2 Not required for ducts used as a part of an approved smoke control system in accordance with Section 909.
3 Not required in sprinklered building of other than Group H for 1-hour walls penetrated by ducted HVAC systems.
4 Not required for steel exhaust subducts extending at least 22 inches vertically in exhaust shafts having continuous airflow upward to the outside.
5 Not required in parking garage supply or exhaust shafts that are separated from other building shafts by a minimum of 2-hour fire-resistance-rated construction.
6 See Section 1019.1.2 for permitted penetrations of exit enclosures.
7 Not required in sprinklered buildings of other than Group H for tenant separation and corridor walls.
8 Not required in buildings of other than Group H where duct penetration is limited to 100 square inches; is of minimum 0.0217-inch steel; does not have communicating openings between a corridor and adjacent spaces; is installed above a ceiling; does not terminate at a wall register of the fire-resistance-rated wall; and a minimum 12-inch-long steel sleeve is centered in each duct opening, approximately secured, and the annular space between the sleeve and the wall opening is filled with mineral wool batting.
9 Not required for corridor penetrations of minimum 0.019-inch steel ducts with no openings into corridor.
10 Not required where openings in steel ducts are limited to a single smoke compartment.
11 General requirement mandates shaft enclosures for openings in floor and roof systems.
12 In other than Group I-2 and I-3, fire dampers are permitted in lieu of shaft enclosures for penetration of fire-resistance-rated horizontal assembly that connects two floors.
13 Where shaft enclosure is not provided, an approved ceiling damper is required at the ceiling line of a fire-resistance-rated floor/ceiling or roof/ceiling assembly.
14 Not required, provided the shaft enclosure, does not connect more than two stories and the annular space around the duct is filled with noncombustible material.
15 Limited to three connected stories without shaft enclosure, provided fire dampers are installed at each floor line and annular space is filled.
16 Not required in ducts within individual dwelling units.
17 Not required in building with a smoke control system if not necessary for operation and control of system.
18 Not required where penetrating up to three floors, provided the steel duct is located within a wall cavity, serves only one dwelling unit or sleeping unit, and is a maximum of 4 inches in diameter and limited to 100 square inches in 100 square feet; and provided the annular space around the duct is protected, and any grille openings in a fire-rated ceiling are protected with ceiling radiation dampers.

There will be times when a fire-resistance-rated assembly is penetrated by a duct or transfer opening that is not required to be protected by a fire or smoke damper. In such situations, the condition will be regulated and protected as a penetration, in accordance with Section 712.

Topic: Fireblocking
Reference: IBC 717.2

Category: Fire-Resistance-Rated Construction
Subject: Concealed Spaces

Code Text: *In combustible construction, fireblocking shall be installed to cut off concealed draft openings (both vertical and horizontal) and shall form an effective barrier between floors, between a top story and a roof or attic space. Fireblocking shall be installed in the locations specified in Sections 717.2.2 through 717.2.7.*

Discussion and Commentary: Experience has shown that the greatest fire damage to conventional light-framed wood buildings occurs when the fire travels unimpeded through concealed draft openings. Virtually any concealed air space within a building will provide an open channel through which high-temperature air and gases can spread. Fireblocking is invaluable to the control of fire prior to active fire suppression activities.

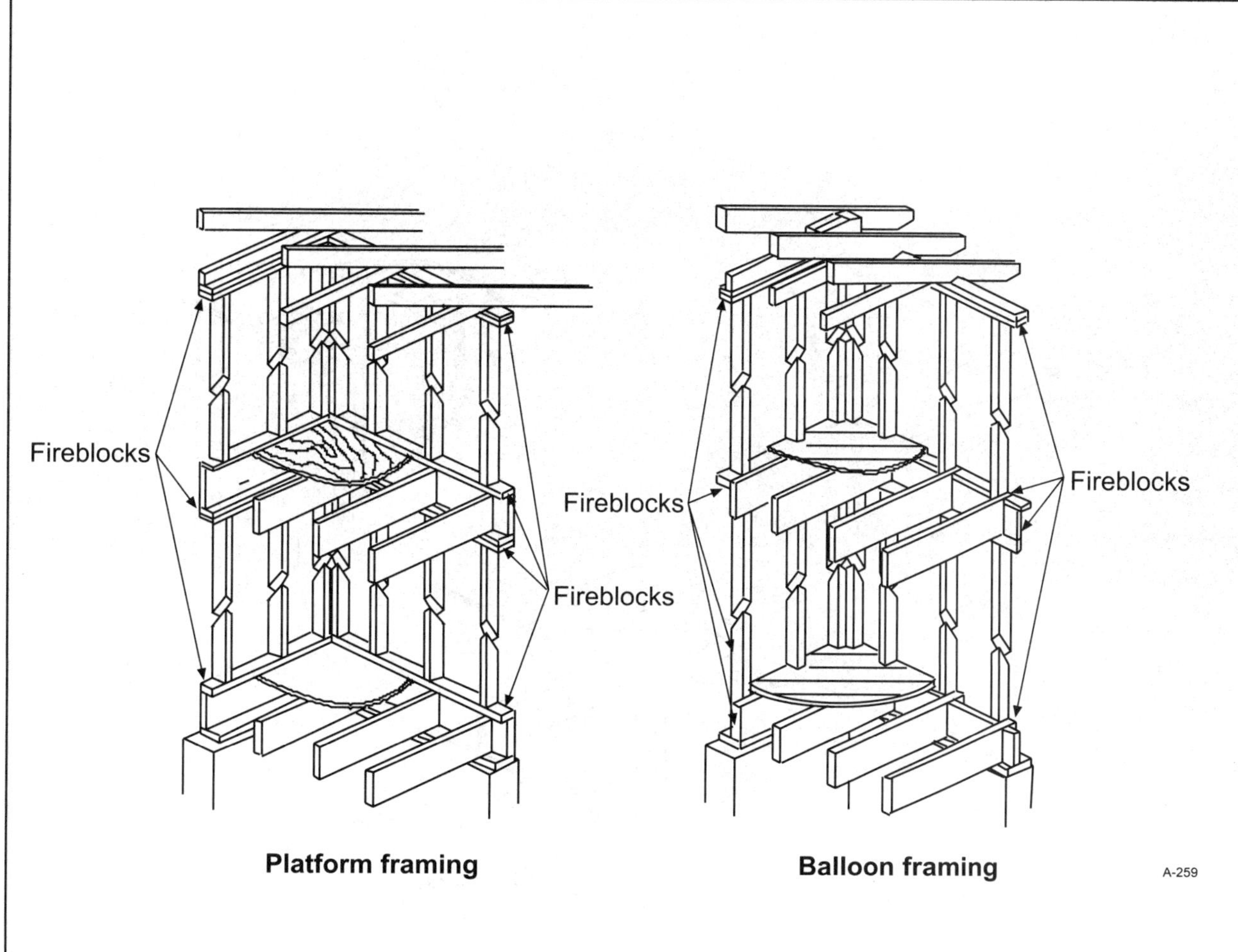

In noncombustible construction, building materials located in concealed areas of the building construction do not contribute to the spread of fire. Therefore, fireblocking and draftstopping are required only in buildings of combustible construction.

Topic: Required Locations
Reference: IBC 717.2

Category: Fire-Resistance-Rated Construction
Subject: Fireblocking

Code Text: *Fireblocking shall be provided in concealed spaces of stud walls and partitions, including furred spaces, and parallel rows of studs or staggered studs, as follows: 1) vertically at the ceiling and floor levels, and 2) horizontally at intervals not exceeding 10 feet. Fireblocking shall be provided at interconnections between concealed vertical . . . and horizontal spaces . . . such as occur at soffits, drop ceilings, cove ceilings and similar locations.* See additional provisions for fireblocking at stairways; openings around vents, ducts and chimneys; concealed spaces of exterior architectural trim; and concealed sleeper spaces in floors.

Discussion and Commentary: The platform framing techniques that are typically used in light-frame wood construction provide adequate fireblocking between stories in the stud walls. However, furred spaces and openings for penetrating elements such as vents should be addressed carefully as avenues for fire transmission between stories or along a wall.

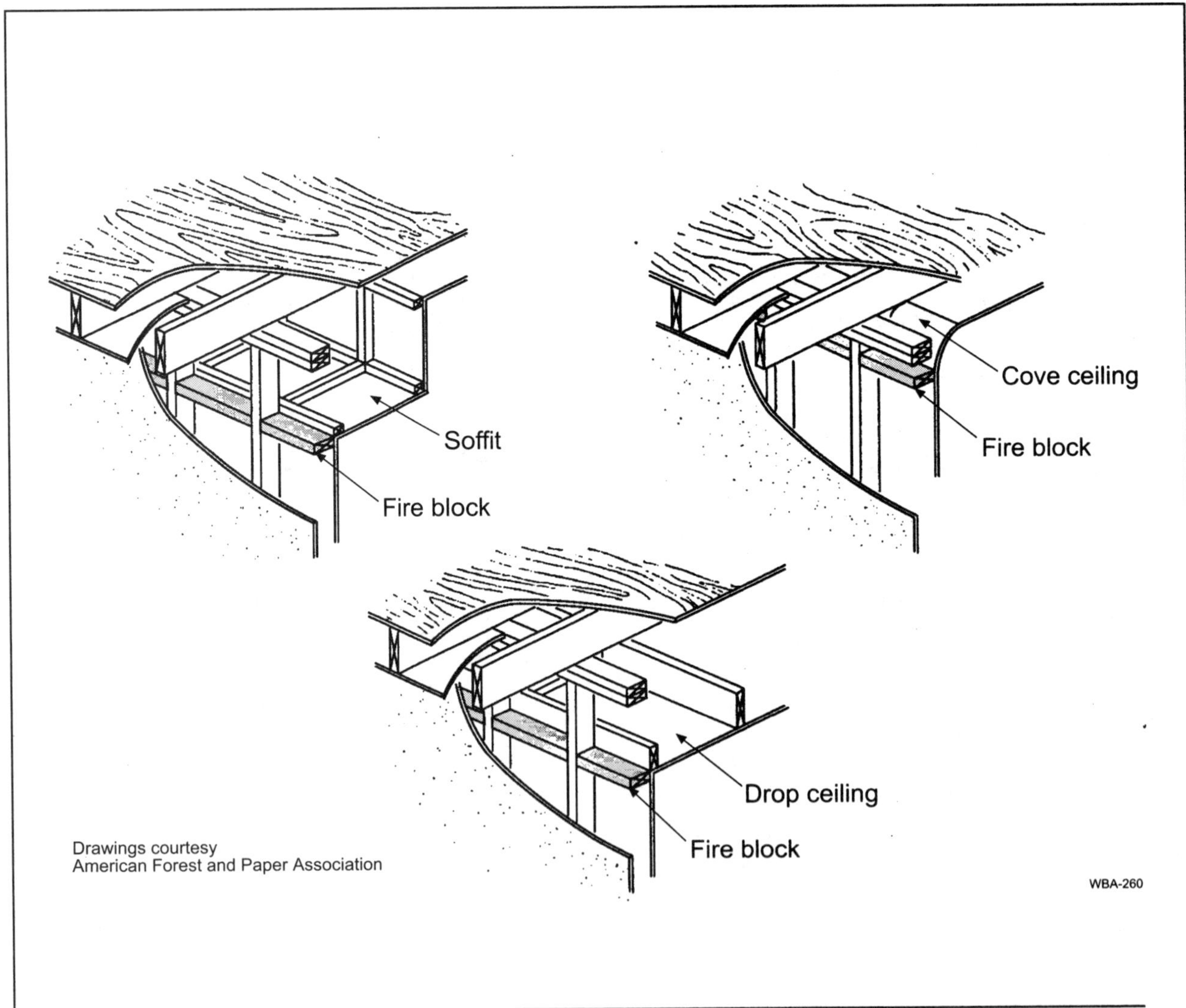

In general, fireblocking materials must consist of lumber or wood structural panels of the thicknesses specified, gypsum board, cement fiber board, batts or blankets of mineral wool or glass fiber, or any other approved materials securely fastened in place.

Topic: Definition and Materials
Reference: IBC 702, 717.3.1

Category: Fire-Resistance-Rated Construction
Subject: Draftstopping

Code Text: *A draftstop is a material, device or construction installed to restrict the movement of air within open spaces of concealed areas of building components such as crawl spaces, floor/ceiling assemblies, roof/ceiling assemblies and attics. Draftstopping materials shall not be less than 0.5-inch gypsum board, 0.375-inch wood structural panel, 0.375-inch particleboard or other approved materials adequately supported. The integrity of draftstops shall be maintained.*

Discussion and Commentary: Draftstopping, like fireblocking, is required only in combustible construction. However, although the role of draftstopping is important, it is less critical than that of fireblocking. Therefore, the protective materials used in draftstopping construction are permitted to be less substantial.

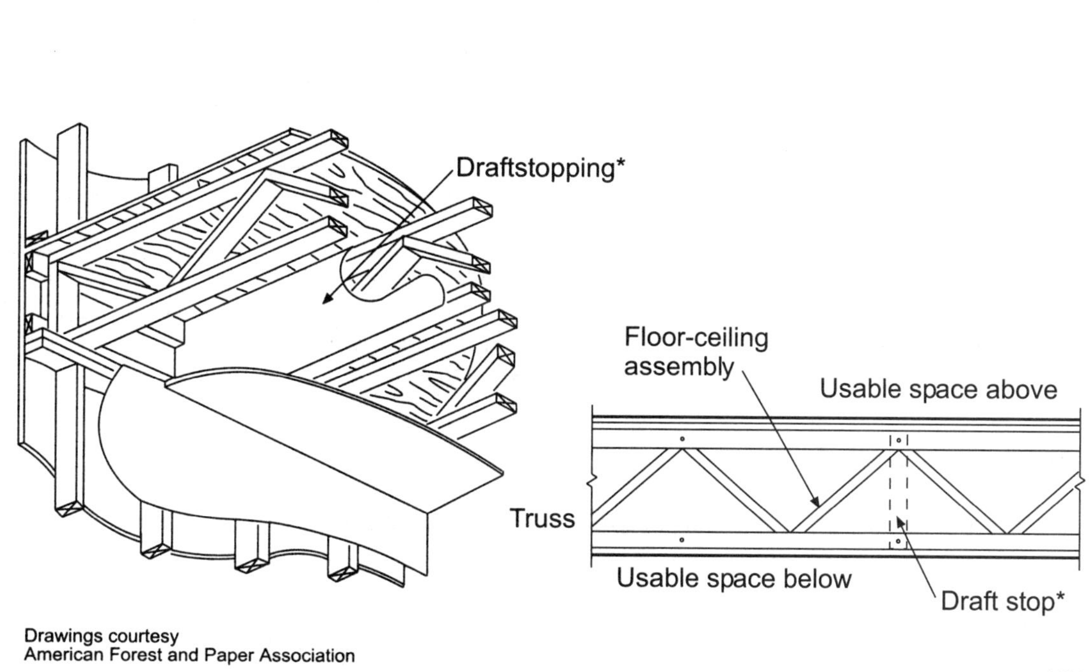

Other than Group R Occupancies - max. 1,000 sq ft.

For SI: 1 square foot = 0.093 m^2.

The provisions for draftstops are categorized for two general occupancy categories: residential and all uses other than residential. Both floor/ceiling assemblies and attics are addressed for each category. Many of the requirements are eliminated in fully sprinklered buildings.

QUIZ

Study Session 7 — Sections 712–719

I. Multiple Choice

1. An approved through-penetration firestop system requires a T rating when which of the following conditions occurs?

   a. a fire wall is penetrated by a combustible penetrating item
   b. a fire barrier wall is penetrated above a nonrated ceiling membrane
   c. a ceiling of a one-hour horizontal assembly is penetrated by a steel conduit
   d. a floor penetration of a fire-rated assembly is not contained within a wall cavity

   Reference_______________

2. Where the annular space is filled with an approved material, noncombustible piping may connect a maximum of __________stories, provided the horizontal assemblies require no fire-resistance rating.

   a. 2
   b. 3
   c. 4
   d. 6

   Reference_______________

3. In which of the following locations is a fire-resistant joint system required to protect all joints?

   a. floors within malls
   b. horizontal exit walls
   c. mezzanine floors
   d. roofs where openings are permitted

   Reference_______________

4. Girders and beams required to have a fire-resistance rating must be individually protected on all sides where supporting a minimum of __________.

   a. a roof only
   b. a floor and a roof
   c. two floors
   d. two floors and a roof

   Reference_______________

5. The edges of lugs, brackets, rivets and bolt heads attached to fire-resistance-rated structural members shall maintain a minimum of __________ inch(es) clearance to the surface of the fire protection.

   a. $^1/_2$
   b. 1
   c. $1^1/_2$
   d. 2

   Reference_______________

6. Stirrups used for concrete reinforcement may extend a maximum of __________ inch into the required thickness of fire protection.

a. $^1/_4$ b. $^3/_8$
c. $^1/_2$ d. 1

Reference________________

7. An opening protective in a 1-hour fire barrier used in a vertical exit enclosure shall have a minimum fire-protection rating of __________ hour.

a. $^1/_3$ b. $^1/_2$
c. $^3/_4$ d. 1

Reference________________

8. Opening protectives in a 2-hour exterior wall shall have a minimum fire-protection rating of __________.

a. 20 minutes b. 45 minutes
c. 1 hour d. 90 minutes

Reference________________

9. Fire doors in smoke barrier walls shall have a maximum air leakage rate of __________cfm per square foot under specified test conditions.

a. 1 b. 2
c. 3 d. 5

Reference________________

10. Where not used as a horizontal exit, what is the maximum amount of glazing permitted in a 11/2-hour fire door located in a 2-hour fire-resistance-rated fire wall?

a. 0, no glazing is permitted b. 100 square inches
c. 144 square inches d. 9 square feet

Reference________________

11. In what location may self-closing and automatic-closing devices be omitted from required fire doors?

a. Group E corridor doors b. doors in walls separating hotel sleeping units
c. doors between vertical exit enclosures and exit passageways d. Group I-2 smoke barrier doors

Reference________________

12. For a fire door that is automatic-closing by smoke detection, the maximum delay before the fire door starts to close is __________ seconds after the smoke detector is actuated.

a. 3
b. 5
c. 10
d. 15

Reference_______________

13. Where automatic-closing fire doors are installed, which of the following locations does not require closing upon actuation of smoke detectors?

a. cross-corridor doors in an office building
b. doors in a fire barrier separating control areas
c. a pair of doors installed in a fire wall
d. a single horizontal exit door

Reference_______________

14. What is the maximum size of wired glass permitted in a fire window assembly?

a. 100 square inches
b. 1296 square inches
c. 54 inches by 54 inches
d. unlimited

Reference_______________

15. In which of the following locations is wired glass prohibited in fire doors?

a. 1-hour vertical exit enclosure
b. 2-hour exterior wall
c. 2-hour vertical exit enclosure
d. 3-hour fire wall used as a horizontal exit

Reference_______________

16. The total area of interior fire window assemblies is limited to a maximum of __________ percent of the area of the common wall within any room.

a. 10
b. 20
c. 25
d. 50

Reference_______________

17. What is the minimum fire damper rating for a damper located in a 1-hour fire barrier?

a. 20 minutes
b. 45 minutes
c. 1 hour
d. $1^1/_2$ hour

Reference_______________

18. Where a spot-type detector is used to actuate a smoke damper installed within an unducted opening in a smoke barrier wall, the detector shall be located a maximum of __________ from the damper.

a. 12 inches vertically
b. 30 inches vertically
c. 3 feet horizontally
d. 5 feet horizontally

Reference_______________

19. Where a duct passes through a fire wall, which of the following dampers is/are required?

a. fire damper only
b. smoke damper only
c. both a fire and smoke damper
d. neither a fire nor smoke damper

Reference_______________

20. In general, which of the following dampers is/are required where an air transfer opening penetrates a shaft enclosure?

a. fire damper only
b. smoke damper only
c. both fire and smoke dampers
d. neither a fire damper or smoke damper

Reference_______________

21. Which of the following materials is not specifically listed by the code as a fireblocking material?

a. 2-inch nominal lumber
b. two thicknesses of 1-inch nominal lumber with broken lap joints
c. one thickness of 0.719-inch wood structural panel with joints backed
d. one thickness of $^1/_2$-inch particleboard with joints backed

Reference_______________

22. The maximum spacing of fireblocking within concealed spaces of exterior architectural elements erected with combustible framing is __________ feet.

a. 10
b. 20
c. 60
d. 100

Reference_______________

23. Which of the following materials is not specifically listed by the code as a draftstopping material?

a. $^1/_2$-inch gypsum board
b. $^3/_8$-inch wood structural panels
c. $^1/_2$-inch particleboard
d. glass fiber batts

Reference_______________

24. In a nonsprinklered Type V office building, the maximum attic area permitted between draftstops is __________.

a. 1,000 square feet
b. 3,000 square feet
c. 100 feet in any direction
d. unlimited

Reference_______________

25. Other than for cellulose loose-fill insulation that is not spray applied, the maximum flame spread index of insulating materials concealed within a Type II building shall be __________.

a. 25
b. 50
c. 75
d. unlimited

Reference_______________

26. A through-penetration firestop system, where used to protect a membrane penetration in a fire barrier wall, shall at minimum have a(n) _____ rating of not less than the rating of the wall penetrated.

a. F
b. L
c. T
d. F and T

Reference_______________

27. A firestop system may not be required for the protection of unlisted steel electrical boxes in a one-hour fire partition, provided the boxes have a maximum individual size of _____ square inches.

a. 16
b. 25
c. 100
d. 144

Reference_______________

28. What is the minimum required fire-protection rating for glazing located in a 1/2-hour fire-resistance-rated fire partition?

a. 0, no rating is required
b. 20 minutes
c. 30 minutes
d. 45 minutes

Reference_______________

29. Where wood sleepers are installed for the installation of wood flooring in a church sanctuary, the maximum size of any open spaces shall be _____ square feet unless the entire underfloor space is filled with an approved material.

a. 10
b. 20
c. 100
d. 144

Reference_______________

30. Where plaster is used for fire-resistance purposes, it shall be provided with an additional layer of approved lath where its minimum thickness exceeds _____ inch.

a. $^3/_8$
b. $^1/_2$
c. $^3/_4$
d. 1

Reference_______________

INTERNATIONAL BUILDING CODE

Study Session 8

Chapter 9 — Fire Protection Systems

OBJECTIVE: To obtain an understanding of the design and installation of fire protection systems, including automatic sprinkler systems, standpipe systems, fire alarm and detection systems, smoke control systems, and smoke and heat vents.

REFERENCE: Chapter 9, 2003 *International Building Code*

KEY POINTS:

- What are the quality standards for fire protection systems?
- How shall fire alarm systems be monitored?
- What are the different classifications for standpipe systems? For other types of systems?
- When may the use of a residential sprinkler system be recognized for exceptions or reductions permitted by the code?
- For Group A-1, A-3 and A-4 occupancies, what size fire area requires the installation of an automatic sprinkler system? How many occupants? What location in the building?
- When must a restaurant or café be sprinklered?
- Which conditions would allow Group E occupancies to be nonsprinklered?
- A sprinkler system is required in Groups F-1, M and S-1 occupancies when the floor area within any fire area exceeds what size?
- Which high-hazard occupancies require installation of a sprinkler system? Institutional occupancies?
- Which residential occupancies require the installation of an automatic sprinkler system? In which portions of the building must the sprinkler system be located?
- Under what conditions must sprinkler protection be provided for exterior balconies and ground-floor patios of dwelling units?
- For the purpose of fire department access, what is considered a "windowless" building?
- In "windowless" buildings, how are basements regulated as compared to above-grade levels?
- When must buildings be sprinklered due to their height?
- Which locations or uses are exempt from the sprinkler requirements?
- When are standpipes required?
- When a standpipe system is mandated, where must the hose connections be located?
- In which occupancies are manual fire alarm systems required? Automatic fire alarm systems?
- Where are smoke alarms mandated?
- Where fire alarms are required, where must visible appliances be installed?
- What is the scope and purpose of a smoke-control system?
- What are the three different methods of mechanical smoke control? Which of the three is the primary means of controlling smoke?
- What are the critical elements for the acceptance of a smoke-control system?
- In which occupancies are smoke and heat vents required?
- When smoke and heat vents are provided, what are their minimum size and spacing requirements?
- What is the minimum distance between curtain boards? What is the maximum permitted size of the curtained area?
- Under which conditions can a mechanical smoke exhaust system be substituted for smoke and heat vents?

Topic: Definition and Scope
Reference: IBC 901, 902

Category: Fire Protection Systems
Subject: Protection Systems

Code Text: *The provisions of Chapter 9 shall specify where fire protection systems are required and shall apply to the design, installation and operation of fire protection systems. A fire protection system is approved devices, equipment and systems or combinations of systems used to detect a fire, activate an alarm, extinguish or control a fire, control or manage smoke and products of a fire or any combination thereof. Fire protection systems shall be installed, repaired, operated and maintained in accordance with the* IBC *and the* International Fire Code.

Discussion and Commentary: The code provides requirements for three distinct systems considered vital to a safe building environment. The first system is intended to control and limit fire spread and to provide building occupants and fire personnel with the means of fighting a fire. The second system provides for detection of a fire condition and a means of notification. The third system is intended to control smoke migration.

General requirements for fire protection systems:

- Systems to be installed, repaired, operated and maintained in accordance with the *International Building Code* and *International Fire Code*.
- Systems not required by the IBC are permitted to be installed for partial or complete protection, provided such systems meet the requirements of the IBC.
- Any system for which an exception to, or reduction in, the provisions of the IBC has been granted shall be considered a required system.
- No person shall remove or modify any system installed or maintained under the provisions of either code without approval of the building official.
- All systems shall be tested in accordance with the requirements of the IBC and IFC, in the presence of the building official and at the expense of the owner or owner's representative.
- It is unlawful to occupy portions of a structure until the required fire protection systems within that portion have been tested and approved.

Unless specifically excepted, approved supervising stations are mandated for automatic sprinkler systems, fire alarm systems, and Group H occupancy manual alarm, automatic fire extinguishing and emergency alarm systems.

Topic: Fire Areas
Reference: IBC 702

Category: Fire Protection Systems
Subject: Automatic Sprinkler Systems

Code Text: *A fire area is the aggregate floor area enclosed and bounded by fire walls, fire barriers, exterior walls or fire-resistance-rated horizontal assemblies of a building.*

Discussion and Commentary: The concept behind fire areas is that of compartmentalization. As a building is subdivided into smaller spaces through the use of fire-resistance-rated elements, the potential hazards tend to be confined to each compartment. Therefore, as the level of hazards decreases, the need for protection diminishes. In the IBC, this reduced level of protection is reflected in the fact that an automatic sprinkler system may not be required. The sole purpose for the creation of fire areas is to address the requirements of Section 903.2 for sprinkler protection. Where sprinkler systems are not an issue, the creation of fire areas is unnecessary.

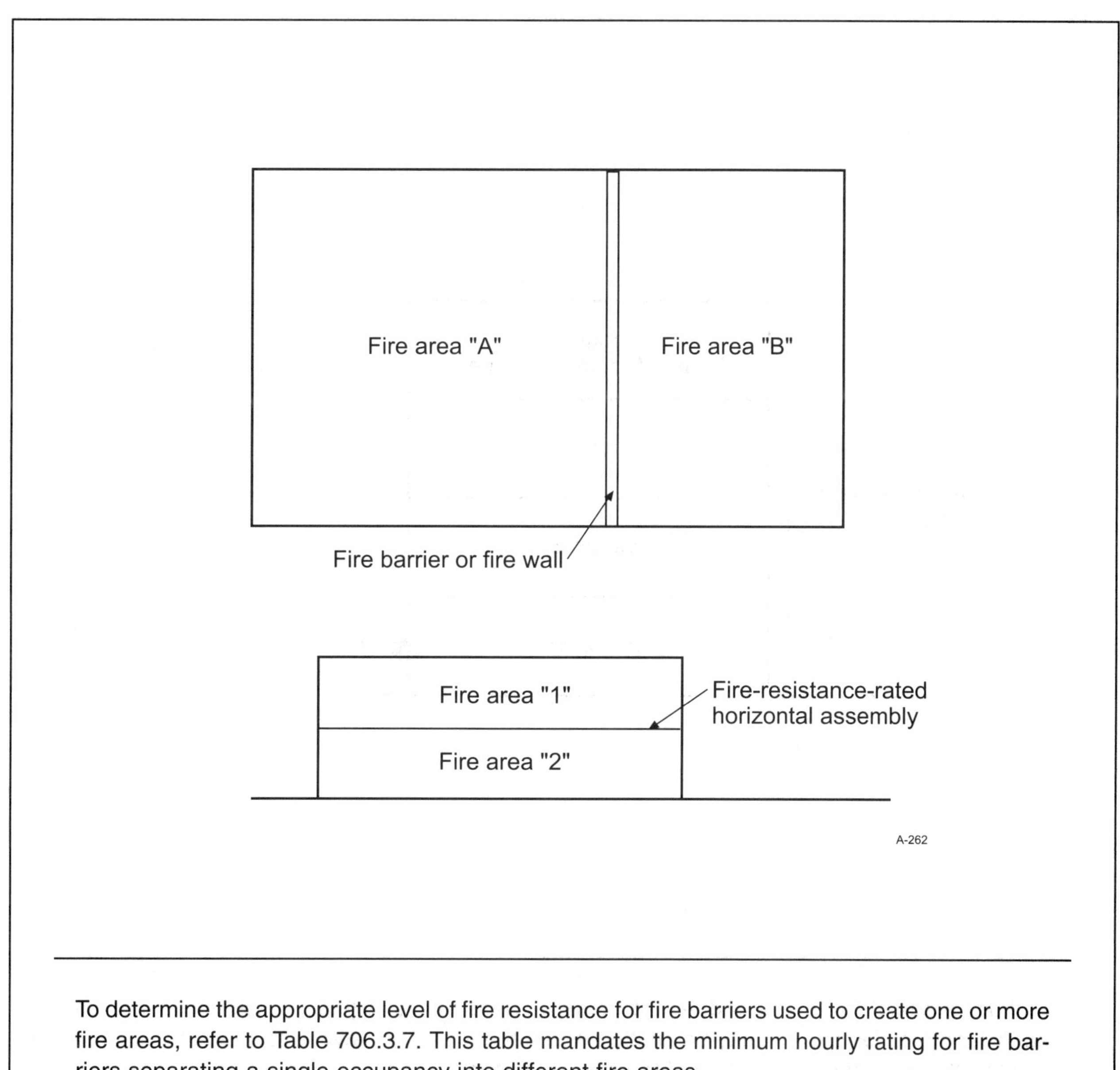

To determine the appropriate level of fire resistance for fire barriers used to create one or more fire areas, refer to Table 706.3.7. This table mandates the minimum hourly rating for fire barriers separating a single occupancy into different fire areas.

Topic: Group A Occupancies
Reference: IBC 903.2.1

Category: Fire Protection Systems
Subject: Automatic Sprinkler Systems

Code Text: *An automatic sprinkler system shall be provided throughout buildings and portions thereof used as Group A occupancies as provided in* Section 903.2.1. *For Group A-1, A-2, A-3 and A-4 occupancies, the automatic sprinkler system shall be provided throughout the floor area where the Group A-1, A-2, A-3 or A-4 occupancy is located, and in all floors between the Group A occupancy and the level of exit discharge. For Group A-5 occupancies, the automatic sprinkler system shall be provided in the spaces indicated in Section 903.2.1.5.*

Discussion and Commentary: Although most Group A occupancies lack the combustible loading that creates a high degree of fire severity, protection provided by an automatic sprinkler system is deemed necessary due to the hazards of having large numbers of people in concentrated areas. Based on varying thresholds, a sprinkler system may be required in any of the five assembly occupancies.

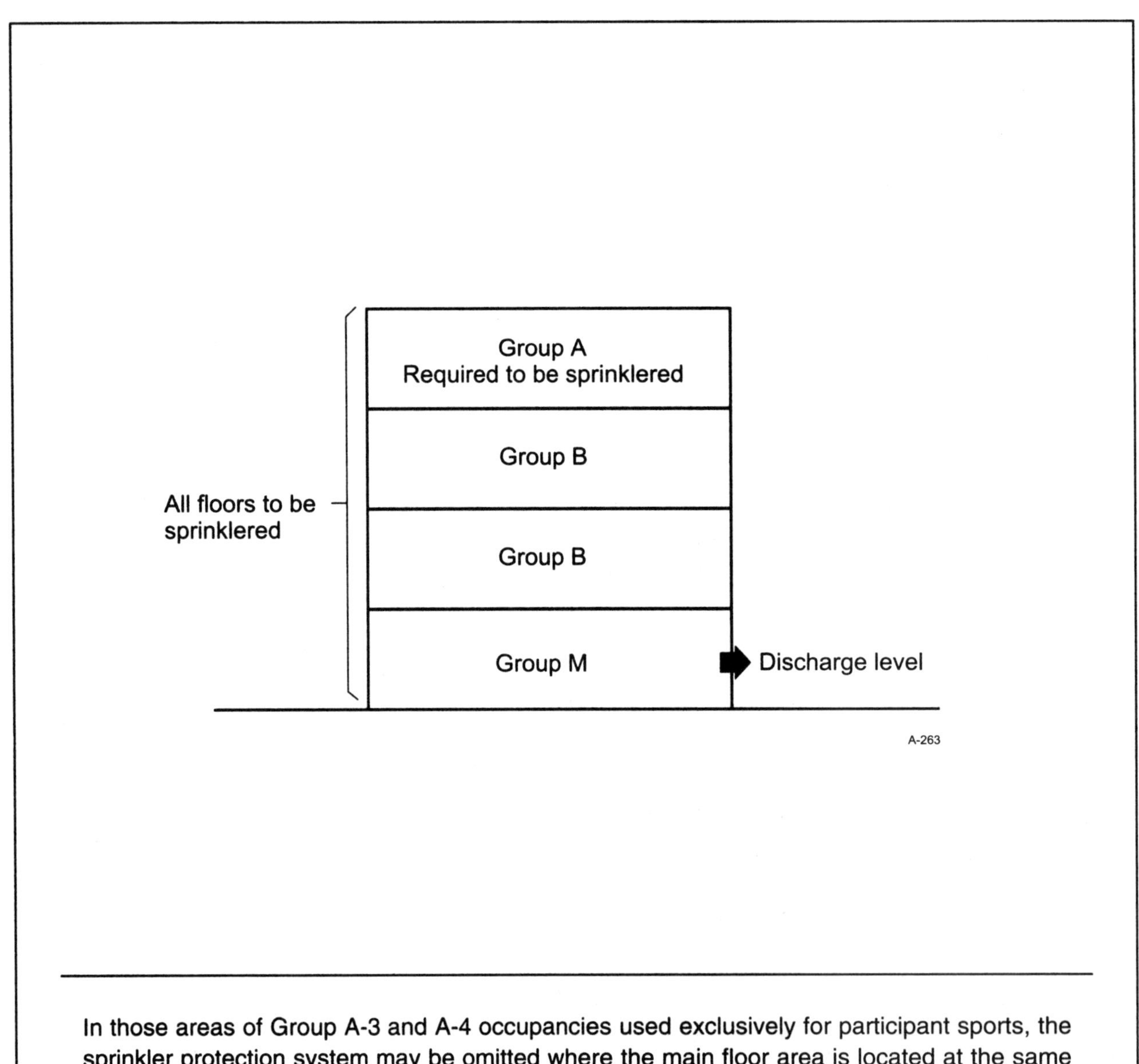

In those areas of Group A-3 and A-4 occupancies used exclusively for participant sports, the sprinkler protection system may be omitted where the main floor area is located at the same level as the level of exit discharge of the main entrance and exit.

Topic: Group E Occupancies
Reference: IBC 903.2.2

Category: Fire Protection Systems
Subject: Automatic Sprinkler Systems

Code Text: *An automatic sprinkler system shall be provided for Group E occupancies as follows: 1) throughout all Group E fire areas greater than 20,000 square feet (1858 m²) in area, and 2) throughout every portion of educational buildings below the level of exit discharge.* See exception for buildings with direct egress at ground level from each classroom.

Discussion and Commentary: As a group, educational occupancies tend to have a very good fire record. This stems from the ongoing supervision of activities in the building, as well as the rapid egress of students in response to emergencies. However, because of the amount of combustibles in Group E occupancies and the potentially high occupant load, it is typically necessary to provide sprinkler systems for those undivided floor areas exceeding 20,000 square feet or in basements.

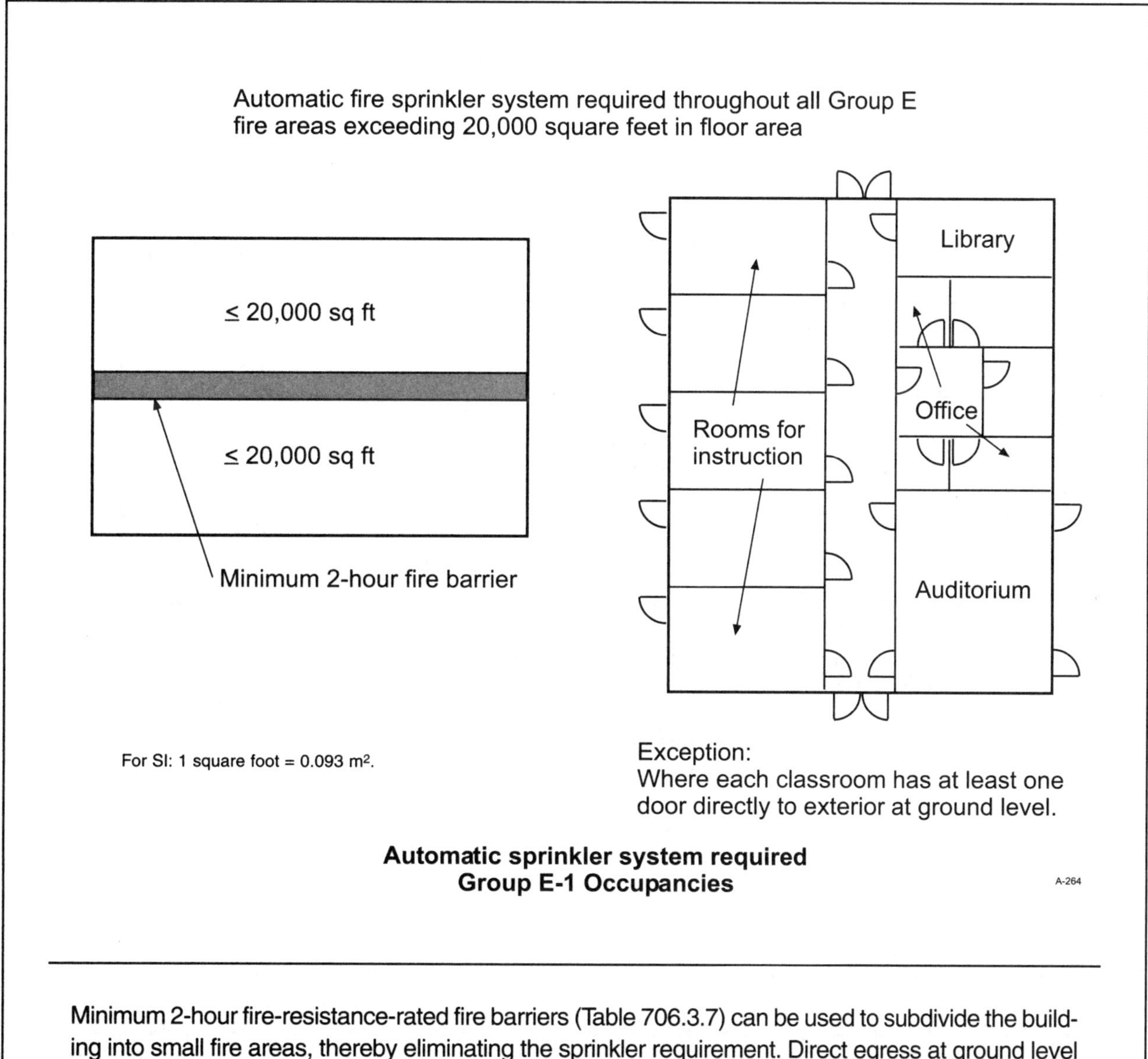

Automatic sprinkler system required
Group E-1 Occupancies

Minimum 2-hour fire-resistance-rated fire barriers (Table 706.3.7) can be used to subdivide the building into small fire areas, thereby eliminating the sprinkler requirement. Direct egress at ground level from each classroom is also deemed to be an equivalent method of ensuring occupant safety.

Topic: Groups F-1, M and S-1 Occupancies **Category:** Fire Protection Systems
Reference: IBC 903.2.3, 903.2.6, 903.2.8 **Subject:** Automatic Sprinkler Systems

Code Text: *An automatic sprinkler system shall be provided throughout all buildings contain a Group F-1 occupancy where one of the following conditions exists: 1) where a Group F-1 fire area exceeds 12,000 square feet (1115 m*^{2}*) or 2) where a Group F-1 fire area is located more than three stories above grade, or 3) where the combined area of all Group F-1 fire areas on all floors, including any mezzanines, exceeds 24,000 square feet (2230 m*^{2}*).* Same criteria applies to Group M and S-1 occupancies.

Discussion and Commentary: Because of the potential presence of high levels of combustible materials in factories, sales buildings and warehouses, the IBC limits the size and location of fire areas not protected by an automatic sprinkler system. If any fire area in the building exceeds the threshold, the sprinkler system must be provided throughout the entire building, not just in the fire area that exceeds the area or height limitations.

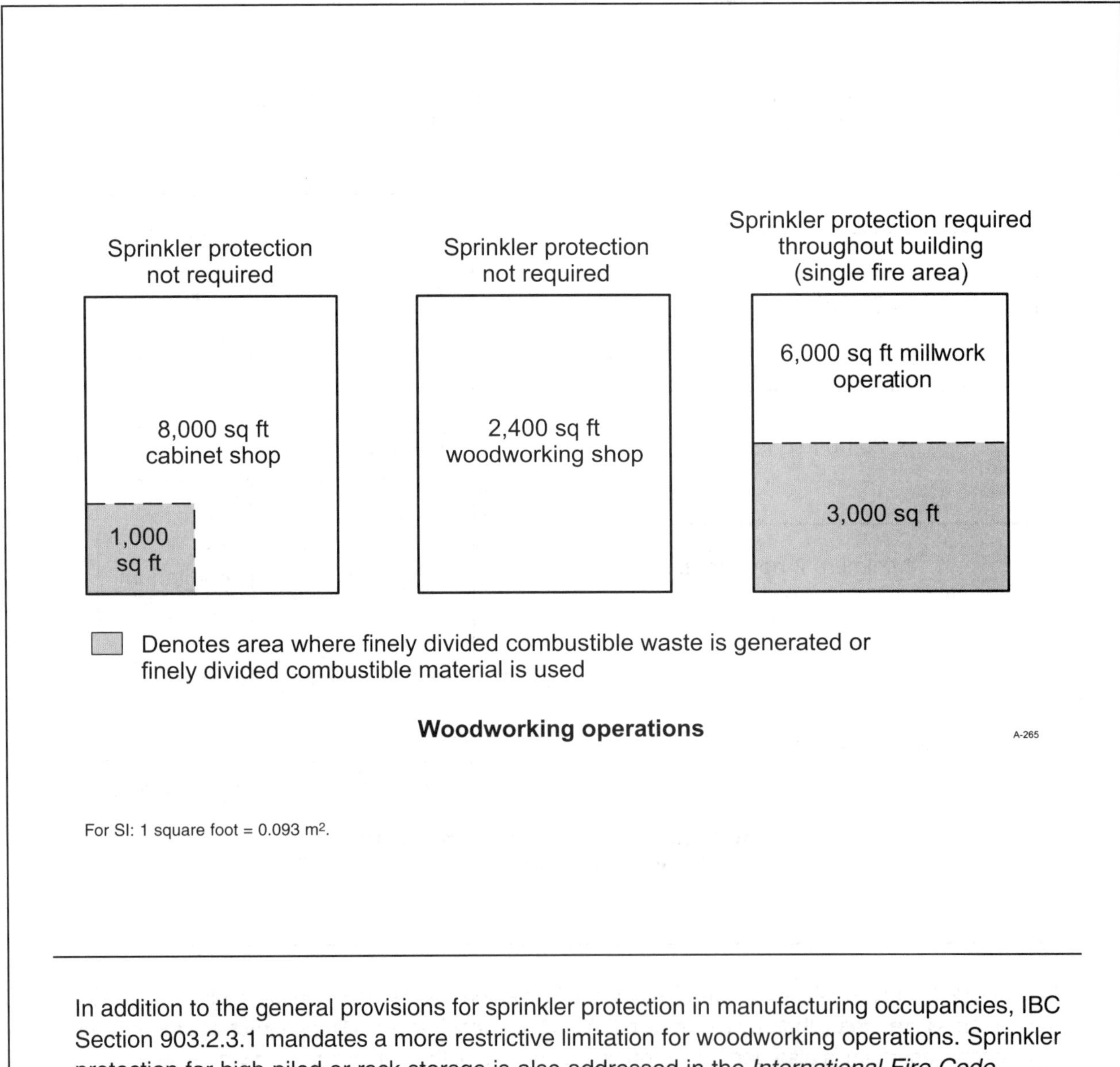

Woodworking operations

In addition to the general provisions for sprinkler protection in manufacturing occupancies, IBC Section 903.2.3.1 mandates a more restrictive limitation for woodworking operations. Sprinkler protection for high-piled or rack storage is also addressed in the *International Fire Code.*

Topic: Groups H and I Occupancies
Reference: IBC 903.2.4.1, 903.2.5

Category: Fire Protection Systems
Subject: Automatic Sprinkler Systems

Code Text: *An automatic sprinkler system shall be installed in Group H occupancies. An automatic sprinkler system shall be provided throughout buildings with a Group I fire area.*

Discussion and Commentary: Hazardous occupancies require automatic sprinkler systems to protect not only the building's occupants and contents, but also the surrounding property. The sprinkler system only need be provided in the portion of the building classified as Group H. Buildings containing institutional uses must be protected throughout due to the lack of mobility of the occupants. The sprinkler system is intended to limit the size and the spread of a fire, thereby allowing extra time for moving occupants of the institutional building into an adjoining smoke compartment or through a horizontal exit.

[F] TABLE 903.2.4.2
GROUP H-5 SPRINKLER DESIGN CRITERIA

LOCATION	OCCUPANCY HAZARD CLASSIFICATION
Fabrication areas	Ordinary Hazard Group 2
Service corridors	Ordinary Hazard Group 2
Storage rooms without dispensing	Ordinary Hazard Group 2
Storage rooms with dispensing	Extra Hazard Group 2
Corridors	Ordinary Hazard Group 2

In a semiconductor fabrication facility classified as a Group H-5 occupancy, the sprinkler system must be installed throughout the entire building. For sprinkler design criteria, the code identifies the occupancy hazard classifications based on the various areas and locations.

Topic: Group R Occupancies
Reference: IBC 903.2.7

Category: Fire Protection Systems
Subject: Automatic Sprinkler Systems

Code Text: *An automatic sprinkler system installed in accordance with Section 903.3 shall be provided throughout all buildings with a Group R fire area.*

Discussion and Commentary: Statistics bear out that the majority of fire deaths and injuries occur in residential occupancies. It has also been statistically shown that buildings provided with sprinkler systems perform quite well under fire conditions. This mandate for the installation of automatic sprinkler systems in all buildings containing any Group R occupancy is based upon the desire to reduce such fire deaths and injuries in all residential buildings regulated by the *International Building Code*. This provision, like most requirements found in Chapter 9, is also found in the *International Fire Code*.

All buildings containing a Group R occupancy to be sprinklered throughout.

The scope of the IBC, Section 101.2, defers certain residential occupancies to the construction regulations of the *International Residential Code*. As such, this provision applies only to those residential structures constructed under the requirements of the *International Building Code*.

Topic: Fire Department Access
Reference: IBC 903.2.10.1

Category: Fire Protection Systems
Subject: Automatic Sprinkler Systems

Code Text: *An automatic sprinkler system shall be installed throughout every story or basement of all buildings where the floor area exceeds 1,500 square feet and* where there are not complying exterior wall openings.

Discussion and Commentary: The IBC considers those structures with inadequate exterior openings for fire department access and/or rescue to be "windowless buildings," which require the installation of an automatic sprinkler system. Two methods of providing appropriate openings are set forth; one method is for openings below grade, and the other is for openings entirely above adjoining ground level. In all cases, at least one side of the building must be provided with complying openings in each 50 lineal feet of exterior wall. Basements are more highly regulated than floors above grade.

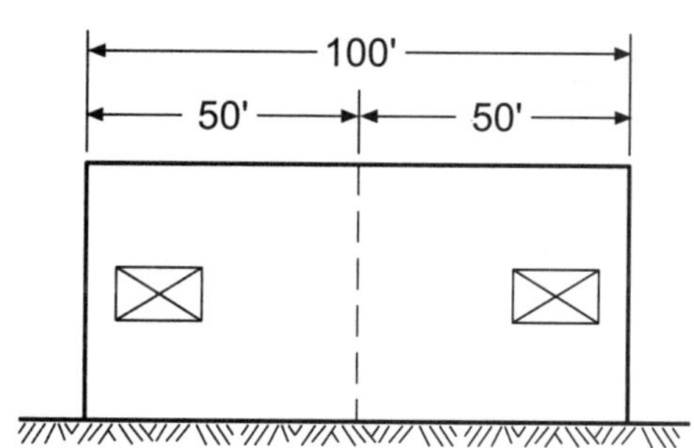

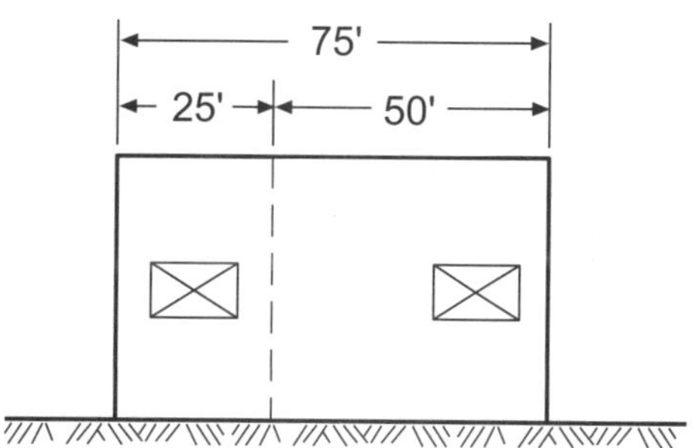

⊠ Required exterior opening:
1. Twenty square feet of opening in each 50 lineal feet or fraction thereof.
2. Minimum dimension of 30 inches.
3. Accessible to the fire department from the exterior.
4. Cannot be obstructed in a manner that prevents firefighting or rescue from the exterior.

For SI: 1 inch = 25.4 mm, 1 foot = 304.8 mm.

A-267

If complying openings are provided on two or more sides of the building, or if an exterior wall is less than 75 feet from an opposing exterior wall provided with complying openings, then an automatic sprinkler system is not required.

Topic: Buildings Over 55 Feet in Height
Reference: IBC 903.2.10.3

Category: Fire Protection Systems
Subject: Automatic Sprinkler Systems

Code Text: *An automatic sprinkler system shall be installed throughout buildings with a floor level having an occupant load of 30 or more that is located 55 feet (16 764 mm) or more above the lowest level of fire department vehicle access.* See exceptions that exempt airport control towers, open parking structures and Group F-2 occupancies.

Discussion and Commentary: Because of difficulties associated with manual suppression of a fire in buildings constructed a substantial height above the fire department's point of attack, an automatic sprinkler system is required throughout the building, regardless of occupancy. Note that buildings that qualify for a sprinkler system by this provision, often termed "mid-rise" buildings, are not necessarily high-rise buildings as defined in Section 403.1.

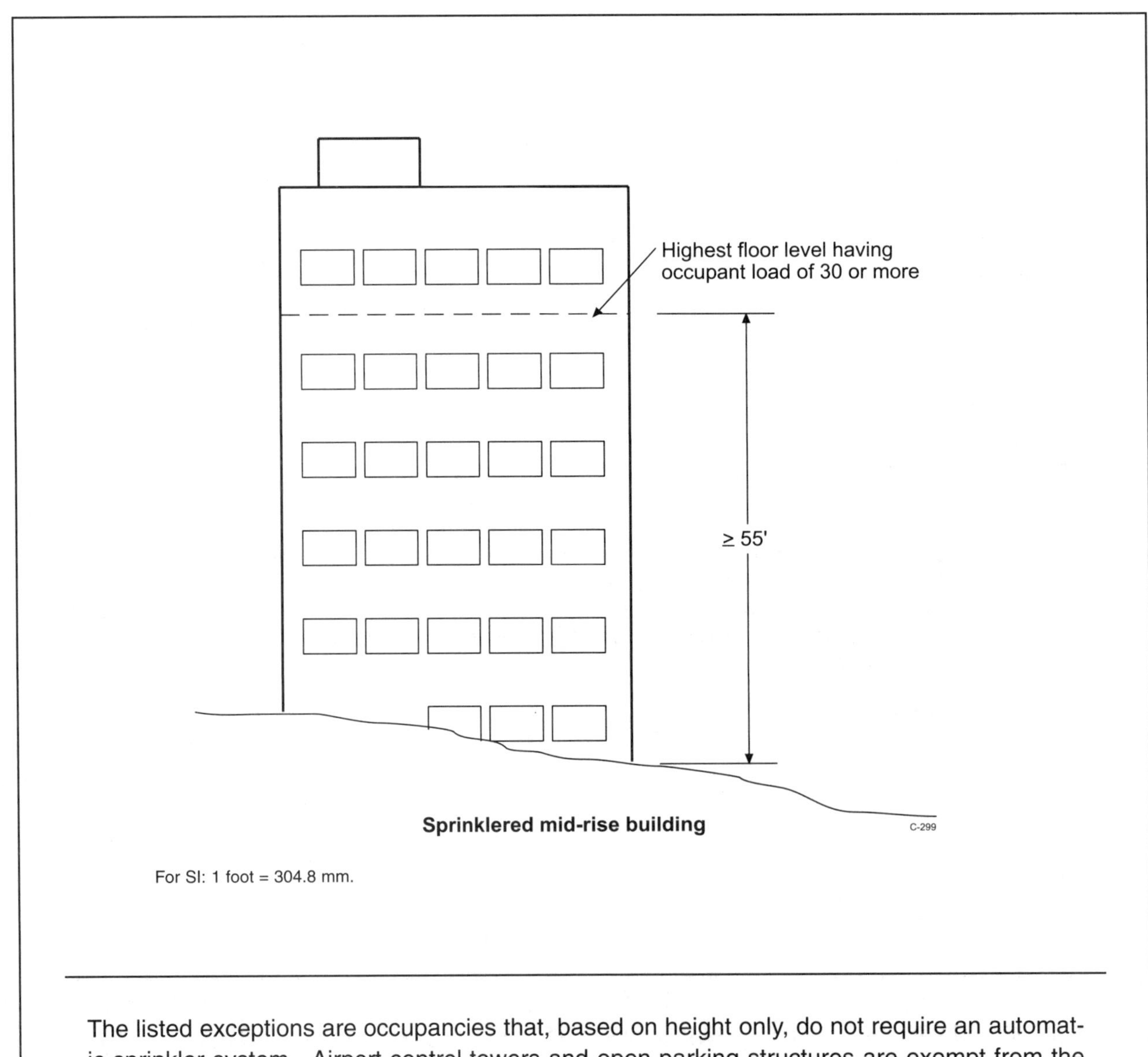

Sprinklered mid-rise building

For SI: 1 foot = 304.8 mm.

The listed exceptions are occupancies that, based on height only, do not require an automatic sprinkler system. Airport control towers and open parking structures are exempt from the high-rise provisions of Section 403 also.

Topic: Required Installations
Reference: IBC 905.3

Category: Fire Protection Systems
Subject: Standpipe Systems

Code Text: *Standpipe systems shall be installed where required by Sections 905.3.1 through 905.3.6 and in the locations indicated in Sections 905.4, 905.5 and 905.6.*

Discussion and Commentary: Installed exclusively for the fighting of fires, a standpipe system is a wet or dry system composed of piping, valves, outlets and related equipment designed to provide water at specified pressures. Standpipe systems are permitted to be combined with automatic sprinkler systems. Divided into Classes I, II and III, standpipe systems are generally required in large-area buildings having combustible contents, or in structures of substantial height. Connections for Class I standpipes, which are solely for use by the fire department, shall be located in protected areas to allow for staging operations. Exit enclosures are typical locations for Class I connections.

REQUIRED STANDPIPE INSTALLATIONS

LOCATION OR USE	NONSPRINKLERED BUILDING	SPRINKLERED BUILDING
Building with highest story located at more than 30 feet above lowest level of fire department vehicle access	Class III [1,2,3]	Class I
Building with lowest story located at more than 30 feet below highest level of fire department vehicle access	Class III [1,2,3]	Class I
Group A occupancies with occupant load exceeding 1,000	Class I [5]	No requirement
Covered mall buildings	—	Class I
Stages more than 1,000 square feet	Class III	Class III [6]
Underground buildings	—	Class I

1 Class I standpipes permitted in basements equipped with automatic sprinkler system
2 Class I manual dry standpipes permitted in open parking garages subject to freezing temperatures, provided hose connections located as for Class II systems
3 Class I manual standpipes permitted in open parking garages where highest floor is less than 150 feet above the lowest level of fire department vehicle access
4 Not required in Groups A-4, A-5, F-2, R-2, S-2 or U occupancies
5 Not required in open-air-seating spaces without enclosed spaces
6 Hose connections permitted to be supplied by sprinkler system

Fire hose cabinets in which hoses are attached to outlets on Class II standpipes (as well as the use of portable fire extinguishers) are provided as a means by which the building occupants can control the fire prior to either sprinkler activation or fire personnel arrival.

Topic: Where Required
Reference: IBC 907.2

Category: Fire Protection Systems
Subject: Fire Alarm and Detection Systems

Code Text: *An approved manual, automatic, or manual and automatic fire alarm system shall be provided in accordance with Sections 907.2.1 through Section 907.2.23. An approved automatic fire detection system shall be installed in accordance with the provisions of the IBC and NFPA 72. The automatic fire detectors shall be smoke detectors, except that an approved alternative type of detector shall be installed in spaces such as boiler rooms where, during normal operation, products of combustion are present in sufficient quantity to actuate a smoke detector.*

Discussion and Commentary: For many of the uses identified by the IBC, it is necessary to provide some level of notification to the building occupants and/or a supervised location reserved for a fire emergency. The threshold at which an alarm and/or detection system is required varies according to the occupancy.

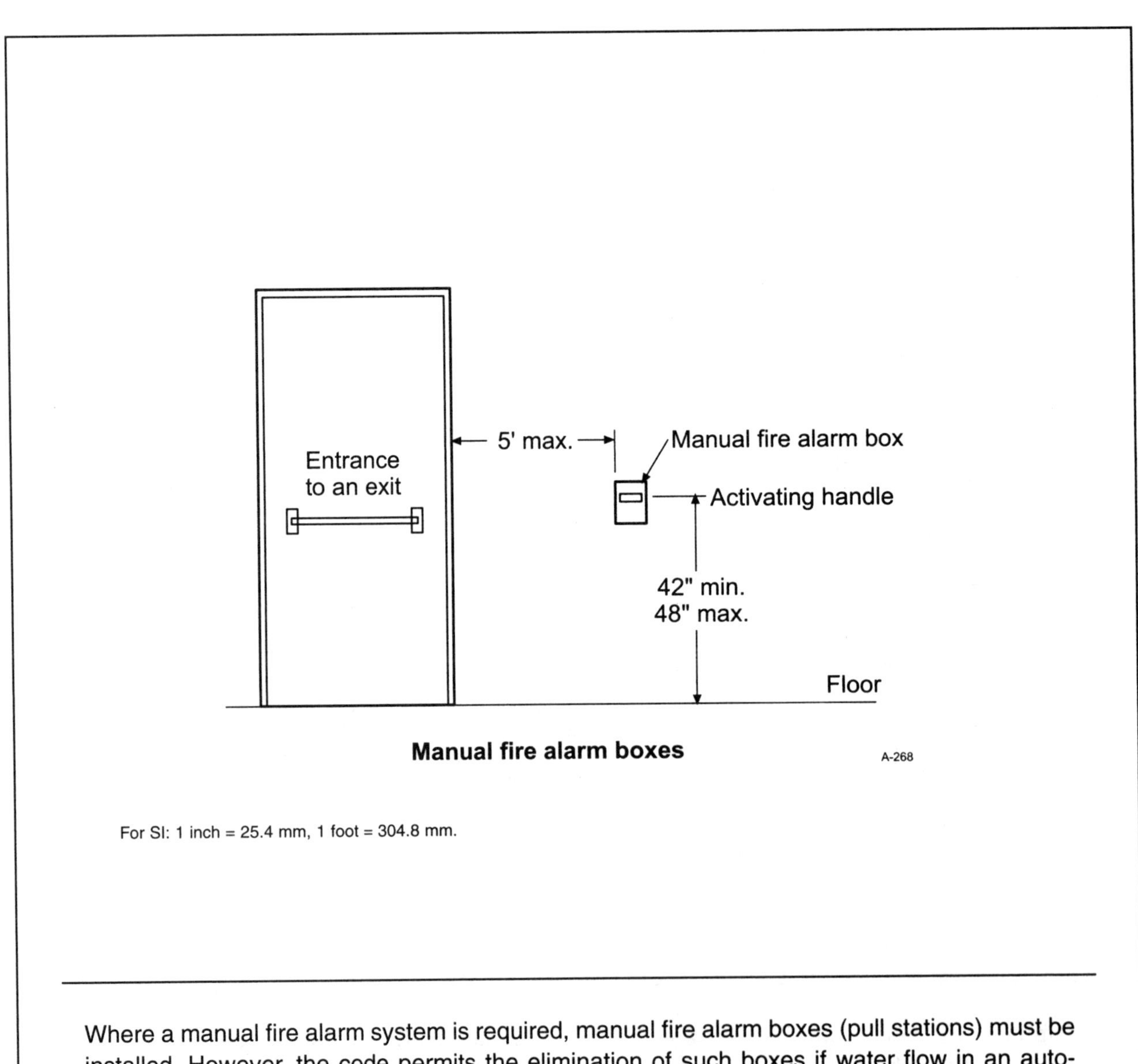

Manual fire alarm boxes

For SI: 1 inch = 25.4 mm, 1 foot = 304.8 mm.

Where a manual fire alarm system is required, manual fire alarm boxes (pull stations) must be installed. However, the code permits the elimination of such boxes if water flow in an automatic sprinkler system installed throughout the building activates the notification appliances.

Topic: Scope
Reference: IBC 909.1

Category: Fire Protection Systems
Subject: Smoke Control Systems

Code Text: *Section 909 applies to mechanical or passive smoke control systems when they are required by some other provision of the IBC. Smoke control systems regulated by Section 909 serve a different purpose than the smoke- and heat-venting provisions found in Section 910.*

Discussion and Commentary: The provisions of this section do not apply unless specifically mandated for a special use, such as an atrium. It is the intent that none of the requirements apply unless directed by other provisions of the code. Where a smoke control system is provided, it may be either passive or mechanical, or a combination of the two systems. A mechanical system is an engineered system that uses mechanical fans either to produce pressure differences across smoke barriers or to establish airflows to limit and direct smoke movement. A passive system is a system of smoke barriers arranged to limit the migration of smoke.

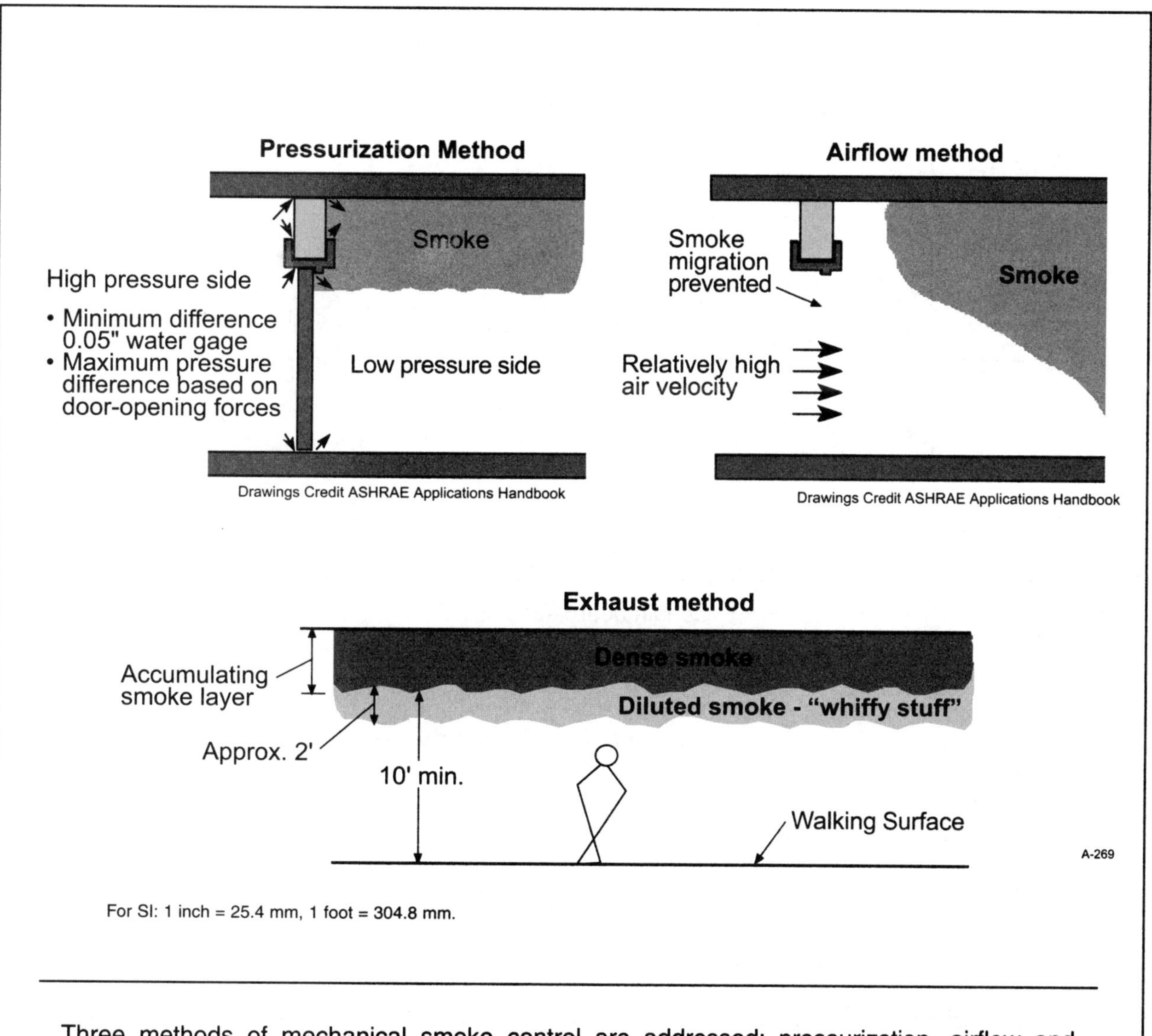

Three methods of mechanical smoke control are addressed: pressurization, airflow and exhaust. Pressure differences across smoke barriers shall be the primary means of smoke control. The building official may accept the airflow or exhaust methods in specific situations.

Topic: Where Required
Reference: IBC 910.2

Category: Fire Protection Systems
Subject: Smoke and Heat Vents

Code Text: *Approved smoke and heat vents shall be installed in the roofs of one-story buildings or portions thereof (1) used as Group F-1 or S-1 occupancies having more than 50,000 square feet in undivided area, or (2) used as a Group H occupancy in accordance with Section 910.2.2, or (3) containing high-piled combustible stock or rack storage in any occupancy group in accordance with Section 413 and the IFC, or (4) used as a Group F-1 or S-1 occupancy where the maximum exit access travel distance is increased in accordance with Section 1015.2.*

Discussion and Commentary: Smoke and heat vents shall be installed in conjunction with curtain boards, which confine the smoke and hot gases so that they are not diluted. Curtain boards thus increase the effectiveness of automatic vents.

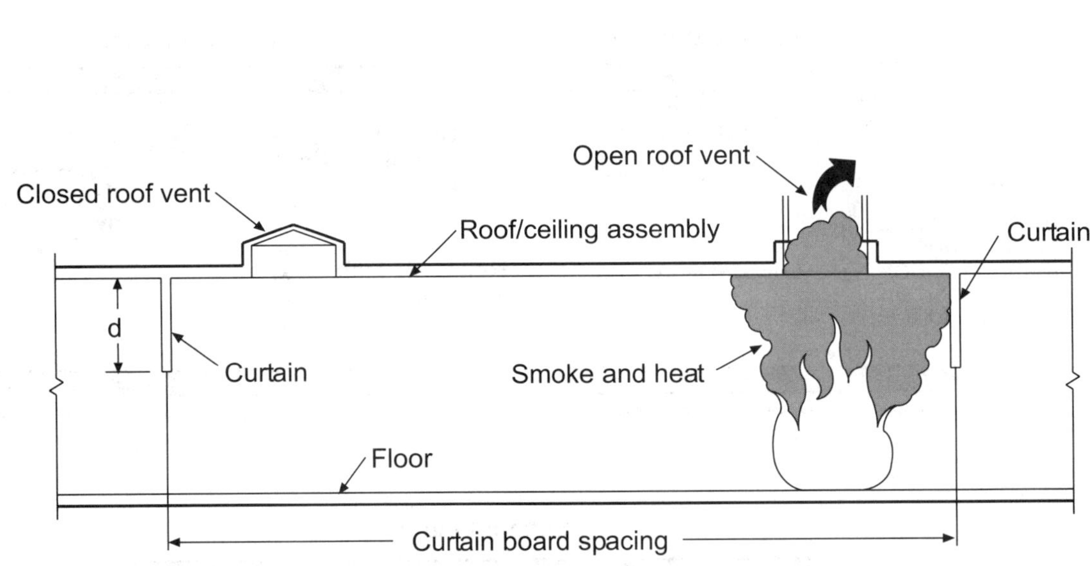

Note: In general, several small vents are more effective than a larger vent of equal area.

Roof vents and curtain boards

A-272

The code permits the building official to approve the use of a mechanical smoke exhaust system to ventilate the building as an alternative to smoke and heat vents. The exhaust fans in such a system are regulated for size, location, operation, wiring, control, supply air and interlocks.

QUIZ

Study Session 8 — Chapter 9

I. Multiple Choice

1. Automatic sprinkler systems shall be monitored by an approved supervising station where the minimum number of sprinklers is __________.

a. 10
b. 20
c. 50
d. 100

Reference_______________

2. Which one of the following classes of standpipe systems is intended primarily for the use of building occupants or the fire department during initial response?

a. Class I
b. Class II
c. Class III
d. Class IV

Reference_______________

3. Which one of the following types of standpipe systems requires water from a fire department pumper to be pumped into the system in order to supply the system demand?

a. automatic dry
b. automatic wet
c. manual wet
d. semiautomatic dry

Reference_______________

4. In a Group A-2 occupancy, an automatic sprinkler system shall be provided throughout any fire area ___________.

a. exceeding a minimum of 12,000 square feet in area
b. used for the consumption of alcoholic beverages
c. located one story above the exit discharge level
d. having a minimum occupant load of 100

Reference_______________

5. Stadium press boxes having a minimum of __________ square feet shall be sprinklered.

a. 400
b. 1,000
c. 5,000
d. 12,000

Reference_______________

6. Unless each classroom has at least one exterior door at grade level, a sprinkler system is required for all Group E fire areas exceeding _________ square feet.

a. 2,500
b. 5,000
c. 12,000
d. 20,000

Reference_______________

7. Where woodworking operations in a Group F-1 occupancy generate finely divided combustible waste, an automatic sprinkler system is required for a minimum size fire area of _________ square feet.

a. 1,000
b. 2,500
c. 5,000
d. 12,000

Reference_______________

8. In a Group H-5 occupancy, which of the following locations requires an occupancy hazard sprinkler classification of Extra Hazard Group 2?

a. fabrication areas
b. service corridors
c. egress corridors
d. storage rooms with dispensing

Reference_______________

9. An automatic sprinkler system shall be provided in a Group M occupancy having a minimum of _________ stories above grade.

a. 2
b. 3
c. 4
d. 6

Reference_______________

10. Which of the following residential occupancies must be sprinklered under all conditions?

a. Groups R-1 and R-2 only
b. Groups R-1, R-2 and R-4 only
c. Groups R-2 and R-4 only
d. All Group R occupancies

Reference_______________

11. A building shall be fully sprinklered where the combined area of all Group S-1 fire areas exceeds _________ square feet.

a. 2,500
b. 5,000
c. 12,000
d. 24,000

Reference_______________

12. A single-story Group S-1 repair garage shall be fully sprinklered where the fire area contains a minimum of __________ square feet.

a. 2,500
b. 10,000
c. 12,000
d. 24,000

Reference_______________

13. A Group S-2 parking garage used to store commercial buses shall be sprinklered where the fire area has a minimum size of __________ square feet.

a. 2,500
b. 5,000
c. 10,000
d. 12,000

Reference_______________

14. Where any portion of a basement exceeds a minimum of __________ feet from complying exterior openings, the basement shall be provided with an automatic sprinkler system.

a. 50
b. 75
c. 100
d. 150

Reference_______________

15. Which of the following NFPA automatic sprinkler systems is designed for installation in one- and two-family dwellings?

a. 13
b. 13D
c. 13R
d. 17A

Reference_______________

16. Which of the following spaces requiring sprinkler system protection is not required to use quick-response or residential sprinklers?

a. light-hazard occupancies
b. sleeping units in Group R-1
c. patient sleeping rooms in Group I-2
d. sales rooms of Group M

Reference_______________

17. A minimum of __________ shall be maintained between automatic sprinklers and the top of piles of combustible fibers.

a. 12 inches
b. 18 inches
c. 3 feet
d. 5 feet

Reference_______________

18. A secondary water supply, where required in high-rise buildings, shall have a minimum duration of __________ minutes.

a. 15 b. 30
c. 60 d. 90

Reference_______________

19. The manual actuation device for a fire-extinguishing system for a commercial cooking system shall be located a minimum of __________ feet and a maximum of __________ feet from the kitchen exhaust system.

a. 3, 6 b. 5, 10
c. 6, 12 d. 10, 20

Reference_______________

20. Connections for Class II standpipe systems shall be located so that all portions of the building are within __________ feet of a nozzle attached to __________ feet of hose.

a. 20, 50 b. 30, 100
c. 40, 125 d. 40, 150

Reference_______________

21. In a nonsprinklered Group B occupancy, a manual fire alarm system shall be installed where there are a minimum of __________ occupants above or below the level of exit discharge.

a. 101 b. 201
c. 301 d. 501

Reference_______________

22. A manual fire alarm system is not required in a Group E occupancy with a maximum occupant load of __________ persons.

a. 49 b. 99
c. 299 d. 499

Reference_______________

23. Manual fire alarm boxes shall be located a maximum of __________ feet from the entrance to each exit.

a. 5 b. 10
c. 12 d. 20

Reference_______________

24. In a Group R-1 hotel providing 220 sleeping units, a minimum of __________ such units shall be provided with visible alarm notification devices.

a. 3
b. 11
c. 17
d. 22

Reference________________

25. The minimum sound pressure level for audible alarm notification appliances in an office building shall be __________ decibels.

a. 60
b. 70
c. 90
d. 105

Reference________________

26. A manual actuation device for an automatic fire-extinguishing system serving a commercial cooking system shall be located a minimum of _____ feet and a maximum of _____ feet from the kitchen exhaust system.

a. 5, 10
b. 5, 20
c. 10, 15
d. 10, 20

Reference________________

27. A Class III wet standpipe is not required for stages having a maximum size of _____ square feet.

a. 100
b. 400
c. 500
d. 1,000

Reference________________

28. Where natural ventilation is utilized for venting a smokeproof enclosure, each vestibule shall be provided with a minimum _____-square-foot opening in the exterior wall.

a. 9
b. 16
c. 24
d. 35

Reference________________

29. Other than for an aircraft repair hangar, a one-story Group S-1 occupancy shall be provided with smoke and heat vents where it exceeds _____ square feet in undivided area.

a. 8,000
b. 10,000
c. 15,000
d. 50,000

Reference________________

30. In a Group F-1 occupancy, smoke and heat vents shall be spaced at maximum intervals of _____ feet when measured center to center.

a. 60

b. 75

c. 100

d. 120

Reference________________

INTERNATIONAL BUILDING CODE
Study Session 9
Sections 1001–1007, 1011–1012 — Means of Egress I

OBJECTIVE: To obtain an understanding of the general system design requirements of a means of egress system, including the determination of occupant load, the required width of egress components, means of egress identification and illumination, accessible means of egress and the provisions regulating guards.

REFERENCE: Sections 1001, 1007, 1011–1012, 2003 *International Building Code*

KEY POINTS:

- What is the definition of a means of egress system? What are its three distinct elements?
- What is the minimum ceiling height permitted along a means of egress?
- What limitations are placed on protruding objects extending below the minimum ceiling height? Projecting horizontally over a walking surface?
- For an elevation change along the egress path, at what point is a ramp required rather than a step or stairway?
- In areas without fixed seats, what is the correct method of determining occupant load?
- What method shall be used to calculate the occupant load in areas with fixed seating, such as benches, pews or booths?
- How may the design occupant load be increased over what is calculated?
- In which types of rooms or spaces must the maximum occupant load be posted?
- How is exiting addressed where exits serve more than one floor?
- How is exiting from a mezzanine regulated?
- Are yards, patios and courts regulated in the same manner as interior areas?
- How shall the minimum width of different egress components be determined?
- What is the maximum allowable encroachment of a door into the required egress width?
- When must the means of egress be illuminated? What is the minimum required illumination at the floor level?
- Which locations must be provided with emergency power for egress illumination?
- For what duration is an emergency power system for means of egress illumination required to provide power?
- What is considered an accessible means of egress? How many are required in a building?
- When is an area of refuge needed? How are they to be constructed?
- How must an accessible means of egress be identified?
- What is the purpose of an exterior area for rescue assistance? How must this area be separated from the interior of the building it serves?
- Where are exit signs required? When must they be illuminated? What level of illumination is required? Which types of power sources are necessary?
- What is the definition of a guard?
- When are guards required? What is the minimum height requirement from the walking surface to the top of a guard?
- How must guards be constructed to limit passage through the protective barrier?

Topic: General
Reference: IBC 1001.1

Category: Means of Egress
Subject: Administration

Code Text: *Buildings or portions thereof shall be provided with a means of egress system as required by Chapter 10. The provisions of Chapter 10 shall control the design, construction and arrangement of means of egress components required to provide an approved means of egress from structures and portions thereof.*

Discussion and Commentary: The *International Building Code* regulates the design, construction and maintenance of an exiting system through two general categories—system design and egress components. Any building elements that are a part of the system must be reviewed for compliance with the criteria for the number, location, width or capacity, height, continuity and arrangement of egress components, and all other applicable provisions.

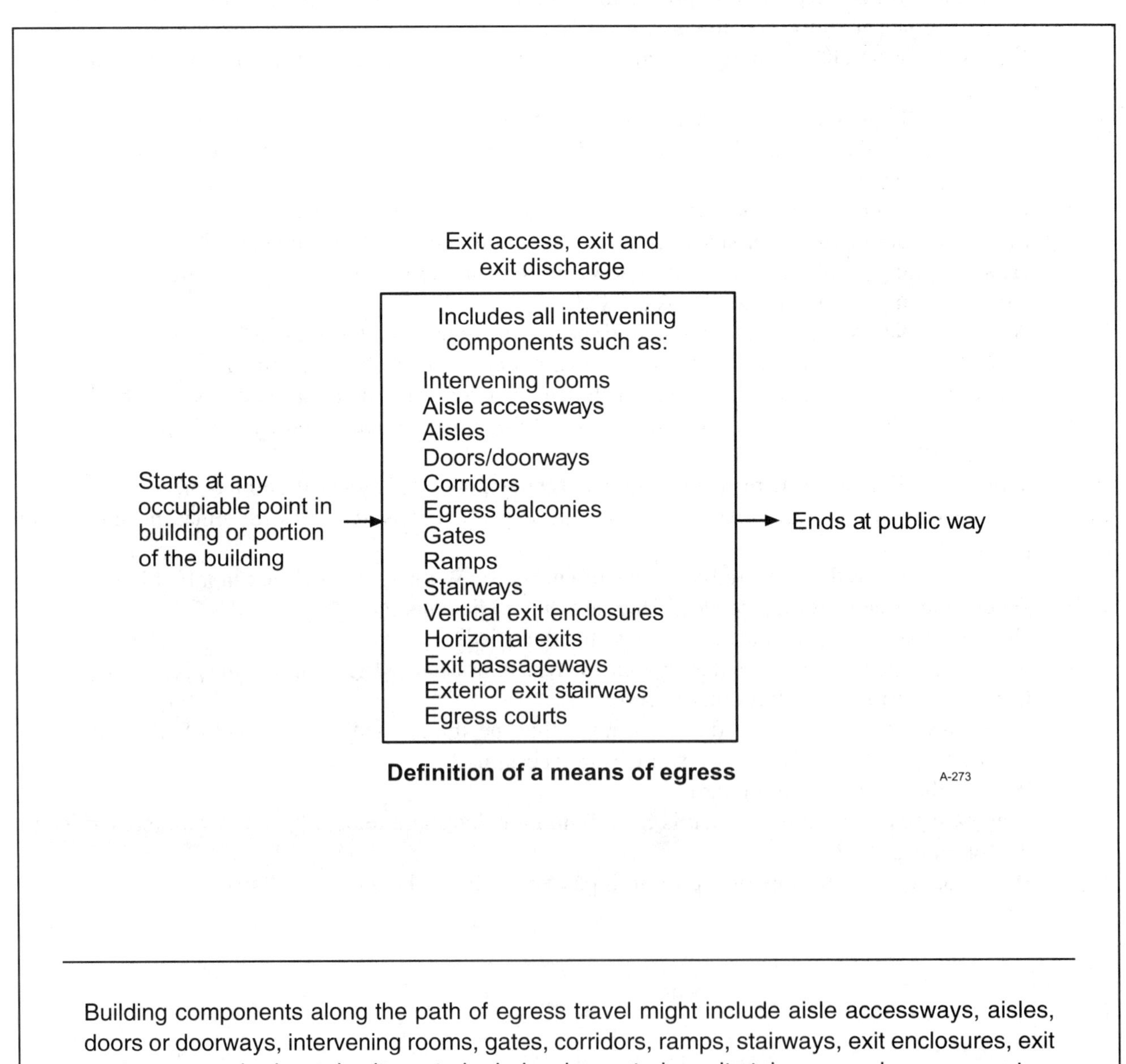

Definition of a means of egress

Building components along the path of egress travel might include aisle accessways, aisles, doors or doorways, intervening rooms, gates, corridors, ramps, stairways, exit enclosures, exit passageways, horizontal exits, exterior balconies, exterior exit stairways and egress courts.

Topic: Three-Part Egress System
Reference: IBC 1002

Category: Means of Egress
Subject: Definitions

Code Text: *A means of egress is a continuous and unobstructed path of vertical and horizontal egress travel from any occupied portion of a building or structure to a public way. A means of egress consists of three separate and distinct parts: the exit access, the exit, and the exit discharge.*

Discussion and Commentary: The exit access begins at any occupied location within the building and does not end until it reaches the door to an exit enclosure, a horizontal exit or exit passageway, an exterior exit stairway or ramp, or an exterior door at ground level. Travel distance is regulated throughout the exit access, and the path of travel is seldom a fire-protected environment. At the exit discharge, which begins where the exit ends, egress remains regulated until the public way is reached.

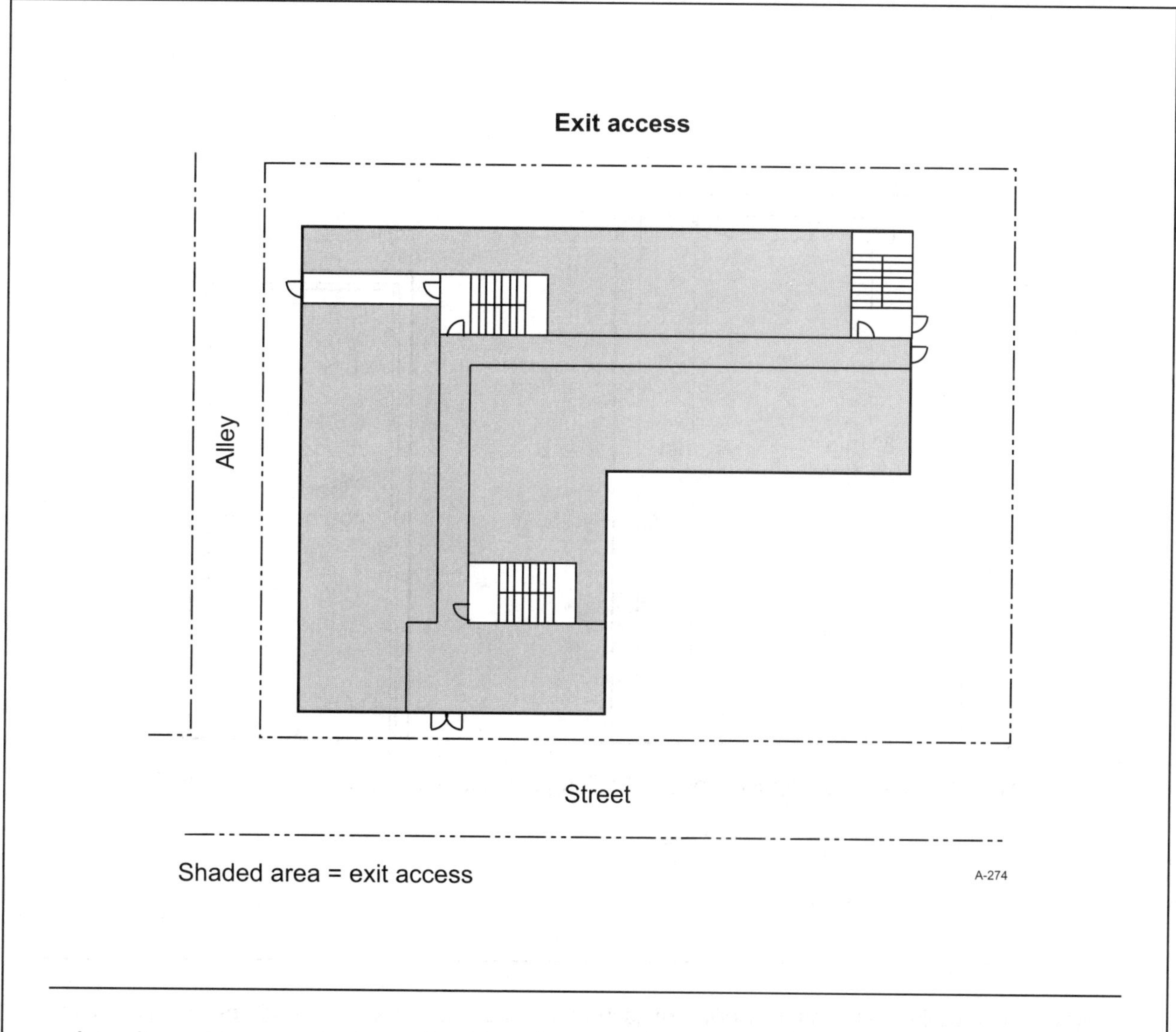

An exit provides a protected path of travel to an exit discharge. Because an exit component affords protection, travel distance is no longer a concern once the exit has been reached. Exit discharge travel distance to the public way is also unlimited.

Topic: Ceiling Height
Reference: IBC 1003.2

Category: Means of Egress
Subject: General Egress

Code Text: *The means of egress shall have a ceiling height of not less than 7 feet.*

Discussion and Commentary: In addition to providing a travel path of adequate width, the code requires that the clear height of the means of egress be maintained at least 7 feet above the walking surface. There are several exceptions to this general requirement that permit limited reductions in the mandated height. Under most conditions, the vertical clearance at a stairway or doorway may be reduced to 80 inches. Protruding objects, such as sprinklers and light fixtures, are also permitted to extend below the minimum required ceiling height for up to 50% of ceiling area of the means of egress, provided such objects maintain a headroom clearance of at least 80 inches. Special provisions are applicable to sloped ceilings.

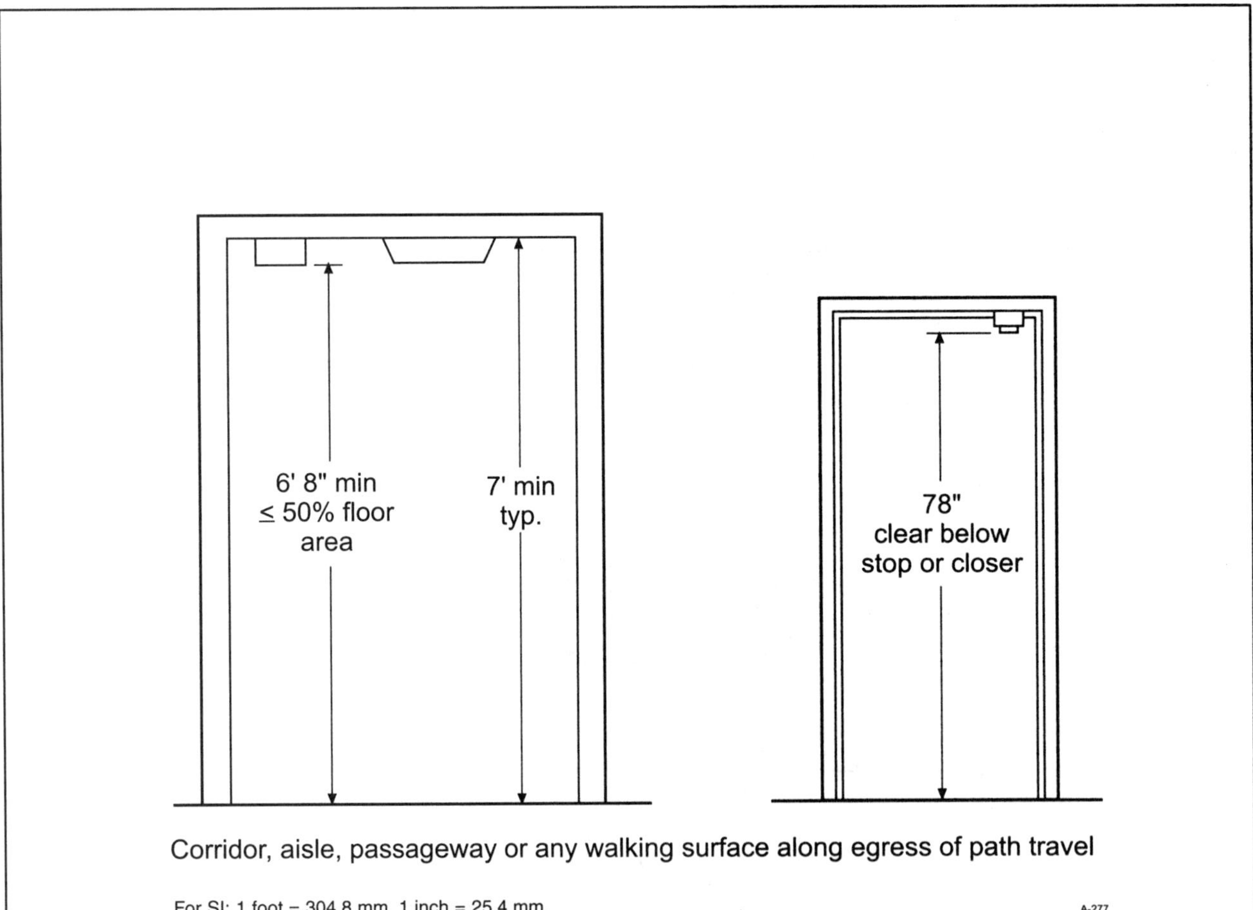

The minimum ceiling heights for dwelling units in residential occupancies are addressed in Section 1208.2. Habitable spaces, such as bedrooms and living rooms, occupiable spaces and corridors must be at least 7 feet 6 inches in height. In other areas, reduced headroom is permitted.

Topic: Elevation Change
Reference: IBC 1003.5

Category: Means of Egress
Subject: General Egress

Code Text: *Where changes in elevation of less than 12 inches exist in the means of egress, sloped surfaces shall be used. Where the slope is greater than 1 unit vertical in 20 units horizontal, ramps complying with Section 1010 shall be used. Where the difference in elevation is 6 inches or less, the ramp shall be equipped with either handrails or floor finish materials that contrast with adjacent floor finish materials.* See exceptions.

Discussion and Commentary: Along the egress path, there is a concern about slight changes in elevation that are not readily apparent to persons seeking to exit under emergency conditions. Therefore, a single riser or a pair of shallow risers is not permitted. Steps used to achieve minor differences in elevation frequently go unnoticed, and as such, can cause accidents.

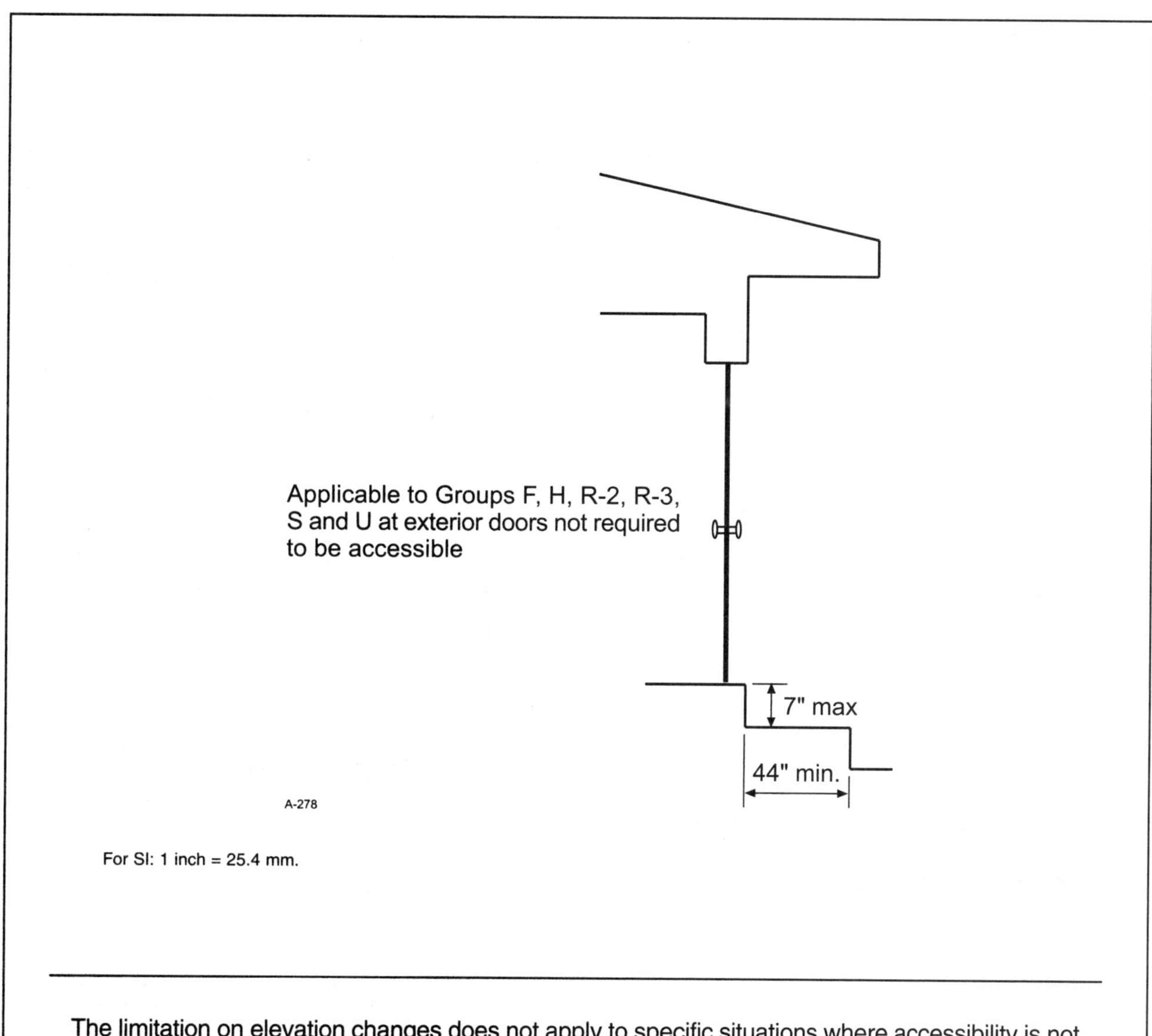

The limitation on elevation changes does not apply to specific situations where accessibility is not required. A maximum 7-inch step is permitted at exterior doors of Groups F, H, R-2, R-3, S and U. In addition, one or two complying steps are allowed when an additional handrail is provided.

Topic: Design Occupant Load
Reference: IBC 1004.1

Category: Means of Egress
Subject: Occupant Load

Code Text: *In determining means of egress requirements, the number of occupants for whom means of egress facilities shall be provided shall be established by the largest number computed in accordance with Sections 1004.1.1 through 1004.1.3. The number of occupants computed at the rate of one occupant per unit of area as prescribed in Table 1004.1.2.*

Discussion and Commentary: For occupant load determination, it must be assumed that under normal conditions all portions of a building are fully occupied at the same time. The density characteristics of the various uses identified in Table 1004.1.2 are considered "occupant load factors." For most occupancies, the gross floor area is to be considered. However, a few of the occupant load factors are based on net floor area, which allows the deduction of areas such as corridors, stairways, toilet rooms, equipment rooms and closets.

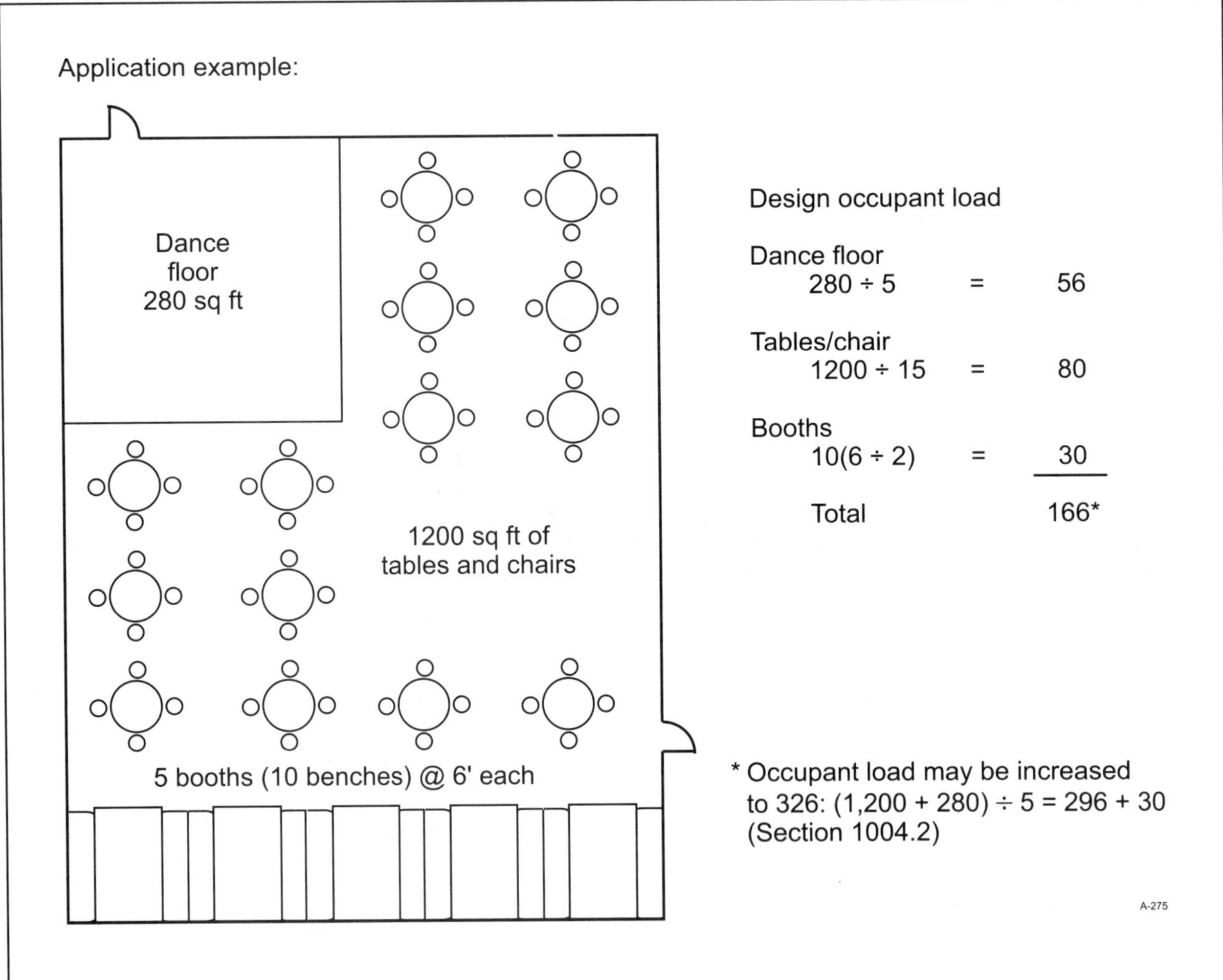

Where fixed seats are installed, Section 1004.7 specifies that the occupant load is determined simply by counting the number of seats. For benches and pews, the factor is one occupant per 18 inches of width. For booth seating, the factor is 24 inches per occupant.

Topic: Outdoor Areas
Reference: IBC 1004.8

Category: Means of Egress
Subject: Occupant Load

Code Text: *Yards, patios, courts and similar outdoor areas accessible to and usable by the building occupants shall be provided with means of egress as required by Chapter 10. Where outdoor areas are to be used by persons in addition to the occupants of the building, and the path of egress travel from the outdoor areas passes through the building, means of egress requirements shall be based on the sum of the occupant loads of the building plus the outdoor areas.* See exceptions for service and dwellings.

Discussion and Commentary: Although not limited in application, this provision primarily addresses the use of outdoor areas for dining and/or drinking in restaurants and similar establishments. The building official is authorized to establish an occupant load for the outdoor space in accordance with its anticipated use and to apply all means of egress provisions that would be appropriate.

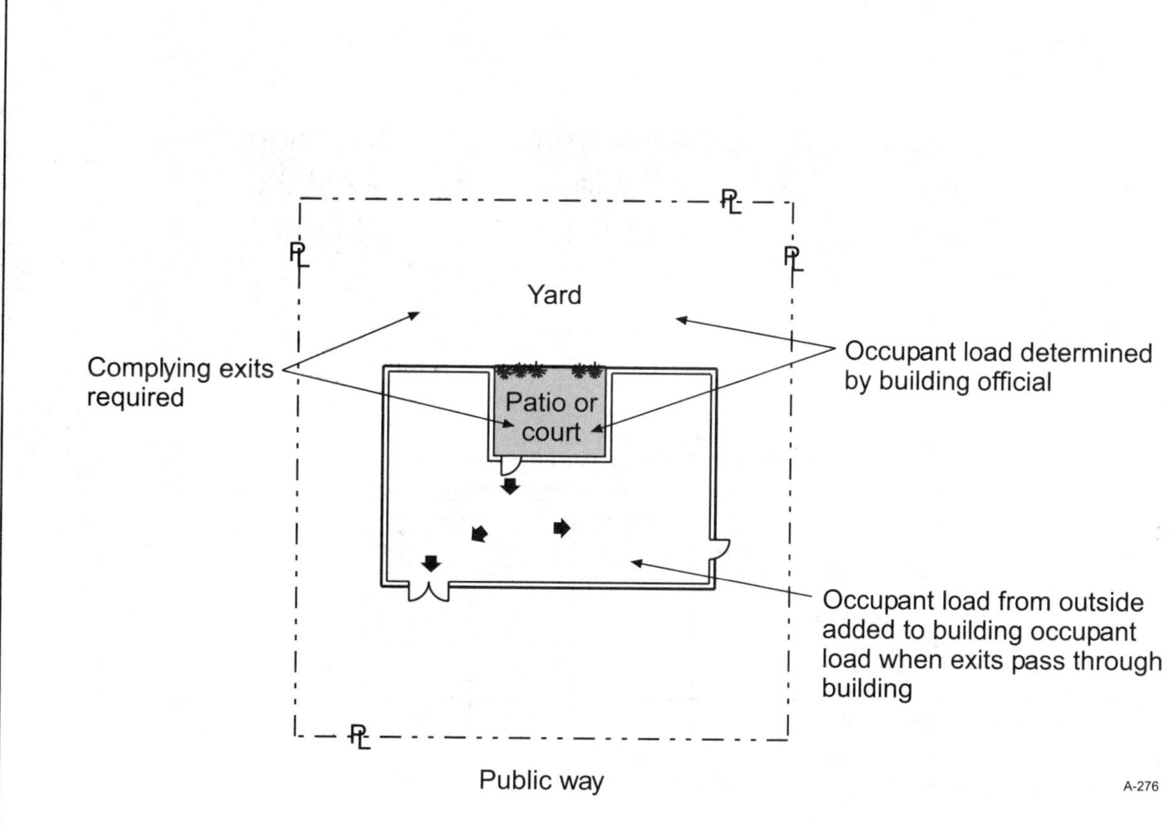

Outdoor reviewing stands, grandstands and bleachers must have their occupant loads calculated according to the specific types of seating arrangements, such as chairbacks, benches, loose chairs, etc. Additional specific requirements are contained in Section 1024.

Topic: Minimum Required Width
Reference: IBC 1005.1, 1005.2

Category: Means of Egress
Subject: Egress Width

Code Text: *The means of egress width shall not be less than required by* Section 1005. *The total width of means of egress in inches (mm) shall not be less than the total occupant load served by the means of egress multiplied by the factors in Table 1005.1 and not less than specified elsewhere in* the IBC. *Doors opening into the path of egress travel shall not reduce the required width to less than one-half during the course of the swing. When fully open, the door shall not project more than 7 inches (178 mm) into the required width.* See exception for doors within units of Groups R-2 and R-3.

Discussion and Commentary: In a given means of egress system, different components will afford different capacities. The most restrictive component will establish the capacity of the overall system. Doorways, aisles, stairways and corridors also have minimum established widths that must be provided.

Occupant Load Served X Factor from Table 1005.1 ≤ Minimum Available Width

TABLE 1005.1
EGRESS WIDTH PER OCCUPANT SERVED

OCCUPANCY	WITHOUT SPRINKLER SYSTEM		WITH SPRINKLER SYSTEM[a]	
	Stairways (inches per occupant)	Other egress components (inches per occupant)	Stairways (inches per occupant)	Other egress components (inches per occupant)
Occupancies other than those listed below	0.3	0.2	0.2	0.15
Hazardous: H-1, H-2, H-3 and H-4	0.7	0.4	0.3	0.2
Institutional: I-2	NA	NA	0.3	0.2

For SI: 1 inch = 25.4 mm. NA = Not applicable.

a. Buildings equipped throughout with an automatic sprinkler system in accordance with Section 903.3.1.1 or 903.3.1.2.

Width, in terms of a means of egress system or component, is the clear, unobstructed usable width afforded along the exit path by the individual components. Unless the code provides for a permitted projection, the minimum clear width may not be reduced throughout the travel path.

Topic: Multiple Means of Egress
Reference: IBC 1005.1

Category: Means of Egress
Subject: Egress Width

Code Text: *Multiple means of egress shall be sized such that the loss of any one means of egress shall not reduce the available capacity to less than 50 percent of the required capacity. The maximum capacity required from any story of a building shall be maintained to the termination of the means of egress.*

Discussion and Commentary: Where two complying means of egress are provided, the occupant load is to be distributed evenly between the two means of egress. However, where three or more means of egress are available, it is permissible to size one of the egress points for up to 50 percent of the occupant load, while distributing the remaining occupant load among the other means of egress. This distribution is not required to be equally applied; however, a dramatic imbalance of egress component capacities relative to occupant load distribution should be avoided.

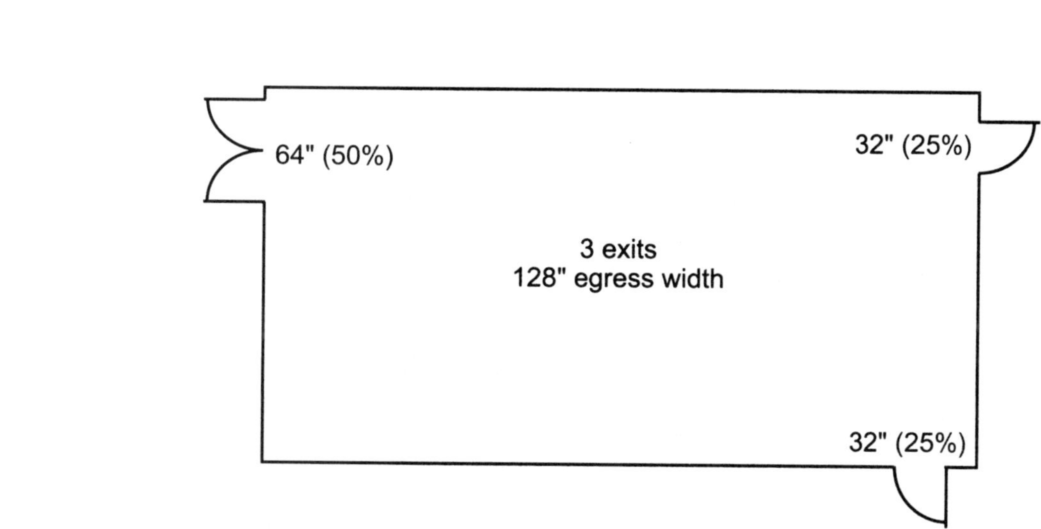

Given: A retail store having 3 exits, with a total required exit width of 128 in.
Determine: The manner in which the exit width may distributed.

Any manner is acceptable that does not assign more than 50% (64 in.) of the required exit.

Egress width distribution

A-187a

For SI: 1 inch = 25.4 mm.

One of the fundamental concepts in the design of the means of egress is that the capacity of the egress path not be diminished until the public way is reached. Regardless of minimum required component width, the calculated width based on the occupant load served must be maintained.

Topic: Emergency Power
Reference: IBC 1006.3

Category: Means of Egress
Subject: Illumination

Code Text: *The power supply for means of egress illumination shall normally be provided by the premises electrical supply. In the event of power supply failure, an emergency electrical system shall automatically illuminate corridors, passageways, and aisles in rooms and spaces which require two or more means of egress, and corridors, exit stairways, exterior egress components above grade, interior discharge elements, and exit discharge doorways in buildings required to have two or more exits.*

Discussion and Commentary: Often identified as "emergency lighting," a completely separate source of power from the premise's wiring system is required when the life-safety risk in a building becomes sufficiently great. This threshold is recognized as the point at which the occupant load of the room, area or building is high enough so that two means of egress are required.

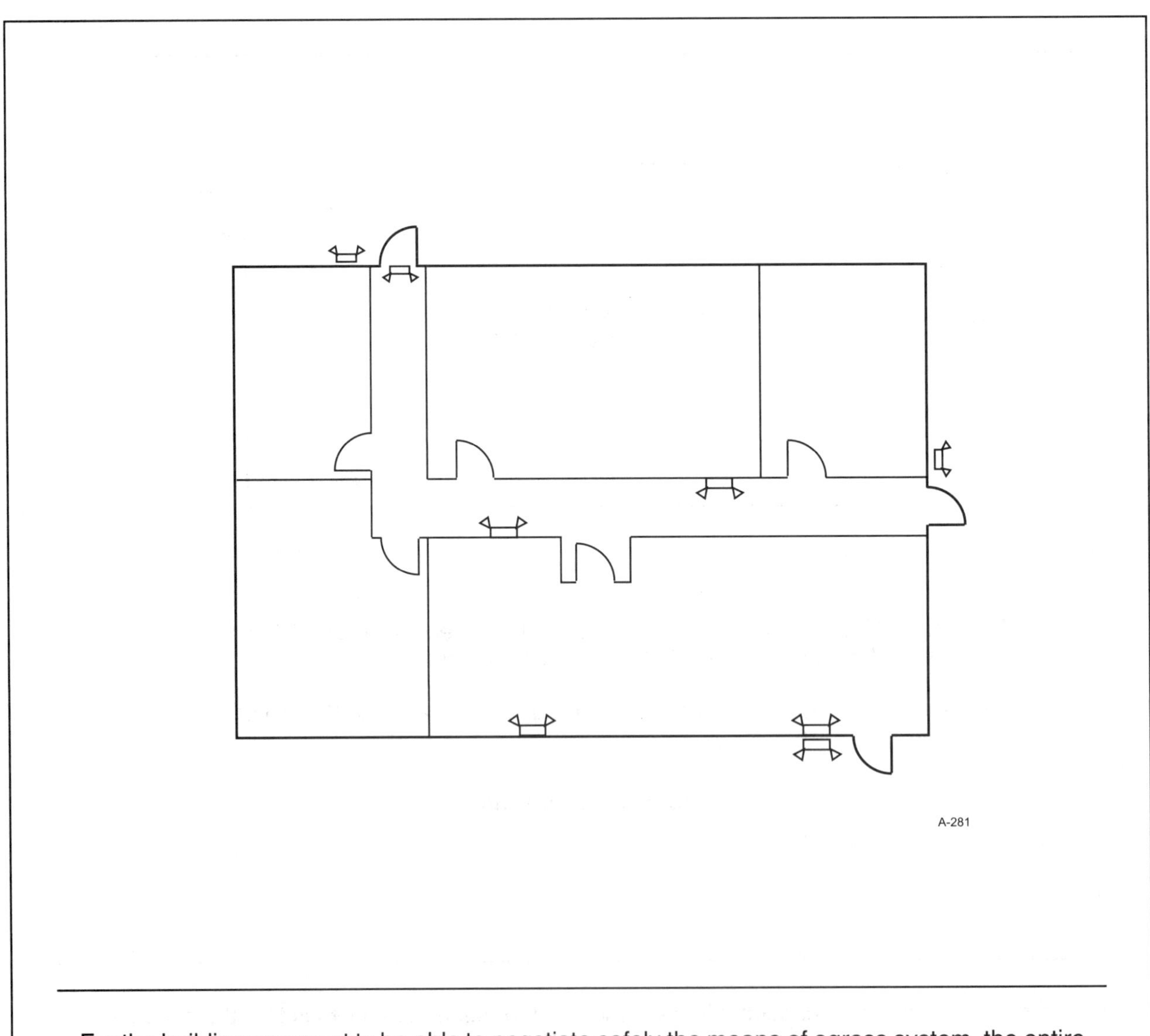

For the building occupant to be able to negotiate safely the means of egress system, the entire system must be illuminated any time the building is occupied. The illumination must provide an intensity of at least one foot-candle at the floor level.

Topic: General
Reference: IBC 1007

Category: Means of Egress
Subject: Accessible Means of Egress

Code Text: *Accessible spaces shall be provided with not less than one accessible means of egress. Where more than one means of egress is required by Sections 1014.1 or 1018.1 from any accessible space, each accessible portion of the space shall be served by not less than two accessible means of egress. See exceptions. Each required accessible means of egress shall be continuous to a public way and shall consist of one or more of the following components: accessible routes, stairways within exit enclosures, elevators, platform lifts, horizontal exits or smoke barriers.* See exceptions for use of exterior areas for assisted rescue.

Discussion and Commentary: An accessible means of egress is *a continuous and unobstructed path of exit travel, usable by a mobility-impaired person, that provides an accessible route from any point to an area of refuge, a horizontal exit or a public way.*

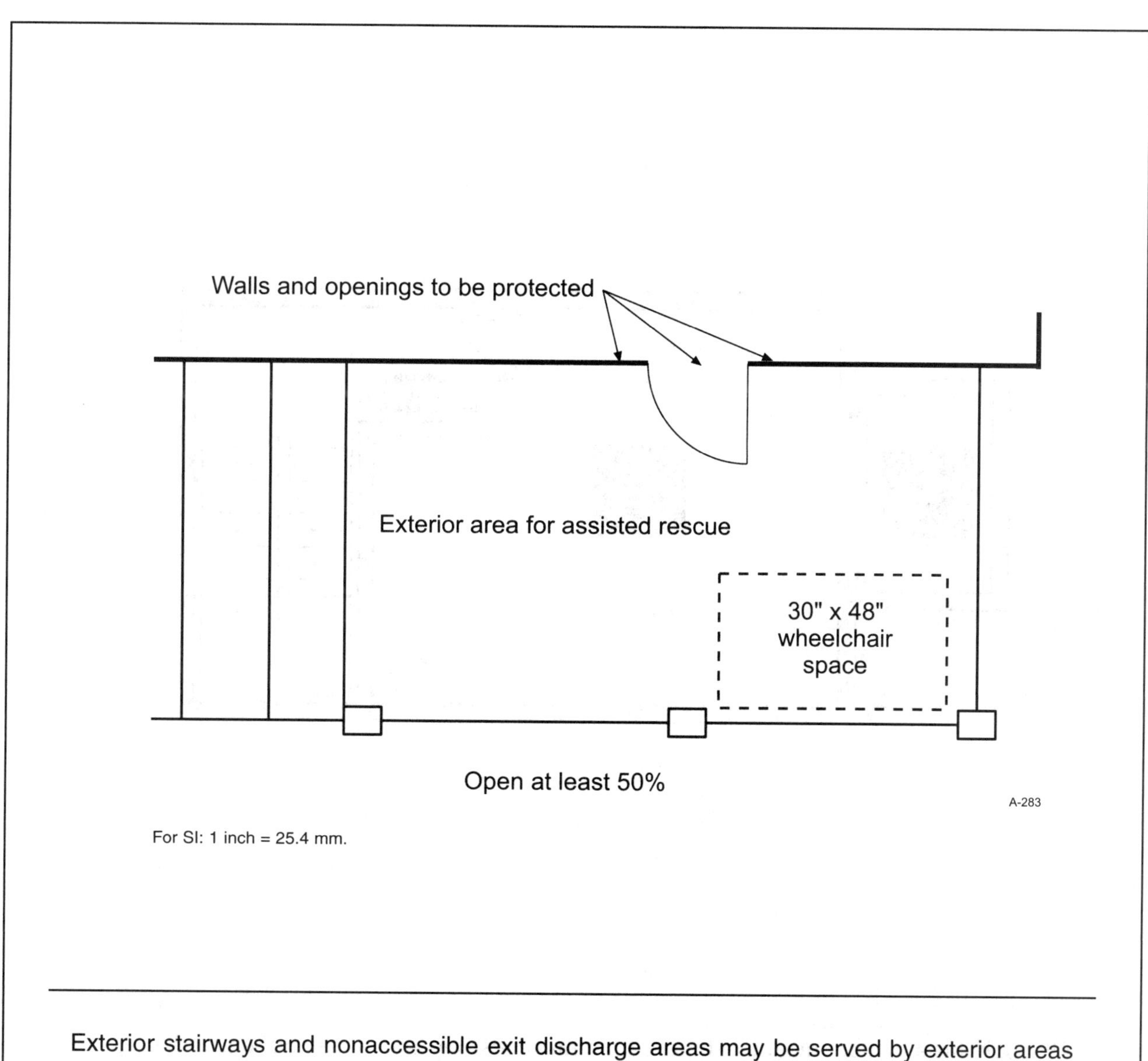

Exterior stairways and nonaccessible exit discharge areas may be served by exterior areas for assisted rescue. These specific exterior refuge areas must be adequately separated from the interior of the building by fire-resistance-rated construction and fire-protected openings.

Topic: Areas of Refuge
Reference: IBC 1007.6

Category: Means of Egress
Subject: Accessible Means of Egress

Code Text: *Every required area of refuge shall be accessible from the space it serves by an accessible means of egress. Every required area of refuge shall have direct access to an enclosed stairway complying with Section 1007.3 and 1019.1 or an elevator complying with Section 1007.4.*

Discussion and Commentary: An area of refuge is defined as *an area where persons unable to use stairways can remain temporarily to await instructions or assistance during emergency evacuation.* Areas of refuge need to be separated from the remainder of the story by smoke barriers unless the building is fully sprinklered or the refuge area is located within a stairway enclosure. A two-way communication system with appropriate instructions must be provided in each area of refuge and must also be identified by complying signs.

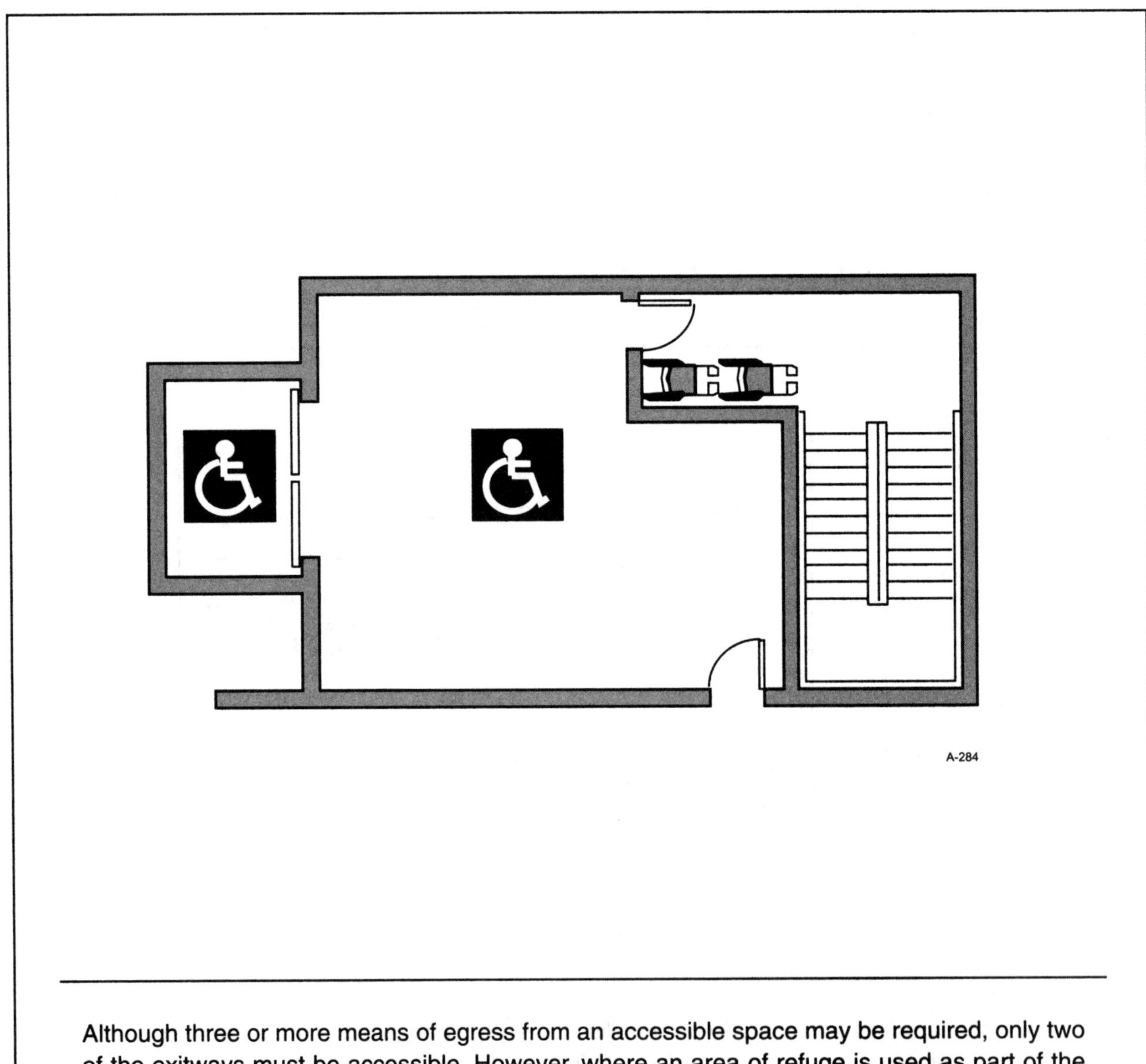

Although three or more means of egress from an accessible space may be required, only two of the exitways must be accessible. However, where an area of refuge is used as part of the egress system, the maximum travel distance set forth in Section 1015.1 must be maintained.

Topic: Where Required
Reference: IBC 1011.1

Category: Means of Egress
Subject: Exit Signs

Code Text: *Exit and exit access doors shall be marked by an approved exit sign readily visible from any direction of egress travel. Access to exits shall be marked by readily visible exit signs in cases where the exit or the path of egress travel is not immediately visible to the occupants.* See exceptions for uses or conditions where exit signs are not required.

Discussion and Commentary: Exit signs are only mandated when the room or area under consideration is required to have multiple exits or exit access doors. Other locations are also specified where the presence of an exit sign is deemed unnecessary, such as clearly identifiable main exterior doors. Although the appropriate locations for exit signs should be identified during the plan review phase of a project, the true evaluation of their effectiveness should be done just prior to occupancy, when the correct location and orientation of the signs can be checked.

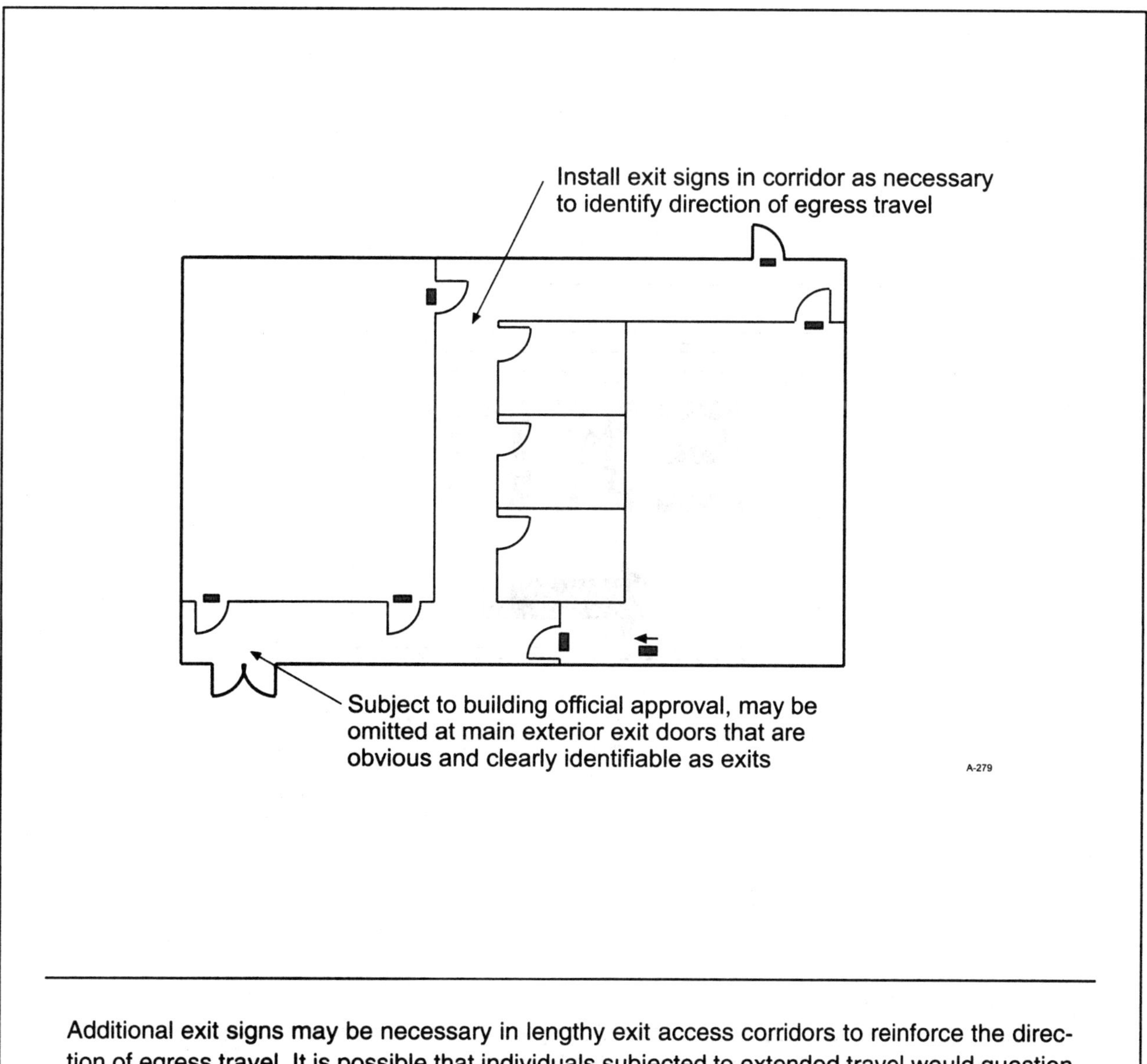

Additional exit signs may be necessary in lengthy exit access corridors to reinforce the direction of egress travel. It is possible that individuals subjected to extended travel would question the availability of an exit and attempt to locate an alternative egress path.

Topic: Illumination and Power Source
Reference: IBC 1011.2, 1011.5.3

Category: Means of Egress
Subject: Exit Signs

Code Text: *Exit signs shall be internally or externally illuminated. To ensure continued illumination for a duration of not less than 90 minutes in case of primary power loss, the sign illumination means shall be connected to an emergency system provided from storage batteries, unit equipment or an on-site generator.*

Discussion and Commentary: To ensure visibility under all conditions, required exit signs must always be illuminated. The building official may approve alternative types of signs or lighting systems to those specified, provided that equivalent light levels can be achieved. A separate source of power shall be provided to all required exit signs, regardless of the occupant load served, much in the same manner as it is required for path of travel illumination.

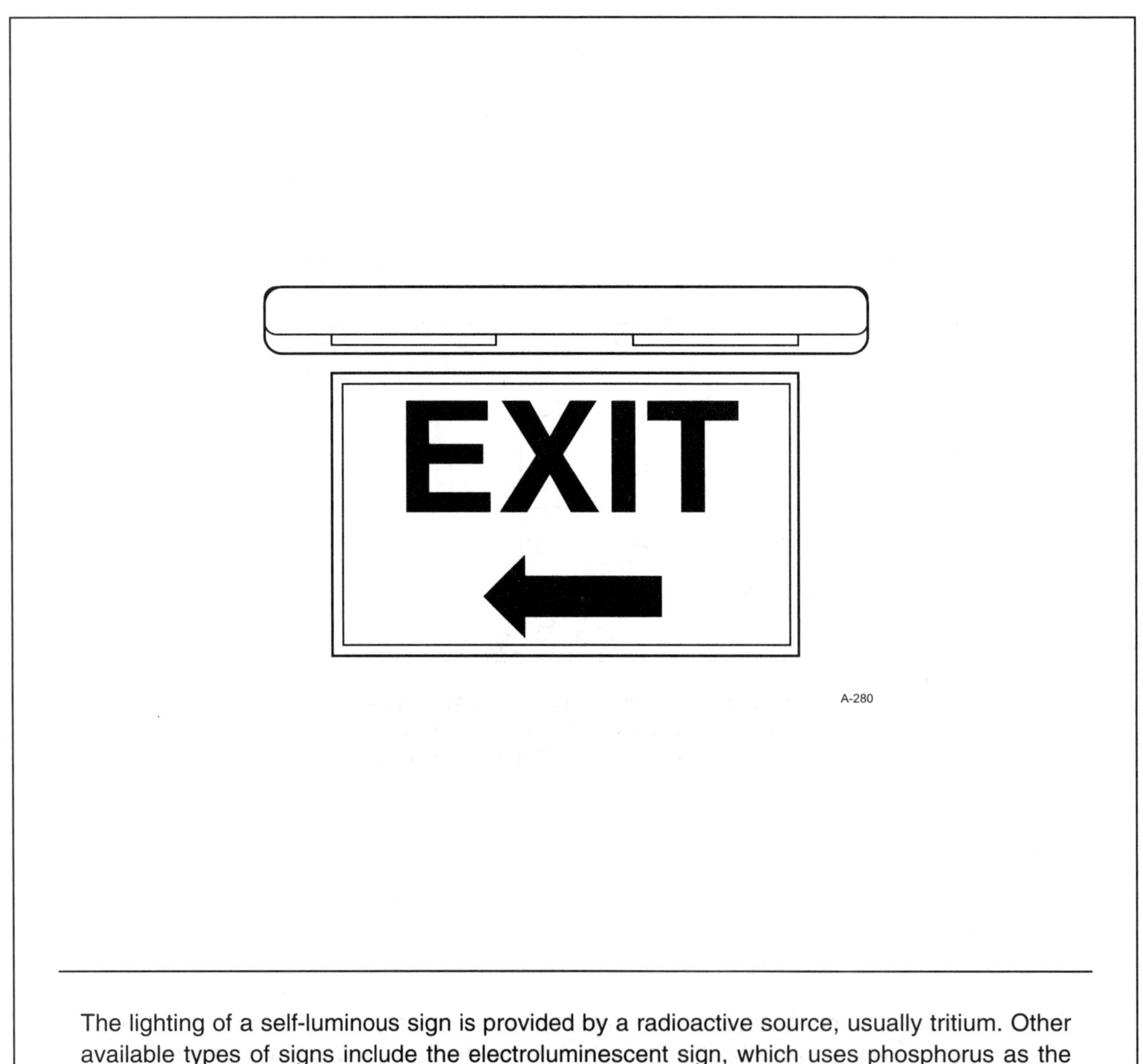

The lighting of a self-luminous sign is provided by a radioactive source, usually tritium. Other available types of signs include the electroluminescent sign, which uses phosphorus as the illuminating element. LED signs are also available as an alternative method.

Topic: Location, Height and Openings
Reference: IBC 1012

Category: Means of Egress
Subject: Guards

Code Text: *Guards shall be located along open-sided walking surfaces, mezzanines, industrial equipment platforms, stairways, ramps and landings that are located more than 30 inches above the floor or grade below. Guards shall form a protective barrier not less than 42 inches high. Open guards shall have balusters or ornamental patterns such that a 4-inch-diameter sphere cannot pass through.* See exceptions.

Discussion and Commentary: Guards must be of adequate height and structural stability to prevent an individual from accidentally falling from the protected area. They must be designed also to prevent small children from intentionally crawling through the barrier. In certain industrial-type areas, the degree of protection is reduced because of the nonpublic uses involved. In addition, guards are not mandated in specific applications relating to loading docks, stages, platforms and vehicle service pits.

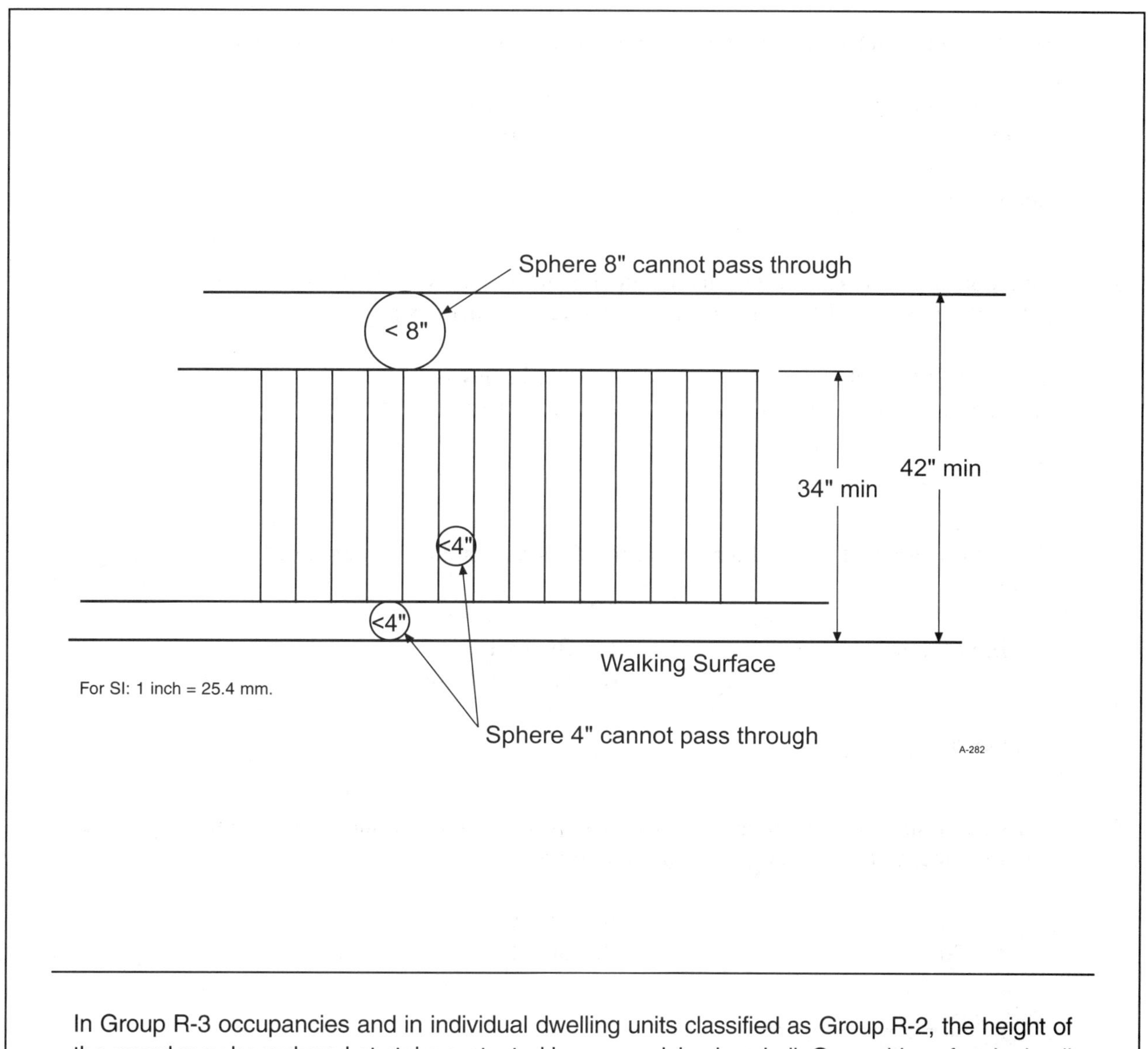

In Group R-3 occupancies and in individual dwelling units classified as Group R-2, the height of the guard may be reduced at stairs protected by a complying handrail. Open sides of stairs in all other occupancies must have minimum 42-inch-high guards in addition to the required handrails.

QUIZ

Study Session 9 — Sections 1001–1007, 1011-1012

I. Multiple Choice

1. A yard that provides access to a public way for one or more exits is considered a(n) __________.

   a. exit accessway
   b. egress court
   c. public way
   d. horizontal exit

   Reference_______________

2. Which of the following elements is not a distinct and separate part of the means of egress?

   a. exit discharge
   b. exit access
   c. exit
   d. exit convergence

   Reference_______________

3. That portion of the exit access that occupants must traverse before two separate and distinct paths of egress travel to two exits are available is defined as a __________.

   a. means of egress
   b. single egress path
   c. common path of egress travel
   d. limited egress travel distance

   Reference_______________

4. Panic hardware that is listed for use on fire door assemblies is considered to be __________ hardware.

   a. fire egress
   b. fire exit
   c. panic
   d. panic and fire

   Reference_______________

5. An alternating tread device has a series of steps that are positioned a minimum of _____ degrees and maximum of _____ degrees from horizontal.

   a. 130, 45
   b. 45, 60
   c. 50, 70
   d. 60, 75

   Reference_______________

6. In a dining room without fixed seating, the occupant load is determined by dividing the floor area by a factor of one occupant per __________ square feet.

a. 7 net
b. 15 net
c. 15 gross
d. 20 net

Reference________________

7. A 1,500-square-foot (net) woodworking shop classroom in a high school is considered to have a design occupant load of __________ persons.

a. 25
b. 30
c. 75
d. 100

Reference________________

8. For areas having fixed seats and aisles, the occupant load for bench seating without armrests is based on one occupant for each __________ inches of seating length.

a. 15
b. 18
c. 24
d. 30

Reference________________

9. In a fully-sprinklered Group B office building having an occupant load of 3,200 occupants, the minimum total calculated means of egress width by egress other than stairways shall be __________ inches.

a. 960
b. 640
c. 480
d. 320

Reference________________

10. A stairway serving 400 occupants in a fully-sprinklered Group I-2 hospital shall be a minimum of __________ inches in width.

a. 60
b. 80
c. 120
d. 160

Reference________________

11. Multiple means of egress shall be sized so that the loss of any one means of egress shall not reduce the available capacity by a maximum of __________ of the required capacity.

a. 10 percent
b. 25 percent
c. $33^1/_3$ percent
d. 50 percent

Reference________________

12. When fully open, a door is permitted to project into the required width of the path of egress travel a maximum of __________.

a. one-half the required width
b. one-half the actual width
c. $3^1/_2$ inches
d. 7 inches

Reference______________

13. Up to 50 percent of the ceiling area of a means of egress may have a minimum ceiling height of __________ where reduced by protruding objects.

a. 78 inches
b. 80 inches
c. 84 inches
d. 90 inches

Reference______________

14. At a doorway, the minimum headroom clearance below any door closer or stop shall be __________ inches.

a. 76
b. 78
c. 80
d. 84

Reference______________

15. Other than handrails serving stairs and ramps, the maximum projection into the travel path of a horizontal projection located 48 inches above the walking surface shall be __________ inches.

a. $1^1/_2$
b. $3^1/_2$
c. 4
d. $4^1/_2$

Reference______________

16. At an exterior door not required to be accessible in a Group F-1 occupancy, what is the maximum permitted elevation change?

a. $^1/_2$ inch
b. 1 inch
c. 7 inches
d. 8 inches

Reference______________

17. Exit signs shall be located so that the maximum distance from any point in an exit access corridor to the nearest visible exit sign is __________ feet, or the listed viewing distance for the sign, whichever is less.

a. 50 b. 75
c. 100 d. 150

Reference_______________

18. Externally-illuminated exit signs shall have a minimum intensity at the face of the sign of __________ foot-candles.

a. 1 b. 5
c. 10 d. 12

Reference_______________

19. Emergency lighting facilities for means of egress illumination shall provide __________ along the path of egress at floor level.

a. at least 1 foot-candle b. an average of 1 foot-candle
c. at least 5 foot-candles d. an average of 0.2 foot-candle

Reference_______________

20. A guard need not be located along an open-sided walking surface located a maximum of __________ inches above the floor below.

a. 15 b. 30
c. 36 d. 42

Reference_______________

21. In a mercantile occupancy, a required guard shall form a protective barrier a minimum of __________ inches in height.

a. 36 b. 38
c. 42 d. 44

Reference_______________

22. In areas of a Group S-1 occupancy not open to the public, horizontal intermediate rails in a required guard shall be constructed so that a minimum __________ sphere cannot pass through any opening.

a. 4-inch
b. 6-inch
c. 12-inch
d. 21-inch

Reference_______________

23. Where a roof-top HVAC unit requiring occasional service and maintenance is located a maximum of __________ from the roof edge, a complying guard shall be provided.

a. 10 feet
b. 5 feet
c. 3 feet
d. 30 inches

Reference_______________

24. In a nonsprinklered building, an enclosed stairway utilized as an accessible means of egress shall be a minimum of __________ inches in clear width between handrails.

a. 36
b. 44
c. 48
d. 60

Reference_______________

25. An area of refuge serving 450 occupants shall be provided with a minimum of __________ wheelchair space(s).

a. 1
b. 2
c. 3
d. 5

Reference_______________

26. Where a barrier is installed below a protruding object having a vertical clearance of less than 80 inches, the maximum height of the barrier shall be _____.

a. 27
b. 30
c. 36
d. 42

Reference_______________

27. In all cases, the occupant load in a room or building shall not be increased beyond a maximum of one occupant per _____ square feet.

a. 3
b. 5
c. 6
d. 7

Reference_______________

28. The means of egress in which of the following areas is required to be illuminated when the space is occupied?

a. aisle accessways in Group A
b. sleeping units in Group I
c. dwelling units in Group R-2
d. aisles in Groups F and S

Reference_______________

29. The exterior wall adjacent to an exterior area for assisted rescue does not require a fire-resistance rating where the area is located a minimum of _____ feet horizontally from the wall.

a. 5
b. 10
c. 15
d. 20

Reference_______________

30. A tactile sign stating EXIT shall be provided adjacent to the door of all of the following means of egress components, except for _____.

a. an egress stairway
b. the exit discharge
c. a horizontal exit
d. an exit passageway

Reference_______________

INTERNATIONAL BUILDING CODE
Study Session 10
Sections 1008–1010 — Means of Egress II

OBJECTIVE: To obtain an understanding of the general component requirements of a means of egress system, including those regulating doors, gates, stairways, ramps and turnstiles located along the egress path.

REFERENCE: Sections 1008–1010, 2003 *International Building Code*

KEY POINTS:

- What is the minimum height and width of an egress door?
- What are the limitations on projections into the required clear door width?
- When must doors swing in the direction of egress travel?
- What is the maximum opening force permitted for an interior side-swinging door without a closer? Other side-swinging doors? Sliding and folding doors?
- What are "special" doors? How are they regulated differently than other doors?
- At a door, what change in elevation is permitted for a landing or floor surface?
- How must landings at doors be sized? What is the maximum allowable amount that doors may encroach into the required landing size?
- What is the maximum height of a threshold at a doorway?
- Which types of locks and latches are required on egress doors?
- When is the unlatching of an egress door permitted to take more than a single operation?
- Why do turnstiles create special egress concerns? What are the limitations on their use?
- When is panic hardware required?
- How are gates regulated differently than doors?
- How is the minimum required width of a stairway determined?
- At a stairway and its landings, what is the minimum headroom clearance?
- What is the minimum rise of a stair riser? Maximum rise? Minimum tread run?
- What degree of tolerance is permitted between the largest and the smallest tread run within a flight of stairs? Between the greatest and the smallest riser height?
- How are stairway landings regulated for size?
- What is the maximum vertical rise permitted between stairway landings?
- Which special limitations apply to winding, circular or spiral stairways? Alternate tread devices?
- What must be the minimum height of a handrail located above the nosing of stairway treads and landings? Maximum height?
- Under which conditions are intermediate handrails required?
- What are the exceptions to the general provision that handrails be continuous and without interruption?
- To what extent must handrails extend beyond the top and bottom risers of a stair flight?
- How much clear space is needed between a handrail and a wall or other surface?
- When is a stairway required to provide access to a roof?
- What is the maximum permissible ramp slope? The maximum permissible rise for a ramp?
- How are ramp landings regulated for width? Length? Construction? Edge protection?
- When are handrails required for ramps?

Topic: Additional Doors and Identification
Reference: IBC 1008.1

Category: Means of Egress
Subject: Doors, Gates and Turnstiles

Code Text: *Doors provided for egress purposes in numbers greater than required by the IBC shall meet the requirements of Section 1008. Means of egress doors shall be readily distinguishable from the adjacent construction and finishes such that the doors are easily recognizable as means of egress doors. Mirrors or similar reflecting materials shall not be used on means of egress doors. Means of egress doors shall not be concealed by curtains, drapes, decorations or similar materials.*

Discussion and Commentary: During a fire or other incident, occupants will attempt to exit through those doors that they believe will eventually lead to the exterior. Accordingly, any doors that would suggest an egress path must meet all of the door requirements. In addition, means of egress doors must be obvious and available for immediate use by the building occupants.

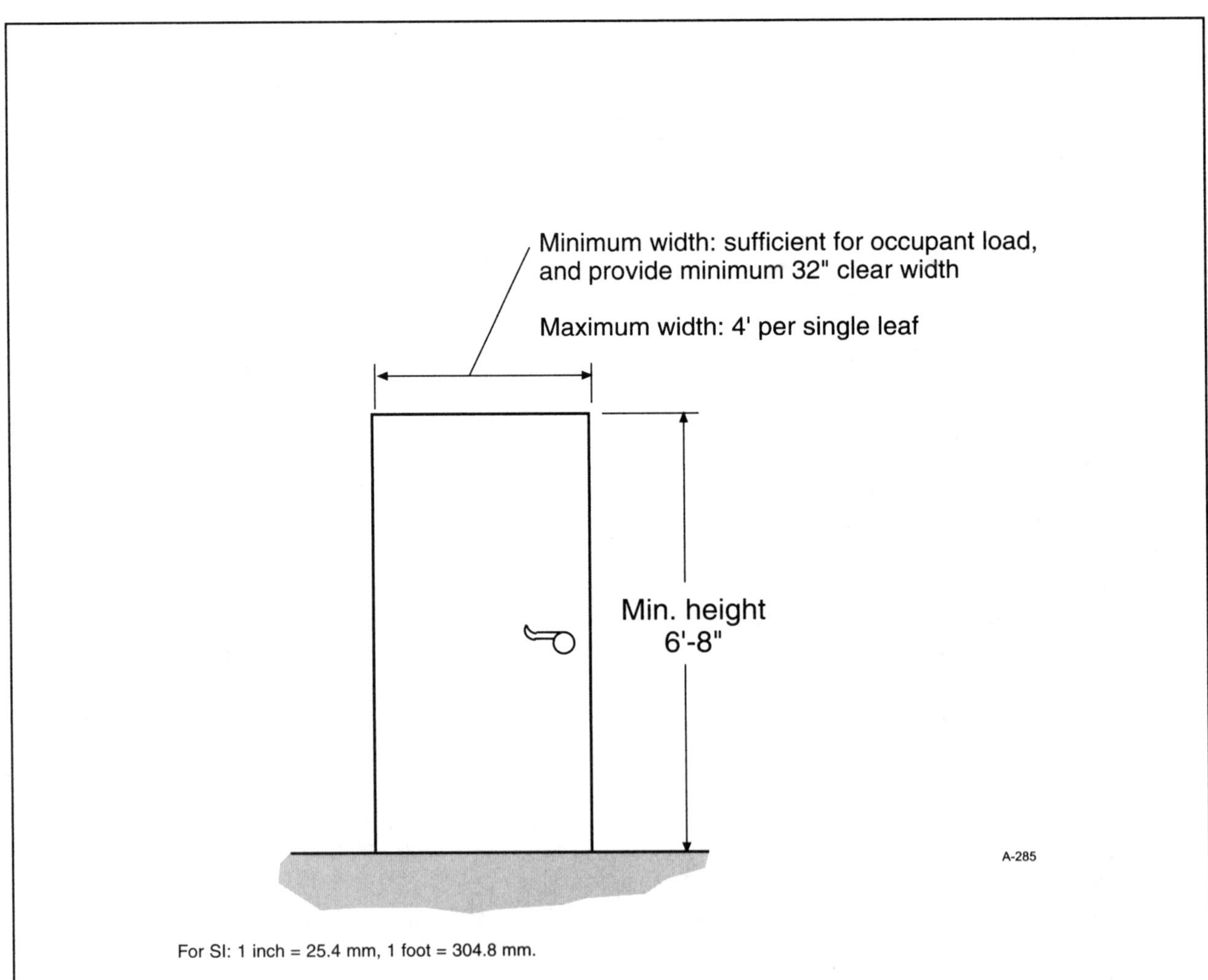

In accordance with Section 1017.2, any building or structure used for human occupancy must have at least one exterior door opening that complies with the minimum width (32 inches) and height (80 inches) requirements of Section 1008.1.1.

Topic: Sizes of Doors
Reference: IBC 1008.1.1

Category: Means of Egress
Subject: Doors, Gates and Turnstiles

Code Text: *The minimum width of each door opening shall be sufficient for the occupant load thereof and shall provide a clear width of not less than 32 inches. Clear openings of doorways with swinging doors shall be measured between the face of the door and the stop, with the door open 90 degrees. The height of doors shall not be less than 80 inches.* See exceptions for both width and height.

Discussion and Commentary: A clear width of 32 inches is required only to a height of 34 inches above the floor or ground. Beyond this point, projections up to 4 inches into the required width are permitted. Although a single doorway is expected to be used for the egress of one individual at a time, it must also be adequate for wheelchair users.

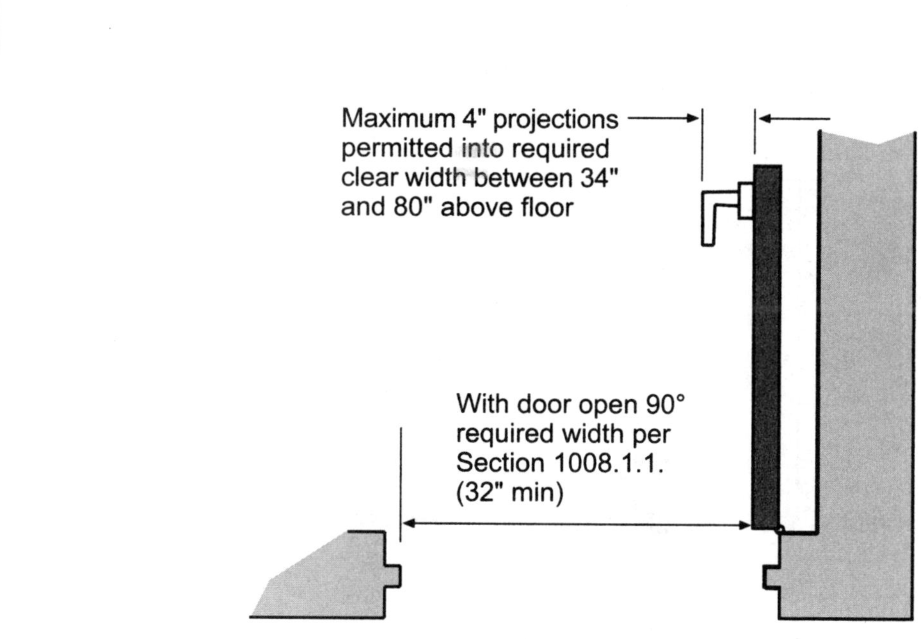

Egress width at doors is net dimension

For SI: 1 degree = 0.745 rad, 1 inch = 25.4 mm.

The maximum width of a door leaf is regulated by the code at 48 inches, mostly because of the greater opening force required and the lack of maintenance necessary to assure reasonable opening effort.

Topic: Door Swing
Reference: IBC 1008.1.2

Category: Means of Egress
Subject: Doors, Gates and Turnstiles

Code Text: *Egress doors shall be side-hinged swinging.* See exceptions. *Doors shall swing in the direction of egress travel where serving an occupant load of 50 or more persons or a Group H occupancy.*

Discussion and Commentary: Numerous fire deaths in buildings have been attributed to improper exit doors, but no single incident is more infamous than the 1942 Coconut Grove fire in Boston. Inward-swinging exterior exit doors were a significant factor in the loss of 492 lives. As a result, doors serving sizable occupant loads or Group H occupancies must swing in the direction of exit flow. For assembly and educational occupancies, the use of panic hardware increases the likelihood that egress doors can be opened easily.

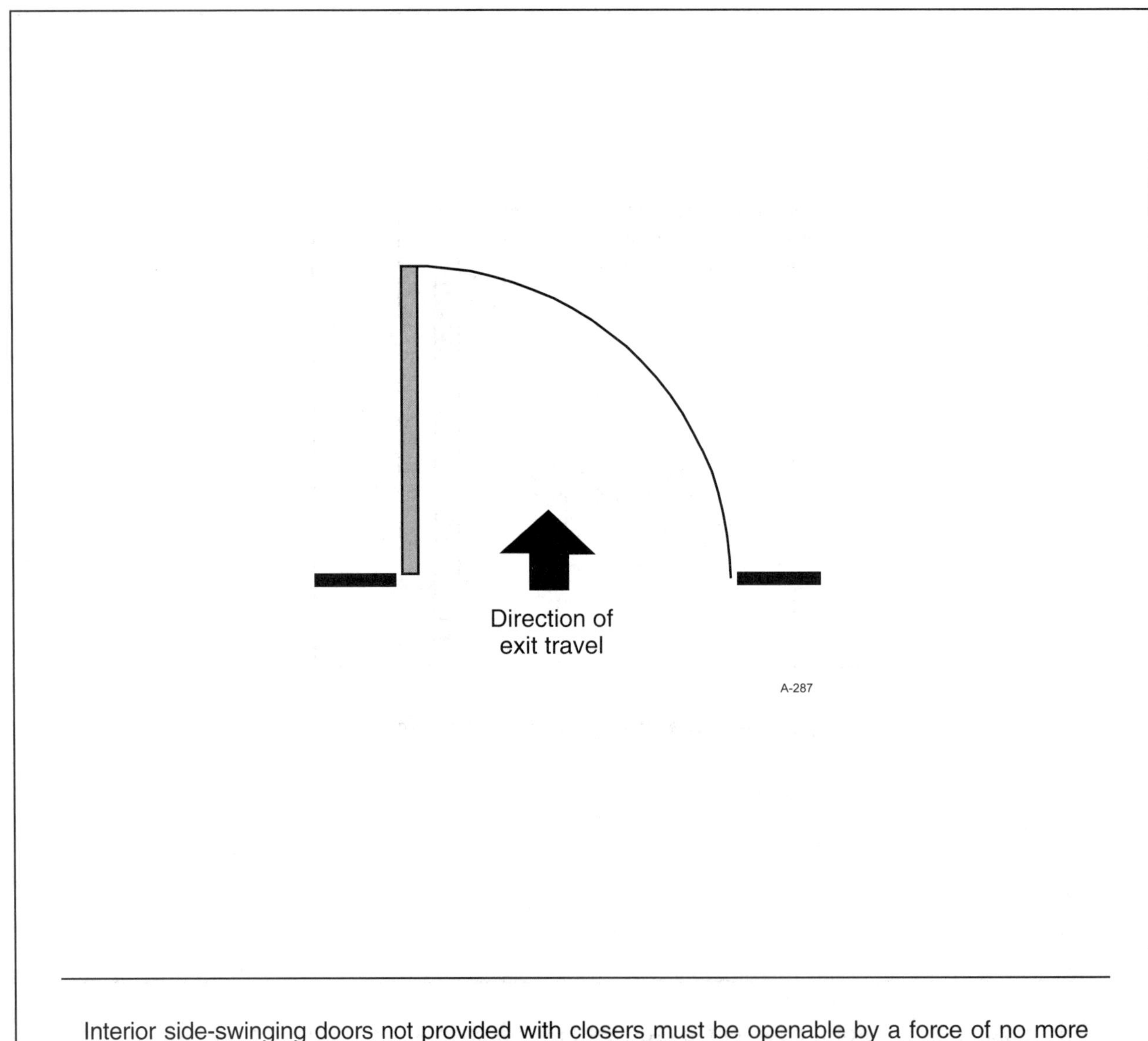

Interior side-swinging doors not provided with closers must be openable by a force of no more than 5 pounds. Where a closer is installed, such as for fire doors or exterior doors, the opening force limitation is increased to ensure that the device can bring the door to a fully closed position.

Topic: Special Doors
Reference: IBC 1008.1.3

Category: Means of Egress
Subject: Doors, Gates and Turnstiles

Code Text: *Special doors and security grilles shall comply with the requirements of Sections 1008.1.3.1 through 1008.1.3.5.*

Discussion and Commentary: In general, doors in means of egress systems must be of the pivoted or side-hinged swinging type. Other doors, identified as special doors, are also addressed in the code. Such doors include revolving doors, power-operated doors, horizontal sliding doors, access-controlled egress doors and security grilles. These types of doors are specifically limited in their use because the difficult or unusual operation of such doors increases the likelihood of obstructed travel in an emergency.

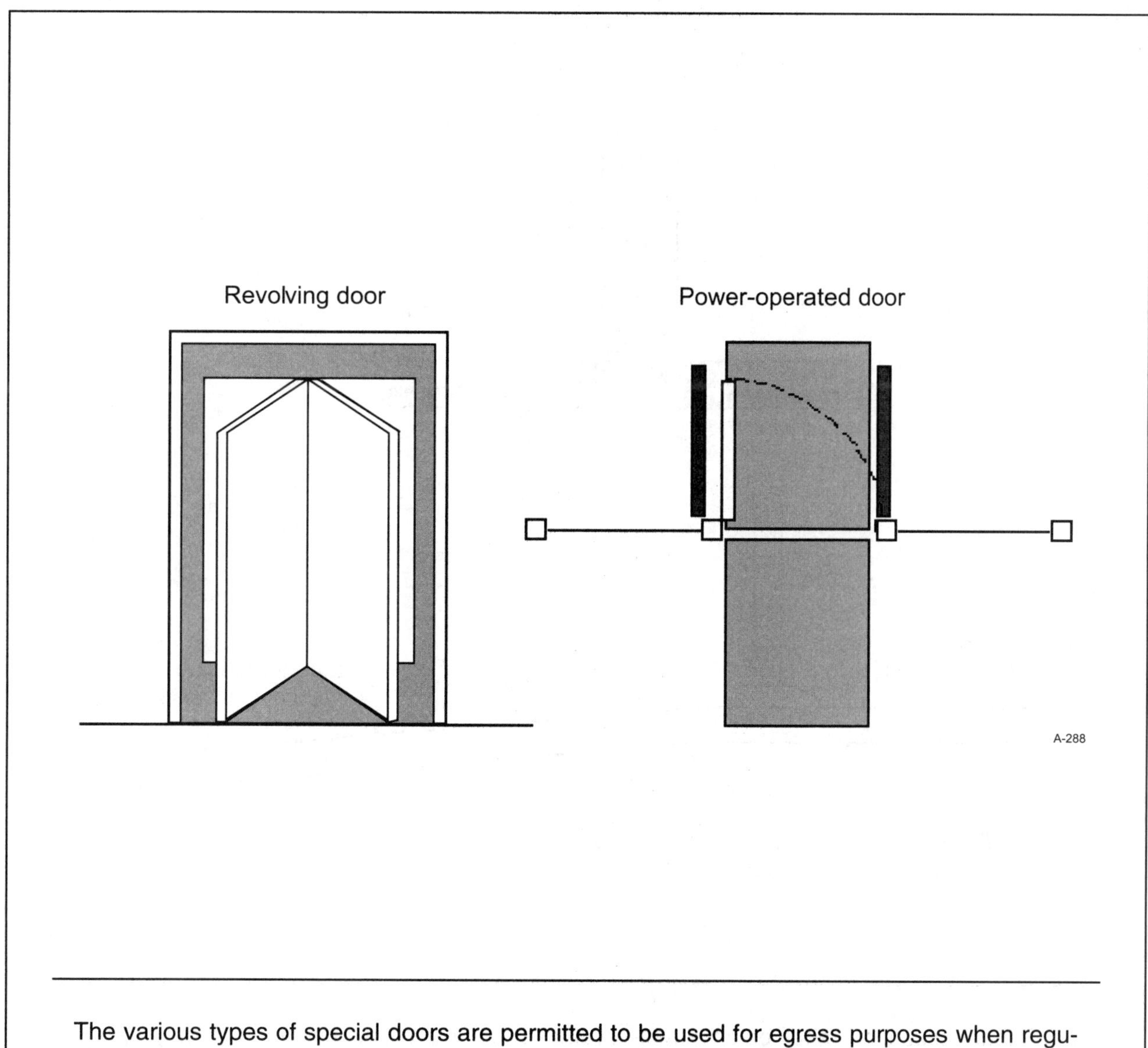

The various types of special doors are permitted to be used for egress purposes when regulated by occupancy, occupant load, operation, opening force, power supply or other factors that contribute to the effectiveness and reliability of the egress door.

Topic: Floor Elevation
Reference: IBC 1008.1.4

Category: Means of Egress
Subject: Doors, Gates and Turnstiles

Code Text: *There shall be a floor or landing on each side of a door. Such floor or landing shall be at the same elevation on each side of the door.* See exceptions.

Discussion and Commentary: To avoid a surprise change in the elevation of a walking surface as it passes through a doorway, limitations have been placed on the height differential. The IBC generally requires that no elevation change occur at a door. In many cases, however, such a change in elevation takes place due to a variation in the type or thickness of floor finish materials. Where this occurs, a difference of no more than $^1/_2$ inch is permitted. Otherwise, only those exceptions that apply to certain dwelling units or to exterior doors not on an accessible route may have an elevation change at a doorway.

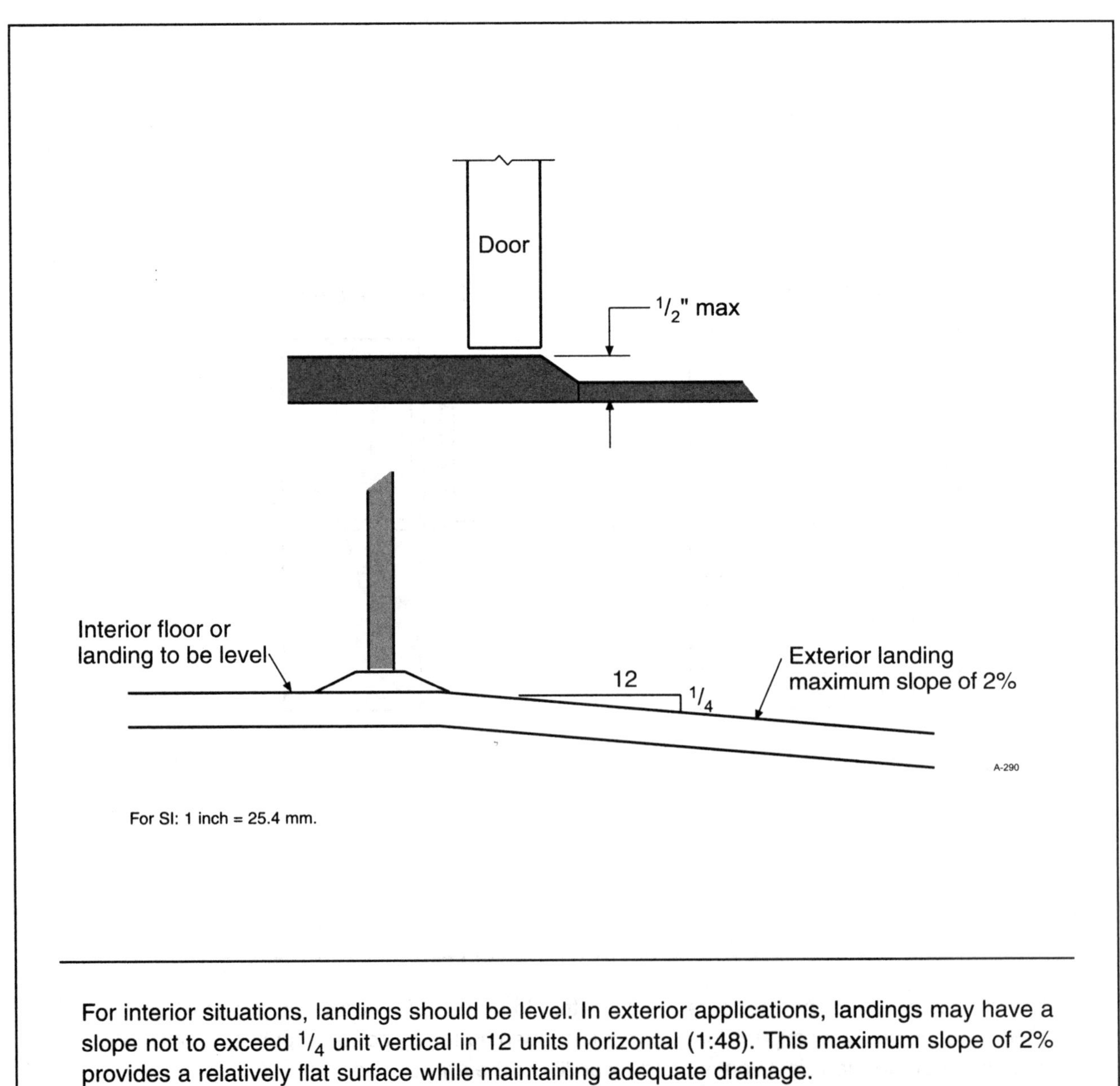

For interior situations, landings should be level. In exterior applications, landings may have a slope not to exceed $^1/_4$ unit vertical in 12 units horizontal (1:48). This maximum slope of 2% provides a relatively flat surface while maintaining adequate drainage.

Topic: Landings at Doors
Reference: IBC 1008.1.5

Category: Means of Egress
Subject: Doors, Gates and Turnstiles

Code Text: *Landings shall have a width not less than the width of the stairway or the door, whichever is the greater. Doors in the fully open position shall not reduce a required dimension by more than 7 inches. When a landing serves an occupant load of 50 or more, doors in any position shall not reduce the landing to less than one-half its required width.*

Discussion and Commentary: This provision, which allows a door to project into the path of exit travel on a stairway's landing, comprises two issues. The first issue is that a door is not a fixed obstruction; it swings across the landing when it is used by occupants of the building. The second issue is that a door in any position is allowed to obstruct only one half of the required width of the landing. The expectation is that the additional width of the landing will be provided for the occupants using the stairway as the door swings toward its fully open or fully closed position.

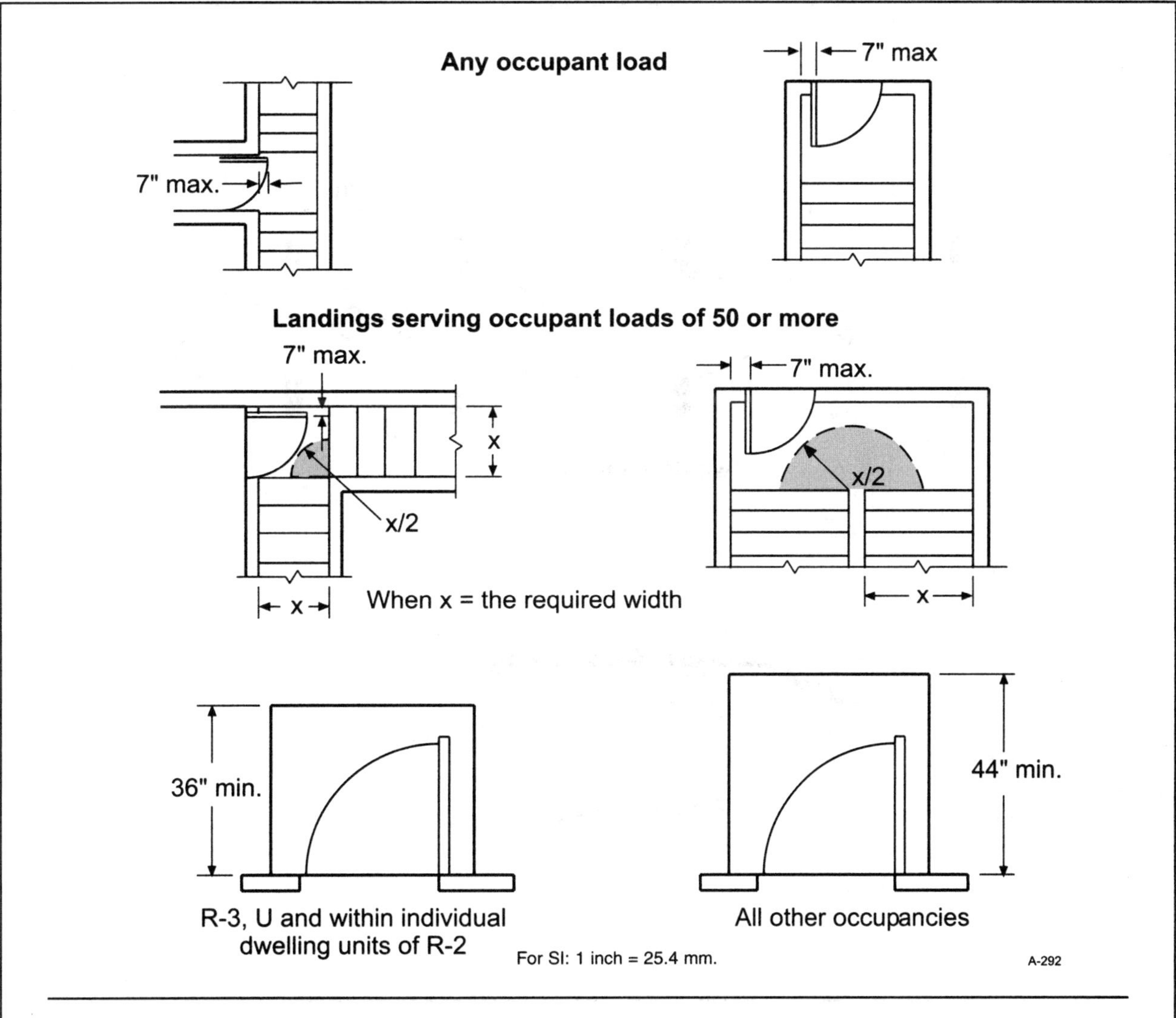

In Group R-3 and U occupancies, and within individual units of Group R-2 occupancies, the length of a landing can be no less than 36 inches. In all other occupancy groups, the minimum landing length is 44 inches, measured in the direction of travel.

Topic: Door Arrangement
Reference: IBC 1008.1.7

Category: Means of Egress
Subject: Doors, Gates and Turnstiles

Code Text: *Space between two doors in series shall be 48 inches minimum plus the width of a door swinging into the space. Doors in series shall swing either in the same direction or away from the space between doors.* See exceptions for dwelling units and horizontal sliding power-operated doors.

Discussion and Commentary: Where two doors are installed in a manner to create a vestibule or similar space, they must be located so to allow building occupants effective and efficient movement through one door prior to continuing through the second door. This is especially true where the person opening the door has limited mobility and is required to make special effort in opening the door and passing through the doorway. The IBC recognizes these concerns by mandating an adequate spatial separation between doors provided in a series.

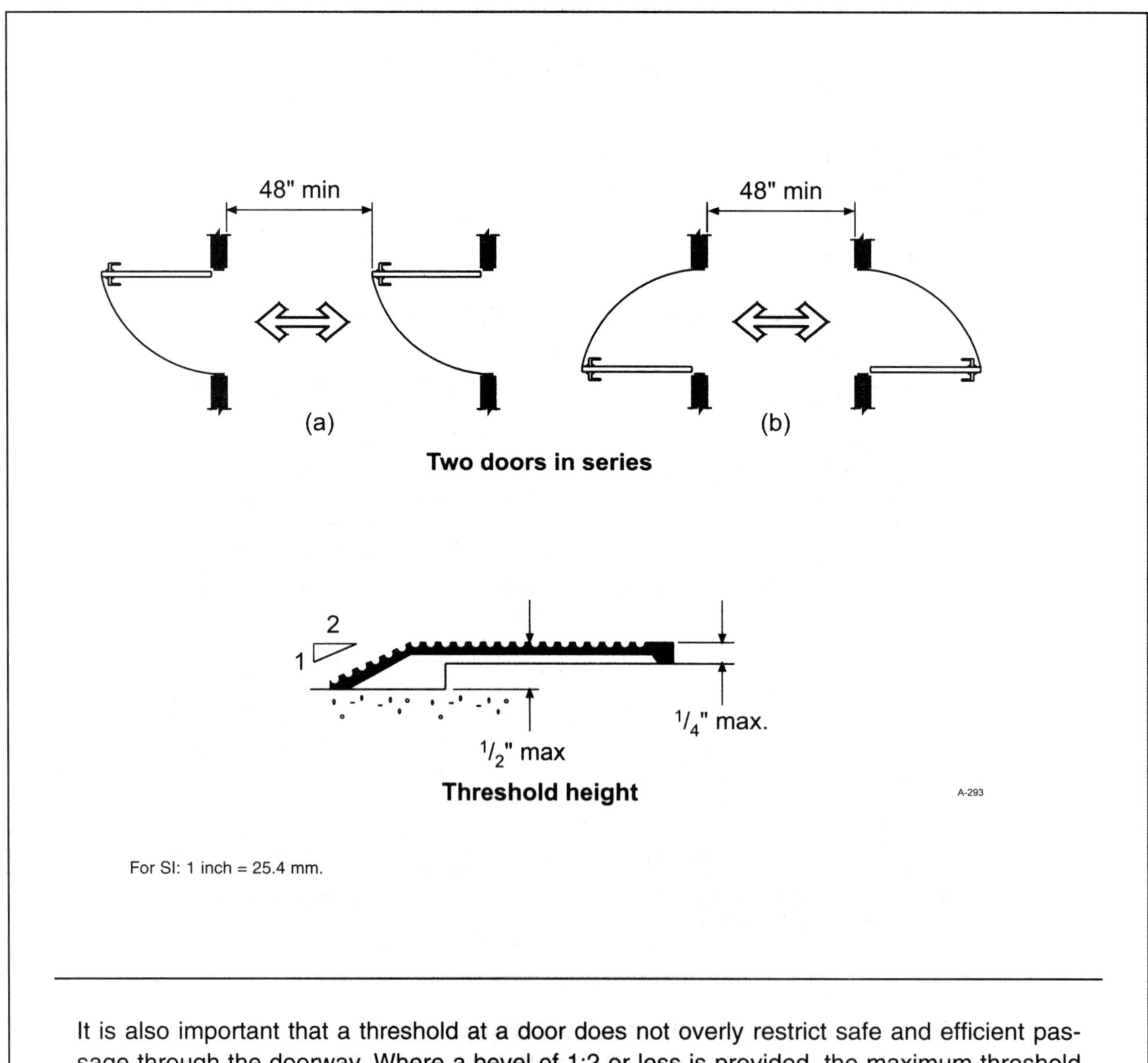

It is also important that a threshold at a door does not overly restrict safe and efficient passage through the doorway. Where a bevel of 1:2 or less is provided, the maximum threshold height is $^1/_2$ inch. Otherwise, an abrupt change in elevation is limited to $^1/_4$ inch.

Topic: Operations
Reference: IBC 1008.1.8

Category: Means of Egress
Subject: Doors, Gates and Turnstiles

Code Text: *Except as specifically permitted by* Section 1008.1.8, *egress doors shall be readily openable from the egress side without the use of a key or special knowledge or effort. Door handles, pulls, latches, locks and other operating devices shall be installed 34 inches (864 mm) minimum and 48 inches (1219 mm) maximum above the finished floor. Locks and latches shall be permitted to prevent operation of doors where* any of four conditions exists. *Manually operated flush bolts or surface bolts are not permitted.* See two exceptions. *The unlatching of any leaf shall not require more than one operation.* See exception identifying four locations that allow for multiple operations.

Discussion and Commentary: Every element along the path of exit travel through a means of egress system, particularly doors, must be under the control of, and operable by, the person seeking egress. The intent is that the hardware installed be of a type familiar to most users, readily recognizable and usable under any emergency conditions.

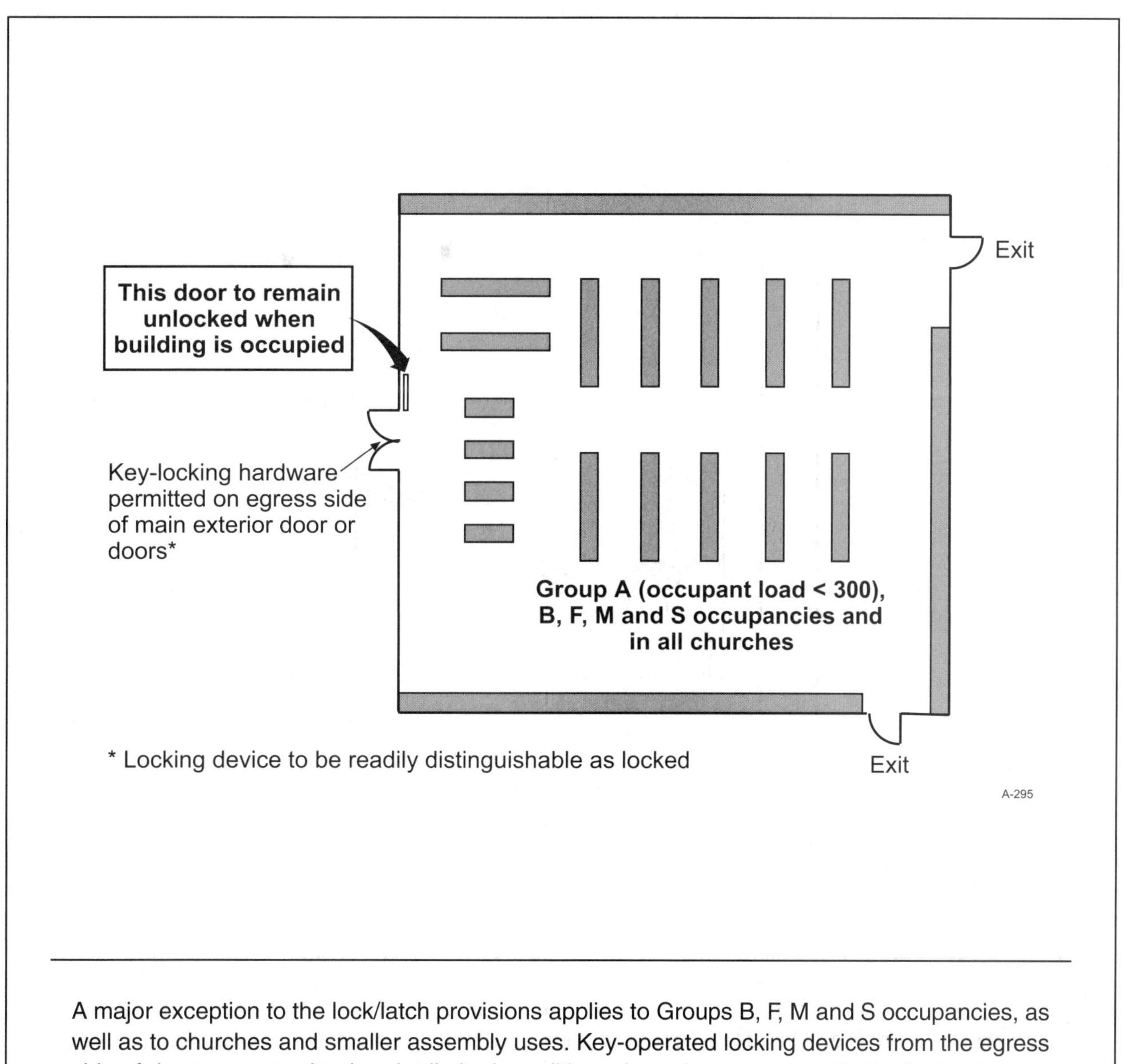

A major exception to the lock/latch provisions applies to Groups B, F, M and S occupancies, as well as to churches and smaller assembly uses. Key-operated locking devices from the egress side of doors are permitted under limited conditions, based on compensating safeguards.

Topic: Panic and Fire Exit Hardware
Reference: IBC 1008.1.9

Category: Means of Egress
Subject: Doors, Ramps and Turnstiles

Code Text: *Each door in a means of egress from an occupancy of Group A or E having an occupant load of 100 or more and any occupancy of Group H-1, H-2, H-3 or H-5 shall not be provided with a latch or lock unless it is panic hardware or fire exit hardware.*

Discussion and Commentary: Panic hardware is a door-latching assembly incorporating a device that releases the latch when force is applied in the direction of exit travel. It is utilized in assembly occupancies because of the hazard that occurs when a large number of occupants reach an exit door at the same instance. In educational occupancies, the same concern is present, along with the need for children to be able to operate the latch of an exit door easily during an emergency. Fire exit hardware is merely panic hardware listed for use on a fire door assembly.

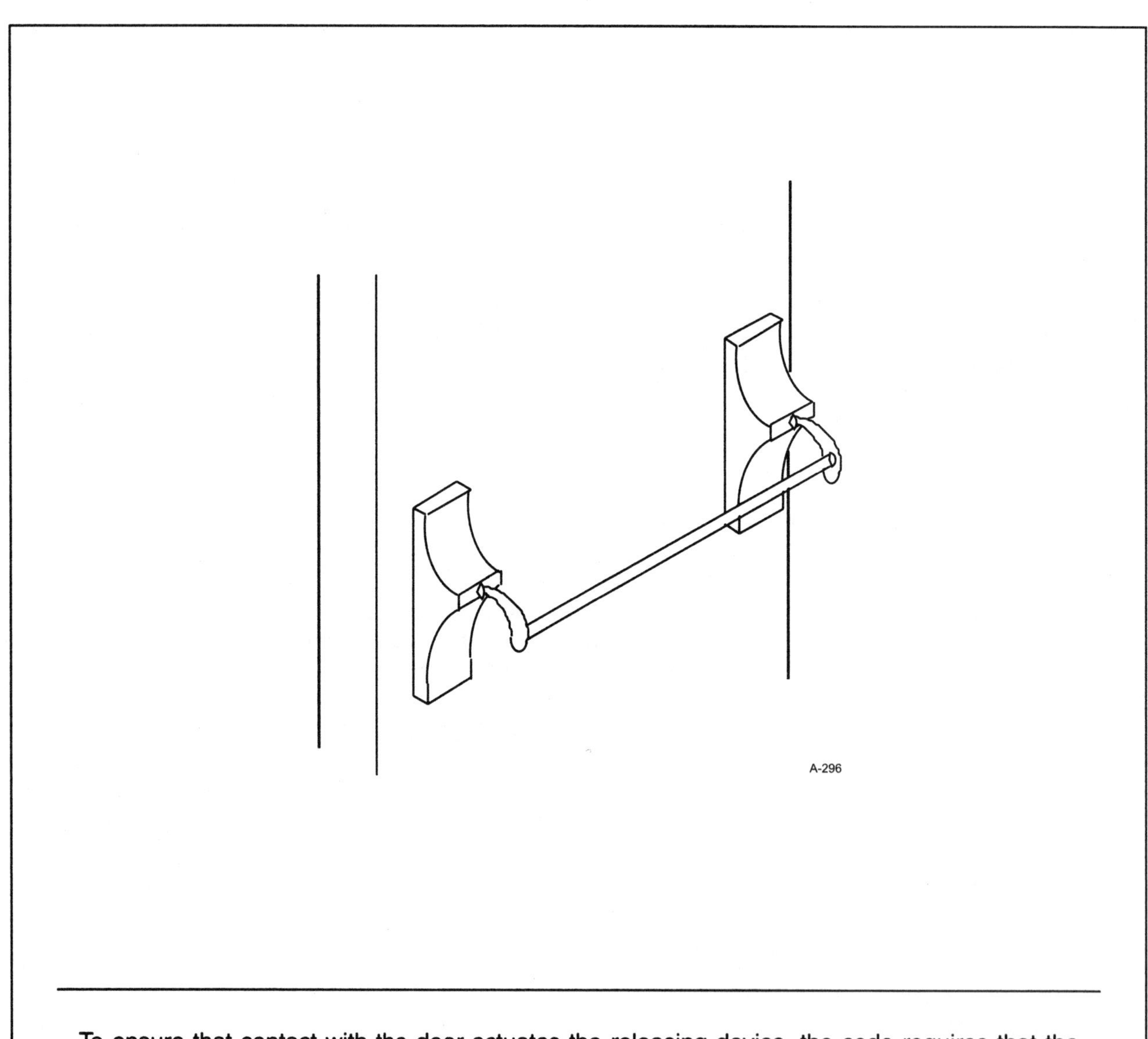

To ensure that contact with the door actuates the releasing device, the code requires that the actuating portion extend for at least one half of the door width. Where balanced or pivoted doors are used, the device width is again limited to one half of the door width for leverage purposes.

Topic: Stairway Width
Reference: IBC 1009.1, 1009.11.7

Category: Means of Egress
Subject: Stairways and Handrails

Code Text: *The width of stairways shall be determined as specified in Section 1005.1* (calculated based on occupant load) *but such width shall not be less than 44 inches.* See exceptions for small occupant loads, spiral stairways, aisle stairs, and where a stairway lift is installed. *Projections into the required width at each handrail shall not exceed 4.5 inches at or below the handrail height. Projections into the required width shall not be limited above the minimum headroom height required in Section 1009.2.*

Discussion and Commentary: A stairway is considered one or more flights of stairs, each made up of one or more risers and any connecting landings. Any change of elevation along a travel path, unless accomplished by a ramp, must include a stair or stairway. Although stairways are generally required to be at least 44 inches in width, a 36-inch-wide stairway is permitted where serving an occupant load of 50 or less.

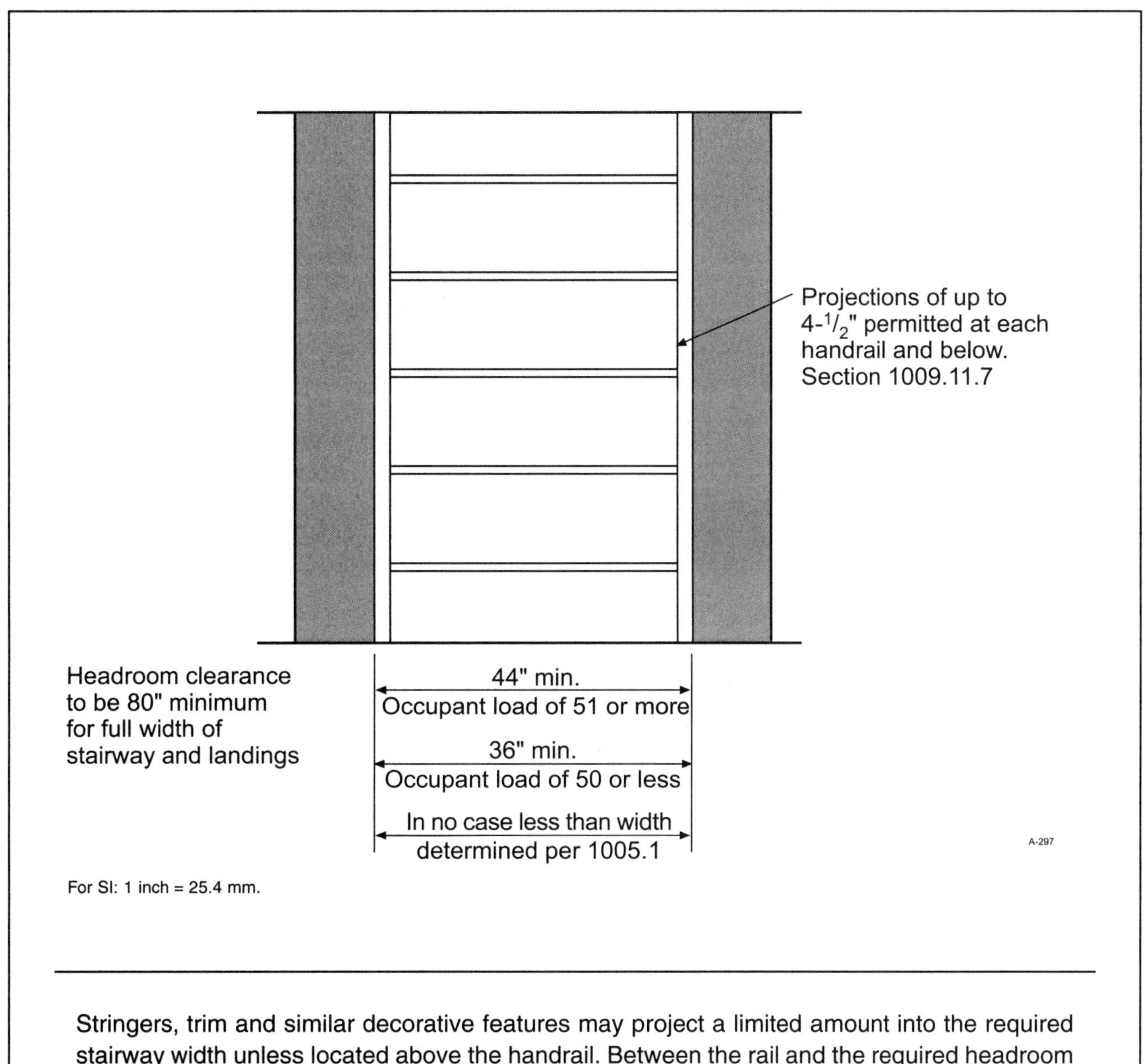

Stringers, trim and similar decorative features may project a limited amount into the required stairway width unless located above the handrail. Between the rail and the required headroom height of 80 inches, no projection is permitted.

Topic: Stair Treads and Risers
Reference: IBC 1009.3

Category: Means of Egress
Subject: Stairways and Handrails

Code Text: *Stair riser heights shall be 7 inches maximum and 4 inches minimum. Stair tread depths shall be 11 inches minimum.* See exceptions, including the allowance for greater riser heights (7.75 inches) and shallower tread depths (10 inches) in Group R-3 and associated Group U occupancies, and within individual dwelling units of Group R-2.

Discussion and Commentary: The stairway 7-11 rule is the result of much research and discussion on stairway design. In addition to the proportional criteria that has been developed, the uniformity of the treads and risers in a flight of stairs is critical. The maximum variation between the highest and lowest risers and between the shallowest and deepest treads is limited to $^3/_8$ inch within any flight, which is intended as a permissible construction tolerance.

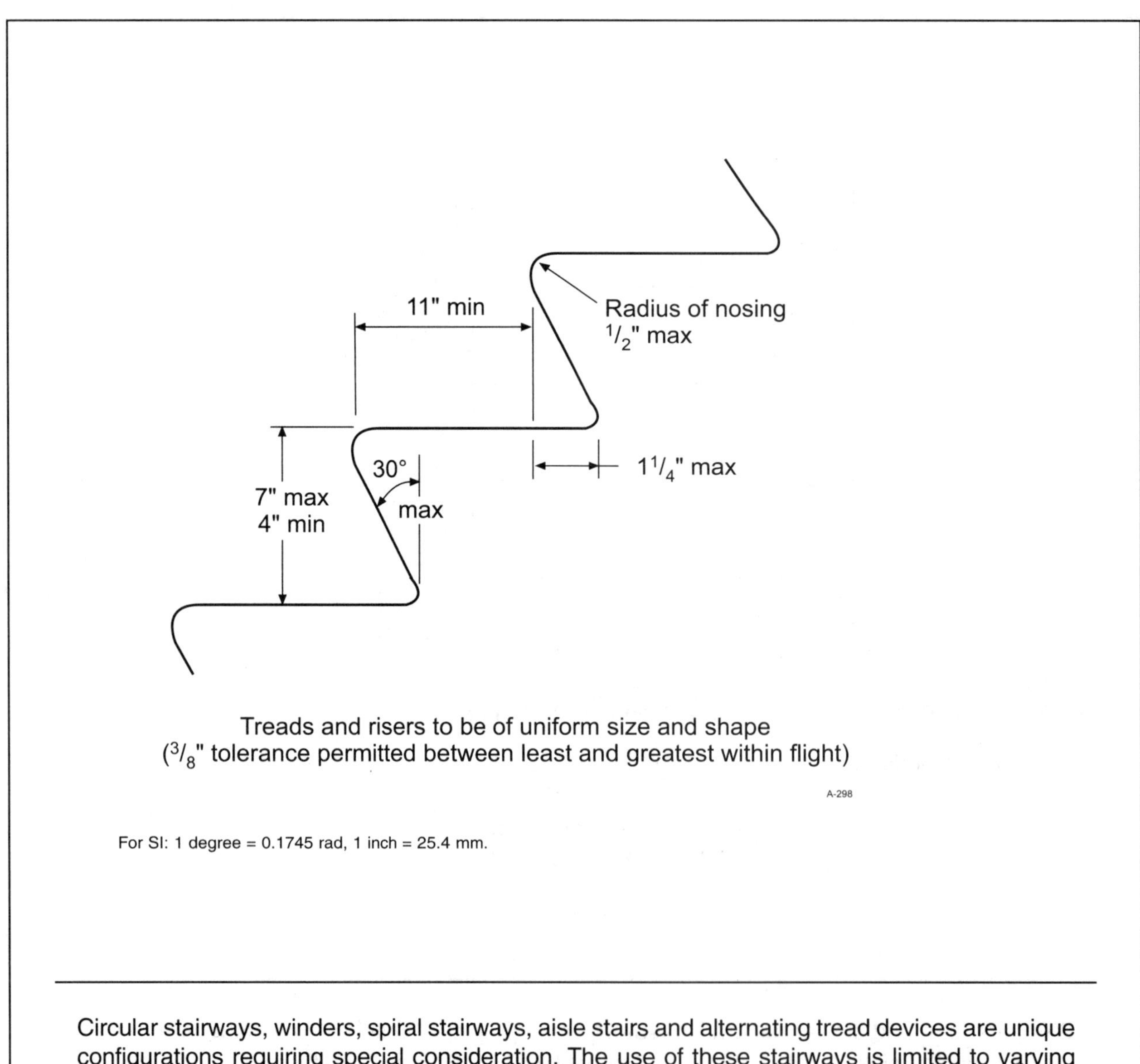

Circular stairways, winders, spiral stairways, aisle stairs and alternating tread devices are unique configurations requiring special consideration. The use of these stairways is limited to varying degrees based on occupancy, occupant load, design and use as a required means of egress.

Topic: Stairway Landings
Reference: IBC 1009.4

Category: Means of Egress
Subject: Stairways and Handrails

Code Text: *There shall be a floor or landing at the top and bottom of each stairway. The width of landings shall be not less than the width of stairways they serve. Every landing shall have a minimum dimension measured in the direction of travel equal to the width of the stairway. Such dimension need not exceed 48 inches where the stairway has a straight run.* See exceptions.

Discussion and Commentary: A landing that serves a stairway is required to have a length equal to or greater than the stairway width unless the stairway has a straight run. This measurement is based on the actual width of the stairway, not the required width. It is important to ensure that the capacity of the stairway is not reduced as occupants travel between stairway flights. A length of 48 inches is acceptable for straight stairway travel, insofar as the capacity is not reduced for travel through the landing.

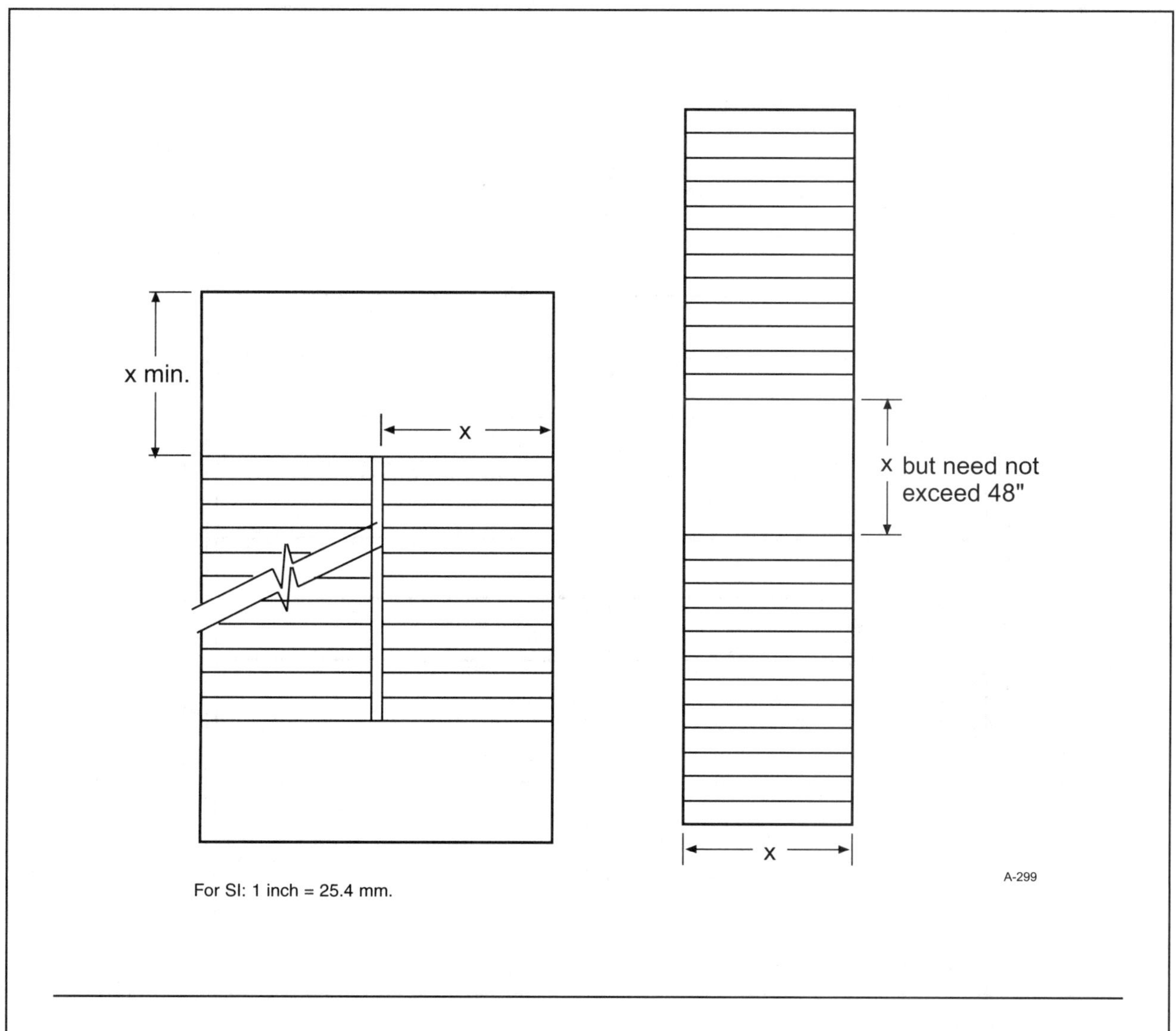

For SI: 1 inch = 25.4 mm.

Because of the difficulty many individuals encounter while negotiating stairs, the code requires a maximum vertical rise between landings of 12 feet. When placed at limited intervals, landings can be used as a resting place for the stair user and can also make stair travel less intimidating.

Topic: Handrail Locations
Reference: IBC 1009.11, 1009.11.2

Category: Means of Egress
Subject: Stairways and Handrails

Code Text: *Stairways shall have handrails on each side.* See five exceptions. *Intermediate handrails are required so that all portions of the stairway width required for egress capacity are within 30 inches of a handrail. On monumental stairs, handrails shall be located along the most direct path of egress travel.*

Discussion and Commentary: The handrail, a very important safety element of a stairway, must be located within relatively easy reach of every stair user. Therefore, in most applications, a rail must be provided on both sides of the stairway. In the case of extremely wide stairways, such as monumental stairs, the requirement for additional rails located throughout the width of the stairway is based on the required stairway width, not the actual width.

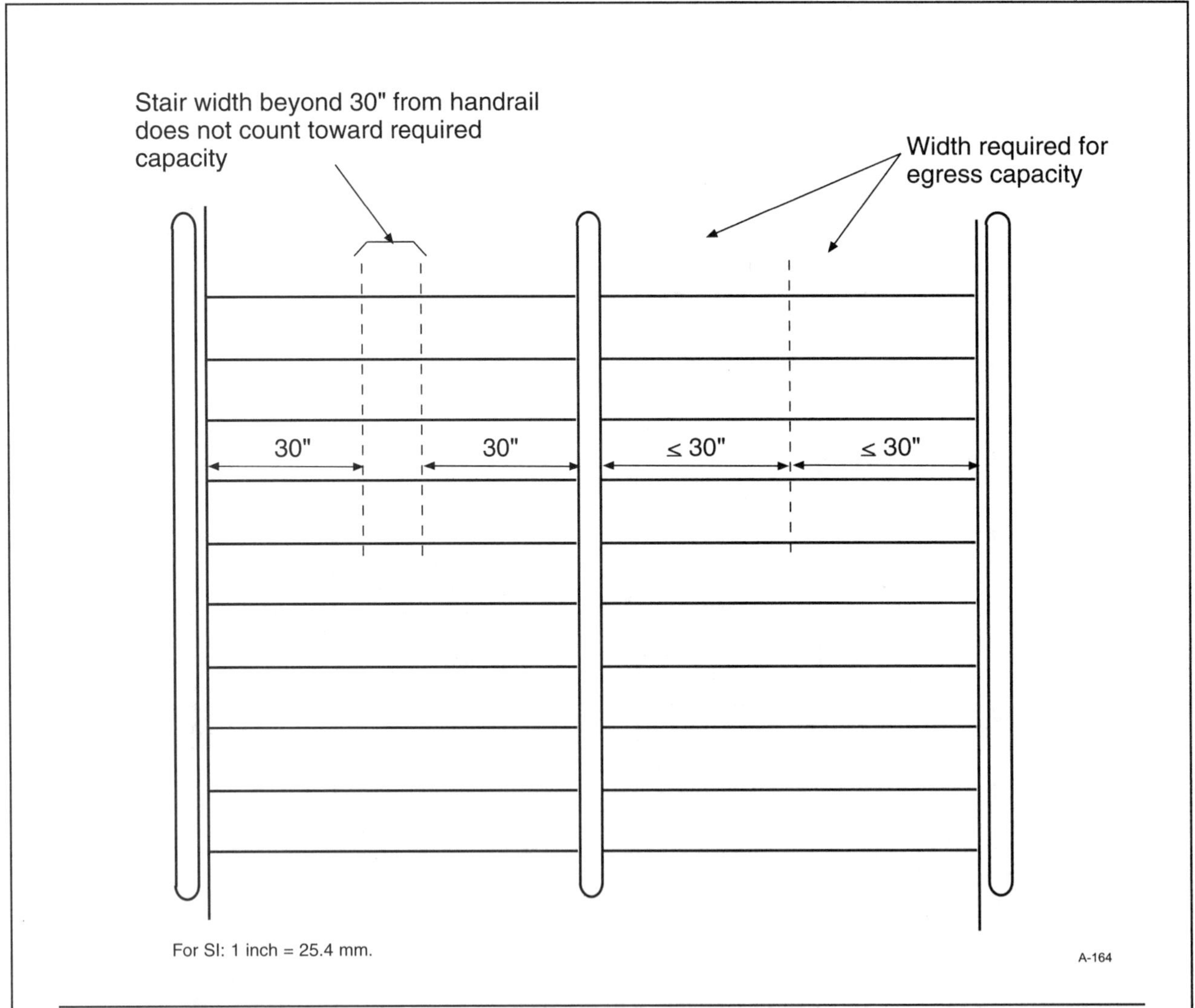

Various exceptions permit the use of a single handrail, and in some cases no rail, within a dwelling unit. In addition, aisle stairs with a center handrail, or those serving seating on only one side, are permitted to use a single handrail.

Topic: Handrail Dimensions
Reference: IBC 1009.11

Category: Means of Egress
Subject: Stairways and Handrails

Code Text: *Handrail height, measured above stair tread nosings, or finish surface of ramp slope, shall be uniform, not less than 34 inches and not more than 38 inches. Handrails with a circular cross section shall have an outside diameter of at least 1.25 inches and not greater than 2 inches or shall provide equivalent graspability. If the handrail is not circular, it shall have a perimeter dimension of at least 4 inches and not greater than 6.25 inches with a maximum cross-section dimension of 2.25 inches.*

Discussion and Commentary: Handrail height shall be measured from the nosing of the treads to the top of the rail. Handrails located above or below this height range are not easily reached by most individuals. The shape of the rail should allow for easy grasping by most users.

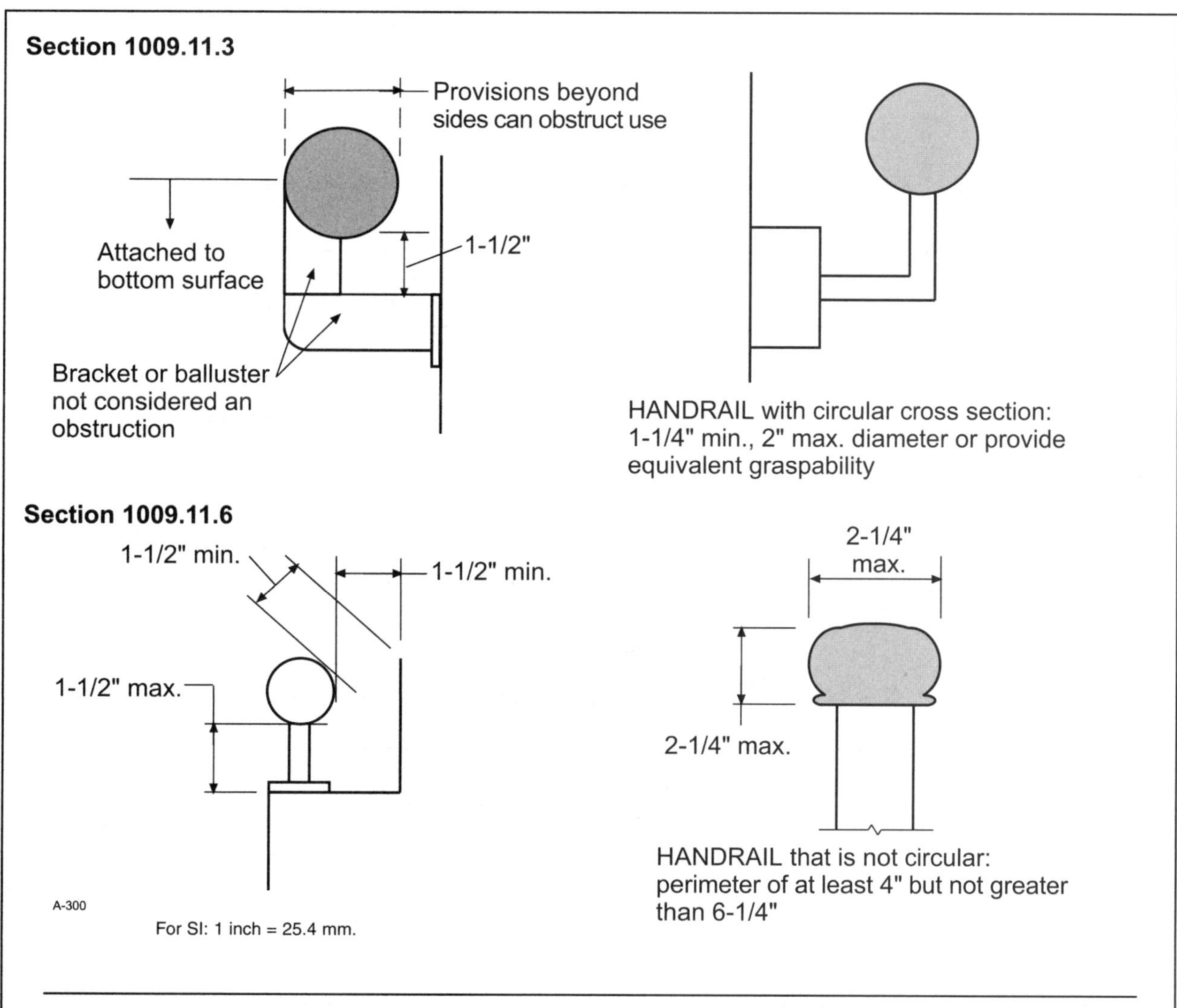

A major goal of handrail design and location is to make it easily graspable; hence, it is mandatory that the rail be placed at least $1^1/_2$ inches from any abutting elements, such as a wall. However, the projection of the rail into the required width is limited to no more than $4^1/_2$ inches.

Topic: Slope, Rise, Width and Handrails
Reference: IBC 1010

Category: Means of Egress
Subject: Ramps

Code Text: *Ramps used as part of a means of egress shall have a running slope not steeper than one unit vertical in 12 units horizontal. The slope of other ramps shall not be steeper than one unit vertical in eight units horizontal. The rise for any ramp run shall be 30 inches maximum. The minimum width of a means of egress ramp shall not be less than that required for corridors by Section 1016.2. The clear width of a ramp and the clear width between handrails, if provided, shall be 36 inches. Ramps with a rise greater than 6 inches shall have handrails on both sides complying with Section 1009.11.*

Discussion and Commentary: Although many of the governing ramp provisions are designed for accessibility purposes, egress capabilities must also be considered. Unlike allowances for corridors, there are no permitted projections into the required height or width of ramps.

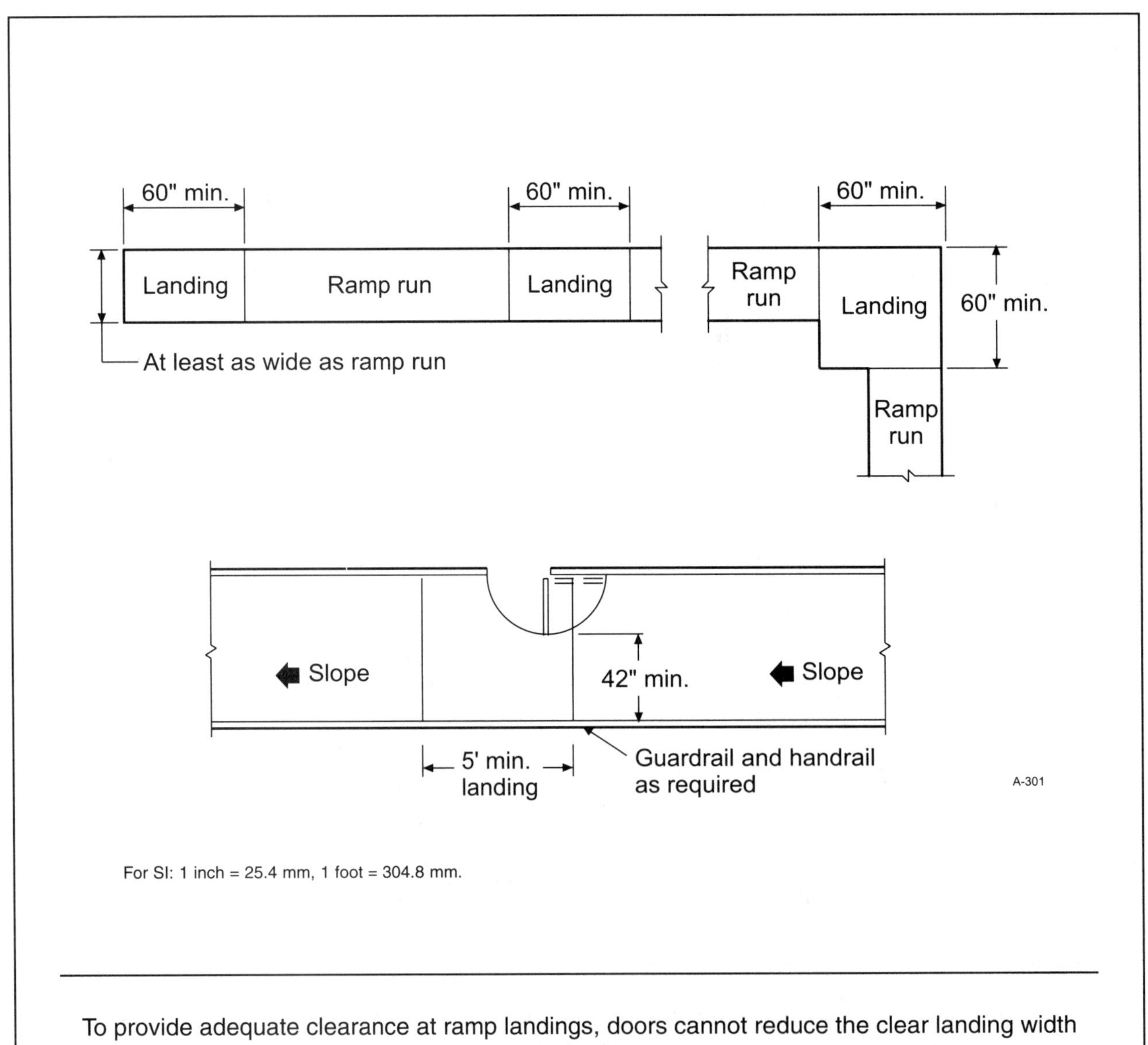

To provide adequate clearance at ramp landings, doors cannot reduce the clear landing width to less than 42 inches. A landing must be at least 60 inches in length and at least as wide as the widest ramp run adjoining the landing.

QUIZ

Study Session 10 — Sections 1008-1010

I. Multiple Choice

1. In general, a door opening shall provide a minimum clear width of __________ inches.

   a. 30 b. 32
   c. 34 d. 36

   Reference________________

2. In a Group I-2 occupancy, means of egress doors used for the movement of beds shall have a minimum width of __________ inches.

   a. 32 b. 36
   c. $41^1/_2$ d. 44

   Reference________________

3. The minimum required width for door openings does not apply to storage closets less than __________ square feet in floor area.

   a. 10 b. 25
   c. 50 d. 100

   Reference________________

4. At a door opening, the maximum permitted projection into the required clear width shall be __________ inch(es) at any point between 34 inches and 80 inches above the floor.

   a. 0, no projections are permitted b. $^1/_2$
   c. 1 d. 4

   Reference________________

5. In which of the following uses must an egress door be a side-hinged swinging door where serving an occupant load of 10 or less?

   a. office b. storage
   c. manufacturing d. retail sales

   Reference________________

6. In a Group F-2 occupancy, egress doors shall swing in the direction of egress travel where serving a minimum occupant load of __________ persons.

a. 10 b. 30
c. 50 d. 100

Reference_______________

7. For a side-swinging fire door provided with a self-closing device, the egress door shall swing to a full-open position when subjected to a maximum __________ force.

a. 5-pound b. 15-pound
c. 30-pound d. 50-pound

Reference_______________

8. A revolving door shall be provided with a side-hinged swinging door located in the same wall and within __________ feet of the revolving door.

a. 5 b. 10
c. 20 d. 50

Reference_______________

9. Entrance doors in a means of egress in a Group B office building may be equipped with an approved entrance and egress access control system under limited conditions, including that any manual unlocking device be located a maximum of __________ feet from the secured doors.

a. 3 b. 4
c. 5 d. 10

Reference_______________

10. Exterior landings at doors shall have a maximum slope of __________ unit vertical in 12 units horizontal.

a. $^1/_8$ b. $^1/_4$
c. $^1/_2$ d. 1

Reference_______________

11. Other than at sliding doors serving dwelling units, the maximum height for thresholds at doorways is __________ inch.

a. $^1/_8$ b. $^1/_4$
c. $^1/_2$ d. 1

Reference_______________

12. Approved, listed delayed egress locks are permitted under specific conditions in all but which of the following occupancies?

a. Group A-2
b. Group I-2
c. Group F-2
d. Group S-2

Reference_______________

13. Door handles, pulls, latches, locks and other operating devices shall be installed a minimum of __________ inches and a maximum of __________ inches above the finished floor.

a. 32, 48
b. 34, 42
c. 34, 48
d. 36, 54

Reference_______________

14. In a Group E occupancy, panic hardware shall be provided on exterior egress doors when serving a minimum occupant load of __________ persons.

a. 1, panic hardware is always required
b. 10
c. 50
d. 100

Reference_______________

15. Stairways shall have a minimum headroom clearance of __________ inches.

a. 76
b. 78
c. 80
d. 84

Reference_______________

16. Within an individual dwelling unit of a Group R-2 apartment building, a stairway shall have a maximum riser height of __________ inches and a minimum tread depth of __________ inches.

a. 7, 11
b. $7^3/_4$, 10
c. 8, 9
d. $8^1/_4$, 9

Reference_______________

17. For a 60-inch-wide stairway having a straight run, any intermediate landing shall be a minimum of __________ inches in length.

a. 36
b. 44
c. 48
d. 60

Reference_______________

18. For winders, the minimum permitted tread depth at the narrow edge shall be __________ inches.

a. 4
b. 6
c. 8
d. 10

Reference_______________

19. Where serving a maximum of five occupants, a spiral stairway may be used as a means of egress component from a space having a maximum floor area of __________ square feet.

a. 200
b. 250
c. 500
d. 1,000

Reference_______________

20. Stairway handrails shall be located a minimum of __________ inches and a maximum of __________ inches above stair tread nosings.

a. 30, 34
b. 30, 38
c. 32, 34
d. 34, 38

Reference_______________

21. Where handrails are not continuous between stair flights, they shall continue to slope for __________ beyond the bottom riser.

a. the depth of one tread
b. a minimum of 12 inches
c. 12 inches plus one tread depth
d. one-half the length of the landing

Reference_______________

22. Projections into the required width at each stairway handrail shall be limited to a maximum of __________ inches at any point at and below the handrail height.

a. 0, no projections permitted
b. $1^1/_2$
c. $3^1/_2$
d. $4^1/_2$

Reference_______________

23. The maximum permitted rise of any ramp shall be __________ inches.

a. 30
b. 44
c. 48
d. 60

Reference_______________

24. Only those ramps having a maximum rise of __________ inches are permitted without complying handrails.

a. 6 b. 12
c. 24 d. 30

Reference________________

25. Unless having a maximum height of __________ inches, turnstiles shall be regulated as for revolving doors.

a. 34 b. 36
c. 38 d. 39

Reference________________

26. Where a power-operated door must be opened manually, the maximum force to set the door in motion shall be _____ pounds.

a. 5 b. 15
c. 30 d. 50

Reference________________

27. The space required between two doors in a series shall be a minimum of _____ inches plus the width of a door swinging into the space.

a. 30 b. 44
c. 48 d. 60

Reference________________

28. A stairway serving an occupant load of 35 in an office suite shall have a minimum width of _____ inches.

a. 30 b. 36
c. 42 d. 44

Reference________________

29. Where a stairway serves an assembly occupancy, handrails having a circular cross section shall have a minimum outside diameter of _____ inches and a maximum diameter of _____ inches.

a. $1^1/_4$, 2 b. $1^1/_4$, $2\,^5/_8$
c. $1^1/_2$, 2 d. $1^1/_2$, $2\,^5/_8$

Reference________________

30. Where a railing is used as edge protection along the side of a ramp run, it must have a rail mounted a minimum of _____ inches and a maximum of _____ inches above the ramp surface.

a. 4, 12
b. 8, 15
c. 15, 18
d. 17, 19

Reference_______________

INTERNATIONAL BUILDING CODE
Study Session 11
Sections 1013–1016 — Means of Egress III

OBJECTIVE: To obtain an understanding of the system design requirements for the exit access, including number of exits, separation of egress doorways and maximum travel distances, as well as the requirements for the exit access components, including aisles, corridors and egress balconies.

REFERENCE: Section 1013–1016, 2003 *International Building Code*

KEY POINTS:

- What portion of the means of egress system is the exit access?
- Is egress permitted through an adjoining or intervening room? If so, under what conditions?
- How must egress be provided where more than one tenant occupies any single floor of a building or structure?
- What is a common path of travel?
- Why is the common path of travel so limiting?
- Where must complying aisles be provided?
- What is the minimum permitted aisle width in public areas of Groups B and M? In nonpublic areas?
- What is an aisle accessway? What is the minimum aisle accessway width where the aisle serves seating arrangements at tables or counters?
- How do the exiting provisions for egress balconies compare with those for corridors?
- When is a fire-resistance-rated separation mandated between the building and an egress balcony?
- When are at least two exits or exit access doorways required from a room?
- At what point is access required to three or more exits?
- Why are multiple exit paths required to be separated at a specified minimum distance from each other?
- At what minimum distance must two exits or exit access doorways be separated? Three or more exits or exit access doorways?
- What benefit is derived from exit separation in a sprinklered building?
- Why is travel distance regulated?
- How is the maximum travel distance measured? Where does it start? Where does it end?
- How is travel distance measured where travel involves stairways?
- Which occupancies permit the least travel distance? The most?
- What are the travel distance limitations for low-hazard storage and manufacturing buildings? Which special conditions must be met?
- To what amount can the travel distance be increased on an exterior egress balcony?
- What is the purpose of a corridor? When must a corridor be of fire-resistance-rated construction?
- What is the minimum required width of a corridor?
- What is a dead-end condition? When are dead ends limited in length?
- How is the use of corridors for supply, return, exhaust or ventilation air regulated?

Topic: Egress Through Intervening Spaces
Reference: IBC 1013.2
Category: Means of Egress
Subject: Exit Access

Code Text: *Egress from a room or space shall not pass through adjoining or intervening rooms or areas, except where such adjoining rooms or areas are accessory to the area served; are not a high-hazard occupancy; and provide a discernible path of egress travel to an exit.*

Discussion and Commentary: A workable means of egress system must be direct, obvious and unobstructed. Therefore, egress may only travel through an intervening room, space or area where the exit path is discernable. Travel must be such that it is readily apparent which direction the occupant must go to continue toward the exit. In addition, access through a high-hazard space is prohibited unless traveling from another high-hazard space. It is expected that any intervening room used for egress will be accessory to the room from which egress begins.

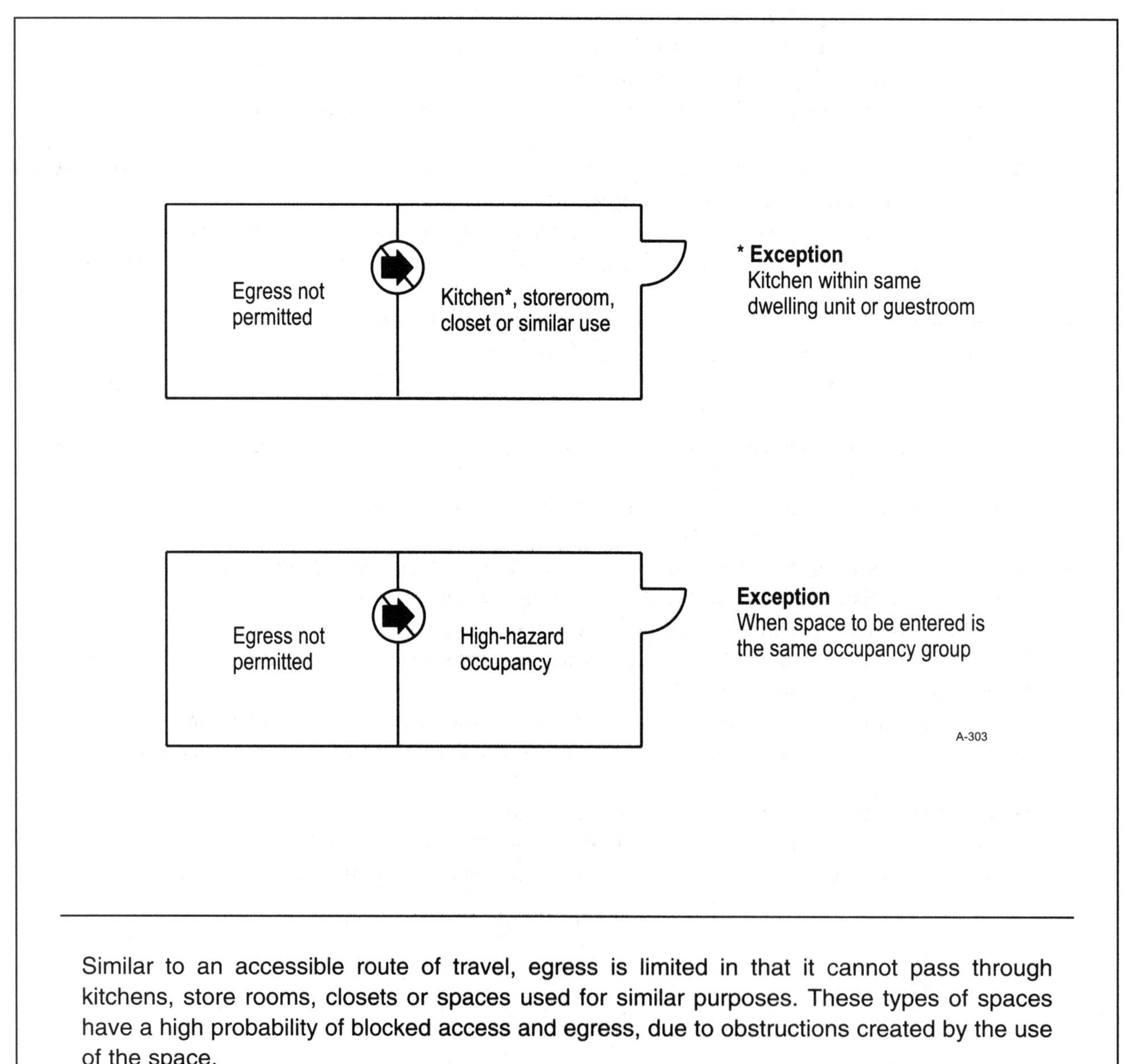

Similar to an accessible route of travel, egress is limited in that it cannot pass through kitchens, store rooms, closets or spaces used for similar purposes. These types of spaces have a high probability of blocked access and egress, due to obstructions created by the use of the space.

Topic: Common Path of Egress Travel
Reference: IBC 1013.3

Category: Means of Egress
Subject: Exit Access

Code Text: *In occupancies other than Groups H-1, H-2 and H-3, the common path of egress travel shall not exceed 75 feet (22 860 mm). In occupancies in Groups H-1, H-2 and H-3, the common path of egress travel shall not exceed 25 feet (7620 mm).* See three exceptions where a 100-foot common path is acceptable.

Discussion and Commentary: A common path of egress travel is defined as *that portion of exit access which the occupants are required to traverse before two separate and distinct paths of egress travel to two exits are available.* The concept of limiting the common path of egress travel addresses the concern that multiple egress options must be available to occupants where the expected egress travel distance becomes excessive. Although the overall travel distance in a building may be of considerable length, such travel is greatly limited where only one egress path is available.

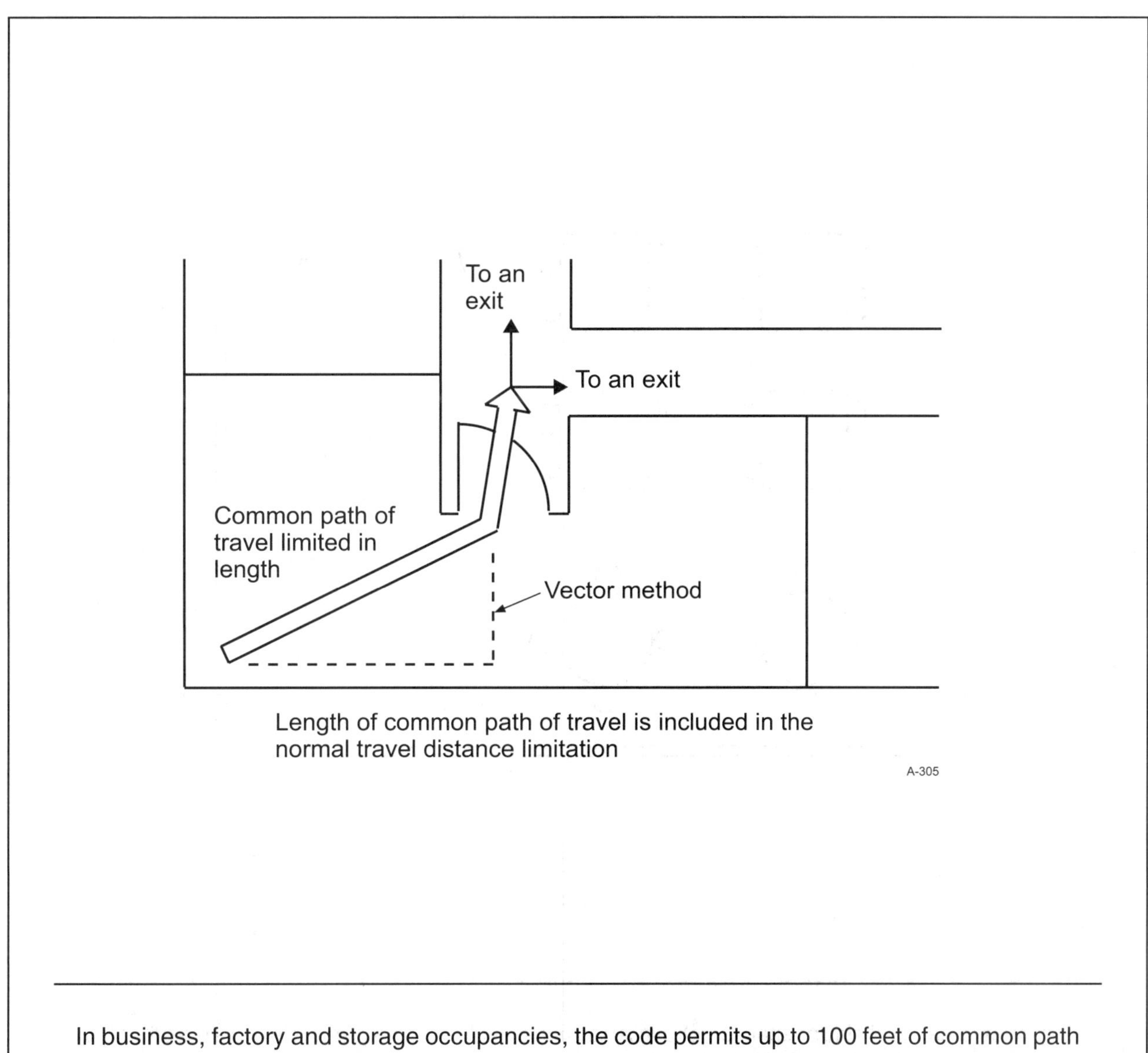

In business, factory and storage occupancies, the code permits up to 100 feet of common path of egress travel where the building is fully sprinklered. The 100-foot limitation also applies to nonsprinklered buildings housing Groups B, S or U with an occupant load of 30 or less.

Topic: Aisles
Reference: IBC 1013.4

Category: Means of Egress
Subject: Exit Access

Code Text: *Aisles shall be provided from all occupied portions of the exit access which contain seats, tables, furnishings, displays and similar fixtures or equipment. Aisles serving assembly areas, other than seating at tables, shall comply with Section 1024. Aisles serving reviewing stands, grandstands and bleachers shall also comply with Section 1024. The required width of aisles shall be unobstructed.* See exception for doors, handrails, trim and decorative features. *In Group B and M occupancies, the minimum clear aisle width shall be determined by Section 1005.1 for the occupant load served, but shall not be less than 36 inches (914 mm).* See exception for nonpublic aisles.

Discussion and Commentary: Well-defined aisles must be provided throughout office spaces, retail stores and similar facilities. The mandated clear width varies based on the presence of obstructions, such as chairs, clothes racks or other items that can easily interrupt the egress flow to an exit.

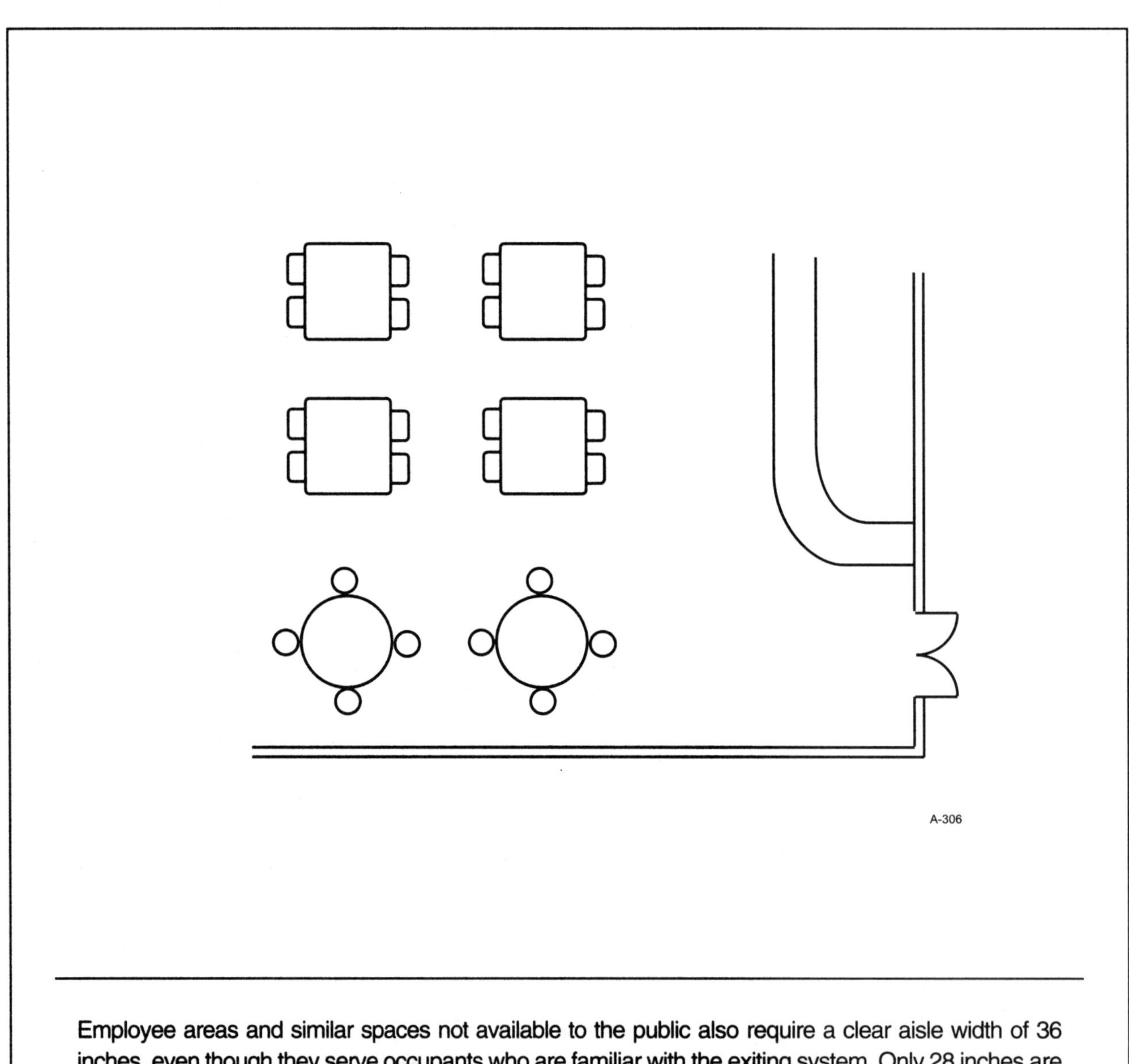

Employee areas and similar spaces not available to the public also require a clear aisle width of 36 inches, even though they serve occupants who are familiar with the exiting system. Only 28 inches are required for nonpublic aisles not required to be accessible and that serve less than 50 persons.

Topic Seating at Tables
Reference: IBC 1013.4.2

Category: Means of Egress
Subject: Exit Access

Code Text: *Aisle accessways serving arrangements of seating at tables or counters shall have sufficient clear width to conform to the capacity requirements of Section 1005.1. Aisle accessways shall provide a minimum of 12 inches plus 0.5 inch of width for each additional 1 foot, or fraction thereof, beyond 12 feet of aisle accessway length measured from the center of the seat farthest from an aisle.* See exception for aisle accessways of limited lengths and occupant loads. *The length of travel along the aisle accessway shall not exceed 30 feet from any seat to the point where a person has a choice of two or more paths of egress travel to separate exits.*

Discussion and Commentary: To facilitate progress toward an established aisle, it is important that a minimum degree of egress width be established within areas furnished with tables and chairs. An aisle accessway, defined as *that portion of an exit access that leads to an aisle*, is thus regulated.

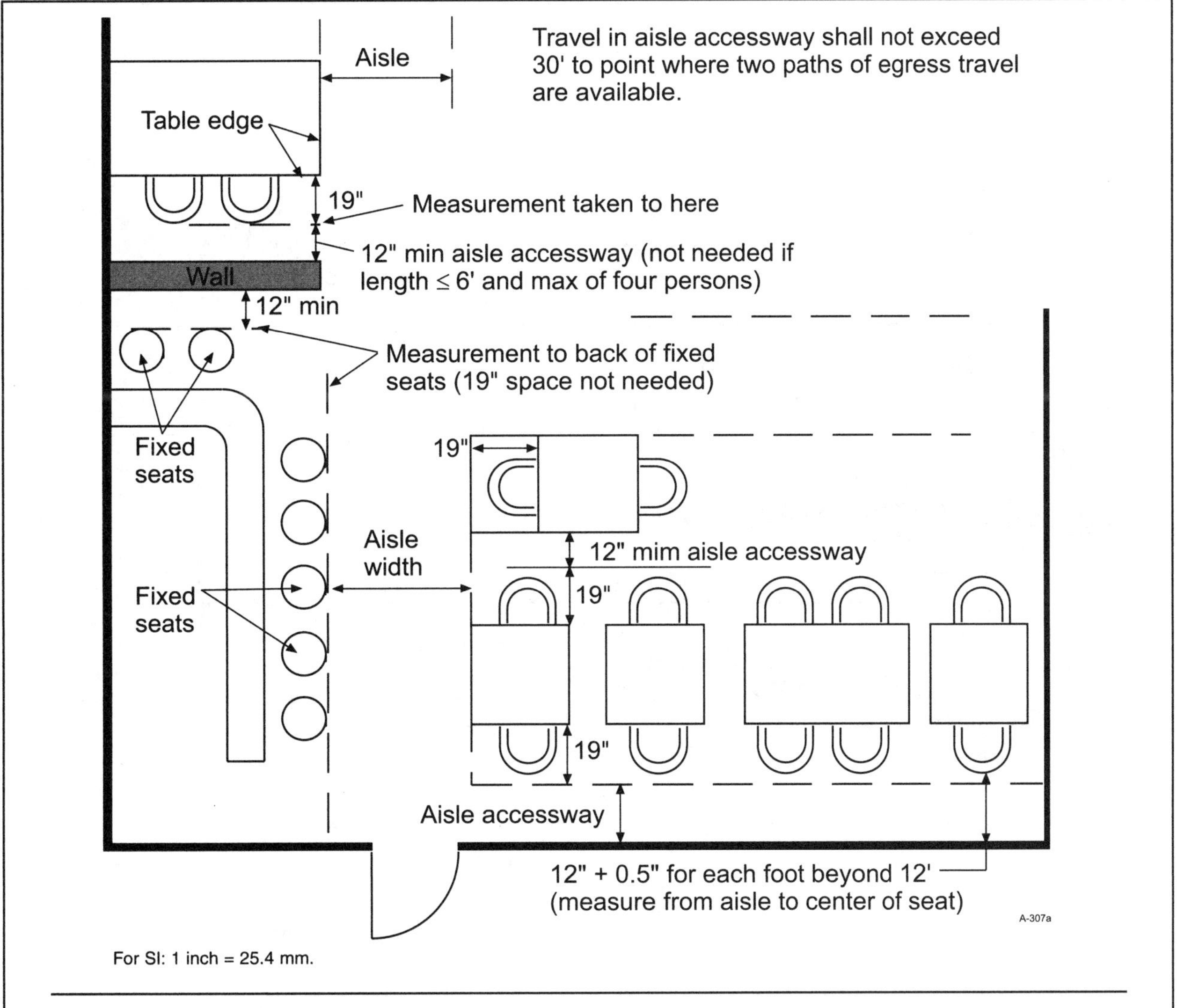

The method of determining the clear width differs based on the type of seating that is provided. For fixed seats, the measurement is made from the back of the seats. Otherwise, the clear width is measured to a line 19 inches from the edge of the table or counter.

Topic: Egress Balconies
Reference: IBC 1013.5

Category: Means of Egress
Subject: Exit Access

Code Text: *Balconies used for egress purposes shall conform to the same requirements as corridors for width, headroom, dead ends and projections. Exterior egress balconies shall be separated from the interior of the building by walls and opening protectives as required for corridors.* See exception for elimination of separation.

Discussion and Commentary: Although the openness of exterior balconies provides some degree of protection from smoke and toxic gases created by a fire, travel along such balconies usually places the occupants at considerable risk. Therefore, the IBC regulates egress balcony travel in a manner consistent with unprotected travel inside the structure. An increase of 100 feet in maximum allowable travel distance is permitted by Section 1015.3 for egress balcony travel.

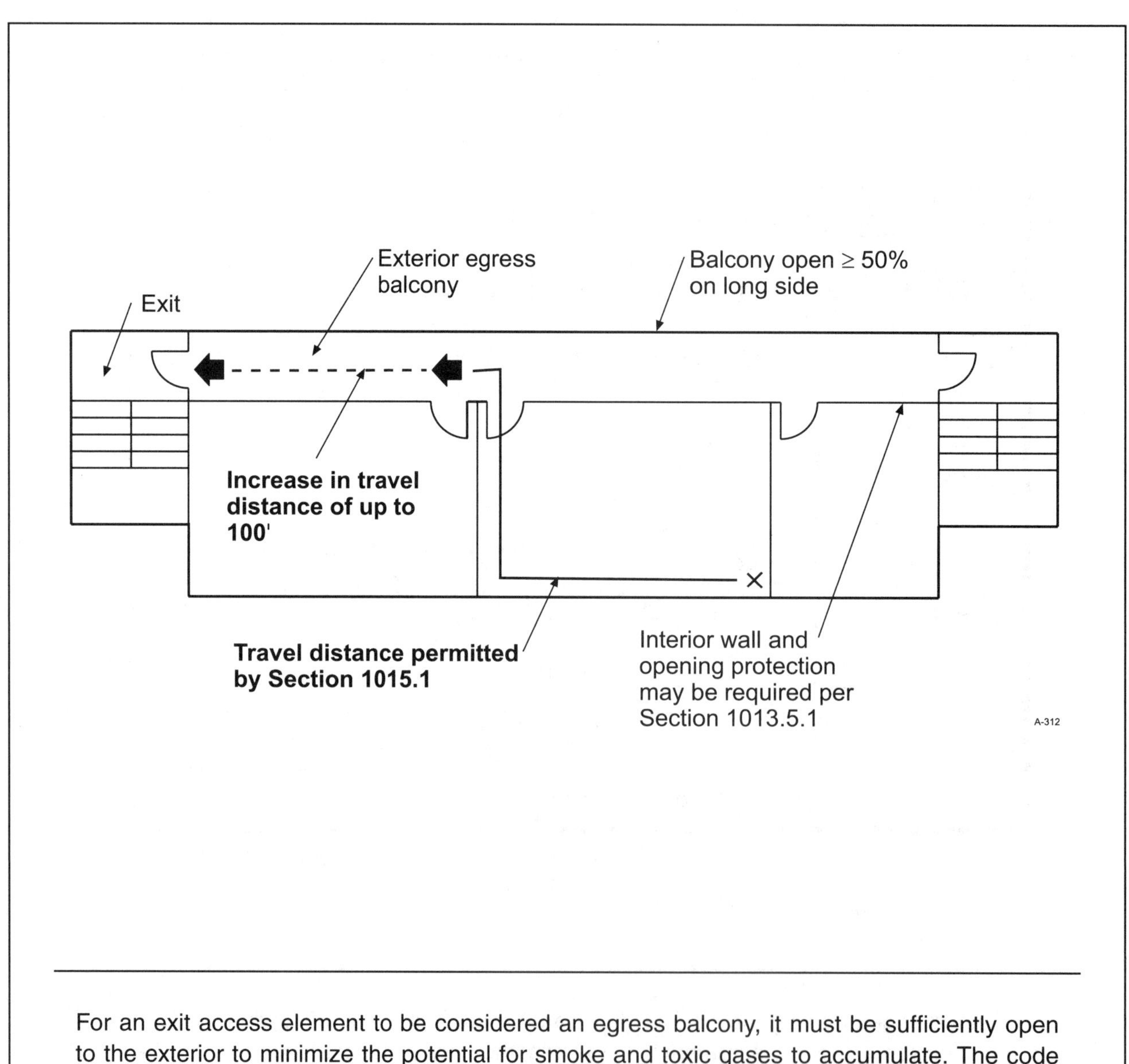

For an exit access element to be considered an egress balcony, it must be sufficiently open to the exterior to minimize the potential for smoke and toxic gases to accumulate. The code considers openings for at least 50 percent of the long side to be adequately open.

Topic: Doorways Required
Reference: IBC 1014.1

Category: Means of Egress
Subject: Exit and Exit Access Doorways

Code Text: *Two or more exits or exit access doorways from any space shall be provided where the occupant load of the space exceeds the values in Table 1004.1, or (2) where the common path of egress travel exceeds the limitations of Section 1013.3, or (3) required by Sections 1014.3, 1014.4 and 1014.5.*

Discussion and Commentary: Two basic criteria establish the point at which it is necessary to provide at least two paths of egress travel from a portion of a building. The first is a function of both the occupancy involved and the occupant load of the space. The second is related to the maximum travel distance an occupant encounters prior to reaching a point where a choice of egress paths is available. Based on the occupancy involved, where the established occupant load or the common travel distance is exceeded, the space must have multiple egress doorways.

TABLE 1014.1
SPACES WITH ONE MEANS OF EGRESS

OCCUPANCY	MAXIMUM OCCUPANT LOAD
A, B, E, F, M, U	50
H-1, H-2, H-3	3
H-4, H-5, I-1, I-3, I-4, R	10
S	30

Requirements for three or four exits are found in Section 1018.1 and are based solely on occupant load. The same criteria applies for access to exits, where a very high occupant load is assigned to a room or space. Multiple exit access doorways must then be provided.

Topic: Doorway Arrangement
Reference: IBC 1014.2

Category: Means of Egress
Subject: Exit and Exit Access Doorways

Code Text: *Required exits shall be located in a manner that makes their availability obvious. Where two exits or exit access doorways are required from any portion of the exit access, the exit doors or exit access doorways shall be placed a distance apart equal to not less than one-half of the length of the maximum overall diagonal dimension of the building or area to be served measured in a straight line between exit doors or exit access doorways. Interlocking or scissor stairs shall be counted as one exit stairway.* See exceptions for sprinklered buildings and where a rated corridor connects two exit enclosures.

Discussion and Commentary: One of the fundamental concepts of exiting is that a single fire incident should not render all means of egress unusable. In this regard, egress doorways are required to be located so as to minimize the probability of such an occurrence. The required separation in sprinklered buildings is reduced to a distance of one third of the overall diagonal.

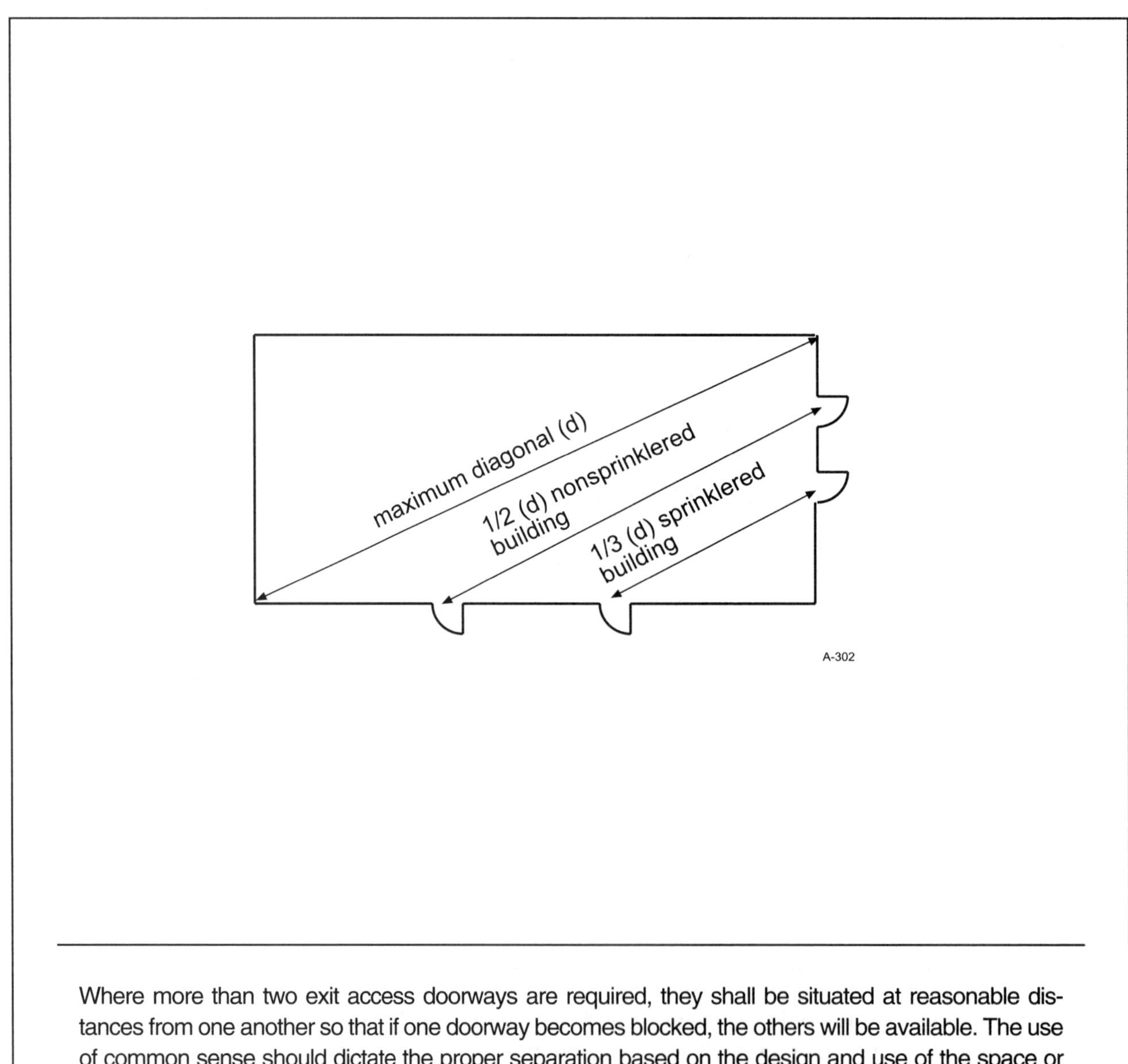

Where more than two exit access doorways are required, they shall be situated at reasonable distances from one another so that if one doorway becomes blocked, the others will be available. The use of common sense should dictate the proper separation based on the design and use of the space or room.

Topic: Travel Distance Limitations **Category:** Means of Egress
Reference: IBC 1015.1 **Subject:** Exit Access Travel Distance

Code Text: *Exits shall be so located that the maximum length of exit access travel, measured from the most remote point within a story to the entrance to an exit along the natural and unobstructed path of egress travel, shall not exceed the distances given in Table 1015.1.*

Discussion and Commentary: Travel distance is considered the portion of egress travel between any occupiable location in a building and the nearest door of an exit. Because quick evacuation from a building is the foremost method of protecting the occupants in many fire incidents, the length of travel is limited until the occupant reaches one of the "protected components." Travel should be measured around any obstruction that is considered fixed or permanent, including low-height office partitions, retail shelving, storage racks, fixed seating, etc.

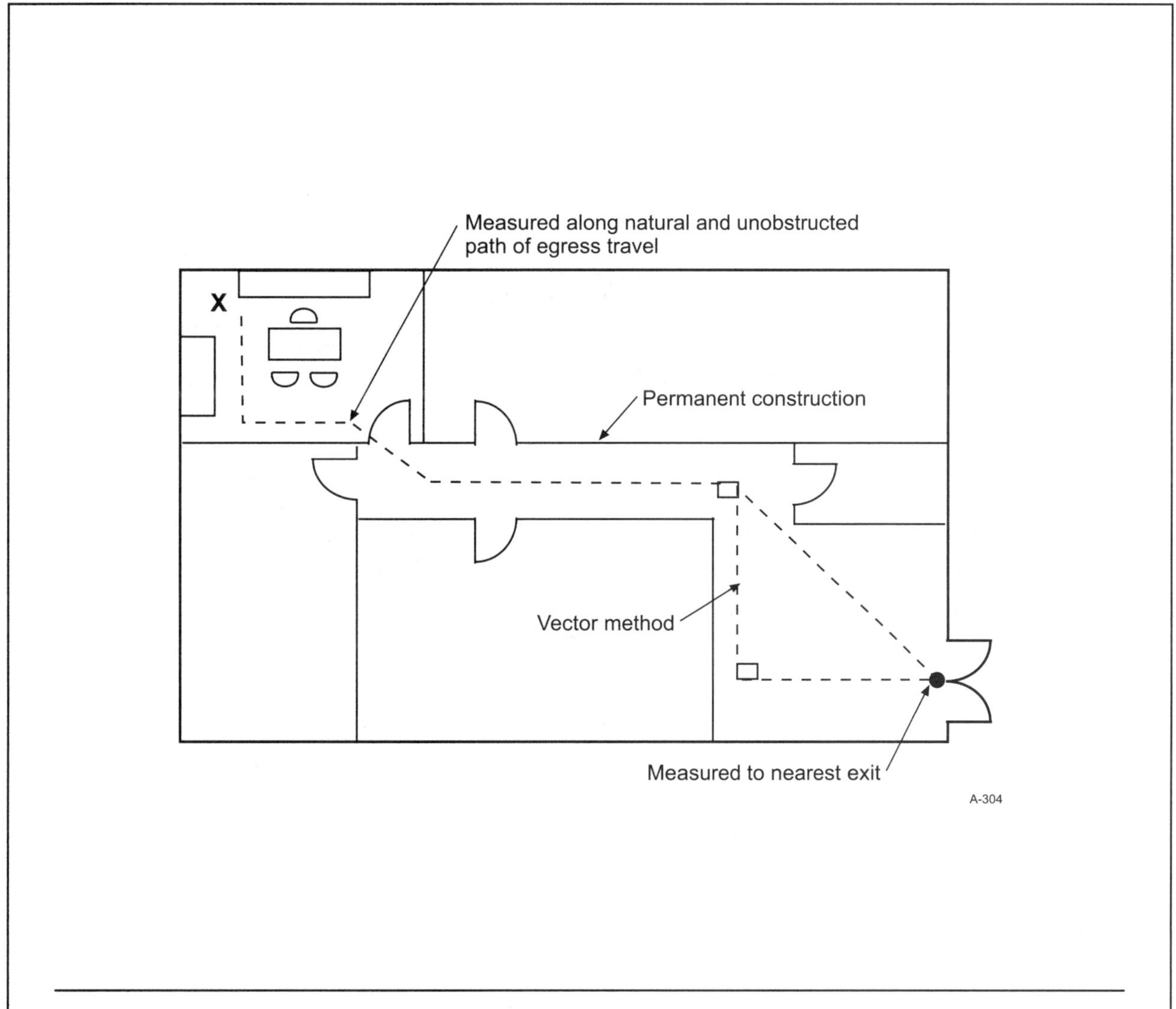

In most sprinklered buildings, the code permits a moderate increase in the permitted travel distance. An increase of 50 feet is typical of most occupancies; however, a travel distance increase of 100 feet is permitted for Group B occupancies protected by a sprinkler system.

Topic: Corridor Construction
Reference: IBC 1016.1

Category: Means of Egress
Subject: Corridors

Code Text: *Corridors shall be fire-resistance rated in accordance with Table 1016.1. The corridor walls required to be fire-resistance rated shall comply with Section 708 for fire partitions.* See four exceptions where a rating is not required.

Discussion and Commentary: A fire-resistance-rated corridor is intended to protect occupants of the corridor during egress travel from an incident in an enclosed space bordering the corridor. The construction of the corridor provides a minimum level of protection from fire and smoke through the use of fire-resistance-rated walls and ceilings, as well as fire-protected openings. Smoke infiltration is limited also by smoke- and draft-control door assemblies and smoke dampers. Occupancy group, occupant load and presence of a fire sprinkler system are the major factors in determining whether or not a corridor must have a fire-resistance rating.

TABLE 1016.1
CORRIDOR FIRE-RESISTANCE RATING

OCCUPANCY	OCCUPANT LOAD SERVED BY CORRIDOR	REQUIRED FIRE-RESISTANCE RATING (hours)	
		Without sprinkler system	With sprinkler system[c]
H-1, H-2, H-3	All	Not Permitted	1
H-4, H-5	Greater than 30	Not Permitted	1
A, B, E, F, M, S, U	Greater than 30	1	0
R	Greater than 10	1	0.5
I-2[a], I-4	All	Not Permitted	0
I-1, I-3	All	Not Permitted	1[b]

a. For requirements for occupancies in Group I-2, see Section 407.3.
b. For a reduction in the fire-resistance rating for occupancies in Group I-3, see Section 408.7.
c. Buildings equipped throughout with an automatic sprinkler system in accordance with Section 903.3.1.1 or 903.3.1.2 where allowed.

Exceptions eliminate the need for a fire-resistance-rated corridor in certain Group E occupancies, in sleeping units or dwelling units of residential occupancies, in open parking garages and in Group B occupancies that are permitted a single means of egress by Section 1014.1.

Topic: Corridor Width
Reference: IBC 1016.2

Category: Means of Egress
Subject: Corridors

Code Text: *The minimum corridor width shall be as determined in Section 1005.1* (calculated width)*, but not less than 44 inches.* See exceptions for specific uses.

Discussion and Commentary: To allow for adequate circulation throughout a building and, more importantly, for egress purposes, a minimum width requirement is established. In addition, complying routes of travel to accessible spaces must be provided. Only in areas used for access to electrical, mechanical or plumbing systems or equipment is the width permitted to be reduced to less than 36 inches. A minimum 36-inch width is mandated for corridors within dwelling units, or for those corridors serving an occupant load of 50 or less. Only specific projections such as doors are permitted to encroach a limited distance into the required corridor width.

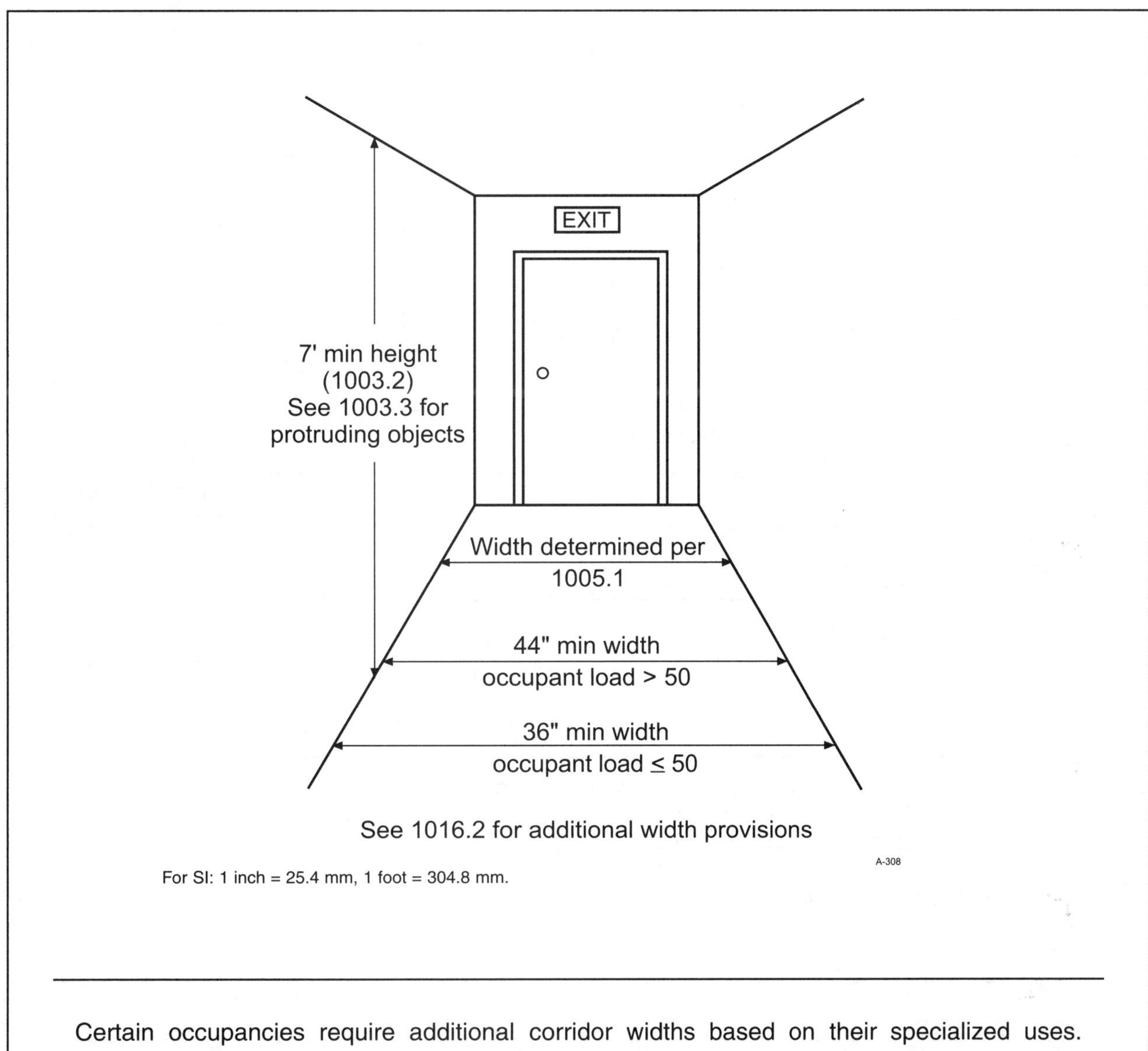

Certain occupancies require additional corridor widths based on their specialized uses. Corridors serving 100 or more occupants in Group E educational occupancies must be at least 72 inches in width, and health-care occupancies require increased widths for bed movement.

Topic: Dead Ends
Reference: IBC 1016.3

Category: Means of Egress
Subject: Corridors

Code Text: *Where more than one exit or exit access doorway is required, the exit access shall be arranged such that there are no dead ends in corridors more than 20 feet in length.* See exceptions for increased dead-end lengths.

Discussion and Commentary: Limitations on dead-end corridors are established where two or more exit or exit access doorways are required. The intent is to limit the distance building occupants must travel before they determine that there is no way out and that they must retrace steps in order to locate an exit or exit access doorway. Where only a single means of egress is permitted, a dead-end condition is not limited in length; however, the provisions of Section 1013.3 for common paths of travel must be considered.

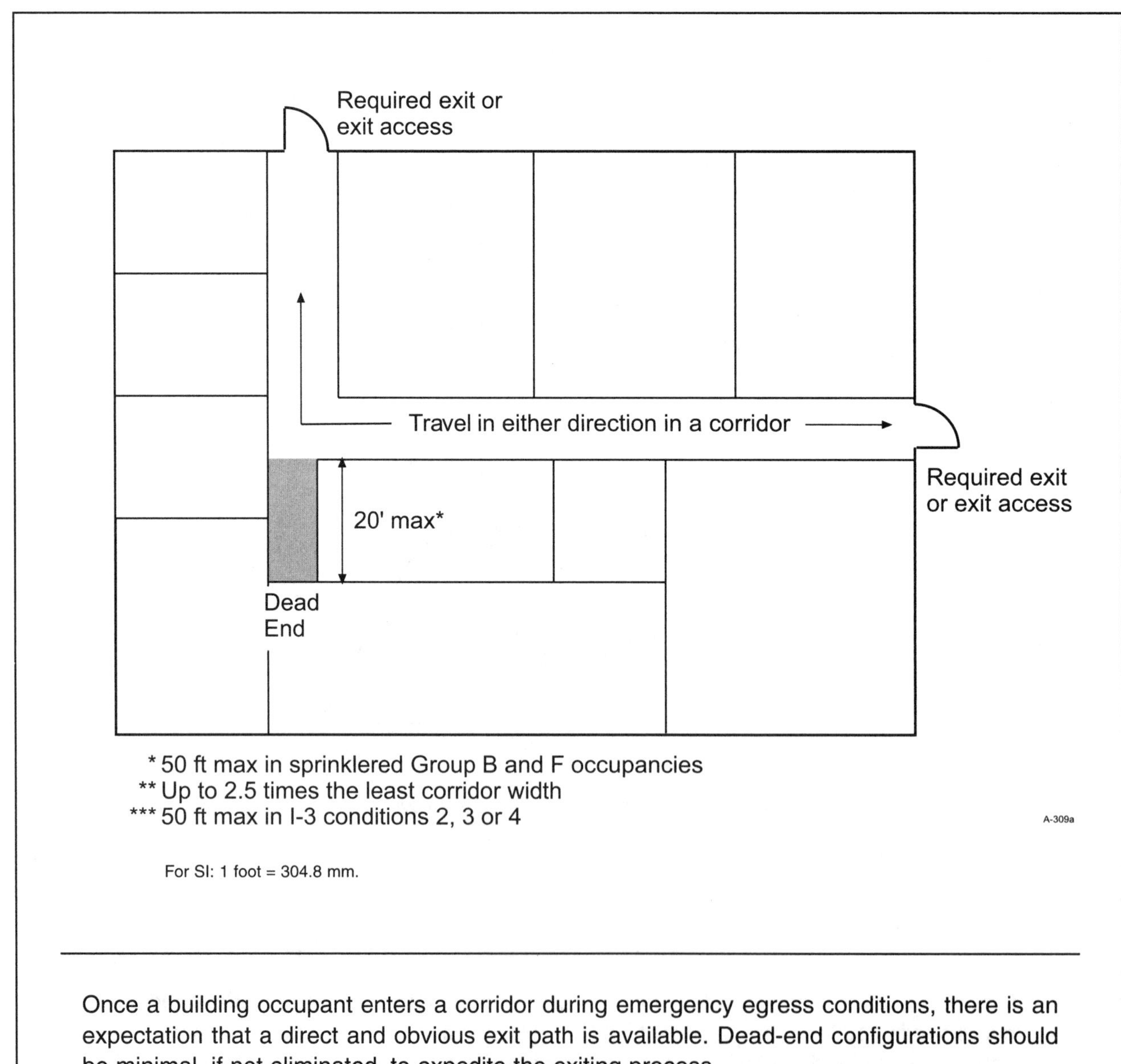

Once a building occupant enters a corridor during emergency egress conditions, there is an expectation that a direct and obvious exit path is available. Dead-end configurations should be minimal, if not eliminated, to expedite the exiting process.

Topic: Air Movement in Corridors
Reference: IBC 1016.4

Category: Means of Egress
Subject: Corridors

Code Text: *Exit access corridors shall not serve as supply, return, exhaust, relief or ventilation air ducts or plenums.* See three exceptions addressing return air and makeup air for exhaust systems. *Use of the space between the corridor ceiling and the floor or roof structure above as a return air plenum is permitted for one or more of the following conditions:* See five conditions.

Discussion and Commentary: The use of corridors for the movement of air is strictly limited by the code. Because a corridor is intended to be a relatively safe environment for occupants exiting a building, it is not advisable to introduce air movement that might increase the potential for fire, smoke or toxic gases to enter the corridor. It is possible, under specific conditions, to use the space above a corridor ceiling as a return air plenum. For example, where the corridor is not required to be of fire-resistance-rated construction, or where the above-ceiling space is isolated from a rated corridor by fire-resistance-rated construction, the upper area may be used for return air.

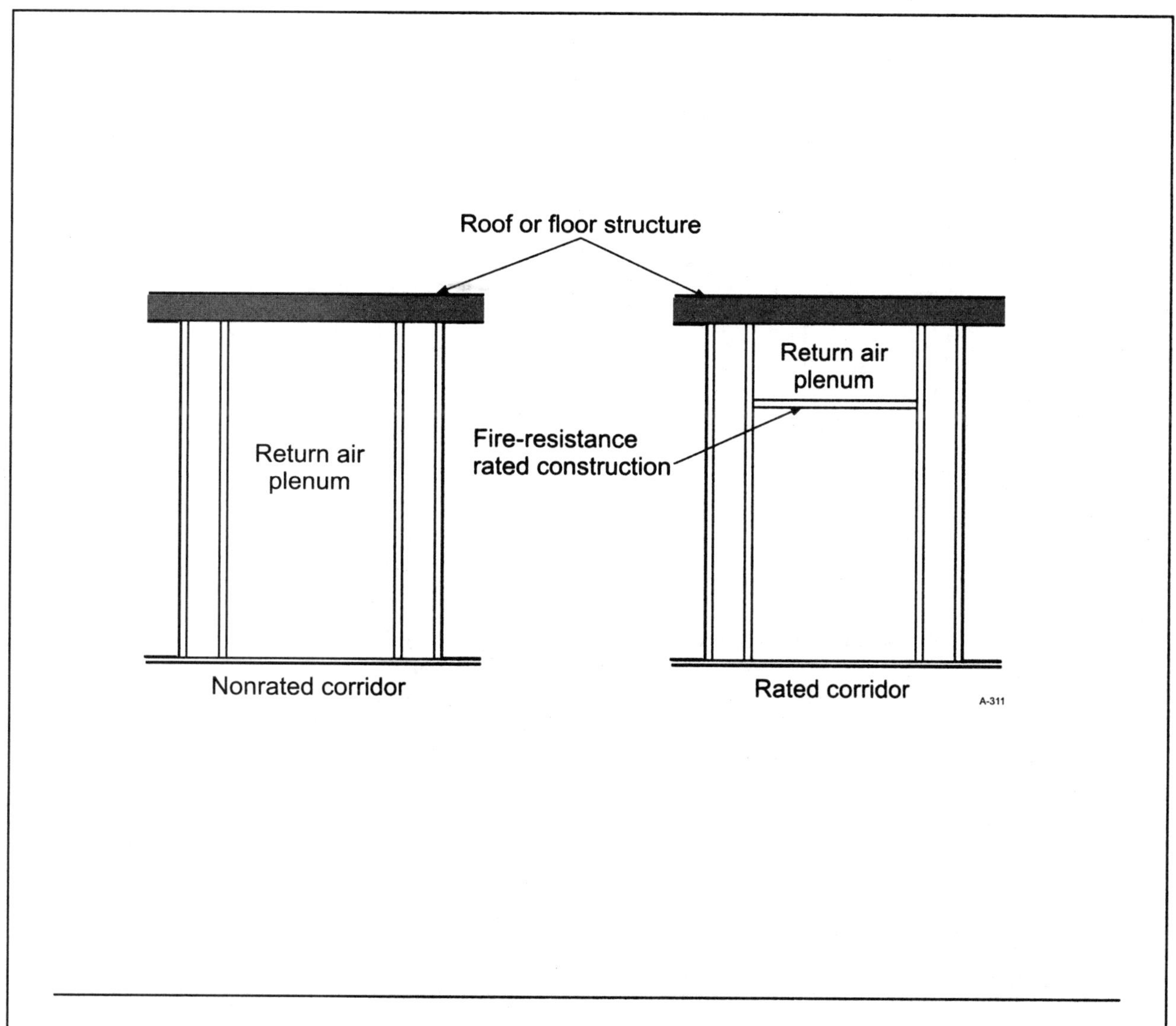

Where a corridor is directly supplied with outdoor air, make-up air for exhaust systems in rooms that open directly into a corridor may be taken from the corridor. The rate at which outdoor air is supplied to the corridor must exceed the rate of makeup air taken from the corridor.

Topic: Corridor Continuity
Reference: IBC 1016.5

Category: Means of Egress
Subject: Corridors

Code Text: *Fire-resistance-rated corridors shall be continuous from the point of entry to an exit. Fire-resistance-rated corridors shall not be interrupted by intervening rooms.* See exceptions for foyers, lobbies and reception rooms.

Discussion and Commentary: Once an occupant enters a corridor required to be of fire-resistance-rated construction, he or she expects that travel to an exit will be direct. The level of protection within the corridor must not be reduced at any point along the egress path. Where an intervening room or space interrupts the corridor, it is quite likely that the exitway will be obstructed or confusing. Where corridor travel includes or terminates at a lobby, foyer or reception room, the condition is considered acceptable, insofar as such spaces are usually an extension of the circulation and egress path.

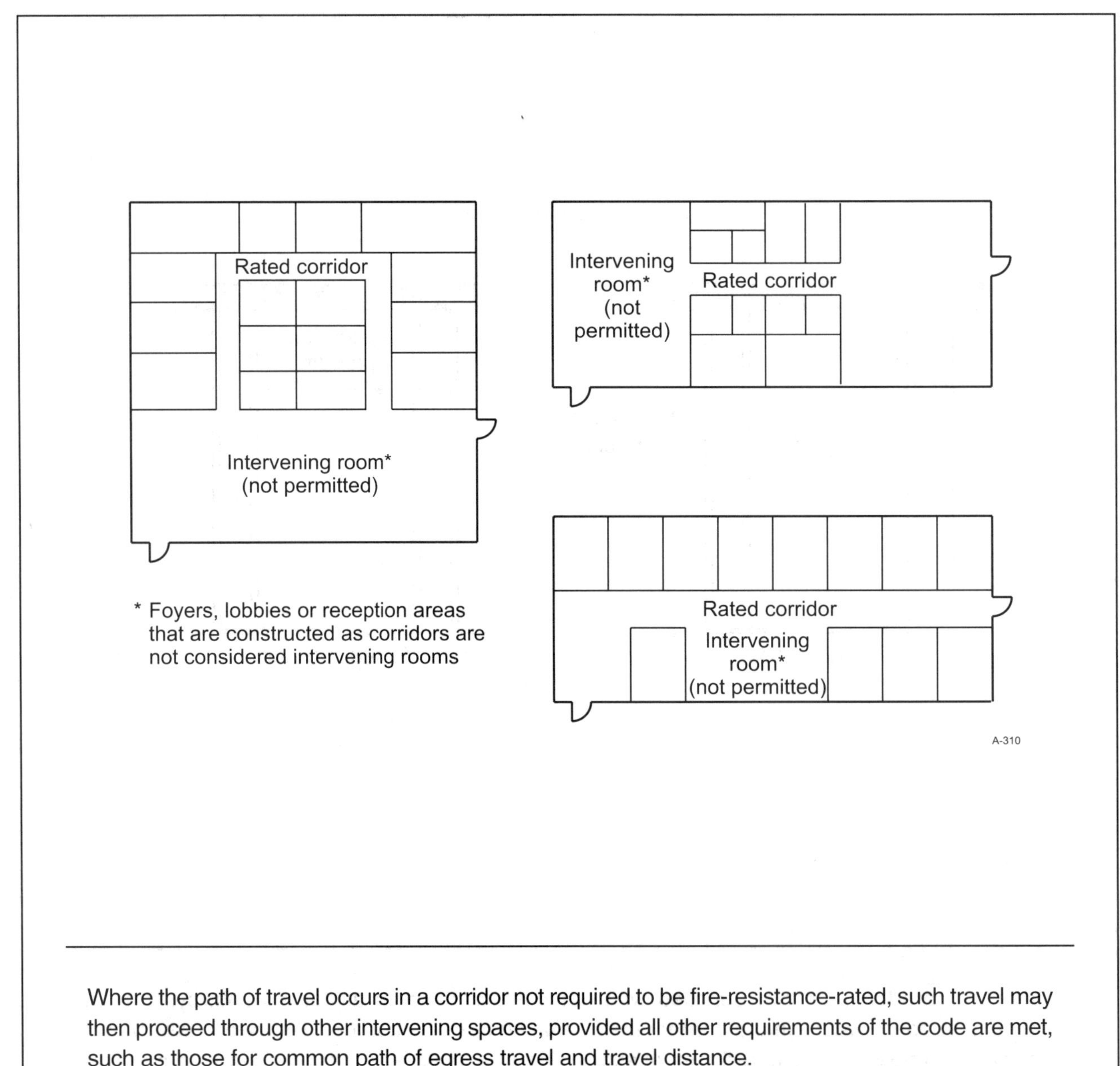

Where the path of travel occurs in a corridor not required to be fire-resistance-rated, such travel may then proceed through other intervening spaces, provided all other requirements of the code are met, such as those for common path of egress travel and travel distance.

QUIZ

Study Session 11 — Sections 1013–1016

I. Multiple Choice

1. Where the common path of travel is within the permitted limits, a Group B occupancy may have a single means of egress where the maximum occupant load is __________.

a. 10 b. 20
c. 30 d. 50

Reference________________

2. In which of the following occupancies having an occupant load of 40 must at least two exits or exit access doorways always be provided?

a. A-2 b. B
c. F-1 d. S-1

Reference________________

3. What is the minimum number of exits required for a Group E occupancy having an occupant load of 1,200?

a. 2 b. 3
c. 4 d. 6

Reference________________

4. Where two means of egress are required from a room in a fully sprinklered building, they shall be separated a minimum of __________ of the length of the maximum overall diagonal dimension of the area served.

a. one-half b. one-third
c. one-fourth d. one-sixth

Reference________________

5. Which of the following conditions is not specifically required where egress from a room passes through an adjoining room?

a. a discernable path of travel must be provided
b. the adjoining room shall be accessory to the area served
c. no more than one means of egress can pass through the adjoining room
d. unless of the same occupancy, the adjoining room cannot be classified as high-hazard

Reference________________

6. Through which one of the following spaces is egress not specifically prohibited?

a. toilet rooms
b. store rooms
c. kitchens
d. closets

Reference_______________

7. In a Group I-2 occupancy, patient sleeping rooms may egress through one intervening room where the intervening room is used as an exit access for a maximum of __________ patient beds.

a. 2
b. 5
c. 8
d. 10

Reference_______________

8. At least two exit access doors are required from a Group I-2 suite of rooms, other than patient sleeping rooms, where the minimum suite floor area is __________ square feet.

a. 1,000
b. 2,500
c. 5,000
d. 10,000

Reference_______________

9. In a Group B occupancy located in a fully-sprinklered building, the maximum permitted exit access travel distance is __________ feet.

a. 200
b. 250
c. 300
d. 400

Reference_______________

10. In a nonsprinklered Group A-3 occupancy, what is the maximum permitted exit access travel distance?

a. 150 feet
b. 200 feet
c. 250 feet
d. 300 feet

Reference_______________

11. Up to an additional 100 feet of travel distance is available where the last portion of exit access travel occurs __________.

a. within a corridor
b. within a one-hour-rated corridor
c. on an exterior egress balcony
d. on an exterior exit stairway

Reference_______________

12. In a Group H-3 occupancy, the common path of egress travel is limited to a maximum of __________ feet.

a. 25 b. 75
c. 100 d. 150

Reference________________

13. In an office tenant space having an occupant load of 30 persons, the maximum length of a common path of egress travel is __________ feet.

a. 25 b. 75
c. 100 d. 200

Reference________________

14. In the public areas of a Group M occupancy, aisles having fixtures or equipment on both sides shall be a minimum of __________ inches in width.

a. 28 b. 36
c. 42 d. 44

Reference________________

15. What is the minimum required width of an aisle serving 60 persons in a nonpublic area?

a. no minimum width is required b. 28 inches
c. 36 inches d. 44 inches

Reference________________

16. In areas of tables and seating, __________ feet is the maximum length of travel along an aisle accessway to the point where a person has a choice of two or more paths of egress travel to separate exits.

a. 12 b. 20
c. 30 d. 50

Reference________________

17. A corridor serving 125 persons in a Group E occupancy shall be a minimum of __________ inches in width.

a. 36 b. 44
c. 60 d. 72

Reference________________

18. A corridor serving an occupant load of 40 persons shall have a minimum width of __________ inches.

a. 36 b. 44
c. 48 d. 60

Reference_______________

19. In a nonsprinklered Group M retail sales building, a corridor serving a minimum occupant load of __________ persons shall be fire-resistance rated.

a. any number of b. 11
c. 31 d. 51

Reference_______________

20. In a fully-sprinklered building, a corridor serving 100 persons in which of the following occupancies must be fire-resistance rated?

a. Group A-2 b. Group I-2
c. Group M d. Group R-1

Reference_______________

21. In a Group I-1 occupancy, corridors requiring more than one exit or exit access doorway may have dead-ends if limited to a maximum of __________ feet in length.

a. 8 b. 20
c. 30 d. 50

Reference_______________

22. In a fully-sprinklered Group B office building, the maximum permitted length of a dead-end condition in a corridor requiring at least two means of egress is __________.

a. 20 feet b. 50 feet
c. twice the corridor width d. four times the corridor width

Reference_______________

23. Utilization of corridors as return air plenums is permitted within tenant spaces having a maximum floor area of __________ square feet.

a. 400 b. 1,000
c. 3,000 d. 5,000

Reference_______________

24. What is the minimum required width of an egress balcony serving an apartment building's occupant load of 55 persons?

a. 36 inches b. 42 inches
c. 44 inches d. 48 inches

Reference_______________

25. The long side of an egress balcony shall be a minimum of _________ percent open.

a. 25 b. 40
c. 50 d. $66^2/_3$

Reference_______________

26. In a Group A-2 dining room having a single exit access door, the common path of egress travel is limited to a maximum of _____ feet.

a. 25 b. 75
c. 100 d. 200

Reference_______________

27. At least two exits or exit access doors are required from a refrigeration machinery room where the room has a minimum floor area exceeding _____ square feet.

a. 0, two exits are always required b. 200
c. 500 d. 1,000

Reference_______________

28. A stairway serving as a means of egress from a catwalk serving a stage shall have a minimum width of _____ inches.

a. 22 b. 28
c. 32 d. 36

Reference_______________

29. What is the maximum permitted travel distance for a single-story Group F-1 factory provided with automatic heat and smoke roof vents and an automatic sprinkler system?

a. 200 feet b. 250 feet
c. 300 feet d. 400 feet

Reference_______________

30. A 16-foot-wide corridor in a Group E high school is permitted to have a dead end condition, provided the dead end is a maximum of _____ feet in length.

a. 20
b. 30
c. 40
d. 50

Reference_______________

INTERNATIONAL BUILDING CODE
Study Session 12
Sections 1017–1025 — Means of Egress IV

OBJECTIVE: To obtain an understanding of the provisions governing the exit and exit discharge portions of the means of egress, the special requirements applicable to egress from assembly occupancies, and the details for emergency escape and rescue openings.

REFERENCE: Sections 1017 through 1025, 2003 *International Building Code*

KEY POINTS:

- What is the definition of an exit? What elements of the building are considered exits?
- For which purposes are exits permitted to be used?
- How many exits from a building are required? From any floor level within a building?
- What degree of fire resistance is required for vertical exit enclosures?
- When is an enclosure not required for an exit stairway?
- How must exterior walls of a vertical exit enclosure be protected?
- Is usable space permitted under an enclosed stairway? An unenclosed stairway?
- Where permitted, how shall usable space under stairways be separated from the remainder of the building?
- How is travel in a vertical exit enclosure that extends beyond the discharge level addressed?
- Where are stairway floor number signs to be located?
- What is a smokeproof enclosure? When is a smokeproof enclosure required?
- What is an exit passageway?
- How is an exit passageway regulated for width?
- What level of fire-resistance-rated construction is mandated for an exit passageway?
- Which types of openings and penetrations are permitted in an exit passageway or a vertical exit enclosure? How are openings and penetrations to be protected?
- In what manner can an exit passageway be provided with ventilation?
- What is the function of a horizontal exit? How is it to be constructed?
- How is the capacity of a horizontal exit refuge area determined?
- What is the maximum height permitted for an exterior exit stairway?
- What is the minimum size exterior opening required for an exterior exit stairway?
- Where does the exit discharge begin? Where does it end?
- What is an egress court?
- What is the minimum size of an egress court? When are egress court walls required to be of fire-resistance-rated construction with protected openings?
- What is a safe dispersal area? What conditions must apply where such an area is utilized?
- What is the minimum capacity of the main exit in an assembly occupancy?
- What is smoke-protected assembly seating?
- What minimum aisle widths are required in assembly occupancies without smoke protection? With smoke protection?
- How is the guard height regulated in assembly areas where the guards interfere with occupant sightlines?
- Where are emergency escape and rescue openings required?
- What is the minimum height and width of an emergency escape and rescue opening? Minimum clear opening size? Maximum sill height from floor?

Topic: Definition
Reference: IBC 1002.1

Category: Means of Egress
Subject: Exits

Code Text: An exit is *that portion of a means of egress system which is separated from other interior spaces of a building or structure by fire-resistance-rated construction and opening protectives as required to provide a protected path of egress travel between the exit access and the exit discharge. Exits include exterior exit doors at ground level, exit enclosures, exit passageways, exterior exit stairs, exterior exit ramps and horizontal exits.*

Discussion and Commentary: The path of travel through the exit access portion of the egress system must be designed to lead to one or more exits, which are locations where some degree of protection or safety from fire hazards is provided. Travel distance is no longer regulated once an exit is reached; therefore, travel within an exit component is virtually unlimited.

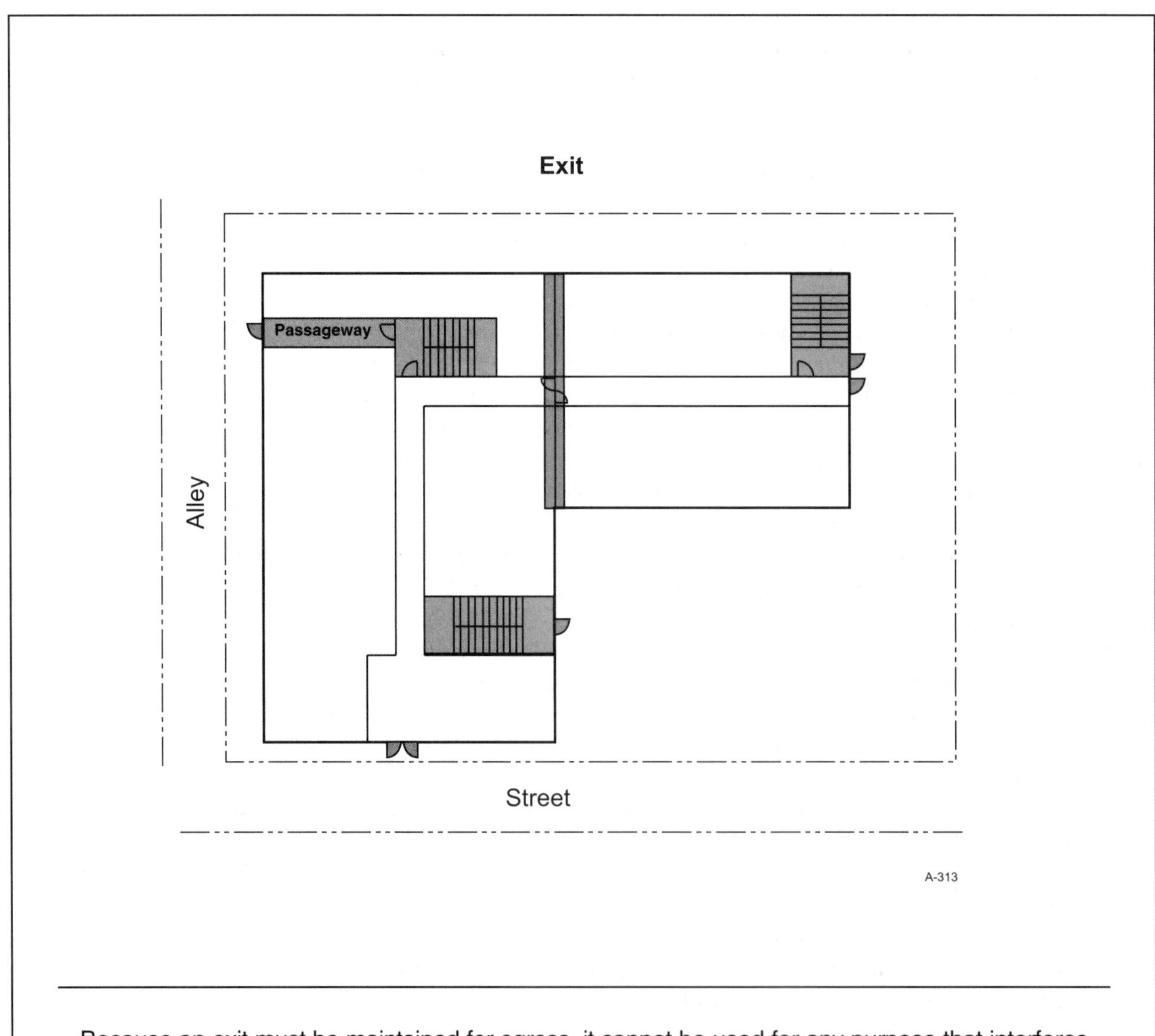

Because an exit must be maintained for egress, it cannot be used for any purpose that interferes with egress. In addition, once a mandated level of protection is provided for occupants reaching an exit, that level cannot be diminished prior to their reaching the exit discharge.

Topic: Minimum Number
Reference: IBC 1018.1

Category: Means of Egress
Subject: Exits

Code Text: *All rooms and spaces within each story shall be provided with and have access to the minimum number of approved independent exits as required by Table 1018.1 based on the occupant load, except as modified in Section 1014.1 or 1018.2. For the purposes of* Chapter 10, *occupied roofs shall be provided with exits as required for stories. The required number of exits from any story, basement or individual space shall be maintained until arrival at grade or the public way.*

Discussion and Commentary: The general provisions call for at least two unique and separate exits from any room, floor area or building. However, in many cases it has been determined that more than one exit provides little, if any, additional protection. Therefore, only one exit is permitted for egress from buildings of limited occupant loads, story heights and travel distances. In all cases, the exit must be continuous to the point where the exit discharge begins.

TABLE 1018.1
MINIMUM NUMBER OF EXITS FOR OCCUPANT LOAD

OCCUPANT LOAD	MINIMUM NUMBER OF EXITS
1-500	2
501-1,000	3
More than 1,000	4

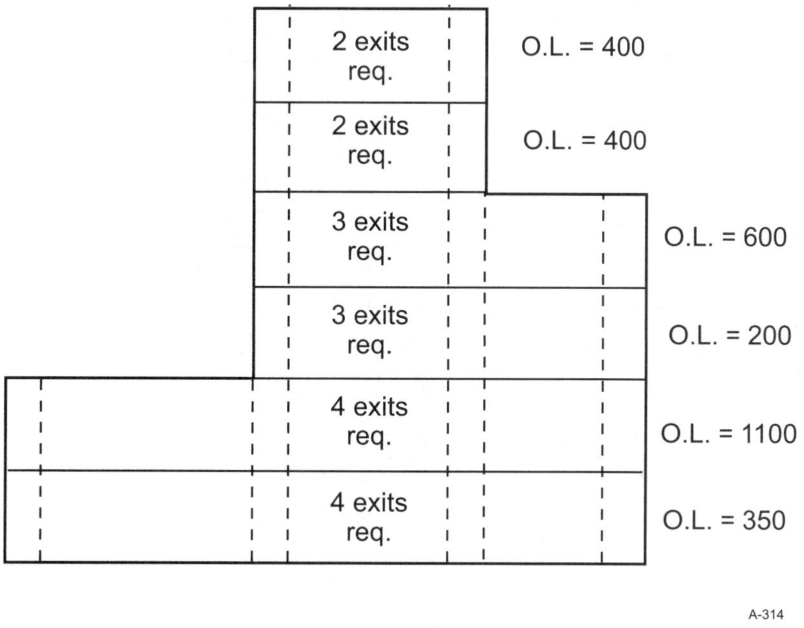

Until all exit paths reach the exterior at grade level, the minimum required number of exits must be maintained. Once exterior grade is reached, the required number of exit paths may be reduced, provided that the required exit width is maintained until arrival at the public way.

Topic: Buildings with One Exit
Reference: IBC 1018.2

Category: Means of Egress
Subject: Number of Exits and Continuity

Code Text: *Only one exit shall be required in buildings as described below: 1) buildings described in Table 1018.2, provided that the building has not more than one level below the first story above grade plane, 2) buildings of Group R-3 occupancy, and 3) single-level buildings with the occupied space at the level of exit discharge provided that the story or space complies with Section 1014.1 as a space with one means of egress.*

Discussion and Commentary: Buildings with one exit are permitted where the configuration and occupancy meet certain characteristics which together do not present an unacceptable fire risk to the buildings' occupants. Those structures that are relatively small in size have a shorter travel distance and fewer occupants; thus, having access to a single exit does not significantly compromise the safety of the occupants.

TABLE 1018.2
BUILDINGS WITH ONE EXIT

OCCUPANCY	MAXIMUM HEIGHT OF BUILDING ABOVE GRADE PLANE	MAXIMUM OCCUPANTS (OR DWELLING UNITS) PER FLOOR AND TRAVEL DISTANCE
A, B[d], E, F, M, U	1 Story	50 occupants and 75 feet travel distance
H-2, H-3	1 Story	3 occupants and 25 feet travel distance
H-4, H-5, I, R	1 Story	10 occupants and 75 feet travel distance
S[a]	1 Story	30 occupants and 100 feet travel distance
B[b], F, M, S[a]	2 Stories	30 occupants and 75 feet travel distance
R-2	2 Stories[c]	4 dwelling units and 50 feet travel distance

For SI: 1 foot = 304.8 mm.

a. For the required number of exits for open parking structures, see Section 1018.1.1.

b. For the required number of exits for air traffic control towers, see Section 412.1.

c. Buildings classified as Group R-2 equipped throughout with an automatic sprinkler system in accordance with Section 903.3.1.1 or 903.3.1.2 and provided with emergency escape and rescue openings in accordance with Section 1025 shall have a maximum height of three stories above grade.

d. Buildings equipped throughout with an automatic sprinkler system in accordance with Section 903.3.1.1 with an occupancy in Group B shall have a maximum travel distance of 100 feet.

The restriction on the number of levels below the first story is intended to limit the vertical travel an occupant must accomplish to reach the exit discharge in a single-exit building. Above the first story, the limitation is more restrictive, with a single exit available to only five occupancies.

Topic: Enclosures Required
Reference: IBC 1019.1

Category: Means of Egress
Subject: Vertical Exit Enclosures

Code Text: *Interior exit stairways and interior exit ramps shall be enclosed with fire barriers. Exit enclosures shall have a fire-resistance rating of not less than 2 hours where connecting four stories or more and not less than 1 hour where connecting less than four stories. The number of stories connected by the shaft enclosure shall include any basements but not any mezzanines.* See nine exceptions that identify where enclosures are not required.

Discussion and Commentary: Also addressed in Section 707, vertical openings created for stairways must typically be enclosed with fire-resistance-rated construction. Two commonly used exceptions permit unenclosed exit stairways between two interconnected floors, though they are limited to no more than 50 percent of the required number of exits. The exception is not applicable to Group H and I occupancies. In fully sprinklered buildings, all stairways serving only the first and second floors may be unenclosed.

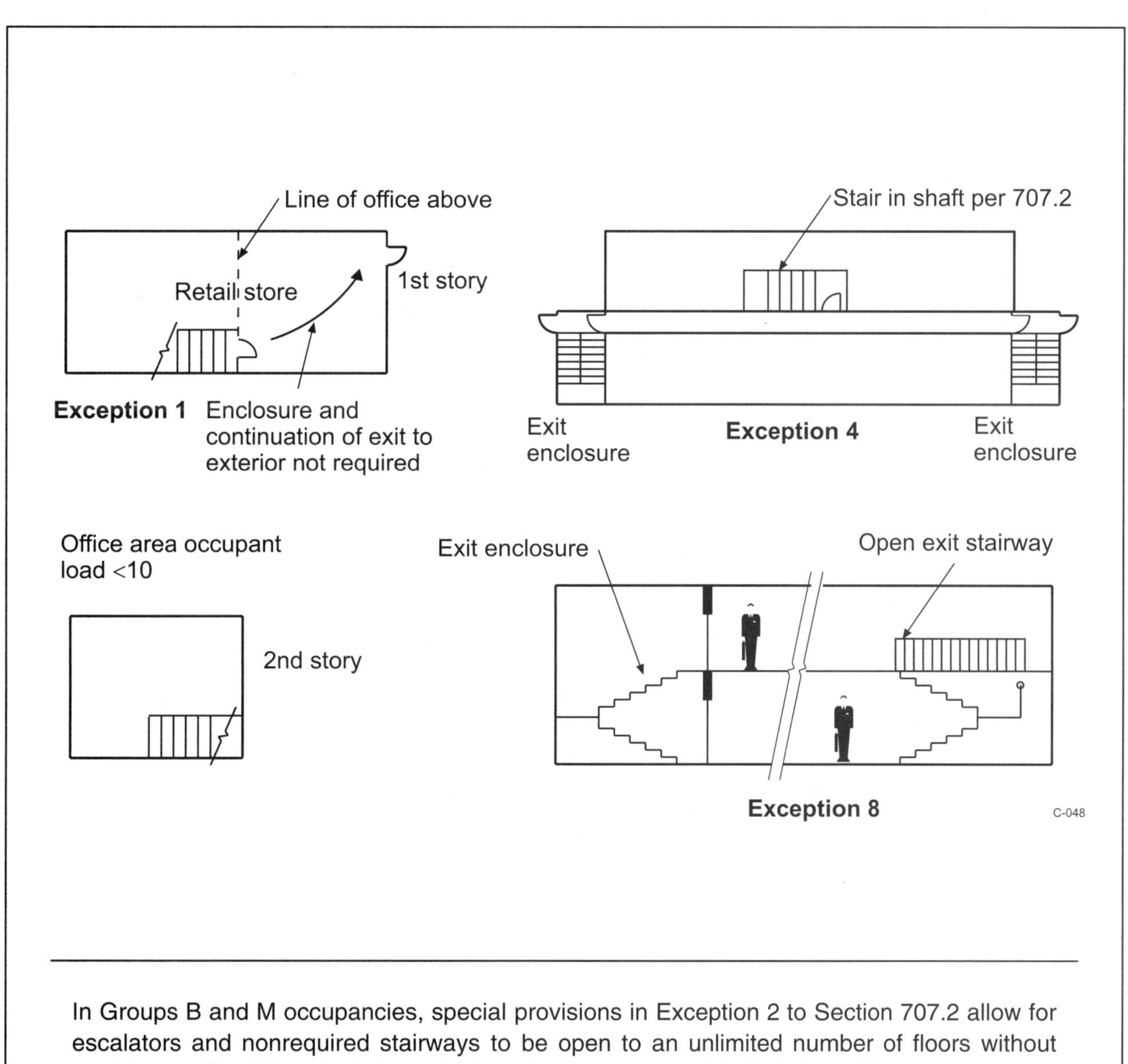

In Groups B and M occupancies, special provisions in Exception 2 to Section 707.2 allow for escalators and nonrequired stairways to be open to an unlimited number of floors without enclosures. Conditions include sprinklers, draft curtains and limited size of floor openings.

Topic: Vertical Enclosure Exterior Walls
Reference: IBC 1019.1.4

Category: Means of Egress
Subject: Vertical Exit Enclosures

Code Text: *Where nonrated walls or unprotected openings enclose the exterior of the stairway and the walls or openings are exposed to other parts of the building at an angle of less than 180 degrees, the building exterior walls within 10 feet horizontally of a nonrated wall or unprotected opening shall be constructed as required for a minimum 1-hour fire-resistance rating with $^3/_4$-hour opening protectives. This construction shall extend vertically from the ground to a point 10 feet above the topmost landing of the stairway or to the roof line, which ever is lower.*

Discussion and Commentary: Unless regulated according to fire separation distance or type of construction, the exterior wall of a vertical exit enclosure usually needs no fire-resistance rating. However, where exposure is possible from other exterior walls of the building in close proximity to the exit enclosure, a limited degree of fire separation is necessary.

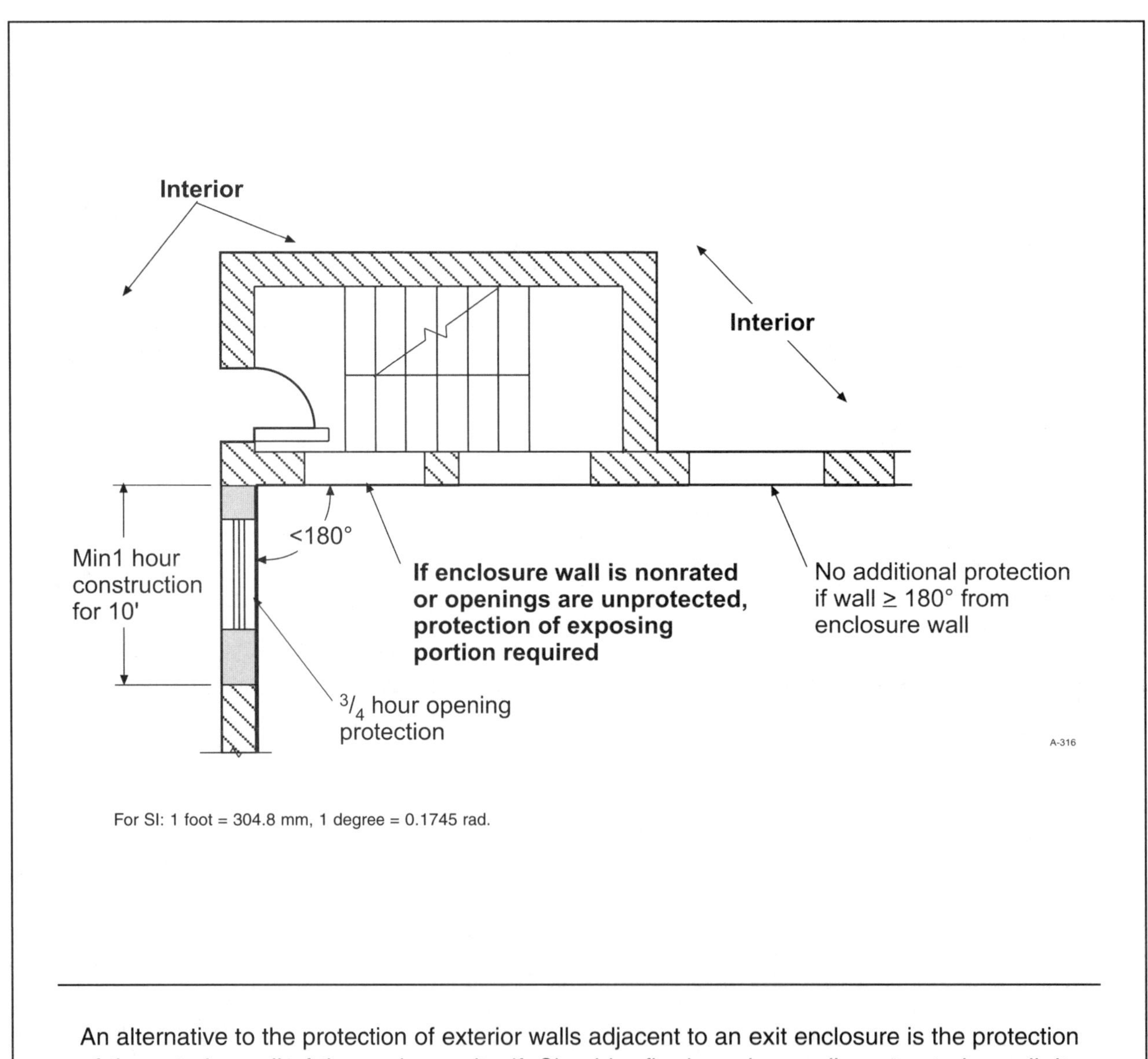

For SI: 1 foot = 304.8 mm, 1 degree = 0.1745 rad.

An alternative to the protection of exterior walls adjacent to an exit enclosure is the protection of the exterior wall of the enclosure itself. Should a fire breach an adjacent exterior wall, its penetration of the exit enclosure would be halted for an acceptable time period.

Topic: Smokeproof Enclosures
Reference: IBC 1019.1.8

Category: Means of Egress
Subject: Vertical Exit Enclosures

Code Text: *In buildings required to comply with Section 403* (High-rise Buildings) *or 405* (Underground Buildings), *each of the exits of a building that serves stories where the floor surface is located more than 75 feet above the lowest level of fire department vehicle access or more than 30 feet below the level of exit discharge serving such floor levels shall be a smokeproof enclosure or pressurized stairway in accordance with Section 909.20.*

Discussion and Commentary: In those buildings where vertical egress travel is extensive, an additional level of protection is mandated, primarily to address the hazard of smoke and toxic gases that are produced in a fire. Through ventilation or pressurization, the potential for smoke and gases to enter the enclosure is dramatically reduced.

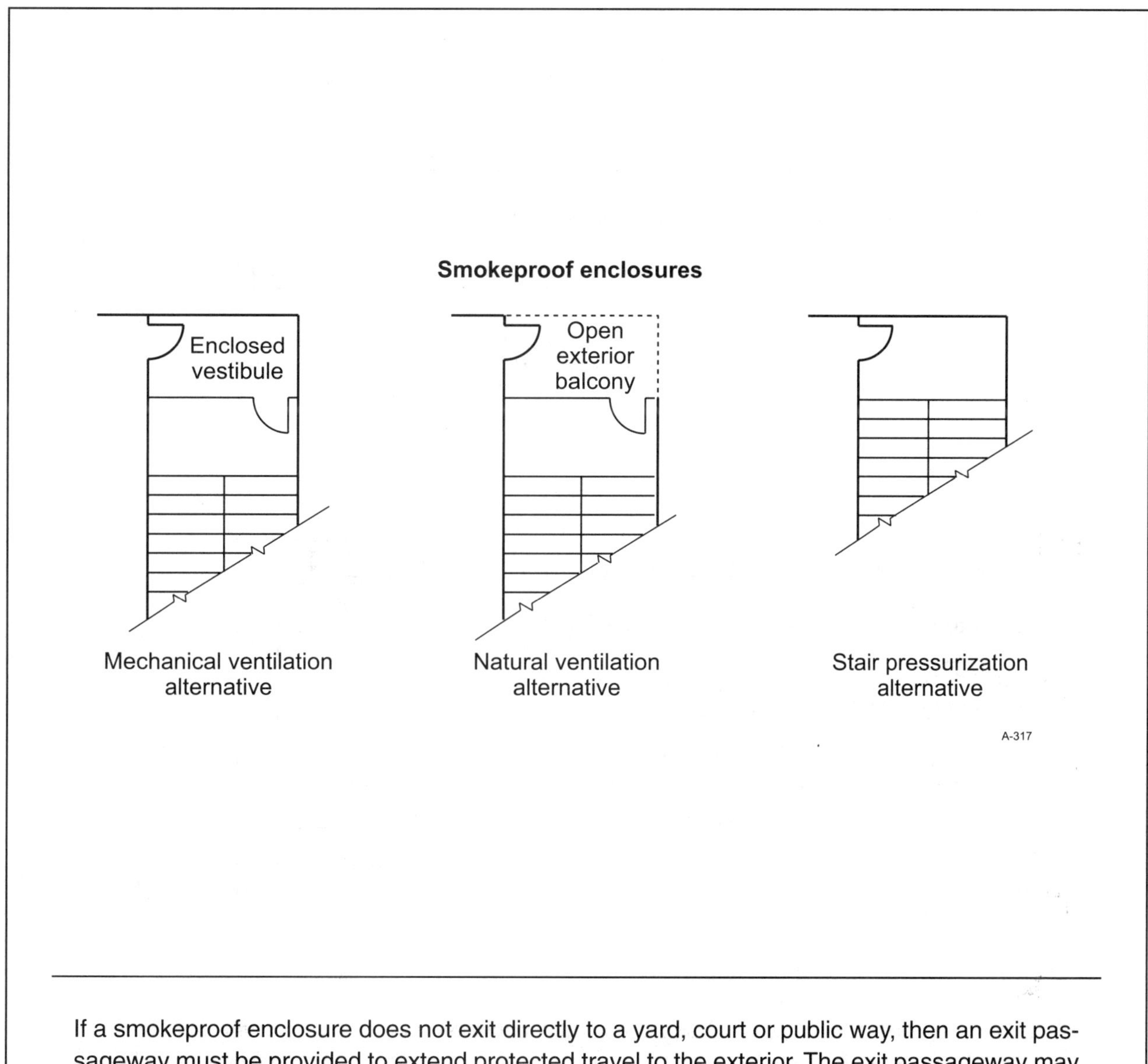

If a smokeproof enclosure does not exit directly to a yard, court or public way, then an exit passageway must be provided to extend protected travel to the exterior. The exit passageway may have no other openings unless it is protected in the same manner as the vertical enclosure.

Topic: Construction
Reference: IBC 1020

Category: Means of Egress
Subject: Exit Passageways

Code Text: *An exit passageway shall not be used for any purpose other than a means of egress. Exit passageway enclosures shall have walls, floor and ceiling of not less than 1-hour fire-resistance rating, and not less than that required for any connecting exit enclosure. Exit passageways shall be constructed as fire barriers in accordance with Section 706.*

Discussion and Commentary: An exit passageway is defined as *an exit component that is separated from all other interior spaces of a building or structure by fire-resistance-rated construction and opening protectives, and provides for a protected path of egress travel in a horizontal direction to the exit discharge or the public way.* It is an egress component of a higher level than a fire-resistance-rated corridor, based primarily on limited openings and penetrations, and increased fire ratings.

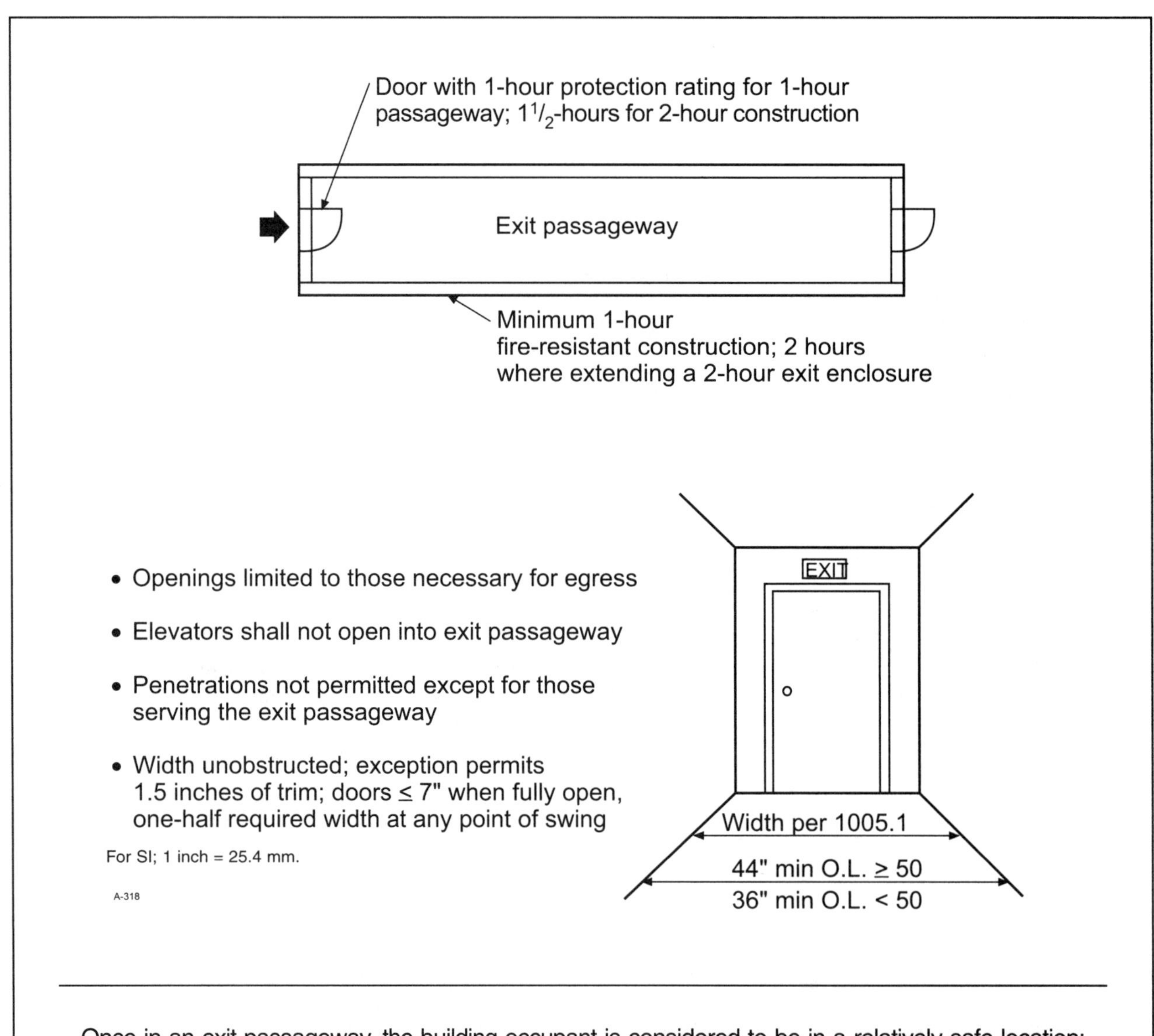

Once in an exit passageway, the building occupant is considered to be in a relatively safe location; thus, travel distances within the exit passageway are unregulated. Simply put, an exit passageway is a horizontal exit enclosure, with conditions and limitations similar to those of a vertical exit enclosure.

Topic: Openings and Penetrations **Category:** Means of Egress
Reference: IBC 1019.1.1, 1020.5 **Subject:** Exits

Code Text: *Except as permitted in Section 402.4.6* (covered mall buildings), *openings in exit enclosures (and exit passageways) other than unexposed exterior openings shall be limited to those necessary for exit access to the enclosure from normally occupied spaces and for egress from the enclosure. Penetrations into and openings through an exit enclosure are prohibited except for required exit doors, equipment and duct work necessary for independent pressurization, sprinkler piping, standpipes, electrical raceway serving the fire department communication and electrical conduit serving the exit enclosure and terminating at a steel box not exceeding 16 square inches.*

Discussion and Commentary: Given the importance of an exit enclosure in the means of egress system, no unnecessary openings or penetrations are permitted to breach the fire-resistant separation. The provisions are essentially the same for both vertical exit enclosures and exit passageways.

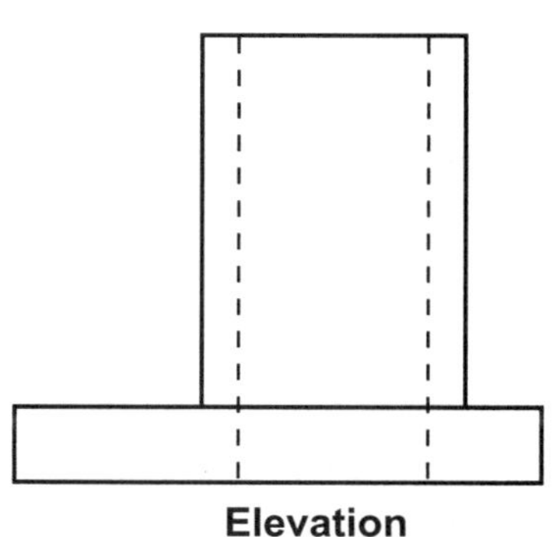

Elevation

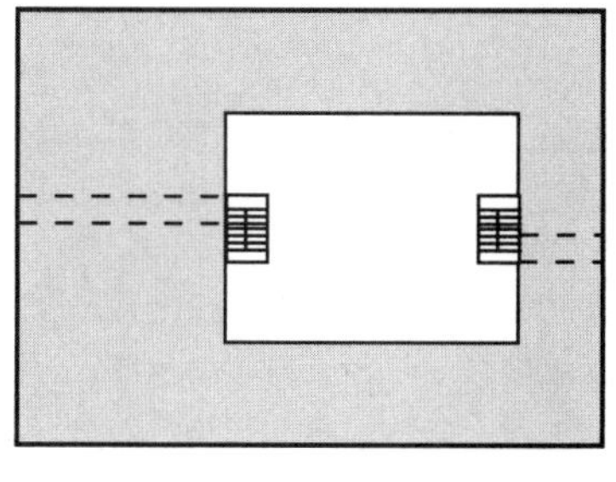

Plan

Enclosure construction:

- Four or more stories-2-hour fire resistance
- Less than four stories-1-hour fire resistance

Openings and penetrations:

- Permitted exterior openings (704)
- Egress from normally occupied spaces
- Egress from enclosure
- Standpipe and sprinklers
- Ductwork for independent pressurization
- Limited electrical conduit

Doors: (715)

- Self-closing or automatic closing
- 1-hour rating in 1-hour construction
- $1^1/_2$-hour rating in 2-hour construction
- Temperature rise limit of 450°F above ambient unless sprinklered buildings

A-319

Several methods are set forth in the code to provide for ventilation of an exit enclosure. In general, penetrations for ductwork must enter directly from the building's exterior or from an interior space separated from the remainder of the building by a shaft enclosure.

Topic: General
Reference: IBC 1021

Category: Means of Egress
Subject: Horizontal Exits

Code Text: *A horizontal exit shall not serve as the only exit from a portion of a building, and where two or more exits are required, not more than one-half of the total number of exits or total width of exit width shall be horizontal exits. The refuge area of a horizontal exit shall be spaces occupied by the same tenant or public areas and each such area of refuge shall be adequate to house the original occupant load of the refuge space plus the occupant load anticipated from the adjoining compartment.*

Discussion and Commentary: A horizontal exit is defined as *a path of egress travel from one building to an area in another building on approximately the same level, or a path of egress travel through or around a wall or partition to an area on approximately the same level in the same building, which affords safety from fire and smoke from the area of incidence and areas communicating therewith.* Constructed as a fire wall or a minimum two-hour fire barrier, a horizontal exit is an exit component of the means of egress system.

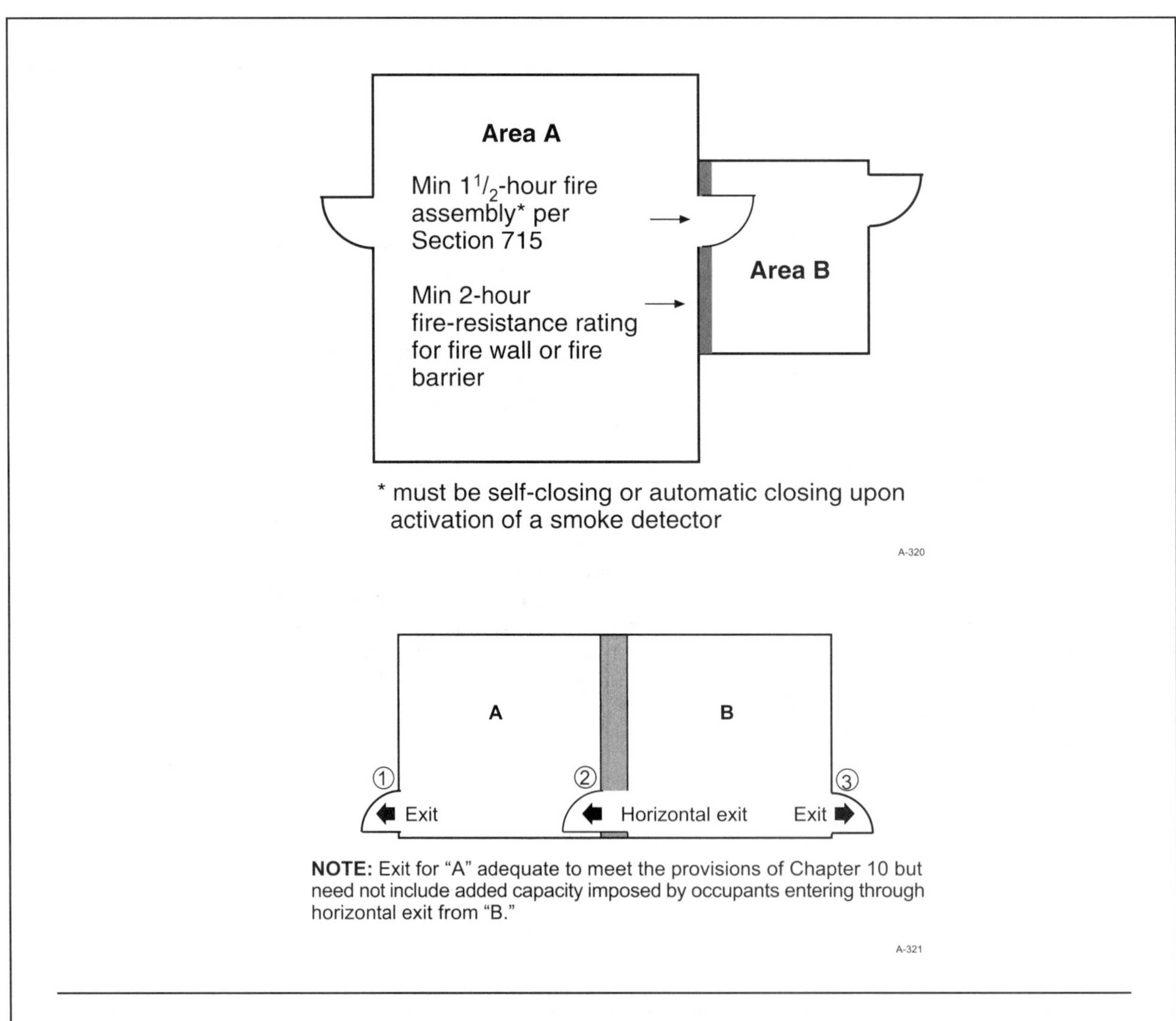

Horizontal exits must extend vertically through all levels of the building, unless minimum two-hour floor assemblies with no unprotected openings are provided. The horizontal exit walls are to extend continuously from exterior wall to exterior wall in order to completely divide the floor.

Topic: Open Side
Reference: IBC 1022.3

Category: Means of Egress
Subject: Exterior Exit Stairways

Code Text: *Exterior exit stairways serving as an element of a required means of egress shall be open on at least one side. An open side shall have a minimum of 35 square feet of aggregate open area adjacent to each floor level and the level of each intermediate landing. The required open area shall be located not less than 42 inches above the adjacent floor or landing level.*

Discussion and Commentary: For a stairway to be considered exterior, it must be open enough to the outside so that smoke and toxic gases will not tend to corrupt the exit route. An exterior exit stairway is considered an exit component and is permitted as an egress element in all occupancies except Group I-2. Where permitted as an element of a required means of egress, an exterior exit stairway is limited to 6 stories and to 75 feet in height.

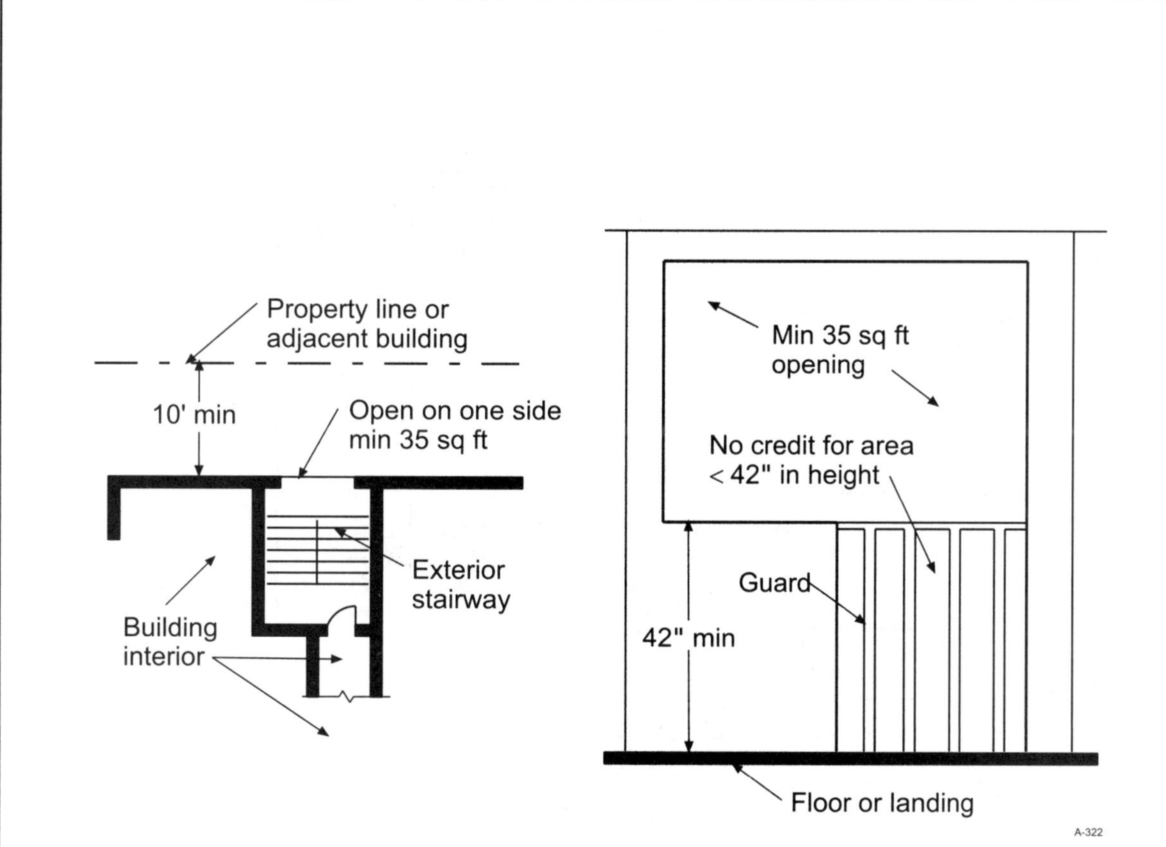

Consistent with the requirements for other exit components, an exterior exit stairway must be separated from the remainder of the building by fire-resistance-rated construction and protected openings. The IBC provides four exceptions where separation is not warranted.

Topic: Definition and Scope
Reference: IBC 1002, 1023.1

Category: Means of Egress
Subject: Exit Discharge

Code Text: The exit discharge is *that portion of a means of egress system between the termination of an exit and a public way. Exits shall discharge directly to the exterior of the building.* See exceptions for discharge level spaces and vestibules. *The exit discharge shall be at grade or shall provide direct access to grade. The exit discharge shall not reenter a building.* See three exceptions.

Discussion and Commentary: Exit discharge travel typically takes place outside of the building, where hazards to the occupants are greatly reduced. Although concern over the accumulation of smoke and toxic gases is eliminated, there is still a risk to the occupants, which is eliminated only at a point of considerable distance from the structure, generally the public way.

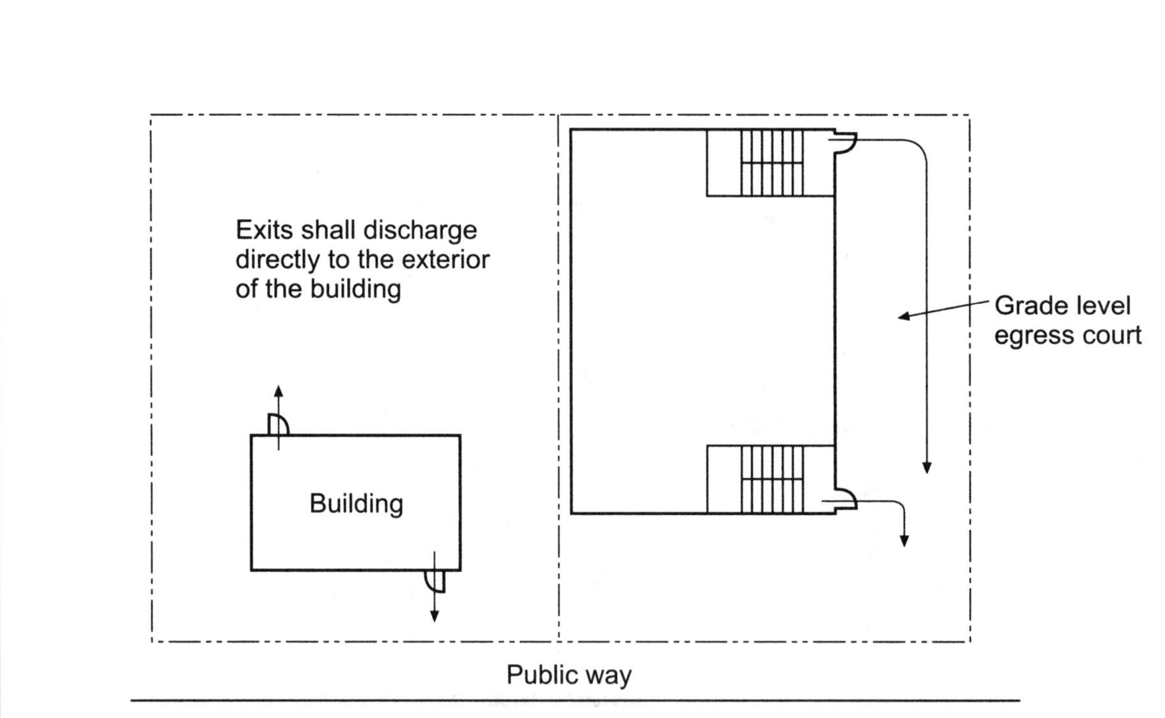

Number of exits maintained until arrival at grade or public way

A-323

When specific conditions are met, up to 50% of the number and capacity of exit enclosures may exit through a vestibule or an area on the discharge level. In addition, stairways in open parking garages may egress through the garage at the discharge level.

Topic: Egress Courts
Reference: IBC 1023.5

Category: Means of Egress
Subject: Exit Discharge

Code Text: *Where an egress court serving a building or portion thereof is less than 10 feet in width, the egress court walls shall be not less than 1-hour fire-resistance-rated exterior walls complying with Section 704 for a distance of 10 feet above the floor of the court, and openings therein shall be equipped with fixed or self-closing, ¾-hour opening protective assemblies.* See exceptions for small occupant loads and dwellings.

Discussion and Commentary: An egress court is defined as *a court or yard which provides access to a public way for one or more exits.* Because an egress court is an element of the exit discharge, occupants must be afforded sufficient protection from a fire within the structure to be reasonably sure that once outside they will reach the safety of a public way.

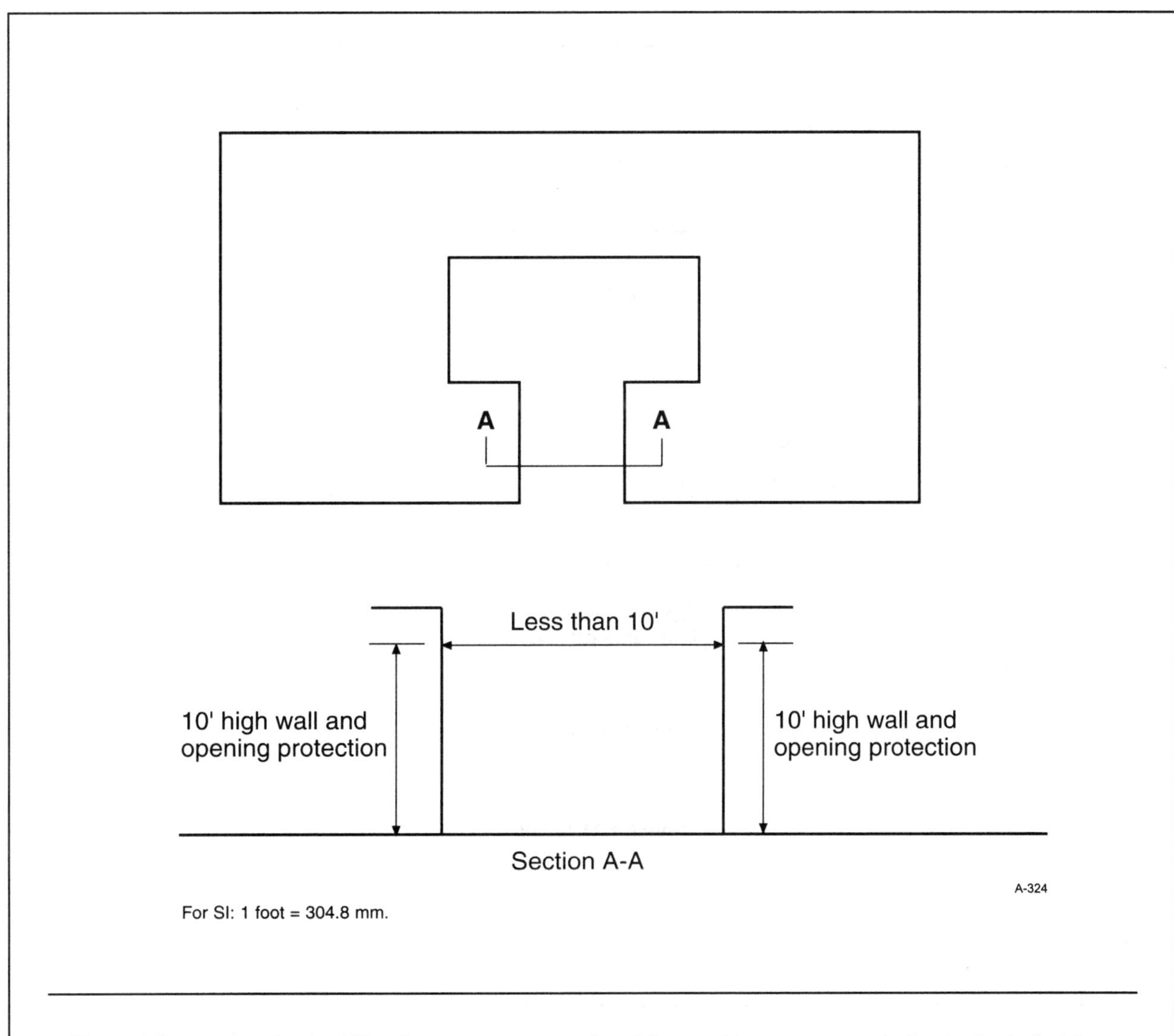

The minimum required width of an egress court is addressed in a manner similar to that of aisles, corridors and stairways. The width must accommodate the calculated capacity, based on occupant load served; however, in no case may it be less than a specified width of 44" (36" in Group R-3).

Topic: Access to a Public Way
Reference: IBC 1023.6

Category: Means of Egress
Subject: Exit Discharge

Code Text: *The exit discharge shall provide a direct and unobstructed access to a public way. See exception for designation of a safe dispersal area where access to a public way cannot be provided.*

Discussion and Commentary: The means of egress is not complete until the occupants of the building have reached a safe place. Such a place is typically a public way, in that it is relatively unobstructed, and more importantly, continuous. It is always possible to continue egress travel along a public way until the necessary level of safety is achieved. The path to reach the public way, as for all other components of the means of egress, must be free of obstructions and other concerns that would cause the occupants' egress travel to be delayed, restricted or unavailable. It is important that the travel path outside of the building be continuously maintained in order to keep the means of egress in a complying condition.

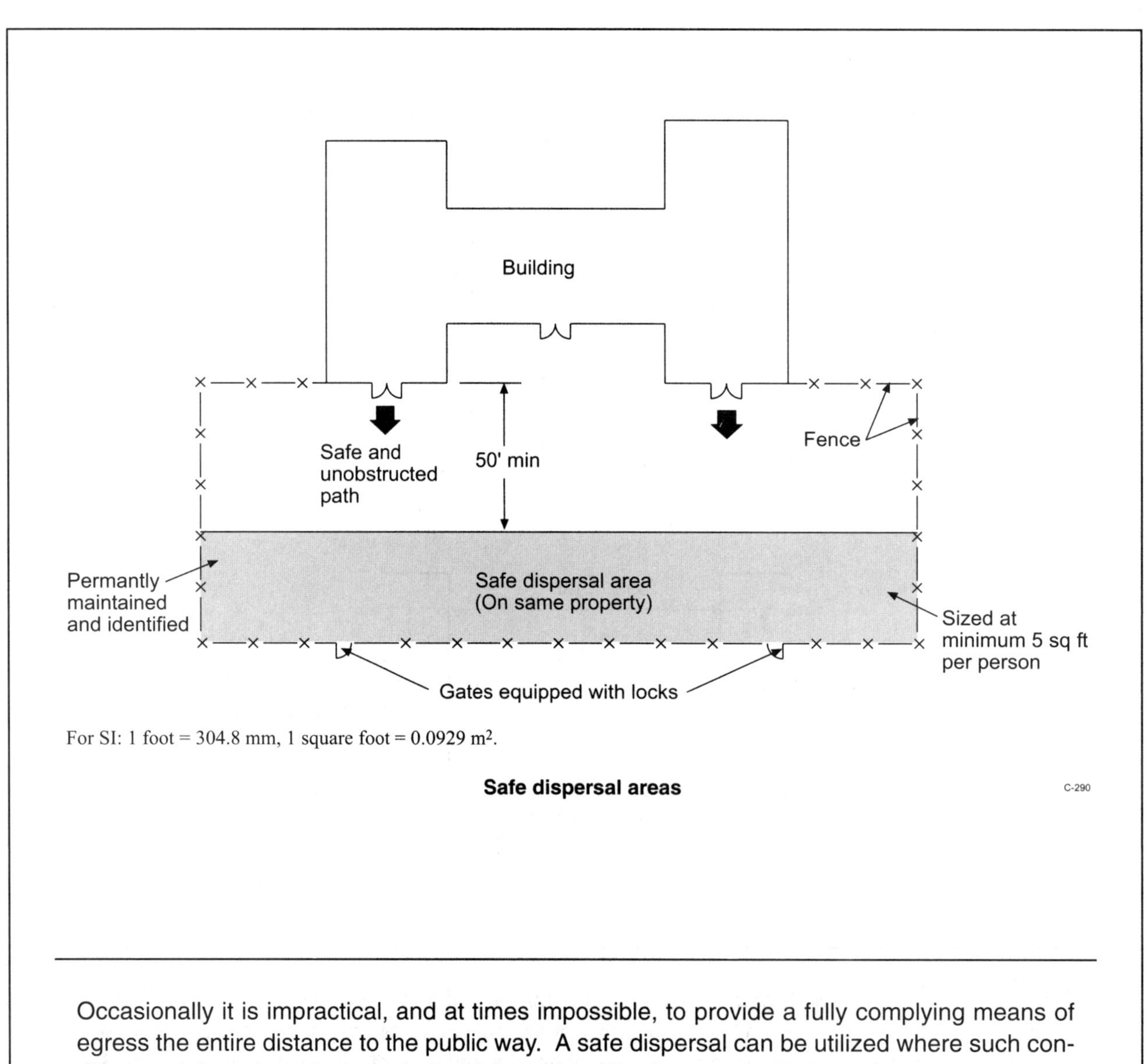

Safe dispersal areas

Occasionally it is impractical, and at times impossible, to provide a fully complying means of egress the entire distance to the public way. A safe dispersal can be utilized where such conditions exist, such as on large industrial or educational campus sites.

Topic: Assembly Main Exit
Reference: IBC 1024.2

Category: Means of Egress
Subject: Assembly

Code Text: *Group A occupancies that have an occupant load of greater than 300 shall be provided with a main exit. The main exit shall be of sufficient width to accommodate not less than one-half of the occupant load, but such width shall not be less than the total required width of all means of egress leading to the exit.*

Discussion and Commentary: In most assembly-type uses, the occupants tend to enter the room or space at a single location. It is expected that under emergency conditions, most of the occupants will attempt to exit at the same point. Therefore, the main entrance/exit must be wide enough to handle a sizeable percentage of the occupants. If there are multiple main entrance/exits, the exit width can be distributed among the exits around the perimeter of the building.

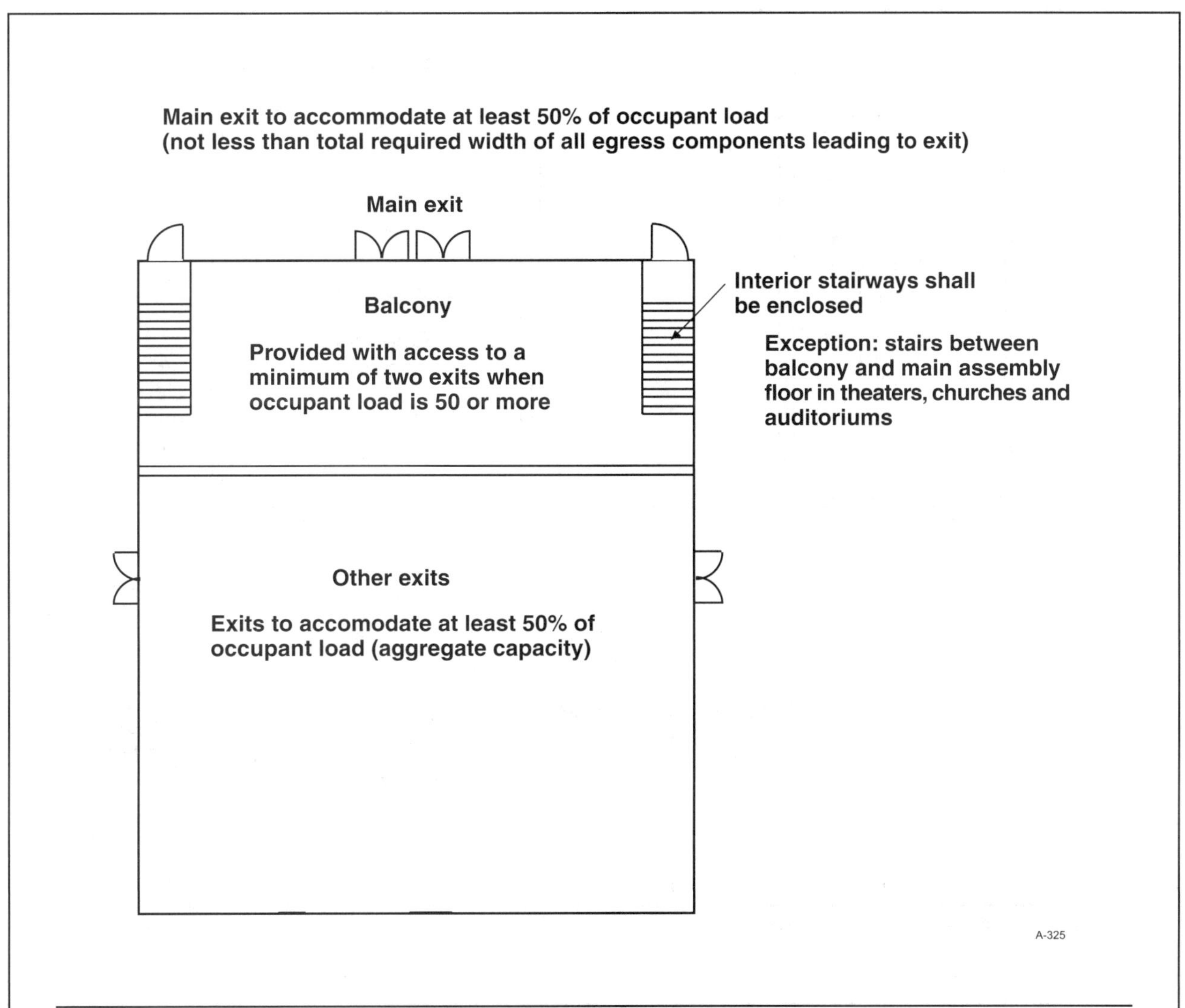

To better define and maintain the egress path through a lobby or foyer to the main entrance/exit, the code mandates that the waiting area be separated from the required egress width. Where seats are not available, the use of railings or partitions is specified.

Topic: Required Openings
Reference: IBC 1025

Category: Means of Egress
Subject: Emergency Escape and Rescue

Code Text: *In addition to the means of egress required by Chapter 10, provisions shall be made for emergency escape and rescue in Group R and Group I-1 occupancies. Basements and sleeping rooms below the fourth story shall have at least one exterior emergency escape and rescue opening in accordance with Section 1025.* See seven exceptions, including those for sprinklered buildings and those with a complying corridor. *Such opening shall open directly into a public street, public alley, yard or court.*

Discussion and Commentary: In those occupancies where persons are sometimes sleeping, a fire will often spread quickly and block the normal egress routes. By requiring a sizeable opening directly from the sleeping room to the exterior, rescue can be more easily accomplished, or alternatively, the occupants may escape without having to travel through the building. In other than Group R-3 occupancies, such openings are not required if the building is fully sprinklered.

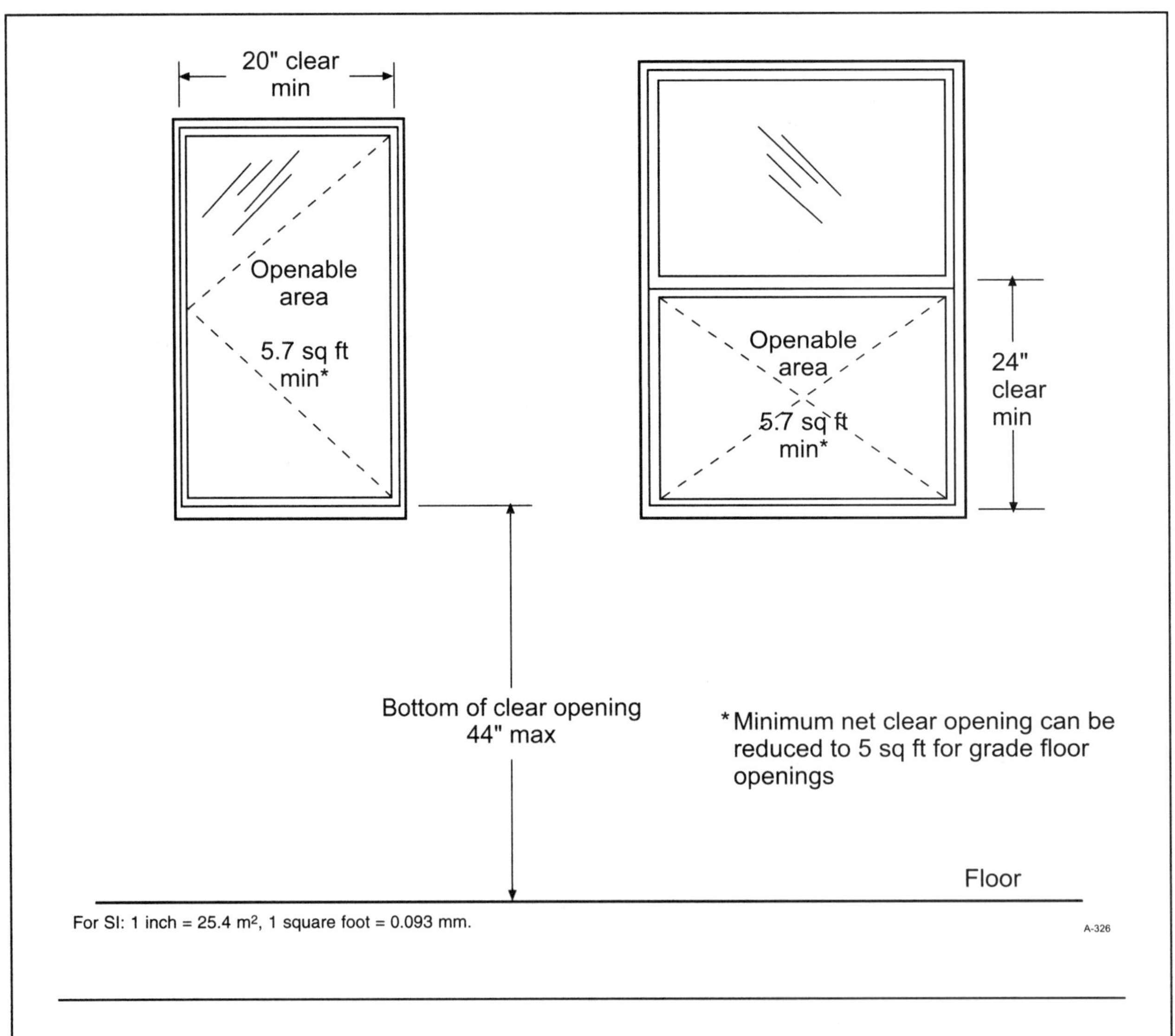

When operable windows are used for egress or rescue purposes, the intent is that they be double-hung, horizontal sliding or casement styles operated by a simple operation. Special types other than those listed must be evaluated for compliance with the operational constraint limitations.

QUIZ

Study Session 12 — Sections 1017–1025

I. Multiple Choice

1. A building having an occupant load of 720 persons shall be provided with a minimum of __________ approved independent exits.

a. two
b. three
c. four
d. five

Reference_______________

2. A single exit is permitted from what type of parking garage?

a. open
b. enclosed
c. commercial trucks and buses
d. vehicles are mechanically parked

Reference_______________

3. A single exit from the second floor of a Group B office building is permitted if the maximum occupant load is __________ persons and the maximum travel distance is __________ feet.

a. 10, 75
b. 30, 75
c. 30, 200
d. 50, 200

Reference_______________

4. Vertical exit enclosures a minimum of __________ stories in height shall be 2-hour fire-resistance rated.

a. three
b. four
c. five
d. six

Reference_______________

5. In other than Group H and I occupancies, a stairway serving a maximum occupant load of __________ persons need not be enclosed where located not more than one story above the level of exit discharge.

a. 9
b. 29
c. 30
d. 50

Reference_______________

6. The open space under exterior stairways shall not be used __________.

a. for any purpose
b. for combustible storage
c. unless fully sprinklered
d. except in Type V construction

Reference________________

7. Stairway floor number signs shall be provided in interior vertical exit enclosures connecting a minimum of __________ stories.

a. 2
b. 3
c. 4
d. 6

Reference________________

8. Smokeproof enclosures shall be provided for exits serving stories a minimum of __________ feet above the lowest level of fire department vehicle access.

a. 30
b. 55
c. 75
d. 160

Reference________________

9. Exit passageways shall be constructed as minimum __________.

a. one-hour fire partitions
b. one-hour fire barriers
c. two-hour fire barriers
d. two-hour fire walls

Reference________________

10. In other than Group I occupancies, a refuge area serving a horizontal exit shall be sized for capacity based on __________ square feet for each occupant to be accommodated.

a. 3
b. 6
c. 15
d. 30

Reference________________

11. In other than a Group I-2 occupancy, exterior exit stairways are permitted as means of egress elements for buildings a maximum of __________ stories in height.

a. 3
b. 4
c. 5
d. 6

Reference________________

12. An exterior exit stairway must be open on at least one side, with such open area a minimum of __________ square feet and located a minimum of __________ inches above the floor or landing level.

a. 9, 36	b. 16, 42
c. 20, 36	d. 35, 42

Reference________________

13. Egress balconies and exterior exit stairways shall be located a minimum of __________ feet from adjacent lot lines.

a. 3	b. 5
c. 10	d. 20

Reference________________

14. What is the minimum width of an egress court serving 40 occupants from an office building?

a. 36 inches	b. 44 inches
c. 48 inches	d. 60 inches

Reference________________

15. Exterior walls enclosing an egress court shall be of minimum one-hour fire-resistance-rated construction to a minimum height of _____ where the egress court is less than 10 feet in width.

a. 6 feet, 8 inches	b. 7 feet, 0 inches
c 8 feet, 0 inches	d. 10 feet, 0 inches

Reference________________

16. A main exit shall be provided for all Group A occupancies having a minimum occupant load of __________ persons.

a. 51	b. 301
c. 501	d. 1,001

Reference________________

17. At least two means of egress shall be provided from balconies having a minimum seating capacity of __________ persons.

a. 10	b. 31
c. 51	d. 100

Reference________________

18. In assembly areas not provided with smoke protection, the minimum width for stairs having 8-inch risers is based on a minimum of __________ inch of width for each occupant served.

a. 0.2 b. 0.22
c. 0.3 d. 0.35

Reference_______________

19. In a 15,000-seat arena provided with smoke-protected assembly seating, the minimum width for a 1:12 ramped aisle is based on a minimum of __________ inch of width for each occupant served.

a. 0.300 b. 0.200
c. 0.120 d. 0.070

Reference_______________

20. The smoke level in a means of egress serving a smoke-protected assembly seating area is intended to be located a minimum of __________ feet above the floor of the means of egress.

a. 6 b. 8
c. 12 d. 15

Reference_______________

21. What is the maximum travel distance for seating in open-air assembly structures of Type I or II construction?

a. 200 feet b. 300 feet
c. 400 feet d. unlimited

Reference_______________

22. What is the minimum required clear width of aisle stairs having seating on only one side?

a. 32 inches b. 36 inches
c. 42 inches d. 44 inches

Reference_______________

23. In aisle stairs, the maximum tolerance permitted between adjacent treads is __________ inch.

a. $^{1}/_{8}$ b. $^{3}/_{16}$
c. $^{1}/_{4}$ d. $^{3}/_{8}$

Reference_______________

24. A railing or fascia system at the foot of aisles in an assembly occupancy shall be a minimum of __________ in height.

a. 26 inches
b. 32 inches
c. 36 inches
d. 42 inches

Reference_______________

25. What is the minimum net clear opening required for emergency escape and rescue grade floor openings?

a. 20 inches by 22 inches
b. 20 inches by 24 inches
c. 5.0 square feet
d. 5.7 square feet

Reference_______________

26. Where horizontal exits are used in the means of egress in a Group I-2 hospital, the horizontal exits can be used for a maximum of _____ of the required exits.

a. one
b. two
c. one-half
d. two-thirds

Reference_______________

27. Along with other limitations, the exit discharge may occur through a vestibule, provided the vestibule has a maximum depth of _____ feet and a maximum length of _____.

a. 8, 15
b. 10, 20
c. 10, 30
d. 15, 30

Reference_______________

28. Egress need not extend to a public way where a safe dispersal area is provided a minimum of _____ feet from the building.

a. 30
b. 50
c. 75
d. 100

Reference_______________

29. An emergency escape and rescue opening shall be located a maximum of _____ inches above the floor surface, measured to the clear opening.

a. 36
b. 42
c. 44
d. 48

Reference_______________

30. Where a window well is provided to serve an emergency escape and rescue opening, it shall have a minimum horizontal area of _____ square feet.

a. 5.0 b. 5.7

c. 9.0 d. 10.0

Reference_______________

INTERNATIONAL BUILDING CODE
Study Session 13
Chapter 11 — Accessibility

OBJECTIVE: To become familiar with the scoping provisions relating to the design and construction of accessible buildings, facilities and elements.

REFERENCE: Chapter 11, 2003 *International Building Code*

KEY POINTS:

- What is the scope of the provisions regulating accessibility and usability?
- How does ICC A117.1 relate to the IBC?
- Are temporary buildings regulated for accessibility?
- How are employee work areas viewed for accessibility?
- Which types of uses are not required to be accessible?
- Where within employee work areas is an accessible route not required?
- What is an accessible route? Which site elements must be connected by an accessible route to an accessible building entrance?
- Which areas within a building must be connected by an accessible route?
- Under which conditions is a vertical accessible route not required?
- How should the accessible route be provided in relationship to the general circulation path?
- How many entrances to a building must be accessible? To a tenant space within a building?
- What percentage of parking spaces must be designed as accessible?
- When is a van-accessible space required?
- Where must accessible parking spaces be located?
- When is an accessible loading zone required?
- What is a Type A dwelling unit? Type B unit? In which types of buildings are such units located?
- Where dwelling units and sleeping units are required to be accessible, what accessible features are required in each Accessible unit, Type A unit and Type B unit ?
- In a theater, auditorium or similar assembly area, how is the minimum number of required wheelchair spaces determined?
- How shall wheelchair spaces be distributed throughout a multilevel assembly facility?
- What is the function of an assistive listening system? Under which conditions are assistive listening systems required?
- Which types of dining areas must be accessible?
- What specific areas of a judicial facility must be accessible?
- What percentage of toilet rooms are required to be accessible? Bathing facilities?
- What are unisex toilet rooms and bathing rooms? When are such rooms required?
- What are the features required in a unisex toilet room? Bathing room?
- Where drinking fountains are provided, how many must be accessible? Storage lockers? Fitting rooms? Check-out aisles?
- Under what conditions is a platform (wheelchair) lift permitted to be a part of a required accessible route?
- Where are detectable warnings required?
- What type of operating mechanisms or controls are regulated for usability?
  When must a stairway be considered an accessible element?
- What is the International Symbol of Accessibility? Where are such signs required?
- Where is directional signage mandated?

Topic: Scope
Reference: IBC 1101

Category: Accessibility
Subject: General Provisions

Code Text: *The provisions of Chapter 11 shall control the design and construction of facilities for accessibility to physically disabled persons. Buildings and facilities shall be designed and constructed to be accessible in accordance with the IBC and ICC A117.1.*

Discussion and Commentary: Chapter 11 of the *International Building Code* sets forth the scoping provisions that identify where and to what degree access must be provided. Once it has been determined that accessible elements are required, the ICC design standard "Accessible and Usable Buildings and Facilities" sets forth the specific technical criteria. As with any other provision of the code, alternative designs, products or technologies that provide equivalent or superior compliance may be accepted by the building official.

Scope
The provisions of Chapter 11 shall control the design and construction of facilities for accessibility to physically disabled persons.

Design
Buildings and facilities shall be designed and constructed in accordance with the IBC and the ICC A117.1-1998 Standard.

A-327

Although space requirements can vary greatly depending on the nature of the disability and the physical functions of the individual, it is generally accepted that spaces designed to accommodate persons using wheelchairs will be functional for most people.

Topic: Where Required
Reference: IBC 1103

Category: Accessibility
Subject: Scoping Requirements

Code Text: *Buildings and structures, temporary or permanent, including their associated sites and facilities, shall be accessible to persons with physical disabilities.* See general exceptions.

Discussion and Commentary: In general, all portions of all buildings are to be provided with elements that will make them fully accessible to individuals with disabilities. There are, however, a number of general exceptions that reduce or eliminate accessibility requirements. Specific areas that are not required to be accessible include: individual employee work areas; detached dwellings and their accessory structures; construction sites; raised security or safety areas, such as observation galleries or fire towers; nonoccupiable spaces and equipment spaces, including elevator pits and transformer vaults; and single-occupant structures accessed at other than grade, such as toll booths.

General Exemptions

Specific requirements. Where not required per Sections 1104 through 1110.

Existing buildings. Existing buildings shall comply with Section 3409.

Employee work areas. Need only comply with fire alarm, accessible means of egress and common use circulation path provisions. Must be able to approach, enter and exit the work area.

Detached dwellings. Detached one- and two-family dwellings and accessory structures, and their associated sites and facilities.

Utility buildings. Group U are exempt except:

1. In agricultural buildings, access is required to paved work areas and areas open to the general public.
2. Private garages or carports that contain required accessible parking.

Construction sites. Structures, sites and equipment directly associated with the actual processes of construction.

Raised areas. Raised areas used primarily for purpose of security, life safety or fire safety.

Limited access spaces. Nonoccupiable spaces accessed only by ladders, catwalks, crawl spaces, freight elevators, very narrow passageways or tunnels.

Equipment spaces. Spaces frequented only by personnel for maintenance, repair or monitoring of equipment.

Single occupant structures. Single occupant structures accessed only by passageways below grade or elevated above grade.

Residential Group R-1. Buildings of Group R-1 containing not more than five sleeping units for rent or hire which are also occupied as the residence of the proprietor.

Day care facilities. Where part of a dwelling unit.

Detention and correctional facilities. Common use areas not serving accessible cells.

Fuel-dispensing systems. Fuel dispensing devices.

Other than those residential occupancies exempt from the accessibility provisions, most buildings will require some level of accessibility. Only those specific areas identified by the code are exempt, whereas the remainder of the structure is regulated for complying accessibility and usability.

Topic: Connected Spaces
Reference: IBC 1104.3

Category: Accessibility
Subject: Accessible Route

Code Text: *When a building, or portion of a building, is required to be accessible, an accessible route shall be provided to each portion of the building, to accessible building entrances, connecting accessible pedestrian walkways and the public way. Where only one accessible route is provided, the accessible route shall not pass through kitchens, storage rooms, restrooms, closets or similar spaces.* See exceptions for accessible dwelling units, fixed-seating assembly areas and mezzanines.

Discussion and Commentary: An accessible route is defined as a continuous, unobstructed path that complies with Chapter 11. It includes corridors, aisles, ramps, elevators, platform (wheelchair) lifts and clear floor space at fixtures. Chapter 4 of ICC A117.1 addresses the design and construction specifications for the elements of an accessible route.

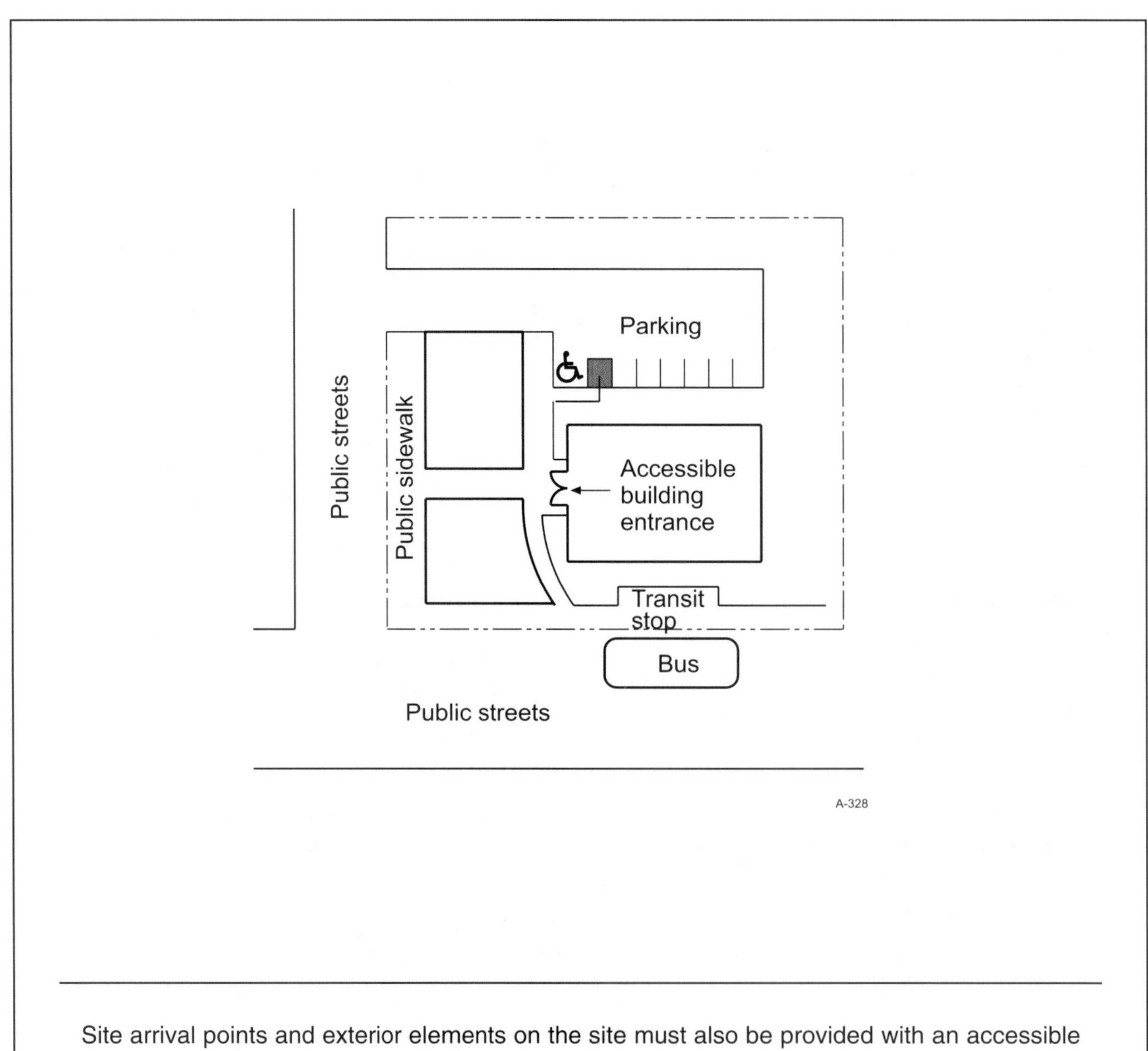

Site arrival points and exterior elements on the site must also be provided with an accessible route to an accessible building entrance. The elements addressed may include public transportation stops, accessible passenger loading zones and accessible parking spaces.

Topic: Multilevel Buildings
Reference: IBC 1104.4

Category: Accessibility
Subject: Accessible Route

Code Text: *At least one accessible route shall connect each accessible level, including mezzanines, in multistory buildings and facilities.* See exceptions for specific occupancies with small floor areas, areas without accessible elements and air traffic control towers.

Discussion and Commentary: Access must be provided both horizontally and vertically throughout a building. Under most conditions, multilevel facilities will contain an accessible elevator to extend an accessible route to the other levels. Ramps also can be used where the elevation change is not excessive. In some occupancies, an accessible route is not required for levels above or below an accessible level, provided that the aggregate size of the inaccessible levels does not exceed 3,000 square feet. It has been determined that it is not feasible to require elevator service for such small spaces.

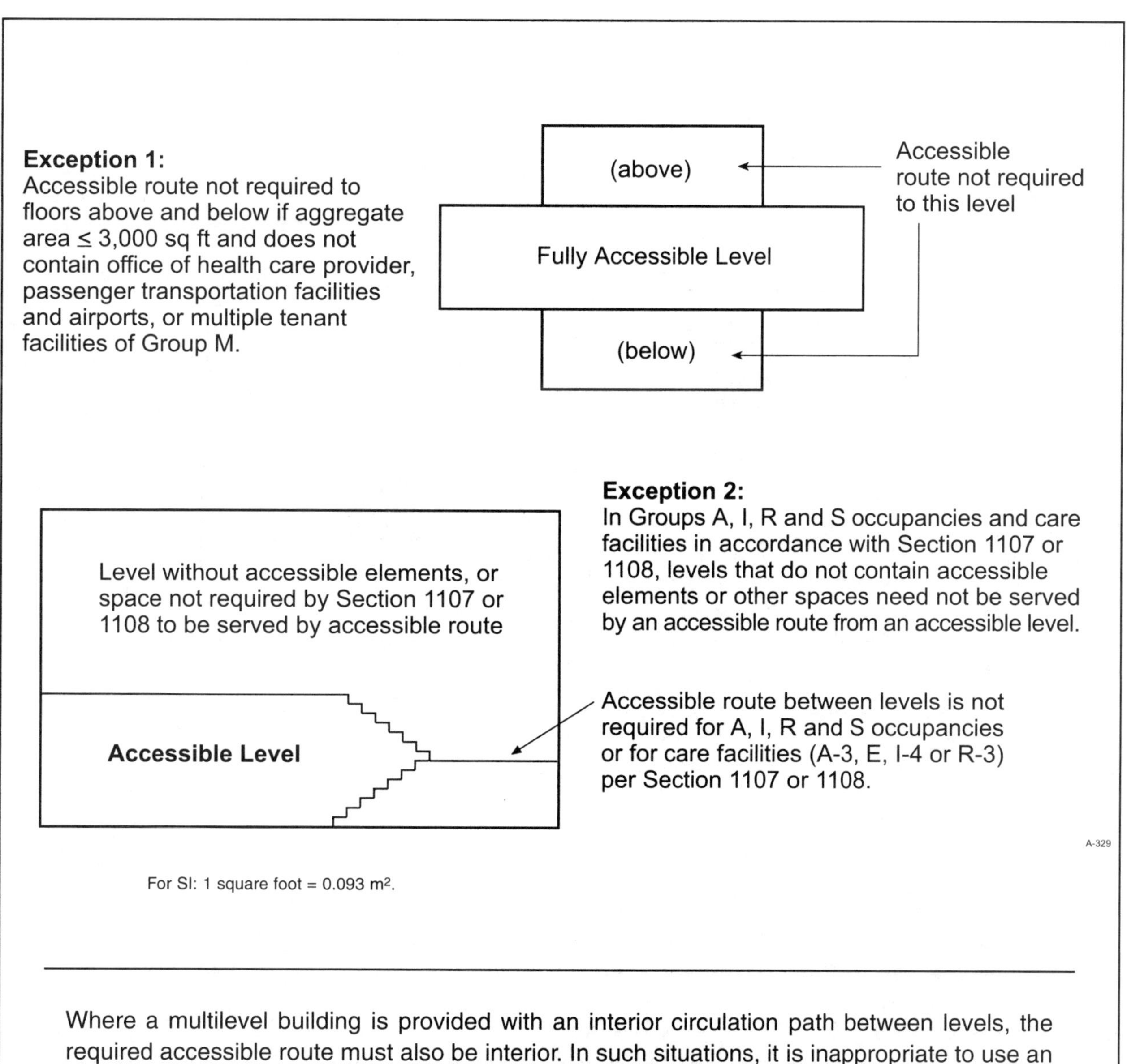

For SI: 1 square foot = 0.093 m².

Where a multilevel building is provided with an interior circulation path between levels, the required accessible route must also be interior. In such situations, it is inappropriate to use an exterior route, such as a series of ramps, as the only accessible means between floor levels.

Topic: Where Required
Reference: IBC 1105.1

Category: Accessibility
Subject: Accessible Entrances

Code Text: *In addition to accessible entrances required by Sections 1105.1.1 through 1105.1.6* (parking garage entrances, entrances from tunnels or elevated walkways, restricted entrances, entrances for inmates or detainees, service entrances, and entrances to tenant spaces, dwelling units and sleeping units), *at least 50 percent of all public entrances shall be accessible.* See exceptions for entrances to areas not required to be accessible and loading/service entrances that are not the only tenant space entrance.

Discussion and Commentary: To provide accessibility to all buildings and tenant spaces, a minimum of one accessible entrance is required. Where additional entrances are provided, often for convenience purposes, at least one half of the total number of entrances must be accessible. Elements to be considered at entrances include the slope of exterior surfaces, door hardware and clear floor space for maneuvering clearances.

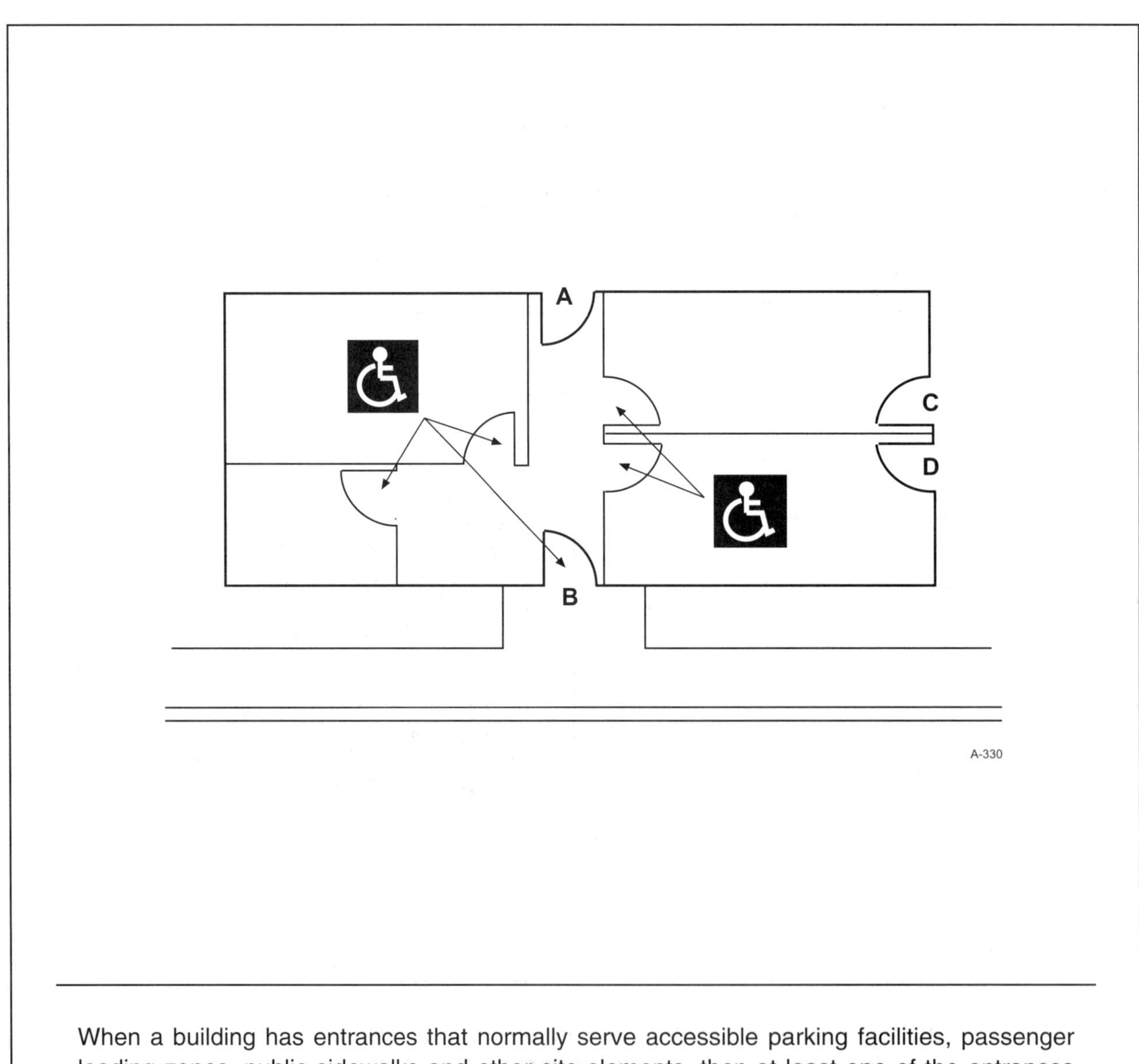

When a building has entrances that normally serve accessible parking facilities, passenger loading zones, public sidewalks and other site elements, then at least one of the entrances serving each of the functions shall comply with the accessible route provisions.

Topic: General Provisions
Reference: IBC 1106

Category: Accessibility
Subject: Parking Facilities

Code Text: *Where parking is provided, accessible parking spaces shall be provided in compliance with Table 1106.1 except as required by Sections 1106.2* (Groups R-2 and R-3)*, 1106.3,* (hospital outpatient facilities) *and 1106.4* (rehabilitation facilities). *For every six or fraction of six accessible parking spaces, at least one shall be a van-accessible parking space. Accessible parking spaces shall be located on the shortest accessible route of travel from adjacent parking to an accessible building entrance.*

Discussion and Commentary: The number of required accessible parking spaces is based on the total number of spaces in the lot or garage. In hospital outpatient facilities where it is anticipated that more accessible spaces will be needed, at least one in ten parking spaces must be accessible. All accessible parking spaces shall be located as close as possible to an accessible building entrance to reduce the distance of travel for those individuals with mobility limitations.

TABLE 1106.1
ACCESSIBLE PARKING SPACES

TOTAL PARKING SPACES PROVIDED	REQUIRED MINIMUM NUMBER OF ACCESSIBLE SPACES
1 to 25	1
26 to 50	2
51 to 75	3
76 to 100	4
101 to 150	5
151 to 200	6
201 to 300	7
301 to 400	8
401 to 500	9
501 to 1,000	2% of total
More than 1,000	20, plus one for each 100 over 1,000

Where parking is provided, accessible parking spaces shall be provided in compliance with Table 1106.1.

Exceptions:

1. Where Group R-2 and R-3 occupancies are required to have accessible dwelling units, 2% of the parking spaces shall be accessible.

   Where parking is provided within or beneath a building, accessible parking spaces shall also be provided within or beneath the building.

2. Where patient and visitor parking spaces serve hospital outpatient facilities, 10% of the spaces shall be accessible.

3. At rehabilitation facilities and outpatient physical therapy facilities, 20% of patient and visitor parking spaces shall be accessible.

Every parking facility with at least one accessible parking space must provide for accessible van parking. Based on a percentage of the total number of accessible spaces, the van space or spaces must have a vertical clearance of at least 98 inches and a minimum 8-foot access isle.

Topic: Group R Occupancies
Reference: IBC 1107.6

Category: Accessibility
Subject: Dwelling Units and Sleeping Units

Code Text: *In occupancies in Group R-1, Accessible dwelling units and sleeping units shall be provided in accordance with Table 1107.6.1.1. In occupancies in Group R-2 containing more than 20 dwelling units or sleeping units, at least 2 percent, but not less than one, of the units shall be a Type A unit. Where there are four or more dwelling units or sleeping units intended to be occupied as a residence in a single structure, every dwelling and sleeping unit intended to be occupied as a residence shall be a Type B unit.* See general exceptions in Sec. 1107.7.

Discussion and Commentary: Both Type A and Type B dwelling units are defined in IBC Section 1102 and described in ICC A117.1. Type A units are considered fully accessible dwelling units, whereas Type B units are only required to have specific accessible elements. A dwelling unit designed and constructed as a Type B unit is intended to comply with the technical requirements for Fair Housing required by federal law.

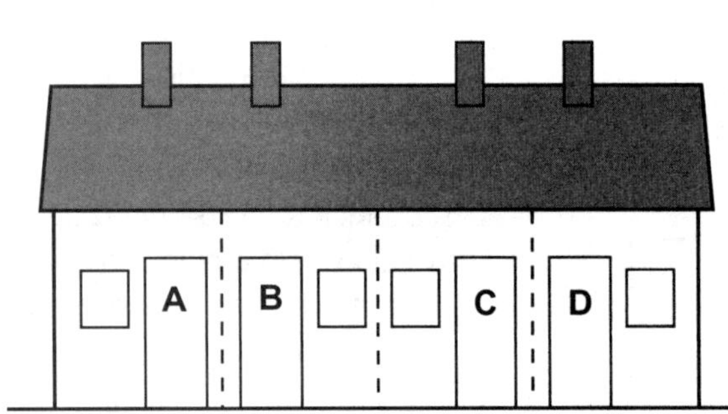

In R-2 and R-3 occupancies where there are ≥ 4 dwelling units in a single structure, every unit shall be a Type B dwelling unit. (Type A units may be substituted for Type B.)

In R-2 occupancies containing > 20 dwelling units, at least 2 percent but not less than 1 shall be a Type A dwelling unit.

Exceptions: Five exceptions are provided that are dependent on elevator service and lowest floor level with respect to base flood elevation.

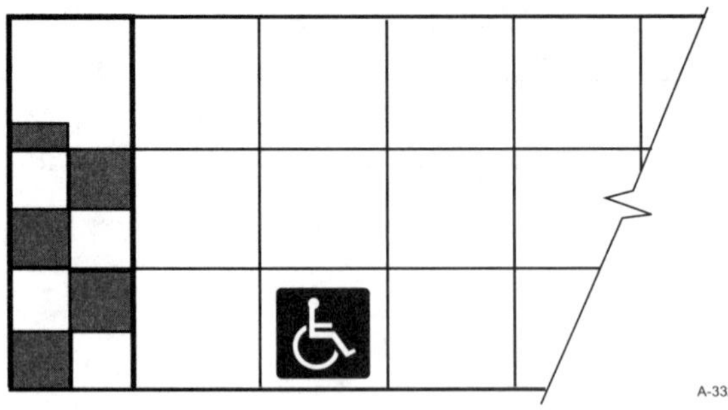

Where Group R-2 and R-3 occupancies contain public or common-use areas, such areas must be accessible if they serve accessible dwelling units. Any recreational facilities serving these occupancies must also must be accessible to a limited degree.

Topic: Assembly Area Seating
Reference: IBC 1108.2

Category: Accessibility
Subject: Special Occupancies

Code Text: *In theaters, bleachers, grandstands, stadiums, arenas and other fixed seating assembly areas, accessible wheelchair spaces complying with ICC A117.1 shall be provided in accordance with Sections 1108.2.2.1 through 1108.2.2.5. Wheelchair spaces shall be provided in accordance with Table 1108.2.2.1. Dispersion of wheelchair spaces shall be based on the availability of accessible routes to various seating areas including seating at various levels in multilevel facilities. At least one companion seat shall be provided for each wheelchair space required by Section 1108.2.2.*

Discussion and Commentary: The unique features of assembly occupancies dictate special accessibility features. In addition to the requirements for wheelchair spaces and assistive listening devices, the code requires accessible seating throughout all dining areas. Specific provisions address fixed seating at booths and tables, as well as at counters.

Section 1108.29

In dining areas, the total floor area allotted for seating and tables shall be accessible.

Exception: In buildings without elevators, an accessible route to a mezzanine seating area is not required, provided that the mezzanine contains less than 25 percent of the total area and the same services are provided in the accessible area.

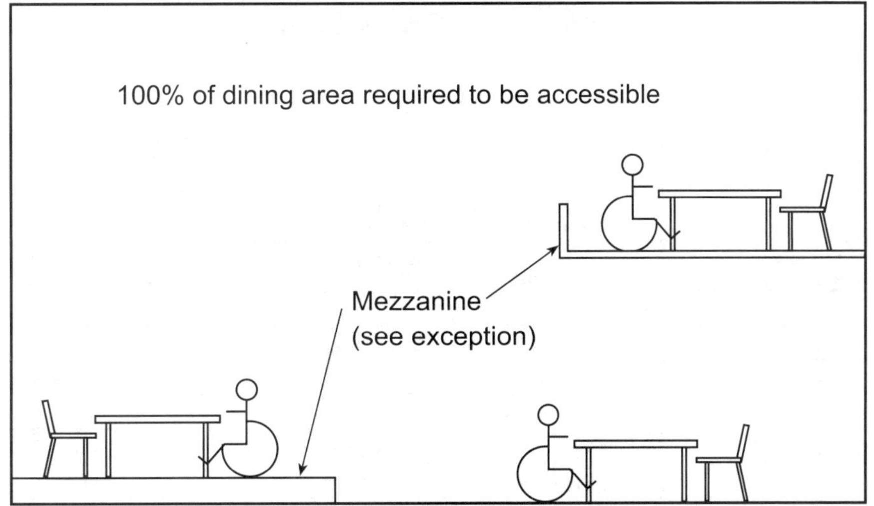

Accessible Dining Areas

Under limited conditions, a dining area may have a mezzanine level that is not served by an accessible route. The mezzanine must be limited in size to 25 percent of the total floor area, and the services provided on the mezzanine must be available on the accessible level.

Topic: Assistive Listening Systems
Reference: IBC 1108.2.7

Category: Accessibility
Subject: Special Occupancies

Code Text: *Each assembly area where audible communications are integral to the use of the space shall have an assistive listening system.* See exception for spaces where no audio amplification system is installed. *Receivers shall be provided for assistive listening systems in accordance with Table 1108.2.7.1. See exception for buildings with multiple assembly areas.*

Discussion and Commentary: These provisions are intended to accommodate people with a hearing impairment. In these assembly areas, audible communication is often integral to the use and full enjoyment of the space. This requirement offers the possibility for individuals with hearing impairments to attend functions in these facilities without having to give advance notice and without disrupting the event in order to have a portable assistive listening system set up and made ready for use.

International symbol of access for hearing loss

A-333b

TABLE 1108.2.7.1
RECEIVERS FOR ASSISTIVE LISTENING SYSTEMS

CAPACITY OF SEATING IN ASSEMBLY AREAS	MINIMUM REQUIRED NUMBER OF RECEIVERS	MINIMUM NUMBER OF RECEIVERS TO BE HEARING-AID COMPATIBLE
50 or less	2	2
51 to 200	2, plus 1 per 25 seats over 50 seats*	2
201 to 500	2, plus 1 per 25 seats over 50 seats.*	1 per 4 receivers*
501 to 1,000	20, plus 1 per 33 seats over 500 seats*	1 per 4 receivers*
1,001 to 2,000	35, plus 1 per 50 seats over 1,000 seats*	1 per 4 receivers*
Over 2,000	55, plus 1 per 100 seats over 2,000 seats*	1 per 4 receivers*

NOTE: * = or fraction thereof

There are three primary types of listening systems available: induction loop, AM/FM and infrared. Each type of system has certain advantages and disadvantages that should be taken into consideration when choosing the system that is most appropriate for the intended application.

Topic: General Provisions
Reference: IBC 1109

Category: Accessibility
Subject: Features and Facilities

Code Text: *Accessible building features and facilities shall be provided in accordance with Sections 1109.2 through 1109.15.* See exception for Type A and Type B dwelling units.

Discussion and Commentary: Where elements such as sinks, drinking fountains, storage lockers, fitting rooms and check-out aisles are provided, a portion, but not less than one of each type of element, must be accessible. In general, all toilet rooms must be accessible. Within each toilet room, at least one water closet and lavatory must be accessible. When other elements are provided, such as mirrors and towel fixtures, at least one must be accessible. Operating mechanisms intended for occupant operation, such as light switches and convenience outlets, shall be useable by persons with physical disabilities.

In other than Type A and Type B dwelling units, accessible building features and facilities shall be provided as required in Section 1109. This includes:

- Toilet and bathing facilities
- Sinks
- Kitchens, kitchenettes and wet bars
- Drinking fountains
- Elevators
- Lifts
- Storage
- Detectable warnings
- Assembly area seating
- Seating at tables, counters and work surfaces
- Service facilities
- Controls, operating mechanisms and hardware
- Recreational facilities
- Stairways

Certain elements addressed in ICC/ANSI A117.1, including telephones and automatic teller machines, have not been included in the scoping provisions of Chapter 11. However, scoping requirements for such features are set forth in Appendix E of the IBC.

Topic: Unisex Toilet and Bathing Rooms
Reference: IBC 1109.2.1

Category: Accessibility
Subject: Features and Facilities

Code Text: *In assembly and mercantile occupancies, an accessible unisex toilet room shall be provided where an aggregate of six or more male and female water closets is required. In recreational facilities where separate-sex bathing rooms are provided, an accessible unisex bathing room shall be provided.* See exception for single-fixture bathing rooms. *Fixtures located within unisex toilet and bathing rooms shall be included in determining the number of fixtures provided in an occupancy.*

Discussion and Commentary: The primary issue relative to unisex toilet/bathing facilities is that some people with disabilities require assistance to utilize them. If the attendant is of the opposite sex, a facility that can accommodate both persons is required. The provisions are applicable only to those types of transient uses where it is expected such facilities are frequently required.

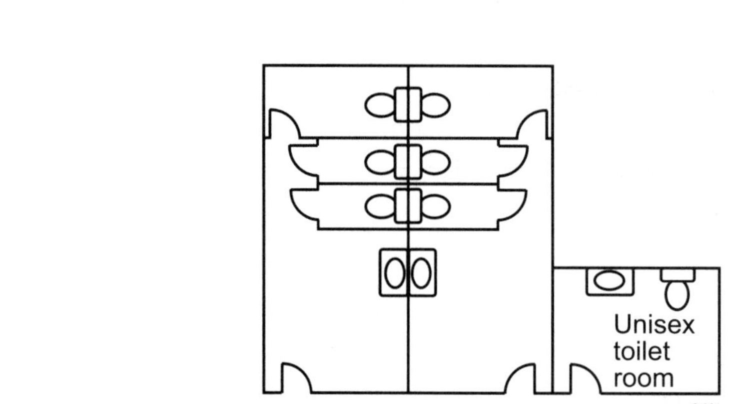

These types of facilities have been identified also as "family bathrooms." For example, a person requiring assistance can also be a small child. A parent shopping or attending an event with a child of the opposite sex can utilize the facility without disrupting the separate-sex toilet rooms.

Topic: Signs
Reference: IBC 1110

Category: Accessibility
Subject: Signage

Code Text: *Required accessible elements shall be identified by the International Symbol of Accessibility at the following locations: (1) accessible parking spaces except where the total number of parking spaces provided is four or less, (2) accessible passenger loading zones, (3) accessible areas of refuge, (4) accessible rooms where multiple single-user toilet or bathing rooms are clustered at a single location, (5) accessible entrances where not all entrances are accessible, (6) accessible check-out aisles where not all aisles are accessible, (7) unisex toilet and bathing rooms, and (8) accessible dressing, fitting, and locker rooms where not all such rooms are accessible.*

Discussion and Commentary: Those site or building elements that need to be identified as accessible for convenience, clarification or life-safety purposes are specified in the code. Special signage is also required for assistive listening capabilities and at every exit stairway door.

International symbol of accessibility

A-333a

Where building entrances are not accessible, directional signage must be installed indicating the travel route to the nearest accessible entrance. Signs must also be provided at inaccessible public toilets directing occupants to the nearest accessible toilet facilities.

QUIZ

Study Session 13 — Chapter 11

I. Multiple Choice

1. For the purpose of accessibility, which of the following areas in a bank is considered an employee work area?

   a. vault
   b. toilet room
   c. corridor
   d. break room

   Reference_______________

2. A continuous, unobstructed path complying with the provisions of IBC Chapter 11 is considered a(n) __________.

   a. accessible route
   b. accessible means of egress
   c. circulation path
   d. public entrance

   Reference_______________

3. Which of the following Group U occupancies is exempt from the accessibility provisions?

   a. paved work areas at agricultural buildings
   b. private garages containing required accessible parking
   c. areas in agricultural buildings open to the public
   d. stables and/or livestock shelters

   Reference_______________

4. When occupied as the residence for the proprietor, Group R-1 occupancies containing a maximum of __________ rooms for rent or hire are not required to be accessible.

   a. 5
   b. 6
   c. 10
   d. 15

   Reference_______________

5. Where only one accessible route is provided, it is permitted to pass through which of the following spaces?

   a. kitchen
   b. laboratory
   c. storage room
   d. toilet room

   Reference_______________

6. Where four public entrances are provided to a building, a minimum of __________ entrance(s) shall be accessible.

a. 1 b. 2
c. 3 d. 4

Reference_______________

7. Where a 1,625-space parking garage serves a covered mall building, a minimum of __________ accessible spaces must be provided.

a. 20 b. 27
c. 33 d. 42

Reference_______________

8. Where a 282-space parking lot serves a cluster of Group R-2 apartment buildings, a minimum of __________ accessible spaces must be provided.

a. 3 b. 6
c. 7 d. 14

Reference_______________

9. A minimum of __________ van-accessible parking space(s) shall be provided for a parking facility containing 16 accessible parking spaces.

a. 1 b. 2
c. 3 d. 6

Reference_______________

10. A theater with a total seating capacity of 840 persons shall be provided with a minimum of __________ accessible wheelchair spaces.

a. 4 b. 8
c. 9 d. 10

Reference_______________

11. Where cubicles are provided in the visiting area of a judicial facility, a minimum of _____ of the cubicles shall be accessible.

a. 5% b. 10%
c. 25% d. 50%

Reference_______________

12. An ambulatory-accessible water closet compartment is not required in a toilet room where the total number of water closet compartments and urinals provided in the room is a maximum of _____ fixtures.

a. 4 b. 6
c. 10 d. 12

Reference_______________

13. In a fraternity house having a minimum of ____ sleeping units, every unit intended to be occupied as a residence shall be a Type B unit.

a. 4 b. 10
c. 16 d. 20

Reference_______________

14. In a 250-seat motion picture theater, a minimum of __________ receivers shall be provided for the assistive listening system.

a. 2 b. 6
c. 10 d. 14

Reference_______________

15. In a Group I-2 nursing home containing 120 patient sleeping units, what is the minimum number of such units that must be accessible?

a. 5 b. 12
c. 60 d. 120

Reference_______________

16. In a 185-room Group R-1 hotel, a minimum of __________ accessible sleeping units shall be provided.

a. 2 b. 4
c. 7 d. 8

Reference_______________

17. A minimum of __________ accessible sleeping units in a 410-room hotel shall be provided with roll-in showers.

a. 4 b. 8
c. 12 d. 13

Reference_______________

18. A Group R-2 apartment building having 16 dwelling units shall be provided with a minimum of __________ Type A dwelling units.

a. 0
b. 1
c. 2
d. 4

Reference_______________

19. A self-storage facility containing 160 storage spaces shall be provided with a minimum of __________ accessible individual self-storage spaces.

a. 1
b. 2
c. 5
d. 8

Reference_______________

20. Unisex toilet rooms may be required in which of the following occupancies?

a. assembly and educational
b. assembly and mercantile
c. business and mercantile
d. factory and storage

Reference_______________

21. The maximum distance of the accessible route from any separate-sex toilet room to a unisex toilet room shall be __________.

a. 200 feet
b. 300 feet
c. 500 feet
d. unlimited

Reference_______________

22. In a large manufacturing plant, a minimum of how many of the 24 drinking fountains shall be accessible?

a. 3
b. 4
c. 12
d. 24

Reference_______________

23. A minimum of __________ percent of seating at fixed tables in an accessible space shall be accessible.

a. 5
b. 10
c. 20
d. 50

Reference_______________

24. A 4,000-square-foot retail sales room with six check-out aisles requires a minimum of __________ accessible check-out aisle(s).

a. 1 b. 2
c. 3 d. 4

Reference_______________

25. An International Symbol of Accessibility sign is not required at an accessible parking space in parking facilities having a maximum of __________ total parking spaces.

a. 1, the sign is always required b. 2
c. 4 d. 5

Reference_______________

26. Permanently-defined common use circulation paths that are located within an employee work area are not required to be regulated as accessible routes, provided the work area has a maximum size of _____ square feet.

a. 300 b. 500
c. 1,500 d. 3,000

Reference_______________

27. A press box serving bleachers is not required to be served by an accessible route where it is a maximum of _____ square feet in floor area and has its points of entry at only one level.

a. 500 b. 1,000
c. 1,500 d. 3,000

Reference_______________

28. What is the minimum number of accessible parking spaces required to be provided in a 40-space parking lot serving an outpatient physical therapy facility?

a. 1 b. 2
c. 4 d. 8

Reference_______________

29. Where 20 dining surfaces are provided at a counter for the consumption of food or drink, a minimum of _____ surface(s) shall be accessible.

a. 0 b. 1
c. 2 d. 4

Reference_______________

30. At which of the following locations is directional signage not required to indicate the route to the nearest like accessible element?

a. inaccessible building entrances
b. elevators not serving an accessible route
c. inaccessible dressing rooms
d. inaccessible public toilet facilities

Reference_______________

INTERNATIONAL BUILDING CODE
Study Session 14
Chapter 4 — Detailed Occupancy Requirements

OBJECTIVE: To obtain an understanding of special building types, features and uses, including covered mall buildings, high-rise buildings, atriums, underground buildings, motor-vehicle-related occupancies, stages and platforms, concealed combustible storage areas, hazardous materials and Groups I-2, I-3 and H.

REFERENCE: Chapter 4, 2003 *International Building Code*

KEY POINTS:

- How are covered mall buildings, anchor buildings and food courts defined?
- In a covered mall building, which special conditions relate to the automatic sprinkler system, standpipe system and smoke-control system?
- How is the occupant load determined for a covered mall building?
- Which specific provisions relate to covered mall buildings in determining the number and arrangement of means of egress?
- What qualifies a structure as a high-rise building?
- In a high-rise building, how are the type-of-construction provisions modified?
- What are the specific provisions relating to smoke detection, fire alarms and communication systems in high-rise buildings?
- What are the various required elements in a fire command center?
- In a high-rise structure, which types of standby power, light and emergency systems are required?
- What defines an atrium? What are the limits of an atrium's use? What fire protection features must be provided in a building containing an atrium?
- How must adjacent spaces be separated from an atrium?
- What is the maximum travel distance when a required exit path enters the atrium space?
- What are the conditions that create an underground building?
- In an underground building, when is compartmentalization required?
- What is the maximum floor area permitted for a private garage?
- How must exterior openings be sized and distributed for a garage to qualify as open?
- How do the provisions differ for an open parking garage in either a single-use or multiple-occupancy building?
- What are the benefits of an open parking garage as opposed to an enclosed garage?
- Which special criteria must be applied to motor vehicle service stations? Repair garages?
- How does a platform differ from a stage?
- What are the minimum construction requirements for stages and platforms?
- When must a stage area be provided with a means for emergency ventilation?
- How shall the proscenium opening between a stage and an auditorium be protected?
- What type of fire separation is required for combustible storage in concealed spaces?
- When are smoke compartments required in Group I-2 occupancies?
- Which special considerations are given to detention facilities because of their unique characteristics?
- How are Group I-3 occupancies classified according to their occupancy condition?
- What is the function of a control area? How many control areas are permitted in a building?
- How must control areas be separated from other portions of the building?
- At what distance must Group H occupancies be set back from property lines?
- Where the spraying of flammable finishes occurs, what special conditions must be met?

Topic: General Requirements
Reference: IBC 402

Category: Detailed Use Requirements
Subject: Covered Mall Buildings

Code Text: *The area of any covered mall building, including anchor buildings of Types I, II, III and IV construction shall not be limited provided the covered mall building and attached anchor buildings and parking garages are surrounded on all sides by a permanent open space of not less than 60 feet and the anchor buildings do not exceed three stories in height. The covered mall building and buildings connected shall be provided throughout with an automatic sprinkler system in accordance with Section 903.3.1.1.*

Discussion and Commentary: A covered mall building is defined as *a single building enclosing a number of tenants and occupants such as retail stores, drinking and dining establishments, entertainment and amusement facilities, passenger transportation terminals, offices, and other similar uses wherein two or more tenants have a main entrance into one or more malls.* Because of its unique character, a covered mall building is more highly regulated for fire protection and egress.

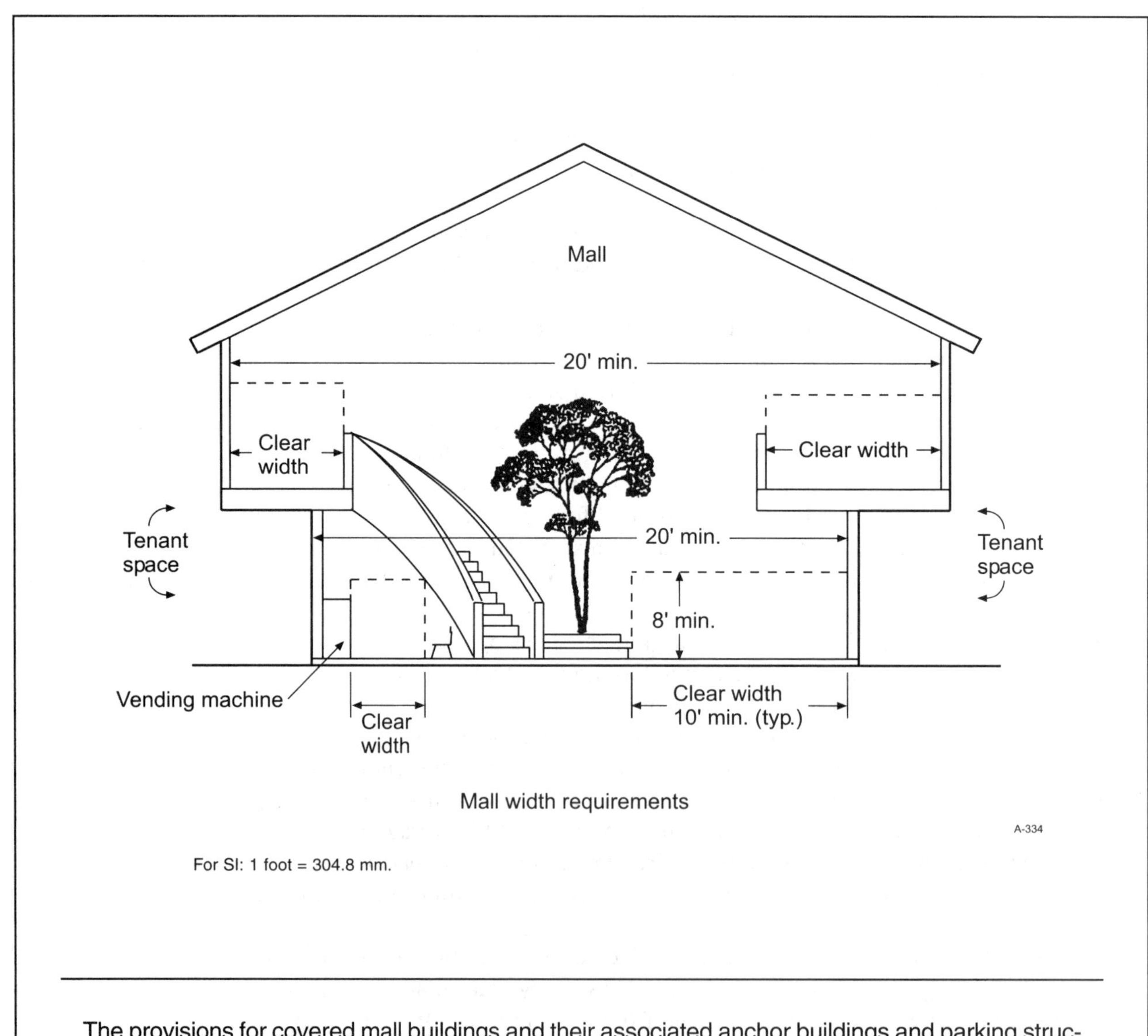

Mall width requirements

The provisions for covered mall buildings and their associated anchor buildings and parking structures allow for an alternative method of design for structures that have these specific features. Where compliant with the provisions of Section 402, similar requirements can be superceded.

Topic: General Requirements
Reference: IBC 403

Category: Detailed Use Requirements
Subject: High-Rise Buildings

Code Text: *The provisions of Section 403 shall apply to buildings having occupied floors located more than 75 feet above the lowest level of fire department vehicle access.* See five exceptions where high-rise provisions are not applicable. *Buildings and structures shall be equipped throughout with an automatic sprinkler system in accordance with Section 903.3.1.1 and a secondary water supply where required by Section 903.3.5.2.*

Discussion and Commentary: A high-rise building is characterized by several features: (1) it is impractical to completely evacuate the building in a timely manner, (2) prompt rescue and firefighting operations are difficult, (3) the occupant load is relatively high, and (4) a potential exists for stack effect. The special provisions of Section 403 are designed to address these concerns.

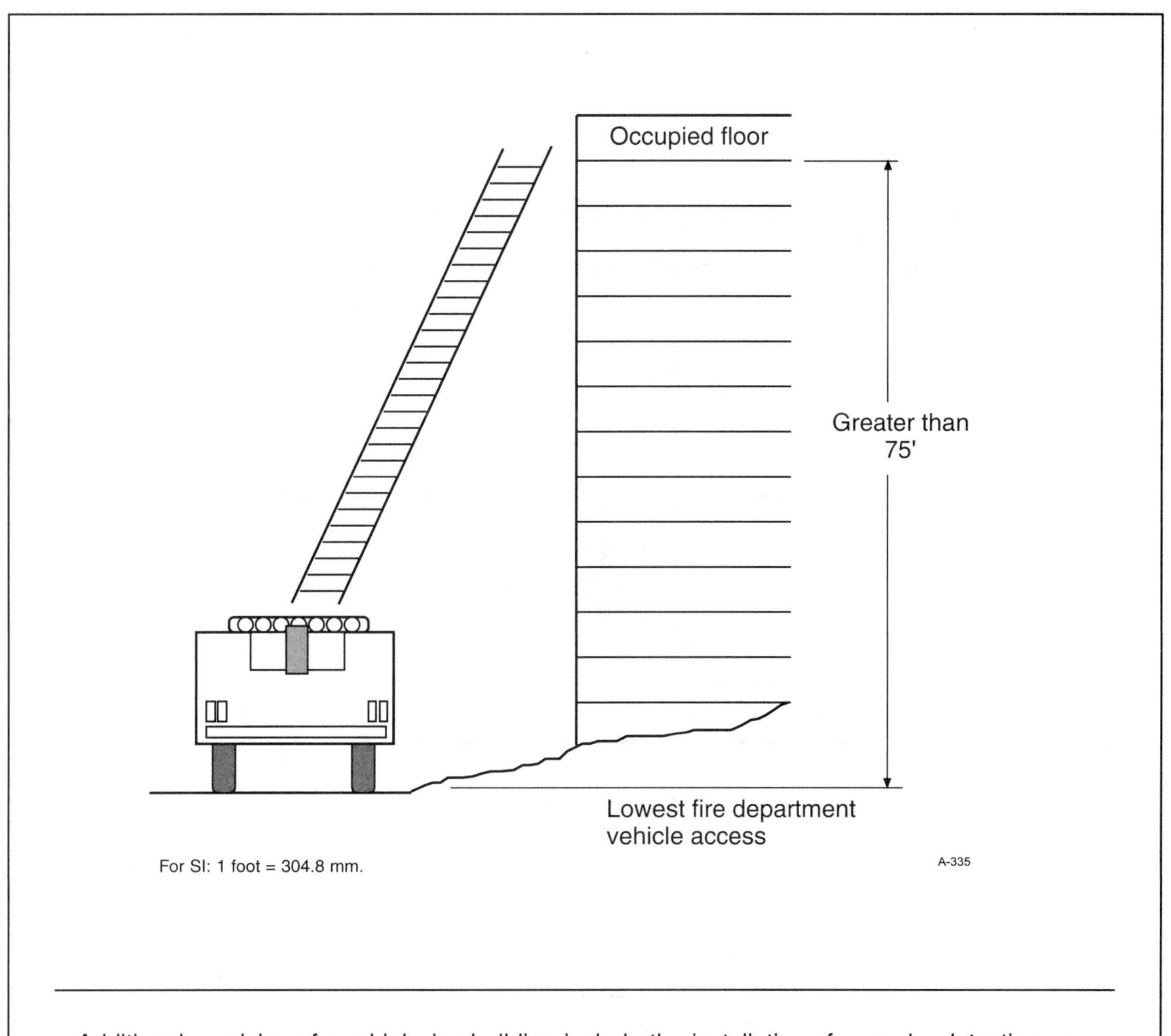

Additional provisions for a high-rise building include the installation of a smoke detection system, emergency voice/alarm and fire department communications systems, a fire command center for use by fire department personnel, and standby power, light and emergency systems.

Topic: General Requirements
Reference: IBC 404

Category: Detailed Use Requirements
Subject: Atriums

Code Text: *Vertical openings meeting the requirements of Section 404 are not required to be enclosed in other than Group H occupancies. An approved automatic sprinkler system shall be installed throughout the entire building. A smoke-control system shall be installed in accordance with Section 909. Atrium spaces shall be separated from adjacent spaces by a 1-hour fire barrier wall.* See exceptions to the sprinkler system, smoke-control system and fire barrier separation requirements.

Discussion and Commentary: An atrium is defined as *an opening connecting two or more stories other than enclosed stairways, elevators, hoistways, escalators, plumbing, electrical, air-conditioning or other equipment, which is closed at the top and not defined as a mall.* The concept of developing atriums is to maintain equivalence in safety to that of an open court, as well as to provide protection of a shaft enclosure.

Sprinkler system throughout - prevents spread of fire.

Smoke-control system - keeps building and atrium clear of smoke so that safe exiting may be accomplished through the atrium.

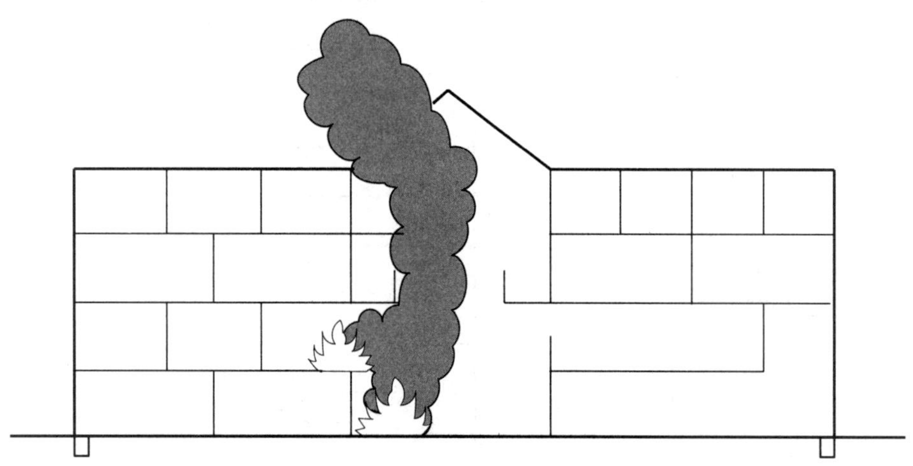

Atrium concept

A-336

Atriums are permitted based on alternative methods of protecting the building from vertical spread of fire, smoke and toxic gases. Additional protection is provided through (1) limited travel distance, (2) standby power, (3) smoke detection and (4) interior finish regulation.

Topic: General Requirements
Reference: IBC 405

Category: Detailed Use Requirements
Subject: Underground Buildings

Code Text: *The provisions of Section 405 apply to building spaces having a floor level used for human occupancy more than 30 feet below the lowest level of exit discharge.* See five exceptions for uses not regulated as underground buildings. *The underground portion of the building shall be of Type I construction. The highest level of exit discharge serving the underground portions of the building and all levels below shall be equipped with an automatic sprinkler system installed in accordance with Section 903.3.1.1.*

Discussion and Commentary: An underground building is highly regulated for many of the same reasons as is a high-rise building. In the case of a structure substantially below ground level, fire department access and firefighting operations are often even more difficult. Therefore, the code mandates the installation of multiple fire protection systems, including a smoke-control system.

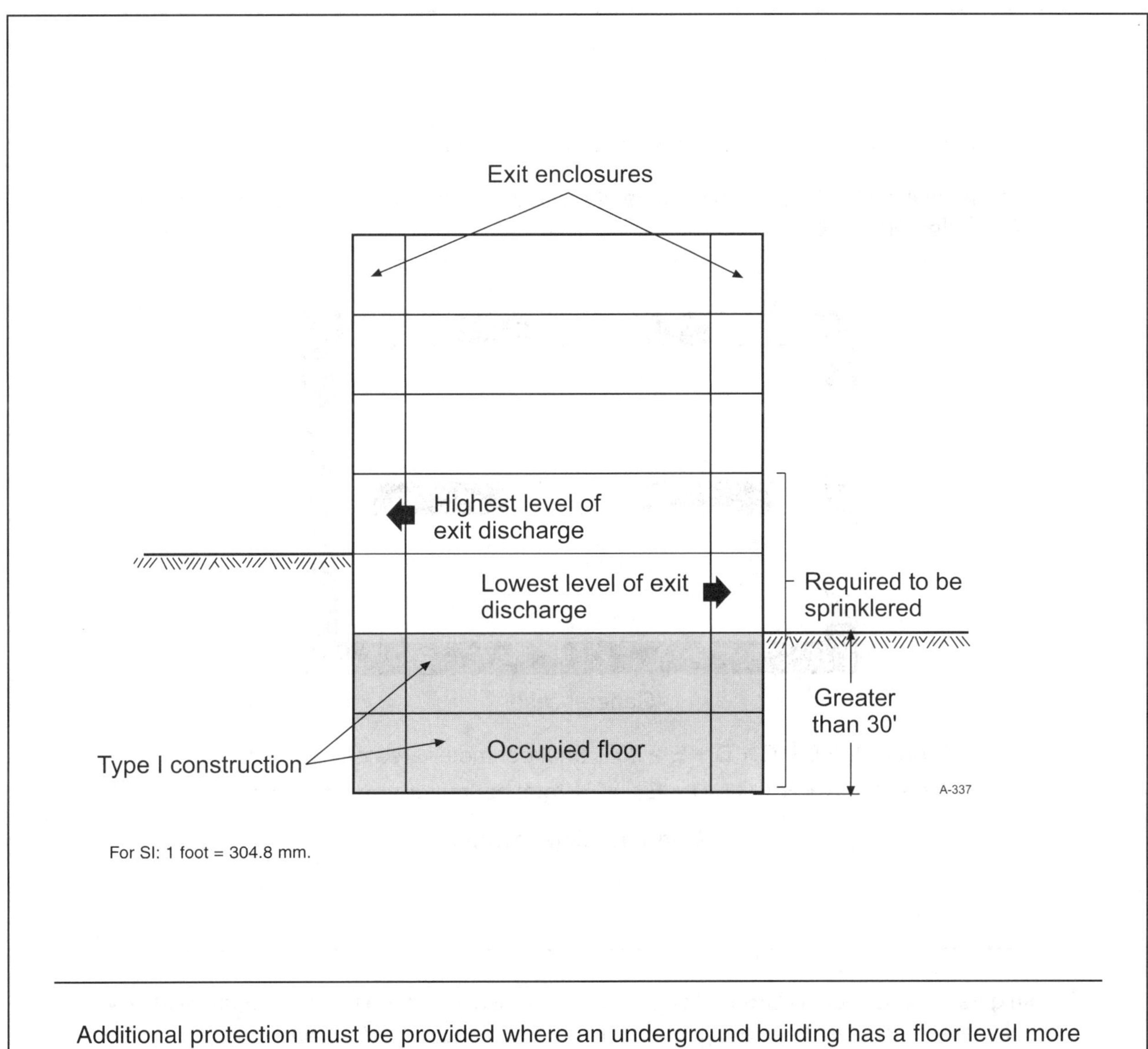

Additional protection must be provided where an underground building has a floor level more than 60 feet below the lowest level of exit discharge. The required creation of multiple compartments assists in both occupant egress and fire department operations.

Topic: General Requirements
Reference: IBC 406

Category: Detailed Use Requirements
Subject: Motor-Vehicle-Related Occupancies

Code Text: *Parking garages shall be classified as either open, as defined in Section 406.3, or enclosed and shall meet the appropriate criteria in Section 406.4. Motor vehicle service stations shall be constructed in accordance with the* International Fire Code *and Section 406.5. Repair garages shall be constructed in accordance with the* International Fire Code and Section 406.6.

Discussion and Commentary: Where motor vehicles are located within a structure, varying degrees of hazard are involved. In a small, private garage or carport, the hazard is relatively low. A moderate level of hazard exists in open parking garages, increasing where the parking garage is enclosed. In structures where vehicles are being fueled or repaired, a relatively high hazard exists. Specific provisions of the IBC address each type of motor-vehicle-related use.

Exterior walls must have uniformly distributed openings on two or more sides.

Interior wall and column lines shall be at least 20 percent open (area) with uniformly distributed openings.

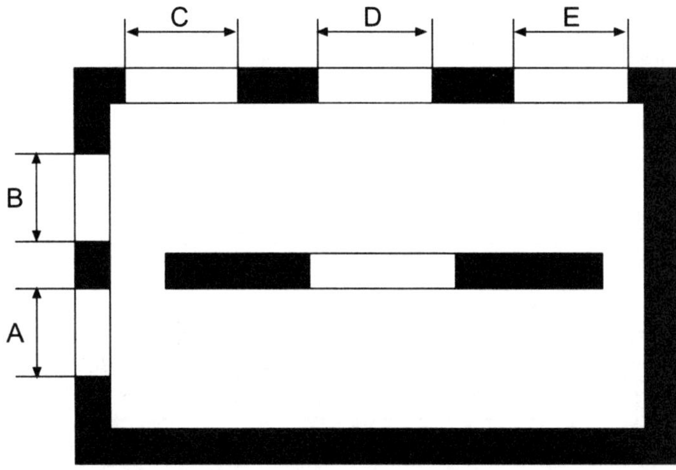

General case

1. Area: A + B + C + D + E ≥ 20% total perimeter area of each tier
2. Length: A + B + C + D + E ≥ 40% total perimeter area of each tier

Open parking garages

A-338

Private garages classified as Group U occupancies are usually limited to 1,000 square feet in floor area. However, such structures are permitted to be 3,000 square feet maximum where no repair work is done and no fuel dispensed, and where the exterior wall and opening protection is increased.

Topic: Smoke Barriers
Reference: IBC 407.4

Category: Detailed Use Requirements
Subject: Group I-2 Occupancies

Code Text: *Smoke barriers shall be provided to subdivide every story used by patients for sleeping or treatment and to divide other stories with an occupant load of 50 or more persons, into at least two smoke compartments. Such stories shall be divided into smoke compartments with an area of not more than 22,500 square feet and the travel distance from any point in a smoke compartment to a smoke barrier door shall not exceed 200 feet.*

Discussion and Commentary: Hospitals, nursing homes and similar uses must have unique life-safety characteristics due to the immobility or limited mobility of most of the occupants. By providing multiple refuge areas on each story of the building, occupants can be moved horizontally into an adjoining smoke compartment that provides protection from adjacent areas.

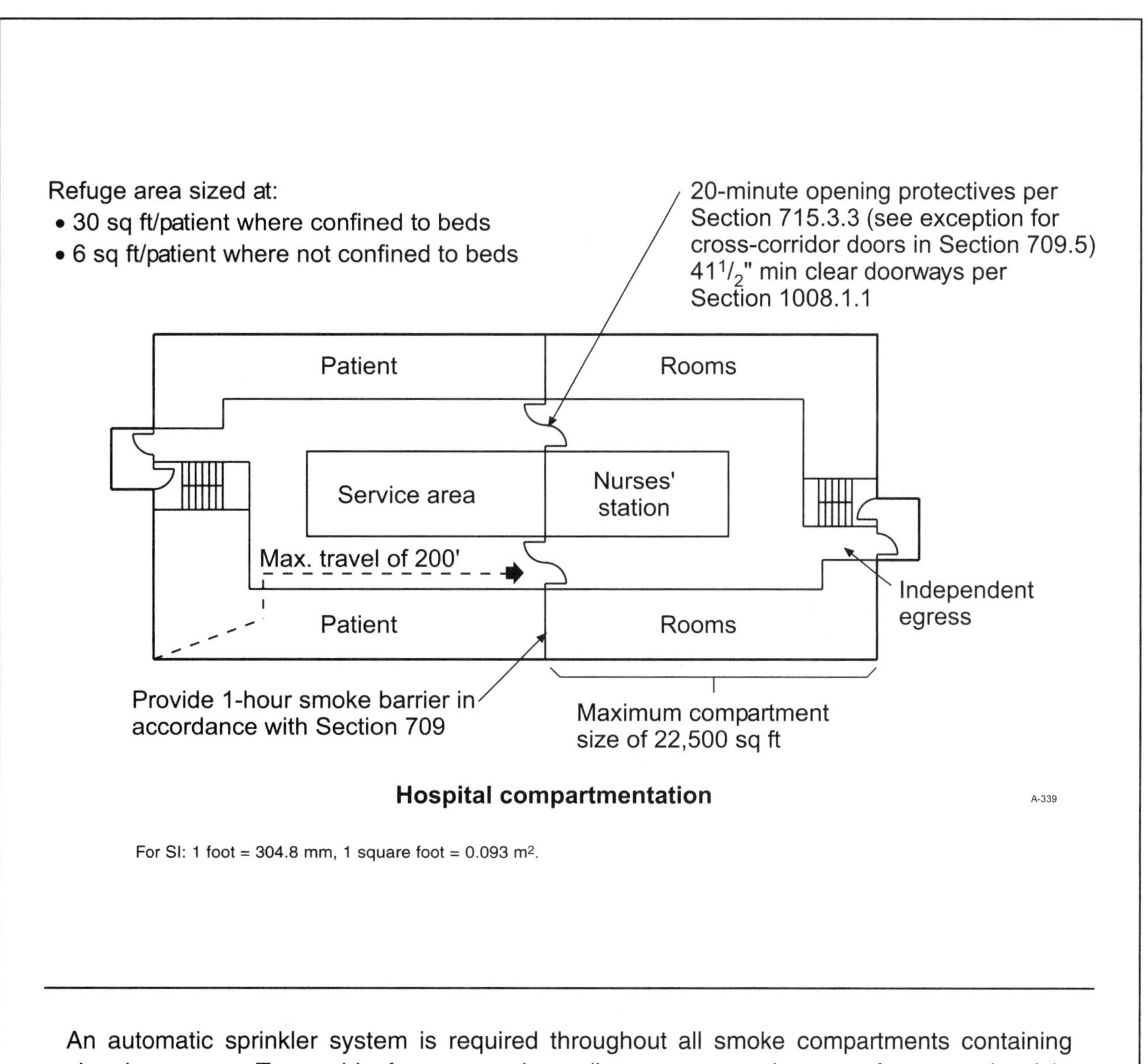

Hospital compartmentation

For SI: 1 foot = 304.8 mm, 1 square foot = 0.093 m^2.

An automatic sprinkler system is required throughout all smoke compartments containing sleeping rooms. To provide for a more immediate response, the use of approved quick-response or residential sprinklers is mandated throughout the smoke compartments.

Topic: General Requirements
Reference: IBC 408

Category: Detailed Use Requirements
Subject: Group I-3 Occupancies

Code Text: *Where security operations necessitate the locking of required means of egress, provisions shall be made for the release of occupants at all times. Egress doors are permitted to be locked in accordance with the applicable use conditions. Exits are permitted to discharge into a fenced or walled courtyard. Enclosed yards or courts shall be of a size to accommodate all occupants, a minimum of 50 feet from the building with a net area of 15 square feet per person.*

Discussion and Commentary: The need for restraint or security in specific types of uses such as jails, prisons and detention centers makes it necessary to install locking devices that are usually unacceptable for a means of egress. The code recognizes such a need and provides alternative design methods to balance the desire for both safety and security.

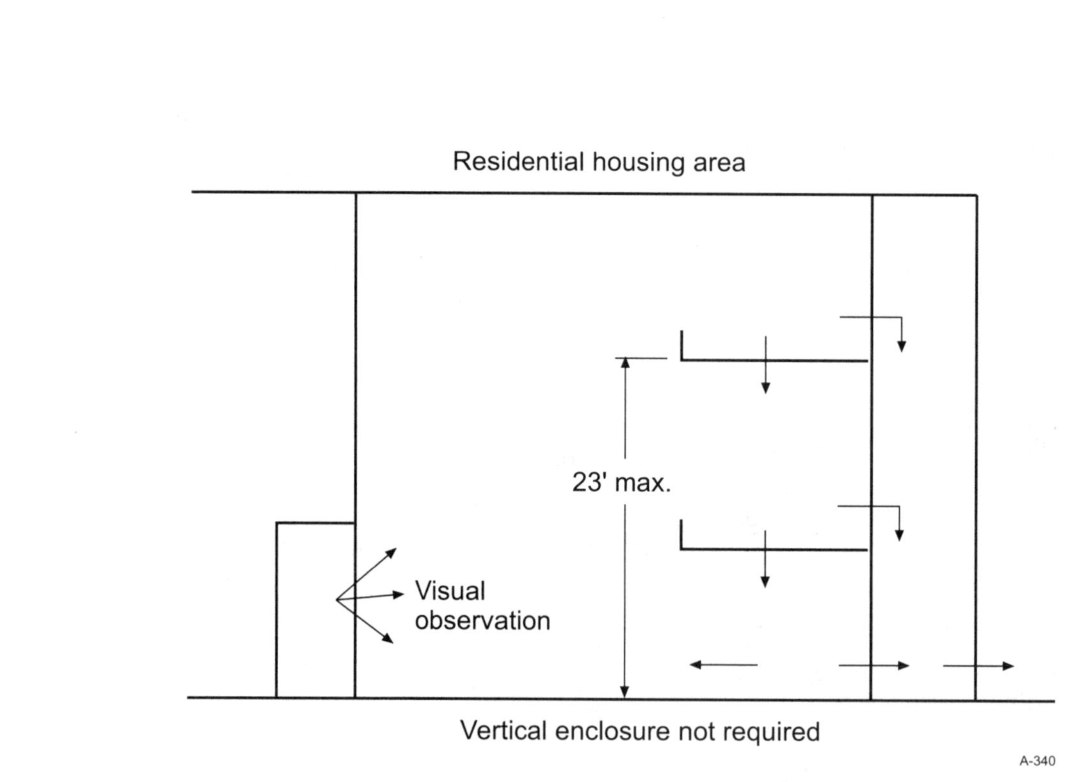

It is often important to ensure that several resident detention areas can be observed from a single location. The code permits the design of a vertical arrangement where several tiers of resident housing areas can be open to each other and to the supervisory area.

Topic: Stages
Reference: IBC 410

Category: Detailed Use Requirements
Subject: Stages and Platforms

Code Text: *A stage is a space within a building utilized for entertainment or presentations, which includes overhead hanging curtains, drops, scenery or stage effects other than lighting or sound . Stages shall be constructed of materials as required for floors for the type of construction of the building in which such stages are located.* See exceptions. *Where the stage height is greater than 50 feet, all portions of the stage shall be completely separated from the seating area by a proscenium wall with not less than a 2-hour fire-resistance rating extending continuously from the foundation to the roof.*

Discussion and Commentary: Given the increased potential for fire hazards in an assembly occupancy with a stage, such a use is regulated for certain elements. The stage must be separated from accessory spaces by fire barriers; ventilation of the stage must be accomplished through smoke control or roof vents; and the proscenium opening must be protected with a curtain of approved materials or an approved water curtain.

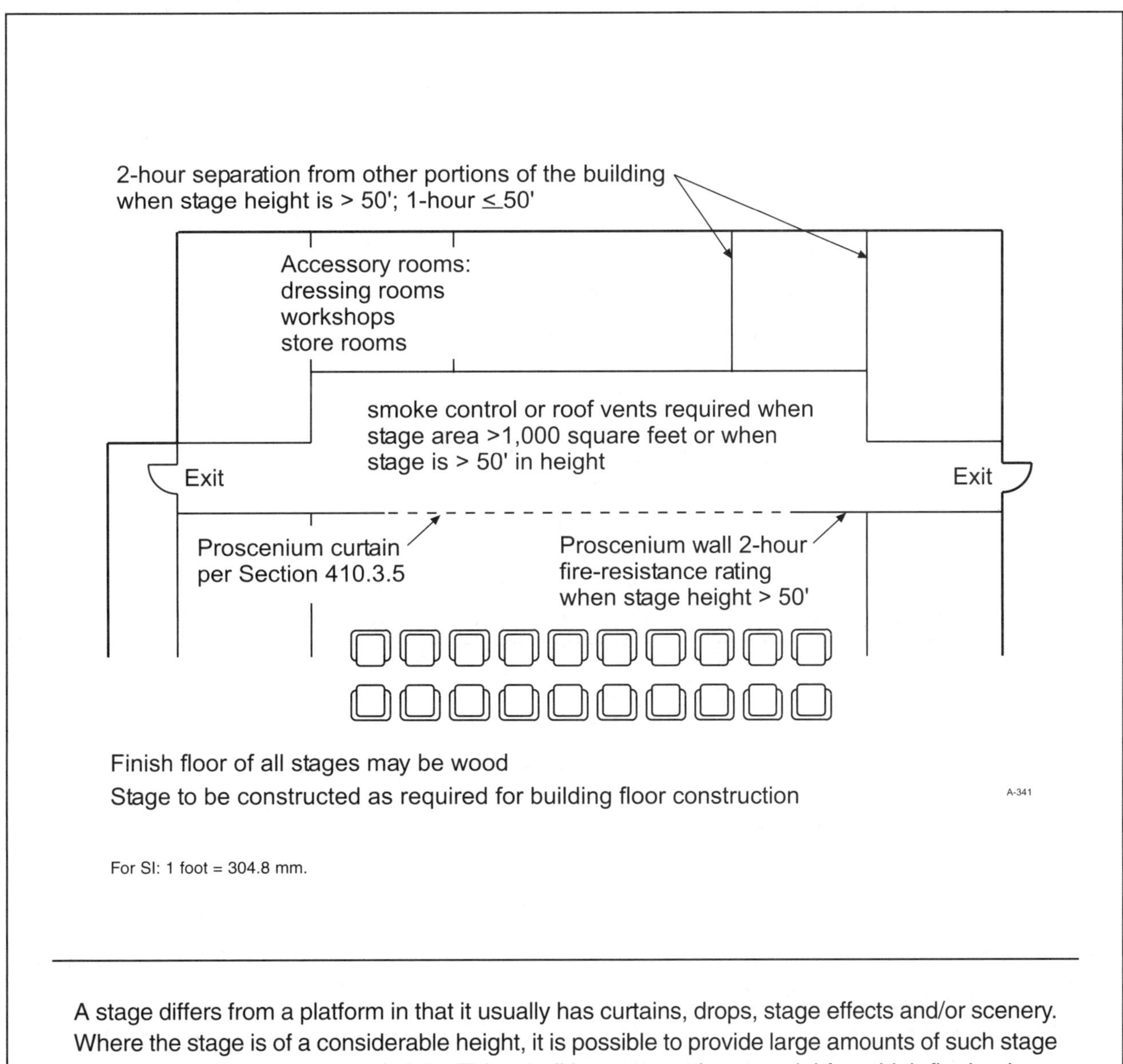

A stage differs from a platform in that it usually has curtains, drops, stage effects and/or scenery. Where the stage is of a considerable height, it is possible to provide large amounts of such stage elements overhead and out of sight. This condition creates the potential for a high fire load.

Topic: Platforms
Reference: IBC 410

Category: Detailed Use Requirements
Subject: Stages and Platforms

Code Text: *A platform is a raised area within a building used for worship, the presentation of music, plays or other entertainment; the head table for special guests; the raised area for lecturers and speakers; boxing and wresting rings; theater-in-the-round stages; and similar purposes wherein there are no overhead hanging curtains, drops, scenery or stage effects other than lighting and sound. Permanent platforms shall be constructed of materials as required for the type of construction of the building in which the permanent platform is located.* See allowances for use of fire-retardant-treated wood for Types I, II or IV construction.

Discussion and Commentary: Few requirements are placed on platforms. However, a minimum 1-hour fire-resistant platform floor construction is required when the area below the platform is used for storage or a similar purpose, because of concern about combustibles being stored within a concealed space below a raised area.

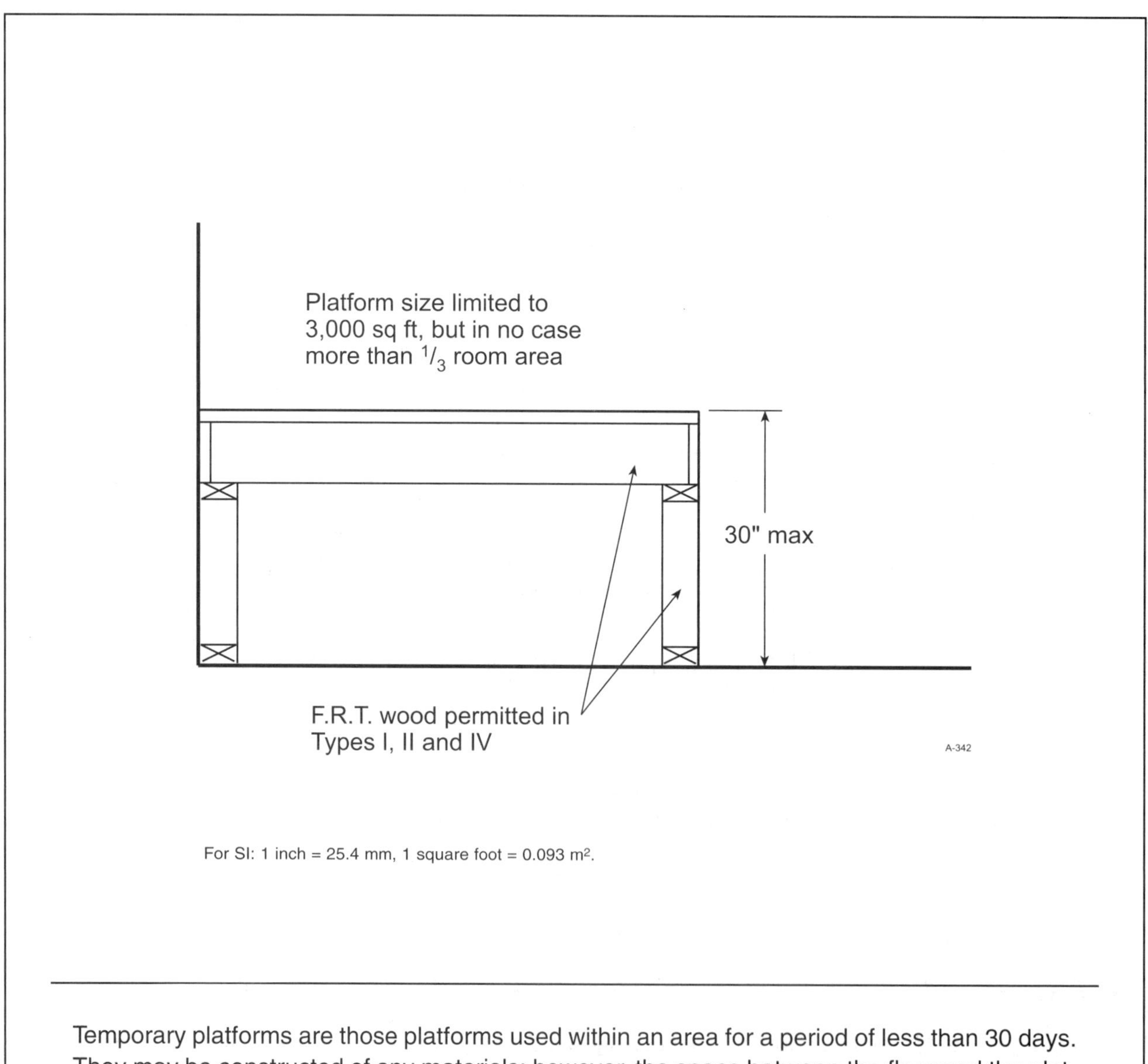

Temporary platforms are those platforms used within an area for a period of less than 30 days. They may be constructed of any materials; however, the space between the floor and the platform cannot be used for any purpose other than wiring or plumbing for platform equipment.

Topic: General Requirements
Reference: IBC 411

Category: Detailed Use Requirements
Subject: Special Amusement Buildings

Code Text: *A special amusement building is any temporary or permanent building or portion thereof that is occupied for amusement, entertainment or educational purposes and that contains a device or system that conveys passengers or provides a walkway along, around or over a course in any direction so arranged that the means of egress path is not readily apparent due to visual or audio distractions or is intentionally confounded or is not readily available because of the nature of the attraction or mode of conveyance through the building or structure.*

Discussion and Commentary: In most cases, an amusement building will be classified as a Group A occupancy. The hazards associated with such a unique use are addressed through provisions for the detection of fire, the illumination of the exit path, the presence of an alarm and emergency voice/alarm communications system and the sprinklering of the structure.

Rapid detection and notification of a fire condition, as well as the discernment of the exit path, are critical in an amusement building. Actuation of either the sprinkler system or the fire detection system shall automatically activate the approved egress directional markings.

Topic: Aircraft Hangars
Reference: IBC 412.2

Category: Detailed Use Requirements
Subject: Aircraft-related Occupancies

Code Text: *Exterior walls located less than 30 feet (9144 mm) from property lines, lot lines or a public way shall have a fire-resistance rating not less than 2 hours. Heating equipment shall be placed in another room separated by 2-hour fire-resistance-rated construction. Entrance shall be from the outside or by means of a vestibule providing a two-doorway separation.* See two exceptions.

Discussion and Commentary: Although most commercial aircraft hangars will not be limited in height (Section 504.1) or in area (Section 507) based on the presence of an automatic sprinkler system, they must be regulated in regards to exterior-wall fire-resistance ratings, basement limitations, floor surfaces, heating equipment separation and finishing restrictions. All of these provisions serve to abate the hazards associated with large aircraft and their integral fuel tanks to acceptable fire-safety levels.

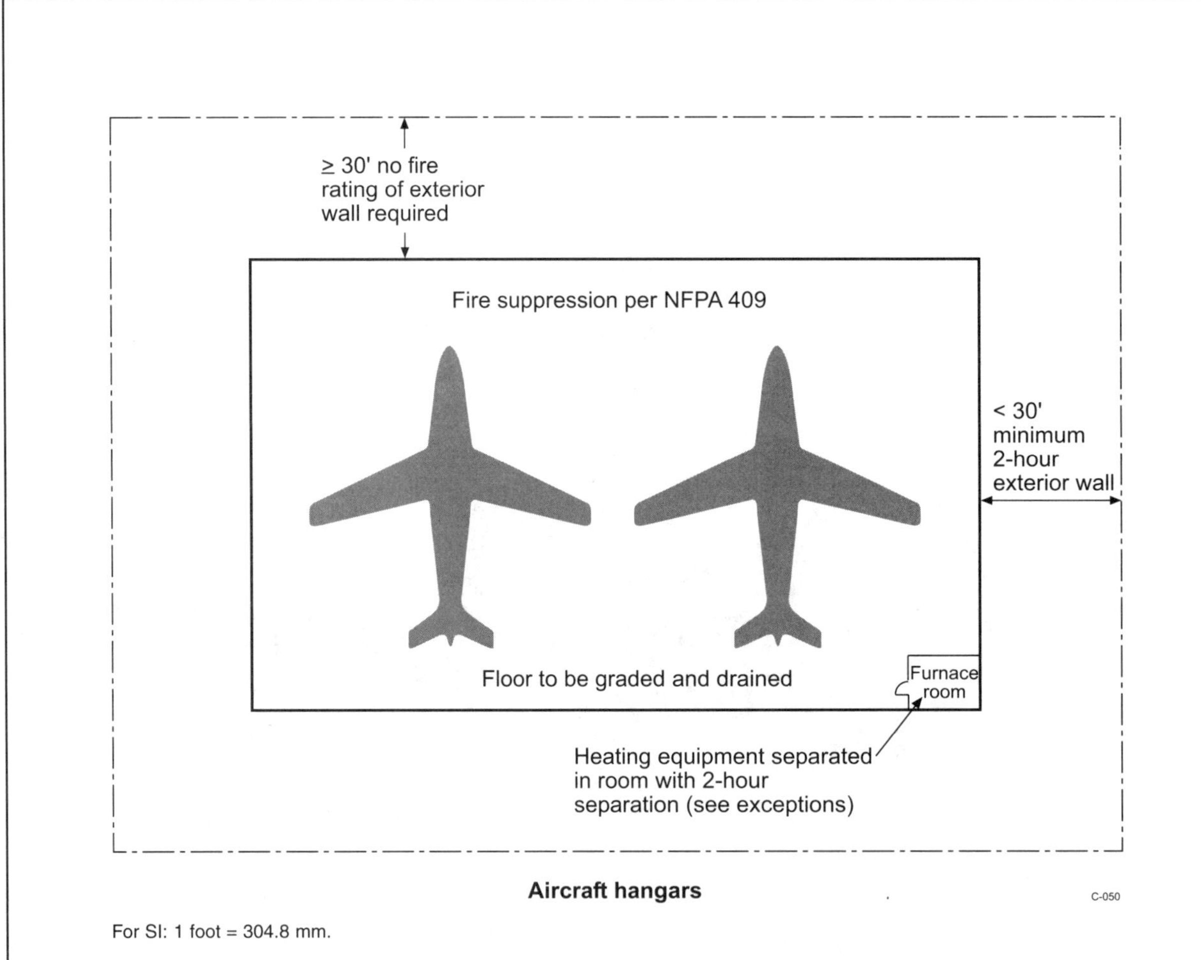

Aircraft hangars

For SI: 1 foot = 304.8 mm.

Although the provisions of Section 903.2.9 do not require automatic sprinkler protection for Group S-2 occupancies (aircraft hangars), a fire suppression system per NFPA 409 is mandated. The foam suppression requirements are exempted where no major maintenance is performed.

Topic: Attic and Under-floor Spaces
Reference: IBC 413.2

Category: Detailed Use Requirements
Subject: Combustible Storage

Code Text: *Attic, under-floor and concealed spaces used for storage of combustible materials shall be protected on the storage side as required for 1-hour fire-resistant construction. Openings shall be protected by assemblies that are self-closing and are of noncombustible construction or solid wood core not less than* $1^3/_4$ *inch in thickness.* See exception for areas protected by an automatic sprinkler system.

Discussion and Commentary: Those areas in a building that tend to be unoccupied present a potential fire hazard where combustible goods are being stored. The presence of a considerable fire load, coupled with the probable delay in recognition of the fire, makes it necessary to provide some degree of protection. A sprinkler system or a fire-resistant separation can provide ample protection.

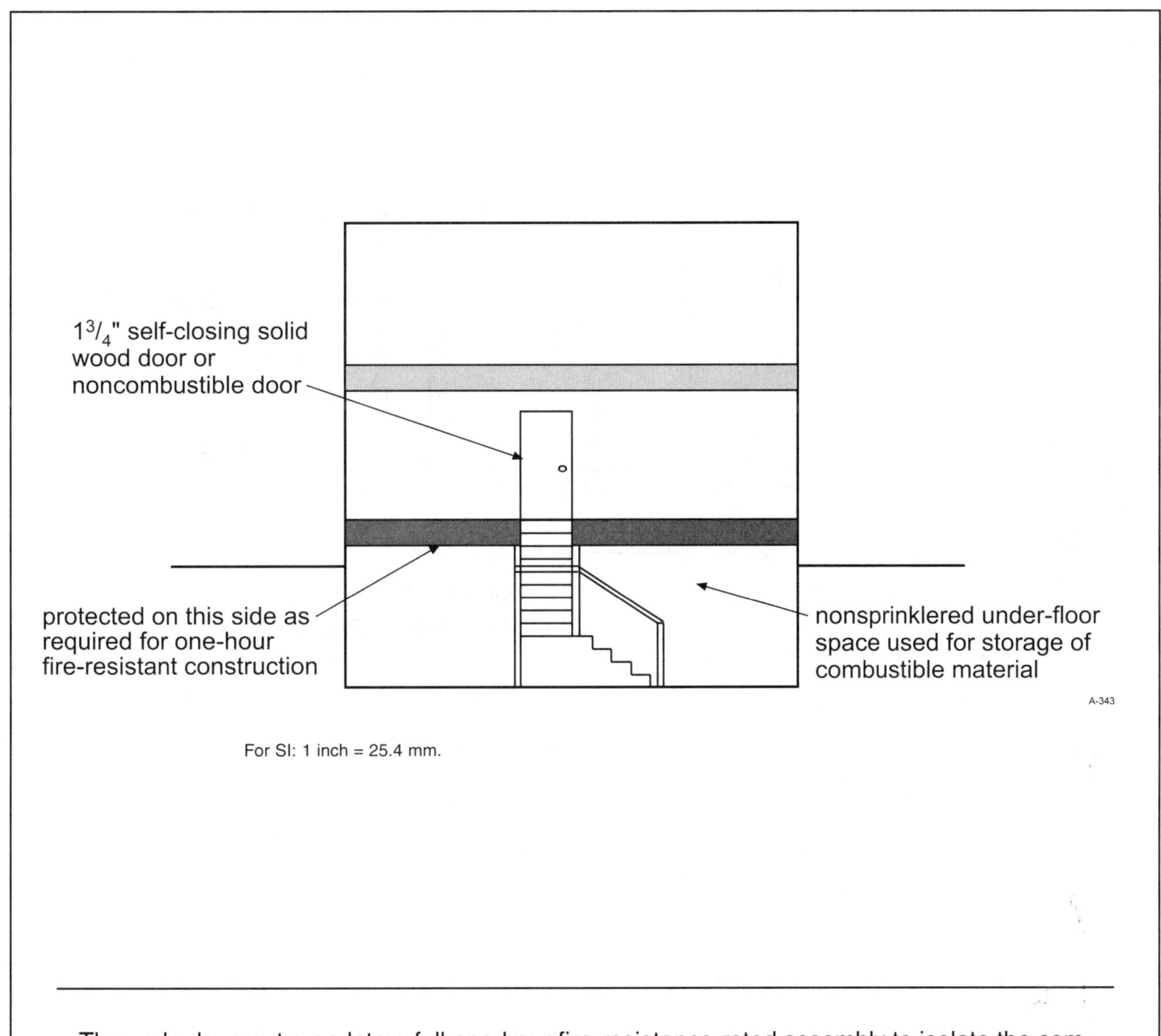

The code does not mandate a full one-hour fire-resistance-rated assembly to isolate the combustible storage area from the unoccupied space. Because the hazard presumably exists only on the inside of the space, that is the only side where the protection is required.

Topic: Control Areas
Reference: IBC 307.2

Category: Detailed Use Requirements
Subject: Hazardous Materials

Code Text: Control areas are defined as *spaces within a building that are enclosed and bounded by exterior walls, fire walls, fire barriers and roofs, or a combination thereof, where quantities of hazardous materials not exceeding the maximum allowable quantities per control area are stored, dispensed, used or handled.*

Discussion and Commentary: The use of control areas provides an alternative method for the use and storage of hazardous materials without classifying the building or structure as a high-hazard (Group H) occupancy. This concept is based on regulating the allowable quantities of hazardous materials per control area rather than per building area by giving credit for further compartmentation through the use of fire-resistance-rated fire barrier walls and horizontal assemblies.

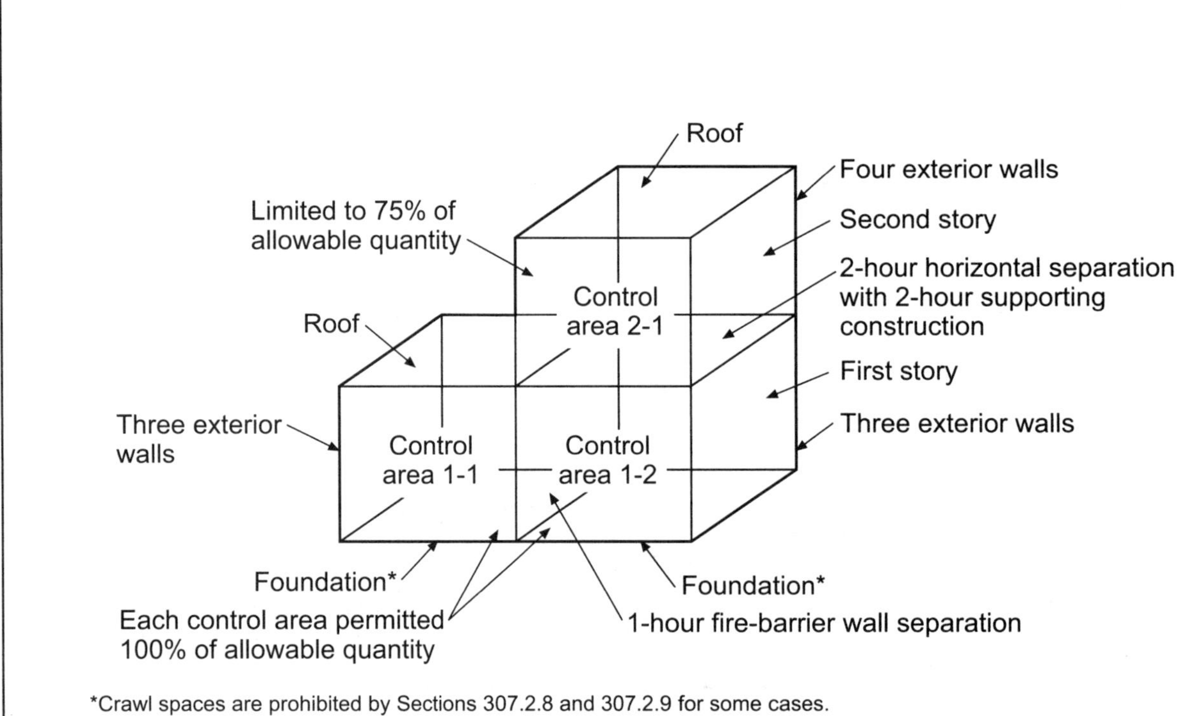

Multi-story control areas

The maximum quantities of hazardous materials within a given control area cannot exceed the exempt amounts for a given material listed in either Table 307.7(1) for physical hazards and Table 307.7(2) for health hazards, as modified by Table 414.2.2 for location within the building.

Topic: Control Areas
Reference: IBC 414.2

Category: Detailed Use Requirements
Subject: Hazardous Materials

Code Text: *Control areas shall be those spaces within a building where quantities of hazardous materials not exceeding the maximum quantities allowed by the IBC are stored, dispensed, used or handled. The maximum number of control areas within a building and the required fire-resistance rating for fire barrier assemblies shall be in accordance with Table 414.2.2. The floor construction of the control area, and the construction supporting the floor of the control area, shall have a minimum 2-hour fire-resistance rating.*

Discussion and Commentary: By distributing hazardous materials in multiple fire-resistant compartments throughout a structure, the amount of material exposed to an immediate fire event is limited. The code allows such limited quantities in buildings of other than Group H occupancy; hence, the use of control areas is an effective method for reducing the occupancy classification by reducing the hazard.

TABLE 414.2.2
DESIGN AND NUMBER OF CONTROL AREAS

FLOOR LEVEL		PERCENTAGE OF THE MAXIMUM ALLOWABLE QUANTITY PER CONTROL AREA[a]	NUMBER OF CONTROL AREAS PER FLOOR[b]	FIRE-RESISTANCE RATING FOR FIRE BARRIERS IN HOURS[c]
Above grade	Higher than 9	5	1	2
	7-9	5	2	2
	6	12.5	2	2
	5	12.5	2	2
	4	12.5	2	2
	3	50	2	1
	2	75	3	1
	1	100	4	1
Below grade	1	75	3	1
	2	50	2	1
	Lower than 2	Not Allowed	Not Allowed	Not Allowed

a. Percentages shall be of the maximum allowable quantity per control area shown in Tables 307.7(1) and 307.7(2), with all increases allowed in the notes to those tables.

b. There shall be a maximum of two control areas per floor in Group M occupancies and in buildings or portions of buildings having Group S occupancies with storage conditions and quantities in accordance with Section 414.2.4.

c. Fire barriers shall include walls and floors as necessary to provide separation from other portions of the building.

The purpose of a control area is to allow the building to be classified according to its general occupancy instead of being classified as a Group H occupancy. A building may comprise a single control area, where the amount of hazardous materials in the entire structure is compliant.

Topic: Distance to Lot Lines
Reference: IBC 415.3.1

Category: Detailed Use Requirements
Subject: Group H Occupancies

Code Text: *Regardless of any other provisions, buildings containing Group H occupancies shall be set back a minimum distance from lot lines as set forth in Items 1 through 4 below.* See specific setback requirements for Groups H-1, H-2 and H-3 occupancies. *Distances shall be measured from the walls enclosing the occupancy to lot lines, including those on a public way.*

Discussion and Commentary: Because of the potentially volatile nature of hazardous materials, specific setback requirements are necessary for Group H occupancies. These provisions take precedence over Table 602 regarding the minimum fire separation distance based on building construction type and exposure. The listed conditions are dependent on the type of materials that are indicative of the specified Group H occupancies, the size of the hazardous material storage area and whether a detached building is required.

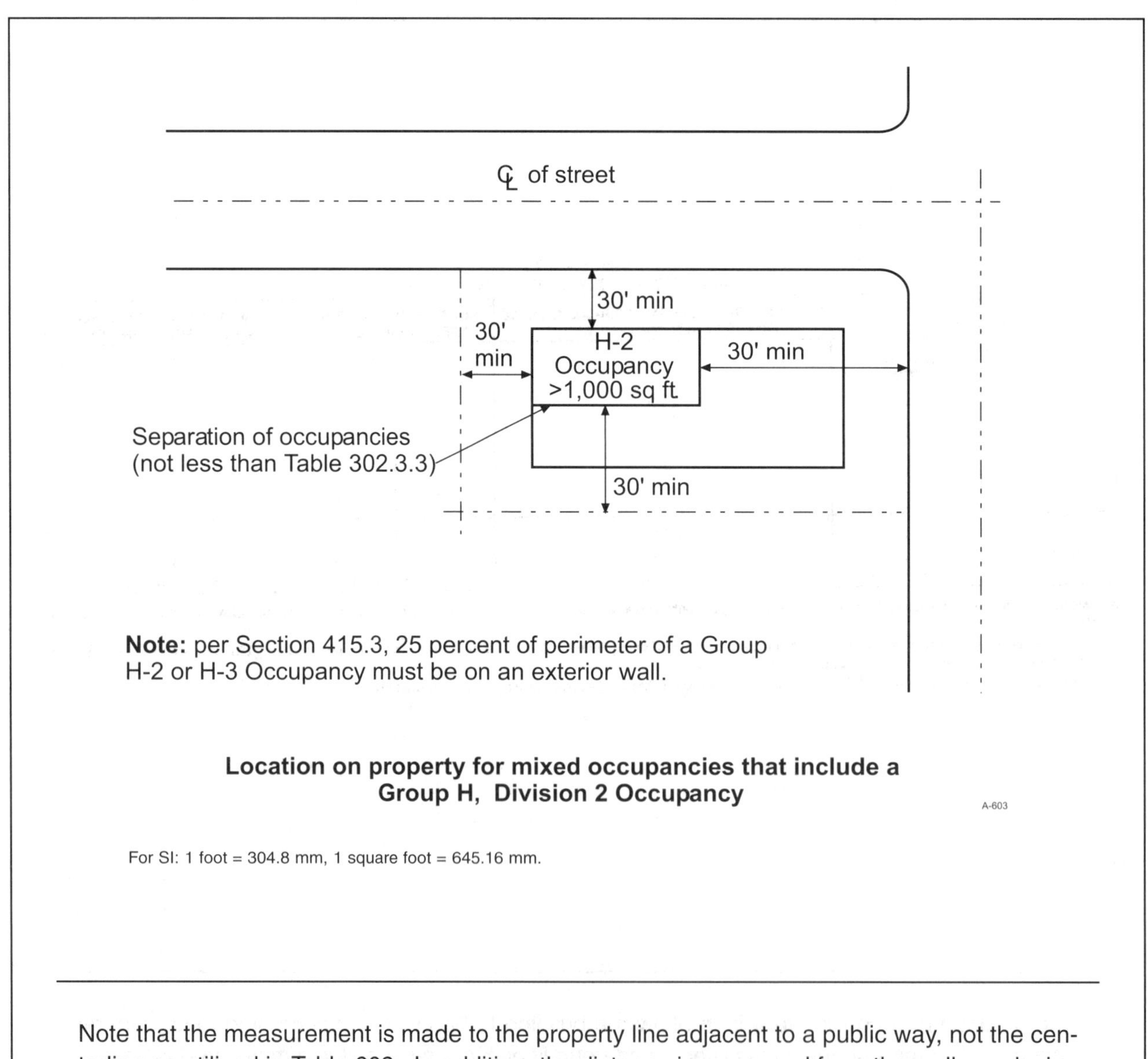

Location on property for mixed occupancies that include a Group H, Division 2 Occupancy

For SI: 1 foot = 304.8 mm, 1 square foot = 645.16 mm.

Note that the measurement is made to the property line adjacent to a public way, not the centerline as utilized in Table 602. In addition, the distance is measured from the walls enclosing the Group H occupancy, which may not necessarily be the exterior wall lines.

Topic: Detached Buildings
Reference: IBC 415.4, 415.5

Category: Detailed Use Requirements
Subject: Group H Occupancies

Code Text: *Group H-1 occupancies shall be in buildings used for no other purpose, shall not exceed one story in height and be without basements, crawl spaces or other under-floor spaces. Group H-2 and H-3 occupancies containing quantities of hazardous materials in excess of those set forth in Table 415.3.2 shall be in buildings used for no other purpose, shall not exceed one story in height and be without basements, crawl spaces or other under-floor spaces.*

Discussion and Commentary: Due to the explosion hazard potential associated with Group H-1 materials, Group H-1 occupancies are required to be in separate detached structures. The limitation of one story is based on the need for a building with a detonation hazard to be exited as soon as possible. Higher-level Group H-2 and Group H-3 occupancies where the quantities of hazardous materials pose an extremely high risk must also be located in buildings with no other uses.

TABLE 415.3.2
REQUIRED DETACHED STORAGE

DETACHED STORAGE IS REQUIRED WHEN THE QUANTITY OF MATERIAL EXCEEDS THAT LISTED HEREIN			
Material	**Class**	**Solids and Liquids (tons)[a,b]**	**Gases (cubic feet)[a,b]**
Explosives	Division 1.1 Division 1.2 Division 1.3 Division 1.4 Division 1.4[c] Division 1.5 Division 1.7	Maximum Allowable Quantity Maximum Allowable Quantity Maximum Allowable Quantity Maximum Allowable Quantity 1 Maximum Allowable Quantity Maximum Allowable Quantity	Not Applicable
Oxidizers	Class 4	Maximum Allowable Quantity	Maximum Allowable Quantity
Unstable (reactives) detonable	Class 3 or 4	Maximum Allowable Quantity	Maximum Allowable Quantity
Oxidizer, liquids and solids	Class 3 Class 2	1,200 2,000	Not Applicable Not Applicable
Organic peroxides	Detonable Class I Class II Class III	Maximum Allowable Quantity Maximum Allowable Quantity 25 50	Not Applicable Not Applicable Not Applicable Not Applicable
Unstable (reactives) nondetonable	Class 3 Class 2	1 25	2,000 10,000
Water reactives	Class 3 Class 2	1 25	Not Applicable Not Applicable
Pyrphoric gases	Not Applicable	Not Applicable	2,000

For SI: 1 ton = 906 kg, 1 cubic foot = 0.02832 M^3.

a. For materials that are detonable, the distance to other buildings or lot lines shall be as specified in Table 415.3.1 based on trinitrotoluene (TNT) equivalence of the material. For materials classified as explosives, see Chapter 33 the *International Fire Code*. For all other materials, the distance shall be as indicated in Section 415.3.1.

b. "Maximum Allowable Quantity" means the maximum allowable quantity per control area set forth in Table 307.7(1).

c. Limited to Division 1.4 materials and articles, including articles packaged for shipment, that are not regulated as an explosive under Bureau of Alcohol, Tobacco and Firearms (BATF) regulations or unpackaged articles used in process operations that do not propagate a detonation or deflagration between articles, providing the net explosive weight of individual articles does not exceed 1 pound.

The need for detached storage is a function of the type, physical state and quantity of material. Because such a single-use structure must be located an adequate distance from surrounding lot lines and other buildings, exterior walls and exterior openings need not be protected for exposure.

QUIZ

Study Session 14 — Chapter 4

I. Multiple Choice

1. The maximum distance from any point within a mall to an exit shall be __________ feet.

   a. 75 b. 200
   c. 250 d. 300

   Reference_______________

2. In a covered mall building, groupings of kiosks shall be separated a minimum of __________ feet from other structures within the mall.

   a. 6 b. 10
   c. 20 d. 30

   Reference_______________

3. A “high-rise” building describes those buildings having occupied floors a minimum of __________ feet above the lowest level of fire department vehicle access.

   a. 55 b. 75
   c. 120 d. 160

   Reference_______________

4. In a “high-rise” building, if standby power is a generator within the building, it shall be located in a separate room enclosed by minimum __________ fire-resistance-rated assemblies.

   a. one-hour fire barrier b. one hour fire-partition
   c. two-hour fire wall d. two- hour fire barrier

   Reference_______________

5. What is the minimum classification for the interior finish of atrium walls and ceilings?

   a. A b. B
   c. C d. DOC FF-1

   Reference_______________

6. At other than the lowest level of the atrium, the maximum permitted travel distance within an atrium space is __________ feet.

a. 75 b. 100
c. 150 d. 200

Reference_______________

7. An underground building must be divided into at least two compartments when a floor level is located a minimum of __________ feet below the lowest level of exit discharge.

a. 30 b. 60
c. 75 d. 120

Reference_______________

8. In parking facilities, vehicle barriers shall be provided where the difference in adjacent floor elevation exceeds __________ inches.

a. 12 b. 30
c. 48 d. 60

Reference_______________

9. Canopies under which fuels are dispensed shall have a minimum clearance of __________ above the surface of the drive-through area.

a. 12 feet, 0 inches b. 13 feet, 6 inches
c. 14 feet, 6 inches d. 16 feet, 0 inches

Reference_______________

10. Unless a permitted increase is applied, what is the maximum number of tiers permitted in a ramp-accessed open parking garage of Type IIA construction?

a. 8 b. 10
c. 12 d. 15

Reference_______________

11. Smoke compartments in a Group I-2 occupancy shall have a maximum floor area of __________ square feet.

a. 5,000 b. 10,000
c. 12,000 d. 22,500

Reference_______________

12. On floors housing patients confined to beds, a minimum of __________ net square feet per patient shall be provided in refuge areas of Group I-2 occupancies.

a. 3
b. 6
c. 15
d. 30

Reference_______________

13. Doors to resident sleeping units in Group I-3 occupancies shall have a minimum width of ___________ inches.

a. 22
b. 26
c. 28
d. 32

Reference_______________

14. In a Group I-3 occupancy, what is the maximum number of residents in any single smoke compartment?

a. 30
b. 50
c. 100
d. 200

Reference_______________

15. The minimum permitted size of a motion picture projection room containing 8 projecting machines shall be ___________ square feet.

a. 320
b. 360
c. 600
d. 640

Reference_______________

16. An approved curtain or water curtain need not be provided at the proscenium opening of stages having a maximum height of __________ feet.

a. 35
b. 50
c. 55
d. 75

Reference_______________

17. Stages exceeding __________ square feet in floor area shall be provided with emergency ventilation.

a. 200
b. 400
c. 500
d. 1,000

Reference_______________

18. What is the minimum interior finish classification for walls and ceilings in a special amusement building?

a. A
b. B
c. C
d. DOC FF-1

Reference_______________

19. What is the occupancy classification of an aircraft paint hangar?

a. Group F-1
b. Group H-2
c. Group S-1
d. Group S-2

Reference_______________

20. How many control areas are permitted on the sixth floor of a research and development building?

a. 0
b. 1
c. 2
d. 4

Reference_______________

21. A Group H-2 liquid use, dispensing and mixing room need not be located on the outer perimeter of a building when limited to a maximum floor area of __________ square feet.

a. 100
b. 200
c. 500
d. 1,000

Reference_______________

22. A Group H-3 occupancy required to be in a detached building shall be located a minimum of __________ feet from all lot lines.

a. 10
b. 20
c. 30
d. 50

Reference_______________

23. Dead ends in service corridors of Group H-5 occupancies shall be a maximum of __________ feet in length.

a. 4
b. 15
c. 20
d. 30

Reference_______________

24. In a drying room, all overhead heating piping shall be located a minimum of __________ inches from combustible contents in the dryer.

a. 1
b. 2
c. 4
d. 6

Reference_______________

25. Nitrocellulose storage located in a building where organic coatings are manufactured shall be enclosed in a room of minimum __________ fire-resistance-rated construction.

a. 1-hour
b. 2-hour
c. 3-hour
d. 4-hour

Reference_______________

26. Where the stage height exceeds 50 feet, workshops and storerooms serving the stage shall be separated from the stage and other parts of the building by minimum _____.

a. one-hour fire partitions
b. one-hour fire barriers
c. two-hour fire barriers
d. two-hour fire walls

Reference_______________

27. In a nonsprinklered office building, an attic space used for the storage of combustible material shall be protected on the storage side with minimum _____.

a. $^1/_2$-inch gypsum board
b. $^1/_2$-inch Type X gypsum board
c. $^5/_8$-inch gypsum board
d. one-hour construction

Reference_______________

28. A minimum _____ fire-resistance rating is required for the floor construction separating multiple control areas within a building.

a. $^1/_2$-hour
b. 1-hour
c. 2-hour
d. 3-hour

Reference_______________

29. Weather protection used to shelter an outdoor hazardous material storage area can only be considered outdoor storage for purposes of the code where the maximum allowable area of the structure is _____ square feet.

a. 1,000
b. 1,500
c. 2,000
d. 3,000

Reference_______________

30. What is the minimum level of construction required to enclose spray rooms used for the application of flammable paints?

a. noncombustible, nonrated
b. one-hour fire partitions
c. one-hour fire barriers
d. two-hour fire barriers

Reference_______________

INTERNATIONAL BUILDING CODE

Study Session 15

Chapters 14, 15 and 18 — Exterior Wall Coverings, Roofs and Foundations

OBJECTIVE: To obtain an understanding of the requirements for exterior wall coverings, including weather-resistant coverings and veneer; roofing assemblies, roof coverings and rooftop structures; and footings and foundations.

REFERENCE: Chapters 14, 15 and 18, 2003 *International Building Code*

KEY POINTS:

- What are the components of a weather-resistant wall envelope?
- When is a vapor retarder not required for an exterior wall?
- What material is considered acceptable as a water-resistant barrier?
- Where is flashing to be installed?
- What is the minimum required thickness of wood veneers on exterior walls of Type I, II, III and IV buildings?
- What is anchored masonry veneer? Adhered masonry veneer?
- How must metal veneers be attached? Glass veneer? Stone veneer?
- Under which conditions is vinyl siding permitted?
- How are combustible exterior wall coverings regulated for ignition resistance? Fireblocking?
- What level of fire resistance is required of combustible balconies and similar projections?
- When is fire-retardant-treated wood permitted for the construction of balconies, porches, decks and exterior stairways in Types I and II construction?
- How shall bay windows and oriel windows be constructed?
- What is a roof assembly? Roof covering?
- What is the purpose of a roof assembly?
- How are roof assemblies classified?
- What is the effectiveness of a Class A roof assembly? Class B? Class C?
- What is a nonclassified roof? A special purpose roof? Where are such roofs permitted?
- How must roof covering materials be identified?
- How shall asphalt shingles be installed? Clay and concrete tile? Wood shakes and shingles? Metal roof panels and roof shingles?
- What is the maximum permitted height of a penthouse? Tower or spire?
- How is reroofing addressed?
- What methods of frost protection are approved for foundation walls, piers and other permanent foundations of buildings?
- What is the minimum depth of a footing below the undisturbed ground surface?
- How shall backfill in the excavated area adjacent to the foundation be placed?
- What special considerations are applicable to footings adjacent to ascending slopes? Descending slopes?
- If not specifically designed, how must footings supporting walls of light-frame construction be constructed?
- How must concrete footings be protected from frost?
- Where is dampproofing required? Waterproofing?

Topic: Weather Protection
Reference: IBC 1403.2

Category: Exterior Walls
Subject: Performance Requirements

Code Text: *Exterior walls shall provide the building with a weather-resistant exterior wall envelope. The exterior envelope shall include flashing, described in Section 1405.3. The exterior wall envelope shall be designed and constructed in such a manner as to prevent the accumulation of water within the wall assembly by providing a water-resistant barrier behind the exterior veneer, as described in Section 1404.2.* See exceptions.

Discussion and Commentary: The code considers it necessary to apply at least one layer of No. 15 asphalt felt, complying with ASTM D 226 for Type 1 felt, in order to provide the weather-resistant barrier between the sheathing and exterior wall veneer. The use of flashing in conjunction with the felt will provide a continuous barrier against water penetration.

TABLE 1405.2
MINIMUM THICKNESS OF WEATHER COVERINGS

COVERING TYPE	MINIMUM THICKNESS (inches)
Adhered masonry veneer	0.25
Anchored masonry veneer	2.625
Aluminum siding	0.019
Asbestos-cement boards	0.125
Asbestos shingles	0.156
Cold-rolled copper[d]	0.0216 nominal
Copper shingles[d]	0.0162 nominal
Exterior plywood (with sheathing)	0.313
Exterior plywood (without sheathing)	See Section 2304.6
Fiberboard siding	0.5
Fiber cement lap siding	0.25[c]
Fiber cement panel siding	0.25[c]
Glass-fiber reinforced concrete panels	0.375
Hardboard siding[c]	0.25
High-yield copper[d]	0.0162 nominal
Lead-coated copper[d]	0.0216 nominal
Lead-coated high-yield copper	0.0162 nominal
Marble slabs	1
Particleboard (with sheathing)	See Section 2304.6
Particleboard (without sheathing)	See Section 2304.6
Precast stone facing	0.625
Steel (approved corrosion resistant)	0.0149
Stone (cast artificial)	1.5
Stone (natural)	2

For all exterior walls other than those constructed of concrete or masonry, the IBC requires the installation of an approved vapor retarder. Any other approved method to resist condensation and moisture leakage is also acceptable.

Topic: Flashing
Reference: IBC 1405.3

Category: Exterior Walls
Subject: Installation of Wall Coverings

Code Text: *Flashing shall be installed in such a manner so as to prevent moisture from entering the wall or to redirect it to the exterior. Flashing shall be installed at the perimeters of exterior door and window assemblies, penetrations and terminations of exterior wall assemblies, exterior wall intersections with roofs, chimneys, porches, decks, balconies and similar projections and at built-in gutters and similar locations where moisture could enter the wall. Flashing with projecting flanges shall be installed on both sides and the ends of copings, under sills and continuously above projecting trim.*

Discussion and Commentary: In general, the code requires that all intersections of exterior surfaces and/or components be flashed to prevent water intrusion. Roof and wall intersections and parapets are especially troublesome, as are exterior wall openings exposed to weather and, in particular, wind-driven rain.

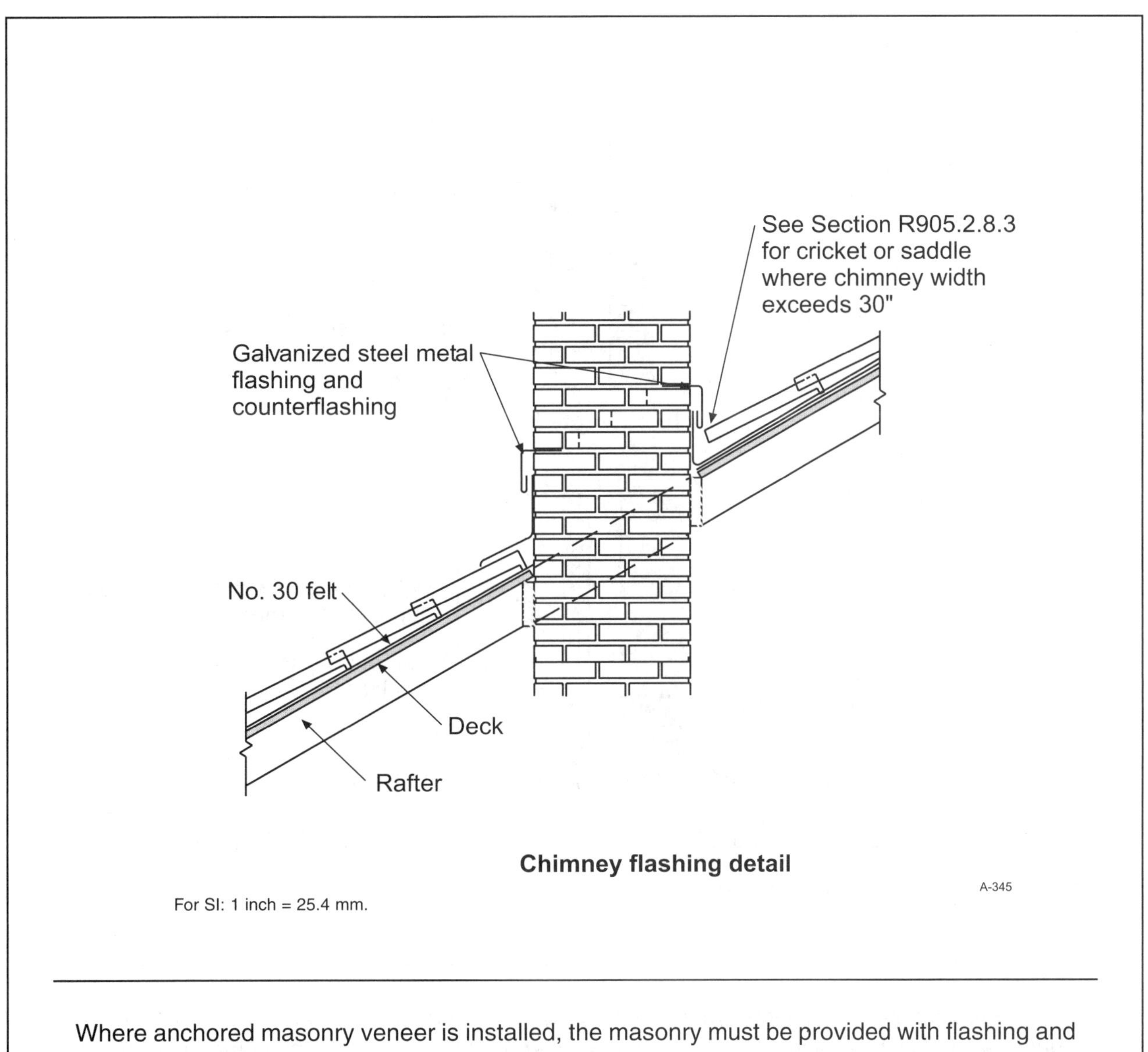

Chimney flashing detail

For SI: 1 inch = 25.4 mm.

Where anchored masonry veneer is installed, the masonry must be provided with flashing and weepholes in the first course above finished ground level above the foundation wall or slab, as well as at other points of support.

Topic: Definitions
Reference: IBC 1402

Category: Exterior Walls
Subject: Veneer

Code Text: *Veneer is a facing attached to a wall for the purpose of providing ornamentation, protection, or insulation, but not counted as adding strength to the wall. Adhered masonry veneer is veneer secured and supported through the adhesion of an approved bonding material applied to an approved backing. Anchored masonry veneer is veneer secured with approved mechanical fasteners to an approved backing.*

Discussion and Commentary: Years ago, veneer was considered an ornamental facing for a masonry wall. Today, the IBC regulates a variety of veneer materials: wood, anchored masonry, stone, slab-type, terra cotta, adhered masonry, metal, glass and, in Chapter 26, plastic. The code regulates material size, type and attachment, as well as other concerns that would cause the veneer to fail.

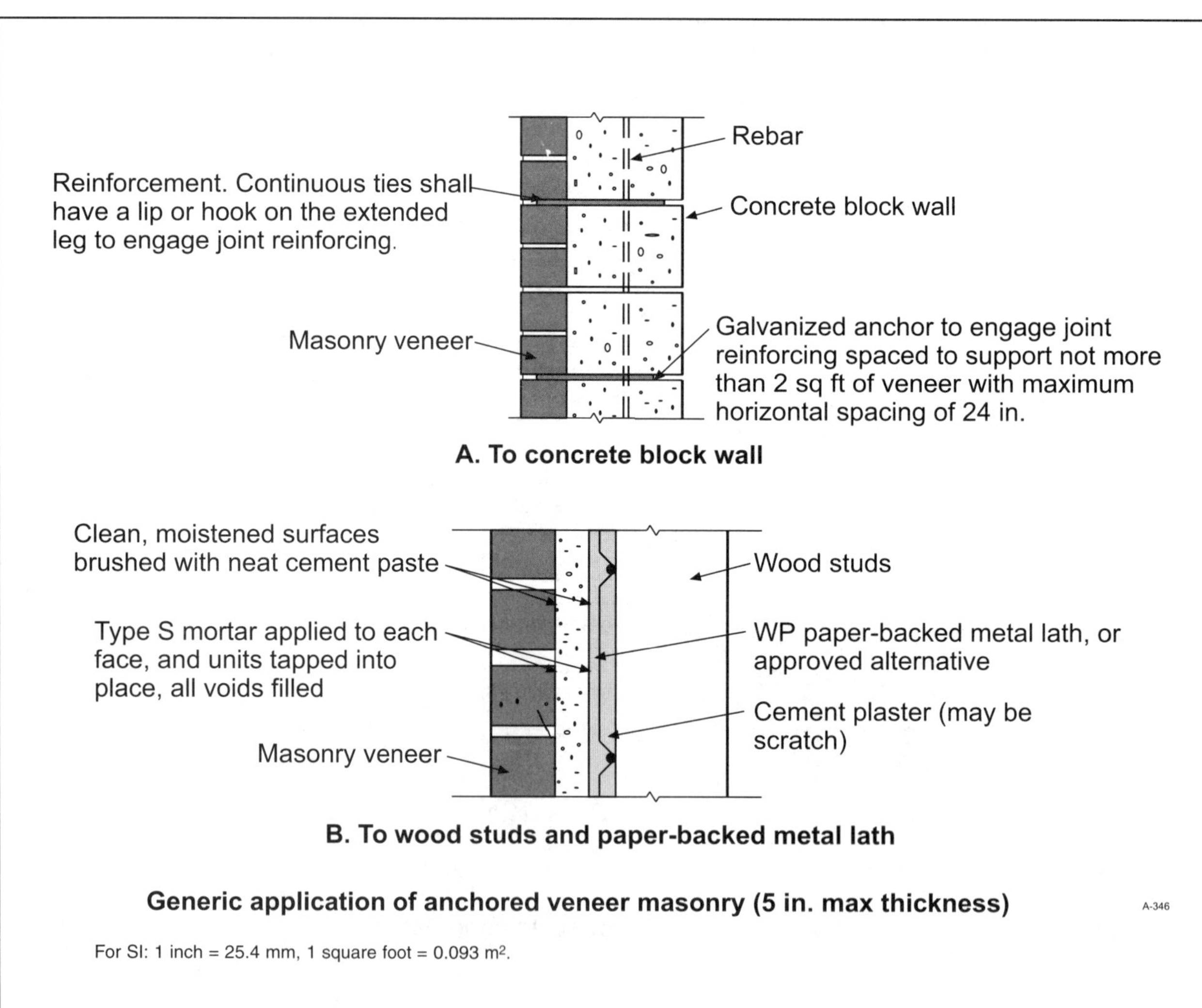

Generic application of anchored veneer masonry (5 in. max thickness)

For SI: 1 inch = 25.4 mm, 1 square foot = 0.093 m^2.

As they are constantly subjected to alternate cycles of wetting and drying, the anchors, ties or supports used in the attachment of veneer must be corrosion resistant. These materials, when used on the exterior of a building, must support the veneer properly for the life of the building.

Topic: Balconies
Reference: IBC 1406.3

Category: Exterior Walls
Subject: Combustible Materials on Exterior Walls

Code Text: *Balconies and similar projections of combustible construction, other than fire- retardant-treated wood, shall afford the fire-resistance rating required by Table 601 for floor construction or shall be of Type IV construction as described in Section 602.4, and the aggregate length shall not exceed 50 percent of the building perimeter on each floor.* See exceptions.

Discussion and Commentary: Although projections may extend beyond the floor area of a building, they still pose some degree of hazard due to their materials of construction. Combustible projections are generally limited to buildings of Types III, IV and V construction; however, fire-retardant-treated wood is acceptable for balconies, porches, decks and exterior stairways not used as required exits in Type I or II buildings that are three stories or less in height.

Balconies and similar projections, when combustible, to have fire-resistive rating as for floor, or be of Type IV construction, except:

- Fire-retardant-treated wood in Types I and II, limited to 3 stories in height, and not used for exiting
- Permitted to be Type V in buildings of Type III, IV or V with no fire rating where sprinkler protection extended to projections
- Guard devices, such as pickets and rails, limited to 42 inches in height

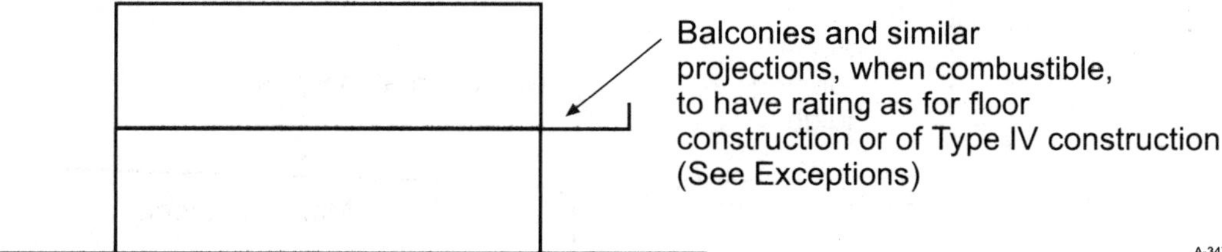

If not constructed of fire-retardant-treated wood, combustible projections must be of heavy-timber or must provide the same degree of fire resistance as the building's floor construction. However, in sprinklered buildings of combustible construction, no fire-resistance rating is required.

Topic: Definition
Reference: IBC 1502

Category: Roof Assemblies and Rooftop Structures
Subject: Roof Assembly

Code Text: *A roof assembly is a system designed to provide weather protection and resistance to design loads. The system consists of a roof covering and roof deck or a single component serving as both the roof covering and the roof deck. A roof assembly includes the roof deck, vapor retarder, substrate or thermal barrier, insulation, vapor retarder and roof covering. Roof covering is the covering applied to the roof deck for weather resistance, fire classification or appearance.*

Discussion and Commentary: There are many components of a roof assembly. Viewed as a unit, a roof assembly is regulated for its resistance to wind, weathering, impact and fire. In addition, roof coverings must be designed, installed and maintained to protect the building from the weather.

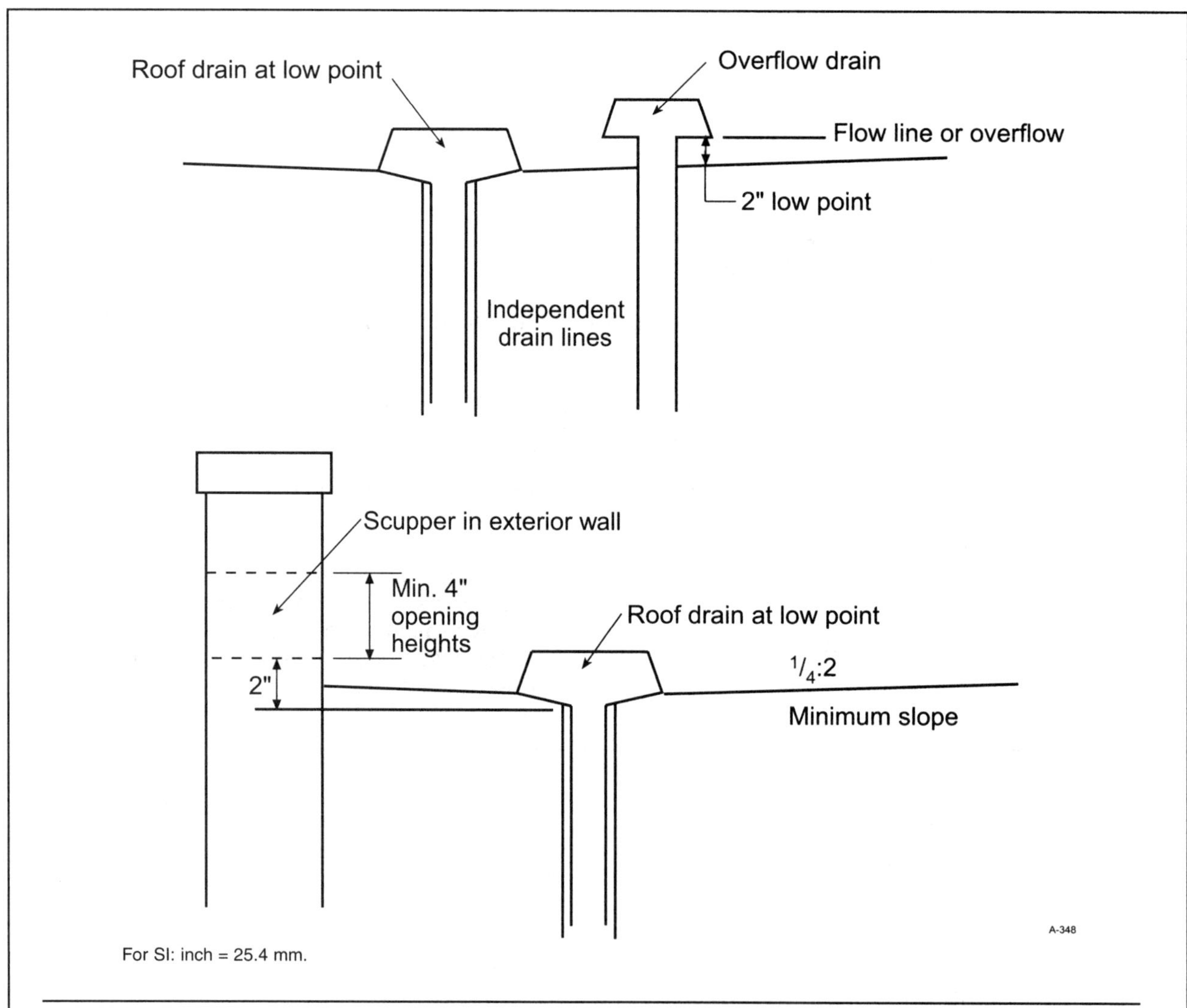

The *International Plumbing Code* is referenced in Section 1503.4 for the design and installation of roof drainage systems. Where water on the roof is not intended to flow over the roof edge, provisions for roof drainage will include primary roof drains supplemented by overflow drains.

Topic: General Requirements
Reference: IBC 1505.1

Category: Roof Assemblies and Rooftop Structures
Subject: Fire Classification

Code Text: *Roof assemblies shall be divided into the classes defined below. Class A, B and C roof assemblies and roof coverings required to be listed by Section 1505 shall be tested in accordance with ASTM E 108 or UL 790. The minimum roof coverings installed on buildings shall comply with Table 1505.1 based on the type of construction of the building.*

Discussion and Commentary: The various required roof covering classifications are related directly to the type of construction of the building. Based on Table 1505.1, a minimum level of fire protection is assigned to address external fire exposures. The exposures are generally created by fires in adjoining structures, wild fires and fire from the subject building that may extend up the exterior wall and onto the top surface of the roof.

TABLE 1505.1[a,b]
MINIMUM ROOF COVERING CLASSIFICATION FOR TYPES OF CONSTRUCTION

IA	IB	IIA	IIB	IIIA	IIIB	IV	VA	VB
B	B	B	C[c]	B	C[c]	B	B	C[c]

For SI: 1 foot = 304.8 mm, 1 square foot = 0.0929 m^2.

a. Unless otherwise required in accordance with the *International Urban Wildland Interface Code* or due to the location of the building within a fire district in accordance with Appendix D.

b. Nonclassified roof coverings shall be permitted on buildings of Group R-3, as applicable in Section 101.2, and Group U occupancies, where there is a minimum fire-separation distance of 6 feet measured from the leading edge of the roof.

c. Buildings that are not more than two stories in height and having not more than 6,000 square feet of projected roof area and where there is a minimum 10-foot fire-separation distance from the leading edge of the roof to a lot line on all sides of the building, except for street fronts or public ways, shall be permitted to have roofs of No. 1 cedar or redwood shakes and No. 1 shingles.

In addition to the Class A, B and C listed roof assemblies, the IBC permits the use of nonclassified roofing and special purpose roofs under limited conditions. These types of roof coverings are limited, respectively, to Group R-3 occupancies and small nonfire-rated buildings.

Topic: Class A, B and C Assemblies
Reference: IBC 1505.2–1505.5

Category: Roof Assemblies and Rooftop Structures
Subject: Fire Classification

Code Text: *Class A roof assemblies are those that are effective against severe fire-test exposure. Class B roof assemblies are those that are effective against moderate fire-test exposure. Class C roof assemblies are those that are effective against light fire-test exposure. Nonclassified roofing is approved material that is not listed as a Class A, B or C roof covering.*

Discussion and Commentary: Traditional Class A roof coverings include masonry, concrete, slate, tile and cement-asbestos. Additionally, any assembly that is tested as Class A in accordance with ASTM E 108 by an approved testing agency and is listed and identified by that agency is included. Traditional Class B roof coverings include metal sheets and shingles, as well as those tested, listed and identified as Class B. There are no specific materials that qualify as Class C; therefore all Class C roof covering are listed as such.

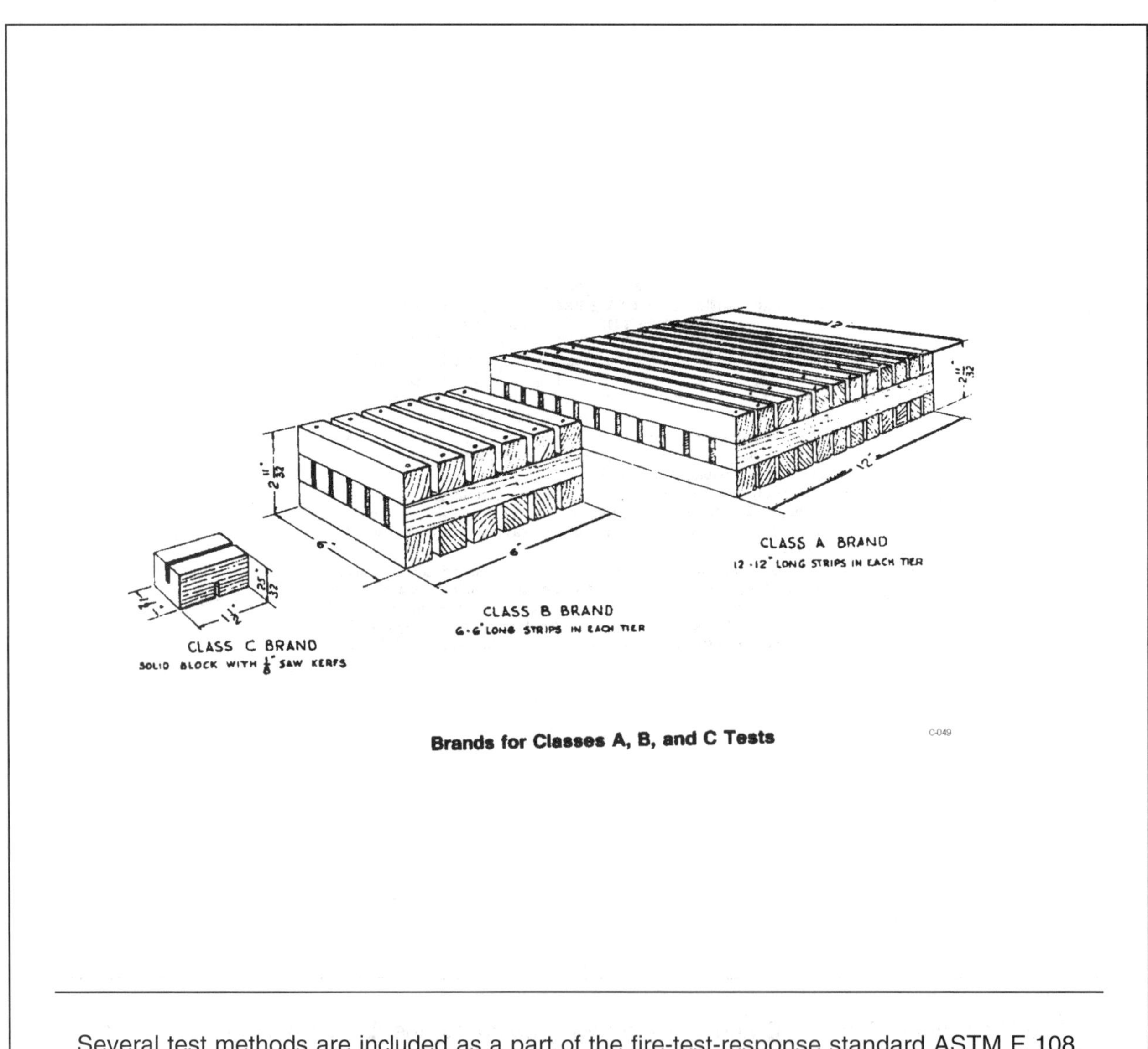

Brands for Classes A, B, and C Tests

Several test methods are included as a part of the fire-test-response standard ASTM E 108, including the intermittent flame exposure test, spread of flame test, burning brand test, flying brand test and rain test. It also is critical that the roof coverings do not slip from position.

Topic: General Requirements
Reference: IBC 1503, 1507

Category: Roof Assemblies and Rooftop Structures
Subject: Roof Coverings

Code Text: *Roof decks shall be covered with approved roof coverings secured to the building or structure in accordance with the provisions of Chapter 15. Roof coverings shall be designed, installed and maintained in accordance with the IBC and the approved manufacturer's installation instructions such that the roof covering shall serve to protect the building or structure. Roof coverings shall be applied in accordance with the applicable provisions of Section 1507 and the manufacturer's instructions.*

Discussion and Commentary: The IBC contains installation requirements for a number of types of roof covering materials and systems. Selectively included in the provisions are deck requirements, limitations on roof slope, underlayment, materials, fasteners and attachment, flashings and application methods.

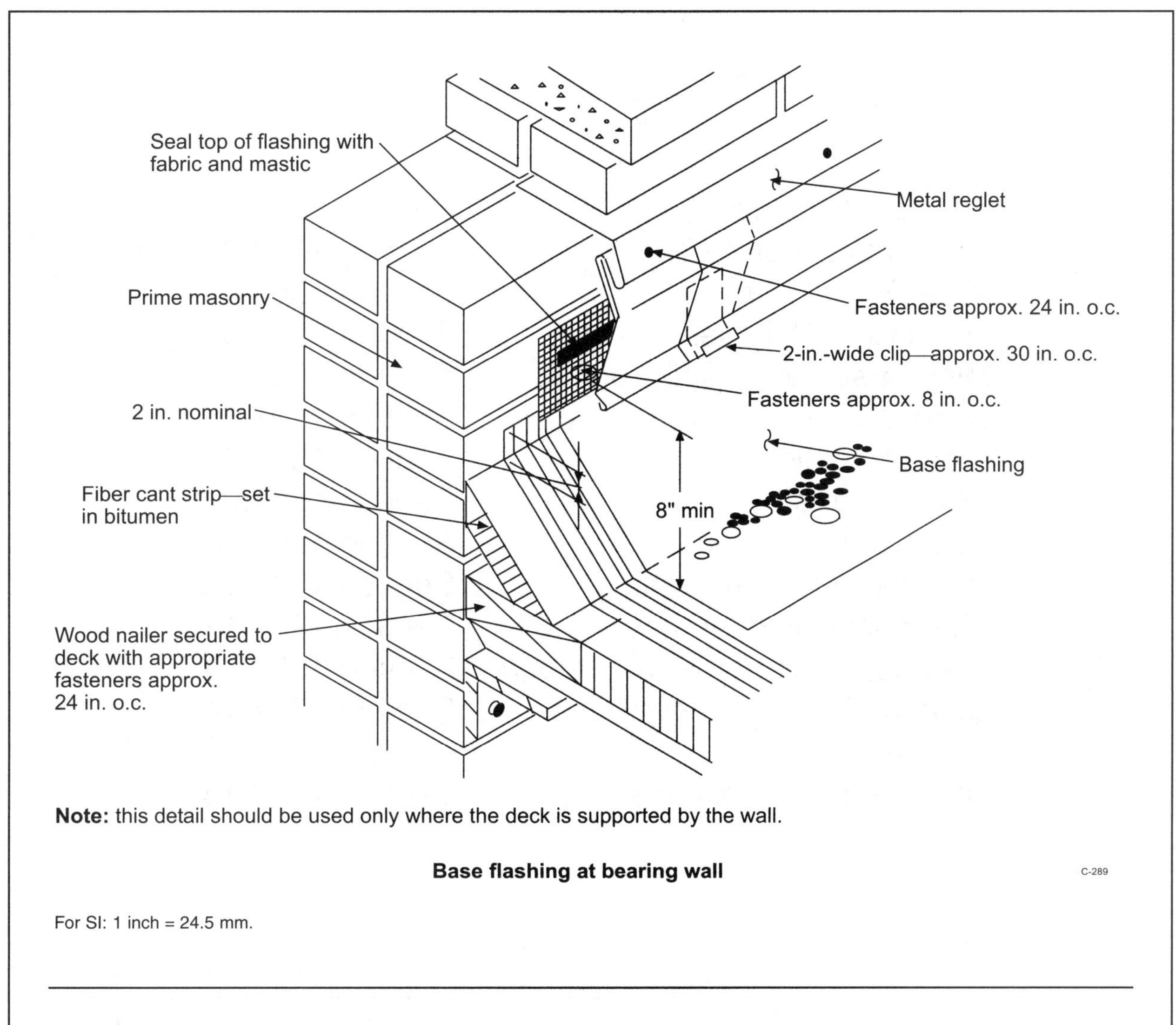

Base flashing at bearing wall

Flashing is essential to a weatherproof roofing assembly. It is required at wall and roof intersections, at gutters, around roof openings such as chimneys and vents, and wherever there is a change in roof slope or direction. Metal flashing shall be minimum No.26 galvanized sheet.

Topic: Materials
Reference: IBC 1506

Category: Roof Assemblies and Rooftop Structures
Subject: Roof Coverings

Code Text: *Roof covering materials shall be delivered in packages bearing the manufacturer's identifying marks and approved testing agency labels required in accordance with Section 1505. Bulk shipments of materials shall be accompanied with the same information issued in the form of a certificate or on a bill of lading by the manufacturer.*

Discussion and Commentary: Roof covering materials must comply with the appropriate quality standards set forth in Section 1507 for each different type of material. The materials must be compatible with the building or structure to which they are applied. In addition, identification of the roof covering materials is mandatory to verify that they comply with the quality standard.

Asphalt Shingles	Section 1507.2
Clay and Concrete Tile	Section 1507.3
Metal Roof Panels	Section 1507.4
Metal Roof Shingles	Section 1507.5
Mineral-surfaced Roll Roofing	Section 1507.6
Slate Shingles	Section 1507.7
Wood Shingles	Section 1507.8
Wood Shakes	Section 1507.9
Built-up Roofs	Section 1507.10
Modified Bitumen Roofing	Section 1507.11
Thermoset Single-ply Roofing	Section 1507.12
Thermoplastic Single-ply Roofing	Section 1507.13
Sprayed Polyurethane Foam Roofing	Section 1507.14
Liquid-applied Coatings	Section 1507.15

Where there are not applicable standards for a specific roof covering material, or where the materials are of questionable suitability, the building official must ask for testing by an approved agency to determine the material's character, quality and limitations of application.

Topic: Asphalt Shingles
Reference: IBC 1507.2

Category: Roof Assemblies and Rooftop Structures
Subject: Roof Coverings

Code Text: *Asphalt shingles shall be fastened to solidly sheathed decks. Asphalt shingles shall only be used on roof slopes of two units vertical in 12 units horizontal or greater. Asphalt shingles shall be secured to the roof with not less than four fasteners per strip shingle or two fasteners per individual shingle. For roof slopes from two units vertical in 12 units horizontal, up to four units vertical in 12 units horizontal, underlayment shall be two layers . . . Provide drip edge at eaves and gables of shingle roofs.*

Discussion and Commentary: There are two fundamental types of asphalt shingles: strip shingles (the most common type) such as three-tab shingles, and individual interlocking shingles such as t-lock shingles. In addition to three-tab, other strip shingles include random or multi-tab, no-cut-out and laminated architectural.

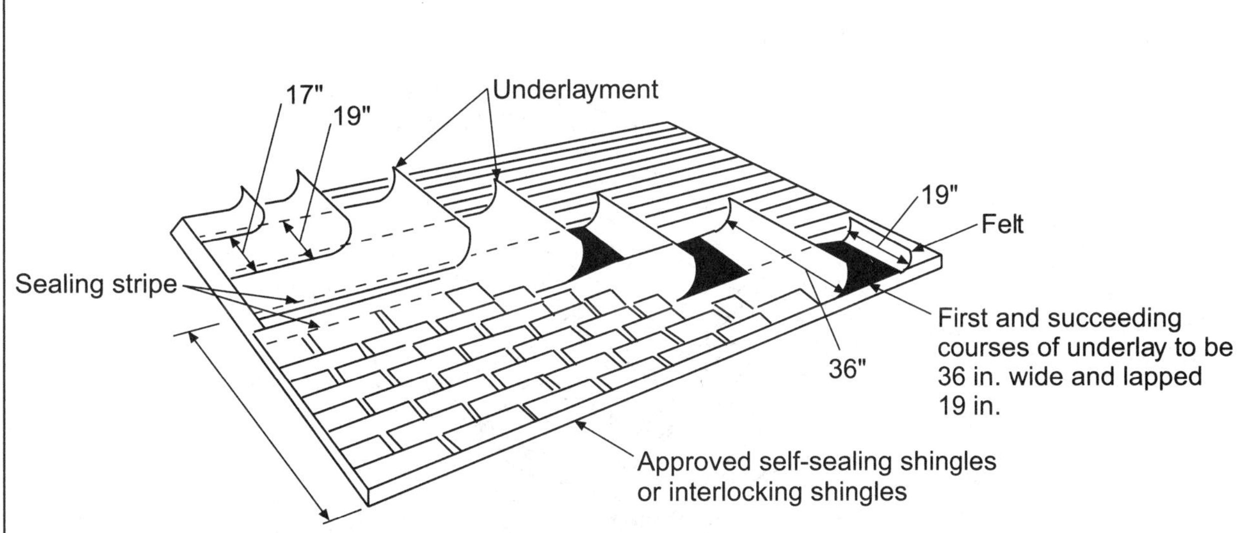

Application of asphalt shingle on slopes between 2:12 and 4:12

Asphalt shingles are typically classified in two types, either cellulose felt reinforced (i.e., organic shingles) and fiberglass mat reinforced (i.e., fiberglass shingles). Although not in the code, the roofing industry recommends the attic space below asphalt shingle roofs be properly ventilated.

Topic: Wood Shakes
Reference: IBC 1507.9

Category: Roof Assemblies and Rooftop Structures
Subject: Roof Coverings

Code Text: *Wood shakes shall only be used on solid or spaced sheathing. Wood shakes shall only be used on slopes of four units vertical in 12 units horizontal. Interlayment shall comply with ASTM D 226, Type I. Fasteners for wood shakes shall be corrosion resistant with a minimum penetration of 0.75 inch (19.1 mm) into the sheathing. Wood shakes shall be laid with a side lap not less than 1.5 inches (38 mm) between joints in adjacent courses. Spacing between shakes in the same course shall be 0.375 to 0.625 (9.5 to 15.9 mm) inches for shakes . . . .*

Discussion and Commentary: Wood shakes, which are defined as roofing products split from logs and then shaped as required by the individual manufacturers, differ from wood shingles in that shingles are defined as sawed wood products featuring a uniform butt thickness per individual length.

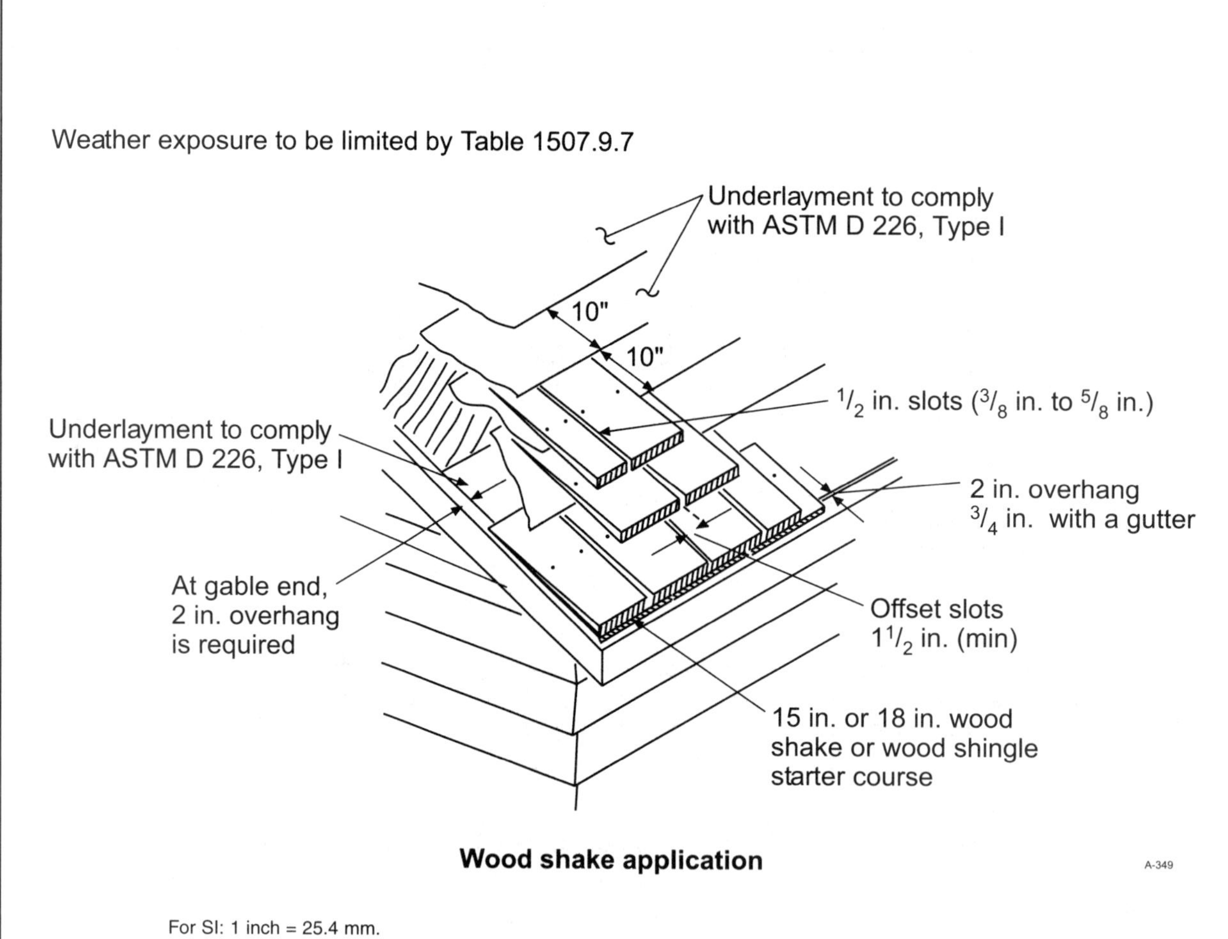

Wood shake application

For SI: 1 inch = 25.4 mm.

Both wood shakes and wood shingles are required to be labeled by an approved third-party inspection agency. The applicable set of grading rules, required of the quality control program, is typically prescribed by the Cedar Shake and Shingle Bureau.

Topic: Penthouses
Reference: IBC 1509.2

Category: Roof Assemblies and Rooftop Structures
Subject: Rooftop Structures

Code Text: *A penthouse or other projection above the roof in structures of other than Type I construction shall not exceed 28 feet (8534 mm) above the roof where used as an enclosure for tanks or for elevators that run to the roof and in all other cases shall not extend more than 18 (5486 mm) feet above the roof. The aggregate area of penthouses and other rooftop structures shall not exceed one-third the area of the supporting roof. A penthouse, bulkhead or any other similar projection above the roof shall not be used for purposes other than shelter of mechanical equipment or shelter of vertical shaft openings in the roof.*

Discussion and Commentary: The general premise is that a penthouse be treated no differently than any other portion of the building. However, the reductions in the general requirements for a story recognize the lack of occupant load or fire loading, as well as the reduced exposure of penthouses when the exterior wall is recessed from the exterior wall of the building.

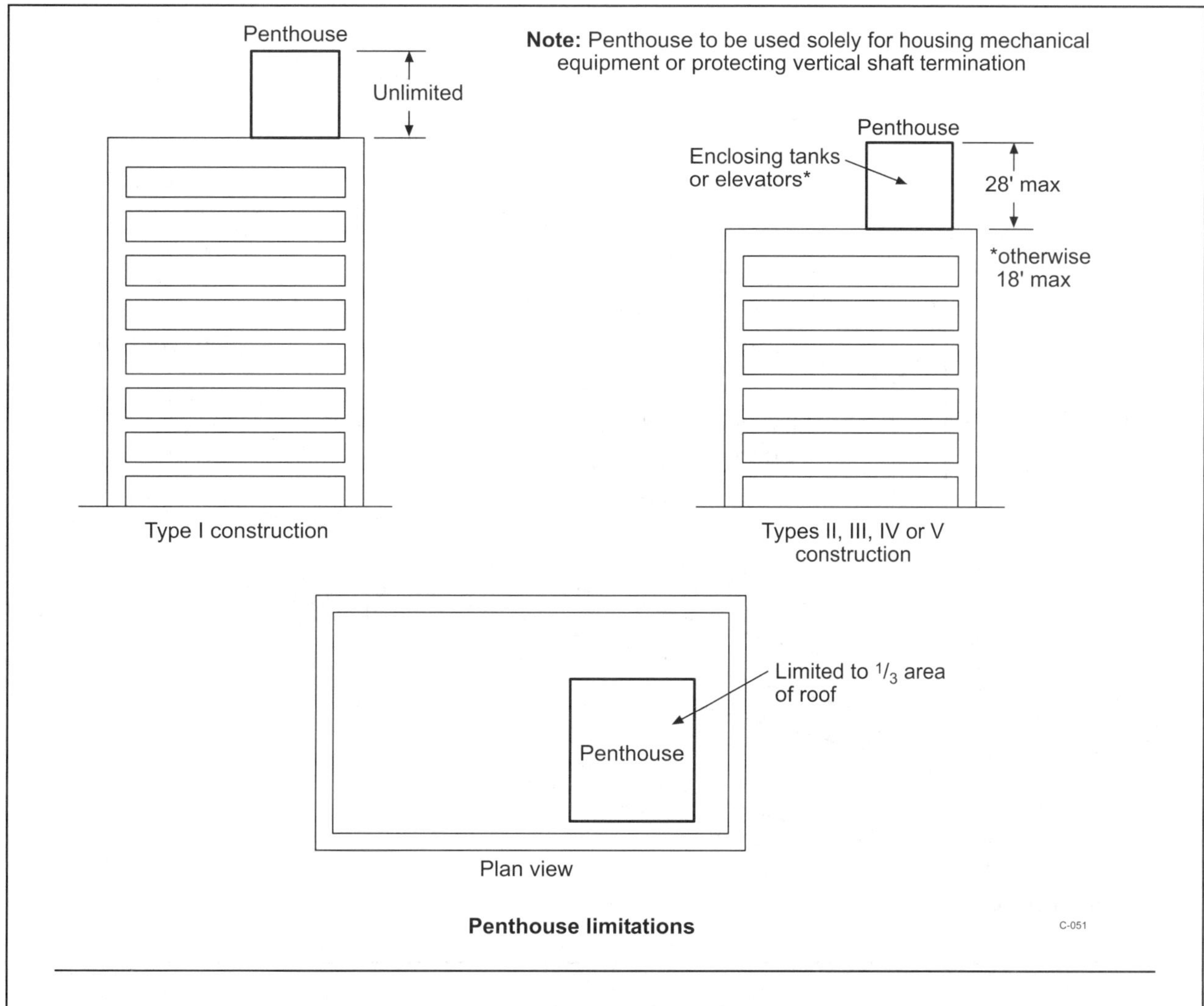

Penthouse limitations

Special allowances are provided for towers, spires, domes and cupolas. It is important, however, to limit the height of such structures where constructed of combustible materials. Limited provisions also regulate the installation of tanks and cooling towers on buildings as well.

Topic: General Requirements
Reference: IBC 1805.1

Category: Soils and Foundations
Subject: Footings and Foundations

Code Text: *Footings and foundations shall be built on undisturbed soil, compacted fill material, or CLSM (controlled low-strength material). The top surface of footings shall be level. The bottom surface of footings are permitted to have a slope not exceeding 1 unit vertical in 10 units horizontal (10-percent slope). Footings shall be stepped where it is necessary to change the elevation of the top surface of the footing or where the surface of the ground slopes more than 1 unit vertical in 10 units horizontal (10-percent slope).*

Discussion and Commentary: If compacted fill material is used to support a footing, the material must be in compliance with the provisions of an approved report. The code identifies seven issues that must be addressed in the report, including specifications for both the site preparation and the material to be used as fill.

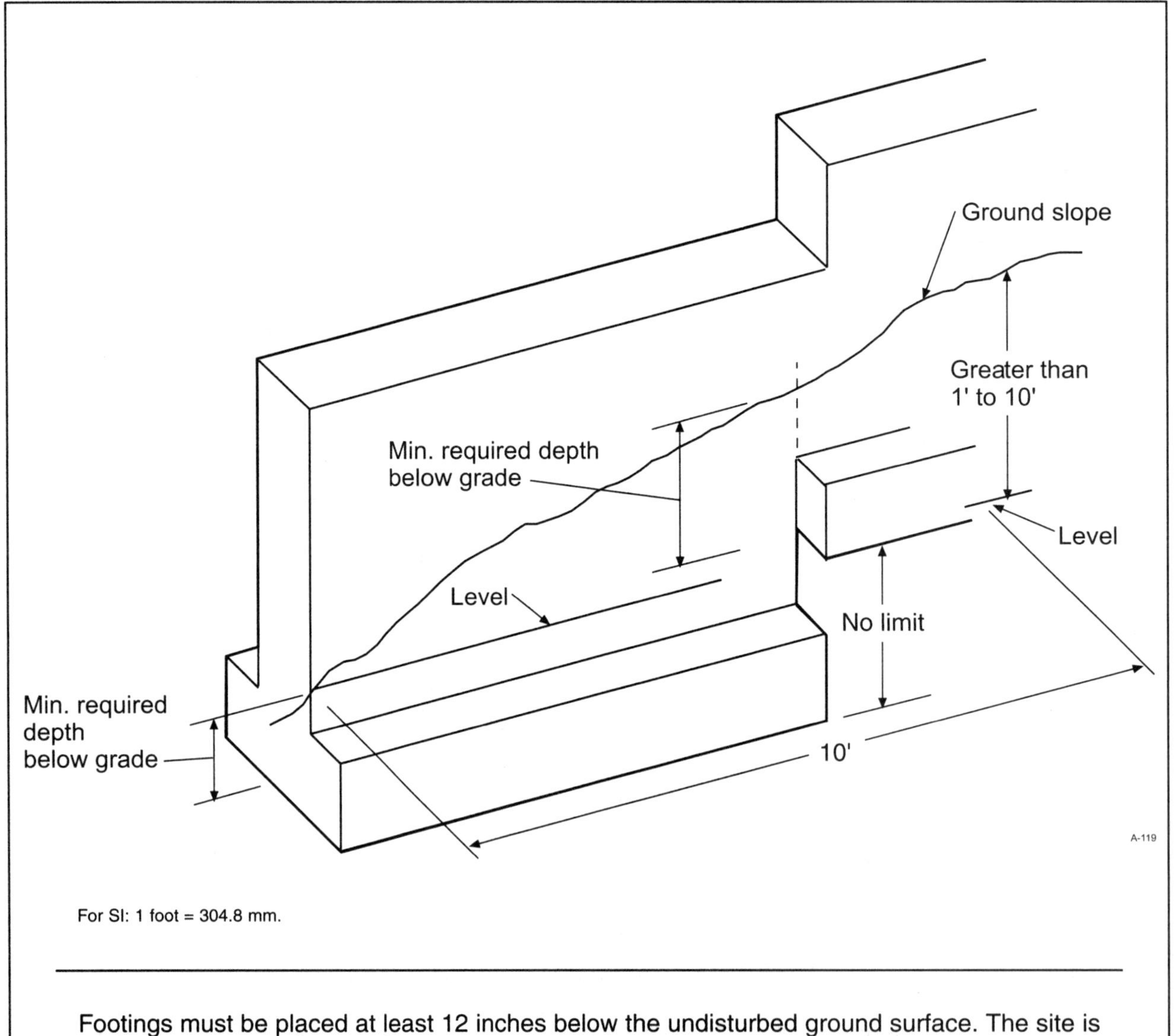

Footings must be placed at least 12 inches below the undisturbed ground surface. The site is recognized to contain shifting or moving soils; the footings must be extended to a sufficient depth to ensure stability.

Topic: Frost Protection
Reference: IBC 1805.2

Category: Soils and Foundations
Subject: Footings and Foundations

Code Text: *The minimum depth of footings below the undisturbed ground surface shall be 12 inches (305 mm). Except where otherwise protected from frost, foundation walls, piers and other permanent supports of buildings and structures shall be protected from frost by one or more of the following methods: 1) extending below the frost line of the locality, 2) construction in accordance with ASCE-32* (Design and Construction of Frost Protected Shallow Foundations), *or 3) erecting on solid rock.* See exception for small free-standing structures. *Footings shall not bear on frozen soil unless such frozen condition is of a permanent character.*

Discussion and Commentary: In winter, frost action can raise the ground level (frost heave), whereas in springtime, the same area will soften and settle back. If foundations are constructed on soils that can freeze, then the heave or vertical movement of the ground, which is rarely uniform, can cause serious damage to buildings and other structures.

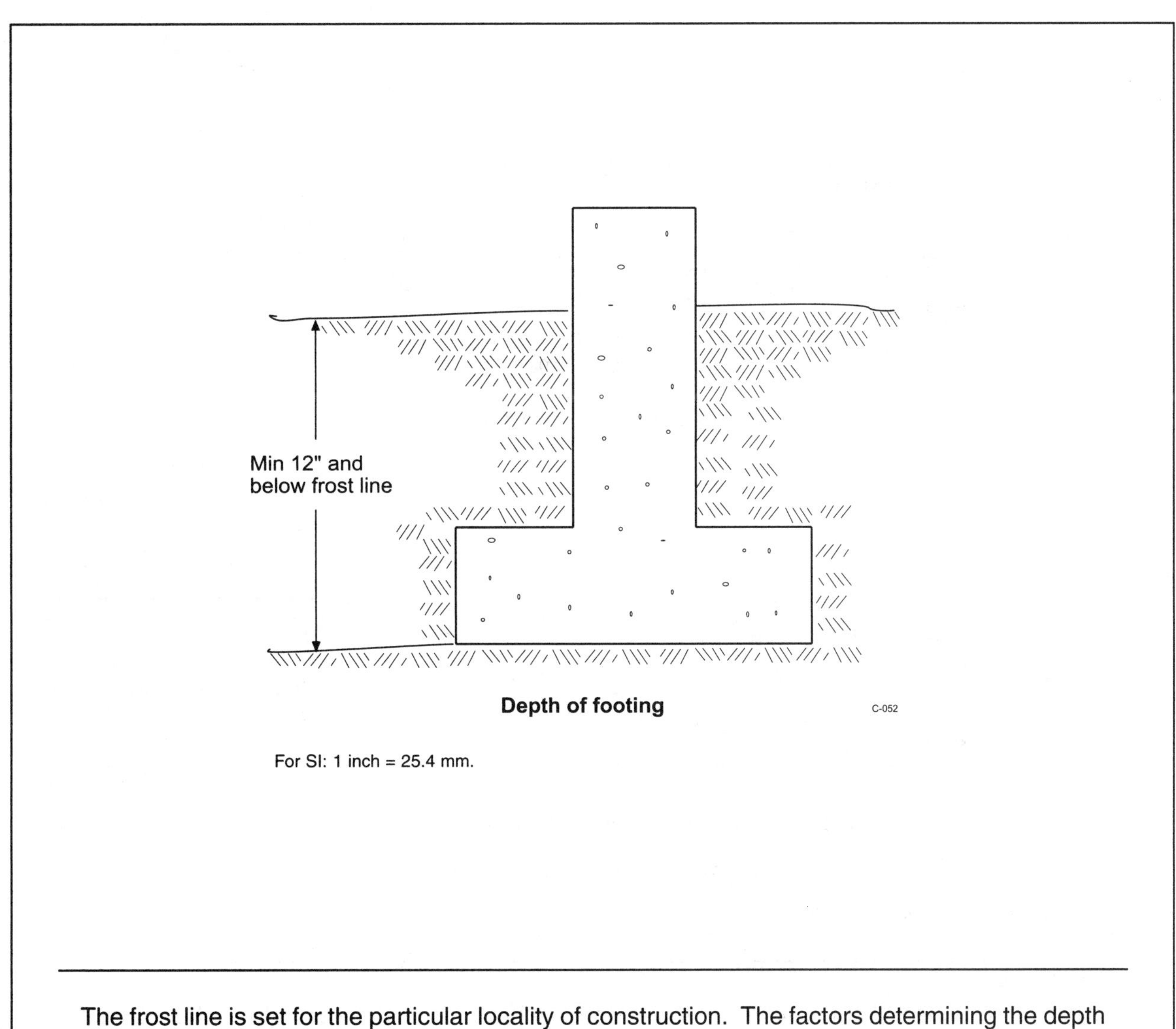

Depth of footing

For SI: 1 inch = 25.4 mm.

The frost line is set for the particular locality of construction. The factors determining the depth of the frost line are air temperature and the length of time it remains below freezing, as well as the soil's level of thermal conductivity and its ability to conduct heat.

Topic: Foundation Elevation
Reference: IBC 1805.3.4

Category: Soils and Foundations
Subject: Foundations

Code Text: *On graded sites, the top of any exterior foundation shall extend above the elevation of the street gutter at point of discharge or the inlet of an approved drainage device a minimum of 12 inches plus 2 percent. Alternate elevations are permitted subject to the approval of the building official, provided it can be demonstrated that required drainage to the point of discharge and away from the structure is provided at all locations on the site.*

Discussion and Commentary: Where natural drainage away from a building is not available, the site must be graded so that water will not drain toward, or accumulate at, the exterior foundation wall. A prescriptive elevation is set forth that will ensure positive drainage to a street gutter or other drainage point; however, any other method that moves water away from the building can be accepted by the building official.

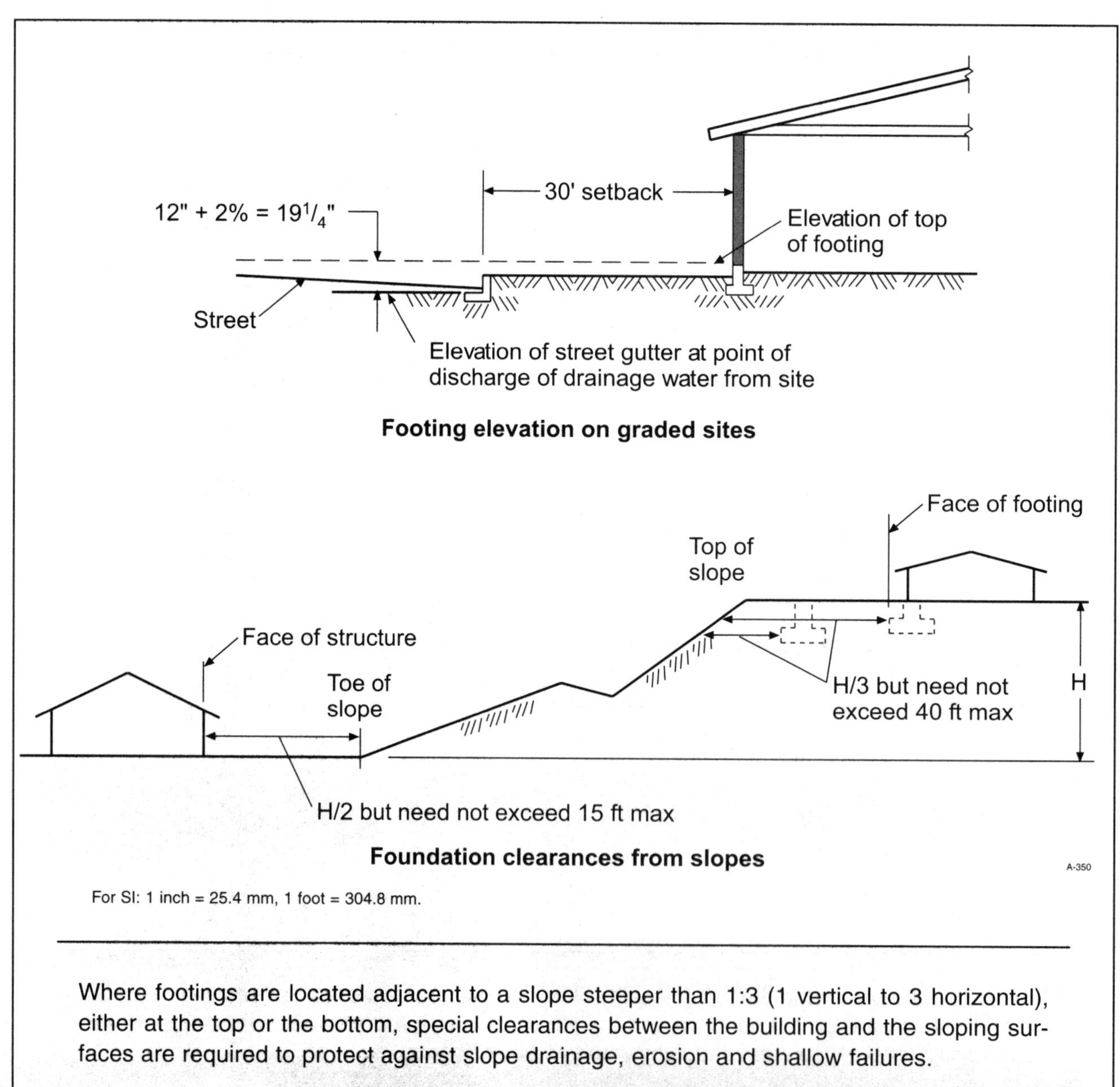

Where footings are located adjacent to a slope steeper than 1:3 (1 vertical to 3 horizontal), either at the top or the bottom, special clearances between the building and the sloping surfaces are required to protect against slope drainage, erosion and shallow failures.

Topic: Concrete Footings
Reference: IBC 1805.4.2

Category: Soils and Foundations
Subject: Footings

Code Text: *Where a specific design is not provided, concrete footings supporting walls of light- frame construction are permitted to be designed in accordance with Table 1805.4.2.*

Discussion and Commentary: In lieu of an engineered design, Table 1805.4.2 provides a prescriptive method for determining footing size criteria that can be used in conjunction with conventional light-framed construction. The minimum thickness of the foundation wall, as well as the minimum width and thickness of the footing, are specified based on the number of floors supported. The minimum depth below undisturbed ground surface is also addressed. Unless protected from frost or erected on solid rock, the footings must also extend below the frost line. The table is based on anticipated loads on the footings and foundations due to wall, floor and roof systems.

TABLE 1805.4.2
FOOTINGS SUPPORTING WALLS OF LIGHT-FRAME CONSTRUCTION[a, b, c, d, e]

NUMBER OF FLOORS SUPPORTED BY THE FOOTING[f]	WIDTH OF FOOTING (inches)	THICKNESS OF FOOTING (inches)
1	12	6
2	15	6
3	18	8[g]

For SI: 1 inch = 25.4 mm, 1 foot = 304.8 mm.

a. Depth of footings shall be in accordance with Section 1805.2.

b. The ground under the floor is permitted to be excavated to the elevation of the top of the footing.

c. Interior-stud-bearing walls are permitted to be supported by isolated footings. The footing width and length shall be twice the width shown in this table, and footings shall be spaced not more than 6 feet on center.

d. See Section 1910 for additional requirements for footings of structures assigned to Seismic Design Category C, D, E or F.

e. For thickness of foundation walls, see Section 1805.5.

f. Footings are permitted to support a roof in addition to the stipulated number of floors. Footings supporting roof only shall be as required for supporting one floor.

g. Plain concrete footings for Group R-3 occupancies are permitted to be 6 inches thick.

Although Table 1805.4.2 is normally used for continuous footings, it can also be used for isolated footings that support interior-stud bearing walls. The footings shall be spaced a maximum of 6 feet on center, with their widths and lengths being twice that shown in the table.

QUIZ

Study Session 15 — Chapters 14, 15 and 18

I. Multiple Choice

1. An exterior wall is defined as a building enclosing wall that has a minimum slope of __________ degrees with the horizontal plane.

   a. 45 b. 60
   c. 75 d. 90

   Reference_______________

2. Veneer secured and supported through the adhesion of an approved bonding material applied to an approved backing is considered __________ masonry veneer.

   a. adhered b. anchored
   c. attached d. spandrel

   Reference_______________

3. A minimum of __________ shall be attached to exterior sheathing in order to provide a continuous water-resistant barrier behind the exterior wall veneer.

   a. one layer of No. 15 asphalt felt
   b. one layer of No. 30 asphalt felt
   c. two layers of No. 15 asphalt felt applied shingle fashion
   d. two layers of No. 15 asphalt felt applied shingle fashion

   Reference_______________

4. Precast stone facing shall be a minimum of __________ inch in thickness in order to be acceptable as an approved weather covering.

   a. $^1/_2$ b. $^5/_8$
   c. $^3/_4$ d. 1

   Reference_______________

5. Interior masonry veneer shall have a maximum weight of _____ psf.

   a. 20 b. 25
   c. 30 d. 40

   Reference_______________

6. What is the minimum permitted thickness for metal veneer mounted on approved sheathing on wood construction?

a. 0.0149 inch
b. 0.0224 inch
c. 0.0478 inch
d. 0.0630 inch

Reference_______________

7. Combustible exterior wall coverings are permitted in Type II buildings having a maximum height of three stories or __________ feet above grade plane.

a. 25
b. 30
c. 35
d. 40

Reference_______________

8. Roofing interlayment shall have a minimum width of __________ inches.

a. 12
b. 18
c. 34
d. 36

Reference_______________

9. What is the minimum roof covering classification for a roof assembly on a building of Type IA construction?

a. Class A
b. Class B
c. Class C
d. nonclassified

Reference_______________

10. Roof assemblies consisting of metal sheets or shingles are considered __________ roof assemblies.

a. Class A
b. Class B
c. Class C
d. special purpose

Reference_______________

11. Double underlayment application is required beneath asphalt shingles on roofs having a maximum slope of __________.

a. 2:12
b. 3:12
c. 4:12
d. 5:12

Reference_______________

12. In areas subject to high winds, underlayment beneath asphalt shingles shall be fastened along the overlap at a maximum spacing of __________ inches.

a. 12
b. 18
c. 24
d. 36

Reference_______________

13. Fasteners for concrete or clay roof tiles shall penetrate the deck a minimum of __________ inch or through the thickness of the deck, whichever is less.

a. $^1/_2$
b. $^5/_8$
c. $^3/_4$
d. 1

Reference_______________

14. What is the minimum permitted roof slope for the installation of metal roof shingles?

a. 2:12
b. 3:12
c. 4:12
d. 5:12

Reference_______________

15. Wood shakes shall be applied to a roof with a minimum side lap of __________ inch(es) between joints in adjacent courses.

a. $^3/_8$
b. $^1/_2$
c. $^3/_4$
d. $1^1/_2$

Reference_______________

16. Where 18-inch-long No. 1 wood shingles are installed on a roof of 12:12 pitch, the maximum weather exposure shall be __________ inches.

a. $3^3/_4$
b. $4^1/_4$
c. $4^1/_2$
d. $5^1/_2$

Reference_______________

17. Sprayed polyurethane foam roofs shall have a minimum design slope of __________ for drainage purposes.

a. $^1/_8$:12
b. $^1/_4$:12
c. 1:12
d. 2:12

Reference_______________

18. In other than Type I construction, a penthouse shall extend a maximum of __________ feet above the roof when used for the protection of rooftop mechanical equipment.

a. 8
b. 12
c. 18
d. 28

Reference________________

19. The bottom surface of footings shall have a maximum slope of __________.

a. $^{1}/_{2}$:12
b. 1:12
c. 1:10
d. 1:20

Reference________________

20. The bottom of a footing shall be located a minimum of __________ inches below the undisturbed ground surface.

a. 6
b. 12
c. 15
d. 18

Reference________________

21. Unless data is submitted that substantiates the use of a higher value, the maximum allowable foundation pressure for silty gravel supporting soil shall be __________ pounds per square foot.

a. 12,000
b. 4,000
c. 3,000
d. 2,000

Reference________________

22. At 28 days, concrete in footings shall have a minimum specified compressive strength of __________ pounds per square inch.

a. 1,500
b. 2,000
c. 2,500
d. 3,000

Reference________________

23. Concrete footings shall be protected from freezing during depositing and for a minimum time period of __________ thereafter.

a. 12 hours
b. 24 hours
c. 3 days
d. 5 days

Reference________________

24. Unless a specific design is provided, concrete footings supporting two floors of light-frame construction shall be a minimum of __________ inches in width and __________ inches in thickness.

a. 12, 6
b. 15, 6
c. 15, 7
d. 18, 8

Reference_______________

25. At the girder supports at the top of hollow masonry foundation walls, a minimum of __________ inches of solid masonry shall be provided.

a. 3
b. 4
c. 6
d. 8

Reference_______________

26. For which of the following types of construction is vinyl siding permitted to be installed on the exterior walls of buildings?

a. Type IIA
b. Type IIB
c. Type IIIB
d. Type VA

Reference_______________

27. The construction of a special purpose wood shake roof mandates a minimum underlayment of _____ placed under the roof sheathing.

a. $^1/_2$-inch wood structural panel
b. $^1/_2$-inch gypsum wallboard
c. $^5/_8$-inch Type X gypsum sheathing
d. $^1/_2$-inch water-resistant gypsum backing board

Reference_______________

28. Slate shingles shall be installed only on roof decks having a minimum slope of _____.

a. 2:12
b. 2 $^1/_2$:12
c. 3:12
d. 4:12

Reference_______________

29. A cupola used as an architectural embellishment, where built of combustible construction, is limited to a maximum height of _____ feet above grade.

a. 45
b. 50
c. 60
d. 85

Reference_______________

30. Unless warranted by climatic or soil conditions, a minimum ground slope of _____ is required away from a building's foundation wall for a minimum distance of _____ feet.

a. 1:48, 10
b. 1:20, 10
c. 1:15, 5
d. 1:12, 5

Reference_______________

INTERNATIONAL BUILDING CODE
Study Session 16
Chapters 16, 17, 19, 21, 22 and 23 —
Special Inspections, Concrete, Masonry and Wood

OBJECTIVE: To identify the provisions relating to general structural forces and engineered design; applicable structural tests; special inspections and structural observation; and specific materials of construction, including concrete, masonry, steel and wood.

REFERENCE: Chapters 16, 17, 19, 21, 22 and 23, 2003 *International Building Code*

KEY POINTS:

- In structural design, what is considered a live load? A dead load?
- How is the minimum design live load for a floor system determined? Concentrated loads? Partition loads?
- How shall design roof loads be determined? When should snow loads be considered?
- What is special inspection? What are the duties and responsibilities of a special inspector?
- Which types of work shall be inspected by a special inspector?
- What is structural observation? When is structural observation required?
- How does Chapter 19 (Concrete) relate to the provisions of ACI 318?
- How shall concrete be evaluated and accepted?
- What are the general requirements for concrete mixing, conveying, depositing and curing?
- Which procedures must be followed when placing concrete during cold weather? During hot weather?
- What requirements address the placement and support of reinforcement in concrete construction? What thickness of concrete cover is required to protect the reinforcement?
- In masonry construction, how shall mortar and grout be regulated?
- How shall masonry be prepared, constructed and protected in cold weather? In hot weather?
- How can the lateral stability of masonry walls be accomplished?
- How must a masonry chimney be designed, anchored, supported and reinforced?
- What are the minimum required thicknesses of masonry fireplace walls and firebox walls?
- What is the minimum clearance required between combustible materials and fireplace or chimney walls? Between combustible materials and the fireplace opening?
- How must the hearth be constructed for a masonry fireplace?
- Hearth extensions must be of what minimum size?
- At what minimum height must a masonry chimney terminate?
- How can the minimum capacity of structural wood framing members be established?
- For decay and termite protection, what manner of under-floor clearance is required between exposed ground and wood girders, joists or structural floors?
- How must structural floor and roof sheathing be designed?
- What is considered "conventional light-frame construction"?
- How shall girders be supported?
- What are the limitations on the notching and boring of holes in floor joists, ceiling joists and roof rafters?
- What are braced wall panels? Where are such panels required?
- How shall rafters be framed at the ridge?
- What is a purlin? How shall a purlin system be constructed?

Topic: Uniform and Concentrated Loads
Reference: IBC 1607.3, 1607.4

Category: Structural Design
Subject: Live Loads

Code Text: *The live loads used in the design of buildings and other structures shall be the maximum loads expected by the intended use or occupancy but shall in no case be less than the minimum uniformly distributed unit loads required by Table 1607.1. Floors and other similar surfaces shall be designed to support the uniformly distributed live loads prescribed in Section 1607.3 or the concentrated load, in pounds, given in Table 1607.1, whichever produces the greater load effects.*

Discussion and Commentary: The anticipated live loads are based on the daily use of the building, as well as any temporary loading conditions such as remodeling activities, large group gatherings and short-term storage. They also reflect that, within the general use category, changes will likely occur in furniture layout, traffic patterns, etc. Concentrated loads take into account more specific types of loading consistent with the use of the building.

TABLE 1607.1
MINIMUM UNIFORMLY DISTRIBUTED LIVE LOADS AND MINIMUM CONCENTRATED LIVE LOADS[g]

OCCUPANCY OR USE	UNIFORM (psf)	CONCENTRATED (lbs.)
1. Apartments (see residential)	—	—
2. Access floor systems		
Office use	50	2,000
Computer use	100	2,000
3. Armories and drill rooms	150	—
4. Assembly areas and theaters		—
Fixed seats (fastened to floor)	60	
Lobbies	100	
Movable seats	100	
Stages and platforms	125	
Follow spot, projections and control rooms	50	
Catwalks	40	
5. Balconies (exterior)	100	—
On one- and two-family residences only, and not exceeding 100 ft.^{2}	60	
6. Decks	Same as occupancy served[h]	—
7. Bowling alleys	75	—
8. Cornices	60	—
9. Corridors, except as otherwise indicated	100	—
10. Dance halls and ballrooms	100	—
11. Dining rooms and restaurants	100	—
12. Dwellings (see residential)	—	—
13. Elevator machine room grating (on area of 4 in.^{2})	—	300
14. Finish light floor plate construction (on area of 1 in.^{2})	—	200
15. Fire escapes	100	—
On single-family dwellings only	40	

OCCUPANCY OR USE	UNIFORM (psf)	CONCENTRATED (lbs.)
25. Office buildings		
File and computer rooms shall be designed for heavier loads based on anticipated occupancy		
Lobbies and first-floor corridors	100	2,000
Offices	50	2,000
Corridors above first floor	80	2,000
26. Penal institutions		—
Cell blocks	40	
Corridors	100	
27. Residential		—
One- and two-family dwellings		
Uninhabitable attics without storage	10	
Uninhabitable attics with storage	20	
Habitable attics and sleeping areas	30	
All other areas except balconies and decks	40	
Hotels and multifamily dwellings		
Private rooms and corridors serving them	40	
Public rooms and corridors serving them	100	
28. Reviewing stands, grandstands and bleachers	Note c	—
29. Roofs	See Section 1607.11	
30. Schools		
Classrooms	40	1,000
Corridors above first floor	80	1,000
First-floor corridors	100	1,000
31. Scuttles, skylight ribs and accessible ceilings	—	200
32. Sidewalks, vehicular driveways and yards, subject to trucking	250[d]	8,000[e]
33. Skating rinks	100	—

The code does not require the concurrent application of uniform live load and concentrated live load. The load to be utilized in the structural design of the building would be of the type that produces the greater stress in the structural elements.

Topic: Definitions
Reference: IBC 1702

Category: Structural Tests and Special Inspections
Subject: Inspections and Observations

Code Text: *Special inspection is inspection as herein required of the materials, installation, fabrication, erection or placement of components and connections requiring special expertise to ensure compliance with approved construction documents and referenced standards. Structural observation is the visual observation of the structural system by a registered design professional for general conformance to the approved construction documents at significant construction stages and at completion of the structural system. Structural observation does not waive the responsibility for the inspection required by Section 109, Section 1704 or other sections of the IBC.*

Discussion and Commentary: In addition to the general inspections called for in Section 109 (footings, frame, final, etc.), it is often necessary to call for a more exacting review of the construction process. Through special inspections and structural observation, the work can be evaluated more closely for compliance with the approved construction documents.

Steel Construction	Section 1704.3
Concrete Construction	Section 1704.4
Masonry Construction	Section 1704.5
Wood Construction	Section 1704.6
Soils	Section 1704.7
Pile Foundations	Section 1704.8
Pier Foundations	Section 1704.9
Wall Panels and Veneers	Section 1704.10
Sprayed Fire-resistant Materials	Section 1704.11
Exterior Insulation and Finish Systems	Section 1704.12
Special Cases	Section 1704.13
Smoke Control	Section 1704.14

Under specific conditions, a quality assurance plan may be required for seismic resistance or wind requirements. The code also sets forth unique provisions for special inspections and structural testing for seismic resistance considerations.

Topic: General Requirements
Reference: IBC 1704.1

Category: Structural Tests and Special Inspections
Subject: Special Inspections

Code Text: *Where application is made for construction as described in Section 1704, the owner or the registered design professional in responsible charge acting as the owner's agent shall employ one or more special inspectors to provide inspections during construction on the types of work listed under Section 1704.* See exceptions for work, components or occupancies where special inspection is not required.

Discussion and Commentary: Most building departments do not have the staff of inspectors to provide detailed inspections on large and complex projects. There are also projects where the nature of construction is such that extra care in quality control must be exercised to assure compliance. For these reasons, the code mandates continuous or periodic inspection by special inspectors for certain types of work.

TABLE 1704.4
REQUIRED VERIFICATION AND INSPECTION OF CONCRETE CONSTRUCTION

VERIFICATION AND INSPECTION	CONTINUOUS	PERIODIC	REFERENCED STANDARD[a]	IBC REFERENCE
1. Inspection of reinforcing steel, including prestressing tendons, and placement.	—	X	ACI 318: 3.5, 7.1-7.7	1903.5, 1907.1, 1907.7, 1914.4
2. Inspection of reinforcing steel welding in accordance with Table 1704.3, Item 5B.	—	—	AWS D1.4 ACI 318: 3.5.2	1903.5.2
3. Inspect bolts to be installed in concrete prior to and during placement of concrete where allowable loads have been increased.	X	—	—	1912.5
4. Verifying use of required design mix.	—	X	ACI 318: Ch. 4, 5.2-5.4	1904, 1905.2-1905.4, 1914.2, 1914.3
5. At the time fresh concrete is sampled to fabricate specimens for strength tests, perform slump and air content tests, and determine the temperature of the concrete.	X	—	ASTM C 172 ASTM C 31 ACI 318: 5.6, 5.8	1905.6, 1914.10
6. Inspection of concrete and shotcrete placement for proper application techniques.	X	—	ACI 318: 5.9, 5.10	1905.9, 1905.10, 1914.6, 1914.7, 1914.8
7. Inspection for maintenance of specified curing temperature and techniques.	—	X	ACI 318: 5.11-5.13	1905.11, 1905.13, 1914.9
8. Inspection of prestressed concrete: a. Application of prestressing forces. b. Grouting of bonded prestressing tendons in the seismic-force-resisting system.	X X	—	ACI 318: 18.20 ACI 318: 18.18.4	—
9. Erection of precast concrete members.	—	X	ACI 318: Ch. 16	—
10. Verification of in-situ concrete strength, prior to stressing of tendons in posttensioned concrete and prior to removal of shores and forms from beams and structural slabs.	—	X	ACI 318: 6.2	1906.2

For SI: 1 inch = 25.4 mm.
a. Where applicable, see also Section 1707.1, Special inspection for seismic resistance.

A statement containing the work requiring special inspection, the specific inspections to be performed, and the individuals or firms to be retained for conducting special inspections must be submitted by the permit applicant prior to issuance of the building permit.

Topic: Inspector Qualifications
Reference: IBC 1704.1

Category: Structural Tests and Special Inspections
Subject: Special Inspections

Code Text: *The special inspector shall be a qualified person who shall demonstrate competence, to the satisfaction of the building official, for inspection of the particular type of construction or operation requiring special inspection. Special inspectors shall keep records of inspections. The special inspector shall furnish inspection reports to the building official, and to the registered design professional in responsible charge.*

Discussion and Commentary: It is the duty of the special inspector not only to observe the work, but also to furnish inspection reports indicating that the work inspected was done in accordance with the approved construction documents. If discrepancies are found in the work, the inspector should bring them to the immediate attention of the contractor for correction. If the discrepancies are not corrected, the building official and registered design professional in responsible charge should be notified.

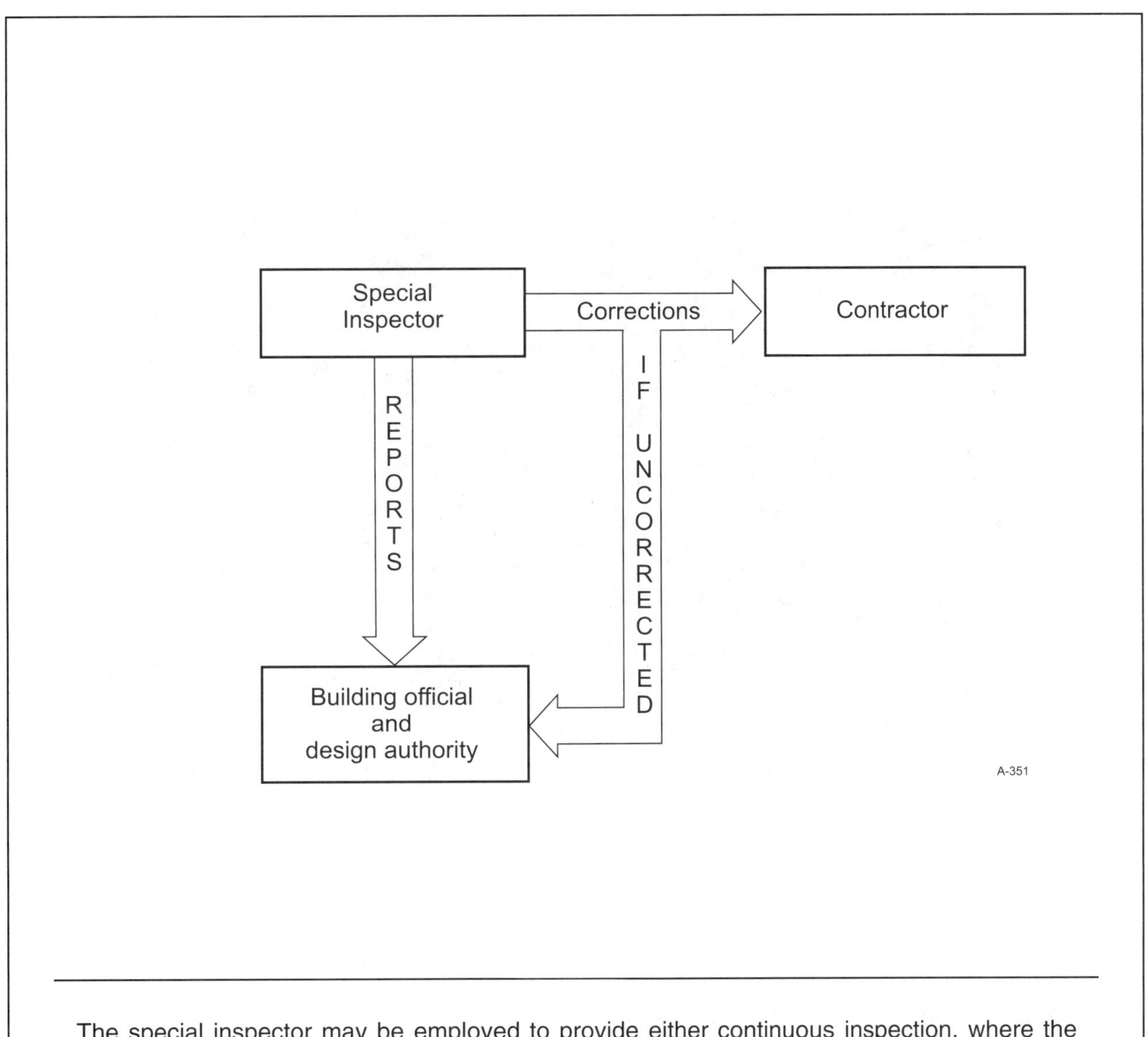

The special inspector may be employed to provide either continuous inspection, where the inspector is present for full-time observation of the work, or periodic inspection, where he or she only intermittently observes the work.

Topic: General Requirements
Reference: IBC 1709.1

Category: Structural Tests and Special Inspections
Subject: Structural Observations

Code Text: *Structural observations shall be provided for those structures included in Seismic Design Category D, E or F, as determined in Section 1616, where one or more of the following conditions exist: (1) the structure is included in Seismic Use Group II or III, (2) the height of the structure is greater than 75 feet above the base, (3) the structure is in Seismic Design Category E and Seismic Use Group I and greater than two stories in height, (4) when so designated by the registered design professional in responsible charge of the design, and (5) when such observation is specifically required by the building official.*

Discussion and Commentary: Structural observations not only are required for the higher Seismic Design Categories but also are required in high-wind areas (basic wind speed > 110 mph) where the structure has a height greater than 75 feet or has an importance factor in category III or IV. The building official or registered design professional in responsible charge can also mandate such observation.

Structural observation is not to be confused with the mandated inspections specified in Section 109, nor with the special inspections listed in Section 1704. This activity is intended to provide an additional level of expertise in the review of structures posing a very high level of complexity.

Topic: Scope
Reference: IBC 1901

Category: Concrete
Subject: Plain and Reinforced Concrete

Code Text: *The provisions of Chapter 19 shall govern the materials, quality control, design and construction of concrete use in structures. Structural concrete shall be designed and constructed in accordance with the requirements of Chapter 19 and ACI 318 as amended in Section 1908 of the IBC. The contents of Sections 1902 through 1907 are patterned after, and in general conformity with, the provisions for structural concrete in ACI 318.*

Discussion and Commentary: Requirements for the design, testing, mixing, placing and protection of concrete construction are essentially reproduced from publications published and copyrighted by the American Concrete Institute. Section 1908 contains the primary modifications to the provisions of ACI 318.

Construction Requirements for Concrete Work

Specifications for Tests and Materials (Chapter 3)	Section 1903
Durability Requirements (Chapter 4)	Section 1904
Concrete Quality, Mixing and Placing (Chapter 5)	Section 1905
Formwork, Embedded Pipes and Construction (Chapter 6)	Section 1906
Details of Reinforcement (Chapter 7)	Section 1907

To make reference to the ACI commentary easier for users of the IBC, the section designations of IBC Chapter 19 have been made similar to those found in ACI 318. Italics are used to indicate that the *International Building Code* differs substantially from the ACI standard.

Topic: Depositing **Category:** Concrete
Reference: IBC 1905.10 **Subject:** Quality, Mixing and Placing

Code Text: *Concrete shall be deposited as nearly as practicable to its final position to avoid segregation due to rehandling or flowing. Concrete that has partially hardened or been contaminated by foreign materials shall not be deposited in the structure. Retempered concrete or concrete that has been remixed after initial set shall not be used unless approved by the registered design professional. Concrete shall be thoroughly consolidated by suitable means during placement and shall be thoroughly worked around reinforcement and embedded fixtures and into corners of the forms.*

Discussion and Commentary: Preparation prior to placing concrete is as critical to quality construction as is the actual concrete placement. Equipment for mixing and transporting concrete must be clean. Debris and ice shall be removed from any areas to be occupied by concrete. All laitance and other unsound material must be removed prior to the placement of additional concrete against hardened concrete.

Possible Effects of Cold Weather

- Permanent damage to early freezing
- Slower setting and slower strength gain
- Freezing of fresh concrete prior to hardening
- Reduced durability . . . same as strength reduction
- Freezing of green concrete at edges and corners
- Dehydrated surface areas due to use of space heaters
- Cracking due to sudden temperature change if strength gain insufficient

Possible Effects of Hot Weather

- Increased water demand
- Difficult to control entrained air
- Rapid evaporation of mixing water if dry and windy
- Rapid slump loss
- Faster set
- Greater dimensional changes on cooling
- Increased tendency to crack or craze
- Reduced long term strength
- Possible "cold joints"
- Increased permeability

In hot weather, proper attention shall be given to any aspect that might impair the required strength or serviceability of the concrete. Adequate equipment must be provided for heating concrete materials and protecting concrete during freezing or near-freezing weather.

Topic: Surface Conditions
Reference: IBC 1907.4
Category: Concrete
Subject: Reinforcement

Code Text: *At the time concrete is placed, reinforcement shall be free from mud, oil or other nonmetallic coatings that decrease bond. Epoxy coatings of steel reinforcement in accordance with ACI 318 are permitted. Except for prestressing steel, steel reinforcement with rust, mill scale or a combination of both, shall be considered satisfactory, provided the minimum dimensions comply with applicable ASTM specifications.*

Discussion and Commentary: Once the surface conditions of the reinforcement are determined to be satisfactory, the placement of the reinforcement must be evaluated for support and securement. To assure adequate free area around reinforcing members for concrete and aggregate consolidation, minimum clearances between bars are mandated. Specific tolerances for the placement of reinforcement are allowed, including those for minimum concrete cover.

TABLE 1907.7.1
MINIMUM CONCRETE COVER

CONCRETE EXPOSURE	MINIMUM COVER (inches)
1. Concrete cast against and permanently exposed to earth	3
2. Concrete exposed to earth or weather	
No. 6 through No. 18 bar	2
No. 5 bar, W31 or D31 wire, and smaller	1 $^1/_2$
3. Concrete not exposed to weather or in contact with ground	
Slabs, walls, joists:	
No. 14 and No. 18 bars	1 $^1/_2$
No. 11 bar and smaller	$^3/_4$
Beams, columns:	
Primary reinforcement, ties, stirrups, spirals	1 $^1/_2$
Shells, folded plate members:	
No. 6 bar and larger	$^3/_4$
No. 5 bar, W31 or D31 wire, and smaller	$^1/_2$

For SI: 1 inch = 25.4 mm.

The minimum level of concrete cover for reinforcement in nonprestressed, cast-in-place concrete is specified in Table 1907.7.1. The minimum thickness of cover is based on bar size, method of concrete placement, exposure to weather and type of concrete structural element.

Topic: Bed and Head Joints
Reference: IBC 2104.1.2

Category: Masonry
Subject: Construction Requirements

Code Text: *Unless otherwise required or indicated on the construction documents, head and bed joints shall be $^3/_8$ inch thick, except that the thickness of the bed joint of the starting course placed over foundations shall not be less than $^1/_4$ inch and not more than $^3/_4$ inch. Units shall be placed while the mortar is soft and plastic. Any unit disturbed to the extent that the initial bond is broken after initial positioning shall be removed and relaid in fresh mortar.*

Discussion and Commentary: During masonry construction, it is important that the units be placed in a manner so as to form a solid bond. Hollow-masonry units must have all face shells of bed joints fully mortared. Solid masonry units must be placed in fully mortared bed and head joints, with the ends of the units completely buttered.

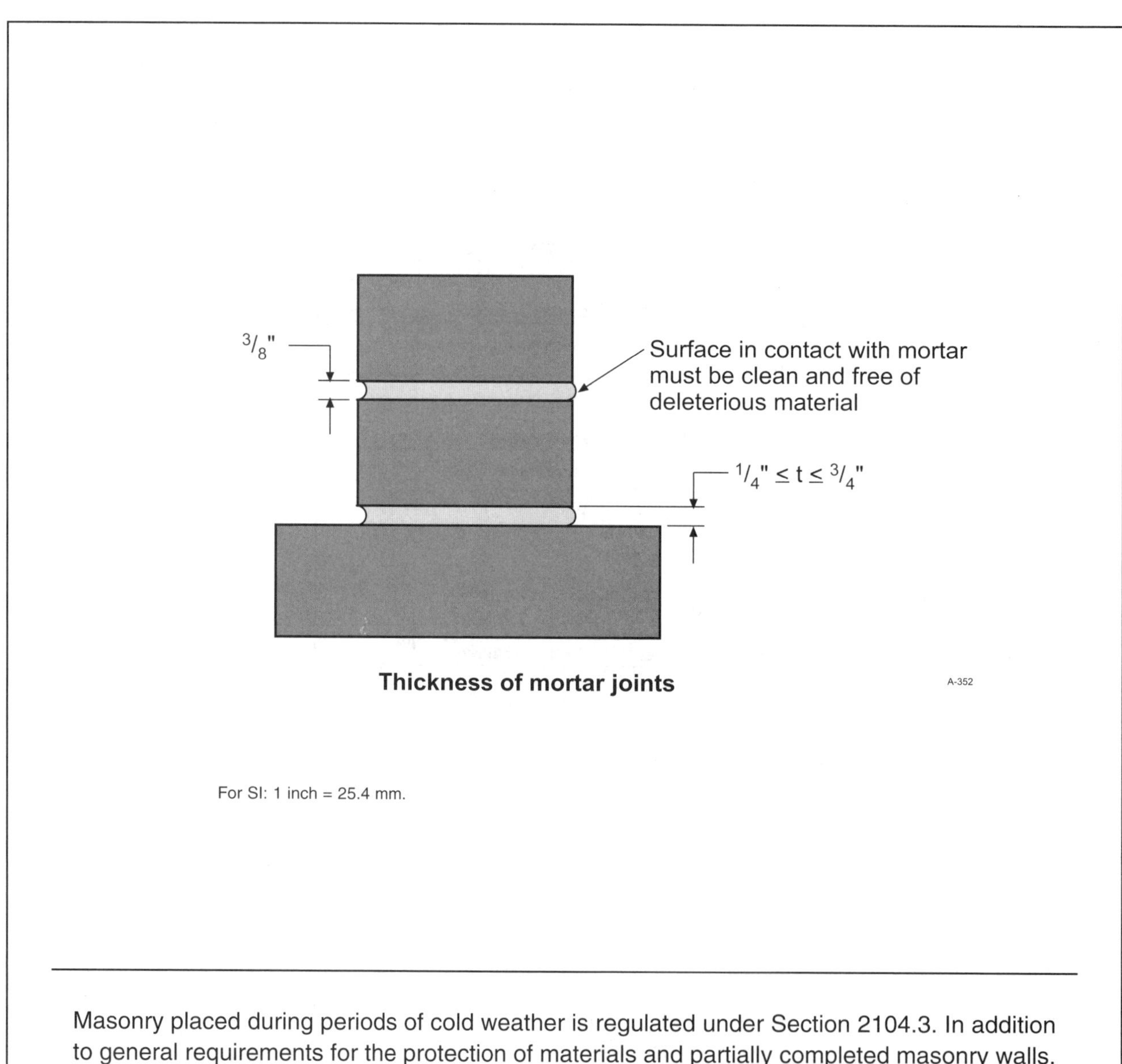

Thickness of mortar joints

Masonry placed during periods of cold weather is regulated under Section 2104.3. In addition to general requirements for the protection of materials and partially completed masonry walls, provisions address procedures for construction spanning various temperature ranges.

Topic: Fireplace Walls
Reference: IBC 2111.5

Category: Masonry
Subject: Fireplaces

Code Text: *Masonry fireplaces shall be constructed of solid masonry units, hollow masonry units grouted solid, stone, or concrete. When a lining of firebrick at least 2 inches in thickness or other approved lining is provided, the minimum thickness of back and sidewalls shall each be 8 inches of solid masonry, including the lining. The width of joints between firebricks shall not be greater than* $^1/_4$ *inch. When no lining is provided, the total minimum thickness of back and sidewalls shall be 10 inches of solid masonry.*

Discussion and Commentary: Fireplace and firebox thickness is regulated in order to insulate surrounding construction, both exposed and concealed, from excessive temperature levels. It is important that the walls be constructed in such a fashion that they are solid throughout.

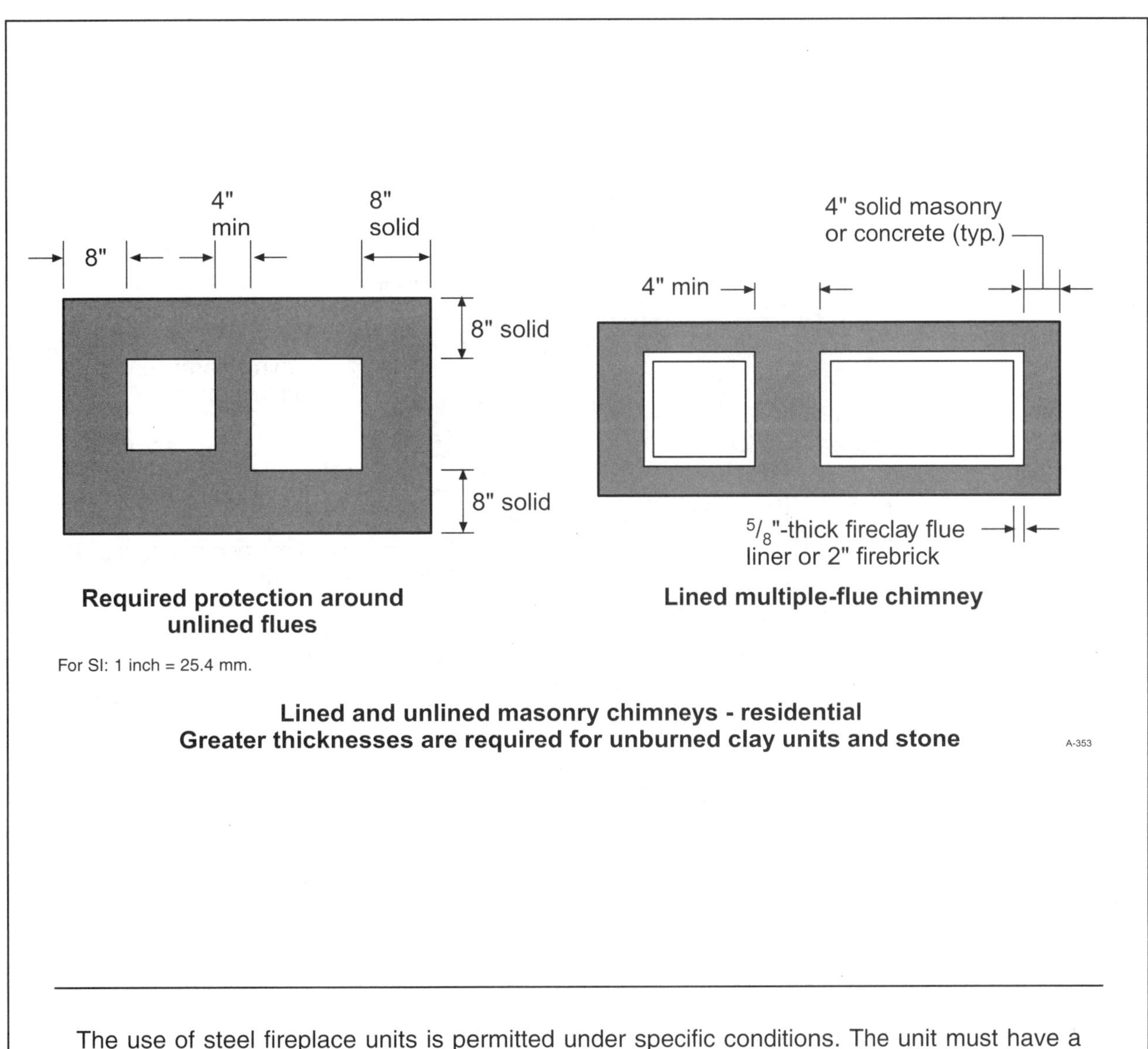

The use of steel fireplace units is permitted under specific conditions. The unit must have a minimum $^1/_2$-inch steel firebox liner and an air chamber. The total thickness at the back and sides must be at least 8 inches, with no less than 4 inches of solid masonry.

Topic: Hearth Extensions
Reference: IBC 2111.9

Category: Masonry
Subject: Fireplaces

Code Text: *Hearth extensions shall extend at least 16 inches in front of, and at least 8 inches beyond, each side of the fireplace opening. Where the fireplace opening is 6 square feet or larger, the hearth extension shall extend at least 20 inches in front of, and at least 12 inches beyond, each side of the fireplace opening. The minimum thickness of hearth extensions shall be 2 inches.* See exception for raised firebox openings.

Discussion and Commentary: Hearth extensions are necessary to keep sparks and embers that fly from the firebox from igniting combustible material, such as carpet, on the floor. Radiated heat from the fireplace can also ignite combustible flooring materials located adjacent to the fireplace opening and adjacent fireplace walls.

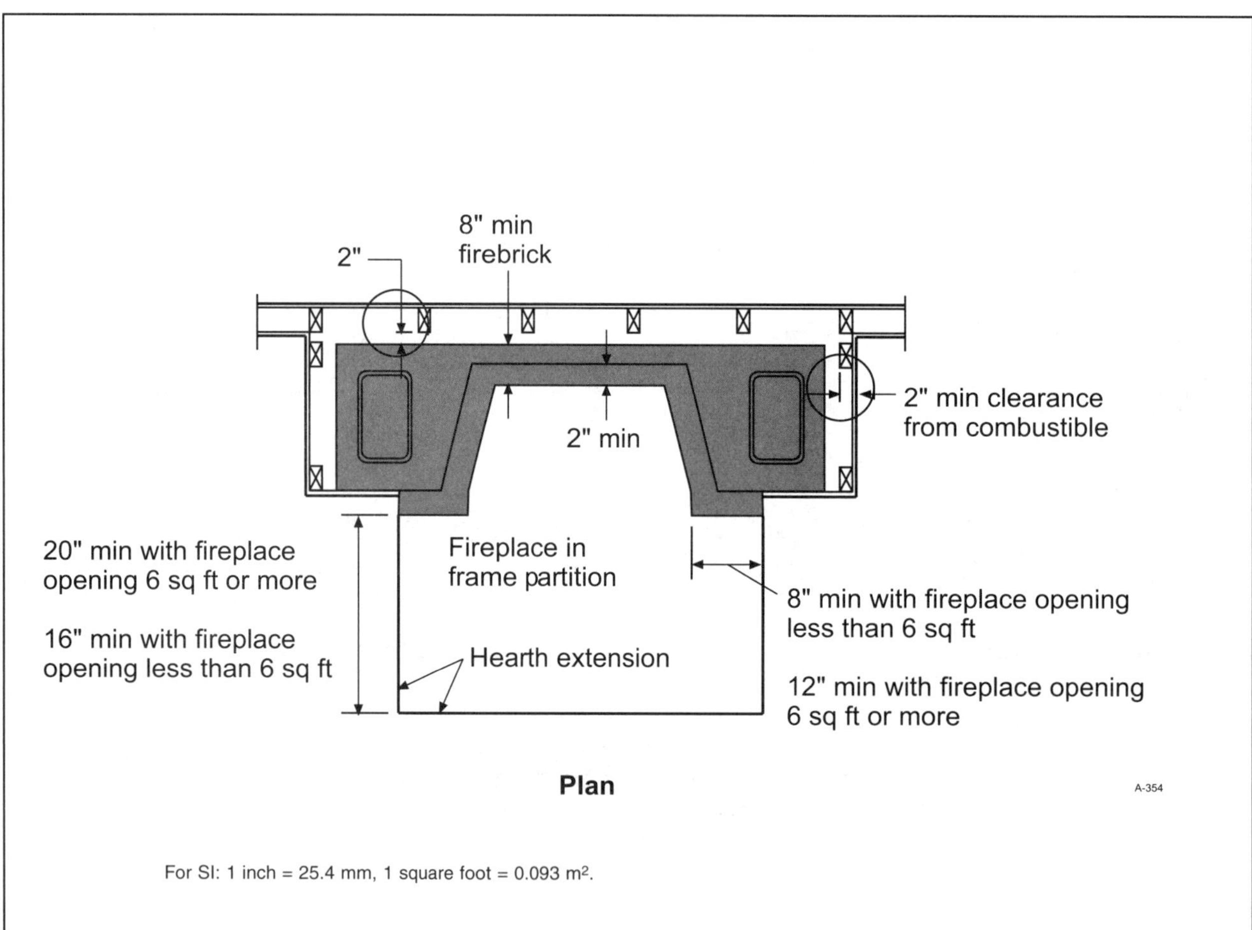

For SI: 1 inch = 25.4 mm, 1 square foot = 0.093 m².

For obvious reasons, the hearth and the hearth extension must be constructed of, and supported by, noncombustible materials. Hearths must be specifically constructed of either concrete or masonry. The minimum thickness of fireplace hearths is 4 inches.

Topic: Clearance to Combustible Material **Category:** Masonry
Reference: IBC 2111.11, 2111.12 **Subject:** Fireplaces

Code Text: *Any portion of a masonry fireplace located in the interior of a building or within the exterior wall of a building shall have a clearance to combustibles of not less than 2 inches from the front faces and sides of masonry fireplaces and not less than 4 inches from the back faces of masonry fireplaces. The air-space shall not be filled, except to provide fireblocking in accordance with* Section 2111.13. See four exceptions for alternate methods to the required clearances.

Discussion and Commentary: The radiant heat transfer through the materials used to construct a masonry fireplace and/or chimney necessitates a minimum separation between the masonry and combustible materials, such as wood floor, wall or ceiling framing. The depth of the noncombustible fireblocking, placed on metal strips or lath, is to be 1 inch.

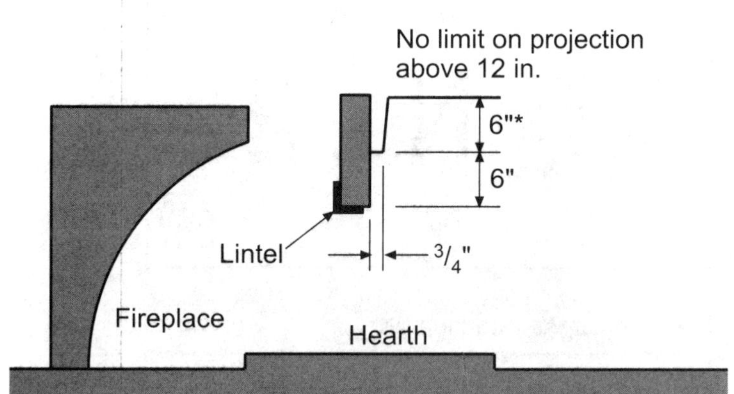

* Combustible materials may project $^1/_8$ in. for each 1 in. clearance.
No combustible materials permitted within 6 in. of opening.

For SI: 1 inch = 25.4 mm.

Combustible materials projection from fireplace

A-355

No combustible materials, such as trim and ornamentation, are permitted within 6 inches of the opening at the face of the fireplace. Combustibles placed less than 12 inches from the opening, while permitted, are very limited in their projection from the fireplace opening.

Topic: Identification
Reference: IBC 2303.1

Category: Wood
Subject: Minimum Standards and Quality

Code Text: *Lumber used for load-supporting purposes, including end-jointed or edge-glued lumber, machine stress rated or machine evaluated lumber, shall be identified by the grade mark of a lumber grading or inspection agency that has been approved by an accreditation body that complies with DOC PS 20 or equivalent. Wood structural panels, when used structurally (including those used for siding, roof and wall sheathing, subflooring, diaphragms and built-up members), shall conform to the requirements for its type in DOC PS 1 or PS 2.*

Discussion and Commentary: Obviously, the proper use of a wood structural member cannot be determined unless it has been identified. Grade marks, identification marks, certificates of inspection and quality marks are various methods of indicating the type and quality of wood members.

Visually Graded Lumber

Machine Stress-rated lumber

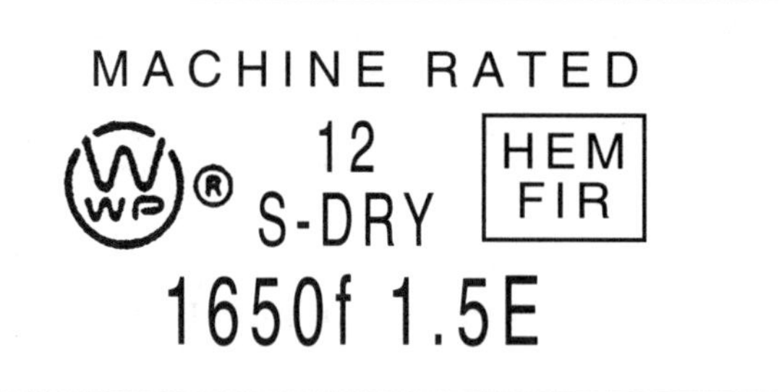

A-356

Lumber and, particularly, wood structural panels are highly variable in strengths and other mechanical properties; hence, such materials must conform to the applicable standards or grading rules specified in the code.

Topic: Protection Against Decay
Reference: IBC 2304.11.2

Category: Wood
Subject: General Construction Requirements

Code Text: *Wood installed above ground in the locations specified in Sections 2304.11.2.1 through 2304.11.2.6 shall be naturally durable wood or preservative-treated wood that uses water-borne preservatives, and shall be treated in accordance with AWPA C2 or C9 or applicable AWPA standards for above-ground use.*

Discussion and Commentary: To protect against decay and termite infestation, the code addresses those members for which care must be taken, including: joists, girders and subfloor adjacent to exposed ground in crawl spaces; framing members and wall sheathing that rest on exterior foundation walls; sleepers and sills on a concrete slab in direct contact with earth; girder ends in masonry or concrete walls; wood siding adjacent to the ground; and posts and columns supported by a concrete slab.

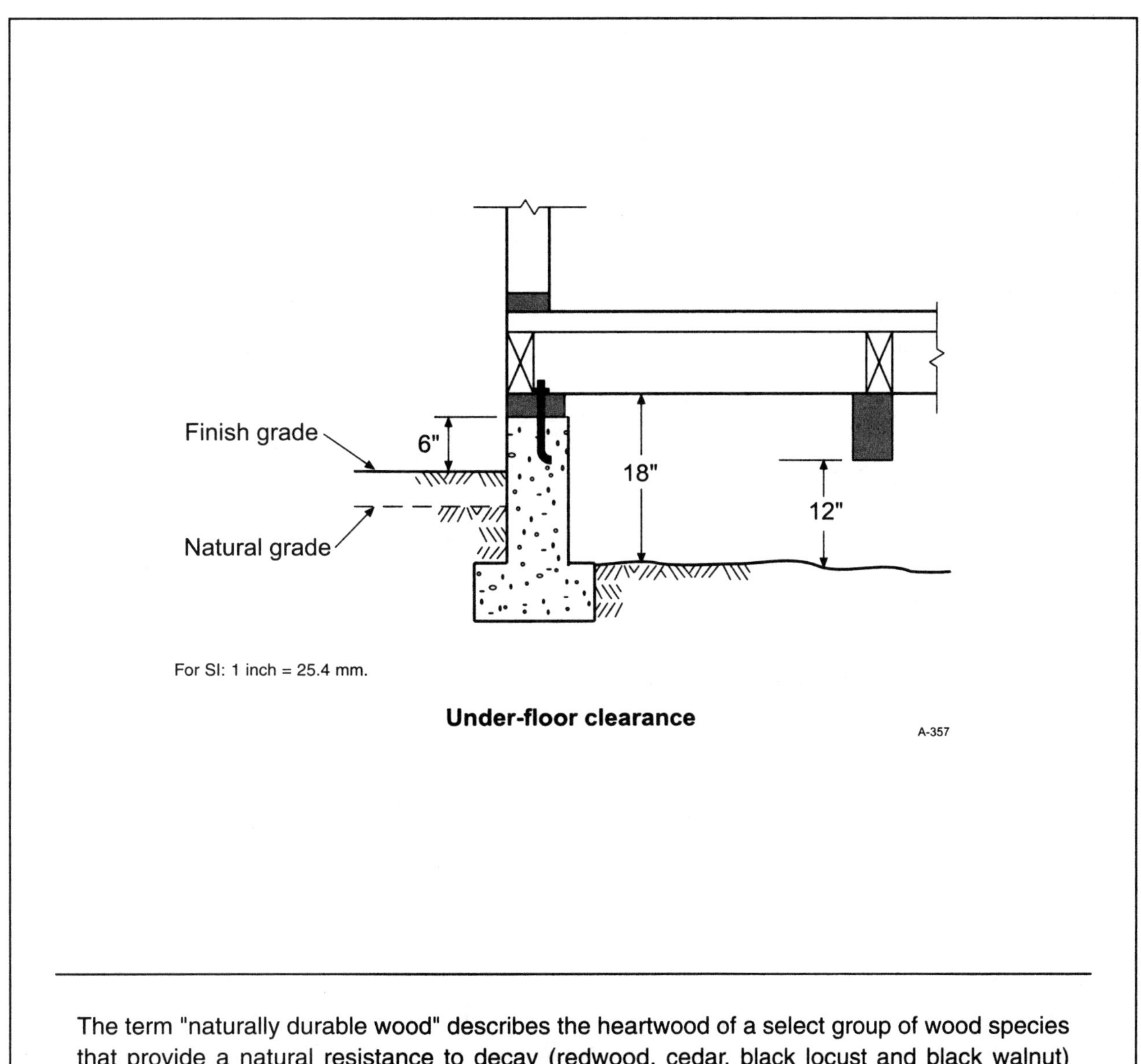

Under-floor clearance

The term "naturally durable wood" describes the heartwood of a select group of wood species that provide a natural resistance to decay (redwood, cedar, black locust and black walnut) and/or termites (redwood and Eastern red cedar).

Topic: Scope
Reference: IBC 2308.1

Category: Wood
Subject: Conventional Light-frame Construction

Code Text: *The requirements in Section 2308 are intended for conventional light-frame construction. Other methods are permitted to be used provided a satisfactory design is submitted showing compliance with other provisions of the IBC. Interior nonload-bearing partitions, ceilings and curtain walls of conventional light-frame construction are not subject to the limitations of Section 2308.*

Discussion and Commentary: Conventional light-frame wood construction is considered *a type of construction whose primary structural elements are formed by a system of repetitive wood-framing members.* The provisions of Section 2308 are based on experience gained over the last several decades. This experience has resulted in the prescriptive requirements contained in this section. Compliance with AF&PA's *Wood Frame Construction Manual* is considered equivalent to Section 2308.

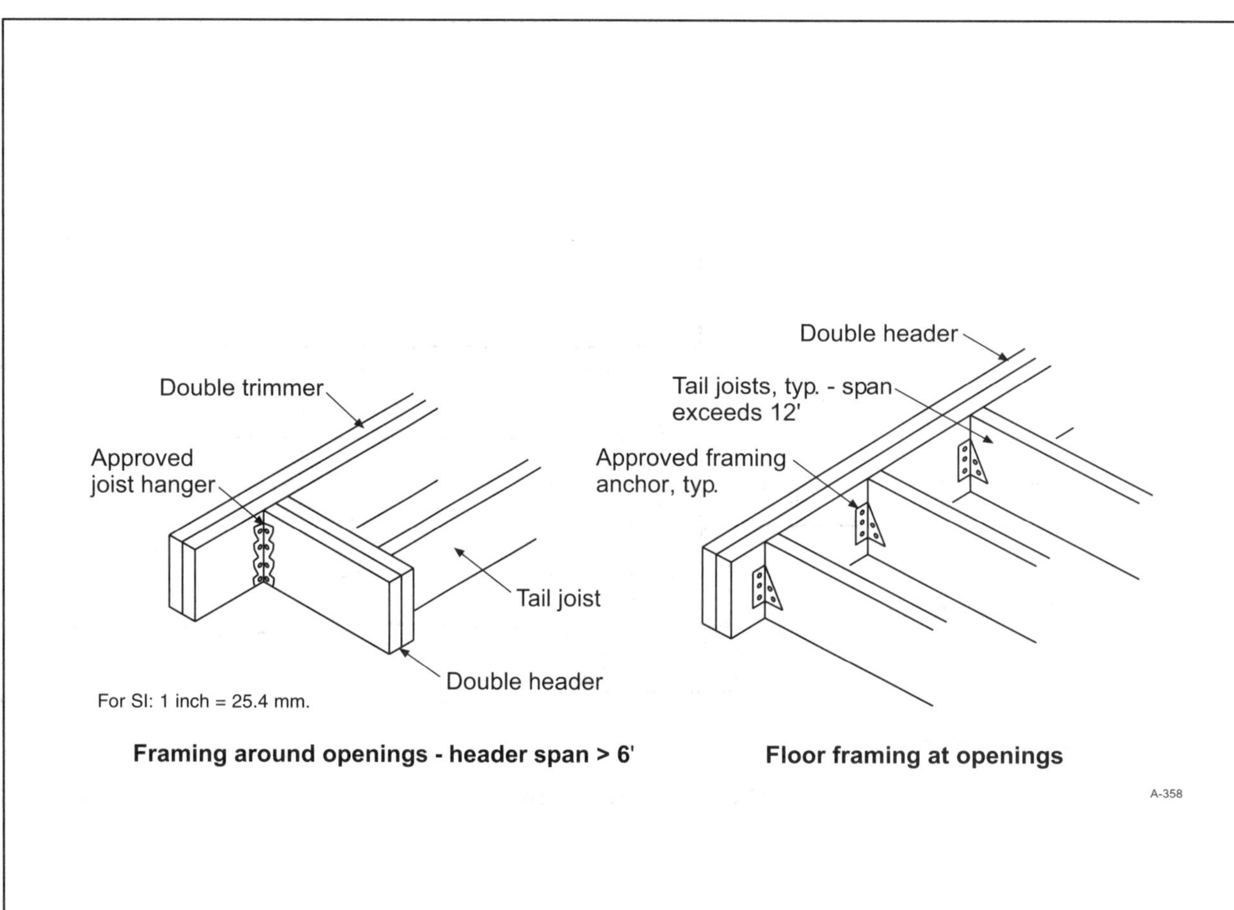

Framing around openings - header span > 6'

Floor framing at openings

The limitations placed on buildings of conventional light-frame construction are based on limits to: number of stories; floor-to-floor height of bearing walls; live, dead and snow loads; wind speeds; rafter span; and Seismic Design Categories.

Topic: Foundation Plates or Sills
Reference: IBC 2308.6

Category: Wood
Subject: Conventional Light-frame Construction

Code Text: *Foundation plates or sills shall be bolted or anchored to the foundation with not less than ½-inch diameter steel bolts or approved anchors. Bolts shall be embedded at least 7 inches into concrete or masonry, and spaced not more than 6 feet apart. There shall be a minimum of two bolts or anchor straps per piece with one bolt or anchor strap located not more than 12 inches or less than 4 inches from each end of each piece. A properly sized nut and washer shall be tightened on each bolt to the plate.*

Discussion and Commentary: The prescriptive requirements for the installation of anchor bolts are applicable to all buildings of conventional light-frame wood construction. The provisions set forth the necessary criteria to adequately tie the framing system to the foundation.

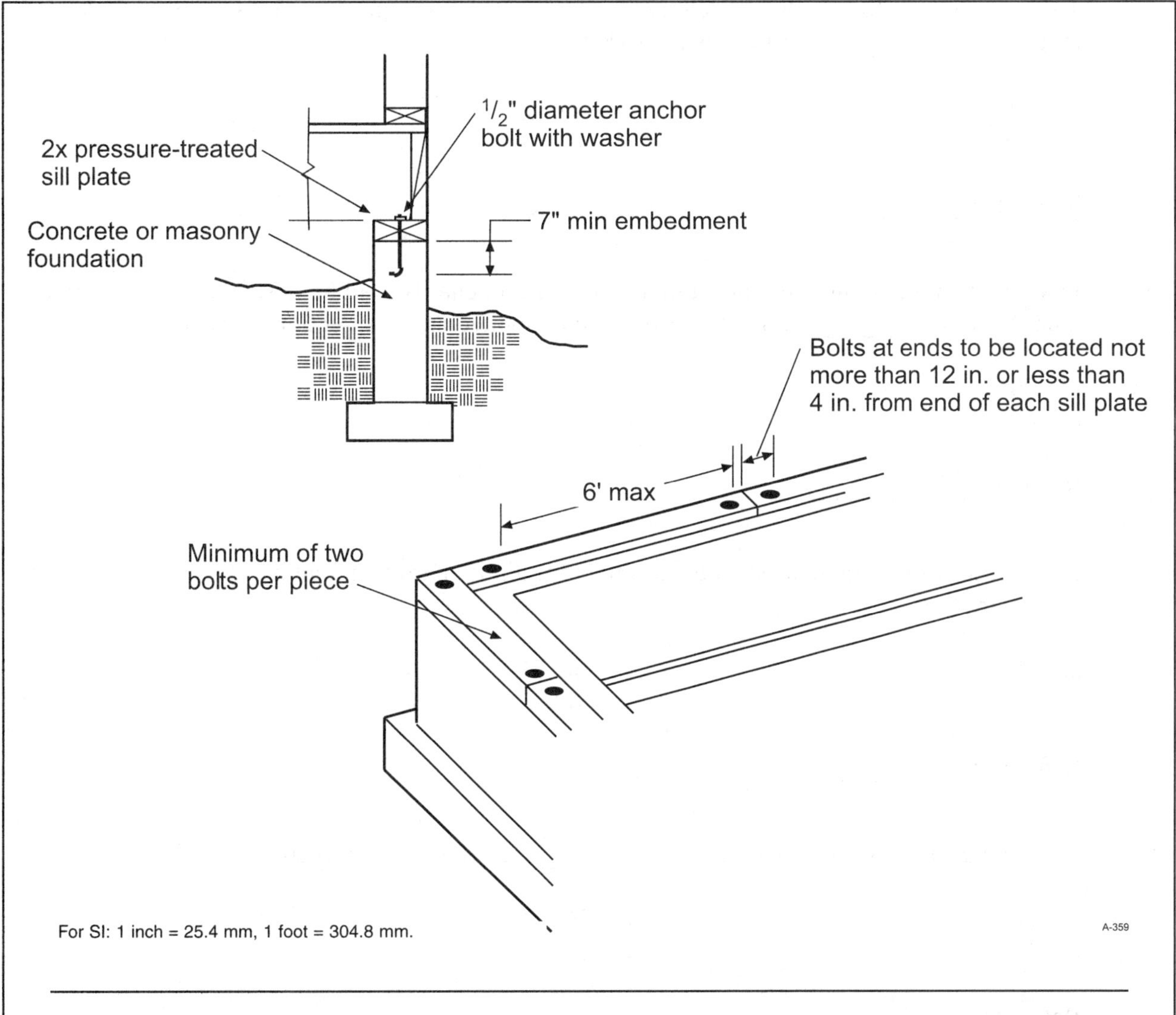

In Seismic Design Categories D and E, it has been shown that additional anchorage methods are necessary to resist the lateral forces being applied at the foundation connection. Thus, minimum $^3/_{16}$-inch by 2-inch by 2-inch steel plate washers are mandated between the sill plate and the nut.

QUIZ

Study Session 16 — Chapters 16, 17, 19, 21, 22 and 23

I. Multiple Choice

1. Live loads exceeding a minimum of __________ pounds per square foot shall be posted in applicable portions of commercial or industrial buildings.

   a. 50 b. 75
   c. 100 d. 125

   Reference________________

2. The minimum uniformly distributed live load used in the design of a fixed-seat arena is determined to be __________ pounds per square foot.

   a. 50 b. 60
   c. 100 d. 125

   Reference________________

3. In a Group B office building, handrail assemblies and guards shall be designed to resist a minimum load of __________ pounds per lineal foot applied at any direction at the top.

   a. 20 b. 30
   c. 40 d. 50

   Reference________________

4. Roofs used for roof gardens shall be designed for a minimum live load of __________ pounds per square foot.

   a. 40 b. 60
   c. 75 d. 100

   Reference________________

5. For wind design purposes, Exposure __________ describes flat open country and grasslands.

   a. A b. B
   c. C d. D

   Reference________________

6. Special inspection for fill placement is not required during placement of fill a maximum of __________ inches in depth.

a. 4
b. 6
c. 12
d. 24

Reference________________

7. Special inspection thickness testing for sprayed fire-resistant material applied to structural framing members shall be performed on a minimum of __________ percent of the structural members on each floor.

a. 10
b. 25
c. 50
d. 100

Reference________________

8. Structural observation shall be provided for structures in Seismic Design Category E and Seismic Use Group I and a minimum of __________ stories in height.

a. 2
b. 3
c. 4
d. 5

Reference________________

9. For curing purposes, high-early-strength concrete shall be maintained above 50°F and in a moist condition for a minimum of the first __________ after placement.

a. 7 days
b. 5 days
c. 3 days
d. 24 hours

Reference________________

10. What is the minimum required concrete cover for #8 bar reinforcement in nonprestressed, cast-in-place concrete exposed to weather?

a. 3 inches
b. 2 inches
c. $1^1/_2$ inches
d. $^3/_4$ inch

Reference________________

11. What is the minimum required thickness of structural plain concrete basement walls?

a. 6 inches
b. $7^1/_2$ inches
c. 8 inches
d. $9^1/_2$ inches

Reference________________

12. The minimum thickness of a concrete floor slab supported directly on the ground shall be __________ inches.

a. $3^1/_2$ b. 4
c. 5 d. 6

Reference_______________

13. What is the term used to describe masonry in which the tensile resistance of the masonry is taken into consideration and the effects of stresses in reinforcement are neglected?

a. ashlar masonry b. plain masonry
c. reinforced masonry d. solid masonry

Reference_______________

14. Wire wall ties for masonry construction shall be embedded a minimum of __________ inch(es) into the mortar bed of solid-grouted hollow units.

a. $^3/_4$ b. 1
c. $1^1/_4$ d. $1^1/_2$

Reference_______________

15. Weep holes provided in the outside wythe of masonry walls shall be located at a maximum spacing of __________ inches on center.

a. 33 b. 48
c. 64 d. 96

Reference_______________

16. A hearth extension for a masonry fireplace with a 24-inch by 42-inch opening shall extend a minimum of __________ inches in front of, and a minimum of __________ inches beyond, each side of the fireplace opening.

a. 16, 8 b. 16, 10
c. 20, 12 d. 24, 12

Reference_______________

17. Combustible materials located 10 inches from the opening of a masonry fireplace shall have a maximum projection of __________ inch(es).

a. 0, no projection is permitted b. $^3/_4$
c. 1 d. $1^1/_4$

Reference_______________

18. Masonry chimneys shall extend at least 2 feet higher than any portion of the building within 10 feet, with a minimum height of __________ feet above the point where the chimney passes through the roof.

a. 2
b. $2^1/_2$
c. 3
d. 4

Reference_______________

19. Unless naturally durable or preservative-treated wood is used, what is the minimum air space required on the top, sides and end of wood girders entering exterior concrete walls?

a. $^1/_2$ inch
b. 1 inch
c. $1^1/_2$ inch
d. 2 inches

Reference_______________

20. Which of the following types of naturally durable wood cannot qualify as decay resistant?

a. redwood
b. Eastern red cedar
c. black walnut
d. red oak

Reference_______________

21. What is the minimum number and size of nails used to connect a wood jack rafter to a hip?

a. 2-10d, face nail
b. 3-10d, toenail
c. 2-16d, toenail
d. 3-16d, face nail

Reference_______________

22. In conventional light-frame construction, buildings shall be provided with exterior and interior braced wall lines at maximum intervals of __________ feet in both the longitudinal and transverse directions in each story.

a. 20
b. 25
c. 35
d. 50

Reference_______________

23. In conventional light-frame construction, trimmer and header joists shall be doubled where the span of the header exceeds a minimum of __________ feet.

a. 4
b. 6
c. 10
d. 12

Reference_______________

24. In conventional light-frame wall construction, the edge of a bored hole shall be a minimum of __________ inch(es) from the edge of the stud.

a. $^5/_8$ b. $^3/_4$
c. 1 d. $1^1/_4$

Reference_______________

25. In conventional light-frame roof construction, the maximum span of a 2-inch by 6-inch purlin shall be __________ feet.

a. 4 b. 6
c. 8 d. 12

Reference_______________

26. In the design of stairway treads, a minimum concentrated live load of _____ pounds must be used, determined on an area of 4 square inches.

a. 40 b. 100
c. 200 d. 300

Reference_______________

27. In climates determined to be of moderate exposure, concrete foundation walls exposed to weather shall have a minimum specified compressive strength of _____ psi at 28 days.

a. 2,000 b. 2,500
c. 3,000 d. 3,500

Reference_______________

28. Type II light-framed shear walls of cold-formed steel shall have a maximum wall height of _____ feet

a. 10 b. 14
c. 16 d. 20

Reference_______________

29. Masonry nonstructural floor surfacing a maximum of _____ inches in thickness is permitted to be supported by wood members.

a. 2 b. 4
c. 6 d. 8

Reference_______________

30. In conventional light-frame construction, cripple walls exceeding a minimum of _____ in height shall be framed of wood studs having the size required for an additional story.

a. 14 inches
b. 20 inches
c. 30 inches
d. 48 inches

Reference_______________

INTERNATIONAL BUILDING CODE
Study Session 17
Chapters 8, 12, 25 and 30 —
Interior Finishes, Interior Environment, Gypsum Board and Elevators

OBJECTIVE: To gain an understanding of the limitations on interior wall and ceiling finishes; the installation requirements for gypsum board, lath and plaster; the important issues concerning the interior environment, including light, ventilation and sound transmission; and the provisions for elevators and their hoistways.

REFERENCE: Chapters 8, 12, 25 and 30, 2003 *International Building Code*

KEY POINTS:

- Which building elements are considered to be interior wall and ceiling finishes?
- Which types of materials are not regulated as wall or ceiling finishes?
- What is the standard of quality that addresses interior wall and ceiling finishes?
- Based on flame-spread index, what are the various classes of finish materials?
- When tested in a manner consistent with their use, what is the maximum smoke density index permitted for finish materials?
- In general, what is the maximum thickness of an interior wall or ceiling finish that must be applied directly against a noncombustible backing?
- How is Table 803.4 used to regulate the finish materials on ceilings and walls?
- Under which conditions are textile wall coverings permitted as wall and ceiling finishes?
- In what portions of a building are the interior floor finishes regulated? In which specific occupancies?
- What are the limitations on combustible trim and decorative materials?
- What are the limitations for gypsum wallboard in regard to exterior installation and weather protection?
- How shall fasteners for gypsum wallboard be applied?
- What type of gypsum board assembly requires treated joints and fasteners?
- Where is water-resistant gypsum backing board required?
- Water-resistant gypsum backing board is not permitted for use in which three locations?
- Where used to provide a horizontal diaphragm, how shall gypsum board be installed in a ceiling application?
- How must the occupiable portions of buildings be illuminated? Ventilated?
- When yards and courts are adjacent to exterior openings providing natural light and ventilation, how shall the openings be located?
- In which type of occupancy is the transmission of sound regulated?
- How is air-borne sound to be controlled? Structure-borne sound?
- What are the minimum room widths of habitable spaces? Minimum ceiling heights?
- How are efficiency dwelling units regulated for interior environment?
- What minimum size access opening is required for a crawl space? An attic?
- How must walls and floors in toilet rooms and bathing rooms be surfaced?
- What level of fire resistance is required for elevator shaft enclosures?
- What is the maximum number of elevator cars that may be located in a single elevator hoistway? At what point are two hoistways required?
- What type of doors is prohibited at the point of access to an elevator car?
- When must elevator hoistways be vented? Where are the vents to be located?

Topic: Definition and Classifications
Reference: IBC 801, 802.1, 803.1

Category: Interior Finishes
Subject: Wall and Ceiling Finishes

Code Text: *Interior wall and ceiling finish includes the exposed interior surfaces of buildings including, but not limited to: fixed or movable walls and partitions; columns; ceilings; and interior wainscotting, paneling, or other finish applied structurally or for decoration, acoustical correction, surface insulation, structural fire resistance or similar purposes, but not including trim. These provisions shall limit the allowable flame spread and smoke development based on location and occupancy classification.* See exceptions for very thin materials (<0.036 inches in thickness) and heavy-timber members.

Discussion and Commentary: It is the intent of the IBC to govern those materials applied to walls or ceilings that could contribute to the spread of flame or the development of smoke. Floor finishes are regulated in Section 804.

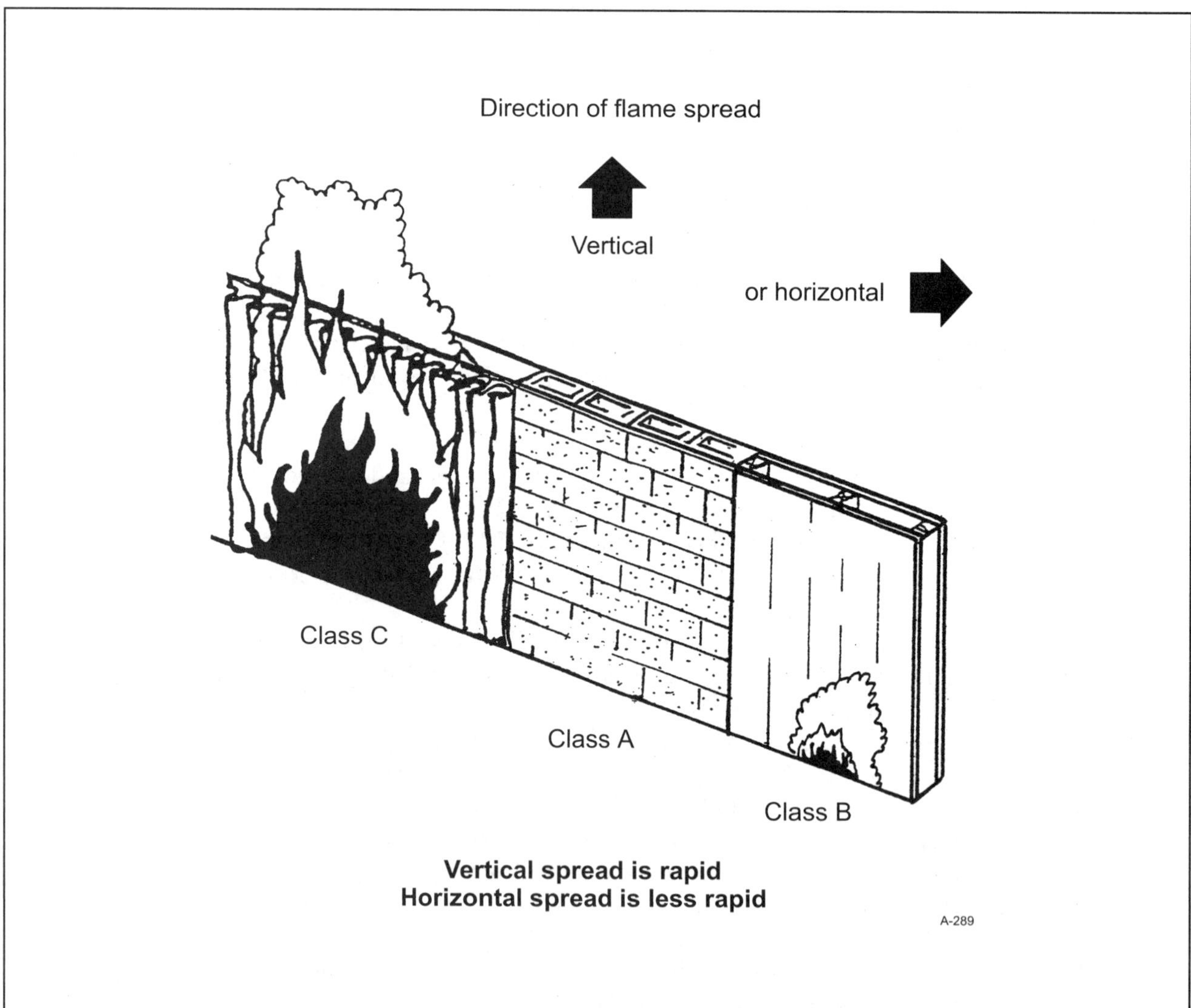

The classification of interior wall and ceiling finishes is based primarily on their flame spread index. Class A has an index of 0 to 25, Class B of 26 to 75, and Class C of 76 to 200. The smoke-developed index for all three classifications is limited to 450.

Topic: Flame-spread Classification
Reference: IBC 803.5

Category: Interior Finishes
Subject: Finish Requirements by Occupancy

Code Text: *Interior wall and ceiling finish shall have a flame spread index not greater than that specified in Table 803.5 for the group and location designated.*

Discussion and Commentary: Based on fire statistics, the rapid spread of fire across an interior finish material has been second only to vertical fire spread through openings between floors as a cause of life loss during building fires. Therefore, limitations are placed on the materials that are used to cover the walls and ceilings of rooms and other enclosed spaces, exit access corridors and other exitways, and vertical exits and exit passageways. The rapid spread of fire and the increased contribution of fuel to the fire are the major reasons why finish materials must meet stringent criteria to gain acceptance.

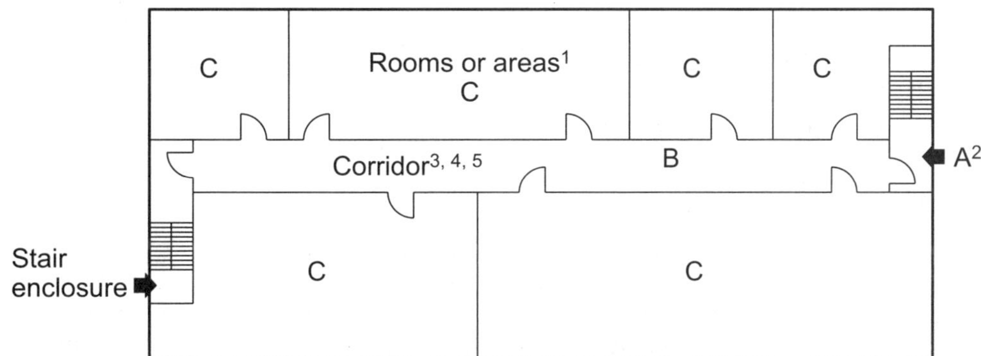

Notes:

1. Class B required for Group A Occupancies exceeding 300 occupants and Groups H and I Occupancies.
2. Class B permitted in group F and Group R-2 occupancies.
3. Class A required in Group I Occupancies, except in Group I-1 where Class B may be used; lobby areas of groups A-1, A-2 and A-3; and Group H occupancies.
4. Class C permitted in Group F Occupancies.

Flame-spread requirements by location within a nonsprinklered building

A-294

Textile materials, where applied to walls or ceilings, must meet additional criteria prior to approval. Finishes that have napped, tufted, looped, nonwoven, woven or similar surface characteristics present a unique hazard on account of their contribution to extremely rapid fire spread.

Topic: Floor Finish Requirements
Reference: IBC 804.5.1

Category: Interior Finishes
Subject: Interior Floor Finish

Code Text: *Interior floor finish in vertical exits, exit passageways and exit access corridors shall not be less than Class I in Groups I-2 and I-3 and not less than Class II in Groups A, B, E, H, I-4, M, R-1, R-2 and S. In all other areas, the interior floor finish shall comply with the DOC FF-1 "pill test."* See exception for the permitted reduction of classification in fully sprinklered buildings.

Discussion and Commentary: Although there are many different types of floor finishes and floor coverings, only those flooring materials composed of fibers are regulated by Section 804. Where required to be classified as Class I or Class II materials, the floor covering materials must be tested by an approved agency in accordance with NFPA 253. In order to verify compliance, the materials must be identified by a hang tag or other suitable method that identifies the manufacturer or supplier, style and finish classification.

Types of classifications: (in terms of heat flux, Sec. 804.2)

- Class I: Minimum 0.45 watts/cm^2 per NFPA 253
- Class II: Minimum 0.22 watts/cm^2 per NFPA 253
- DOC FF-1: Minimum 0.04 watts/cm^2

Required classifications: (Sec. 804.5)

	Nonsprinklered[a]		Sprinklered (NFPA 13 only)	
	Exits/Corr.[b]	Other Areas	Exits/Corr.[b]	Other Areas
Groups I-2 and I-3	Class I	DOC FF-1	Class II	DOC FF-1
Groups F, I-1, R-3, R-4 and U	DOC FF-1	DOC FF-1	DOC FF-1	DOC FF-1
Other Groups	Class II	DOC FF-1	DOC FF-1	DOC FF-1

Note: [a]Section 903.2 requires sprinklers in various occupancies
[b]Includes vertical exits, exit passageways, exit access corridors and rooms or spaces not separated from corridors by full-height partitions.

DOC FF-1, often referred to as the Methenamine Pill Test, essentially evaluates the floor covering when subjected to a cigarette-type ignition by using a small methenamine tablet. All carpeting sold in the United States is required by federal law to pass this test procedure.

Topic: General Requirements
Reference: IBC 805.1

Category: Interior Finishes
Subject: Decorations and Trim

Code Text: *In occupancies of Groups A, E, I, R-1 and dormitories in Group R-2, curtains, draperies, hangings and other decorative materials suspended from walls or ceiling shall be flame resistant in accordance with Section 805.2 and NFPA 701 or noncombustible. In Groups I-1 and I-2, combustible decorations shall be flame retardant unless the decorations, such as photographs and paintings, are of such limited quantities that a hazard of fire spread or development is not present. In Group I-3, combustible decorations are prohibited.*

Discussion and Commentary: In occupancies where large, concentrated occupant loads are expected, or where occupants have limited mobility due to physical limitations or restraint, the contribution of decorative materials to a fire condition is of concern. Therefore, the amount and characteristics of such materials are regulated to limit their impact on the fire severity.

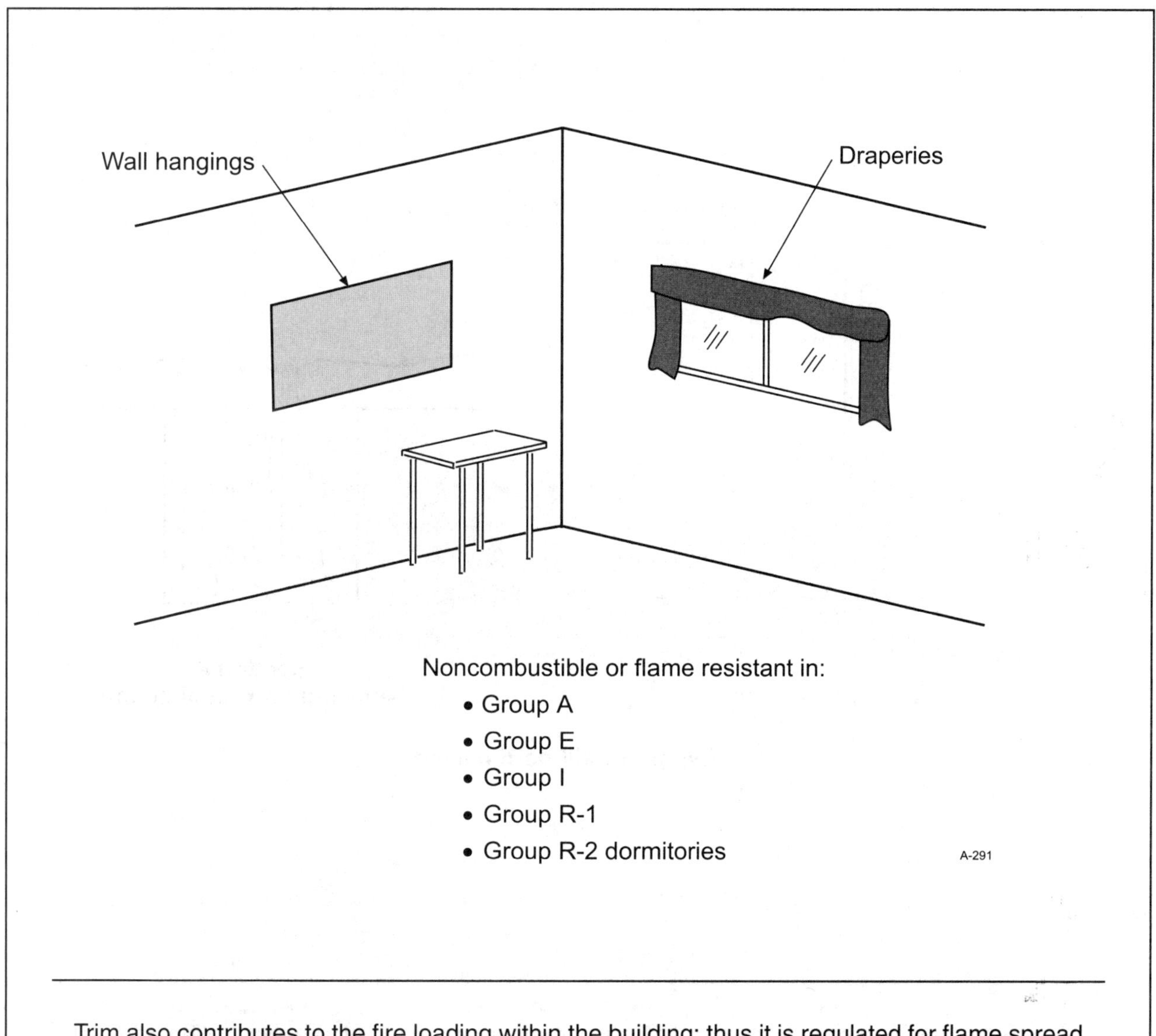

Trim also contributes to the fire loading within the building; thus it is regulated for flame spread and smoke contribution. Where trim consists of combustible materials, except for handrails and guardrails, its surface area is limited to 10 percent of the aggregate wall or ceiling area.

Topic: Installation
Reference: IBC 2508.2, 2508.3

Category: Gypsum Board and Plaster
Subject: Gypsum Construction

Code Text: *Gypsum wallboard or gypsum plaster shall not be used in any exterior surface where such gypsum construction will be exposed directly to the weather. Gypsum wallboard, gypsum lath or gypsum plaster shall not be installed until weather protection for the installation is provided. Edges and ends of gypsum board shall occur on the framing members, except those edges and ends that are perpendicular to the framing members.*

Discussion and Commentary: Gypsum wallboard, like gypsum plaster, is subject to deterioration from moisture. Accordingly, the code does not permit such gypsum materials to be installed on weather-exposed surfaces, as defined in Section 2502. Gypsum materials shall not be installed on interior surfaces until adequate protection from the weather has been provided.

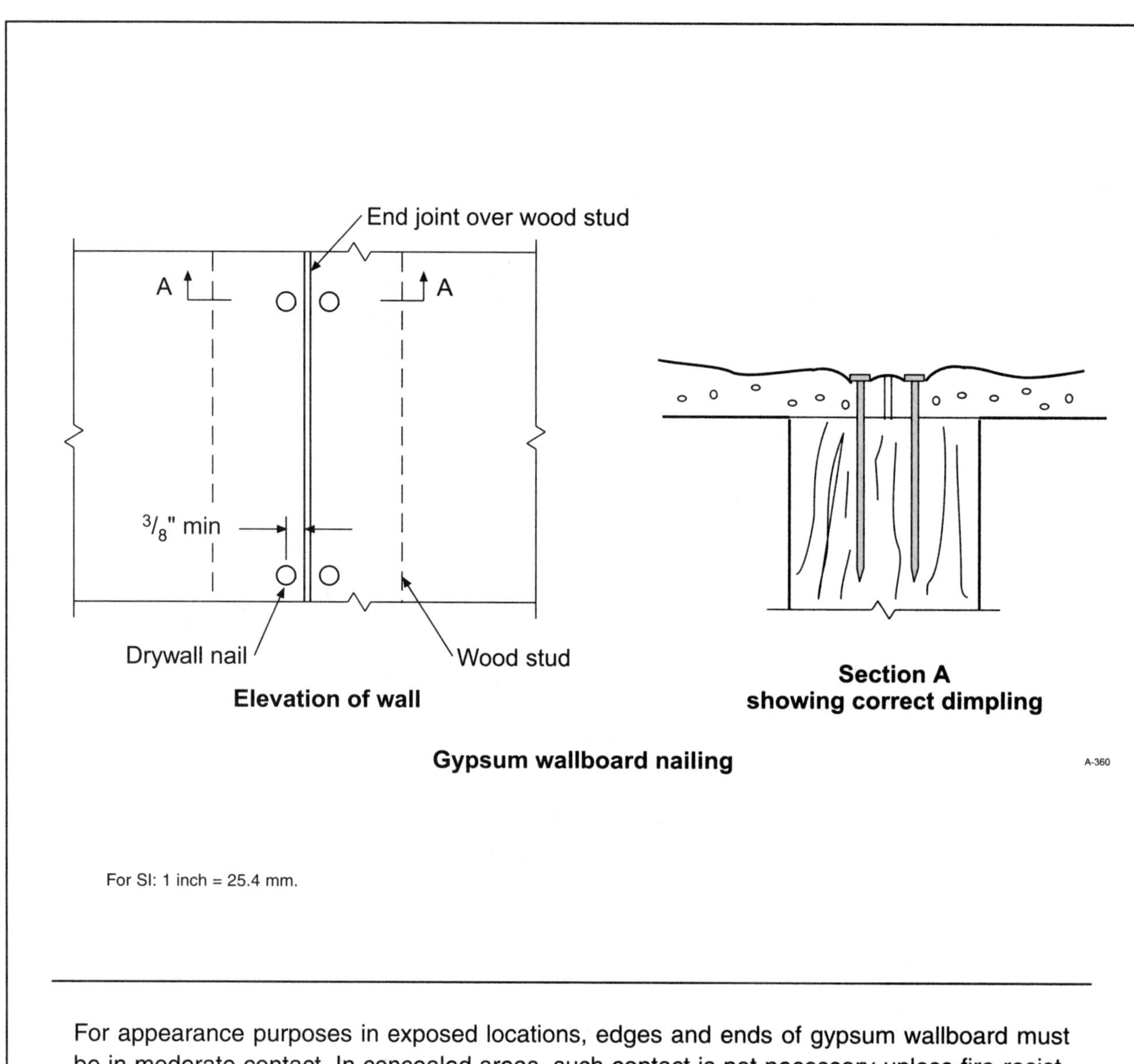

For appearance purposes in exposed locations, edges and ends of gypsum wallboard must be in moderate contact. In concealed areas, such contact is not necessary unless fire-resistance-rated construction or diaphragm action is required.

Topic: Base for Tile
Reference: IBC 2509.2

Category: Gypsum Board and Plaster
Subject: Gypsum Board in Showers

Code Text: *When gypsum board is used as a base for tile or wall panels for tubs, shower or water closet compartment walls, water-resistant gypsum backing board shall be used as a substrate. Regular gypsum wallboard is permitted under tile or wall panels in other wall and ceiling areas when installed in accordance with GA-216 or ASTM C 840.*

Discussion and Commentary: Because of its moisture-resistant qualities, water-resistant gypsum board is required when used as a backing material for tile or wall panels in high-moisture areas. However, evidence of unacceptable performance has caused such gypsum board to be prohibited for use in three locations: (1) over a vapor retarder in tub or shower compartments, (2) in areas subject to continuous high humidity or where there will be direct exposure to water, and (3) on ceilings with excessive spacing between framing members.

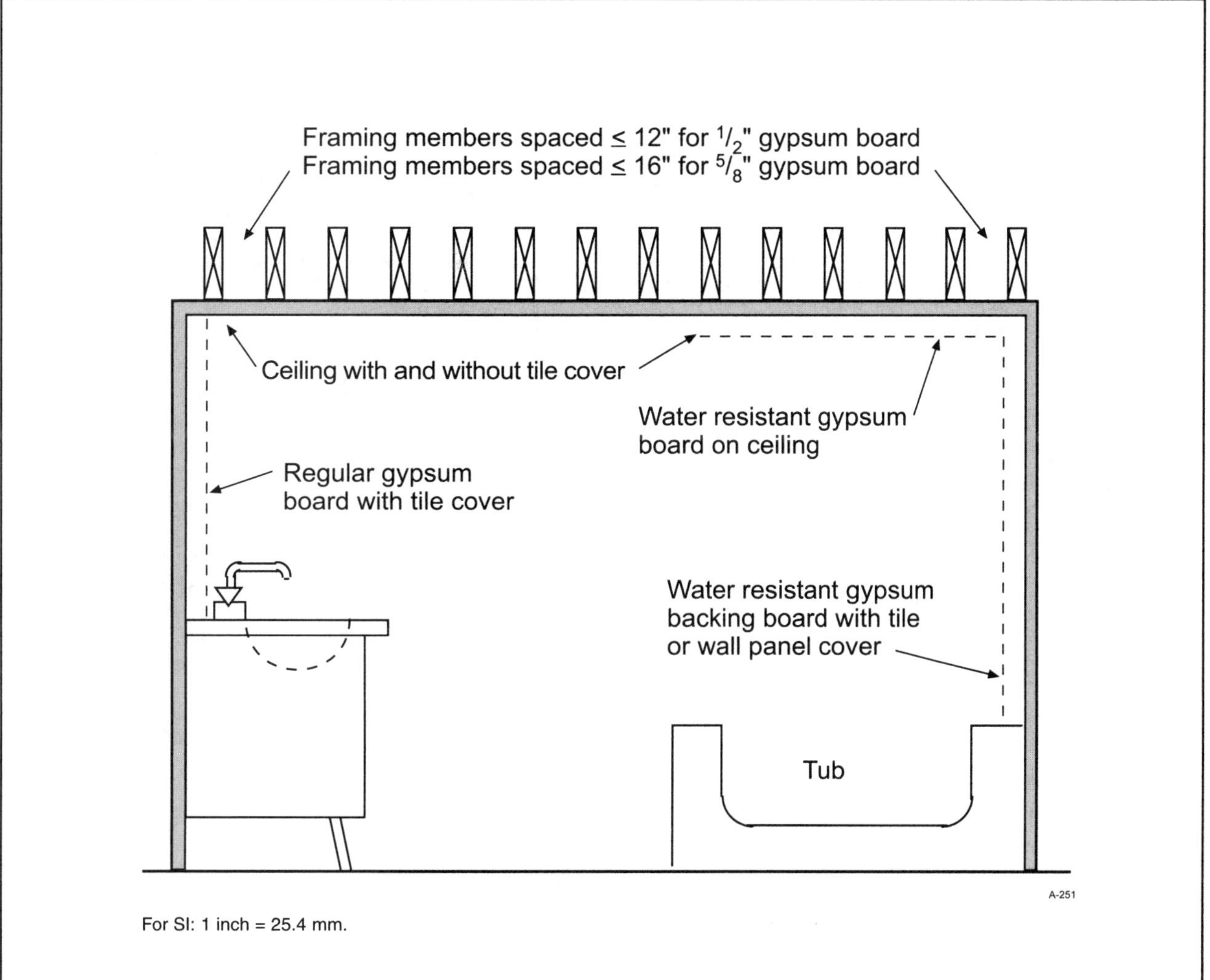

Water-resistant gypsum board tends to sag when installed as ceiling material; therefore, its use is limited only to those applications where the ceiling framing is spaced at no more than 12 inches on center for $^{1}/_{2}$-inch board, or a maximum of 16 inches on center for $^{5}/_{8}$-inch board.

Topic: General Requirements
Reference: IBC 1203.1, 1203.4

Category: Interior Environment
Subject: Ventilation

Code Text: *Buildings shall be provided with natural ventilation in accordance with Section 1203.4 or shall be provided with mechanical ventilation in accordance with the* International Mechanical Code. *Natural ventilation of an occupied space shall be through windows, doors, louvers or other openings to the outdoors. The minimum openable area to the outdoors shall be 4 percent of the floor area being ventilated.*

Discussion and Commentary: To obtain a minimum level of environmental comfort, as well as to maintain sanitary conditions, some form of ventilation must be provided to portions of a building that are normally occupied. The *International Mechanical Code*® (IMC®) will usually be used to determine the minimum acceptable ventilation methods and quantities.

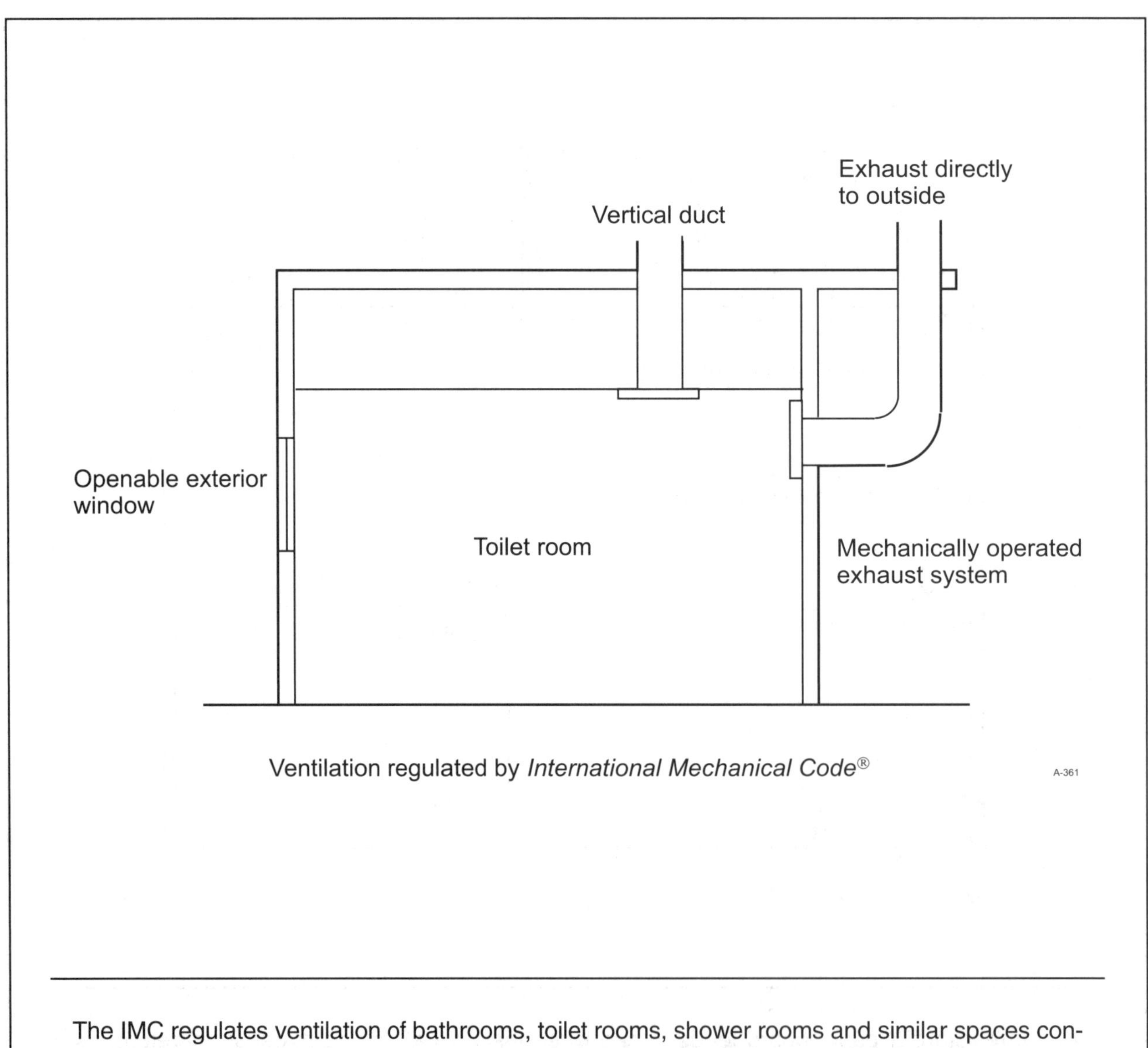

Ventilation regulated by *International Mechanical Code*®

The IMC regulates ventilation of bathrooms, toilet rooms, shower rooms and similar spaces containing bathtubs, showers and spas. The *International Fire Code,* in addition to the IMC, addresses ventilation and exhaust systems where flammable and combustible hazards are present.

Topic: Attic and Under-floor Ventilation
Reference: IBC 1203.2, 1203.3

Category: Interior Environment
Subject: Ventilation

Code Text: *Enclosed attics and enclosed rafter spaces formed where ceilings are applied directly to the underside of roof framing members shall have cross ventilation for each separate space by ventilating openings protected against the entrance of rain and snow. The space between the bottom of the floor joists and the earth under any building except spaces occupied by a basement or cellar shall be provided with ventilation openings through foundation walls or exterior walls. Such openings shall be placed so as to provide cross-ventilation of the under-floor space.* See exceptions for reductions and eliminations of required ventilation.

Discussion and Commentary: Ventilation of the attic and under-floor spaces prevents moisture condensation, which can have adverse effects on the materials of construction located in those spaces. Various exceptions are available that provide equivalent results.

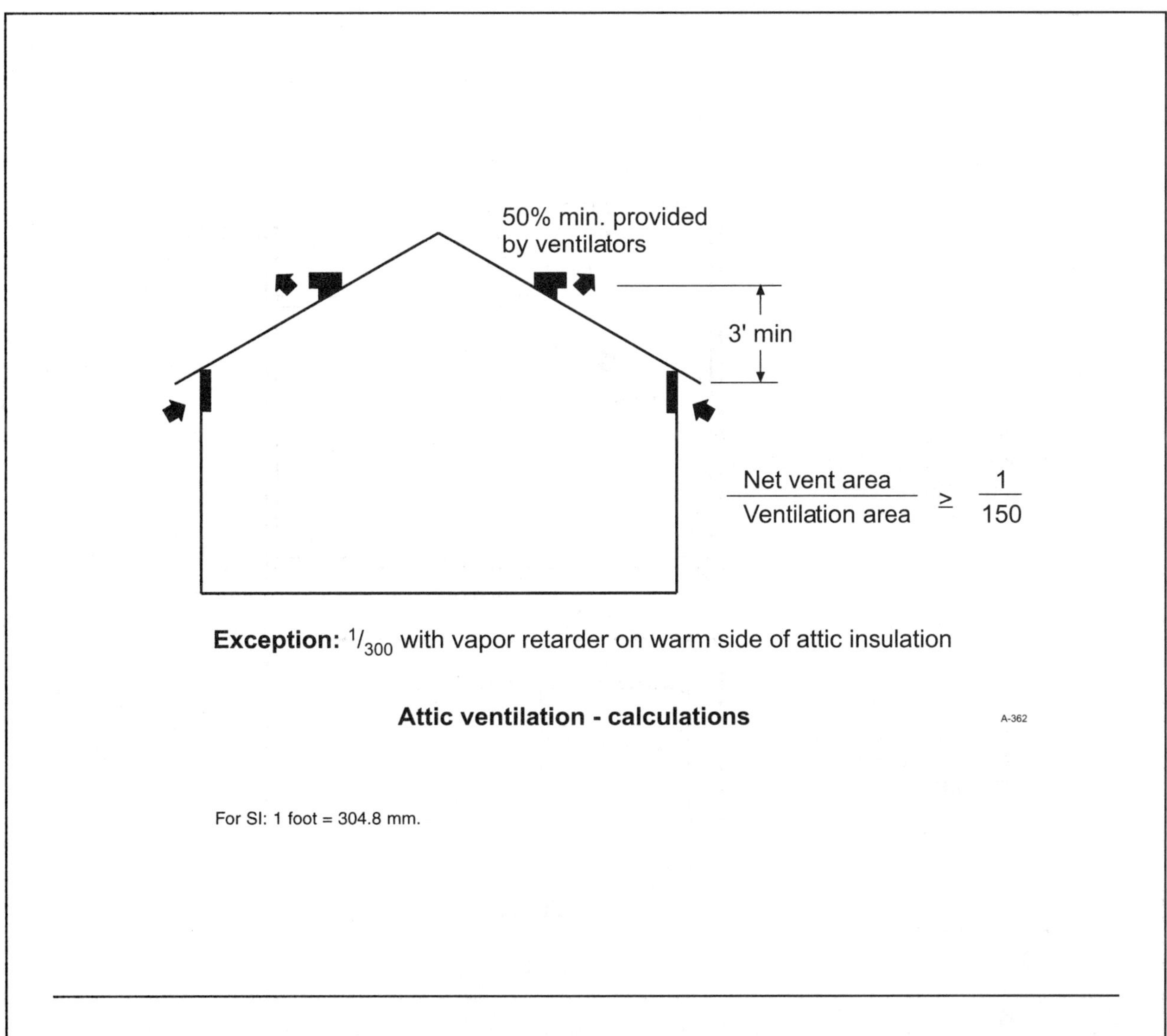

Attic ventilation - calculations

The general requirements for both attic and under-floor ventilation mandate a minimum net area of ventilation openings of $^1/_{150}$ of the area of the space ventilated. In addition, all openings to the exterior must be screened to prevent the entry of birds, rodents and similar creatures.

Topic: General Requirements
Reference: IBC 1205

Category: Interior Environment
Subject: Lighting

Code Text: *Every space intended for human occupancy shall be provided with natural light by means of exterior glazed openings in accordance with Section 1205.2 or shall be provided with artificial light in accordance with Section 1205.3. Exterior glazed openings shall open directly onto a public way or onto a yard or court in accordance with Section 1206. The minimum net glazed area shall not be less than 8 percent of the floor area of the room served. Artificial light shall be provided that is adequate to provide an average illumination of 10 foot-candles over the area of the room at a height of 30 inches above the floor level.*

Discussion and Commentary: It is fundamental that all occupiable areas of a building be provided with adequate illumination. The use of artificial light to satisfy the code is acceptable because it can produce the light necessary for occupancy at any time of the day or night.

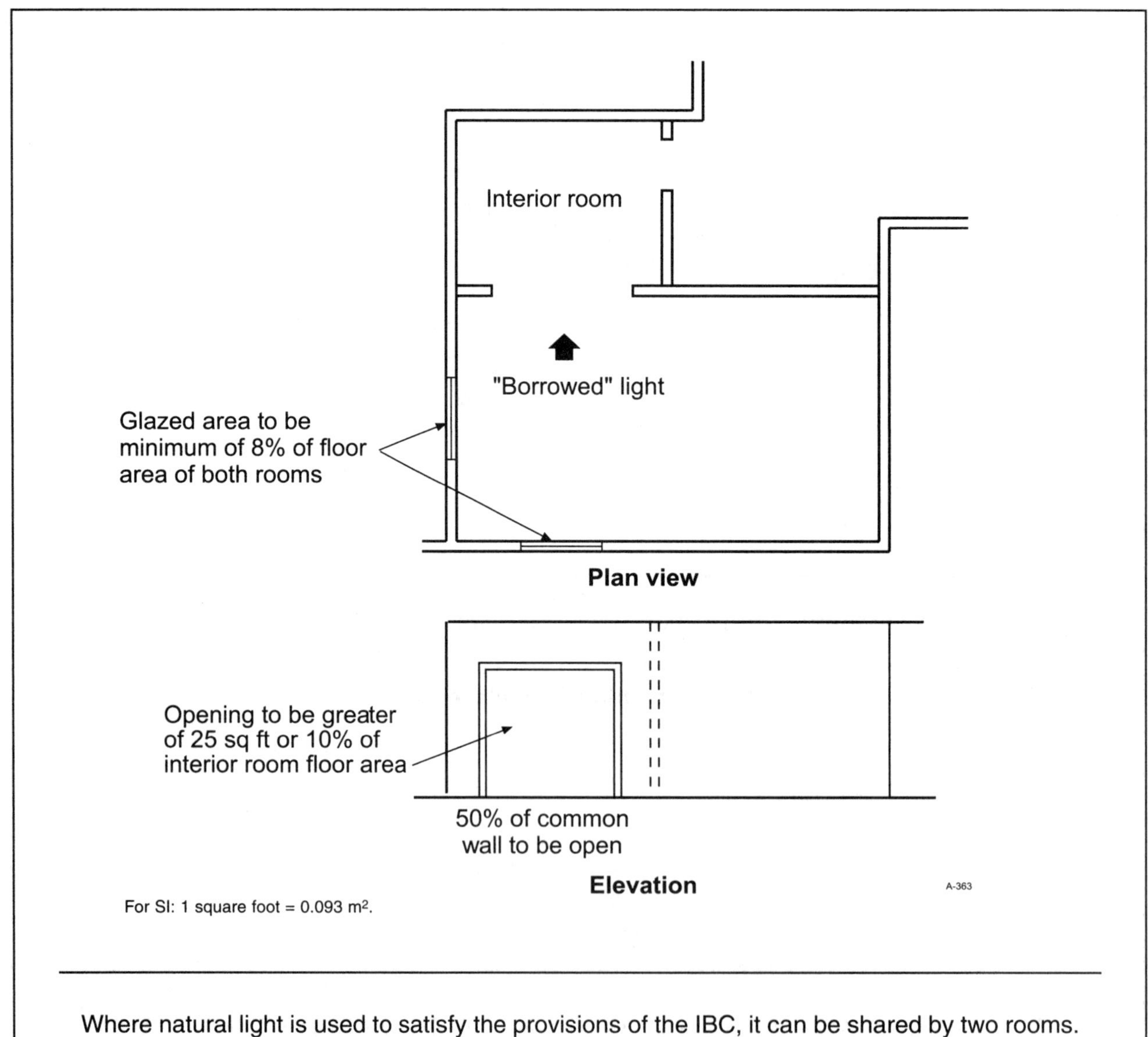

Where natural light is used to satisfy the provisions of the IBC, it can be shared by two rooms. The common wall between the rooms must be adequately open, and the total floor area of both rooms shall be used to calculate the minimum glazed area.

Topic: General Requirements
Reference: IBC 1207

Category: Interior Environment
Subject: Sound Transmission

Code Text: *Walls, partitions and floor/ceiling assemblies separating dwelling units from each other or from public or service areas shall have a sound transmission class (STC) of not less than 50 (45 if field tested) for air-borne noise. Floor/ceiling assemblies between dwelling units or between a dwelling unit and a public or service area within the structure shall have an impact insulation class (IIC) rating of not less than 50 (45 if field tested).*

Discussion and Commentary: To control sound transmission between areas of a residential building, insulated walls and floor/ceiling assemblies are necessary. The regulations address airborne sound that may be carried throughout the structure, as well as impact noise created on the floor of a floor/ceiling assembly.

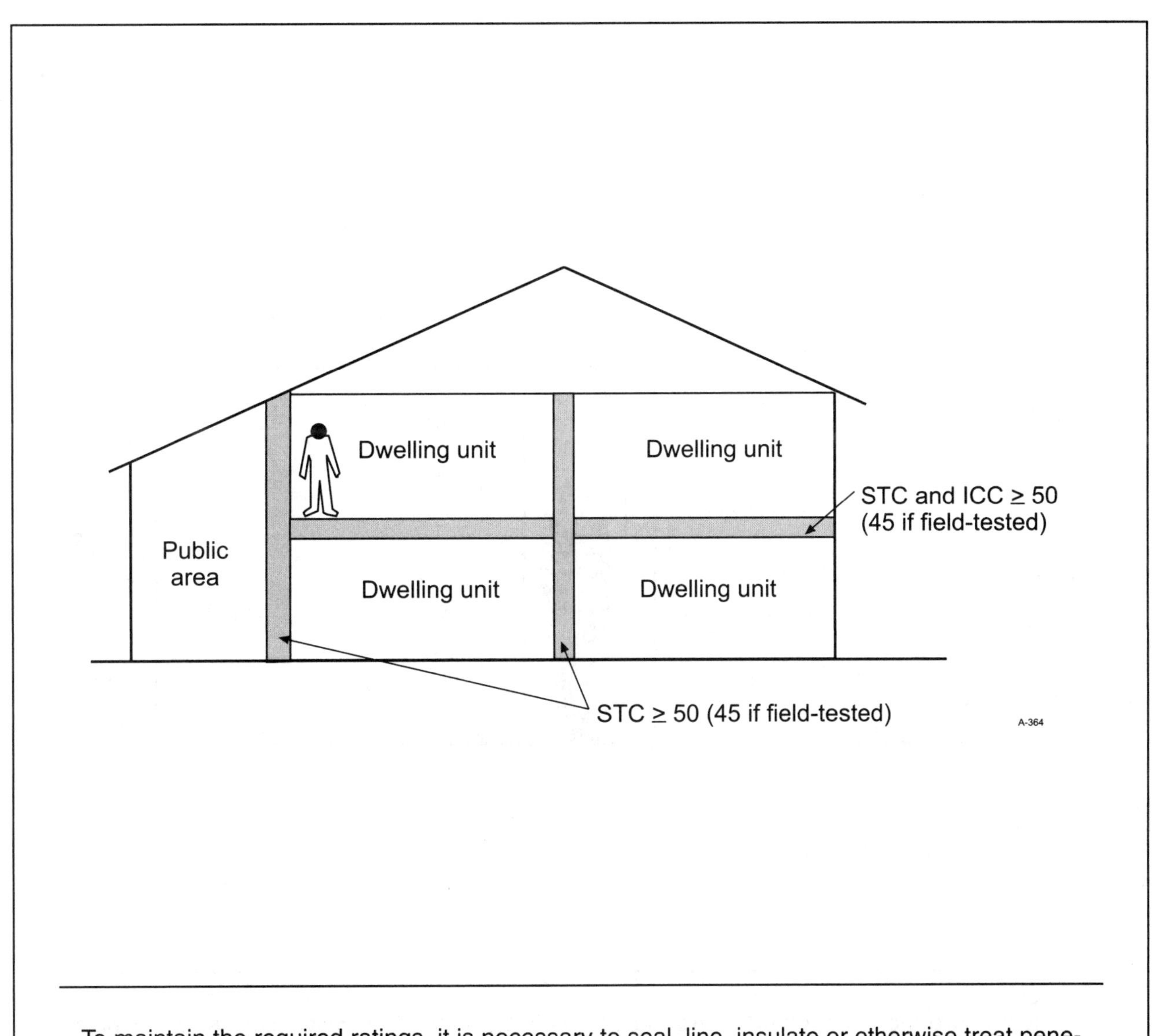

To maintain the required ratings, it is necessary to seal, line, insulate or otherwise treat penetrations through the sound transmission assemblies. The code exempts dwelling unit entrance doors from transmission limits, provided that they are tight fitting to the frame and sill.

Topic: Room Size and Ceiling Height
Reference: IBC 1208

Category: Interior Environment
Subject: Interior Space Dimensions

Code Text: *Habitable spaces, other than a kitchen, shall not be less than 7 feet (2134 mm) in any plan dimension. Kitchens shall have a clear passageway of not less than 3 feet (914 mm) between counter fronts and appliances or counter fronts and walls. Occupiable spaces, habitable spaces and corridors shall have a ceiling height of not less than 7 feet 6 inches (2286 mm). Bathrooms, toilet rooms, kitchens, storage rooms and laundry rooms shall be permitted to have a ceiling height of not less than 7 feet (2134 mm).* See exceptions for exposed beams, sloped ceilings and mezzanines. *Every dwelling unit shall have at least one room that shall have not less than 120 square feet (13.9 m^2) of net floor area. Other habitable rooms shall have a net floor area of not less than 70 square feet (6.5 m^2).*

Discussion and Commentary: For fundamental usability and environmental purposes, it is necessary to mandate minimum requirements for the size and height of occupiable spaces.

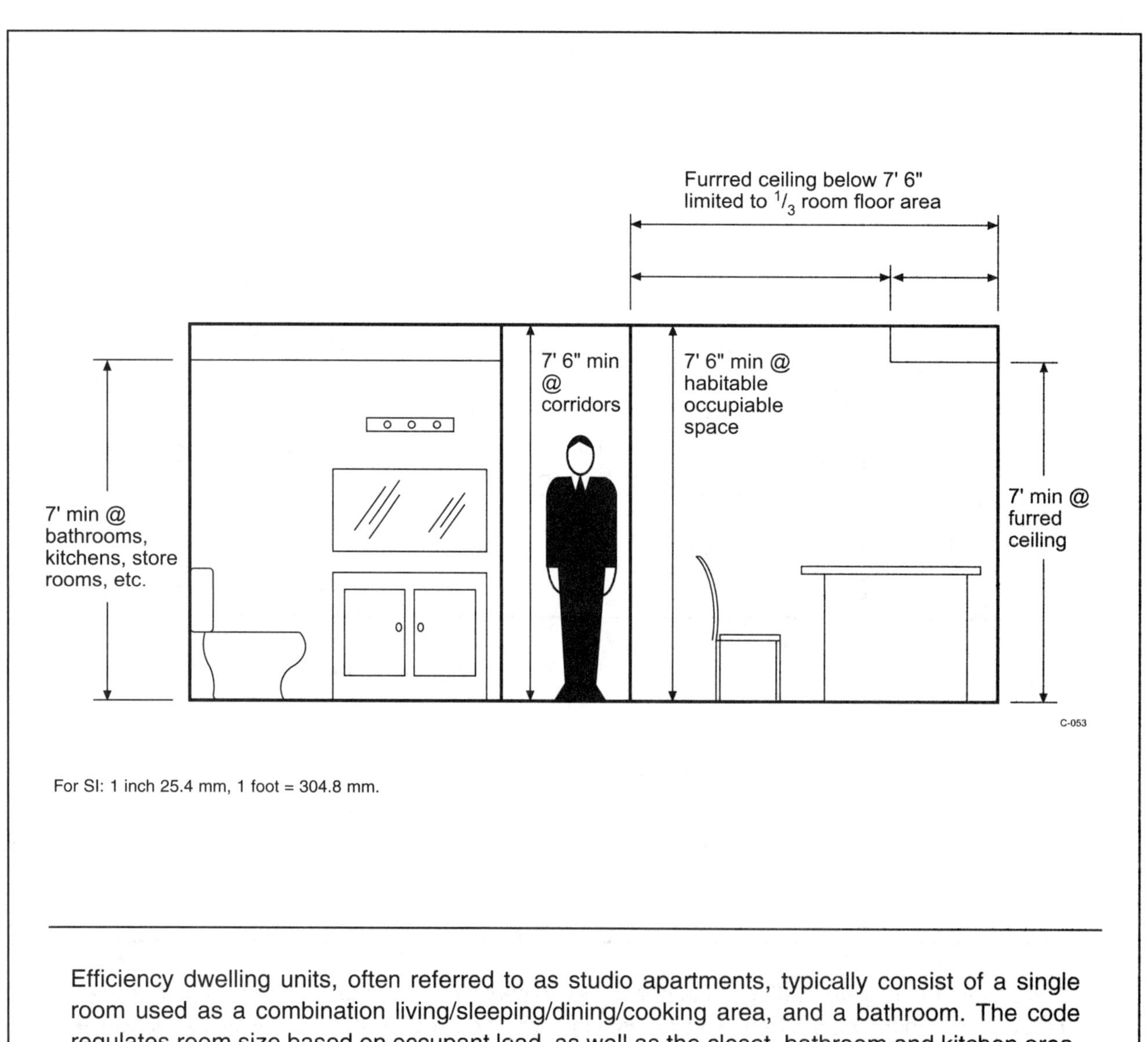

Efficiency dwelling units, often referred to as studio apartments, typically consist of a single room used as a combination living/sleeping/dining/cooking area, and a bathroom. The code regulates room size based on occupant load, as well as the closet, bathroom and kitchen area.

Topic: Attics and Crawl Spaces
Reference: IBC 1209

Category: Interior Environment
Subject: Access to Unoccupied Spaces

Code Text: *Crawl spaces shall be provided with a minimum of one access opening not less than 18 inches by 24 inches (457 mm by 610 mm). An opening not less than 20 inches by 30 inches (559 mm by 762 mm) shall be provided to any attic area having a clear height of over 30 inches (762 mm). A 30-inch (762 mm) minimum clear headroom in the attic space shall be provided at or above the access opening.*

Discussion and Commentary: Items such as plumbing and wiring installations pass through crawl space at times. Required initial and periodic inspections and maintenance and repairs cannot be carried out without access to such crawl spaces. Attic access is also required for similar reasons. Although uncommon, access to the attic for fire department purposes can also be accomplished through such openings. The required openings are a convenient and nondestructive means for any user to access such concealed spaces.

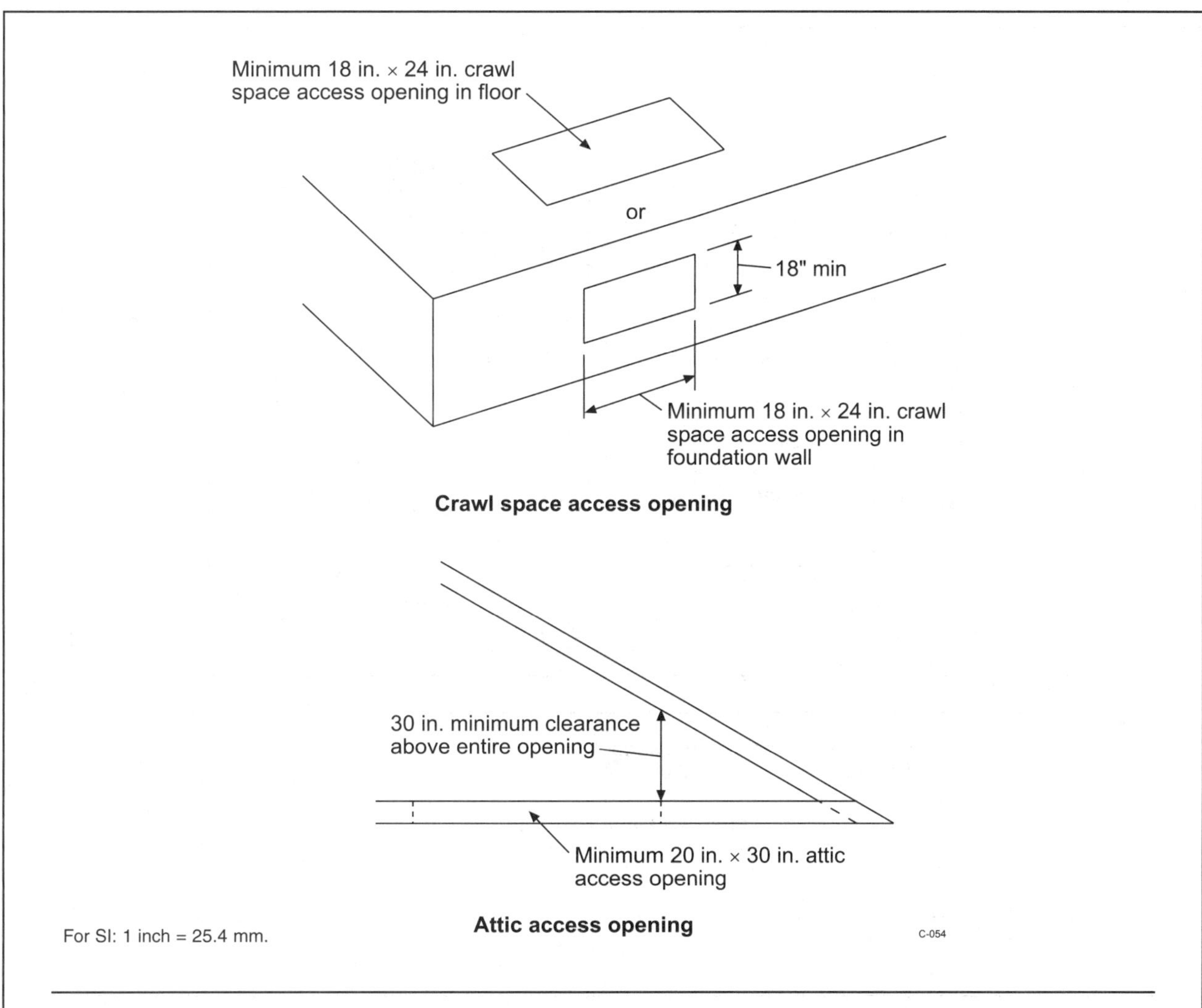

Crawl space access opening

Attic access opening

For SI: 1 inch = 25.4 mm.

Section 306 of the *International Mechanical Code* regulates access to both underfloor and attic spaces for the inspection, service, repair or replacement of any mechanical equipment. In addition to the access opening, the passageway and service area sizes are also addressed.

Topic: Wall and Floor Finishes
Reference: IBC 1210

Category: Interior Environment
Subject: Surrounding Materials

Code Text: *In other than dwelling units, toilet and bathing room floors shall have a smooth, hard, nonabsorbent surface that extends upward onto the walls at least 6 inches (152 mm). Walls within 2 feet (610 mm) of urinals and water closets shall have a smooth, hard, nonabsorbent surface, to a height of 4 feet (1219 mm) above the floor, and except for structural elements, the materials used in such walls shall be of a type that is not adversely affected by moisture.* See exceptions for dwelling units and private toilet rooms. *Accessories such as grab bars, towel bars, paper dispensers and soap dishes, provided on or within walls, shall be installed and sealed to protect structural elements from moisture.*

Discussion and Commentary: For obvious sanitary reasons, it is necessary to provide surfaces in bath and toilet areas that are easily cleaned and maintained.

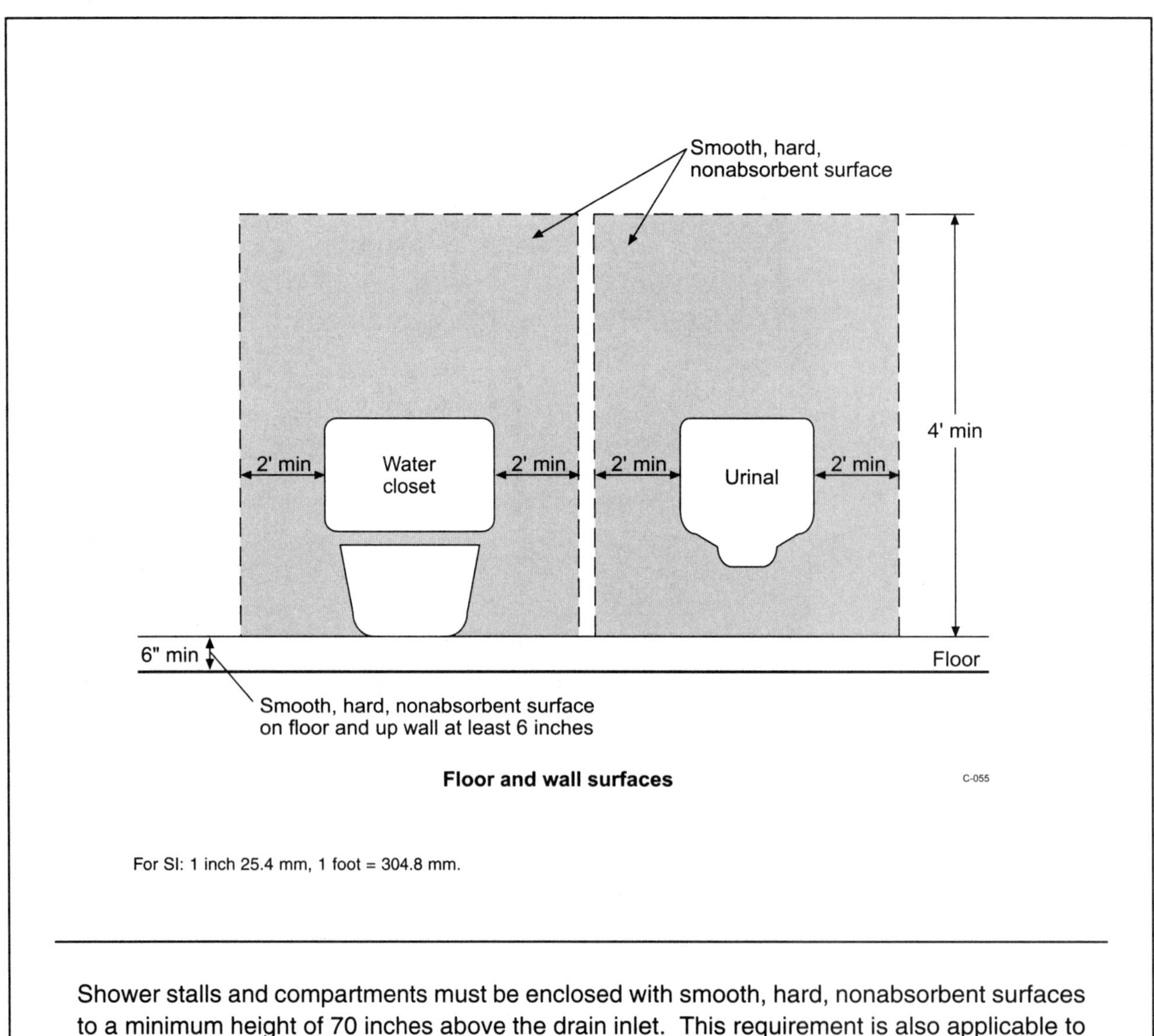

Floor and wall surfaces

For SI: 1 inch 25.4 mm, 1 foot = 304.8 mm.

Shower stalls and compartments must be enclosed with smooth, hard, nonabsorbent surfaces to a minimum height of 70 inches above the drain inlet. This requirement is also applicable to those bathtubs that are provided with shower heads.

Topic: Protection
Reference: IBC 3002.1

Category: Elevators and Conveying Systems
Subject: Hoistways Enclosures

Code Text: *Elevator, dumbwaiter and other hoistway enclosures shall have a fire-resistance rating not less than that specified in Chapter 7. Openings in hoistway enclosures shall be protected as required in Chapter 7. Doors, other than hoistway doors and the elevator car door, shall be prohibited at the point of access to an elevator car unless such doors are readily openable from the car side without a key, tool, special knowledge or effort.*

Discussion and Commentary: An elevator shaft is regulated under the shaft enclosure provisions of Section 707. Generally, an elevator enclosure must be of two-hour fire-resistance-rated construction in Type I buildings or where four or more stories are connected. A one-hour rating is permitted where the shaft enclosure connects three stories or less.

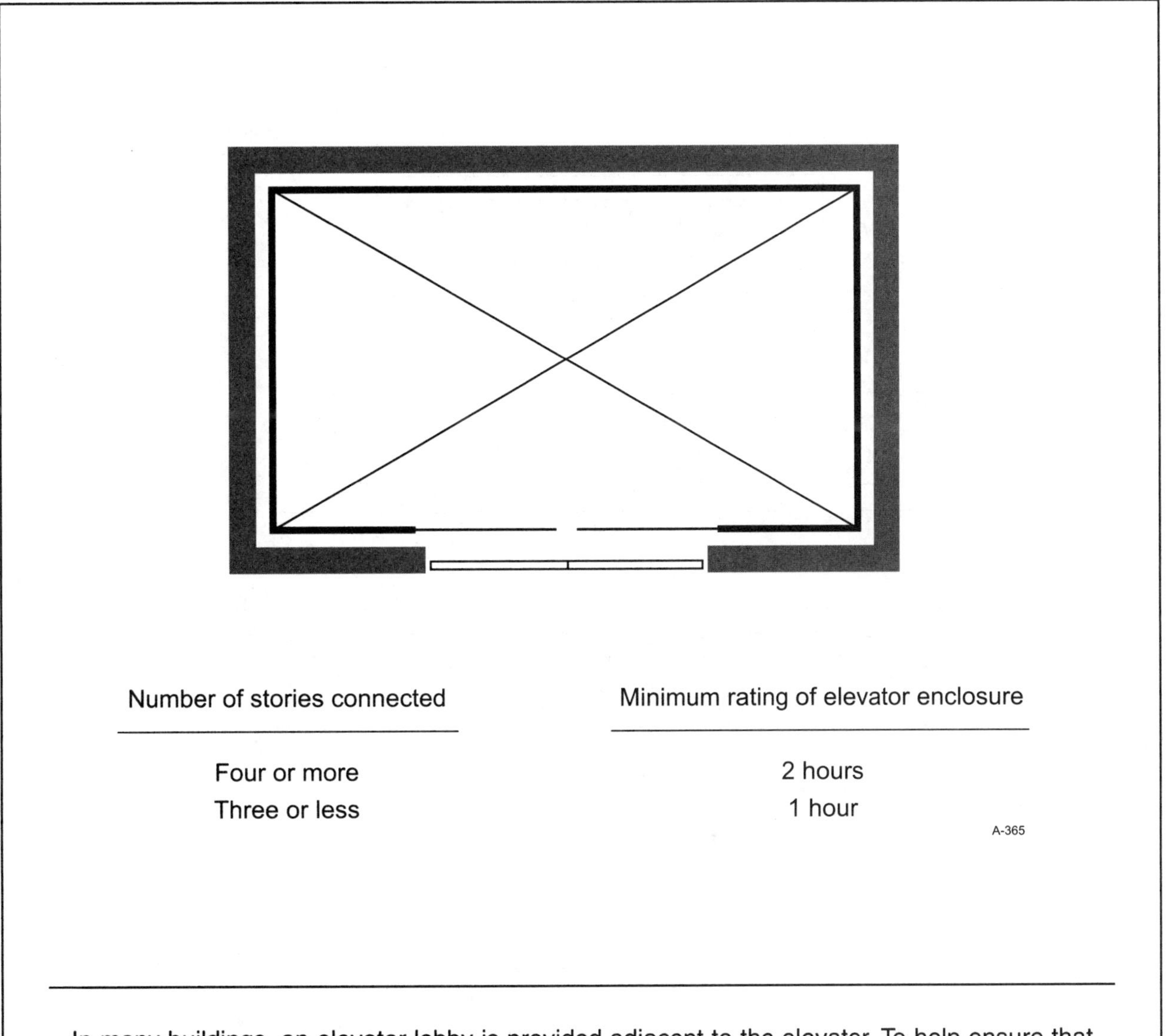

Number of stories connected	Minimum rating of elevator enclosure
Four or more	2 hours
Three or less	1 hour

In many buildings, an elevator lobby is provided adjacent to the elevator. To help ensure that an individual does not become trapped within such a lobby, the lobby door must be openable without the use of a key.

Topic: Number of Cars in Hoistway
Reference: IBC 3002.2, 3002.7

Category: Elevators and Conveying Systems
Subject: Hoistway Enclosures

Code Text: *Where four or more elevator cars serve all or the same portion of a building, the elevators shall be located in at least two separate hoistways. Not more than four elevator cars shall be located in any single hoistway enclosure. Elevators shall not be in a common shaft enclosure with a stairway.*

Discussion and Commentary: The basis for limiting the number of elevator cars in a single hoistway is to provide a reasonable level of assurance that a multilevel building served by several elevators would not have all of its elevator cars disabled by a single fire incident. The provisions increase the chance that some of the elevators would remain operational during an emergency situation.

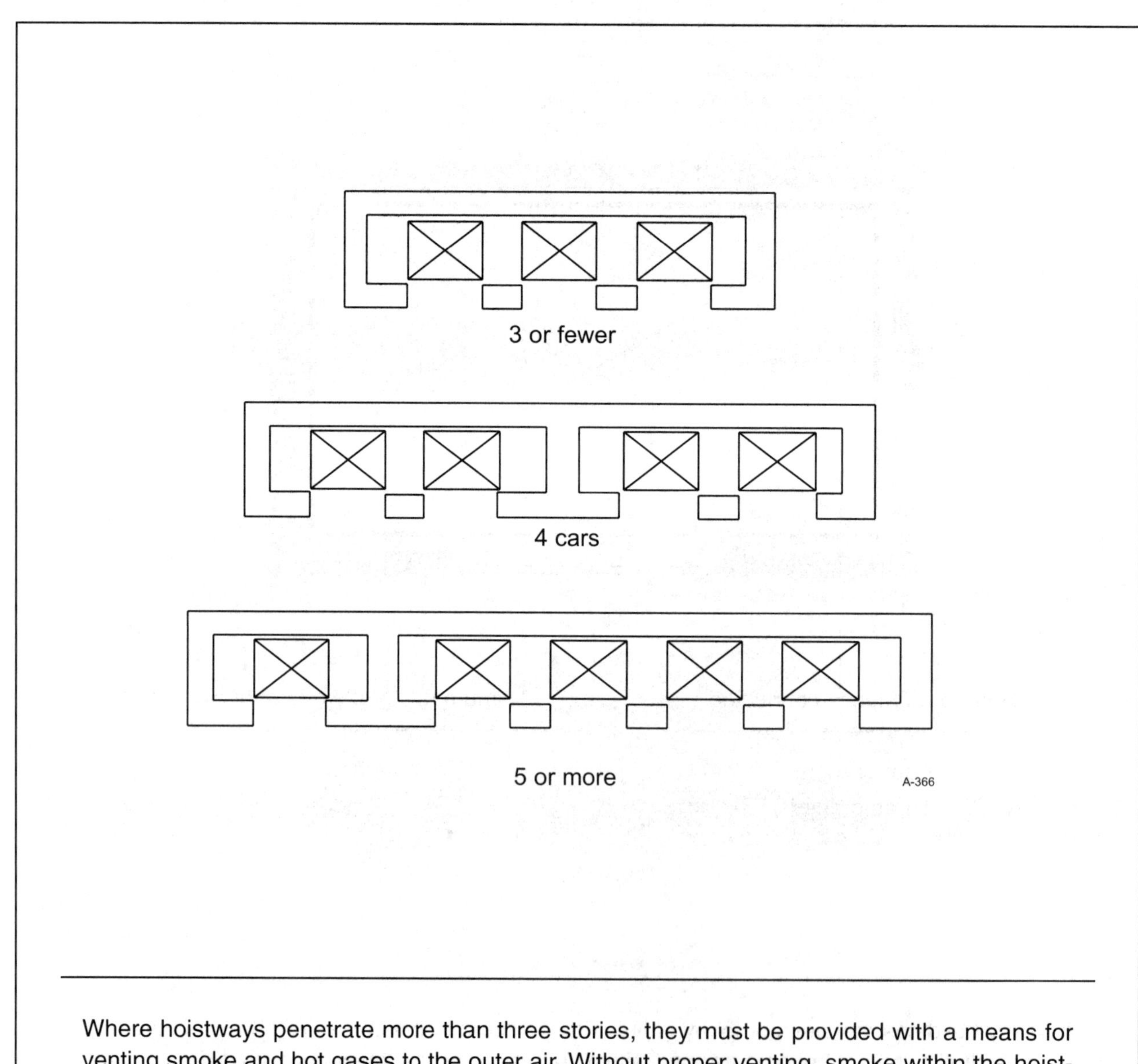

Where hoistways penetrate more than three stories, they must be provided with a means for venting smoke and hot gases to the outer air. Without proper venting, smoke within the hoistways would render the elevator cars useless and be able to spill out into the upper floors.

QUIZ

Study Session 17 — Chapters 8, 12, 25 and 30

I. Multiple Choice

1. Where classified in accordance with ASTM E 84, Class B interior wall and ceiling finishes have a flame spread index of __________ and a smoke developed index of 0-450.

   a. 0-25 b. 26-75
   c. 76-200 d. 201 and greater

   Reference_______________

2. Unless a Class A material or qualified by tests, an interior wall or ceiling finish that is a maximum of __________-inch thick shall be applied directly against a noncombustible backing.

   a. 0.036 b. 0.125
   c. 0.25 d. 0.5

   Reference_______________

3. The wall finish in a dining room classified as Group A-2 in a sprinklered building shall have a maximum flame spread index classification of Class __________.

   a. A b. B
   c. C d. no restrictions

   Reference_______________

4. The wall finish in a vertical exit enclosure of a nonsprinklered Group B office building shall have a maximum flame spread index classification of Class __________.

   a. A b. B
   c. C d. no restrictions

   Reference_______________

5. In a patient room of a fully-sprinklered Group I-2 occupancy, the interior finish materials are permitted to be a maximum of Class C when the room has a maximum capacity of __________ persons.

   a. 1 b. 2
   c. 3 d. 4

   Reference_______________

6. Textile wall coverings shall have a maximum Class __________ flame spread index where installed in a fully-sprinklered art gallery.

   a. A
   b. B
   c. C
   d. not permitted

   Reference_______________

7. In a fully-sprinklered Group I-2 occupancy, carpet installed as an interior floor finish in an exit passageway shall be a minimum __________.

   a. Class I
   b. Class II
   c. Class A
   d. DOC FF-1 "pill test"

   Reference_______________

8. Combustible trim, excluding handrails and guardrails, shall be limited to a maximum of __________ percent of the aggregate wall or ceiling area.

   a. 5
   b. 10
   c. 25
   d. 50

   Reference_______________

9. In a fully-sprinklered Group A auditorium, flame-resistant decorative material shall be limited to a maximum of __________ percent of the aggregate area of walls and ceilings.

   a. 5
   b. 10
   c. 25
   d. 50

   Reference_______________

10. What is the minimum permitted flame-spread index and smoke-developed index for materials used as interior trim?

   a. Class A
   b. Class B
   c. Class C
   d. unlimited

   Reference_______________

11. Within a sleeping unit of a Group R-1 hotel, a space-heating system shall be provided that is capable of maintaining a minimum indoor temperature of __________ at a point 3 feet above the floor on a design heating day.

   a. 65 degrees F
   b. 68 degrees F
   c. 70 degrees F
   d. 72 degrees F

   Reference_______________

12. Where natural light by means of exterior glazed openings is utilized as the required lighting for an occupied space, the minimum net glazed area shall not be less than __________ percent of the floor area of the room served.

a. 4 b. 5
c. 8 d. 10

Reference_______________

13. A stairway within a dwelling unit of a Group R-2 apartment building shall be provided with a minimum illumination level on tread runs of __________ foot-candles.

a. 1 b. 2
c. 5 d. 10

Reference_______________

14. A floor/ceiling assembly between a dwelling unit and a public area within the structure shall have a minimum impact insulation class (IIC) rating of __________ when field tested.

a. 40 b. 45
c. 50 d. not regulated

Reference_______________

15. Occupiable spaces in an office building shall have a minimum ceiling height of __________.

a. 6 feet, 8 inches b. 7 feet, 0 inches
c. 7 feet, 6 inches d. 8 feet, 0 inches

Reference_______________

16. Every dwelling unit shall have at least one room with a minimum floor area of __________ square feet.

a. 70 b. 120
c. 150 d. 220

Reference_______________

17. The minimum size of the access opening to a crawl space shall be __________.

a. 18 inches by 24 inches b. 20 inches by 24 inches
c. 22 inches by 30 inches d. 22 inches by 30 inches

Reference_______________

18. The minimum size of the access opening to an attic area over 30 inches in clear height shall be __________.

a. 18 inches by 24 inches
b. 20 inches by 24 inches
c. 20 inches by 30 inches
d. 22 inches by 30 inches

Reference_______________

19. Shower compartments shall be finished with a smooth, nonabsorbent surface to a minimum height of __________ inches above the drain inlet.

a. 60
b. 66
c. 70
d. 72

Reference_______________

20. Roof soffits are considered weather-exposed surfaces except for those portions located a minimum horizontal distance of __________ feet from the outer edges of the soffit.

a. 3
b. 5
c. 8
d. 10

Reference_______________

21. Water-resistant gypsum backing board that is $^5/_8$-inch-thick is permitted for use on ceilings having a maximum frame spacing of __________ inches on center.

a. 12
b. 16
c. 19.2
d. 24

Reference_______________

22. For exterior plastering, the second coat shall have a maximum variation of __________ inch in any direction under a 5-foot straight edge.

a. $^1/_8$
b. $^3/_{16}$
c. $^1/_4$
d. $^3/_8$

Reference_______________

23. A maximum of __________ elevator car(s) shall be located in any single hoistway enclosure.

a. 1
b. 2
c. 3
d. 4

Reference_______________

24. Holes in the elevator machine room floor for the passage of cables or other moving elevator equipment shall be limited so as to provide a maximum clearance of _________ inch(es) on all sides.

a. $^1/_2$ b. 1
c. $1^1/_2$ d. 2

25. In buildings four or more stories in height, at least one elevator car shall be of such a size to accommodate a minimum _________ ambulance stretcher in the horizontal, open position.

a. 24-inch by 72-inch b. 24-inch by 76-inch
c. 28-inch by 78-inch d. 30-inch by 78-inch

Reference_______________

26. A fibrous floor covering installed in the dining area of a Group A-2 nonsprinklered restaurant shall have a minimum classification of _____.

a. DOC FF-1 "pill test" b. Class I
c. Class II d. Class A

Reference_______________

27. As a general rule, the minimum net area of ventilation openings for under-floor ventilation shall be based on 1 square foot for each _____ square feet of crawl-space area.

a. 100 b. 120
c. 150 d. 300

Reference_______________

28. Where a court is adjacent to exterior openings on both sides of the court that provide for the required natural ventilation, the minimum court width shall be _____ feet if the building is five stories in height.

a. 3 b. 6
c. 9 d. 10

Reference_______________

29. In the construction of a gypsum board fire-resistance-rated assembly, for which of the following applications is joint and fastener treatment required?

a. above a fire-rated ceiling b. where joints occur over wood framing
c. assemblies tested without joint treatment d. tongue-and-groove edge gypsum board

Reference_______________

30. In a single-elevator building where standby power is provided to operate the elevator, the transfer to standby power shall occur automatically within a maximum of _____ seconds after failure of normal power.

a. 10 b. 15
c. 30 d. 60

Reference_______________

INTERNATIONAL BUILDING CODE

Study Session 18

Chapters 24 and 26 — Glazing, Skylights and Plastics

OBJECTIVE: To gain an understanding of the installation requirements for glass and glazing, glazing support and framing, safety glazing, skylights, foam plastics, light-transmitting plastics and plastic veneers.

REFERENCE: Chapters 24 and 26, 2003 *International Building Code*

KEY POINTS:

- How is the installation of replacement glass regulated?
- How must a pane of glass be identified? Tempered glass?
- How must glazing be supported?
- What are the limitations for louvered windows and jalousies?
- Sloped glazing provisions for skylights, roofs and sloped walls apply when the glazing material is installed at what minimum slope from the vertical plane?
- Which materials are permitted for sloped glazing? What limitations are placed on these materials?
- For which sloped glazing installations are screens mandated?
- Skylight frames must be constructed of noncombustible materials in which types of construction?
- When are curbs required for the mounting of skylights?
- How are unit skylights regulated?
- What is safety glazing? What are the standards that regulate safety glazing?
- How shall safety glazing be identified? What information must be included as a part of the identifying mark?
- Which types of doors are exempt from the glazing requirements for hazardous locations?
- When glazing is located adjacent to a door, how is it determined if safety glazing is required?
- Which areas of tub and shower enclosures are considered hazardous locations for glazing?
- Individual fixed or operable glazed panels exceeding nine square feet in area must be safety glazed unless which three conditions exist?
- How is glazing adjacent to stairways and landings to be addressed?
- What are the seven glazing products, materials and uses that are exempt from the requirements for hazardous locations?
- What are the three types of glass permitted to be used as structural balustrade panels in rails?
- What is the maximum flame spread index for foam plastic insulation used in building construction? What is the maximum smoke-developed index?
- When is a thermal barrier necessary to separate the interior of a building from foam plastic insulation?
- Under which conditions may foam plastic insulation be incorporated as a part of a roof covering assembly?
- What are the limitations for the use of plastic veneer within a building? On the exterior wall of a building?
- How are light-transmitting plastics used as wall or roof panels regulated?
- Which specific provisions apply to plastic used as exterior wall panels? As roof panels? In skylights? In light-diffusing systems?

Topic: Allowable Glazing Materials
Reference: IBC 2405.1, 2405.2

Category: Glass and Glazing
Subject: Sloped Glazing and Skylights

Code Text: *Section 2405 applies to the installation of glass and other transparent, translucent or opaque glazing material installed at a slope more than 15 degrees from the vertical plane, including glazing materials in skylights, roofs and sloped walls. For monolithic glazing systems the glazing material shall be laminated glass with a minimum 30-mil polyvinyl butyral (or equivalent) interlayer, wired glass, light-transmitting plastic materials, heat-strengthened glass or fully tempered glass.*

Discussion and Commentary: The provisions for skylights are intended to protect such glazed openings from flying firebrands, to provide adequate strength to carry the load normally attributed to roofs and to protect the occupants of a building from falling glazing materials.

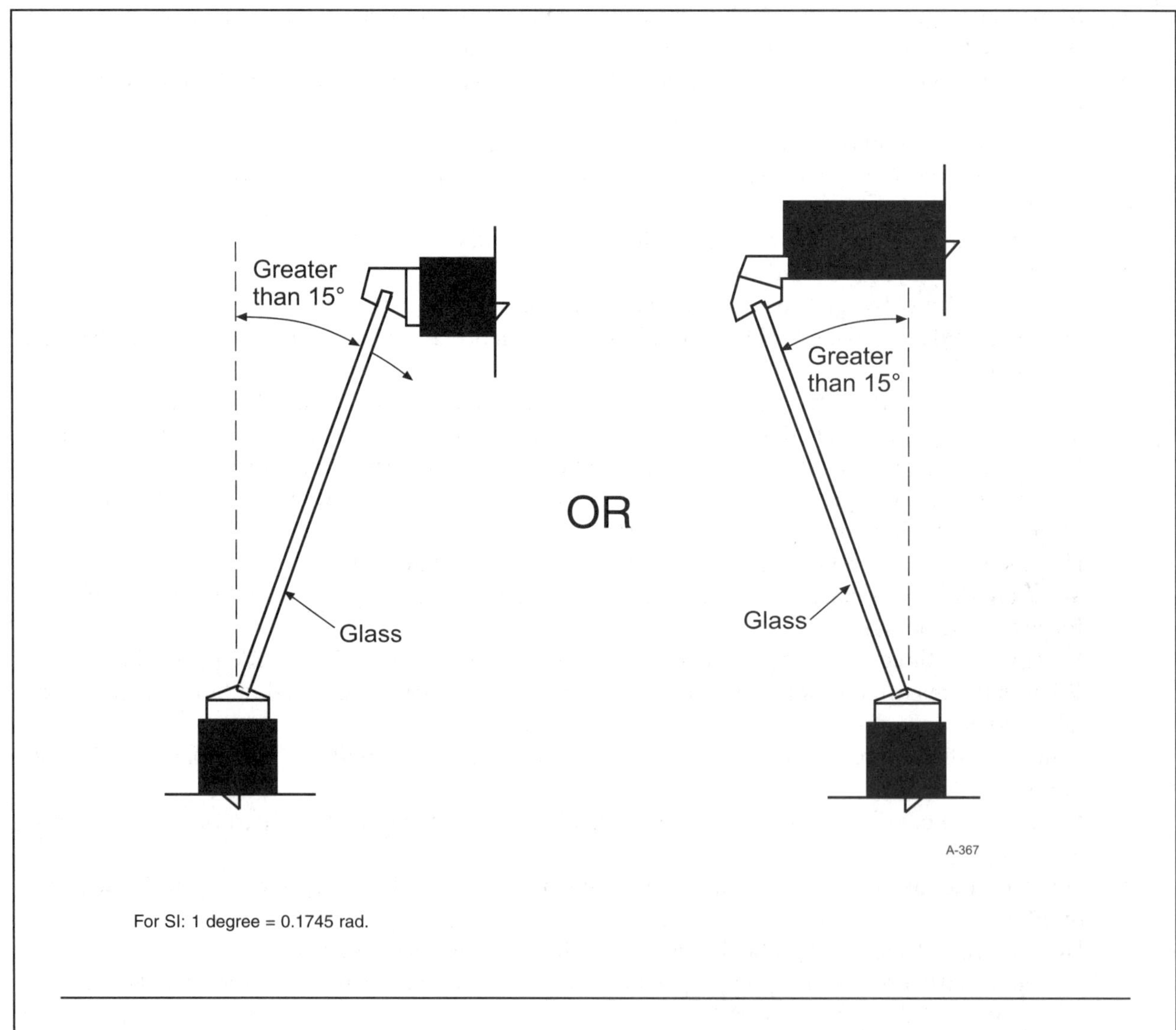

Annealed glass is limited to those areas where the walking surface below is isolated or protected from the risk of falling glass, or to specified greenhouses. Multiple-layer glazing systems must be glazed with only those materials permitted for single-layer glazing systems.

Topic: Screening
Reference: IBC 2405.3

Category: Glass and Glazing
Subject: Sloped Glazing and Skylights

Code Text: *Where used in monolithic glazing systems, heat-strengthened glass and fully tempered glass shall have screens installed below the glazing material.* See exceptions. *The screens and their fastenings shall: (1) be capable of supporting twice the weight of the glazing; (2) be firmly and substantially fastened to the framing members; and (3) be installed within 4 inches of the glass.*

Discussion and Commentary: Heat-strengthened glass has the undesirable characteristic of breaking into shards, whereas tempered glass has been shown to break spontaneously such that large chunks of glass may fall unexpectedly. Thus, these two types of glass require screen protection below the skylight to protect the occupants below.

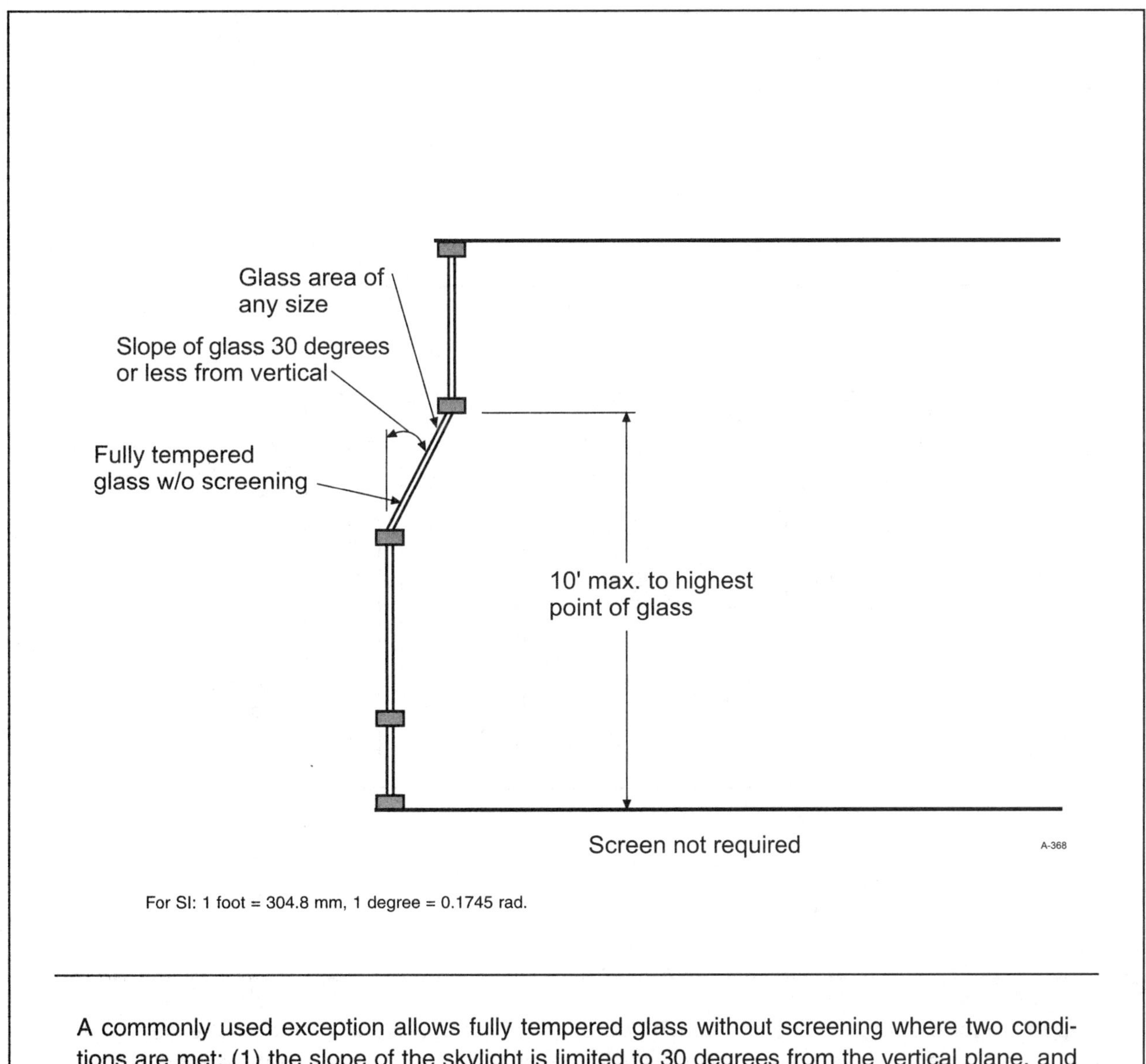

A commonly used exception allows fully tempered glass without screening where two conditions are met: (1) the slope of the skylight is limited to 30 degrees from the vertical plane, and (2) the highest point of the glass is no more than 10 feet above the walking surface.

Topic: Identification
Reference: IBC 2406.2

Category: Glass and Glazing
Subject: Safety Glazing

Code Text: *Except as indicated in Section 2406.1.2, each pane of safety glazing installed in hazardous locations shall be identified by a label specifying the labeler, whether the manufacturer or installer, and the safety glazing standard with which it complies, as well as the information specified in Section 2403.1. The label shall be acid etched, sand blasted, ceramic fired, or an embossed mark, or shall be of a type that once applied cannot be removed without being destroyed.* See exceptions for certifications of compliance and tempered spandrel glass.

Discussion and Commentary: Improper glazing installed in areas subject to human impact can create a serious hazard. Accordingly, it is critical that glazing in such locations be appropriately identified to ensure that the proper glazing is in place.

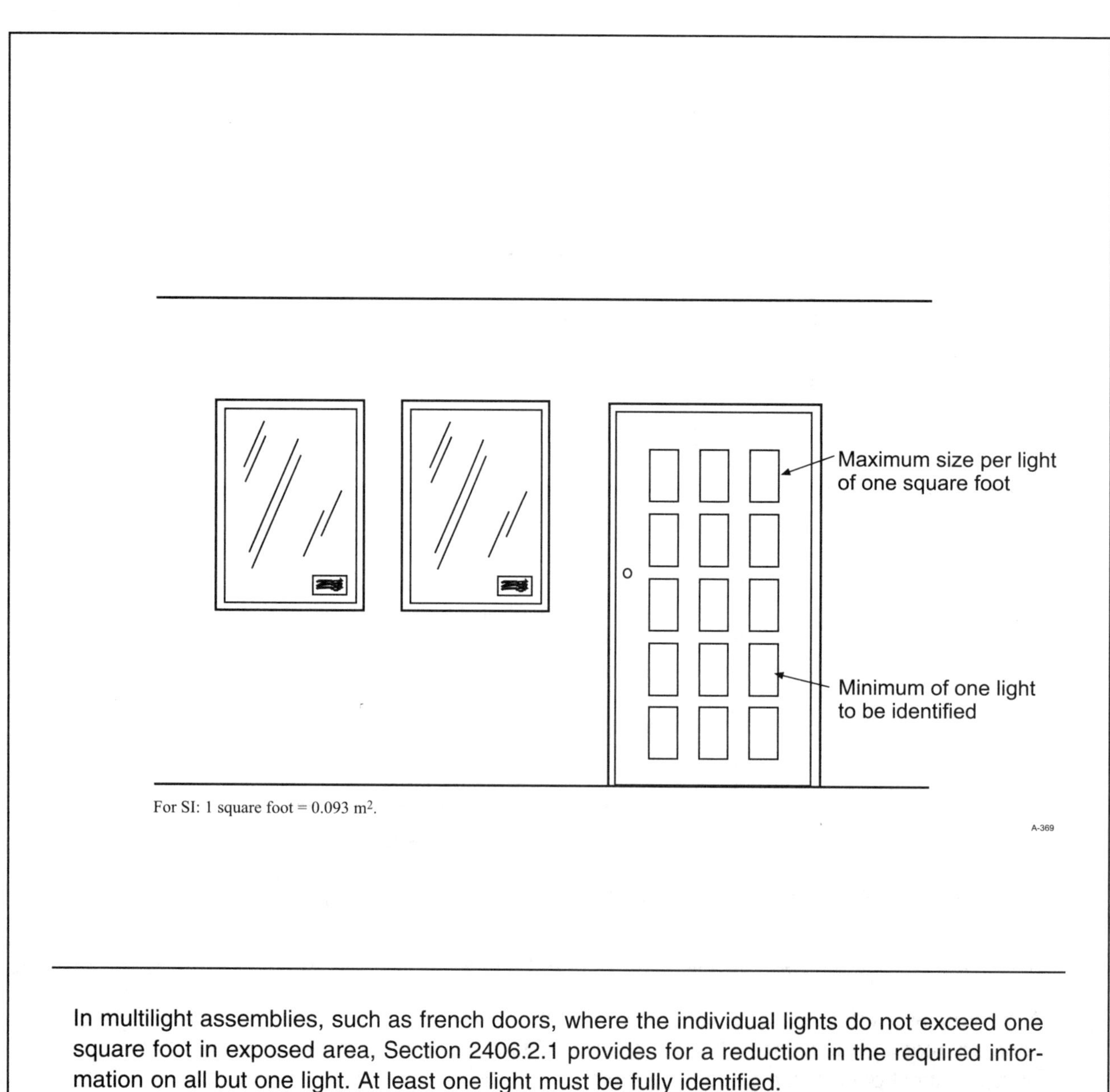

In multilight assemblies, such as french doors, where the individual lights do not exceed one square foot in exposed area, Section 2406.2.1 provides for a reduction in the required information on all but one light. At least one light must be fully identified.

Topic: Glazing in Doors
Reference: IBC 2406.3, #1-4

Category: Glass and Glazing
Subject: Hazardous Locations

Code Text: *The following shall be considered specific hazardous locations requiring safety glazing materials: (1) glazing in swinging doors except jalousies, (2) glazing in fixed and sliding panels of sliding door assemblies and panels in sliding and bifold closet door assemblies, (3) glazing in storm doors, and (4) glazing in unframed swinging doors. Collectively, Items 1 through 4 can be summarized by saying that any door containing glazing must be glazed with safety glass or other safety glazing material recognized by the code for that intended purpose.*

Discussion and Commentary: Glazing in doors is of particular concern due to the increased likelihood of accidental impact by individuals operating or opening the doors. In addition, a person may push against a glazed portion of the door to gain leverage in pushing it open. Therefore, it is important that only safety glazing materials be used for glazing in doors.

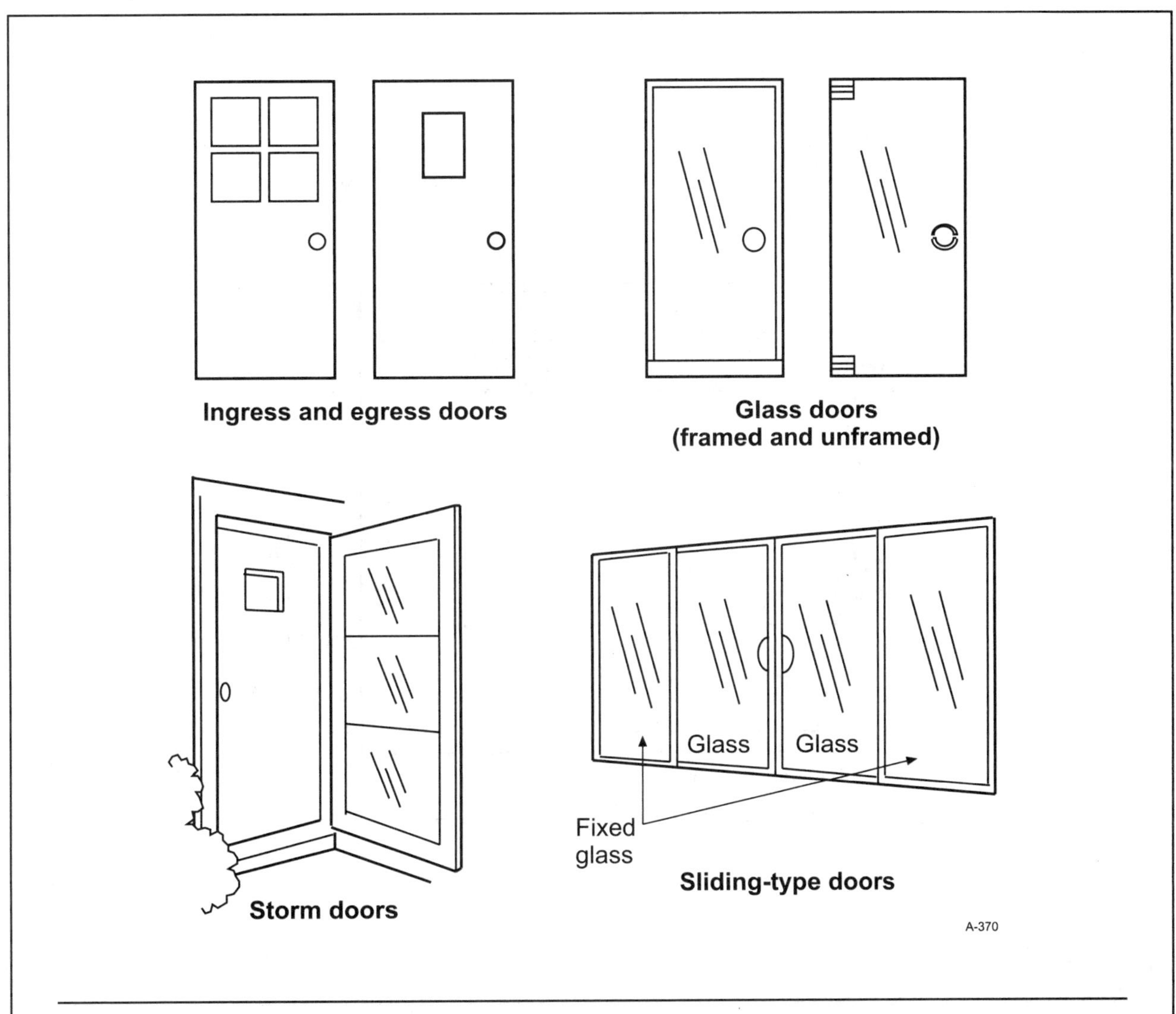

There are a limited number of products and applications that are exempt from the requirements for hazardous locations, including small openings in doors through which a 3-inch-diameter sphere will not pass, and specific decorative assemblies, such as leaded, faceted or carved glass.

Topic: Glazing in Tub and Shower Areas
Reference: IBC 2406.3, #5

Category: Glass and Glazing
Subject: Hazardous Locations

Code Text: *The following shall be considered specific hazardous locations requiring safety glazing materials: (5) glazing in doors and enclosures for hot tubs, whirlpools, saunas, steam rooms, bathtubs and showers. Glazing in any portion of a building wall enclosing these compartments where the bottom exposed edge of the glazing is less than 60 inches (1524 mm) above a standing surface.*

Discussion and Commentary: Because the standing surfaces of bathtubs, showers, hot tubs and similar elements are wet and slippery, glazing adjacent to these elements must be regulated due to the potential for human impact. It is not uncommon for the user to slip while trying to enter or exit. Safety glazing is mandated where any of the glazing within the enclosed area extends to within 60 inches vertically of the standing surface.

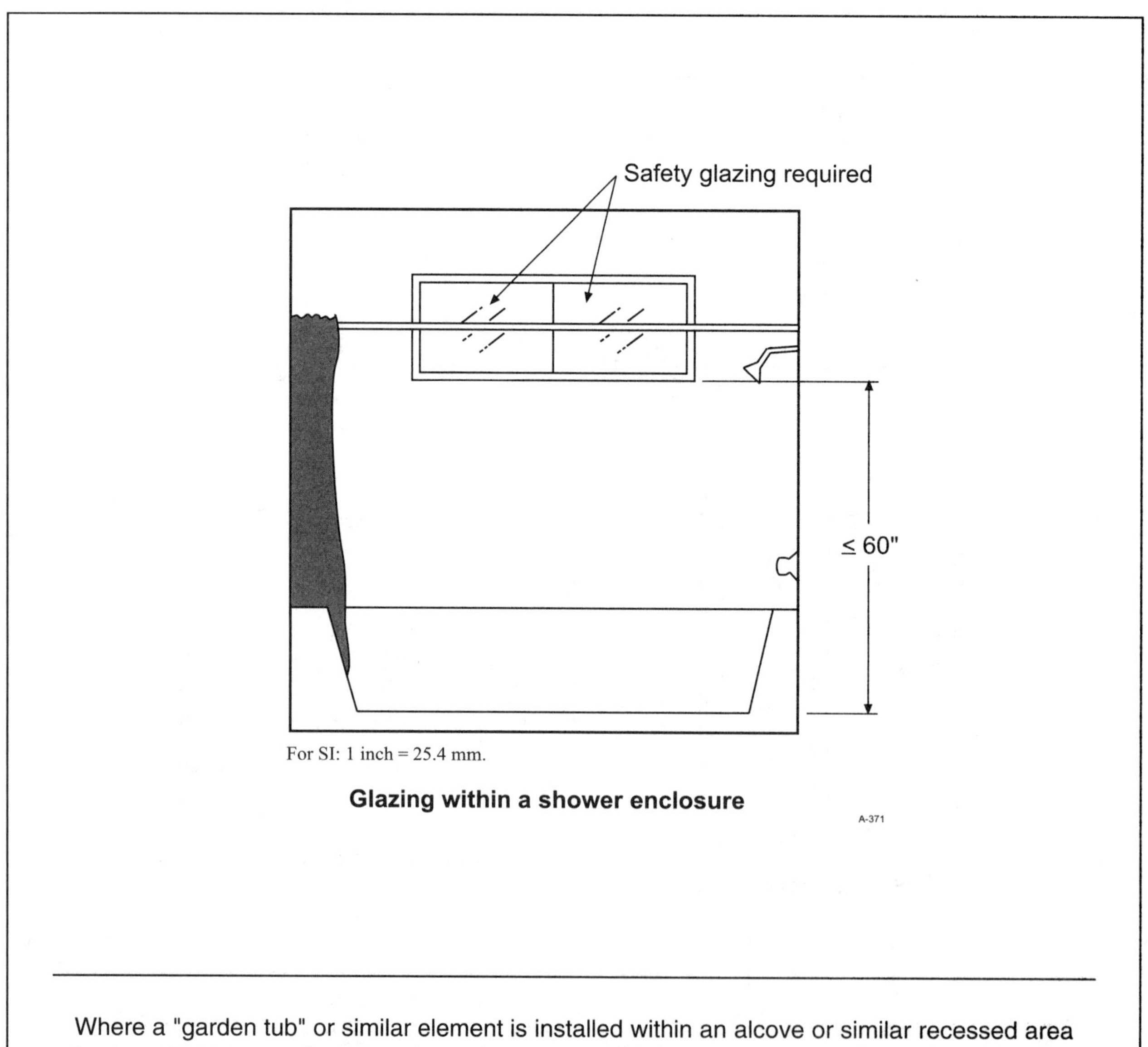

For SI: 1 inch = 25.4 mm.

Glazing within a shower enclosure

Where a "garden tub" or similar element is installed within an alcove or similar recessed area having windows or other glazed openings, the glazing in the walls of the alcove are considered a portion of the enclosure and are thus regulated.

Topic Glazing Adjacent to Doors
Reference: IBC 2406.3, #6

Category: Glass and Glazing
Subject: Hazardous Locations

Code Text: *The following shall be considered specific hazardous locations requiring safety glazing materials: (6) glazing in an individual fixed or operable panel adjacent to a door where the nearest exposed edge of the glazing is within a 24-inch arc of either vertical edge of the door in a closed position and where the bottom exposed edge of the glazing is less than 60 inches above the walking surface. See three exceptions where safety glazing is not mandated.*

Discussion and Commentary: When an individual approaches a doorway, areas adjacent to the door pose a risk when glazing is within 60 inches vertically of the walking surface. A person may slip or mistake the glass panel adjacent to a door for a passageway and walk into the glass, or a person may push against the sidelight with one hand for support while opening the door with the other hand. Therefore, safety glazing is required for any glazed opening located within 24 inches horizontally of the vertical edge of the door.

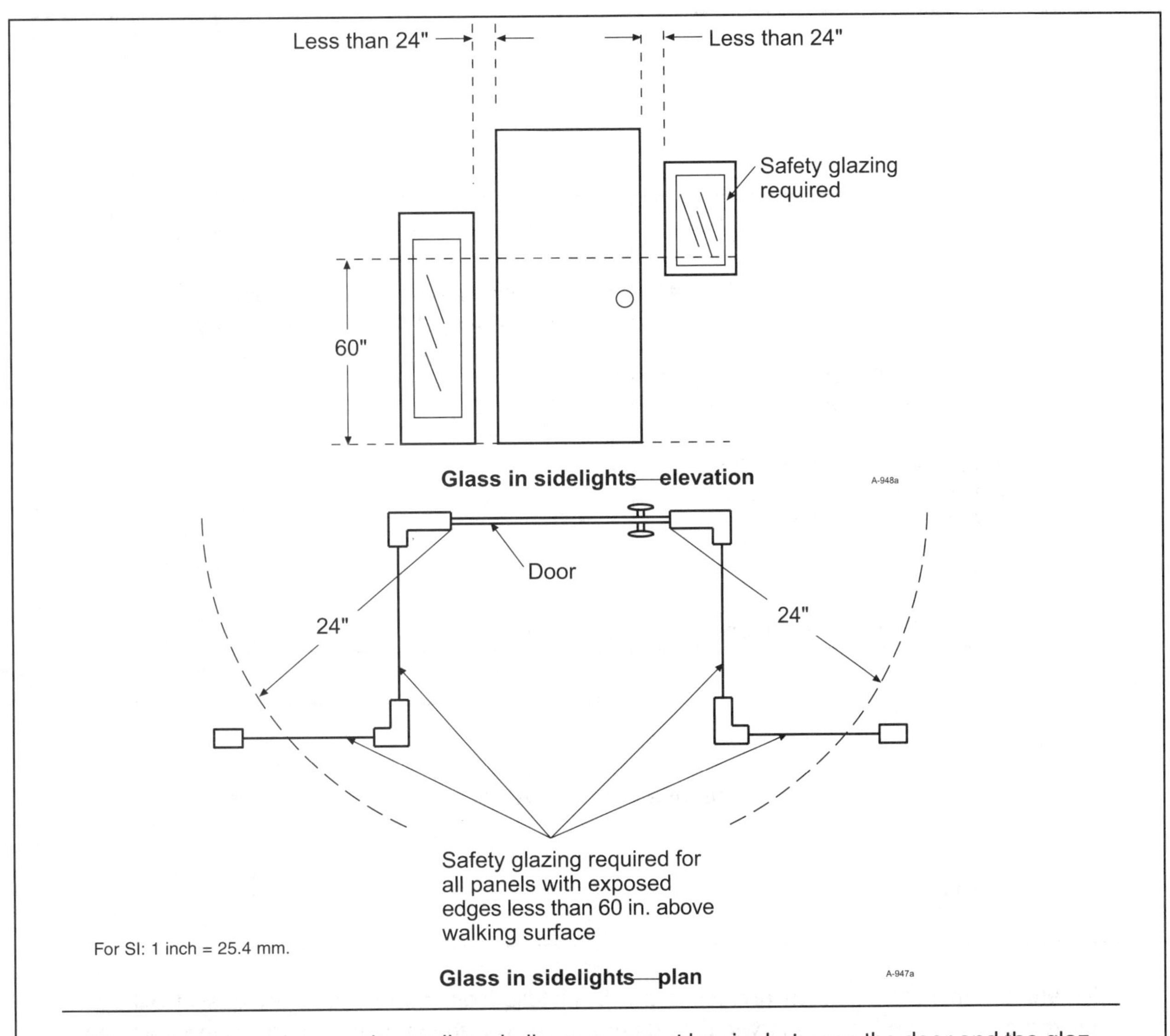

Glass in sidelights—elevation

Glass in sidelights—plan

Where there is an intervening wall or similar permanent barrier between the door and the glazing, or where access through the door is to a closet or similar storage area of limited depth, safety glazing is not required, as the potential for contact is greatly reduced.

Topic: Glazing in Fixed or Operable Panels
Reference: IBC 2406.3, #7

Category: Glass and Glazing
Subject: Hazardous Locations

Code Text: *The following shall be considered specific hazardous locations requiring safety glazing materials: (7) glazing in a fixed or operable panel, other than in those locations described in preceding Items 5 and 6, which meets all of the following conditions: (7.1) exposed area of an individual pane greater than 9 square feet, (7.2) exposed bottom edge less than 18 inches above the floor, (7.3) exposed top edge greater than 36 inches above the floor, and (7.4) one or more walking surface(s) within 36 inches horizontally of the plane of the glazing.*

Discussion and Commentary: Large pieces of glass create a hazard where located close to a travel path because it is possible to impact glazing where no obstacle or barrier is provided as an alternative impact area. Expansive glazing may also be mistaken for a clear opening in the wall.

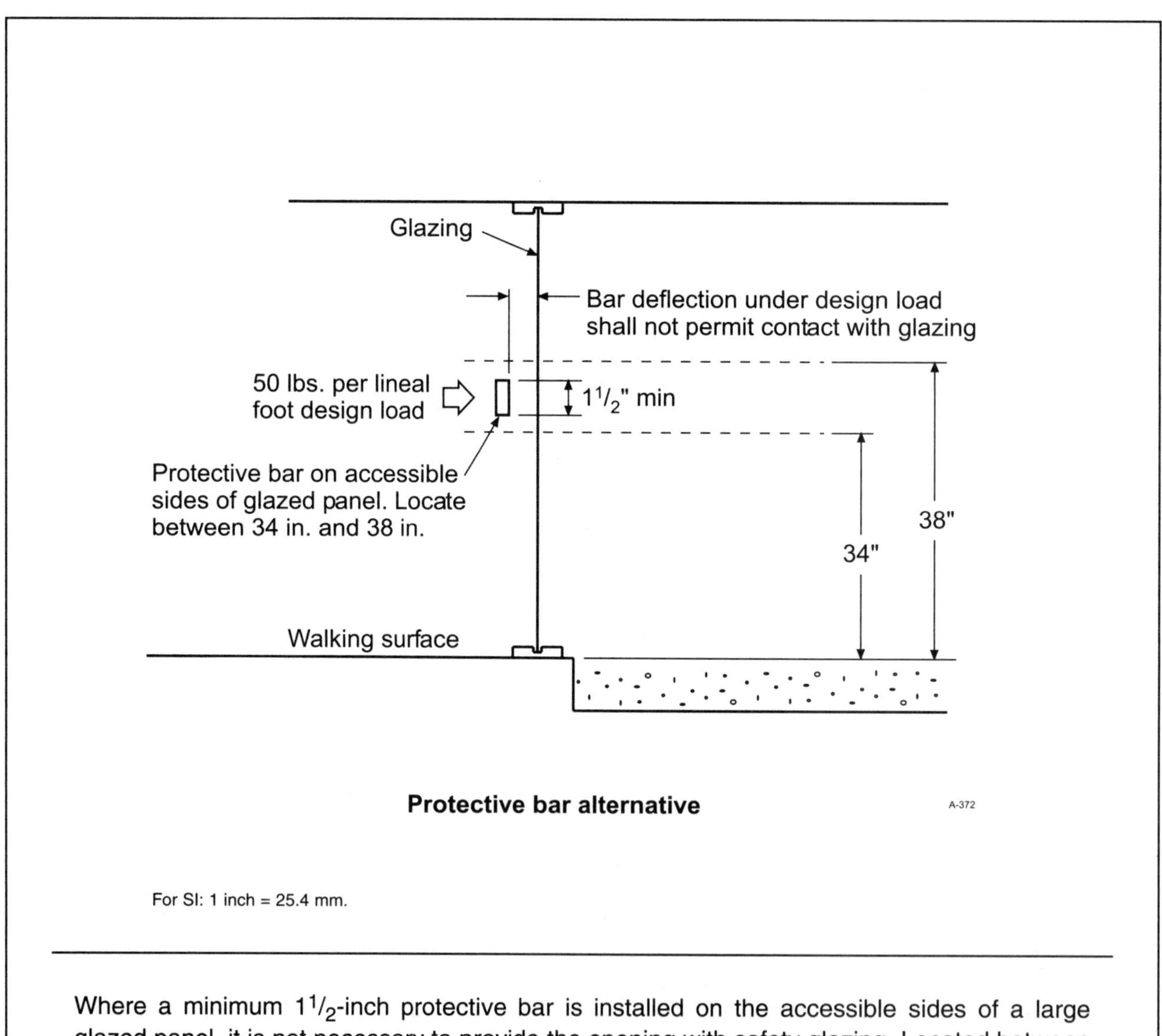

Protective bar alternative

For SI: 1 inch = 25.4 mm.

Where a minimum $1^1/_2$-inch protective bar is installed on the accessible sides of a large glazed panel, it is not necessary to provide the opening with safety glazing. Located between 34 inches and 38 inches above the floor, the bar must be capable of withstanding a 50 plf horizontal load.

Topic: Glazing in Guards or Railings
Reference: IBC 2406.3, #8

Category: Glass and Glazing
Subject: Hazardous Locations

Code Text: *The following shall be considered specific hazardous locations requiring safety glazing materials: (8) glazing in guards and railings, including structural baluster panels and nonstructural in-fill panels, regardless of area or height above a walking surface.*

Discussion and Commentary: Both intentional and unintentional contact with guards and railings are expected to occur; therefore, the IBC mandates that glazing used in such applications always be safety glazing. Safety glazing is required when the glazed infill panel is nonstructural and is supported by a structural frame system. Occasionally, glazing is used as a structural guard rail system without any other means of support. In this case, the glazing is required to be safety glazing.

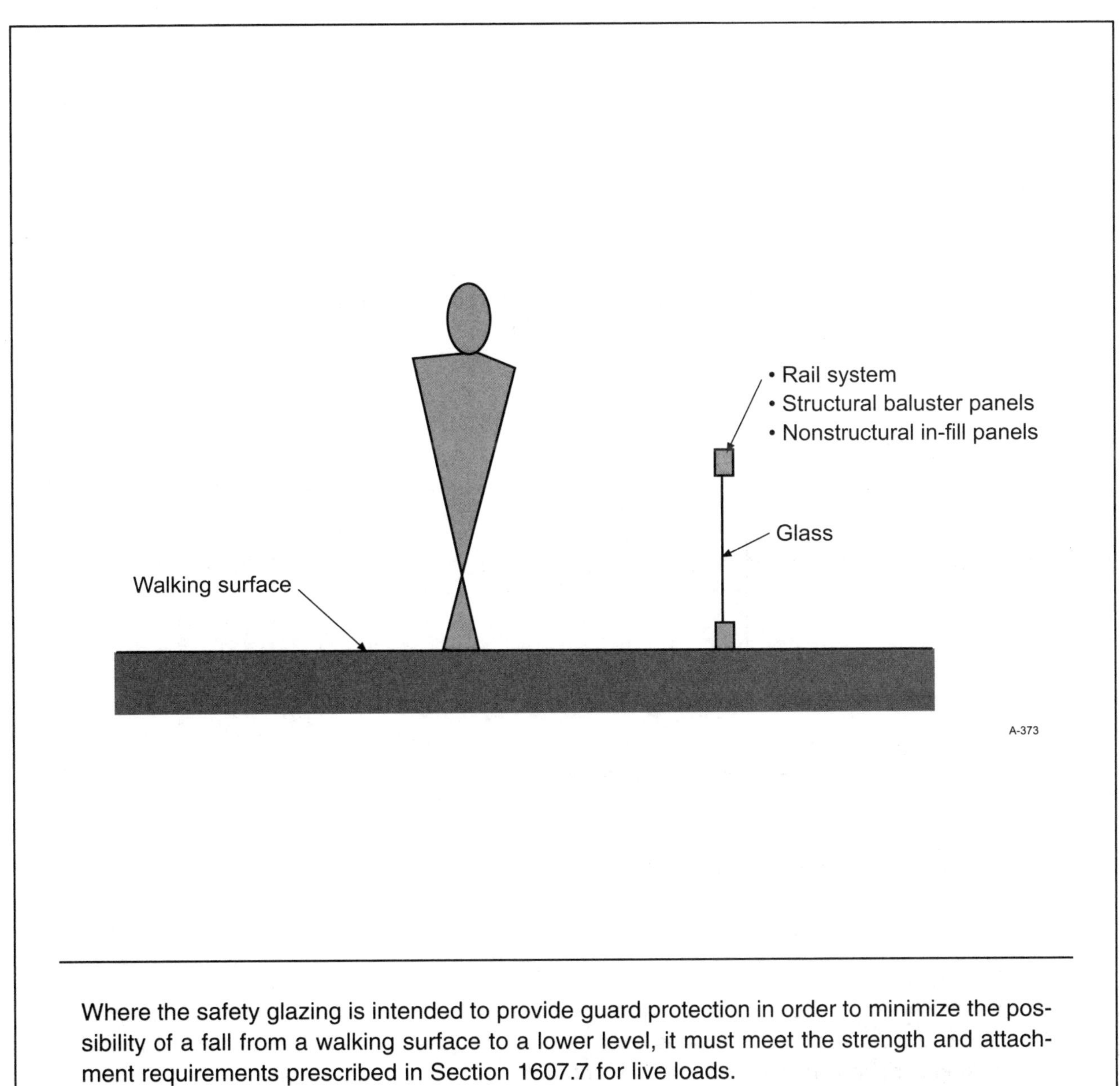

Where the safety glazing is intended to provide guard protection in order to minimize the possibility of a fall from a walking surface to a lower level, it must meet the strength and attachment requirements prescribed in Section 1607.7 for live loads.

Topic: Glazing in Pool Enclosures
Reference: IBC 2406.3, #9

Category: Glass and Glazing
Subject: Hazardous Locations

Code Text: *The following shall be considered specific hazardous locations requiring safety glazing materials: (9) glazing in walls and fences enclosing indoor and outdoor swimming pools, hot tubs and spas where all of the following conditions are present: (9.1) the bottom edge of the glazing on the pool or spa side is less than 60 inches above a walking surface on the pool or spa side of the glazing, and (9.2) the glazing is within 60 inches horizontally of the water's edge of a swimming pool or spa.*

Discussion and Commentary: The deck or similar area adjacent to a swimming pool or spa is often wet when the pool or spa is in use. The walking surface typically becomes slippery and causes a considerable number of slips and falls. It is important that any adjacent glazed area that is susceptible to human impact be provided with safety glazing.

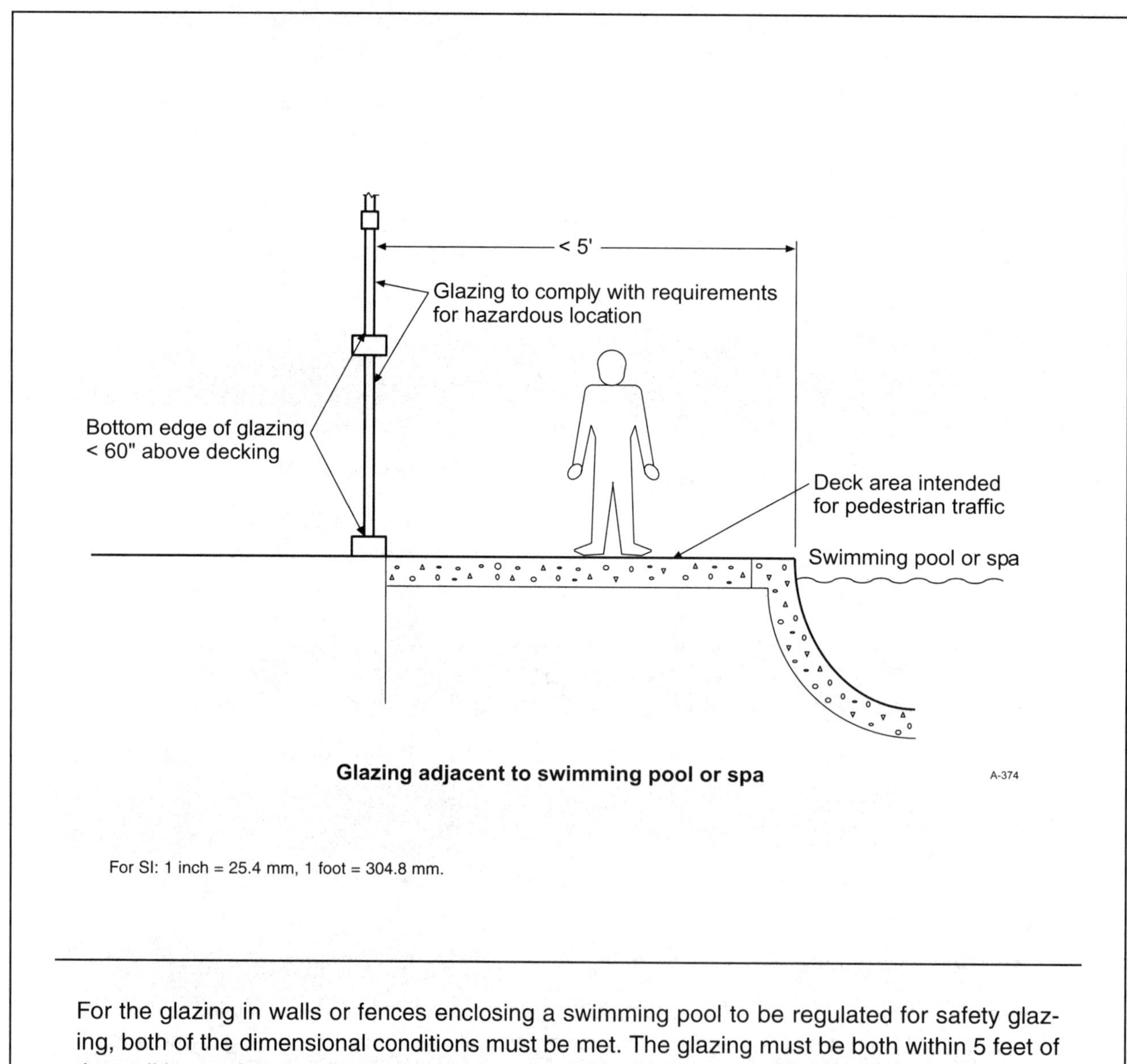

Glazing adjacent to swimming pool or spa

For SI: 1 inch = 25.4 mm, 1 foot = 304.8 mm.

For the glazing in walls or fences enclosing a swimming pool to be regulated for safety glazing, both of the dimensional conditions must be met. The glazing must be both within 5 feet of the walking surface vertically and within 5 feet of the pool or spa edge horizontally.

Topic: Glazing Adjacent to Stairways
Reference: IBC 2406.3, #10

Category: Glass and Glazing
Subject: Hazardous Locations

Code Text: *The following shall be considered specific hazardous locations requiring safety glazing materials: (10) glazing adjacent to stairways, landings and ramps within 36 inches (914 mm) horizontally of a walking surface; when the exposed surface of the glass is less than 60 inches (1524 mm) above the plane of the adjacent walking surface.* See exception where safety glazing is not required.

Discussion and Commentary: Stairways and ramps present users with a greater risk for injury caused by falling than does a flat surface. Not only is the risk of falling greater when using a stair, but the injuries are generally more severe. Unlike falling on a flat surface where the floor will break a person's fall, there is nothing to stop someone from continuing to fall until he or she reaches the bottom of the stair.

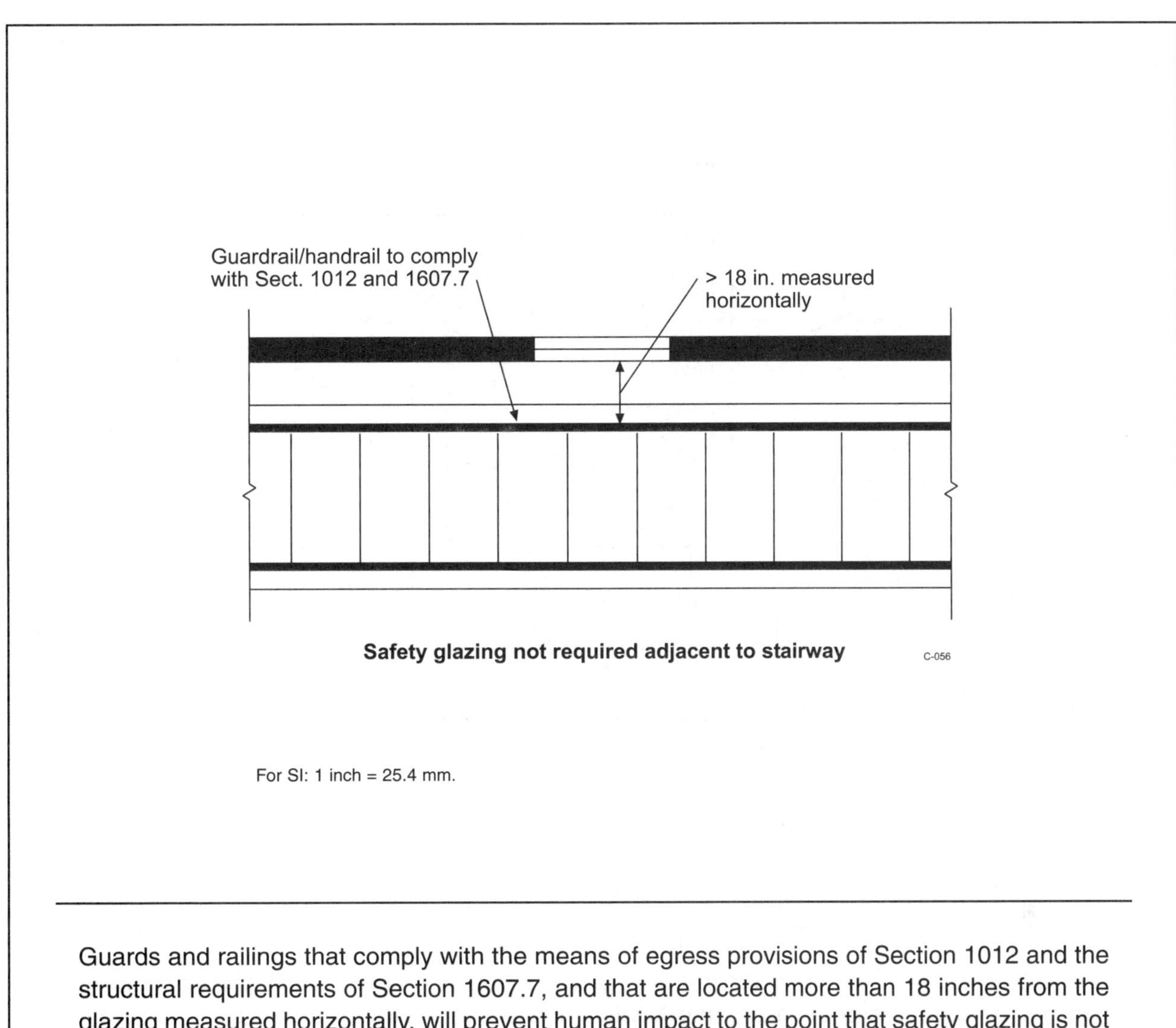

Safety glazing not required adjacent to stairway

Guards and railings that comply with the means of egress provisions of Section 1012 and the structural requirements of Section 1607.7, and that are located more than 18 inches from the glazing measured horizontally, will prevent human impact to the point that safety glazing is not required.

Topic: Glazing Adjacent to Stairways
Reference: IBC 2406.3, #11

Category: Glass and Glazing
Subject: Hazardous Locations

Code Text: *The following shall be considered specific hazardous locations requiring safety glazing materials: (11) glazing adjacent to stairways within 60 inches (1524 mm) horizontally of the bottom tread of a stairway in any direction when the exposed surface of the glass is less than 60 inches (1524 mm) above the nose of the tread.* See exception where safety glazing is not required.

Discussion and Commentary: Historically, stairways have been considered one of the most dangerous elements of a building. Missteps and falls on stairways are quite common; therefore, it is important that any glazing that may be impacted is made of safety glazing materials. Where a complying guard rail or handrail is provided and the glazing is located a sufficient distance from the railing, safety glazing is not mandated.

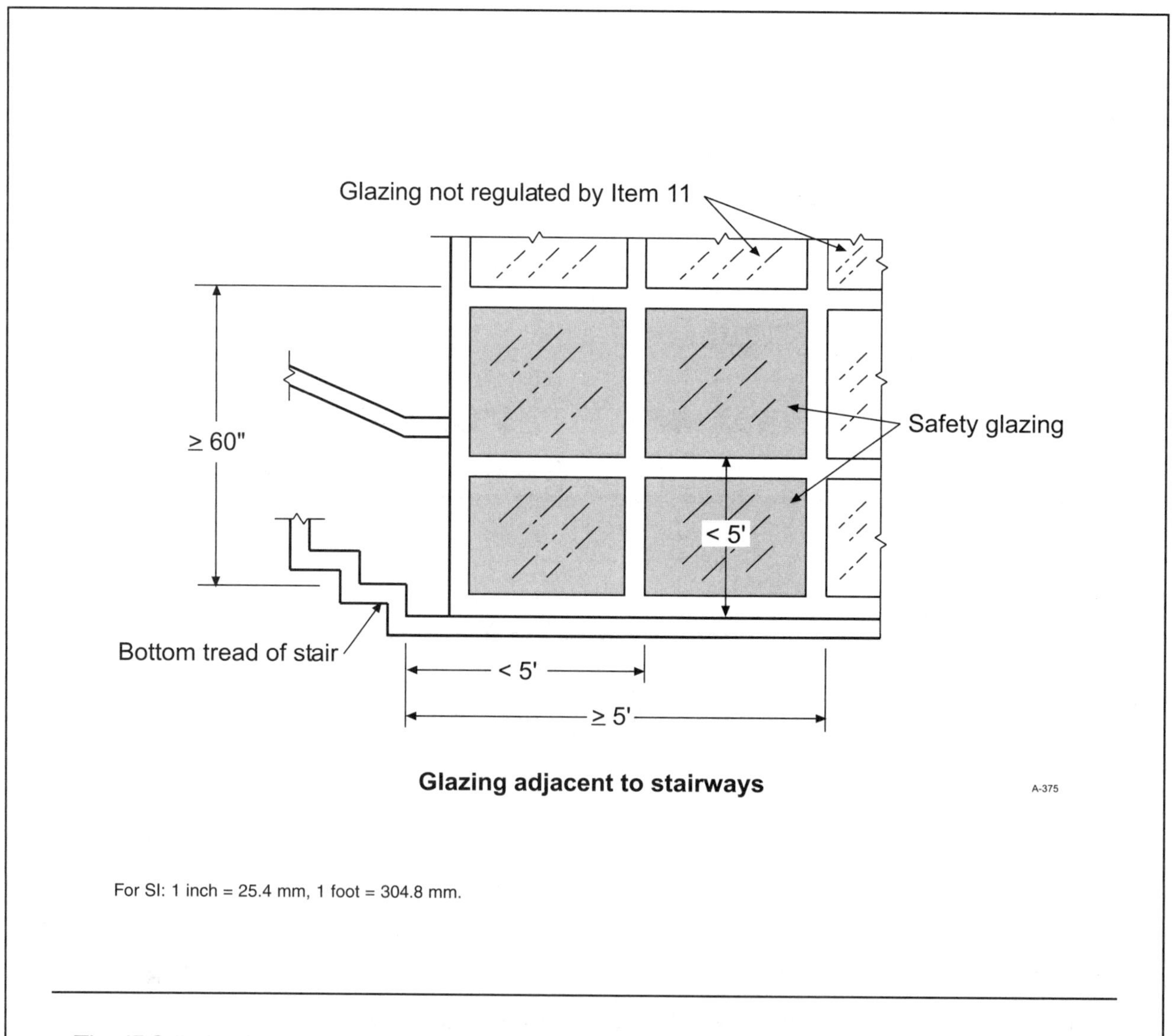

Glazing adjacent to stairways

For SI: 1 inch = 25.4 mm, 1 foot = 304.8 mm.

The IBC limits the area of concern in this item to the bottom of a stair flight and its adjacent landing. As with most of the hazardous location provisions, glazing that is located at least 60 inches vertically above the walking surface is not considered an impact risk.

Topic: Scope and Definition
Reference: IBC 2602, 2603

Category: Plastic
Subject: Foam Plastic Insulation

Code Text: *The provisions of Section 2603 shall govern the requirements and uses of foam plastic insulation in buildings and structures. Foam plastic insulation is a plastic that is intentionally expanded by the use of a foaming agent to produce a reduced-density plastic containing voids consisting of open or closed cells distributed throughout the plastic for thermal insulating or acoustical purposes and that has a density less than 20 pounds per cubic foot.*

Discussion and Commentary: Two basic concepts address the hazards created when foam plastic is exposed to fire conditions: (1) limitation of flame spread and smoke development, and (2) separation from the interior of the building by an approved thermal barrier.

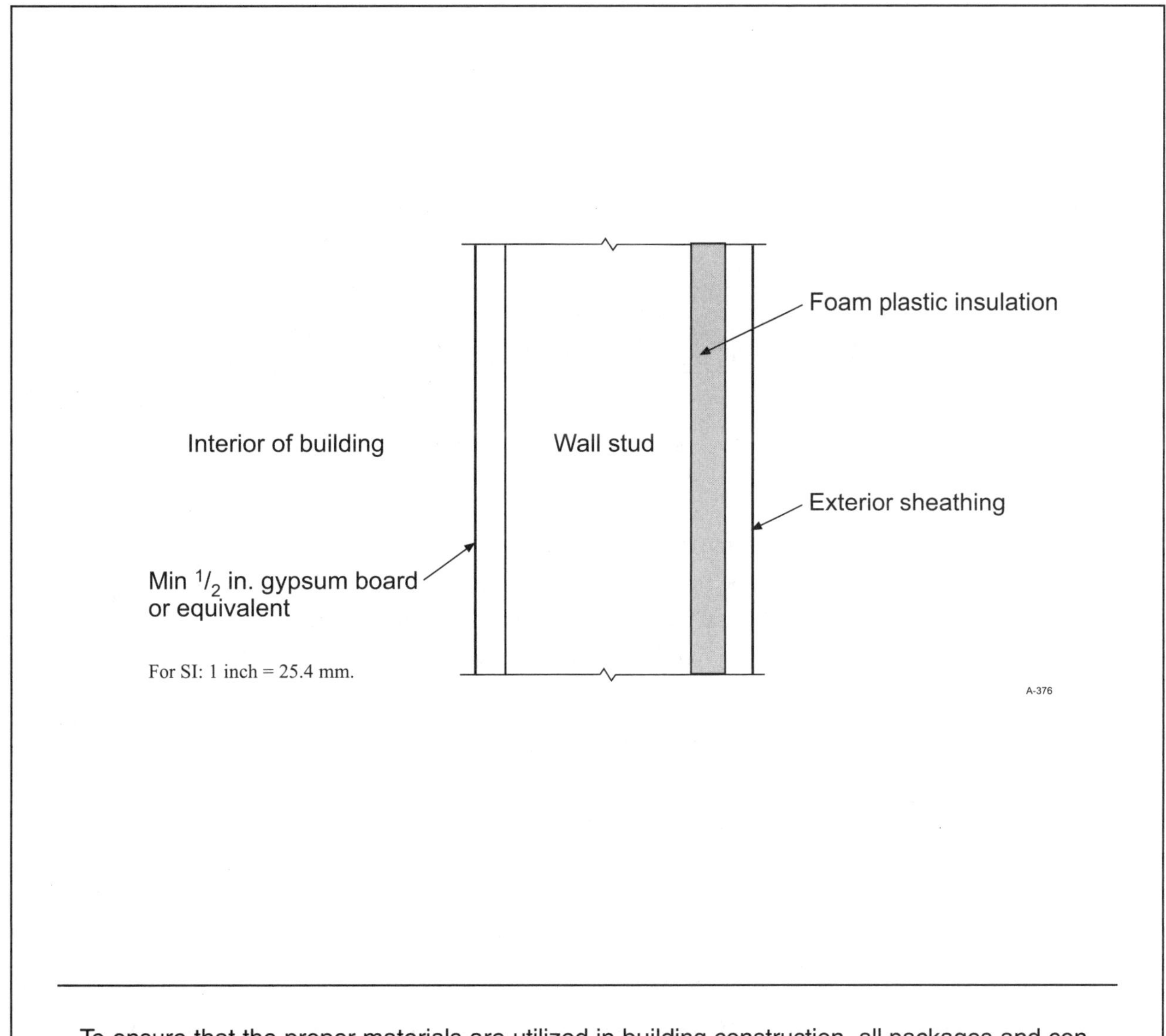

To ensure that the proper materials are utilized in building construction, all packages and containers of foam plastic insulation must be properly identified. Such identification must include information to show that the final use of the product complies with the code requirements.

Topic: Thermal Barrier
Reference: IBC 2603.4

Category: Plastic
Subject: Foam Plastic Insulation

Code Text: *Except as provided for in Sections 2603.4.1 and 2603.8, foam plastic shall be separated from the interior of a building by an approved thermal barrier of 0.5 inch gypsum wallboard or equivalent thermal barrier material that will limit the average temperature rise of the unexposed surface to not more than 250 degrees F. after 15 minutes of fire exposure, complying with the standard time-temperature curve of ASTM E 119. The thermal barrier shall be installed in such a manner that it will remain in place for 15 minutes.*

Discussion and Commentary: A barrier is mandated to provide a minimum degree of protection between foam plastic materials and a building's occupants. Any type of separation equivalent to that provided by $^{1}/_{2}$-inch gypsum board is considered acceptable.

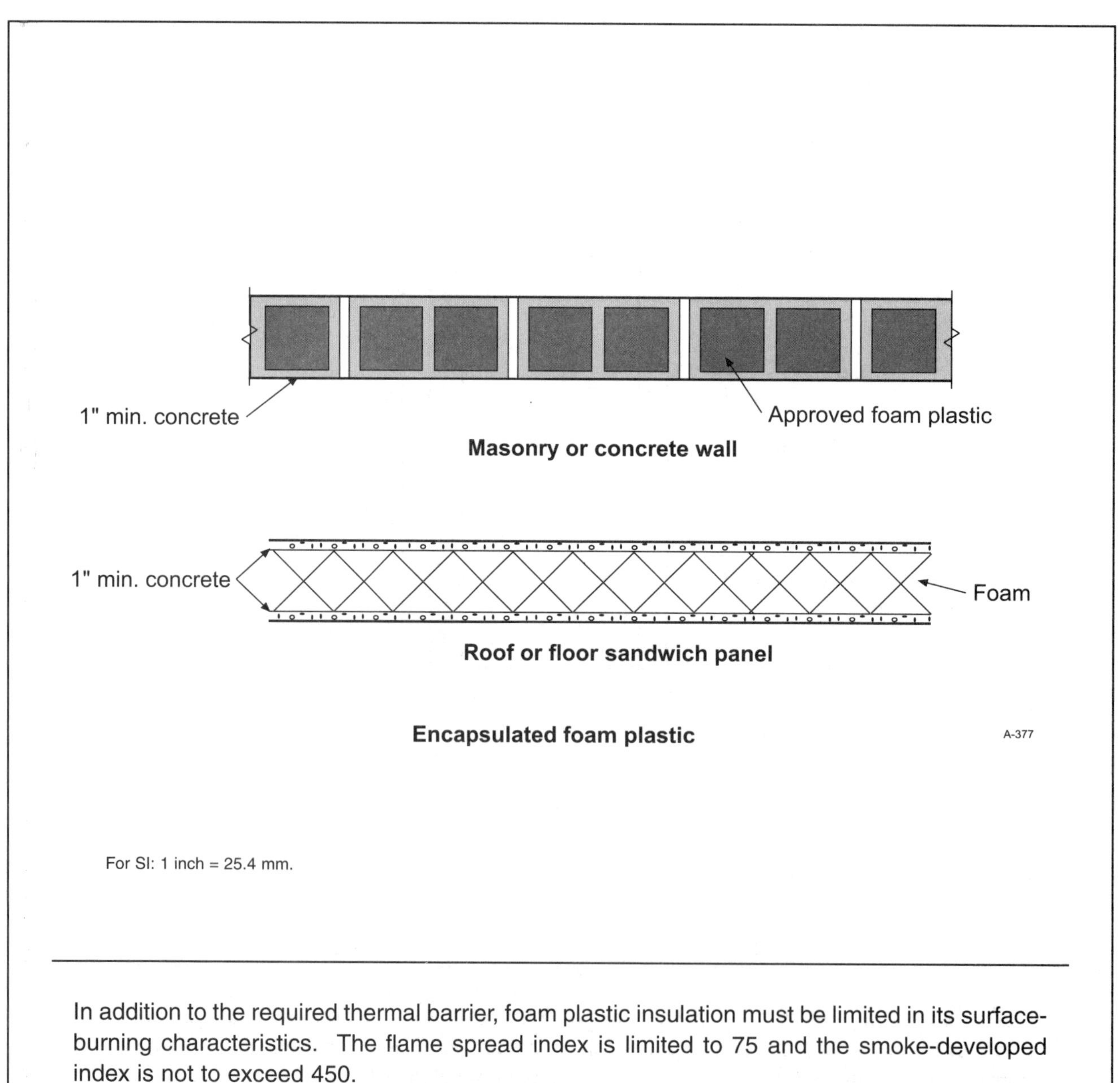

In addition to the required thermal barrier, foam plastic insulation must be limited in its surface-burning characteristics. The flame spread index is limited to 75 and the smoke-developed index is not to exceed 450.

Topic: Interior Finish and Trim
Reference: IBC 2604.2

Category: Plastic
Subject: Foam Plastic

Code Text: *For foam plastics used as interior trim: (1) the minimum density of the interior trim shall be 20 pounds per cubic foot, (2) the maximum thickness of the interior trim shall be 0.5 inch and the maximum width shall be 8 inches, (3) the interior trim shall not constitute more than 10 percent of the aggregate wall and ceiling area of any room or space, and (4) the flame spread index shall not exceed 75 where tested in accordance with ASTM E 84. The smoke-developed index shall not be limited.*

Discussion and Commentary: The general provisions regulating the use of decorations and trim in buildings are found in Section 805. They include plastics materials, other than foam plastics, used as interior trim. All foam plastic trim must comply with the provisions of Section 2604.2.

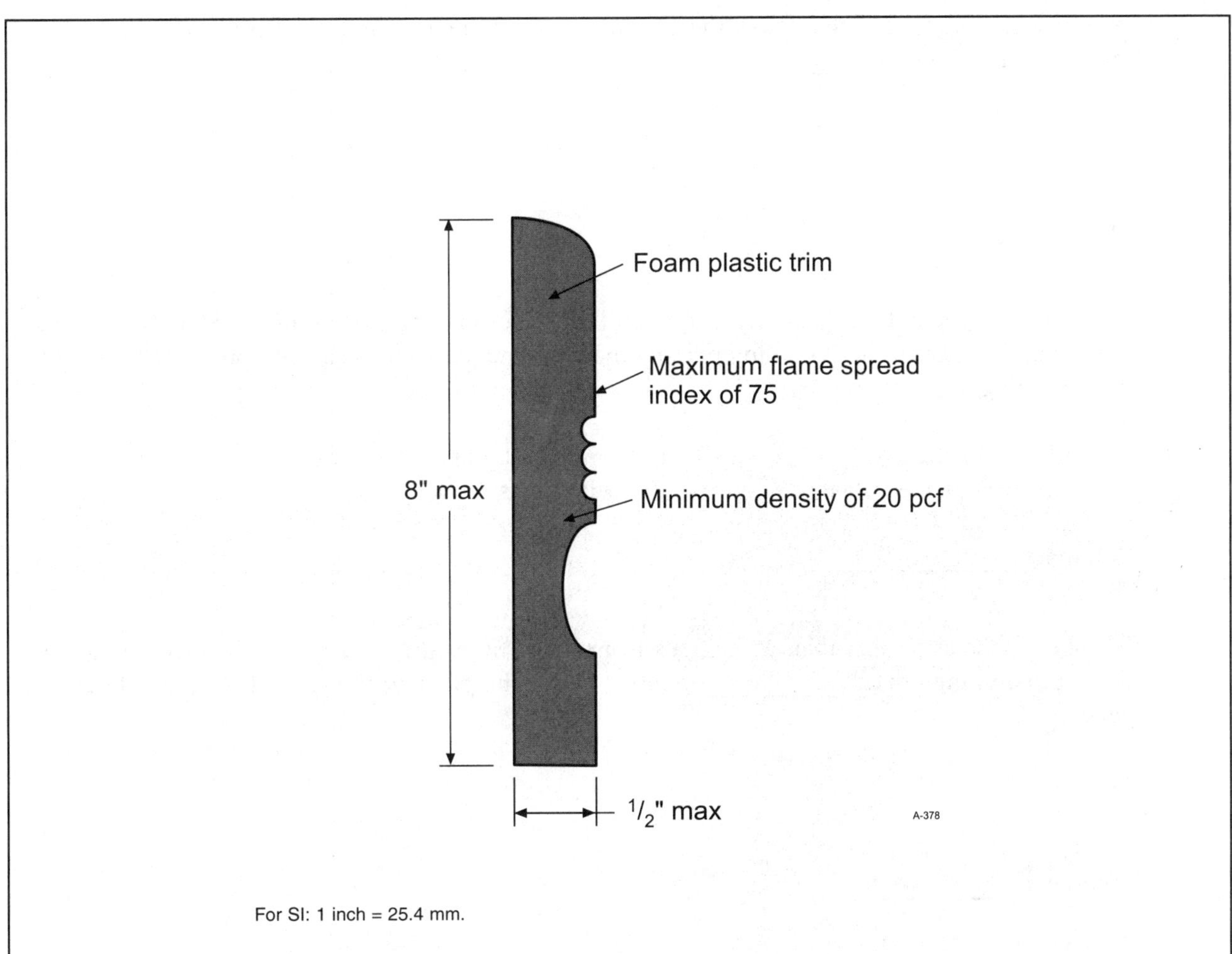

The use of foam plastics as interior finish is limited to applications that comply with Section 2603.8. This provision allows special approval based on the use of large-scale tests. Foam plastic finishes accepted by testing must also conform to Chapter 8 flame spread requirements.

QUIZ

Study Session 18 — Chapters 24 and 26

I. Multiple Choice

1. Wired glass in louvered windows and jalousies shall have a minimum thickness of __________ inch.

a. $^3/_{16}$
b. $^1/_4$
c. $^5/_{16}$
d. $^3/_8$

Reference_______________

2. Where screening is required below the glazing material in a skylight, the screen shall be installed a maximum of __________ inch(es) below the glass.

a. 1
b. 3
c. 4
d. 6

Reference_______________

3. When used as the bottom glass layer in a multiple-layer glazing system installed above a walking surface, which of the following glazing materials never needs to be equipped with complying screening?

a. fully tempered glass
b. laminated glass
c. heat-strengthened glass
d. wired glass

Reference_______________

4. When set at an angle less than 45 degrees from the horizontal plane, a skylight shall be mounted on a curb a minimum of __________ inch(es) above the plane of the roof of a Group B occupancy.

a. 1
b. 2
c. 3
d. 4

Reference_______________

5. Class I safety glazing with a maximum size of __________ per light is permitted in doors.

a. 0 square inches (not permitted of any size)
b. 100 square inches
c. 144 square inches
d. 9 square feet

Reference_______________

6. Which one of the following types of safety glazing materials cannot be identified by a certificate or affidavit?

a. tempered glass
b. wired
c. laminated glass
d. plastic glazing

Reference_______________

7. Glazing within a shower enclosure shall be safety glazing where the bottom exposed edge of the glazing is within __________ inches above a standing surface.

a. 60
b. 66
c. 72
d. 78

Reference_______________

8. Where located less than 60 inches above the walking surface, glazing adjacent to a door within what horizontal distance of either vertical door edge must be safety glazing?

a. 12
b. 18
c. 24
d. 36

Reference_______________

9. When a protective bar is permitted as protection in lieu of safety glazing, the bar must be capable of withstanding a minimum horizontal load of __________ pounds per linear foot.

a. 15
b. 20
c. 40
d. 50

Reference_______________

10. Glazing in walls enclosing a swimming pool need not be safety glazing where located a minimum of __________ feet from the water's edge.

a. 5
b. 6
c. 8
d. 10

Reference_______________

11. Glazing adjacent to stairways does not need to be safety glazing where the plane of the glass is a minimum of __________ inches horizontally from the walking surface.

a. 12
b. 18
c. 24
d. 36

Reference_______________

12. Glazed openings in doors are not considered hazardous locations for glazing purposes, provided the openings will not allow passage of a __________-inch sphere.

a. 3 b. 4
c. 6 d. 9

Reference_______________

13. Fire department glass access panels shall be of __________ glass.

a. heat-strengthened b. tempered
c. laminated d. annealed

Reference_______________

14. Unless otherwise adequately supported, each handrail or guard section shall be supported by a minimum of __________ glass balusters.

a. 2 b. 3
c. 4 d. 6

Reference_______________

15. Foam plastic insulation shall have a density less than __________ pounds per cubic foot.

a. 2 b. 4
c. 10 d. 20

Reference_______________

16. __________ is considered to be a plastic material that is capable of being changed into a substantially nonreformable product when cured.

a. Approved plastic b. Glass fiber reinforced plastic
c. Thermoplastic material d. Thermosetting material

Reference_______________

17. Unless otherwise specified, foam plastic shall have a maximum flame spread index of __________ and a maximum smoke-developed index of __________ where tested in the maximum thickness intended for use.

a. 25, 200 b. 25, 450
c. 50, 200 d. 75, 450

Reference_______________

18. What material is specifically identified as an approved thermal barrier for separating foam plastic from the interior of a building?

a. $^1/_2$-inch gypsum wallboard
b. $^3/_8$-inch Type "x" gypsum wallboard
c. $^3/_8$-inch gypsum sheathing
d. $^1/_2$-inch wood structural panel

Reference_______________

19. Within a concrete floor system, all foam plastic insulation shall be covered on each face by a minimum of a __________-inch thickness of concrete.

a. $^1/_2$
b. 1
c. $1^1/_2$
d. 2

Reference_______________

20. The maximum thickness of foam plastic interior trim shall be _________ inch(es), with a maximum width of _________ inches.

a. 4, 12
b. 2, 12
c. 1, 8
d. $^1/_2$, 8

Reference_______________

21. Plastic veneer may be attached to any exterior wall to a maximum height of _________ feet above grade.

a. 25
b. 35
c. 50
d. 75

Reference_______________

22. In a nonsprinklered Group **B** building, Class CC2 light-transmitting wall panels used in an exterior wall with a fire separation distance of 18 feet are limited to a maximum of _________ percent of the exterior wall.

a. 10
b. 15
c. 25
d. 50

Reference_______________

23. In a sprinklered building, what is the maximum height light-transmitting plastic glazing may be installed above grade level?

a. 35 feet
b. 55 feet
c. 75 feet
d. unlimited

Reference_______________

24. In which one of the following occupancies may light-transmitting plastic roof panels be installed?

a. Group A-1 b. Group H-1
c. Group I-2 d. Group I-3

Reference_______________

25. An interior wall sign of light-transmitting plastic is limited in size to __________ square feet.

a. 16 b. 24
c. 48 d. 100

Reference_______________

26. Glass in window walls sloped a maximum of _____ degrees from the vertical shall be designed to resist the required wind loads for components and cladding.

a. 15 b. 30
c. 45 d. 60

Reference_______________

27. For which of the following applications is the use of a removable paper label permitted for identifying tempered glass for safety glazing purposes?

a. storm doors b. spandrel panels
c. unframed swinging doors d. structural balustrade panels

Reference_______________

28. Only one individual light in a multilight glazed door assembly requires safety glazing identification where each light is a maximum of _____ in size.

a. 64 square inches b. 100 square inches
c. 1 square foot d. $1^1/_2$ square feet

Reference_______________

29. All glazing subject to human impact located in a(n) _____ shall comply with Category II of CPSC 16 CFR 1201.

a. school classroom b. detention facility
c. multipurpose gymnasium d. manufacturing building

Reference_______________

30. Foam plastic spray applied to a sill plate of Type V construction shall have a maximum thickness of _____.

a. 1 inch
b. $1^1/_2$ inches
c. 3 inches
d. $3^1/_4$ inches

Reference_______________

ANSWER KEY

Study Session 1

1.	c	Sec. 101.2, Exception 1
2.	c	Sec. 101.2.1
3.	b	Sec. 102.1
4.	a	Sec. 103.1
5.	d	Sec. 104.1
6.	a	Sec. 104.9.1
7.	b	Sec. 104.10
8.	b	Sec. 104.11
9.	c	Sec. 104.11.2
10.	b	Sec. 105.2, #1
11.	c	Sec. 105.2, #13
12.	b	Sec. 105.5
13.	a	Sec. 105.7
14.	d	Sec. 106.3.1
15.	b	Sec. 106.5
16.	c	Sec. 109.3
17.	a	Sec. 109.5
18.	d	Sec. 110.2
19.	d	Sec. 110.3
20.	b	Sec. 112.2
21.	b	Sec. 3403.2
22.	c	Sec. 3404.3
23.	a	Table 3409.7.5
24.	d	Sec. 3410.5
25.	a	Chapter 35
26.	b	Sec. 105.2, #9
27.	d	Sec. 105.2, #12
28.	d	Sec. 105.6
29.	b	Sec. 107.1
30.	c	Sec. 3410.2

Study Session 2

1.	c	Sec. 302.1, #6
2.	d	Sec. 302.1, #10
3.	a	Sec. 302.1.1
4.	c	Table 302.1.1
5.	d	Table 302.1.1
6.	d	Table 302.1.1
7.	d	Sec. 302.1.1.1
8.	c	Sec. 302.2
9.	a	Sec. 302.3.1
10.	c	Table 302.3.2
11.	c	Table 302.3.2
12.	c	Sec. 302.2.1
13.	a	Sec. 302.2.1
14.	d	Sec. 303.1
15.	a	Sec. 304.1
16.	b	Sec. 306.3
17.	c	Sec. 307.2
18.	b	Sec. 307.4
19.	c	Sec. 308.3.1
20.	d	Table 307.7(1)
21.	a	Sec. 308.2
22.	c	Sec. 309.1, 304.1
23.	b	Sec. 310.1
24.	d	Sec. 310.2. 308.3
25.	d	Sec. 311.3, 312.1
26.	a	Sec. 302.2
27.	b	Sec. 302.3.2, Exception
28.	a	Sec. 303.1
29.	d	Sec. 307.6
30.	c	Sec. 307.9, #13

ANSWER KEY

Study Session 3

1.	a	Sec. 602.2
2.	c	Sec. 602.3
3.	b	Sec. 602.4
4.	a	Sec. 602.3, 602.4
5.	d	Sec. 602.4.1
6.	c	Sec. 602.4.2
7.	c	Sec. 602.4.5
8.	d	Sec. 602.5
9.	b	Table 601
10.	d	Table 601, Note a
11.	a	Table 601
12.	b	Table 601
13.	b	Table 601, Note b
14.	d	Table 601, Note c3
15.	b	Table 601, Note c1
16.	c	Table 602
17.	c	Table 602
18.	b	Table 601
19.	d	Table 602
20.	b	Table 602
21.	d	Sec. 603.1, #1.1
22.	b	Table 602, Note b
23.	a	Sec. 603.1, #1.2
24.	a	Sec. 603.1, #6
25.	d	Sec. 603.1, #4
26.	a	Sec. 602.4.6
27.	a	Table 601
28.	a	Table 601, Note c3iii
29.	c	Table 601
30.	d	Table 601, Note c2

Study Session 4

1.	a	Sec. 501.2
2.	c	Sec. 502.1
3.	c	Table 503
4.	c	Table 503
5.	b	Sec. 503.1.1
6.	a	Sec. 503.2
7.	b	Sec. 506.4
8.	b	Sec. 504.2
9.	c	Sec. 504.2, Exception 1
10.	b	Sec. 504.3
11.	b	Sec. 505.1
12.	b	Sec. 505.1
13.	c	Sec. 505.2
14.	a	Sec. 505.4, Exception 3
15.	a	Sec. 505.4, Exception 1
16.	b	Sec. 506.2
17.	b	Sec. 506.2
18.	c	Sec. 506.2, 506.2.1
19.	b	Sec. 506.2, 506.2.1
20.	c	Sec. 506.3
21.	d	Sec. 506.3
22.	c	Sec. 507.1
23.	d	Sec. 507.4
24.	d	Sec. 507.7
25.	b	Sec. 508.7
26.	d	Sec. 504.3
27.	b	Sec. 507.3
28.	a	Sec. 507.5
29.	b	Sec. 507.6, Table 503
30.	c	Sec.508.6

ANSWER KEY

Study Session 5

1.	a	Sec. 702.1
2.	b	Sec. 702.1
3.	b	Sec. 702.1
4.	d	Sec. 702.1
5.	a	Sec. 702.1
6.	a	Sec. 702.1, 705.2
7.	b	Sec. 702.1
8.	b	Sec. 702.1
9.	c	Sec. 703.2
10.	d	Sec. 703.4
11.	d	Sec. 703.4.2
12.	d	Sec. 704.2
13.	b	Sec. 704.2, #2
14.	d	Sec. 704.2.2
15.	c	Sec. 704.3
16.	b	Sec. 704.5
17.	a	Table 704.8
18.	c	Table 704.8
19.	b	Sec. 704.8.1, Table 704.8
20.	c	Sec. 704.8.2
21.	c	Sec. 704.9
22.	c	Sec. 704.9
23.	b	Sec. 704.11, Exception 2
24.	a	Sec. 704.11.1
25.	b	Sec. 704.11.1
26.	d	Sec. 703.2.1
27.	c	Sec. 704.2.3
28.	c	Table 704.8
29.	a	Sec. 704.11, #6; 704.8.1
30.	d	Table 704.8, Note d

Study Session 6

1.	d	Sec. 705.3, Exception
2.	c	Table 705.4
3.	b	Table 705.4, Note a
4.	a	Sec. 705.5
5.	b	Sec. 705.6
6.	b	Sec. 705.6.1, Exception
7.	c	Sec. 705.7
8.	b	Sec. 705.8
9.	d	Sec. 706.3
10.	c	Sec. 706.4
11.	c	Sec. 706.7
12.	a	Sec. 706.7, Exception 2
13.	c	Sec. 707.2, Exception 2.1
14.	c	Sec. 707.2, Exception 7
15.	c	Sec. 707.4
16.	c	Sec. 707.14.1
17.	c	Sec. 708.1
18.	c	Sec. 708.3
19.	b	Sec. 708.4, Exc. 3
20.	d	Sec. 709.3
21.	b	Sec. 709.4
22.	b	Sec. 709.5, 715.3.3
23.	a	Sec. 711.3.1
24.	d	Sec. 711.3.3
25.	c	Sec. 711.4
26.	b	Table 706.3.7
27.	c	Sec. 707.13.4
28.	a	Sec. 710.3
29.	a	Sec. 710.5
30.	b	Sec. 708.3, Exc. 2; 711.3, Exc.

Study Session 7

1.	d	Sec. 712.4.1.2
2.	b	Sec. 712.4.3.1
3.	b	Sec. 713.1
4.	d	Sec. 714.2.1
5.	b	Sec. 714.2.4
6.	c	Sec. 714.2.5
7.	d	Table 715.3
8.	d	Table 715.3
9.	c	Sec. 715.3.3
10.	d	Sec. 715.3.6.1, Exception 1
11.	b	Sec. 715.3.7, Exception
12.	c	Sec. 715.3.7.3
13.	b	Sec. 715.3.7.3
14.	b	Table 715.4.3
15.	b	Table 715.4.3
16.	c	Sec. 715.4.7.2
17.	d	Table 716.3.1
18.	d	Sec. 716.3.2.1, #3
19.	a	Sec. 716.5.1
20.	c	Sec. 716.5.3.1
21.	d	Sec. 717.2.1
22.	b	Sec. 717.2.6
23.	d	Sec. 717.3.1
24.	b	Sec. 717.4.3
25.	a	Sec. 719.3
26.	a	Sec. 712.3.1.2
27.	a	Sec. 712.3.2, Exception 1
28.	b	Sec. 715.4, Exception 2
29.	c	Sec. 717.2.7
30.	d	Sec. 718.4

Study Session 8

1.	b	Sec. 901.6.1, Exception 2
2.	b	Sec. 902.1
3.	c	Sec. 902.1
4.	c	Sec. 903.2.1.2, #3
5.	b	Sec. 903.2.1.5
6.	d	Sec. 903.2.2
7.	b	Sec. 903.2.3.1
8.	d	Table 903.2.4.2
9.	c	Sec. 903.2.6
10.	a	Sec. 903.2.7
11.	d	Sec. 903.2.8
12.	c	Sec. 903.2.8.1, #2
13.	b	Sec. 903.2.9.1
14.	b	Sec. 903.2.10.1.3
15.	b	Sec. 903.3.1.3
16.	d	Sec. 903.3.2
17.	c	Sec. 903.3.3
18.	b	Sec. 903.3.5.2
19.	d	Sec. 904.11.1
20.	b	Sec. 905.5
21.	a	Sec. 907.2.2
22.	a	Sec. 907.2.3, Exception 1
23.	a	Sec. 907.3.1
24.	c	Table 907.9.1.3
25.	a	Sec. 907.9.2
26.	d	Sec. 904.11.1
27.	d	Sec. 905.3.4
28.	b	Sec. 909.20.3.3
29.	d	Sec. 910.2.1
30.	d	Table 910.3

ANSWER KEY

Study Session 9

1.	b	Sec. 1002.1
2.	d	Sec. 1002.1
3.	c	Sec. 1002.1
4.	b	Sec. 1002.1
5.	c	Sec. 1002.1
6.	b	Table 1004.1.2
7.	b	Table 1004.1.2
8.	b	Sec. 1004.7
9.	c	Table 1005.1
10.	c	Table 1005.1
11.	d	Sec. 1005.1
12.	d	Sec. 1005.2
13.	b	Sec. 1003.3.1
14.	b	Sec. 1003.3.1, Exception
15.	c	Sec. 1003.3.3
16.	c	Sec. 1003.5, Exception 1
17.	c	Sec. 1011.1
18.	b	Sec. 1011.5.2
19.	b	Sec. 1006.3
20.	b	Sec. 1012.1
21.	c	Sec. 1012.2
22.	d	Sec. 1012.3, Exception 3
23.	a	Sec. 1012.5
24.	c	Sec. 1007.3
25.	c	Sec. 1007.6.1
26.	a	Sec. 1003.3.1
27.	b	Sec. 1004.2
28.	d	Sec. 1006.1
29.	b	Sec. 1007.8
30.	c	Sec. 1011.3

Study Session 10

1.	b	Sec. 1008.1.1
2.	c	Sec. 1008.1.1
3.	a	Sec. 1008.1.1, Exception 3
4.	d	Sec. 1008.1.1.1
5.	d	Sec. 1008.1.2, Exception 1
6.	c	Sec. 1008.1.2
7.	b	Sec. 1008.1.2
8.	b	Sec. 1008.1.3.1
9.	c	Sec. 1008.1.3.4
10.	b	Sec. 1008.1.4
11.	c	Sec. 1008.1.6
12.	a	Sec. 1008.1.8.6
13.	c	Sec. 1008.1.8.2
14.	d	Sec. 1008.1.9
15.	c	Sec. 1009.2
16.	b	Sec. 1009.3, Exception 5
17.	c	Sec. 1009.4
18.	b	Sec. 1009.3
19.	b	Sec. 1009.9
20.	d	Sec. 1009.11.1
21.	a	Sec. 1009.11..5
22.	d	Sec. 1009.11.7
23.	a	Sec. 1010.4
24.	a	Sec. 1010.8
25.	d	Sec. 1008.3.1
26.	d	Sec. 1008.1.3.2
27.	c	Sec. 1008.1.7
28.	b	Sec. 1009.1, Exception
29.	a	Sec. 1009.11.3
30.	d	Sec. 1010.9.1

Study Session 11

1.	d	Table 1014.1
2.	d	Table 1014.1
3.	c	Sec. 1014.1.1
4.	b	Sec. 1014.2.1, Exception 2
5.	c	Sec. 1013.2
6.	a	Sec. 1013.2
7.	c	Sec. 1013.2.2, Exception 2
8.	b	Sec. 1013.2.2
9.	c	Table 1015.1
10.	b	Table 1015.1
11.	c	Sec. 1015.3
12.	a	Sec. 1013.3
13.	c	Sec. 1013.3, Exception 2
14.	b	Sec. 1013.4.1
15.	c	Sec. 1013.4.1
16.	c	Sec. 1013.4.2.3
17.	d	Sec. 1016.2 Exception 4
18.	a	Sec. 1016.2, Exception 2
19.	c	Table 1016.1
20.	d	Table 1016.1
21.	b	Sec. 1016.3
22.	b	Sec. 1016.3, Exception 2
23.	b	Sec. 1016.4, Exception 3
24.	c	Sec. 1013.5, 1016.2
25.	c	Sec. 1013.5.2
26.	b	Sec. 1013.3
27.	d	Sec. 1014.4
28.	a	Sec. 1014.6.1
29.	d	Sec. 1015.2
30.	c	Sec. 1016.3, Exception 3

Study Session 12

1.	b	Table 1018.1
2.	d	Sec. 1018.1.1
3.	b	Table 1018.2
4.	b	Sec. 1019.1
5.	a	Sec. 1019.1, Exception 1
6.	a	Sec. 1019.1.5
7.	c	Sec. 1019.1.7
8.	c	Sec. 1019.1.8
9.	b	Sec. 1020.3
10.	a	Sec. 1021.4
11.	d	Sec. 1022.2
12.	d	Sec. 1022.3
13.	c	Sec. 1023.3
14.	b	Sec. 1023.5.1
15.	d	Sec. 1023.5.2
16.	b	Sec. 1024.2
17.	c	Sec. 1024.5
18.	d	Sec. 1024.6.1, #1,#2
19.	d	Table 1024.6.2
20.	a	Sec. 1024.6.2.1
21.	d	Sec. 1024.7, Exception 2
22.	b	Sec. 1024.9.1, #2
23.	b	Sec. 1024.11.1, Exception
24.	c	Sec. 1024.14.3
25.	c	Sec. 1025.2, Exception
26.	d	Sec. 1021.1, Exception 1
27.	c	Sec. 1023.1, Exception 2
28.	b	Sec. 1023.6, Exception
29.	c	Sec. 1025.3
30.	c	Sec. 1025.5.1

ANSWER KEY

Study Session 13

1.	a	Sec. 1102.1
2.	a	Sec. 1102.1
3.	d	Sec. 1103.2.5
4.	a	Sec. 1103.2.11
5.	b	Sec. 1104.3
6.	b	Sec. 1105.1
7.	b	Table 1106.1
8.	b	Sec. 1106.2
9.	c	Sec. 1106.5
10.	c	Table 1108.2.2.1
11.	a	Table 1108.4.3.1
12.	b	Sec. 1109.2.2
13.	a	Sec. 1107.6.2.2.2
14.	c	Table 1108.2.7.1
15.	c	Sec. 1107.5.2.1
16.	d	Table 1107.6.1.1
17.	a	Table 1107.6.1.1
18.	a	Sec. 1107.6.2.1.1
19.	d	Table 1108.3
20.	b	Sec. 1109.2.1
21.	c	Sec. 1109.2.1.4
22.	c	Sec. 1109.5
23.	a	Sec. 1109.11
24.	a	Sec. 1109.12.2, Exception
25.	c	Sec. 1110.1, #1
26.	a.	Sec. 1104.3.1, Exception 1
27.	a	Sec. 1104.3.2, Exception 1
28.	d	Sec. 1006.3
29.	b	Sec. 1108.2.9.1
30.	c	Sec. 1110.2

Study Session 14

1.	b	Sec. 402.4.4
2.	c	Sec. 402.10, #3
3.	b	Sec. 403.1
4.	d	Sec. 403.10.1
5.	b	Sec. 404.7
6.	d	Sec. 404.8
7.	b	Sec. 405.4.1
8.	a	Sec. 406.2.4
9.	b	Sec. 406.5.2
10.	b	Table 406.3.5
11.	d	Sec. 407.4
12.	d	Sec. 407.4.1
13.	c	Sec. 408.3.1
14.	d	Sec. 408.6.1
15.	b	Sec. 409.2
16.	b	Sec. 410.3.5
17.	d	Sec. 410.3.7
18.	a	Sec. 411.8
19.	b	Sec. 412.4.1
20.	c	Table 414.2.2
21.	c	Sec. 415.3, Exception 1
22.	d	Sec. 415.3.1, #3
23.	a	Sec. 415.9.4.4
24.	b	Sec. 417.2
25.	b	Sec. 418.5
26.	c	Sec. 410.5.1
27.	d	Sec. 413.2
28.	c	Sec. 414.2.3
29.	b	Sec. 414.6.1, #3
30.	c	Sec. 416.2

Study Session 15

1.	b	Sec. 1402.1
2.	a	Sec. 1402.1
3.	a	Sec. 1404.2
4.	b	Table 1405.2
5.	a	Sec. 1405.9.1.1
6.	a	Sec. 1405.10
7.	d	Sec. 1406.2.2
8.	b	Sec. 1502.1
9.	b	Table 1505.1
10.	b	Sec. 1505.3, Exception
11.	c	Table 1507.2
12.	d	Sec. 1507.2.8.1
13.	c	Sec. 1507.3.6
14.	b	Sec. 1507.5.2
15.	d	Sec. 1507.9.7
16.	d	Table 1507.8.6
17.	b	Sec. 1507.14.1
18.	c	Sec. 1509.2
19.	c	Sec. 1805.1
20.	b	Sec. 1805.2
21.	d	Table 1804.2
22.	c	Sec. 1805.4.2.1
23.	d	Sec. 1805.4.2.5
24.	b	Table 1805.4.2
25.	b	Sec. 1805.5.4
26.	d	Sec. 1405.13
27.	c	Sec. 1505.7
28.	d	Sec. 1507.7.2
29.	d	Sec. 1509.5
30.	b	Sec. 1803.3

Study Session 16

1.	a	Sec. 1603.3
2.	b	Table 1607.1
3.	d	Sec. 1607.7.1
4.	d	Sec. 1607.11.2.2
5.	c	Sec. 1609.4, #3
6.	c	Sec. 1704.7, Exception
7.	b	Sec. 1704.11.3.2
8.	b	Sec. 1709.1, #3
9.	c	Sec. 1905.11.2
10.	b	Table 1907.7.1
11.	b	Sec. 1909.6.1
12.	a	Sec. 1911.1
13.	b	Sec. 2102.1
14.	d	Sec. 2104.1.3
15.	a	Sec. 2104.1.8
16.	c	Sec. 2111.10
17.	d	Sec. 2111.12
18.	c	Sec. 2113.9
19.	a	Sec. 2304.11.2.4
20.	d	Sec. 2302.1
21.	b	Table 2304.9.1
22.	c	Sec. 2308.3.1
23.	a	Sec. 2308.8.3
24.	a	Sec. 2308.9.11
25.	b	Sec. 2308.10.5
26.	d	Table 1607.1, Note f
27.	c	Table 1904.2.2(2)
28.	d	Sec. 2211.3.1, #6
29.	b	Sec. 2304.12, Exception 1
30.	d	Sec. 2308.9.4

ANSWER KEY

Study Session 17

1.	b	Sec. 803.1
2.	c	Sec. 803.4.4
3.	c	Table 803.5
4.	a	Table 803.5
5.	d	Table 803.5, Note i
6.	a	Sec. 803.6.1
7.	b	Sec. 804.5.1, Exception
8.	b	Sec. 805.5
9.	d	Sec. 805.1.2, Exception
10.	c	Sec. 805.5
11.	b	Sec. 1204.1
12.	c	Sec. 1205.2
13.	a	Sec. 1205.4
14.	b	Sec. 1207.3
15.	c	Sec. 1208.2
16.	b	Sec. 1208.3
17.	a	Sec. 1209.1
18.	c	Sec. 1209.2
19.	c	Sec. 1210.3
20.	d	Sec. 2502.1
21.	b	Sec. 2509.3, #3
22.	c	Sec. 2512.5
23.	d	Sec. 3002.2
24.	d	Sec. 3004.2
25.	b	Sec. 3002.4
26.	a	Sec. 804.5.1
27.	c	Sec. 1203.3.1
28.	c	Sec. 1206.3
29.	a	Sec. 2508.4
30.	d	Sec. 3003.1.2

Study Session 18

1.	a	Sec. 2403.5
2.	c	Sec. 2405.3
3.	b	Sec. 2405.3
4.	d	Sec. 2405.4
5.	d	Table 2406.1
6.	a	Sec. 2406.2, Exception 1
7.	a	Sec. 2406.3., #5
8.	c	Sec. 2406.3., #6
9.	d	Sec. 2406.3., #7
10.	a	Sec. 2406.3., #9
11.	d	Sec. 2406.3., #10.1
12.	a	Sec. 2406.3.1, #1
13.	b	Sec. 2406.4
14.	b	Sec. 2407.1.2
15.	d	Sec. 2602.1
16.	d	Sec. 2602.1
17.	d	Sec. 2603.3
18.	a	Sec. 2603.4
19.	b	Sec. 2603.4.1.1
20.	d	Sec. 2604.2.2
21.	c	Sec. 2605.2, #2
22.	b	Table 2607.4
23.	d	Sec. 2608.2, #3, Exception
24.	a	Sec. 2609.1
25.	b	Sec. 2611.3
26.	a	Sec. 2404.1
27.	b	Sec. 2406.2, Exception 2
28.	c	Sec. 2406.2.1
29.	c	Sec. 2408.3
30.	d	Sec. 2603.4.1.13